SKI Magazine's ENCYCLOPEDIA OF SKIING

SKI Magazine's

1817

ENCYCLOPEDIA OF SKIING

Edited by Robert Scharff

UPDATED

HARPER & ROW, PUBLISHERS

New York, Evanston, San Francisco, London

The excerpt in Section III, pages 222–225, on ski safety is taken from *The Skier's Bible* by Morten Lund. Copyright © 1968 by Morten Lund. Reprinted by permission of the publisher, Doubleday & Company, Inc.

The excerpt appearing in Section IV, pages 317–320, on jumping technique is taken from *Expert Skiing* by David Bradley, Ralph Miller, and C. Allison Merrill. Copyright © 1960 by David Bradley, Ralph Miller, and C. Allison Merrill. Reprinted by permission of the publisher, Holt, Rinehart and Winston.

The excerpt appearing in Section V, pages 386–387, on favorite ski areas is taken from *Ski North America* by Abby Rand. Copyright © 1969 by Abby Rand. Reprinted by permission of the publisher, J. B. Lippincott Company.

Portions of this work first appeared, in somewhat different form, as contributions to *Ski Magazine*. Copyright 1960, 1961, 1962, 1963, 1964, 1965, 1966, 1967, 1968, 1969, 1970, 1971, 1972 by Universal Publishing and Distributing Corporation.

ISBN: 0–06–013918–8 (cloth)
ISBN: 0–06–013919–6 (paper)

LIBRARY OF CONGRESS CATALOG CARD NUMBER: 78–123963

Contents

*and Headwalls—Catwalk Skiing—*Other Ski Teaching Techniques—*Canadian Ski Instructors' Alliance—The Modern French Method—The Austrian System—Graduated-length Method (GLM)—Comparison of Ski Systems—Ski Schools—*Teaching Children to Ski—*Ten Positive Rules to Follow with Children—*Lift and Tow Technique—*Rope Tows—The T-Bar or J-Bar Lifts—Pomalifts—Chair Lifts—Other Lifts—*Ski Touring *—Touring Techniques—Ski Mountaineering—*Ski Safety and Courtesy—*The Ski Patrol —Ten Tips for Safer Skiing—Injured Skiers—Avalanches—Etiquette—*Conditioning *—Warm-ups*

Section IV. Ski Competition, 233

Alpine Ski Competition—*Slalom—Downhill—Giant Slalom—Alpine Combined—Watching Alpine Races—Head-to-head Racing—*Nordic Ski Competition—*Jumping—Ski Flying—Cross-country Racing—Nordic Combined—Biathlon—*International Ski Competition—Winter Olympic Games—Nordic Events (Men)—*15-kilometer Cross-country—18-kilometer Cross-country—30-kilometer Cross-country—50-kilometer Cross-country—Nordic Combined (Cross-country and Jumping)—Biathlon—Jumping—Jumping ("Normal" Hill, 70 meters)—Jumping ("Big" Hill, 90 meters)—40-kilometer (4 × 10 kilometers) Cross-country Relay—30-kilometer (4 × 7.5 kilometers) Biathlon Relay—Alpine Events (Men)—Downhill—Slalom—Giant Slalom—Alpine Combined —Nordic Events (Women)—5-kilometer Cross-country—10-kilometer Cross-country—15-kilometer (3 × 5 kilometers) Cross-country Relay—Alpine Events (Women)—Downhill—Slalom—Giant Slalom—Alpine Combined—*Winter Olympic Games Sites —Ski Championships Won by Nations Year by Year—Medals Won by Nations 1924–1968—FIS Ski World Championships—*Men—Women—*FIS Alpine Championship Medals—FIS Nordic Championship Medals—*FIS Championship Sites—World Cup—*Men—Women—*World Cup Races—*Men—Women—*The Nations Cup—Other Major Ski Events—*Arlberg-Kandahar—Hahnenkamm Races—Lauberhorn—Holmenkollen Competition: The Kings Cup—*United States National Champions—*National Men's Downhill—National Men's Slalom—National Men's Giant Slalom—National Men's Alpine Combined—National Women's Downhill—National Women's Slalom—National Women's Giant Slalom—National Women's Alpine Combined—National Men's Cross-country—National Nordic Combined—National Men's Jumping—*National Junior Championships—*Boys' Downhill—Boys' Slalom—Boys' Giant Slalom—Girls' Downhill—Girls' Slalom—Girls' Giant Slalom—Boys' Cross-country—Boys' Nordic Combined—Boys' Jumping—*NCAA Ski Championships—*Championship Results—Coaches of Team Champions—*National Ski Hall of Fame—*Athlete-of-the-Year Awards—*United States National Competitive Trophies—*Beck International Trophy—Paul Bietila Trophy—Julius Blegen Memorial Plaque and Medal—Gale Cotton Burton Memorial Trophy—Sally Deaver Award—Finlandia Award—Paul Nash Layman, Jr., Trophy—Sons of Norway Junior Jumping Trophy—Torger Tokle Memorial—United States Ski Club Award—White Stag Trophy—Wallace "Bud" Werner Award—Ski Writers Award—*Professional Racing—*Professional Skier of the Year Award—*The

Contents

Section V.   Where to Ski, 331

Section VI.   Glossary, Lexicon, and Ski Associations, 413

Acknowledgments

In the winter of 1935–1936, a young Seattle newspaperman named Alf Nydin published his first editorial in a new magazine called *Ski*. He had sensed the coming growth of the sport and, with it, the start of a new industry. In a sense, the first issue of *Ski* marked the beginning of modern skiing. Earlier years had seen its birth among the snowshoe runners of the High Sierras, the Scandinavian jumpers of the Midwest, and the madcap collegians of the East. But it was in the thirties that the sport really began to grow in the United States.

Throughout the past thirty-five years in which skiing has developed both as a sport and as an industry, *Ski* was there, entertaining, enlightening, challenging, influencing, leading, scolding, encouraging—and always serving American skiing. *Ski* is proud of its latest contribution to the sport—*The Encyclopedia of Skiing*.

As with the magazine, the compilation of this volume required the help of many people. Members of the staff of *Ski* who were exceedingly cooperative were John Fry, Morten Lund, Patricia Doran, Linda Wasserman, and Marje Raab. Writers and technical editors of this publication who were also helpful include Ernie McCulloch, Willy Schaeffler, Junior Bounous, Dixi Nohl, Georges Joubert, Abby Rand, Tom Corcoran, Gloria Chadwick, Martha Miller, Michael Brady, and Robert Beattie.

Although the vast majority of the material in this book appeared in one form or another in *Ski* during the more than thirty-five years of its publication, some material was contributed from other sources. We would like to thank, for instance, Bjorn Kjellstrom of the International Ski Federation, Rita Cavner of the United States Ski Association, Joan Parker, the Austrian National Tourist Office, Edward Champagne of the Canadian National Ski Team, Charles Gibson, John Jay, the Waterville Company, Inc., Elina Burgh of the Norwegian Consulate, Elizabeth Morrish of the Canadian Travel Office, Suzan Irwinson of the Aspen Ski Club, William B. Berry of the National Ski Hall of Fame, Bill Riley of Stowe, Vermont, W. Schwartz of Sugar Bowl, the French Information Office, Jakob Vaage and the Oslo Ski Museum, the Swiss National Tourist Office, Robert Loughrey of Bogus Basin, Enzo Serafini of U.S. Eastern Amateur Ski Association, Taos Ski Valley, Bonne Bell, Raichle of Switzerland, Al Merrill, Jim Reinecke of the Vail Ski Club, and Bill Tanler of *Ski Racing*. In addition, we want to thank our typists, Alice Bauerfeind and Barbara Shalvey, who had the task of typing this huge manuscript.

Special thanks are due to William Davies of Harper & Row, and to Frances Krupka, who compiled most of the competition results and acted as coordinator of the book, for their toil and zest in making this project possible.

SKI Magazine's ENCYCLOPEDIA OF SKIING

SECTION I

The History of Skiing

Skiing on the North American continent today is plainly a burgeoning phenomenon: not much social importance can be attached, say, to the increase of fishermen because the increase roughly parallels the increase of population, but *skiing* has grown from a sport involving less than 30,000 ski jumpers and woodsy outdoor college-club types in the 1920's to 4 million today. For every skier active in the 1920's, we have more than a thousand active skiers in the 1970's.

The physical plant serving these millions has grown still more startlingly: even though recently the annual increase of the number of skiers has remained constant, skiers, individually, have had more money to spend; the construction of lifts, lodges, and ski mountains has *accelerated*. Back in the 1930's it was easy to name the resorts with major ski lift installations—Sun Valley, Alta, Sugar Bowl, Belnap, Stowe, Cannon, Mont Tremblant, North Conway, Aspen—North America now has approximately eight hundred ski areas beyond the rope tow class. What's more, the areas have lift capacities far beyond the two- to three-hundred skiers an hour that used to pass for efficiency: lifts with a capacity of a thousand skiers an hour are legion.

Skiers ride up the hill faster and in greater numbers; they go farther—they fly by the tens of thousands to the Rockies—getting at least one week's winter vacation every year or so, unheard-of in the 1920's. The skier is willing to spend anywhere from $100 to $300 to achieve comfort and enjoyment for his week. As a result, spending for recreational skiing in the United States recently broke the billion dollar barrier. Golfers still outnumber skiers three to one, but in Colorado, where skier-tourists concentrate, the state has more outside income from tourist skiers.

The modern trend from spectator sport toward participant sport contains a second trend: toward more *active* participant sport. The glamor of a seat behind the dugout of the Brooklyn Dodgers faded in the 1940's when compared to the thrill of sinking a ten foot putt on the local golf links with your own hands. In turn, the electric golf cart now signals the fading of the glamor of golf relative to negotiating one's way down Ruthie's Run at Aspen. Progress overtakes and dims the luster and adventure of long-established sports; the need for newer, more glamorous sport then creates a trend toward something more challenging. In the past twenty years, this growth sport has been skiing.

WHERE DID SKIING START?

To find the roots of skiing as we know it today, we will have to go back a few thousand years.

> In skiing's early Golden Age,
> No arguments made skiers rage.
> The ski was used for transportation
> In every snow-bound northern nation.

Skiing may well be more than 5,000 years old—not many sports can make that claim. The word *ski* is the Norwegian name for a snowshoe that was used by the northern nations of the Old World. The name is derived from an Indo-Germanic root. It is found in the English words *skid, skip, skiff, slide,* and *skate*. The Norwegian word *Skilober* refers to a snowshoe. However, Dr. William Fowler wrote in *The Year Book of the Ski Club of Great Britain,* in 1909, that the word *ski* came from a Germanic and Latin word implying splitting. Thus, ski referred to a split or splitting of wood into the ski shape. The Indian snowshoe is different from the ski; thus, the English term *snowshoe* has never been popular in reference to skis and skiing.

No doubt about it, however, that the first skis were made to move on, not play on. Skis dating back to 2500 B.C. have been found in the Altai Mountains of Siberia, and they bear a startling resemblance to those in use today. Some were pointed on both ends, but they had the shovel and tip, and even the thong binding is plainly shown on a Runic stone 3,000 years old. Actually, the earliest ski runners presumably were bones from large animals, strapped to the shoes with leather thongs, as were snowshoes. When man sought a faster way of proceeding over frozen wastes where the land was flat, or progressing over the icy surface of lakes or rivers, he no doubt used smaller bones, and those probably were the pioneer skates, the joints of the bones being smoothed so as to produce a flat surface which permitted a swift, gliding motion.

There appears to be basis for the conclusion that skis were used in the northern part of Europe and in Asia prior to the Christian Era, but there is little in the way of definite fact to substantiate the date. A pair of skis pronounced the oldest known to the world is in the Djugarden Museum at Stockholm,

Sweden. Guesses have been made that the skis might be at least 4,000 years old. In fact, the analytical method of determining the ages of ancient ski finds was developed by the Swedish scholars Lennart von Post and Erik Granlund. Through research by famous ethnologists, the ages of many skis found in the bogs of Norway, Sweden, and Finland have been determined. A few of those finds and their determined ages establish that the ski found at Hoting in Angermanland, Sweden, is between 4,000 and 5,000 years old; the Riihimäki ski found in southern Finland dates back to the Bronze Age; the Arnas ski found in Arnas, Dalarna, Sweden, is estimated to be about 2,500 years old; skis from Kalvtrask in Västerbotten, Sweden, date back to 2000 B.C., while the Ovrebo ski is presumed to be about 2,500 years old.

Most of the very early prehistoric skis were more like snowshoes than like the skis we use today. The Swedish Hoting ski, for instance, is an excellent example of this snowshoe-like construction. The 2,500-year-old Ovrebo ski from southern Norway, on the other hand, has a turned-up, pointed tip and resembles a modern ski. Many of these old skis are preserved in museums—the Hoting ski in Umea, Sweden, and the Ovrebo ski in Oslo, Norway.

One of the first written accounts of skiing appears in the *Sagas*—the classic literature of the Viking period. The Norwegian Vikings were said to be excellent skiers, and the *Sagas* describe several kings living around A.D. 1000 as superb skiers. Skiing was so much a part of Viking life that a god and goddess of skiing, Uller and Skada, were objects of worship. That is, Skada, the giant goddess who in legend was married to Njord, one of the Scandinavian gods, is known as the Goddess of Ski (Odurrdis) in the northern countries of Europe. Uller, the god of winter, always is pictured walking on skis with curved toes, which created the idea that he was so huge that he trod the snow with ships lashed to his feet.

With skis being widely used for hunting and travel, it seems strange that before A.D. 1200 they were not routinely used in warfare. That year, during the Battle of Oslo, King Sverre of Norway equipped his scouts

Painting by K. Bergslien, 1853, of the flight of the "Birchlegs" with the infant King Haakon Haakonson in the 1206 Norwegian Civil War. "Birchlegs" referred to the custom of wrapping legs with birch bark as protection against snow.

with skis and sent them to reconnoiter the Swedish enemy, camped in deep snow, which had marooned him. This makes it appear that skis were not numerous even then, else the entire armies on both sides would have been equipped with them, enabling the troops to navigate through snow and over ice in flat countries.

Six years later, during the Norwegian Civil War, skis again played an important part in Norway's history when the king sent two scouts, called "Birchlegs" because they wrapped their legs with birch to protect them against the cold, to carry the infant royal son Haakon Haakonsson over the mountains in the middle of winter. This feat is commemorated in Norway today by the annual Birkebeinerrennet (Birchleg race), a cross-country marathon ski race which follows the same 35-mile course taken by the king's scouts more than seven and a half centuries ago.

Skiing has played such a large part in Scandinavian life that it is sometimes difficult to separate sport from history. Norway's Birkebeinerrennet has its counterpart in Sweden—the annual 53-mile Vasaloppet cross-country race. At the beginning of the sixteenth century, when rich Denmark controlled Sweden, Gustav Vasa, a young revolutionary, was trying without success to arouse the natives to fight for their freedom. But he was forced to flee, and set out for Norway. After he had left, however, the Dalecarlians had second thoughts, and two woodsmen were sent to bring him back. At Sälen, only 25 kilometers from the border, they caught up with him. Back in Mora, he started raising an army, later beat the Danes and was finally elected King on June 6, 1523, going down in the books as Gustavus Eriksson I.

Some 400 years later, newspaper editor Anders Pers proposed that Gustav Vasa's trip be revived as a modern ski race salute to the past and a reminder of what Dalecarlia and its people have meant to Sweden. "It may seem long," Pers wrote, "but that is as it should be: a real test of man's ability to stand up to hardship."

A popular event, the Vasaloppet race, a distance of 8.5 Swedish miles (85 kilometers or about 53 English miles) skiing between Sälen and Mora in northern Sweden. The Vasa race is connected with Swedish history. Gustav Vasa, a Swedish hero king, was forced to flee in 1521 toward the border of Norway. Two of his supporters followed their king in the tracks and caught up with him in the village of Sälen, 2½ Swedish miles (some 15 English miles) from the Norwegian border. Today's popular event, the Vasaloppet, follows practically the same track, although reversed for practical reasons, beginning in Sälen and ending up in the city of Mora. Our picture shows the "takeoff" at Sälen.

Everyone thought Pers' idea was a good one. The sports club in Mora agreed to sponsor the race. *Dagens Nyheter,* the big Stockholm daily, donated 1,000 kronor ($265) for expenses. The King offered a cup. Only two out of the 119 starters failed to finish the first Vasaloppet, held on March 19, 1922. Ernst Alm, a 22-year-old woodcutter from Norsjö, did it in 7 hours 32 minutes and 49 seconds, to win the cup and cheers. The Vasaloppet has been held every year since, except in 1932 and 1934, when there was no snow. It became an international event in 1948 when three Finnish skiers competed. Now entries come from all over the world. A Canadian and a pearl diver from Japan were among recent contestants. To qualify for the race, entrants must be at least 22 years of age, sponsored by a recognized sports club, and physically fit. The Vasalop-

pet cross-country race follows the original route, celebrating Gustav's victory. Today more than 9,000 skiers participate in this grueling test, making it one of the great sights in sports as the skiers all surge forward in a mass start.

Apparently the Swedes, after 1200, must have learned a lesson as to the value of skis in warfare. Going into war in 1521 and in later conflicts in 1576, 1590, and 1610, they equipped all the troops with either skis or snowshoes. In the 1521 war, the Swedes stretched animal skins between two skis, placed injured comrades on them, and in this fashion carried them off the fields—the first known stretchers.

The bone-runner ski had no standard size. It was not turned up at the ends, this being impossible. Centuries after the beginning of the Christian Era wood was substituted. The standard length of the wooden ski was about 7 feet 6 inches. The runners were about 2 inches thick and 5 inches wide, and about 1 foot of the front end of the ski was turned up, just the way the ski is shown in drawings that deal with legendary gods of the north countries. Obviously, the drawings were not made until long after wooden skis came into existence, although the gods and goddesses predate them by many centuries. Although skiing is several thousand years old, very little improvement occurred in ski technique until the nineteenth century. This lack of progress was due chiefly to the early boots and bindings. The latter were just single, loose toe-straps of leather or willow, while boots were usually simple leather shoes. Because of this loose connection between the skis and the boots, it was not possible to jump or turn while in motion. Skis, therefore, were simply a means of transportation and were employed primarily by woodsmen and hunters. They were also used by doctors, midwives, clergymen, and undertakers during the nineteenth century in the Scandinavian countries.

In 1721 a ski company was organized in the Norwegian army, and some twelve years later regular ski drills were held as part of

Norwegian "ski trooper," circa 1747, showing the short ski "pusher" and the long ski "slider."

maneuvers. These soldiers of the unit are generally credited as being the first to use a leather strap around their heel, in addition

Lithograph by J. Pettersen, Trondheim, 1822, of Norwegian ski company winter maneuvers in 1822.

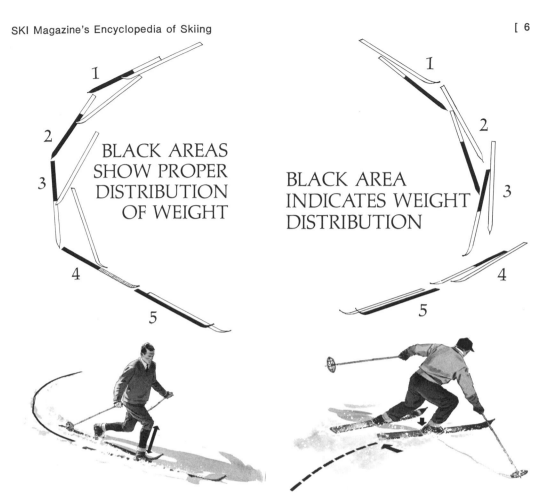

BLACK AREAS
SHOW PROPER
DISTRIBUTION
OF WEIGHT

BLACK AREA
INDICATES WEIGHT
DISTRIBUTION

The telemark turn (left) and Christiania (right). The skiers are in 1930's ski dress. Black areas indicate weight distribution.

to the toestrap, to keep their skis from falling off when skiing downhill. But even these bindings were too loose to permit full control of their skis. So a single solid pole was employed as a brake when skiing downhill and as a "pusher" to increase speed on flat surfaces.

Skis of the late eighteenth century were as much products of local fancy as of technique. Every valley and country village had its own particular type of ski. The most common type, generally used by armies of Norway and Sweden, was the Osterdal, which had one short ski (4 to 6 feet) and one long ski (8 to 10 feet). The long ski provided the glide, while the short one, called the *andor,* was used to push-off or kick (much as one kicks a scooter). The long ski was often grooved, just like a modern ski, to help it keep its direction

while gliding. The andor was generally fur-covered on the underside to give the ski better bite.

Although many areas in the Scandinavian countries had special types of skis suitable for jumping or turning, it was in the late 1830's that skiing as a sport first entered the picture—and naturally enough, it was in Norway. In order to race, it was necessary, of course, to devise some means of changing direction. A young man from the town of Telemark, Sondre Norheim, developed a turn for stopping at the end of ski jump run-outs. The turn began by pushing the uphill or outside ski of the turn ahead of the inside ski. Maintaining weight on the inside ski, the lead ski was angled toward the fall line. Bindings allowing as much as five or six inches of heel lift enabled the skier to push the outside ski even further ahead so that the skier's lead ski and boot were actually in contact with the inside ski's tip during part of the turn. Increased forward lean, edging of the outside ski, and weight shift accompanied by hip and shoulder rotation finally brought the skis around. For increased balance, the skier spread his arms. Modern step-in and latch-in bindings used by today's skiers hold a ski boot heel down so tightly on the ski that the execution of a telemark is almost impossible.

Norheim's major rivals in jumping events, from the town of Christiania (the old name for Oslo), Torjus and Mikkel Hemmestveit, came up with a skidded turn that kept the skis wide apart and more or less parallel. This became known as the "Christiania." Meanwhile, other Norwegians were propelling themselves off bumps through the air to see how far they could jump. Ski jumping was born, and the crutch makers began to see a good thing.

By the earlier 1870's, ski carnivals were common events in Norwegian towns. The earliest events were a cross-country race called the *langlauf,* or "long run," and jumping contests. At this time, skis were held to the feet with toestraps, and skiers used a long stick as a brake when skiing downhill, or to ride on when going over jumps. (Today cross-country and jumping events are called Nordics in ski competition.) Later, as skiers learned both the Christiania (or Christie) and Telemark turn techniques, slalom or downhill races were possible. (Today slalom events are called Alpine in ski competition. In the dialect of Telemark, the tracks on the hillside on a downhill race were known as slalom— sla-slope.) By the late 1800's there were written rules for ski competition in Norway and thousands of spectators viewed contests that are still being repeated today.

The Norwegians who were keen about their sport soon spread it around the world with the zeal of missionaries. Mostly they were miners—a rough lot. Gold was discovered in eastern Australia in 1851, and the Norwegians sailed down under to dig. About twenty years later the Kiandra Ski Club was formed in Australia—considered by many to be the oldest in existence. Meanwhile, across the Atlantic in the snow-packed gold camps of La Porte, Alturas, and Onion Valley, high

1889 painting by Carl Hansen of a girl in Setesdal national costume skiing, Setesdal, Norway.

in the California Sierras, men like Jim Mullen and "Quicksilver" Handel were arranging "the first organized ski competition the world has ever known" and claimed their Union Hotel headquarters as the "first ski hostel." Here, for a bucket of lager beer, a hundred silver dollars, or a gold-mine claim, bearded and crusty miners poured out of their glory holes, strapped on their 12-foot skis (some were made out of solid oak and weighed 25 pounds), and went hell-for-leather down the Sierra race courses at speeds up to 80-plus miles an hour, riding a long pole that looked like a cross between a barber pole and a plumber's helper. Everyone from the Chinese to the Scandinavians was either racing or out there to cheer them on. Even the horses clumped around on foot-long snowshoes with leather bindings. There were portable bars at the "finish" gates to provide the cup-thumping along with an occasional fistfight. The side bets went into the thousands.

About this time—the winter of 1856— John A. "Snowshoe" Thompson, another Norwegian of course, started to provide the only winter land communication between the East and California, tracing the route of Kit Carson and John Fremont from Placerville to Carson Valley, a 90-mile link on skis. It was

Norwegian skiers in Red Wing, Minnesota, 1891 (first team in United States). Left to right: Paul Hønningstad, Mikkel Hemmestveit, Torjus Hemmestveit, Ludvig Hjermstad.

rugged duty, skiing over 30 to 50 feet of snow, with up to 120 pounds of mail (at $2 a letter), but Thompson did it for twenty years. As a matter of fact, after thirteen years he felt Congress owed him a debt of $6,000 or so for underpayment. He filed a claim. Congress sent him a nice letter of thanks—but no check. Citizens, many of whom owed their lives to Thompson's daring rescues when he was not on the mail run, subscribed a small sum for him to show gratitude. Thompson, broken up because of the Congressional rebuff, never recovered from the blow. He died a short time later and is buried in Genoa, California.

Far and wide the Scandinavians spread their doctrine of skis, from Poker Flat and Whiskey Diggings in California to Alta, Utah, and Aspen, Colorado, and all the camps strung along the high rib of the Continental Divide. Preacher John Dyer used his skis, called "snowshoes of Norwegian pattern," to keep the mail moving in Colorado snow coun-

try in the 1860's. And by the 1880's, the Norwegians allowed some Swedes to help them carry the mail over the high Andean Passes from Chile to Argentina—at one time, 300 of them carrying the mail on skis from hut to hut. Nor did they move over, either, until the railroads arrived. But there was no stopping the "Scandihoovians," and by the 1890's, Norwegian immigrants like the Hemmestveits and the Nordheims, who came to the United States, got North American skiing really moving. At Ishpeming, Michigan; at Revelstoke, Canada; and at Berlin, New Hampshire, as well as many other spots in Wisconsin, Minnesota, and elsewhere, crowds of paying spectators gathered to watch the airborne circus. The competitors were professional, salaried jumpers who competed for "large" cash prizes—and they really earned the money. For example, a Dominion champion named Ragnar Omtvedt arrived at an Ottawa jumping hill to open the competition before the governor general and a

The first major jump meet in Switzerland, organized by Christof Iselin.

crowd of thousands. He was told that the hill (he had never seen it before) was an official 200-foot jump, whereupon he strapped on his boards, soared through the air for 203 feet in flawless style—and landed with a crash on the flats of the river ice beyond the outrun, breaking both ankles! The hill, it turned out, was 150 feet.

In Revelstoke they used a 200-foot steel tower, with an elevator, and an adjacent warehouse roof for a takeoff. They even had a woman jumper, Isabel Courier, who leaped 140 feet. This led to the famous jump of Countess Alma Stang in eastern Canada, who made a tremendous leap and transfixed the spectators until the wind blew off her wig and exposed a man! The enraged crowds trampled the ticket booth down in their efforts to get their money back. The fate of Countess Stang is unknown.

A SKI TECHNIQUE IS BORN

It was not until a few years before the turn of this century that central Europe began to realize what a good thing the Scandinavians had going. Then they looked around and saw they had better mountains lying unused right in their back yard than Norway and Sweden had. But, unlike the Scandinavians, who seemed to be interested mainly in cross-country touring and "yoomping," the Europeans, with steeper slopes to navigate, began

Mathias Zdarsky is, according to most ski historians, the father of Alpine skiing.

Hannes Schneider combined safety and speed in organizing a logical system of ski instruction.

to develop downhill racing. This, they soon discovered, as the Norwegians had before them, was not so easy.

In the early 1890's a martinet named Mathias Zdarsky, of Austria, experimented with the various Norwegian ski methods, and in 1896 he announced his own technique based on the theory that with one ski extended out at an acute angle to the fall line, one could slow down and even steer that out-of-control rush to the valley floor.

The Lilienfeld technique, as Zdarsky's method was known, involved a long pole and a low crouch for balance—not very graceful, but it worked. The Norwegians took a dim view of Zdarsky; they said the crouch was not a technique but a sign of cowardice (*they* stood body erect). Back came the retort from the Alps, clear as a mountain echo, "*You* can't keep your skis on the snow long enough to *use* a technique!" Zdarsky then challenged the Norwegians to come down and put it to a test, which they did, sending another Christiania lad, Hansa Horn, to Lilienfeld, where he soundly defeated Zdarsky, despite the latter's precaution of setting the course and giving himself racing position number one. Horn went home in triumph, and Zdarsky went back to the drafting board.

Finally, however, the Europeans won out. Enlisting the aid of a skilled technician,

Colonel Georg Bilgeri, Zdarsky deepened his crouch, used two poles for better balance, shortened his 8 foot skis, and introduced the snowplow. He even began to sniff out the stem Christiania, thus laying the groundwork for future disciples like Hannes Schneider. Incidentally, Zdarsky was the first person in Austria to have taught skiing on a regular basis.

Schneider, a native of Steuben in the Arlberg, was fascinated with the new sport of skiing and had been befriended by Victor Sohm, who taught him the rudiments of the snowplow and stem turn. His father wanted him to be a cheesemaker. Hannes had other ideas. He applied for a job at the Hotel Post in the village of St. Anton in December, 1907, as a ski teacher. His father, like so many fathers after him, thought his son crazy—but he agreed, on the condition that if the ski-teaching business failed to show a profit that winter, young Hannes was to become apprenticed to a cheesemaker in the spring.

It was cheese's loss and skiing's gain. Gradually Schneider worked out a teaching technique that was easy and fun. He studied Zdarsky, improved on his methods. His ski school grew, and so did the number of winter visitors to St. Anton. Delighted, his townspeople sent him to a race in St. Moritz,

Taken around 1910, this historic photograph shows some of the pioneers of Arlberg skiing. Left to right: Herr Ikle, Swiss mountain guide; Herr Schallert, from Bludenz; "Avalanche Franz-Josef" Mathies, so named because he was buried beneath the snow for thirty-six hours and survived to tell about it; Engelbert Strolz, Zürs; Hannes Schneider, Stuben, founder of the Arlberg ski technique; Albert Mathies, the first ski teacher at Zürs; Frau Theresia Sohm, Mathies' sister, one of the first women skiers in Austria.

Switzerland, where the telemark was still very much "in." Schneider won the race easily—and put an end to telemark method.

During World War I, Schneider fought with the Mountain troops on the 12,000-foot Königspitze, firing away at his former climbing and skiing buddies, the Italians, across a glacial abyss. The near-misses were extremely accurate on both sides. It took the lethal barrages of lightning bolts, which crackled away almost daily, to drive them all into their blue-ice "fox holes." Avalanches roared down and wiped out whole battalions. Schneider's respect for the mountains grew, along with his desire to ski in them once again, in peacetime.

The war over, Schneider went home to pick up the pieces and regroup the ski school. He put together a teaching staff of such sterling pros as Luggi Foeger, Otto Lang, Benno Rybizka and others, who launched a meteoric campaign to make the Hannes Schneider Ski School world-famous. Schneider's military precision in the school delighted the British and many other foreigners who were

climbing on the Arlberg (as Schneider's technique was known) bandwagon, for at least there was a way to learn how to control speed and have fun doing it. Almost anyone who tried could learn. Actually, the Schneider, or Arlberg, technique consisted of learning the snowplow, snowplow turn, stem turn, stem Christiania, and parallel swing. It also consisted of "rotation," that is, rotating the body in the direction of the turn. The Tyrolean Professional Ski Teachers, founded in 1925, and the German Ski Association adopted the Schneider method, and it was taught throughout the Tyrol. Two movies of Schneider in action demonstrating his complete control were shown throughout Europe and aroused great interest in the sport. Thanks to Schneider, the ski fever in Europe was nearing epidemic pitch.

The time clock now called for the skiing genius of Hannes Schneider and the imagination and sporting inventiveness of Britain's Arnold Lunn, who by 1920 had checked out every Swiss resort in the Alps and was enthusiastically looking for an excuse to honor

The two men who made the Arlberg-Kandahar meet in St. Anton possible: Hannes Schneider (left) and Sir Arnold Lunn.

the exciting sport of skiing with a downhill race—a race which would put some emphasis on these fine turns that Schneider was teaching. Lunn went to the Norwegians, as usual, and borrowed their "slalom." A whole new chapter of ski racing was opened. The race was a huge success and was called the Arlberg-Kandahar (after Lord Roberts of Kandahar, who kindly donated the trophy). Today the winning of the coveted gold A-K is rated by many of the world's racers as equal to either an Olympic or an FIS medal, and Arnold Lunn was knighted for his contribution to the sport of skiing.

In Canada, where some say they have only two seasons, winter and August, the Nor-

wegians did it again. Men like Herman "Jack Rabbit" Johannsen took advantage of the rolling hills in the Laurentians to set up the Maple Leaf Trail, a 90-mile high route to heaven for the purist touring skier who wanted to get away from the crowds, which had begun to form even then. It was not long before there was more traffic on the Maple Leaf than on Drummond Street in Montreal. And rightly so, for it ran through the "Alouette Belt," stretching from the fringes of Montreal all the way to Mont Tremblant, highest peak in the Laurentians. "So near and yet so foreign" was the catch phrase to lure their skiing neighbors across the border. It was. It had a charming "habitant" atmosphere, inviting open slopes like so many in Europe, the dry snow, the frequent snow train with steaming coffee and yellow wicker seats with slots for your skis; Mrs. Marshall's boarding house in Shawbridge offering brown bread and beans and a friendly warmth; the many-colored habitant *fermes* in St. Sauveur smelling of maple logs and birch in the Quebec Heaters, pea soup, pork, *syrup érable,* mattresses of corn husks, and, always within reach, a lively pub offering quart bottles of stout Canadian ale. This was the fabric of early ski days north of the border.

Skiing in eastern Canada and the northeastern sections of the United States was not

Émile Cochand, hotel man and early promoter of Laurentian skiing, giving first ski lesson in the Laurentians (1911).

a matter of rivalry to be first. Rather, it was a pleasant situation of growing up together in an atmosphere of spirited rapport. When H. Percy Douglas borrowed ideas from the U.S. National Ski Association (founded in 1904) for helping the young and growing Canadian Amateur Ski Association (founded in 1921) to ward off the creeping taint of professionalism, Fred Harris down at Dartmouth College in Hanover, New Hampshire, was already outward bound from those winter dormitory blues. He had looked into the Montreal Ski Club (1904) and liked what he heard about their high boots, mackinaws, Hagen skis, Huitfeldt bindings, fur hats, tallow wax, telemark turns, and swing Christianias. In 1909 he wrote his letter to the college newspaper suggesting a "ski and snowshoe club." Half the boys on the campus voted "Aye!" The Dartmouth Outing Club was formed and exploded into the surrounding hills, which year by year called out Charles Proctor, the Durrances, the Bradleys, the Chivers, Johnny Litchfield, Percy Rideout, A. L. Washburn, Ted Hunter, and many other racing stars. Otto Schniebs and Walter Prager followed the dashing Colonel Dietrich and Gerry Rabb as coaches of the great Dartmouth ski teams. Dietrich's Hapsburg éclat, "Pleas, it vass a pleasur!"— Schniebs' "Vell, chentlemen, I'm going down now . . . it is not that ve vin the race, inschted dot ve ski it . . . ski, no fall . . . dot's the most important dinks of the dinks!" —Prager's "We take the schsteep schstuff schstraight—let's go—okay?"—all of this in the face of blue ice and 40-degree pitches on the Taft downhill run.

The skiing fever grew and grew. Indefatigable Roland Palmedo started the Williams Outing Club in 1915, and Williams College became a ski power among the small colleges. The United States Eastern Amateur Ski Association was formed at Saranac Lake in 1922. The Norsemen Ski Club, the Nansen Ski Club, the Amateur Ski Club of New York, and the Sno Birds of Lake Placid—the list goes on and on. Skiing had indeed come a long way from the days of the 1919 Dartmouth-McGill meet.

The real advent of skiing in America, however, waited until 1932, and it took America's obligation as the Winter Games host of that year to make it a reality. Even at that, the Great Depression almost caused cancellation of the '32 contest. But more than $1 million was raised to transform the upstate New York resort of Lake Placid into the Winter Games site.

In 1924, twenty-six countries participated in the founding of the Fédération Internationale de Ski (FIS). This organization persuaded the Olympic Games Committee to add competition in winter sports to the program. While the modern Olympic era began with the Summer Games at Athens in 1896, another twenty-eight years elapsed until the first Winter Games were staged at Chamonix, France, in 1924. Since then, the Winter Games have become a brilliant ornament in the Olympic tapestry, laced with great moments, drama, pageantry, and spectacular individual performances.

The first Winter Games got off to a modest start with a program that included cross-country skiing, jumping, skating, hockey, and a military ski race that probably was the forerunner of the present-day biathlon. This was also the Olympics in which an eleven-year-old girl named Sonja Henie skated her way to international fame, in the process getting the Winter Games off on a high note.

Norway, which was to dominate the Winter Games through the first seven Olympiads, swept virtually everything in sight at Chamonix. Thorleif Haug, that country's premier skier, won three gold medals and was acclaimed as a national hero.

When the Games moved to St. Moritz in 1928, the United States was represented by the grand total of three skiers. Reporting on the event at the time, the American coach sounded a now familiar refrain: "Perhaps in time we can win when our skiers develop to match the many generations of European developments, but today, except for grit and perseverance, we are outclassed. At every Olympic Games we learn much and grow better."

Grit it was indeed. Charles Proctor of Dartmouth suffered a badly injured knee, hobbled up the landing, and made sixth in the jumping. In the cross-country, the American trio distinguished themselves by taking the last three places. But the worst accident in 1928 was reserved for a Norwegian who jumped 43 meters on a 40-meter hill. His landing on the flat was crushing, but not fatal.

"There is growing in the International Ski Federation (FIS)," wrote an observer after the accident, "a definite movement to restrict championship jumps to a range of 50 meters for the best interests of the sport." Somewhere along the line, however, the movement ran off the trail. The size of the big jumping hill at Grenoble, France, in the 1968 Olympic was 90 meters. For the most part, the fledgling Winter Games were still suffering from growing pains.

The Olympic Committee, in settling on Lake Placid, New York, for the III Olympic Winter Games, found a well-established tradition of all-around winter sports—dating back to 1895. For it was that year which ended Melvil and Annie Godfrey Dewey's twelve-year search for what they termed "a vacation home characterized by simplicity, wholesome . . . and exceptional high standards, authoritatively maintained." These were the precepts of the Deweys in founding the Lake Placid Club, which in 1904–5 remained open for the winter and featured a program with what was billed "the sport of skiing, only recently imported from the Scandinavian countries," along with the already popular winter sports of skating, tobogganing, and snowshoeing. In this history-making decision to test out the possibilities of skiing as a resort type of recreational sport, the result was the birth of commercialized skiing in this country. With confidence in the venture, they imported forty pairs of hickory skis, fitted out with simple toestrap bindings, from Norway. The equipage included poles (one to a customer)—long, stout, and heavy. The instructions recommended their usage as a rudder. This, no doubt, is what kept the ladies leaning in favor of the toboggans for a time.

The Lake Placid Club "idea" was a success from the beginning, for the club has never missed a winter season. Even before World War I, it had become established as the leading winter-sports center of the United States. The ever-expanding facilities included, along with skiing, all other types of winter sports—even sail-skating and ice-boating.

After World War I, a new surge of interest in skiing brought about the formation of the Sno Birds of the Lake Placid Club in order to gain formal recognition of regional and national winter-sport regulator bodies. Through the agency of the Sno Birds, the Lake Placid Club expanded its program to include ski jumping, with additional construction of related facilities. As skiing grew, so did the need for regional organization. It was the Sno Birds who took a leading part in organizing the U.S. Eastern Amateur Ski Association. Veteran Sno Bird secretary Harry Wade Hicks became active in the National Ski Association. And it was with Sno Bird backing that Godfrey Dewey, son of the Lake Placid Club founder, performed the herculean job of securing the III Olympic Games for Lake Placid in 1932.

The 1932 Olympics *did* open on schedule and might have finished on schedule, too, had it not been for the bob run. Mild weather played havoc with the great icy curves, the long, steeply dropping straightaways. A week's extension granted by special approval of the International Committee solved this dilemma. The bobsled races were then run off as planned, and they proved to be one of the most exciting and colorful events of the entire schedule.

Who won the III Winter Olympics? When all was over, when the cheers and excitement had begun to subside, when the throng of spectators that included such notables as Rear Admiral Richard E. Byrd, Gene Tunney, and Mayor Jimmy Walker, such stalwarts of press and radio as Westbrook Pegler, O. O. McGeehan, Ted Husing, and Graham McNamee, were moving for the exits, the host country had scored a notable triumph. We—a nation thought to be relatively unfamiliar with winter sports—had garnered no fewer than six gold medals. Our best previous record—two at Chamonix in 1924.

United States speed skaters, led by nineteen-year-old Jack Shea of Lake Placid, a sophomore at Dartmouth in those days, had won two events—the 500-meter and the 1,500-meter races; his teammate Irving Jaffee accounted for two more by winning the 5,000-meter and the 10,000-meter races. American rules, the Europeans said angrily, gave us a big advantage, and the speed skat-

Governor Franklin D. Roosevelt of New York conducts the opening ceremonies at the 1932 Winter Olympics at Lake Placid.

ing produced the nearest thing to unpleasantness seen during the Games. Nevertheless, American rules—each man skating against every other man, rather than merely against the clock as is done abroad—prevailed. So did the final results.

So four of our six gold medals came from the speed skaters alone. It remained for the bobsledders to claim the others. Handsome, dark-haired Billy Fiske did his part when he piloted his big four-man sled to a thrilling victory at Mount Van Hoevenberg. Riding just behind Fiske was that renowned Rhodes scholar and former amateur heavyweight boxing champion of the world—Eddie Eagan. Behind Eagan, Clifford Gray; at the brakes, another internationalist, Jay O'Brien.

Our sixth gold medal? Another great performance, by an all-around sportsman— the late J. Hubert Stevens, one of the famed four Stevens brothers of Lake Placid, with his younger brother Curtis at the brakes, was entered in the event for two-man sleds. Four heats on two successive days. At the midway

point even his most ardent supporters were ready to count the United States entry as finished. The brilliant, daring Swiss youth— he was only eighteen at the time—Reto Capadrutt held a commanding lead. Some four and a half seconds! Bobsled races are won or lost in a mere fraction of that—a flick of an electric timer. But Hubert Stevens refused to admit defeat. The morning came for the final two heats. With all the skill, courage, and canny knowledge of the sport that he possessed, the Lake Placid racer came roaring down the treacherous icy chute. Once, twice, he slithered around the final curve, bounced across the finish line in a plume of snow and ice. When it was all over, when the accumulated times for both days were added, Hubert Stevens was the winner. Not only had he overcome Capadrutt's lead, but Stevens had added a winning margin of more than a full second over his Swiss rival. The two-man bobsled event was one of the great thrills of the Olympic program.

As everyone expected, the Scandinavians,

and especially the Norwegians, dominated the skiing events, although ending second to the United States in total points scored—77 for the stalwart sons and daughters from the land of the fjords. But in the United States the most far-reaching result of the 1932 Winter Olympics was the wave of interest and enthusiasm generated for winter sports—and especially for skiing—which is now benefitting millions of men, women, and children across the land.

SKIING IN THE THIRTIES

In 1929, several years before the boost from the 1932 Olympics at Placid, an enterprising young girl from Franconia, New Hampshire, by the name of Katherine Peckett, already had a small but enthusiastic fraternity of sports people climbing, schussing, falling, and clumsily performing their pioneering efforts to turn skis on American snow. Katherine Peckett had what might be called the first bona fide ski school in the United States, headed by Sig Buchmayr and Kurt Thalhammer, whom she lured to her Sugar Hill slopes from Europe. As Norman Vaughan in his book *Ski Fever* said, "Katherine Peckett of Franconia, New Hampshire, has perhaps contributed more to skiing in the United States than any other girl. She established the first large ski school, bringing expert instructors from Europe."

Sig Buchmayr and Kurt Thalhammer on the poster they made famous when they were the main attractions at Peckett's-on-Sugar-Hill, New Hampshire.

Sig Buchmayr, barely over five feet tall, literally turned backflips to get attention for skiing. He promoted races, performed in Madison Square and Boston Gardens, and fired literary salvos about his students at the *New York Times'* society pages. Above all, Buchmayr added a note of fashion to a sport which badly needed it. He always looked elegant whether performing on the borax slide at Saks Fifth Avenue or doing a jump turn on the Headwall at Tuckerman Ravine. But at Peckett's, and everywhere else at this time, skiers still had to herringbone, sidestep, or crawl uphill, woolly-suited and panting, to slide downhill.

After almost a century of struggling uphill, it took the inventive genius of a skier to come up with a mechanical device that would propel skiers back up the hill—if not effortlessly, then at least faster and less laboriously than had ever been possible before. It was simple, like so many great inventions, but it worked, and it changed the whole course of the sport's history overnight. It was called a *rope tow*.

The first patent on record was issued in 1932 to a young Swiss engineer (and skier) named Gerhard Mueller, who had tired of climbing a mountain near Zurich for his skiing. He came up with Switzerland's first usable ski tow, a contraption consisting mainly of a one-inch-diameter hemp rope and some old motorcycle parts. It soon became such an attraction among skiers that the hotel where it was installed was able to keep its doors open all winter and do a good business. Mueller went on to bigger and better lifts, and his firm of the same name has now built more than 500 lifts of various kinds at winter and summer resorts the world over.

In 1932 the first rope tow in North America appeared on Foster's Hill at Shawbridge, Canada, in the Laurentians; it was an

North America's first rope tow on Foster's Hill at Shawbridge, Canada.

old Dodge chassis, a series of pulleys and wheels, and a rope, spliced head to tail, running endlessly—or until the splice or motor broke, both of which were frequent occurrences in those days.

In 1934 the first American version appeared in Woodstock, Vermont, spawned by a former Dartmouth ski team captain, Bunny Bertram, in conjunction with the midwifery of Doug Burden and Robert Royce and the surgical skill of David Dodd, a sawmill mechanic. Royce was the owner of the White Cupboard Inn, and he proceeded to set up his infernal contraption on a sheep pasture belonging to a farmer named Gilbert, from whom he rented the land for $10. Gilbert's Hill thus became the Kitty Hawk of the American ski scene. A Model T Ford was jacked up and a grooved wheel set onto one rear wheel, with the other bolted down. The rope was 1,000 feet long, giving the skier a 500-foot ride. There were certain drawbacks—the rope was heavy (about one-inch manila), it was hard to hold if no other skiers were on the tow ahead of one, and it

persisted in twisting for reasons best known to itself. But these were minor problems compared to its tremendous potential. It offered its users up to ten times the amount of downhill running than had heretofore been possible—at a cost of $1 a day.

The news spread like wildfire. Woodstock soon found itself the boom town of American skiing, and for good reason. The terrain was a natural, with many round-topped hills, free of forests. Writing in the *British Ski Year Book* as long ago as 1932, Daniel L. Brown found such ideal skiing that he was moved to rave: ". . . there are plenty of ski tours around Woodstock that give an abundance of downhill, open-slope running and fairly open-wood running, something which is available to this extent in no other section east of the Rockies that I have visited."

Suicide Six at Woodstock is a name which has long held a fascination in skiers' imaginations. According to Bunny Bertram, who owned and operated the area until selling it to Laurance Rockefeller in 1961, the hill was originally designated simply as "Hill 6" on topographical maps. The word "Suicide" was added to pep it up and instantly became part of the skier's vocabulary. It drops 600 feet through islands of sugar maples at an average grade of 20 degrees with occasional drops of 45 degrees to end at Barnard Brook below. Like the Tuckerman Headwall, the bottom of the slope is invisible from the top.

Countless skiers remember it as the site of their first competitive lumps. Its proximity to Hanover proved to be a boon to Dartmouth College, and many of the Big Green greats trained here—Dick Durrance, Ted Hunter, Ed Wells, Charles McLane, and the like. Bunny used to amuse himself and others by running the rope at a fast clip—around 25 miles per hour—which would shorten the agonizing time it took to get to the top. It also had the side effect of spewing unwary skiers of low avoirdupois off into orbit at the top of the hill.

Bertram ran weekly time trials, a sort of wild downhill race with no control gates other than the start and the finish. Winners received metal pins in the shape of the numeral 6, and there were gold, silver, and bronze classifications. The spring was the best time, when the snow was just "corning" (crystallized snow). In the thirties a Gold 6 was as good as a diamond A-K in this neck of the woods. The wearer of such a pin was looked upon as one who had flouted death or, at the very least, risked personal injury and had come out a winner.

Rope tows were to skiing what Henry Ford's Model T was to the nation a couple of decades earlier; they provided a cheap, fairly reliable method of uphill transportation. The ubiquitous manila strands proliferated across the country like a spider web, all the way to the West Coast, where Jim Parker installed some on Mount Rainier and Mount Baker. Within a few years every ski slope worthy of the name had one or more of the infernal contraptions; Stevens Pass outside Seattle, which became known as the "eliminator system," put in six in a series, each faster and steeper than the last, and only the hardy survived. Wilmot Hills, just across the Wisconsin state line from Illinois, put in eleven, and this area soon became known as "The Alps of Chicago"—despite its 198-foot vertical drop! With rope tows rolling merrily from coast

to coast in the middle thirties, and cash registers clanging, the Eastern railroads (which in those days were interested in carrying passengers and offering extra services) came up with the happy idea of "snow trains." Their first effort chugged as far north as Norfolk, Connecticut, on January 27, 1935, and was deemed a moderate success, considering that no uphill facilities were available. The fare was certainly reasonable: $2.00 round trip. The very next month the officials of the New York, New Haven & Hartford ordered an all-out attack on New England. Pittsfield, Massachusetts, was to be the target area. Price: $2.00 round trip. No tows were available there yet, either, but the open slopes of a farmer named Clarence J. Bousquet beckoned—and they were bigger than Norfolk's. As the long train snorted to a stop on a little-used siding at the edge of this city, some 3,000 natives gawked in ill-concealed amazement at 447 fledgling skiers. Special buses, private cars, and even horse-drawn sleighs were pressed into service to take the skiers to the nearby farm of Bousquet, a husky entrepreneur who, after a busy career in numerous fields, had settled down to raising mink and cutting logs on his Tamarack Road property. Here the big-city visitors cavorted all day to the point of exhaustion as some of the grinning townspeople lined the trails and slopes to watch. But after that historic day, Claire Bousquet, as he was known to his legions of friends, took a long, hard look at his minks and weighed them against the skiers. The skiers showed the most potential, and that summer he hustled to Woodstock, Vermont, to study the pioneer rope tows in that community. By the start of the 1935–36 season, he had constructed his own version, with many improvements. Each year saw additional trails, slopes, and tows until Bousquet's had the East's highest capacity with seven rope tows at the start of World War II.

As operator of Claire and Charlie's Sporting Goods Store in Pittsfield with his three brothers, Claire Bousquet soon added a ski shop and a branch at his ski area, and Charlie Parker, former Amherst College coach who was largely responsible for the introduction of modern skiing in the Berkshires, was engaged as ski instructor. "I charged a dollar a head," Parker recalled, "and I taught from

Snow trains did a great deal to popularize skiing in the thirties.

seventy-five to one hundred persons on a good day and that wasn't hay, brother!"

The indomitable snow trains continued to feed into Eastern ski areas, and on Washington's Birthday, 1937, the snow trains hauled 3,000 skiers from Grand Central Station to the Berkshires. On February 1 and 2, 1942, six snow trains from New York and Boston dumped 12,000 skiers into northwest Massachusetts, where the natives were now too busy working at the ski resorts to laugh. All told, the New York, New Haven & Hartford Railroad alone hauled nearly 40,000 skiers on one-day trips to the Berkshires between 1935 and 1942, when the war ended the junkets. Accordionists played rollicking ski songs as the trains lumbered north, and early-day versions of the "schlitzen-frug" were danced in the narrow aisles. A group of New Yorkers formed the Ski-Dreiverin Club in honor of their habitual revels in the third car from the front and elected all ninety charter members "vice-presidents." Unfortunately the war years ended the snow trains, and they never resumed again. The Berkshires turned into one vast snowmaking machine, served by pomalifts, T-bars, and chair lifts. Places like Catamount and Jiminy

Peak boomed, and though the character changed, no one can say the Berkshires were bypassed with the passing of the snow trains.

But even before the end of the snow-train era, the 1930's saw racing history in the making in the Berkshires. Mount Greylock, just outside of Williamstown, Massachusetts, climbs to the highest elevation (3,491 feet) in Massachusetts. The Mount Greylock Club helped lay out the great Thunderbolt racing trail down the steep face of the mountain. The Taft trail at Franconia and the Thunderbolt were at that time the only trails developed solely for racing.

In 1938 the Eastern Downhill Championships were held on Thunderbolt, Mount Greylock, and this event claimed an astounding record of spectator interest. Six thousand ski enthusiasts climbed the steep pitches to watch the University of Munich's visiting ski team battle it out with the Dartmouth team and other top racers. Munich's Fritz Demhel won the race, with Dartmouth's Ted Hunter, second, and Dick Durrance, fifth.

Owing to pressures from conservation supporters all blueprints to date for lift development on Greylock have been blocked, and no important national races have been held since old Greylock's days of glory in the 1930's. But locals and others who remember the great potential of her terrain still hope things will one day pull together and bring this great mountain into the limelight it deserves in Eastern recreational skiing and in the racing circuit.

It was inevitable that skiers would soon begin to look for a more comfortable way of cheating the law of gravity. In 1936 a tall Wisconsin skier and jumper named Fred Pabst invented the J-bar, which cradled the posterior of a skier and let him or her ride to the top in comparative comfort. This was the same year that some nonskiing engineers of the Union Pacific were busy developing the world's first chair lift for the as yet unbuilt Sun Valley.

In many ways, Sun Valley was a generation ahead of its time. Certainly, when it was built by the Union Pacific Railroad in 1936, it startled the fledgling American ski scene, springing full grown out of an isolated Idaho sheep pasture. For a quarter of a century it was regarded by many as the queen of them all.

The adventure came to an end for the Union Pacific in 1964, when they sold their multi-million-dollar queen dowager—lock, stock, and chair lifts—to the Janss Corporation of Los Angeles. It was the end of an era —and the beginning of a new future for "The Valley"—as Bill Janss, no stranger to skiing, immediately announced plans to invest upwards of $30 million in the rejuvenation of the world-famous resort. Writing in a reminiscent vein at the time of the sale, Dorice Taylor, longtime member of Sun Valley's public relations department, described its conception, birth, and early years of glory:

> The success of Sun Valley was assured by its first blueprints. When Averell Harriman, then chairman of the board of the Union Pacific railroad, sent an Austrian Alpine expert, Count Felix Schaffgotsch, West to locate the spot for America's— in fact, the world's—first resort built primarily for winter sports, there were no strings attached. He had the entire West to choose from.
>
> His six-weeks' odyssey took him to Mount Rainier, Mount Hood, the San Bernardino Mountains, Yosemite, the area around Salt Lake City and around Lake Tahoe. He saw many places in Colorado and crossed the Teton Pass in winter in a sleigh for a view of Jackson Hole. One by one, he turned these places down as—too high—too windy—too near a city—too remote from a railroad—too many weekend skiers.
>
> He knew what the great resorts of Europe had to offer and he wasn't going to stick his noble neck out and select a place unless, after a million or so had been spent, it would measure up.
>
> He had seen the eastern part of Idaho and was on his way back to tell Harriman that he had not found a spot, when someone remembered Ketchum.
>
> Ketchum, a village a mile from where Sun Valley would be built, had been a boomtown in the mining days of the 1880's and at one time had a population of 2,000.
>
> In 1936 the population, with many residents hard hit by the Depression, had declined to 270. In wintertime half that number left the valley. The road was not plowed and the only communication with the outside world was by the little train that twice a week puffed up the branch line from Shoshone.
>
> It was in a blizzard late on the afternoon of January 19 that the Count, escorted by a Union Pacific representative and the county supervisor of roads, reached this hamlet in the wake of the county snowplow.
>
> After about three days, word began to get around that the stranger in town was an Austrian count and that he was skiing on the surrounding hills every day to select a place for a million-dollar hotel.
>
> The reaction of Jack Lane, one of the town's prominent sheepmen, when someone phoned the news to him at his lambing headquarters south of Shoshone, was typical. "Don't cash any of his checks," he said.
>
> When a mile north of Ketchum the Count found the little windless basin, surrounded by treeless, sun-drenched slopes and with great wooded Baldy Mountain towering at the end of the valley, he wrote Harriman, "It contains more delightful features than any other place I have seen in the U.S., Switzerland or Austria for a winter sports center." Harriman arrived ten days later in his private car and Ketchum stopped laughing.

The Union Pacific purchased 4,300 acres, and on this vast, snow-covered area, like a blank piece of paper, the architects set out to write the name "Sun Valley" into ski history. They had perfect terrain and they had what was almost a blank check to work with, for everything was to be uncompromisingly "the best." Almost $3 million were spent in the first two years on the original installations at a time just after the Depression when a million was a million.

It was the engineers of the Union Pacific Railroad, lacking any previous experience with skiing, who designed and built the first chair lifts in the world. While most of the engineering department was busy on adaptations of means of uphill transportation already in use—rope tows, J-bars, and cable cars—one young engineer went off on a tangent. Jim Curran, now chief bridge engineer of the railroad, had had experience in building trams for loading bananas in the tropics. He saw that handling a skier and a bunch of bananas presented much the same problem. If, on a monocable, he could re-place the hooks (that carried the bunches of bananas) with chairs, he would have a comfortable and fast lift for skiers. When he presented his plan, his superiors vetoed it. "Too hazardous."

Sometime later the famous old-time Dartmouth skier, Charlie Proctor, who had been called in as a consultant, stopped in Omaha. Curran had a call to bring in "all" the plans. He took this as authority to slip his pet plan back into the pile. When the blueprint for the chair lift came into view, the chief engineer frowned and flipped it over. His flip wasn't fast enough. Sun Valley got its chair lifts. One on 6,780-foot Dollar Mountain and one on 7,500-foot Proctor.

Sun Valley's Ski School began with five Austrian ski instructors, hand-picked by Count Schaffgotsch and headed by Hans Hauser, three times Austrian champion. Under Sigi Engl, also a former Austrian champion but one of the true executives in the world's ski schools, the staff has increased to more than 75 instructors. Proof of the quality of the ski school is that 85 per cent of the

One of the first two chair lifts in the world was built at Sun Valley in 1936.

Dick Durrance receiving the first Harriman Cup from Mrs. Averell Harriman, 1937.

that made "ski bum" a fashionable phrase, with its farsighted policy—new at the time —of allowing its employees free lift passes and a certain amount of spare time during the workday to ski. Many a good skier got his or her start by working as a busboy in the Challenger Inn or a waitress at Trail Creek. It was Sun Valley that held the first East-West college meet over Christmas, 1937, when a formidable Dartmouth team that included Dick Durrance, Steve Bradley, Warren Chivers, and John Litchfield defeated a strong University of Washington squad.

Competition was very much a part of Averell Harriman's creed, and he fostered it in every way. He built a beautiful jumping hill and served it with a chair lift, which also serviced a long, perfectly graded slalom slope. He donated a silver bowl for an annual race, and the Harriman Cup races became a traditional event—and the most important one—on the American racing calendar until 1965 when it was discontinued. Many of the great names in ski racing the world over won this traditional event.

guests—experts and beginners—ski in the school.

It was Sun Valley that helped to develop some of North America's great racers like Gretchen Fraser, Shirley McDonald, Clarita Heath, Grace Lindley, Nancy Reynolds, Wendy Cram, Barney McLean, Ernie Mc-Cullough, and many more. It was Sun Valley

More people raced in those days, and the weekly running of the Diamond Races over a fixed course on Mount Baldy drew large crowds of contestants and spectators. Those who finished within certain prescribed time limits were entitled to wear silver, gold, or "diamond" pins, and wear them they did, with pride. Gretchen Fraser won the first diamond pin ever awarded to a woman and went on to win the first gold medal ever won by an American skier in the Olympics.

EARLY SKI TECHNIQUES

By bringing more people to skiing, the lifts also changed the condition of the snow. Whereas one major run a day used to be par, four, five, or more runs were the rule with a lift. The resulting traffic packed down the runs, requiring new technical skills on the part of the skier. Changes in equipment also were important. Steel edges had just been extended from the tip to tail of the ski. Kandahar cable bindings had replaced Bildstein's heel spring. The hooks of the Kandahar cables were set back toward the heel, tying the heel down so that skiers could lean

forward. These inventions doubled the average speed for standard ski runs. Skiers were no longer afraid of speed. Never before— or since—in the history of Alpine skiing has there been so much progress made in two or three winters as in the winters of 1935 to 1936.

The developments permitted unprecedented control over the skis, and the result was the introduction of new ski-teaching techniques. The first was proposed by two Austrians, Dr. F. Hoschek and Friedl Wolfgang. They rejected the snowplow and the stem in favor of the "direct way to swing-ing," emphasizing shoulder rotation and up-ward unweighting. This approach would not have caused the sensation it did had it not been for the racing successes of Anton (Toni) Seelos, an Austrian ski instructor. Actually, Seelos revolutionized slalom tech-nique by skiing the way Hoschek and Wolf-gang advocated. He was so far ahead of his time that his slalom victories by 10 seconds or more were not at all unusual. Because of his superiority in this event, the rules were rigged in such a way that he could not (al-ways) also win the combined; in figuring combined, downhill was worth about one-third more than the slalom. Seelos' technique was characterized by upward unweighting, rotation and vorlage, and most important of all, parallel skis throughout the turn.

The Hoschek-Wolfgang-Seelos ideas had a cool reception in Austria, but struck a re-sponsive chord in France, then emerging as a major ski power in Europe. Seelos was brought to Chamonix, where he coached the French team, which under the leadership of Émile Allais and Paul Gignoux further re-fined the parallel technique. It differed from the Austrian version primarily by unweight-ing with a down-and-forward motion and by what is called the ruade, a lifting of the tails of the skis in a horse-kick-type motion.

Even while rotational skiing was reaching its peak, a small but prophetic group of Swiss and Austrian ski technicians were de-veloping a parallel system based on counter-rotation—that is, the twisting of the upper body in a direction opposite to the legs and skis. The system was invented by the Austri-ans, Toni Ducia and Kurt Reindl, and by the Swiss, Giovanni Testa and Dr. Eugen Mat-thias. Ducia and Reindl published their counterrotational thesis, *Le Ski d'Aujour-d'hui,* in France in 1935. Testa and Matthias published their first edition of *Naturliches Skilaufen* (Natural Skiing) in Munich the following year.

Going through Matthias's and Testa's book, you find the familiar comma position demonstrated by a skier with a plumbline on a cap mounted on his head. (Somewhere through the years this analogy was lost.) Comma, as advocated by Matthias, was an

Austrian Toni Seelos was the unchallenged master of slalom in the mid-thirties. His tech-nique was characterized by parallel skis through-out the turn.

asymmetrical position discussed in countless battles by the most able ski theorists of that time. Their consensus was that the asymmet-rical position was the best position to take, whenever possible. An expert named Buyten-dijk explained: "The asymmetrical position is assumed for two reasons; first, we are subconsciously striving for the propriocep-tively most comfortable position and second, we are striving for the most stable position." Matthias used an analogy: a traversing skier is like a skier who has a rope tied around his waist. The rope (representing centrifugal force) is being pulled down the slope. If the skier wants to resist the pull, the asym-metrical position with the upper ski ahead is the one in which he could most easily do so.

Despite important slalom victories by Ru-dolf Rominger, who became the world's best slalom racer with the Matthias-Testa tech-nique, an attempt made to institute reverse shoulder of so-called St. Moritz school just before World War II was only partially suc-cessful. The emphasis of the day was too greatly on pure parallel, and counterrota-

Émile Allais was one of the forerunners of the French rotational technique.

tion still based its beginning maneuvers on the passé stem and snowplow.

In the thirties Émile Allais, fresh from his triumph as a racer in international competition, introduced his "French technique." His technique consisted of gathering speed before a turn, then just before making the turn rolling forward on the tips of the skis while rotating the body in the direction of the turn and contracting the stomach muscles to lift the heels off the snow. The skis could then be easily twisted in the desired direction. The method was tried and had a brief rage, but it was too difficult for the average skier.

At first we in the United States stabbed wildly at the sport—tasting the fun, the exuberance, the beauty. We had learned to get to the slopes by way of the riotous snow trains and to get to the top by way of sundry lethal contraptions, but we were still bashing and crashing our way downhill, more horizontal than vertical 90 per cent of the time. Except for the small, fortunate groups exposed to the Austrian boys at Peckett's, Erling Strom at Placid, and Otto Schniebs at Dartmouth, ski technique was a phrase alien to all of us. And so when the first disciples of technique trickled in from Europe, they found a ready seedbed for their teaching systems and we

followed them with a trusting eagerness approaching adoration. Schneider, Rybizka, Foeger, Ruschp, Buchmayr, Lang, Pfeifer, and others from Austria, and Prager, Iselin, Thorner, and Loosli from Switzerland, were some of the first who formed the ski school line-ups from coast to coast.

On February 11, 1939, Hannes Schneider, no longer welcome in his native, Nazi-annexed Austria, stepped off the train at North Conway, New Hampshire, into the infant world of American skiing. It is easy in retrospect to smile at the almost childlike faith American skiers (and they were far from alone in the ski countries of the world) had in Schneider. But then, few can remember the impact he made on the sport, even before it was really recognized as such. It was an impact to be made only once. Schneider had that rare combination of vision, analytical ability, leadership, and horse sense which enabled him almost single-handedly to change the character of skiing from a gingerly used tool of the winter mountaineer to a sport in its own right.

Zdarsky, Bilgeri, and their compatriots, although they evolved such turns as the stem, also had a strong aversion to speed (*gefaerlich*) and therefore developed such maneuvers as the *Schenkelsitzbremse* (which was as ghastly as it sounds) for unavoidable steeper pitches. Schneider's particular contribution was to liberate skiing from this strait jacket and to develop the technique that made controlled high-speed skiing possible. But ingenuity and an original turn of mind were not the only Schneider attributes. Alice Kiaer, who herself performed prodigious feats of leadership in developing the American women's ski team to the point where it brought home important silverware with regularity, called Schneider "a natural leader." Others rightly called him "the father of modern skiing." He was a father figure in more ways than one. He would chastise his students like children, even if the object of his wrath happened to be King Albert of Belgium. His instructors were subject to and dispensers of a discipline which gave the ski instructor, particularly the Austrian ski instructor, a unique status in the world of sport.

In Schneider's scheme of things, the instructor was king of the slopes, the dispenser of mountain wisdom, the ultimate authority on questions of ski technique. In the dawn of American skiing, he was. And having gained his status on the strength of the Arlberg system and mystique, he was not about to let heretics spoil a good thing. Not only he, but his students as well, preached the gospel according to St. Anton (Austria). Even in Schneider's last years (he died in 1955), when pure Arlberg was in steep decline, Rick Earle, one of Schneider's first American instructors, recalls his "personal magnetism" which made disciples out of all of those who came into contact with him. In trying to analyze the compelling Schneider personality, he recalls that "Hannes had to call us only once. It was enough." Today, thanks to Hannes, the snow has only to fall once—and millions heed the call of the mountains.

Hannes Schneider in no small measure owed his touching welcome at North Conway to those of his lieutenants who had made the long journey from the Alps to *Amerika* before him. Like evangelists, they crisscrossed the land, and Arlberg was the word. But the first Arlberger to come to the United States was not a native of the Arl-

Otto Eugen Schniebs—"Skiing is a way of life"—was one of the strongest disciples of Hannes Schneider.

berg, nor did he plan to become a ski instructor. Otto Schniebs' intentions may have been to come here as a watchmaker, but his niche proved to be in making thousands believe that, indeed, skiing is "a vay uf life."

Schniebs learned to ski while hauling a mortar around the Alps as a mountain trooper in World War I ("Dot's not hexectly schporrt, I can dell you!"), later fell under the Schneider spell, and then ran his own ski school in Bavaria. He could ski and teach skiing, let there be no doubt about that, but more important, he was a super-salesman for the sport—in his own inimitable way.

Today the charms of skiing are extensively expounded in newspapers, magazines, movies, and television. Schniebs had no such support. Only one who could tell Smith College girls in all innocence that "I am here tonight to tell you how to do it and how not to do it . . . on skis" could get people to go out into the New England winters to see for themselves what was going on in those hills. Schniebs, although not the first European instructor, was the prototype for all those who were to

Four of the better-known European ski instructors who helped make skiing popular in the United States. Top, left to right: Friedl Pfeifer and Luggi Foeger. Bottom, left to right: Fred Iselin and Walt Prager.

follow in his footsteps. He imbued American skiing with its characteristic Austro-Bavarian flavor which it retains to this day; to fracture the English language into a telling aphorism was as important as knowing how to ski. If nothing else, he certainly created a demand for instructors in controlled skiing à la Arlberg.

After the mid-thirties, with "Ben' ze knees" something of a national rallying cry, the trickle turned into a stream. It was almost as if Hannes Schneider had staked out the country and had awarded franchises to the most faithful of his disciples. Benno Rybizka went to North Conway and the Eastern Slope; Luggi Foeger, to Yosemite; Otto Lang, to Mount Rainier; Friedl Pfeifer, to Sun Valley; Sepp Ruschp, to Stowe. These men were more than superb skiers. They were truly great teachers who could impart more with

a well-timed "Do like so, ja!" than months of dubbing around without such help. But not all of the European ski instructors were Austrians. Switzerland sent its share, including Hans Thorner, Walt Prager, and Fred Iselin.

There were, however, many European skiing instructors who were not too competent. These were the ones who gave rise to the phrase "Bend zee knees, two dollars pleez." In 1937 skepticism about American ski instruction had developed to the point where the Eastern Amateur Ski Association ordered the first certification examinations held in the United States. These were conducted at Suicide Six at Woodstock in February, 1938. Of the seventeen candidates who took this certification examination, only six passed, "showing all too clearly," as reported by certification chairman Ford K. Sayre, "that many of those now giving instruction need further training in skiing as well as in teaching." The certification idea spread rapidly, but did not really solve the problem of instruction. This was because no attempt was made to establish a unified system of ski instruction. The only requirement for certification was that an instructor demonstrate skiing competence in his chosen technique, plus an ability to explain it to his students. Each technique, or system, had its own group of advocates. Prager and Thorner, for instance, taught the traditional Swiss method. Fritz Loosli was an early advocate of the all-parallel school of Émile Allais. Hans Georg and Louis Cochand had brought over the reverse shoulder of St. Moritz school. But despite these various heresies, Schneider's Arlberg method was still *the* accepted standard of good technique. His disciples— Rybizka, Pfeifer, Foeger, and Lang—were not only excellent skiers and fine teachers but also highly articulate, and their message during this early era of technique confusion was upheld by the majority of American skiers.

Actually, the years leading up to World War II were vigorous ones in America for the lusty infant called skiing. They were the years of the great Dartmouth ski team under Walt Prager which swept away all opposition, East and West, and even invaded Chile and New Zealand. Names like Dick Durrance, the Bradleys, the Chivers, et al. became household words in the ski fraternity. The United States sent its first downhill and slalom teams to the Winter Olympics at Garmisch-Partenkirchen, where except for Dick Durrance they made absolutely no impression whatsoever, but Alice Kiaer's "Red Stockings" team of American girl skiers let the world know that America, although still far behind, had every intention and capability of catching up fast. On the home front Americans were dreaming up Bunyanesque races like the Silver Skis down Mount Rainier and the Inferno down Mount Washington.

In 1925, the Fédération Internationale de Ski—the world-wide ruling body of skiing that was founded in 1910—held its first international ski competition. Up to 1930, the FIS World Championships were restricted to Nordic events; from then on, Alpine events were included. Except during 1928 and 1932, they were held annually until 1939. Since World War II, World Championships have been held only in even-numbered years between Olympics.

In 1936, the United States, for the first time, decided to send a full team of skiers to compete against the seasoned Europeans in the IV Winter Olympics at Garmisch-Partenkirchen. Also for the first time, slalom and downhill competition—known as Alpine events—were to be included.

However, United States Alpine skiers were regarded at that time as completely unproven and were ranked below the flatlanders of England, Holland, and Belgium. Members of the United States men's team were selected informally on the basis of their results in the previous spring's National Championships at Mount Rainier in Washington, where Robert Livermore of Boston was second in the combined. He did not even know that he was selected until that fall when he received a certificate signed by Avery Brundage, perennial president of the United States Olympic Committee.

If the Depression almost interfered with the 1932 Games, a far more ominous roadblock had appeared by 1936. It was the black-mustached countenance of Adolf Hitler. With Berlin selected as the site of the 1936 Summer Olympiad, Germany's mountain resort of Garmisch-Partenkirchen, in the Bavarian Alps, won approval as the Winter Games locale. But Germany did not win approval at all among many outstanding liberals around the world. In an anti-Hitler article in *The Nation* in 1935, Heywood Broun advocated that America boycott the '36 Games. The Committee on Fair Play in Sports in New York issued a statement against American participation entitled "Preserve the Olympic Ideal." Westbrook Pegler waxed furious. The skiing team ran short of money because of the controversy. When the Winter Games were about to open, an observer wrote: "Thousands of troops and brownshirts in khaki uniforms, armed with shovels with which they presented arms on every and any occasion, roamed the streets. The S.S. Black Guard was very much in evidence."

Yet despite the opposition, the Garmisch-Partenkirchen Games developed into the biggest staged up to then. More than 1,000 athletes from 28 nations participated. The United States team boasted 90 members; Germany, 143. Each day brought 75,000 visitors, mostly from Munich. (In comparison, the 1968 games at Grenoble, France, had a daily visitor list of about 7,000.) The jumping event alone attracted 150,000 onlookers. Chancellor Hitler himself declared the IV Olympic Winter Games open as snow fell in blinding flurries.

From those with a less acute understanding of the Fascist threat, the Germanic efficiency at the '36 Games at least brought grudging admiration. Wrote skiing manager Joel Hildebrand after the Games: "I believe the decision to participate in the Winter Games was wise. If we refused to participate for the sake of political protest which could not possibly have the desired effect, then other nations would, in the future, avoid the United States because we are not always above reproach, and so the Olympic Games would come to an end and one of the few existing opportunities would be destroyed for young people to learn that young people in other countries are mostly rather decent and not eager to go to war against them, despite

any propaganda of their governments and munitions makers."

Whatever America's young winter athletes may have learned about the political feelings of their contemporaries from other lands, they got an incisive lesson in winter sports. Norway swept the affair; host Germany was second. Only in bobsledding did the United States win a gold medal.

In 1936, the downhill and the slalom became official Olympic events for the first time. Describing the pre-Games prospect, a writer for *Collier's* said: "If we should happen to win the downhill race it will probably be because at a critical point some wild Indian forgets about telemarks and christianias, kicks his skis downhill and lets it rip."

In fact, America's Dick Durrance, who also acted as coach for the United States skiers, registered a commendable tenth place in the combined. The event was won by two Germans: Christel Cranz and Franz Pfnür. But probably the most dramatic competition of the games was provided by Birger Ruud, the most successful of three brothers who were Norway's top ski family for a decade. Birger was not only an outstanding jumper; to this day he is the only competitor who has

The 1936 Winter Olympics at Garmisch-Partenkirchen marked the first time that the Alpine events had been incorporated in the games. Franz Pfnür of Germany won the combined event that year.

won Olympic events in both Nordic and Alpine disciplines. This unusual feat took place in the 1936 Olympics, when he won the downhill over highly touted German, French, and Austrian racers and then went on to win the jumping. Unfortunately, no gold medal was given for the downhill event that year. (Only winners of the Alpine combined received medals, and Ruud finished fourth.) But Ruud holds the Winter Olympic longevity record, at least as far as medal winners are concerned. He won his first medal in 1932, a gold for jumping, then repeated in 1936 as noted above. He was still good enough in 1948 to win a silver medal, also in jumping.

In the IV Winter Games, Betty Woolsey led the American girls with a fourteenth in the downhill, while Clarita Heath, Helen Boughton, and Leigh and Mary Bird were in the last bracket. But in 1937, American women had made rapid strides under the managership of Alice Kiaer. Clarita Heath and Marion McKean could be counted upon to finish in the top ten in any European race they entered. Miss Heath was fourth in the World Championship downhill, fourth in slalom, and fourth in the combined. The following year, Miss McKean was sixth in the World Championship downhill and eighth in the combined.

While tilting at the windmills of skiing abroad, Americans were also jumping on our steeds and running off in all directions at home. It was the age of bash and crash, and hell bent. New races were being dreamed up, and there were plenty of takers. One of the most famous was the "Silver Skis" on Mount Rainier in the Pacific Northwest.

Like its Eastern counterpart, Mount Washington's "Inferno," it spawned legends of daring deeds—and they were that. In 1936 Otto Lang, one of Hannes Schneider's disciples who taught skiing for three years in the Pacific Northwest, told a newspaper correspondent, "It certainly holds a unique position in America's racing courses. It is without any doubt the fastest and longest course, although it may not be technically the most difficult. But what it demands more than anything else is courage and stamina. The stretches to relax are few and the going is sometimes rough when the wind has blown

and built up rolling waves." However, it says something for the hardiness of the Pacific Northwest variety of the breed that the first Silver Skis in 1934 didn't wipe out the few practitioners who could honestly call themselves skiers.

"All races on the Silver Skis program," the race instructions directed, "will use the simultaneous start. Skier Number-One will line up at the extreme left of the line looking down the slope. Number-Two shall be immediately on his right and so on. On the starting line competitors shall line up at least one yard apart."

If you said "geschmozzle start" before finishing the above paragraph, you are a genuine old-timer. Only four years later, this type of start belonged to ancient history.

Meanwhile, back in the high Sierras of California, another race of a different sort was being brewed. Soon after the Sugar Bowl was opened to the skiing public in 1939, John Wiley, co-founder of the Bowl with Hannes Schroll, received a telephone call from San Francisco lawyer Sherman Chickering, one of the original investors. He said he had stumbled upon an old copy of *Crofutt's New Overland Tourist and Pacific Coast Guide,* published in 1883, which had a description of an old California ski-racing event way back in 1854. Then he quoted from the description: "In Sierra County, California, where snow often falls to a depth of ten or twelve feet, the snow-skate is a great favorite, becoming a source of pleasant recreation on moon-lit evenings—visits from ten to fifteen miles being made after tea and returning the same evening. Here, too, snow-skating forms one of the most popular pastimes—racing. A belt, studded and set with silver, becomes the prize of the successful racer." Before the telephone conversation was over, they both agreed it would be a great idea to revive the "belt" race and call it the Silver Belt Trophy.

The first Silver Belt was held in April, 1940, on Mount Lincoln. The first winners were Friedl Pfeifer and Gretchen Fraser. Through the years the annual meet was turned into a renowned ski-racing classic. Many skiing greats such as Alf Engen, Christian Pravda, Buddy Werner, Clarita Heath, Starr Walton, and Linda Meyers have become the proud owners of the coveted silver belts. As a matter of tradition, the Silver Belt was a spring race, usually held a week after Easter. Some say it was a sporting excuse for the season's last blast. The racing was serious, but all else that went with it was gay, lusty springtime fun. The Silver Belt was continued until the 1971 season but was then dropped from regular racing schedules because of the lateness in the season. The last official winners of the Silver Belt were Pat Simpson and Cheryl Bechdolt.

Ski jumping was popular in the thirties, and no single ski jumper ever caught the public fancy as did Torger Tokle, who came from Norway in 1939 and, after shattering hill records from coast to coast, died for his adopted country in World War II.

Only a few hours after his arrival in New York City in January, 1939, Tokle was inducted into the Norway Ski Club of Brooklyn and rushed to nearby Bear Mountain, where he was entered in the Class B competition. Riding his borrowed skis with a style and a vigor which immediately set him apart, Tokle not only won the Class B event but outjumped the whole field in Class A.

In four seasons of competition, Tokle won an unparalleled 42 of the 48 tournaments in which he competed, breaking no fewer than 24 hill records. Tokle dominated the field, but he also brought the competitive level to a new high as American jumpers like Alf Engen, Harold Sorensen, Mezzy Barber, and Arthur Devlin were spurred to greater heights. In Tokle's first season here, he clashed head-on with Reidar Andersen, renowned Norwegian and Holmenkollen champ at the Eastern Championships in Laconia, New Hampshire. Although not as stylish as the older man, Tokle's powerful takeoff and his ability to get the last bit of ride gave him longer flights and a tie for first place with the great Andersen.

Tokle was beaten by a Norwegian airman from the Little Norway training camp in Canada for the 1942 National and Eastern titles, but in Lake Placid and in Brattleboro, he put even more fire into his performances and beat his rivals soundly both times.

At Brattleboro in early 1942, he also retired the famed Winged Trophy. And at Iron Mountain, Michigan, he added another foot to his American record with a jump of 289 feet.

Tokle, along with thousands of other skiers, joined the United States Army. In October, 1942, he was assigned to the ski troops of the 87th Regiment. There was no time for jumping or public adulation, and Tokle skied with a heavy pack and rifle on his shoulders and was promoted to sergeant. In the spring of 1945, the 87th Regiment was locked in mountain warfare with the Germans in the Italian Apennines. Leading his men into action on March 3, at the battle for Monte Terracia, Tokle was killed by enemy machine-gun fire. As a lasting tribute to this great and beloved jumper, the Norway Ski Club established a Torger Tokle Memorial Trophy for the annual competition of the National Jumping Championships. The trophy is housed in the National Ski Museum in Ishpeming, Michigan.

North American skiing made impressive strides in the 1936 to 1940 period. In spite of technique confusion, thousands were learning to ski under competent instructors. Major lift installations were built at such locations as Mont Tremblant (Quebec), Belknap (New Hampshire), Alta (Utah), and Sugar Bowl (California), and hundreds of rope tows were installed on less imposing slopes in every snow region of the United States. And American ski racers were improving steadily, too. An excellent group, led by Dick Durrance, planned to go to the FIS World Championships in Norway in 1940. As it turned out, most of them, as well as hundreds of others, volunteered for the ski troops instead.

"WE CLIMB TO CONQUER"

Wherever skiers gather, the words "Tenth Mountain" are sure to be heard, for its members and its fame have spread far and wide across the ski world. Pete Siebert at Vail, Friedl Pfeifer at Aspen, Bud Phillips at Mad River, Ralph Townsend at Williams

. . . the list could go on and on, and it reads like the *Who's Who* of skiing. It was an elite group, with great loyalty; at their recent twentieth reunion at Vail, more than 1,000 showed up. Yet because of wartime censorship, their brilliant battle record is still little known to the outside world. Often one hears the question, "Did they ever use the ski troops in World War Two?"

Did they ever! To quote one of their famous songs, put on your "ninety pounds of rucksack, and a pound of grub or two, and we'll schuss the mountain like our daddy used to do."

The rapid-strike capabilities of the Finnish patrols in the Russo-Finnish War made a deep impression on certain tacticians in the U.S. War Department. In the bitter winter of 1939–40, the Finns, taking maximum advantage of the mobility of skis, were able to bring the Russian army to a complete halt, using hit-and-run raids on vulnerable supply and communications lines. Not until the snow left the ground were the Russians able to bring superior fire and manpower to bear and to break the Finnish resistance. With these thoughts in mind, Charles Minot Dole, who had formed the National Ski Patrol System in 1938, approached some United States Army officers at Governor's Island in June, 1940. His plan: to mobilize the skiers of America into a highly trained winter striking force, using the 3,000 members of the National Ski Patrol as a nucleus. He was promptly advised to take his ideas to Washington, D.C., where the subject was treated, in his own words, "with polite derision." Dole persisted, however, and received an appointment with Chief of Staff General George C. Marshall. This far-seeing man admitted that the Army was weak in winter warfare, and in the fall of 1940 sent two colonels from his staff up to New York for further discussions with Dole.

A year later the 87th Infantry Mountain Regiment was activated at Fort Lewis, Washington—the first tangible evidence that "Minnie" Dole's work had borne fruit. Shortly thereafter the National Ski Patrol System was hired by the War Department to recruit picked men for this new outfit—the first time in American history that a civilian agency had been given full military recruit-ing powers. The 87th's objective: to train men for mountain warfare, in winter and in summer.

With funds available at last, the National Ski Patrol System headquarters moved out of Dole's Greenwich, Connecticut, residence and into a New York office. "Immediate Action" bulletins went out from the War Department to the commanding generals of the various armies training within the United States, informing them of this unprecedented liaison and "directing development of this relationship with local patrolmen to the end that national defense receive the full benefit and technical knowledge of the patriotic civilians concerned."

Under the command of Colonel Onslow S. Rolfe, a former cavalry officer who learned mountain warfare (and skiing) along with his troops, the 87th trained eight hours a day, six days a week. They worked on the art of military skiing—until the boys from the South who had been drafted into this outfit began to address their skis each morning as "mah torture boahds!" But their muscles grew strong and their faces turned coppery brown in the blazing sun and stinging snow, and they became an outfit. "We Climb to Conquer" was their motto, and they set out to prove it. A patrol scaled the 14,408-foot summit of Rainier, the fourth-highest peak in the country, carrying extra test equipment that averaged more than 85 pounds per man. It was the first such winter ascent that had ever been made, and it was significant that it was guided by a corporal—Peter Gabriel, former head of the Franconia Ski School and a Swiss mountaineer of international fame.

The art of winter warfare was so new to the Army that no place existed in the military "Tables of Organization" for skiers and mountaineers. As this badly needed talent flowed in through the efficient National Ski Patrol System, it stayed bottled up in the ranks, unable to rise to proper levels of leadership because of the Army's antiquated setup for "flatland fighting." Crack ski instructors like Walter Prager and Gordon Wren (who later became coach and contestant on the 1948 U.S. Olympic Team) remained enlisted men, in the ranks—while nevertheless called upon to teach the high-ranking officers how to ski. Top-notch moun-

The Tenth Mountain Division in training at Mount Rainier, Washington.

taineers like Eldon Metzger of Seattle had to become company clerks in order to win chevrons. These were indeed times of trial, but the work went on, and Dole's men continued to pour in.

It soon became apparent that mountain and winter warfare must expand, and Camp Hale was constructed astride the Continental Divide in Colorado, at a cost of $28 million. Here at the highest Army Camp in America (almost 10,000 feet), the Tenth Mountain Division was activated in the fall of 1942. Technicians trained in snow and mountains were needed to organize the special troops now being added—engineers to erect aerial tramways, signal corps to lay wire on skis, artillery to emplace the 75 mm. pack-howitzers on mountain heights, medical corps personnel to evacuate wounded from deep snows. Then it was that the War Department went again to Minot Dole in New York and said, "We need twenty-five hundred qualified men in sixty days. Can you get them for us?" Could he? Red tape was slashed on every side, and the National Ski Patrol Sys-

tem secured 3,000 hand-picked men in the allotted two months.

In the ensuing years, more than 25,000 applications for the Tenth Mountain Division passed over Dole's desk—and of these 12,000 men and officers were processed. As a result of this careful selection, the I.Q. of the division at Camp Hale rose to the astounding average of 135. Since 130 is the requirement for entry into Officer Training School, this meant that by the law of averages every single man at Camp Hale was potential officer material!

But more than that, it meant that out of the necessities of war an incredible collection of sportsmen had been fused together into one great unit. They came from far and near—from Franconia, Stowe, and North Conway, from Moon Valley and Iron Mountain and Ishpeming, from Yosemite and Mount Rainier and Sun Valley, to name a few. And there were some from Finland, Norway, Switzerland, and Austria. Seldom had there been such a fraternity of skiers and mountaineers as those who came together at

Camp Hale during the early war years. Despite bumbling Army inefficiency which at first throttled constructive leadership and confined skilled technicians to menial tasks, morale in this unique outfit remained as high as the peaks on which they skied and climbed and worked for two and a half long years, while the War Department made up its official mind where to use them. But they never lost this esprit de corps, even through dreary weeks of flatland training in Texas. They just let off steam by rappelling down the outside of eight-story Austin hotels with climbing ropes to the street below. Finally came the call they had been waiting for— and the Tenth Mountain, some 12,000 strong, embarked on the ship *West Point,* the former *United States,* and sailed to Naples and combat. On their arrival in the wreck-strewn harbor on January 15, 1945, an Australian soldier from a ship nearby hailed them. "Hey, myte," he shouted, "what ship is that?" Quick as a flash shot back the reply in a good Brooklyn accent: *"The Staten Island ferry!"* The Tenth had arrived! The long months of testing were over, and the grim days of combat lay just ahead. Both friend and foe alike were waiting to see if they could live up to their proud motto: *"Vires montesque vincimus"*—"We Conquer Mountains and Men."

Conquer they did. The Tenth Mountain Division will go down in history as one of the most amazing military outfits ever to fight under the Stars and Stripes—or any other flag for that matter. Perhaps because it was the first and, therefore, the oldest unit of the Tenth, the 87th Mountain Infantry Regiment seemed to set the keynote.

In the summer of 1945, their mission accomplished, the Tenth Mountain returned home. Behind them they left almost 1,000 of their comrades killed in action. Ahead of them lay inactivation; the famous crossed bayonet insignia would never be worn in combat again.

"Did they ever use the ski troops?" Ask General Mark Clark: "I look upon the action of the Tenth Mountain as one of the most vital and brilliant in the Italian campaign. Nothing could stop your drive. This is the aggressive spirit of which victory is made. It was a privilege to have you in this command. Good luck to you."

And today it is not an overstatement to say that the Mountain Troops are the rooftree of American skiing. There is hardly a ski area on the North American continent that does not have a Mountain Troop man in the ski school, ski patrol, on its executive or management staff, or heading up the whole show.

SKIING POSTWAR BOOM

The end of World War II saw old-timers and a new generation of skiers ready to hit the slopes but not too well equipped or clothed. The all-out war effort had diverted the creative minds in the ski business for more serious, deadly projects, and for five years all ski and clothing manufacture had been for the ski troops and other winter-weather servicemen. Fortunately, a variable flood of Army surplus material was released for private consumption soon after the Japanese Armistice was signed. While vast crowds of ski enthusiasts took to the hills on long, white, surplus Army skis and in baggy military ski suits, a handful of imaginative and courageous individualists passed up the skiing fun to hole up in workshops and designing rooms to produce a whole new con-

cept in ski clothing and equipment.

For instance, for 5,000 years, from the peat-bog skis unearthed in Scandinavia to the top racing skis at the 1950 World Championships at Aspen, all skis were made of wood. For the first 4,900 years or so, they were made from single pieces of wood. Actually, the first ski of importance was the Telemarken ski from Telemark, Norway. This ski was shorter and wider than skis used previously. It was similar to the shape of skis today; it had a curved tip, and the boot was held with a thong. Modern-day skis are a product of the Telemarken ski. An important advance in skis, of course, was the introduction of the steel edge in the 1930's. This made possible the skiing of packed slopes and affected the evolution of ski technique.

Hickory and ash had always been the best wood for skis. But, by the beginning of World War II, it was becoming increasingly difficult to find sufficient quantities of high-grade hickory and ash for the continued construction of one-piece skis, and improved glues made possible the laminated ski. Plastic running surfaces were added for greater speed and durability, and elaborate plastic and paint combinations were used to produce colorful models, varying not only in name but in competitive record. All of this, plus the advertising wars for the skier market, added to the cost of skis. And it was discovered with dismay that the improved skis did not last nearly as long as the clumsier one-piece hickories of the previous generation. The more violent racers discovered that their favorite skis were going soft, if not dead, after a month or so on the circuit.

Wood remained popular until the mid-1950's, when metal skis received a good share of the market in the United States. The earliest commercially available metal skis were the Dow Metal Air Ski, invented by Dr. T. H. McConica, and the Trueflex, nee Alu 60, which was the product of the inventive minds of Wayne Pierce, Art Hunt, and Dave Richey, all employees of the Chance-Vought Aircraft Company. Both the Air Ski and the Alu 60 had the same basic problems. They had no steel edges, and in wet snow the skis came practically to a dead stop because of the suction created by the bare metal running surfaces, which would not hold wax. At the time there seemed to be no commercially feasible solution to prevent metal skis from taking an abrupt and permanent set, and skier interest in the "tin cans" subsided in a temporary wave of equipment conservatism.

In Baltimore an aviation engineer, Howard Head, was also intrigued with producing a ski out of twentieth-century materials. His original idea was to use thin layers of aluminum on the top and bottom of a lightweight wooden core and bond the sandwich together under high heat, boiling it in the oil tank to set the glue. It took him nearly six months to make one ski, and once he had a pair, Head found out that they were as strong as wood and only half as heavy. But the aluminum bottom froze repeatedly and the edges were not good. Now Head had a

ski that did not break—but he himself was broke. He had to take a part-time job for his only source of income, and his skeleton crew worked for more than a year without receiving any pay.

Using plastic bottoms and steel edges, Head finally came up with a ski which would provide satisfactory running. He added black plastic to the top to reduce the metallic glare, and in 1950, his first year of production, he sold 300 pairs of skis at the unheard-of price of $85 a pair! Instructors and racers were not too impressed, but doctors, housewives, and tired businessmen were delighted. They could make their turns at moderate speeds so easily that they called the skis "cheaters." Head skis, made in the United States, suddenly became prestige skis in Europe.

In 1960, Head roamed the pre-Olympic training races and went to Squaw Valley with a supply of new yellow-bottom racing skis, but none of the racers was willing to use them in the actual events. So it was with mixed feelings that Head saw the Squaw Valley downhill race won with metal skis— the first time metal skis had ever been used by an Olympic winner. But he was disappointed that it was a French-made Allais 60, used by Jean Vuarnet. Austrian Kastle metal skis were also used in the Olympics. The next year the racers switched to metal skis in large numbers, but none of the top skiers would use the Head models. When the professional racing circuit was established, Head was one of the sponsors and the pros began riding to victory on his skis. The big breakthrough came in 1963 when Switzerland's Josl Minsch won the International Olympic downhill tryout race at Innsbruck on Heads. After that, more and more racers used the Heads. A dream of nearly two decades came true for Howard Head in the 1964 Olympics when he saw his skis carry an American skier to a silver medal.

The revolution in the production of skis reached a high point in 1965 when some leading shops offered only epoxy, fiberglass, and metal skis, with wooden skis relegated to children's inexpensive models. Nevertheless, except in the United States, the wood ski is predominantly utilized in the world today.

The design of bindings has changed

rapidly since 1890. The first metal binding was made in 1894 by Fritz Huitfeldt in Norway. It was so successful that it was employed in skiing for more than twenty-five years. The binding consisted of a piece of iron slipped through a mortise under the ball of the foot and bent up around the toe. An adjustable strap was laced across the toe. Various combinations of long thongs and buckles were utilized to hold the heel from turning back and forth across the ski. No attempt was made to hold the heel to the ski. Since 1925, many modern advances in bindings have evolved. Probably the development and promotion of the safety binding is the most important safety advancement in equipment.

Early boots were of the moccasin type. The boots have advanced with the bindings in direct demand to the needs and/or the limitations of existing equipment. In other words, as technique became better understood, better equipment was designed to meet the requirements. At the present time, plastic boots are popular.

The Lapps used a single heavy pole as a weapon. One pole was common until the early 1900's. The pole was placed between the legs. After 1907, two poles became part of the ski technique. The early poles had no rings on the ends. The trend in lengths of poles has changed many times; poles were long until about 1942; short poles became popular and remained so until 1949, and the trend was then toward long poles. The first commercial bamboo poles were introduced about 1900. Since World War II, many advances in pole design and materials have helped the evolution of modern ski technique.

The increased interest in skiing changed the character of ski areas. The day of the rugged outdoorsmen became a thing of the past. The new skier began to demand better facilities—better food, better lodging, better entertainment. And to handle the growing lift lines, high-capacity, high-speed lifts were developed. It was also during the early postwar period that slopes were first mechanically groomed. Less-experienced skiers found the going much easier at those ski areas that were cleared and whose slopes were packed, and they flocked to them.

Ski clothing styles also changed. Baggy pants became less baggy, and the parkas—they were still called jackets then—were almost fit to wear in public. Although the potato-sack-tied-in-the-middle look was still widely in vogue, a few skiers who had been to Europe started to appear in closely tailored pants. Actually, improvements in materials and clothing design have helped to popularize skiing as a style sport. After World War II, manufacturers of clothing recognized the postwar revolution in skiing. The shift from mountain touring to downhill skiing demanded a design of clothing suited to the new ski techniques. Famous racers have been the trend setters. The racer's style in skiing and ski wear often has become the gospel. Lightweight, warm clothing has been an important factor in the evolution of ski technique. Because of these new concepts in ski wear, elegance grew out of functional design.

For a time after the war there was a period of status quo as far as skiing technique and instruction was concerned. True, the Austrians, while employing many of the fundamental maneuvers of the Arlberg technique, had adopted sideslipping and an increased amount of rotation from the French. And while the French still emphasized their no-stem approach, they were not nearly as dogmatic about it as in prewar years. The rivalry between the two basic techniques flared briefly in 1948 when Émile Allais came to the United States, but generally there was not too much difference between the top practitioners of the two systems.

In the early forties, however, technique ideas began to split. While the French improved their rotationary technique through intensive research and tests, the Austrians experimented with thrusting of the feet. In 1955, the New Official Austrian Ski System was shown at the International Ski Instructors' Congress held in Val d'Isère, France. Its ultimate form—continuous turning down the fall line—was called *wedeln*.

The new system, although seemingly more complex than the older rotation, spread rapidly throughout the ski world. There were three basic reasons for this quick acceptance. First, there were a number of skiers who had advanced sufficiently to be capable of wedeln. Second, metal skis, easier to turn than the old skis, were readily available. Third, precise control of the skis had been

Dr. Stefan Kruckenhauser of St. Christoph, Austria, directed the creation of the official Austrian teaching system in the postwar era.

considerably enhanced by the improvement in boots. By the time wedeln became "official," even the lowliest skier had a better linkage with his skis than the super-experts of the prewar period.

The battle of techniques, which started in the postwar decade, continues. For further information on the various techniques and systems, see Section III.

Ski racing underwent some important changes in the postwar era, too. Winning racers in international meets were acclaimed with worldwide publicity. As competition gained in intensity, technique was refined and improved over and over again. Coaching and training became major factors, and new equipment made extreme high speeds possible. With one or two exceptions, the new heroes of the Olympics, the World Championships, the A-K's, and the Hahnenkamms were products of systems whose only objective was to turn out champion skiers, no matter the cost.

In the first postwar competition, the 1948 Olympics at St. Moritz, Switzerland, the United States and Canadian teams offered a combination of native and imported competitors. And coaches such as Walter Prager, a Swiss, coached the U.S. Alpine team, and Émile Allais, a Frenchman, coached the Canadian team. The competitors ranged from

prewar "retreads" to dewy-eyed youngsters, and the results were gratifying, but not conclusive.

The prospects looked a little better, yet when eighty-three competitors skied over the 18-kilometer cross-country course, it seemed like the same old story again. America's five entries wound up among the last eighteen places. Our achievements in the Nordic events (jumping and cross-country) began to look slightly improved when Gordon Wren leaped to a fifth place in the jumping. Then in the august company of the great French team (Henri Oreiller and James Couttet), and of Switzerland's Karl Molitor and Austria's Franz Gabl, America's Jack Reddish skied to a seventh place in the slalom. But it remained for the ladies to demonstrate just how far U.S. skiing had progressed after the war. Twisting and poling to a first place in the women's special slalom, Gretchen Fraser won the first gold medal in the history of American participation in the skiing events.

Cheers, flowers, gifts, and telegrams showered on the popular Gretchen. But to the astonished Europeans, she did not wholly overshadow the equally amazing pre-Olympic victory they had witnessed that winter of '48 when fifteen-year-old Andrea Mead swept the combined honors at Pontresina. As it turned out, the achievement merely proved a preface to Andy's capture of two gold medals four years later at Oslo.

"It will be the greatest flop in the skiing world," the leader of the French team said during the snow famine that preceded the Oslo Games in 1952. He had occasion later to eat his words. From the opening day, when the flaming Olympic torch arrived at the stadium after a 120-mile ski relay, until the final lowering of the Olympic flag with its five intertwined circles, the '52 Winter Games —the only ones ever staged in a capital city —rank among the most successful yet held.

Host Norway swept the 1952 Games, and no other competitor more closely symbolized the spirit of his country's victory than Alpine champion Stein Eriksen. Up to that time, Norway had always been a power in the Nordic skiing events. But Eriksen's gold medal in the giant slalom brought Scandinavian skiing achievement into a new era. Overnight the blond Norwegian, who now

Gretchen Fraser (left) won the first gold medal in the history of American participation in the skiing events during the 1948 Olympic games. Gordon Wren (right) one of the United States' best jumpers in the forties and fifties.

teaches in the United States, became a national hero. This notoriety also enabled some American newspapers to create a "petit scandale." Eriksen's name was romantically linked with United States skier Katy Rodolph. As a result, Katy and teammate Paul Wegeman revealed that they were secretly married. The marriage had not been revealed because it meant Wegeman's discharge from the Naval Aviation Cadet program.

Eriksen was not the only skiing star to emerge from the Oslo Games. A slalom gold medal went to Othmar Schneider of Austria. And thirty-three-year-old Zeno Colo of Italy streaked to victory in the downhill. Winner of the exhausting 30-mile cross-country race was Finland's Veikko Häkulinen.

Stein Eriksen of Norway was that country's first great Alpine champion.

Henri Oreiller of France swept all events during 1949 Harriman Cup.

The Olympic scene shifted to Cortina, Italy, in 1956, but the change of locale and poor snow conditions did little to help the United States. Not a single American medal was won at the VII Winter Games, although Brookie Dodge and Andrea Mead Lawrence both placed fourth in events. The Cortina

Games, however, will be remembered for the herculean feats of Anton (Toni) Sailer, a young Austrian plumber who astounded the ski world by winning all three Alpine events. The Scandinavian countries again dominated the Nordic events, with the U.S.S.R. making a strong bid, especially in the jumps, that

Othmar Schneider (left) and Christian Pravda (right), both of Austria, were leading skiers just after World War II.

Andrea Mead Lawrence (center) is congratulated by runners-up after her victory in the women's giant slalom ski race at the opening of the 1952 Winter Olympic Games. Dagmar Rom (right) of Austria was second, and Annemarie Buchner of Germany was third.

marked it as a potential power in future Olympics.

Actually, the 1956 Olympic team was more than usually promising. Ralph Miller, Tom Corcoran, Buddy Werner, Bill Beck, Marvin Melville, and Brookie Dodge were first-rate competitors, but the team was badly handicapped by low morale, poor organization, and lack of European race experience. At that, it came tantalizingly close to a medal —which instead, went to the American team's Japanese rival, Chiharu Igaya.

Igaya went on to win the silver medal, but he was almost deprived of it—by, of all people, the Americans. In his second run he caught a tip only six gates from the start but managed to make "an extraordinary recovery." Had the U.S. protest been upheld, Dodge, who ended up in fourth place, would have won a bronze medal.

Igaya won a third-place medal in the 1958 FIS World Championships at Bad Gastein, Austria, but the going was tough for the American team. There was hope for the future when Sally Deaver took second place in the giant slalom, but the men were a disappointment. Buddy Werner was fourth in the slalom and fifth in the giant slalom, and

Chiharu "Chick" Igaya (left), trained in the United States, won a silver medal for Japan in the 1956 Winter Olympics. Among those he beat was former collegiate teammate Brookie Dodge of the United States (right).

lost his bid for a medal in the combined by falling only a few feet from the finish in the downhill.

If the American Alpine teams felt that they were slipping in the 1950's, the Nordic competitors must have been convinced they were in a tailspin. What was worse, very few people cared. Up until the years immediately after World War II, the United States could lay claim to some better than average jumpers. But the breed fizzled, except for those especially talented ones like Art Devlin, dark, handsome king of American ski jumpers, whose career of trophy collecting spanned twenty years in his heyday, more eagle than man. When the big 60-meter jump was built for the 1932 Olympics in his native Lake Placid, Devlin was just a kid. But already he was outgrowing the practice hill with a natural style and a longing for the big, long, soaring jumps that were soon to win him a berth on four Olympic teams, first place in every major jumping competition in America, plus the proud owner of the 1963 Hall of Fame Award for "Devoted Service to the Sport of Skiing." Even his war career, which temporarily interrupted his jumping career, was spent soaring through the skies—as a fighter pilot with the Army Air Force.

Devlin climbed out of his fighter plane and onto his jumping skis in 1946 to win the Nationals at Steamboat Springs, Colorado, and two years later made the 1948 Olympic Team with a jump that almost killed him. He outjumped the hill by 40 feet at Leavenworth, Washington. A knee injury, as a result of this jump, took him out of the St. Moritz events. But the 1950 FIS gained him a fourth place. Though he outdistanced the winner by 24 feet, he missed first place on style points. That same year, Devlin set a spectacular new North American distance record at Steamboat Springs, Colorado, when he passed the 300-foot mark for the first time in jumping history—which was comparable to bettering the four-minute mile in track. He soared to a distance of 307, with Gordy Wren right behind him with a jump of 297 feet. This, of course, had been done in Europe years before.

Nineteen-fifty was Devlin's peak year, but he went on to take eleventh place at the 1952 Olympics at Oslo, tenth at the 1954 FIS, and tied for ninth at the 1956 Olympics (top

Art Devlin was the king of American ski jumpers during the fifties.

American in each case). He retired from jumping competition when he missed a berth on the Olympics at Squaw Valley by one point, but Devlin will be remembered as consistently one of the greatest of them all in North America, and any visitor to his Olympic Motel in Lake Placid will be dazzled by his 15-foot showcase full of trophies—well earned by a marvelous athlete!

Commenting on the general Nordic picture, Coach Al Merrill said, "In 1954 we were so bad that even the Scandinavian girls beat our time over ten kilometers!"

Maybe because things could not get worse, they gradually got better. Sven Wiik, coach at Western State College in Colorado, had the particular talent to cajole the most likely of material into a reasonable resemblance of the required product. By 1960 something of a Nordic dawn had arrived. Mack Miller of Western State put on an inspiring performance at Squaw Valley, competing in the 15-kilometer, 30-kilometer, and 50-kilometer races and the relay. There were no medals, but at least there was strong hope for the future.

If medals proved to be elusive to the North American men in both the Nordic and Alpine events, they were far from that for the women. Since Olympic and FIS World Alpine Championship competition resumed

Buddy Werner (left) and Tom Corcoran (right) were the United States' best in the early sixties.

after World War II, American and Canadians have failed only twice to bring home medals—in 1950 and in 1956. After 1956, Lucille Wheeler of Canada stunned the world by winning the downhill and the giant slalom in the 1958 FIS. In 1960, it was another Canadian, Anne Heggtveit, who captured a gold medal in slalom at the Squaw Valley Olympics. Anne also was the first North American to win the Arlberg Kandahar, in 1959. But most of the attention at that time was focused on two plucky American women, Betsy Snite and Penny Pitou, who campaigned in Europe for three years for the

invaluable experience that comes only from racing against the world's best week after week. Penny was strong in downhill and Betsy a demon in slalom. There were weeks in Europe when the Europeans wondered if they had any women racers at all. The American girls swept all honors.

America's broad hopes for the 1960 Games at Squaw Valley, California, were jolted when Bud Werner broke his leg in pregame training. Nevertheless, Tom Corcoran took a surprising fourth in the giant slalom, and Penny Pitou won two silver medals in the downhill and giant slalom, while Betsy Snite

During the 1960 Winter Games, Penny Pitou (left) won silver medals in the downhill and giant slalom, while Betsy Snite (right) won a silver in the slalom.

Marielle Goitschel of France (left) congratulates Austria's Christl Haas, winner of ladies' downhill at 1962 FIS championships.

won a silver in the slalom. Combined with Anne Heggtveit's gold medal in slalom, it was the biggest racing setback the Europeans had ever received. But 1960 was also notable for the great French renaissance. Using metal skis for the first time in international competition and with their egg position, the French swept to victory in almost every downhill in 1960 and 1961. In the Olympics, the hero was Jean Vuarnet, a journeyman racer from whom little had been expected. Yet there was justice in his surprise victory. He and the French ski theoretician Georges Joubert were primarily responsible for developing the egg position that carried the French to victory.

In 1961, the French had a new hero, Guy Périllat. Périllat managed the unprecedented feat of winning every major race he entered that season, something that even Sailer had not managed to do. But just as it seemed that French domination was assured, the Austrians staged a strong comeback in the 1962 FIS. The man who led the comeback was Karl Schranz, who was thought to be over the hill after he had failed to crack the first ten in the 1960 Winter Olympic Games.

At the 1964 Olympics in Innsbruck, Austria, it was the same story all over again for the Americans. The women were winning the medals (Joan Hannah and Barbara Ferries had taken third in the giant slalom and downhill at Chamonix), then Jean Saubert won a bronze in the slalom and tied for a silver in the giant slalom—and the men were trying too hard and getting nowhere. But on February 8, 1964, almost thirty years of frustration came to an end. Billy Kidd and Jimmy Heuga came through for silver and bronze medals respectively in the slalom.

The Austrians with Egon Zimmerman, Josef "Pepi" Stiegler, and Christl Haas, and the French with François Bonlieu and Christine and Marielle Goitschel, walked off with all the Alpine events at the '64 Olympics. The results at Innsbruck perhaps were not quite as much as Americans at home hoped for. But it was more than enough for the Europeans, who realized that the old order in Alpine racing had changed for good—even if not for their own. Reflecting on those elusive gold medals—in the men's division— Bud Werner put it very bluntly, "If you want to be first, you have to take chances . . . there are only two places in a race . . . first and last!"

This was the philosophy of competition expressed by a young racer who, above all others here or abroad, had been eulogized by the press, his teammates, and the whole skiing fraternity, not only for his prowess as a racer but for his instincts, compassion, and inspiration as a man. Bud Werner, of Steamboat Springs, who flashed to his first spectacular international victory at the Holmenkollen in Norway at age seventeen, went on from there to become known as "the fastest man in the world on skis"—when he stood. Actually, Werner was the first of the American men racers to put to test, and win the

Billy Kidd (left) and Jimmy Heuga (right) at 1964 Winter Olympics after capturing the silver and bronze medals in slalom. Bob Beattie (center) was the United States team ski coach.

respect of, the top European and Scandinavian racers. His list of victories, nationally and internationally, is well known—Harriman Cup twice, Roch Cup twice, National Championships, FIS teams, Olympic teams, and "the big ones" in Europe—Holmenkollen Downhill, Lauberhorn Combined, Grand Prix de Chamonix Downhill, Hahnenkamm Downhill, and many others.

Before his big chance in the 1960 Olympics, Werner, starting with the Lauberhorn in Switzerland, had won major races in every country in Europe. Despite his periodic falls he was, by all standards, the world's unofficial number one racer. The pressure was on in 1960. Then, with a snap heard around the ski world, his leg broke and with it America's hopes for the Olympics. Tough luck followed him to the 1962 FIS at Chamonix, where he lost his way and spun out in a blinding blizzard, and to the 1964 Olympics at Innsbruck, where his teammates, Heuga and Kidd, came out in the money (Werner was eighth) with medals in slalom —partly owing to Werner's encouragement and side-coaching of these younger and less experienced boys. But on April 12, 1964, Bud Werner and Barbi Henneberger pointed their skis straight down a mountainside for the last time and skied for their lives as a thundering avalanche bore down on them. Both were killed, and the entire ski racing world lost that race.

The men's world Alpine racing scene in 1966 to 1968 was dominated by Jean-Claude Killy. Not only did he win the first World Cup in 1967 with a perfect score, but he repeated again in 1968 with a near-perfect score. He also swept all three Alpine gold medals in the 1968 Olympics at Grenoble, France. The only other triple winners in *one* Winter Games history were Thorleif Haug of Norway in 1924 Nordic events and, of course, Toni Sailer in 1956 for the three Alpine titles. Johan Grøttumsbraaten was the winner of three gold medals in two games (1928 and 1932) in Nordic events. Sixten Jernberg of Sweden, however, ruled Nordic ski competition for twelve years. Actually, Jernberg is the all-time Olympic Nordic medalist. From 1956 until 1964, he won a total of nine medals, which explains why the Scandinavians called him "The King" without any modifiers whatsoever. Four of those medals were gold—in the 50-kilometer in 1956 and 1964, in the 30-kilometer in 1960, and in the relay in 1964. Three were silver—in the 15-kilometer in 1956 and 1960, and the 30-kilometer in 1956; and two were bronze— in the relay in 1956 and in the 15-kilometer in 1964. Veikko Häkulinen of Finland— Jernberg's great rival—participated in four Olympics between 1952 and 1964 and won seven medals, four of which were gold. Only the Russian Pavel Kolchin could come close to challenging them and then only over a period of about four years.

Nancy Greene of Canada was Killy's counterpart among the women in the late 1960's. She won the World Cup in both 1967 and 1968, as well as winning the giant slalom in the Winter Olympics. At these, Marielle Goitschel (France) and Olga Pall (Austria) won the ladies' Alpine titles. The United States obtained no medal in skiing during the 1968 Olympics. Both Killy and Greene turned professional after the games.

At the twenty-eighth FIS Alpine World Ski Championships in 1970, Betsy Clifford of Canada won the women's giant slalom, while Anneroesli Zryd of Switzerland, Ingrid Lafforgue of France, and Michèle Jacot of France won the downhill, slalom, and combined gold medals, respectively. Bernhard Russi of Switzerland took the men's downhill, while Karl Schranz (Austria) and Jean-Noël Augert (France) captured the giant slalom

Jean-Claude Killy of France (left) and Toni Sailer of Austria (center) are the only two to ever win three gold medals in Alpine ski events during one Olympic. Thorleif Haug of Norway (right) won three in 1924 Winter Games in the Nordic events. J. Grøttumsbraaten of Norway won three gold medals in two games (1928 and 1932).

and slalom. But for Americans and for sentimentalists all over the world, Val Gardena, Italy, will always be remembered as the place where Billy Kidd—after eight grueling years on the international racing circuit, his ankles taped and his sore back corseted—became the first North American man to win a gold medal in world Alpine championship skiing. Kidd took the FIS combined title with a slalom run the equal of his Olympic medal performance in 1964 and the best downhill run by an American in eighteen years—despite a spoiled first run in the giant slalom. Except for Kidd, the Americans put on a generally disappointing performance. Yet no one—including the racers and coaches, sad to say—seemed surprised. But equally important was Kidd's announcement the following day that he was turning professional.

At the 1972 Olympic games in Japan, Barbara Cochran captured the gold medal given for the slalom event, while Susan Corrack took home a bronze medal for her downhill efforts. The Russians dominated the Nordic events with six gold medals, while Switzerland was the big winner in the Alpine contests with three. The United States has never won a medal in any of the Nordic contests. The United States men have yet to win a gold medal in Winter Olympic games.

However in 1968, John Bower became the first American ever to win a European cross-country race. He captured history's most prestigious ski trophy: the King's Cup, given every year for best combined jumping and cross-country score at Norway's Holmenkol-len. This is the original Holmenkollen cup, tougher to win than the Olympic Nordic combined gold medal. (In the Olympics, countries are limited to four entries; at Holmenkollen, they can have any number.)

The early 1970's have brought along a host of new men stars, including David Zwilling, Hansi Hinterseer, Franz Klammer, and Karl Cordin of Austria; Gustavo Thoeni (winner of the 1971, 1972, and 1973 World Cups), Piero Gros, Illario Pegorari, and Rolando Thoeni of Italy; Jean-Noël Augert, Henri Duvillard, and Claude Perrot of France; Walter Tresch, Bernhard Russi, Roland Collombin, and Adolf Roesti of Switzerland; Bob Cochran and Don Rowles of the United States. The women Alpine stars of the early 1970's are Annemarie Proell (three-time winner of the World Cup), Monika Kaserer, Wiltrud Drexel of Austria; Patricia Emonet, Daniele Debernard, and Jacqueline Rouvier of France; Marie-Theres Nadig and Bernadette Zurbriggen of Switzerland; Barbara and Marilyn Cochran, Sandra Poulsen, and Susan Corrock of the United States; Judy Crawford and Betsy Clifford of Canada; and Rosi Mittermaier of West Germany. Add to this list the professional skiing stars, such as Hugo Nindle, Spider Sabich, Harold Stuefer, Otto Tschudi, Tyler Palmer, Ken Corrock, Jean-Claude Killy and Malcolm Milne. Other names, of course, will reach ski stardom in the years ahead. Victory in the great races is usually essential for a racer to be ranked among the great. But sometimes—not often—a man's legend is bigger than his records. Such a racer was Toni Matt. He was a good racer, no question about that. He won the Harriman Cup in 1939, the U.S. Nationals in 1949, and several other important races. But this is not what he is remembered for.

In the 1938–39 season, Matt cut 5, 10, and sometimes 30 seconds off American course records, one after another. The climactic race that year was the Inferno, the marathon run from the top of the 6,000-foot peak of New England's highest mountain. Just after the start the course goes over fearful Tuckerman's Headwall, a pitch 1,000 feet high, with a 60-degree incline at the top. The course finishes at the end of the zigzag Sherburne trail, four miles away. The first racers who ran the Inferno that April 22 took a good three or four swinging, high-speed turns on the Headwall to check their speed. But when Matt came bolting over the edge, he schussed the wall like a lead plummet, hitting 85 miles per hour as he came streaming off the bottom, his skis shattering the icy snow. Matt hit the Sherburne trail at timber line riding a fantastic head of speed, and the strain began to tell. The effort at each turn was increasingly exhausting. Finally, he hit the last S-turn; losing his grip on the snow, skis chattering, he went straight at a tree. But Matt gave a great, last-ditch scrambling lurch, missed the tree by a hair, and blitzed across the finish. He was down in 6 minutes, 29.4 seconds, *one minute* faster than the number two man, Dick Durrance. It was, and still is, the largest winning margin in the history of modern American skiing. It is interesting to note, however, that Matt's accomplishment received little attention at the time. Newspaper accounts of the event and an article in the *Ski Annual* of the following fall only detail that Matt won the race in record time. Perhaps because of this oversight, the story of how Toni Matt schussed the Headwall has become legend—lovingly passed on from skier to skier until it became one of the greater moments in American skiing history.

HIGHLIGHTS OF SKIING

Ski Magazine has been reporting news and events of the ski world since 1935—a period that is generally regarded as the "modern era" of the sport in this country. During these three decades, *Ski*'s growth has directly paralleled and influenced almost every facet of skiing. Calling on our own records, the history books, and the memories of the people who have made this sport, *Ski Magazine* has compiled this list of firsts and highlights in the dynamic development of the skiing sport.

1849 Discovery of gold attracts Scandinavian sailors from West Coast ports to the California mountains.

1850–51 First early "snowshoe" clubs appear among prospectors, in the "Lost Sierras" of California. John "Snowshoe" Thompson arrives in West from Norway.

1853 Early races staged by "ski runners" in Onion Valley, California.

1854 The first recorded ski race in the United States was held in Sierra County, California. It was straight downhill—no turns —on 15-foot skis. The prize was a silver belt trophy.

1856 "Snowshoe" Thompson, a Norwegian immigrant, makes the first 90-mile mail runs on skis between Placerville, California, and Genoa, Nevada, setting off a "snowshoe" rage. He continued the runs until 1869.

1860 Sondre Norheim makes the first officially measured jump (30.5 meters) in Morgedal, Norway.

1866 First Alturas Snowshoe Club race staged at La Porte, California, in heart of Plumas County skiing country. Prospectors race for prize money on 8- and 12-foot skis.

1866–75 Peak of racing enthusiasm in California. Races are of the downhill type with money prizes for the winners. "Dope" (wax) becomes a factor in racing.

1868 The first public discussion of ski technique (in Norway) following the use of the telemark turn by the skiers of Telemark in a competition with skiers from Christiania (Oslo). Sondre Norheim introduces his so-called telemark bindings.

1877 Christiania Ski Club, formed in Norway, claims to be first formal ski organization in world. (Kiandra Ski Club of Australia is said to have been the first "club"

Slalom winners at 1968 Winter Olympics were (left to right) Annie Famose, Marielle Goitschel (both of France), and Nancy Greene of Canada.

formed in 1871.) Christiania ski turn introduced.

1879 First systematic ski-jumping meet conducted at Christiania (Oslo), Norway, between Christiania and Telemark ski clubs.

1882 Nansen Ski Club of Berlin, New Hampshire, first official ski club formed in the United States. (The Alturas Snowshoe Club of LaPorte, California, conducted racing events in 1866, but it is not generally accepted as an "official" ski club.)

1887 First jumping competition in America won by Mikkel Hemmestveit at Red Wing, Minnesota.

1888 Skis first reported used in New York City during blizzard of '88. Fridtjof Nansen, a Norwegian, traverses southern Greenland using skis. The event itself and the book he subsequently published resulted in a tremendous interest in skiing throughout Europe. The two combined are usually considered responsible for opening the Alpine skiing era.

1891 Group of eleven clubs forms Central Organization in Michigan. Though unsuccessful, it was forerunner of U.S. Ski Association.

1892 First Holmenkollen jumping meet held in Norway.

1894 Fritz Huitfeldt produces the first toe irons, a significant invention which made positive control over the skis feasible and greatly speeded the development of skiing on the more difficult Alpine slopes. Colonel Georg Bilgeri introduces military skiing to the Austrian Tiroler Corps.

1896 Austrian Mathias Zdarsky experimented with the sport with Norwegian skis in the early 1890's, and in 1896 writes the first illustrated ski manual, *Lilienfeld Schilauf Technik.* He used short skis and one pole.

1901 Zdarsky is first person in Austria to teach skiing on a regular basis. He has 612 pupils.

1901–2 French army organizes first military ski classes with Norwegian instructors. Italian ski club formed at Turin.

1903 Ski Club of Great Britain is formed.

1904 National Ski Association founded at Ishpeming, Michigan. Carl Tellefsen is elected its first president. Montreal Ski Club, Canada's first, is founded and a few days later conducts first Canadian jumping meet.

1905 Zdarsky sets first slalom course; requires competitors to go around a single pole, not through a gate made up of two poles.

1907 First United States cross-country championships held at Ashland, Wisconsin, won by Asario Autio. Hannes Schneider starts ski school at St. Anton, Austria.

1909 Dartmouth Outing Club is founded; Fred Harris elected first president.

1910 First International Ski Congress is held at Christiania, Norway, and the Fédération Internationale de Ski (FIS), the first world-wide ruling body for the sport, was founded.

1911 First Dartmouth Winter Carnival. First ski factory in the United States is opened by C. A. Lund in St. Paul, Minnesota. It remains in continuing operation as the Northland Ski Company. The stem Christiania is first described as such by Carl Luther, a German writer, although Hannes Schneider had developed the turn as early as 1908.

1913 Dartmouth defeats McGill in the first intercollegiate ski meet at St. Saveur, Quebec.

1917 First community winter carnival held at Newport New Hampshire. First Canadian cross-country championships are staged by the Montreal Ski Club.

1920–24 Hannes Schneider formalizes his technique into an instructional system, which subsequently became known as the Arlberg technique. It was the first truly Alpine technique and advocated the abandonment of the telemark.

1921 Canadian Amateur Ski Association formed. First Canadian national championships in jumping and cross-country held.

First modern slalom set at Mürren, Switzerland, by Arnold Lunn. The first systematic exposition, complete with diagrams, of two-gate slalom is published by Arnold Lunn. Dr. Arnold Franck, a German documentary film maker, makes the first ski movie. Hannes Schneider is the major participant in the film.

1922 United States Eastern Amateur Ski Association formed. The first Vasaloppet is held in Sweden.

1923 First American slalom set by Professor Charles Proctor of Dartmouth College.

1924 First Olympic Winter Games held at Chamonix, France, with Nordic ski events only. The International Ski Congress is made into a permanent organization: the Fédération Internationale de Ski (FIS); Colonel Ivar Holmquist is named first president. Cash prizes outlawed by NSA in American amateur competitions.

1925 NSA recognizes U.S. Eastern Amateur Ski Association as an affiliate.

1926 First modern downhill race in the United States held at Mount Moosilauke, New Hampshire, and won by G. Michelson of the University of New Hampshire. First ski shop opened in the United States by Oscar Hambro in Boston. NSA recognizes U.S. Western Ski Association as affiliate.

1927 First snow train in North America from Montreal to the Laurentians by the Canadian Pacific Railroad.

1928 First Arlberg-Kandahar race held at St. Anton, Austria. Second Olympic Winter Games held at St. Moritz, Switzerland; ski events are confined to Nordic competition. Central U.S. Ski Association founded with Julius Blegen as president (recognized as NSA affiliate in 1928). FIS provisionally recognizes Ski Club of Great Britain downhill and slalom rules.

1928–30 Rudolph Lettner, an engineer from Salzburg, invents and patents the steel edge, which provides narrow-tracked running and turning. Skiing is started in the Pacific Northwest of the United States.

1929 The first ski school in the United States is in operation at Peckett's Inn on Sugar Hill in Franconia, New Hampshire. The school is begun in December of 1929, by Sig Buchmayr and Kurt Thalhammer, and $1 is charged for a lesson. First ski train in the United States runs from Boston to Warner, New Hampshire. An experimental downhill race, run in connection with the 1929 FIS World Championships at Zakopane is won by B. Czech of Poland.

1930 The first speed trail is inaugurated, the so-called Flying Kilometer, at St. Moritz, Switzerland. Gustav Lantschner of Austria is the winner at an average speed of 66.4 miles an hour. (Ralph Miller of Dartmouth College was clocked at over 109 miles per hour at Portillo, Chile, in 1955, but this speed was unofficial because there was no electric timing. The figure has been approached by both American and European racers in speed trails at Cervinia, Italy, and at Portillo since that time.) Pacific Northwest Ski Association formed and recognized by NSA. California Ski Association, predecessor of the Far West Ski Association, recognized by NSA. FIS gives full recognition to downhill and slalom.

1931 First official FIS World Championships in downhill and slalom at Mürren, Switzerland, won by Walter Prager and David Zogg, downhill and slalom respectively; and Esmé Mackinnon, both women's downhill and slalom.

1932 III Olympic Winter Games held at Lake Placid, New York, with downhill and slalom still excluded from the ski events. The first rope tow installed by Alex Foster at Shawbridge, Quebec, Canada. This invention was to have a major effect on the development of skiing in North America. First Quebec-Kandahar is held at Mont Tremblant, Quebec.

1933 First National Downhill Championship is held at Mount Moosilauke, New Hampshire, and won by Henry Woods. Hollis Phillips wins first American Inferno race at Tuckerman's Ravine on Mount Washington, New Hampshire. . . . The first Kandahar cable binding holding the skier's heel to the ski is introduced.

1934 The first rope tow is installed in the United States on Clint Gilbert's farm at Woodstock, Vermont. Dick Durrance wins second American Inferno race. First public ski shows held at Madison Square Garden and Boston Gardens. These events draw thousands. Otto Fürrer becomes first three-time winner of Arlberg-Kandahar.

1934–36 Anton Seelos, Austrian racer and trainer, coaches the French team, which

The "king" of Nordic events from 1956 to 1964, Sixten Jernberg of Sweden.

includes Émile Allais. Seelos uses a technique with complete body rotation and counterrotation with an up-unweighting.

1935 American women participate for the first time in FIS World Championships at Mürren, Switzerland. First U.S. National Downhill and Slalom Championships held at Mount Rainier, Washington, and won by Hannes Schroll. First counterrotational technique is introduced by Toni Ducia and Kurt Reindl, two Austrians who worked as trainers for the French team. First snow reports published in New York City. *Ski Magazine* founded by Alf Nydin in Seattle, Washington.

1936 First time Alpine events became part of Winter Olympics. Ski flying was born at Planica, Yugoslavia, when Joseph Bradle of Austria landed at 100 meters (328 feet).

1936–46 During the war and just prior to it the development of skiing slackens. Some is done in Switzerland, Austria, France, and the United States, but it is limited. Skiing plays a military role in some combat areas and is used for recreation and the transportation of troops. Skiing is introduced to thousands of troops during and immediately after the war. It serves as postwar recreation for Allied Occupational Forces in Europe and Japan.

1937 First American ski team visits Chile. First chair lift installed in the East at Belknap, New Hampshire. First parallel technique introduced to North America by Fritz Loosli. Dick Durrance wins first Harriman Cup race at Sun Valley.

1938 First aerial tramway in the United States installed at Cannon Mountain, Franconia, New Hampshire. First Canadian chair lift built by Joseph Ryan at Mont Tremblant, Quebec. National Ski Patrol established with C. Minot Dole named as chairman of national committee. First certification examination of ski instructors held at Woodstock, Vermont. Sepp Ruschp becomes the first certified instructor in the United States. Canadian Ski Instructors Alliance formed. Arlberg-Kandahar canceled when Germany annexes Austria and Hannes Schneider is imprisoned by the Nazis.

1939 Hjalmar Hvam introduces first workable release bindings. Hannes Schneider arrives in the United States and takes over leadership of the ski school at Mount Cranmore. Schneider also developed the first groomed slope by cutting down trees and completely clearing the south slope of Mount Cranmore. First National Women's Downhill and Slalom Championship at Stowe, Vermont, won by Marian McKean and Grace Carter Lindley, respectively.

Franco Nones (left) of Italy became the first Italian to win a gold medal in a Nordic event, in 1968 Games. Toini Gustafsson (right) of Sweden won her second gold at the same Games.

1940 Chair lifts installed at Stowe, Vermont, and Cannon Mountain, New Hampshire. First Alpine lift (thirty-fifth in world) installed at Pico Peak, Vermont. By now, Canada has thirty-two lifts and rope tows. Other U.S. nonrope devices operating at Alta, Utah; Flathead and Lolo Forests, Montana; Jackson Hole and Medicine Bow, Wyoming; Payette Lake, Idaho; Snowqualmie, Washington; Mount Hood, Oregon; Hanover, New Hampshire; Cisco, Snow Valley, Soda Springs, Sugar Bowl, and Yosemite, California.

1941 The war years in U.S. start; 87th Mountain Infantry Regiment forms at Fort Lewis, Washington, then Tenth Mountain Division at Camp Hale, Colorado. NSA severs with FIS. Snow Valley and Bromley open in Vermont despite wartime shortages.

1952 Ski Union of the Americas formed in New York City. Sun Valley initiates "Learn to Ski Weeks."

1946 Twenty-one new T-bars and chairlifts open during first postwar season, including those at Aspen, Colorado; Mittersill, New Hampshire; and North Creek, New York. Aspen opens for first season. Pomalift developed in Europe by Jean Pomagalski.

1947 First double chair lift in North America installed at Berthoud Pass, Colorado. Walter Paepcke forms Aspen Skiing Corporation. The ALU 60, first aluminum ski, appears on the market. Howard Head experiments with a metal ski.

1948 Gretchen Fraser becomes first American to win a medal at Olympic Winter Games, placing first in slalom at St. Moritz, Switzerland. She also places second in ladies'

combined scoring. For first time, downhill and slalom are recognized as separate events in Winter Games. First ski flight to Europe conducted by KLM. First Midwestern chair lift opens as original Sun Valley lift is transplanted to Boyne Mountain, Michigan. Howard Head produces an aluminum alloy ski. *Ski Magazine* merges with three other publications under Bill Eldred. Nicholas Stumpf of Switzerland becomes the first non-Scandinavian to finish in the first three in the Nordic combined in the Holmenkollen. A sharp swing toward reverse-shoulder technique is noted among the younger racers of Europe.

1949 Roland Palmedo establishes Mad River Glen, Vermont; C. V. Starr organizes Mount Mansfield Company at Stowe, Vermont. Squaw Valley opens in California. Platterpull lift, double boots, and the fiberglass ski make their debut. Howard Head produces the first modern metal "sandwich" ski. *Ski Magazine* introduces *gegenschultertecknik,* forerunner of modern reverse-shoulder skiing.

1950 FIS World Championships held at Aspen, Colorado (Alpine); Lake Placid, New York (Jumping); and Rumford, Maine (Nordic). Eastern Intercollegiate Ski Association replaces Intercollegiate Ski Union. First International Ski School Congress held at Zürs, Austria.

1952 Giant slalom first recognized at Winter Olympics in Oslo, Norway. Andrea Mead Lawrence of U.S.A. wins gold medals in giant slalom and slalom. Olympic racers use turntables and thongs. Grossinger's resort in New York uses machine-made snow;

Billy Kidd at 1970 FIS World Alpine Ski Championship at Val Gardena, Italy, became the first North American man to win a gold medal in world Alpine championship skiing. He did it in Alpine combined event. Kidd won the combined event at the 1968 Olympic Winter Games, but no gold medal is now awarded for this event.

two years later, Fahnestock, New York, becomes first ski area to make snow on regular basis.

1953 Modern Austrian Technique (wedeln) first introduced in Austria by Professor Stefan Kruckenhauser and his disciples. First pomalifts in U.S. installed at Arapahoe Basin, Colorado; Snow Ridge, New York; and Suicide Six, Vermont.

1954 Ski Hall of Fame dedicated at Ishpeming, Michigan. NCAA recognizes skiing as intercollegiate sport. Mount Snow opens in Vermont.

1955 Modern Austrian Technique first demonstrated at III International Ski School Congress at Val d'Isère, France. Hannes Schneider dies. Henke introduces first buckle boot in America. First Hart metal skis introduced. Kofix base (plastic finish) appears on skis.

1956 Toni Sailer "grand-slams" at Winter Olympics in Cortina d'Ampezzo, Italy, winning all three Alpine gold medals and combined. *Ski* introduces new wedeln technique of Austrians to American skiers.

1958 Canadian Lucille Wheeler wins gold medals in giant slalom and downhill at FIS

Games in Bad Gastein, Austria; Sally Deaver wins silver medal in giant slalom for U.S.; metal skis first used in downhill competition by French team. Wildcat Mountain, New Hampshire, opens with first gondola in America. Sugarbush Valley opens in Vermont at start of next season.

1959 Buddy Werner becomes first American male to win a major European downhill, winning at the Hahnenkamm in Kitzbühel, Austria.

1960 French become the first team to use metal skis successfully in winning several major European downhills prior to the Olympics. VIII Olympic Winter Games at Squaw Valley, California. Canada's Anne Heggtveit wins slalom; Penny Pitou wins silver medals in downhill and giant slalom; and Betsy Snite wins a silver medal in slalom. France's Jean Vuarnet wins men's downhill on metal skis. The French—Jean Vuarnet, James Couttet, Paul Gignoux, and Émile Allais—develop a natural ski style called *Christiania léger* in which the body remains square over the skis at all times.

1961 Professional Ski Instructors of America (PSIA) organized at Whitefish, Montana. William Lash of Salt Lake City is named first president. Christian Pravda wins first professional ski race at Aspen, picking up $1,500 in prize money. (The pros have raced annually since that time, but have had difficult going against the more spectacular amateurs.) Ski Industries of America (SIA), the first nationwide trade organization, opens New York City offices. Bob Beattie, University of Colorado ski coach, is named head coach of the U.S. Alpine team for the 1962 FIS World Championships. (Two years later he became the first American coach to succeed himself when he was named to lead the 1964 Olympic team.)

1962 Joan Hannah places third in giant slalom and Barbara Ferries third in the downhill at the FIS World Championships in Chamonix, France. Chuck Ferries wins Hahnenkamm slalom. NSA changes name to United States Ski Association (USSA). PSIA formulates American Ski Technique (described in Section III).

1963 National Ski Areas Association (NSAA) founded. Jim Balfanz and Gene Kotlarek finish second and fourth, respectively, at Holmenkollen, the highest placing Americans have achieved in major international Nordic competition. USSA recognizes Alaska Division as affiliate with Russ Read first president. Boyne Mountain, Michigan, installs world's first triple chair lift.

1964 Billy Kidd and Jimmy Huega become the first American men to win Olympic medals for skiing, being second and third, respectively, in the slalom at the IX Olympic Winter Games at Innsbruck, Austria. Jean Saubert ties for second in the giant slalom and places third in the slalom. Buddy Werner killed in a Swiss avalanche shortly after announcing his retirement from racing. Uniform trail-marking system adopted by NSAA. National Professional Ski League formed. Luigi di Marco of Italy sets men's speed record at 108.35 miles per hour at Cervinia, Italy. Kristl Stafner of Austria sets women's speed record, 88.67 miles per hour, at Cervinia. Boyne Highlands, Michigan, installs world's first quadruple chair lift. Robert Beattie appointed first United States National Alpine ski coach.

1965 First American International Team Races (a memorial to Buddy Werner) held at Vail, Colorado, and won by Austria (men) and France (women). David Jacobs named first full-time Canadian ski coach. Ernst Hinterseer wins first *Ski Magazine* Professional Racing Cup in league competition. Ski industry celebrates first National Ski Week. USSA maps $450,000 fund-raising campaign. Snow drought hits East. Ski instructors from around the world demonstrate technique at Interski, Bad Gastein.

1966 The first FIS World Championships (Alpine) are held in the southern hemisphere, at Portillo, Chile.

1967 Nancy Greene (Canada) and Jean-Claude Killy (France) win the first World Cup of Alpine Skiing. France wins Nations Cup.

1968 France wins first Nations Cup of Alpine Skiing. Greene and Killy become first repeat winners of the World Cup. Killy becomes second man to win three gold medals in Alpine competition during Winter Olympics. John Bower, at Holmenkollen, Norway, becomes first American to win a European Nordic competition. *Ski the Outer Limits* filmed.

1969 Nastar (a recreational ski-racing program) is formed. Bob Beattie retires as U.S. Alpine team director. Record snowfalls. Sierra Club holds up Mineral King ski development. Over-the-boot pants grow popular.

1970 At Planica, Yugoslavia, Manfred Wolf of East Germany becomes first skier to jump 165 meters (over 542 feet). At the FIS championships at Val Gardena, Italy, William Kidd becomes first North American man to win a gold medal in world Alpine championship skiing. The first $40,000 pro race staged. Willy Schaeffler named U.S. Alpine team director. Fiberglass ski sales exceed metal for first time. Nastar at 40 ski areas.

1971 First race ever in the Canadian-American Trophy held at Waterville Valley, New Hampshire, in early January. Jerry Martin sets a North American distance record off the 90-meter hill, soaring 345 feet. Vladimir "Spider" Sabich becomes the all-time official one-season money winner with $21,188.77 in prize money.

1972 Barbara Ann Cochran wins the women's slalom at the Winter Olympic games in Supporo, Japan, while Susan Corrock picks up a bronze medal in the downhill. Spider Sabich breaks his previous year's prize money record with earnings of over $50,650. First National Championship of Exhibition Skiing held at Vail, Colorado. Scott Brooksbank wins the overall championship, but Wayne Wong named Hotdogger (exhibition skier) of the Year. Marty Hall named head United States Nordic coach. Colorado voters reject 1976 Winter Olympic Games in referendum vote. Avery Brundage resigns as president of International Olympic Committee.

1973 Annemarie Proell of Austria and Gustavo Thoeni become first three-time winners of the World Cup. Jean-Claude Killy joins the pro circuit and becomes top-money winner with some $68,625. John Clendevin wins National Exhibition Championship at Sun Valley, but Eddie Ferguson named Hotdogger of the Year. World Cup events (other than Olympic Games) held in Japan for the first time. Mickey Cochran replaces Willy Schaeffler as head coach of the U.S. Ski Team. U.S. Ski Training Headquarters opens at Park City, Utah. Innsbruck, Austria, selected as site of the XII Winter Olympic Games in 1976.

SECTION II

Ski Equipment

The selection of proper equipment is a step that demands a skier's most careful consideration. It involves not only formidable expenditure but also a knowledge of what equipment is available and what will be best suited to the skier. Proper selection of ski equipment will have a direct bearing on the ease and speed with which you progress to advanced skiing and on the enjoyment that you will experience from the sport.

OBTAINING SKI EQUIPMENT

Although there are several rules of thumb that a skier may use to guide him, choosing equipment is largely a matter of individual preference, guided by the skier's taste, temperament, budget, and physical characteristics. There is seldom only one correct item of equipment for any particular skier. Rather, there is usually a choice to be made from several similar items. To obtain the needed equipment, there are three ways that may be employed to obtain it: borrowing, renting, or buying.

Borrowing

Since most new skiers are introduced to the sport by their friends, the most economical solution is to borrow equipment from them. If such equipment is suitable—and beware of the friend who assures you that you can get by with an oversize pair of boots or skis— everything is fine. But remember that the usual reason for spare equipment is that it is not worth trading in or selling. If the equip-

ment requires minor repairs, go to the nearest ski shop and have them made, along with any needed adjustments.

It is possible, though more difficult, to borrow ski clothing. However, one can usually get away with long, preferably thermal, underwear under blue jeans and a couple of sweaters. Although this kind of outfit may draw a few smiles, it is not unusual.

Even if you are not sure how you feel about skiing, a small investment in ski clothing will not be wasted. Sweaters, stretch pants, and parkas are acceptable wear for many activities and can serve for various kinds of informal social occasions.

Renting

If ski equipment cannot be borrowed from friends, it can be rented from a ski shop. Rental fees range anywhere from $4 to $15 a day, depending on the type of equipment you rent and the region from which it is rented. Generally, rentals tend to be slightly less in cities than in ski areas; but remember, particularly if you are traveling any distance to a resort, that you will be paying for the equipment while you are transporting it back and forth. Of course you may find that the rental equipment at the resort is not suitable to your needs, particularly when there is a large demand for it during the so-called high seasons. Also remember that any rental service is only as good as the person who operates it. It takes time to pick out the proper length in skis, to adjust the release bindings, and to fit the right boots. If a horde of skiers seeking rentals descends at once on a harried shop operator, the service will be slow and mistakes are more than possible. If you are renting at home, it is best to visit the ski shop days before the ski trips begins. They will usually put the equipment aside for you. If you are renting at a ski area, go early, even the afternoon before, if possible. In some cases, deposits are required.

Many ski shops will credit the rental cost if you decide to purchase equipment from them. It is a good idea to check into this matter before renting. But, it should be pointed out that beginners are not the only ones who rent equipment. Experienced skiers who live in regions where there is no weekend skiing and who take an annual ski vacation are often renters. So are casual skiers—those who ski fewer than three or four weekends a year. The decision whether to rent or to buy often depends on the amount of skiing you plan to do in any given season. More on renting equipment can be found later in this section.

Buying

If, after a ski trip or two, you find that you enjoy the sport, it is time to consider the purchase of equipment. Your budget should bear some relation to the amount of skiing you plan to do. For instance, lift tickets, lodging, and meals must be taken into consideration in determining how many ski trips are feasible each season. Figuring an average of $10 a day for meals, $8 for lodging, and $6 for lifts, for a total of about $24 a day, how many such days can you afford?

It is safe to say that if you ski ten days or more a season, it will pay you to invest in your own equipment. Assuming that a $200 outfit—consisting of metal skis, medium-high-quality boots, good bindings, and poles—has a life of at least five years, you will save a good deal over this period by buying rather than renting. In addition, you have something to sell or trade if you decide to give up skiing or step up to more costly equipment. But even if you ski fewer than ten days a year, you should definitely consider the purchase of boots. Rental boots are not always of high quality, and the fact that they are worn by dozens of different feet in the course of a season is bound to stretch them out of shape. Foot shape is as personal as fingerprints, and a boot not broken to a particular foot will never provide a perfect link between skier and skis, the major justification for the price and construction of ski boots.

When selecting boots, it is important that maximum leeway be given in your budget. In order to get that perfect fit, it may be necessary to go into a price bracket higher than originally anticipated. Only after boots have been purchased is it time to decide on skis, bindings, and poles—preferably in that order.

In buying skis, keep in mind that although metal and fiberglass skis are more expensive than wood skis, they have a longer life and are virtually impervious to humidity. Furthermore, metal and fiberglass skis can be reconditioned readily and can be counted on to have a trade-in value, even after several years of use. However, if you have any doubts about your "love" for skiing, settle for a pair of medium-priced wood skis.

In the case of bindings, it is wise to purchase the best you can afford. Bindings can last a lifetime and can be taken off when you change skis. Even the best are not excessively expensive, and their release features, when properly adjusted, can save you from a bad accident.

When buying ski poles, your budget has a great deal of latitude. Although it is a distinct joy to handle a modern, lightweight pole, such a pole is not essential for the average skier.

In planning your purchase of equipment you should not overlook ski clothing and such accessories as Arlberg straps, goggles, and ski racks. They should be considered by even the budget-conscious skiers. In any case, all equipment should be purchased from a reputable ski shop. Selling ski equipment requires a great deal of specialized knowledge not only about the equipment itself but also about its suitability for each individual skier, its servicing, and its maintenance. For example, mounting a pair of bindings is not merely a case of putting some screws into a pair of skis; it is a precision operation if the binding is to function properly.

It is foolish to buy "hot shot" racing equipment that is beyond your capabilities. The glamor of name-brand racing skis is totally lost on the slope if you do not know how to handle them. Remember that you will only hurt yourself by trying to make the salesman believe that you are better than you really are.

Finally, a few thoughts about children's equipment. There is a tendency, even on the part of experienced skiing parents, to skimp on children's equipment on the grounds that "they'll grow out of it by next year." This is wrong. Generally speaking, the price range in children's equipment is a good deal narrower than in adult equipment. For very few dollars extra, you can get the equipment they should have. And one of the advantages of

getting better-than-average equipment for children is that it can be sold or traded after the children have outgrown it. There are many parents in a similar situation. Because of this, a good source of children's equipment is the ski swaps staged by some ski clubs.

If you are operating on some sort of budget, keep in mind an overall balancing of costs among skis, boots, bindings, and poles, even though boots have the first priority. This table can be used as a rough guide, whether you are buying for adults or children.

Guide to Balancing Costs of Ski Equipment

Total Expenditure	Boots	Bindings*	Skis	Poles
$155	$ 55	$20	$ 65	$15
175	60	20	80	15
200	65	25	95	15
225	70	25	110	20
255	75	30	125	25
275	80	35	135	25
300	90	35	150	25
Up to 415	140	40	200	35
Up to 510	200	55	210	45

* Includes installation.

SKI BOOTS

The proper fit of your ski boots is one of the most important factors in selecting equipment. The boots are your means of communication with your skis, and if subtle changes of weight distribution are not faithfully transmitted by your boots to your skis, your efforts cannot be effective. That is, the boots are the vital link between skier and skis. If the boots are imperfect, turns will be imperfect.

The human foot and ankle joints are designed by nature to walk, run, jump—barefoot. Mechanically, the foot is a complicated ball-joint arrangement swiveling in all directions, with a complex arch, many small bones and ligaments, a few strong muscles, and relatively poor blood circulation. This design hardly matches the requirements of skiing: some flexion, mainly forward and back; very strong, almost rigid, resistance laterally which can sustain the weight of the body (plus centrifugal force) while standing on only the

edge of the foot; extreme insulation against cold and dampness. The ski boot must fill in for the deficiencies of the human foot, and this is the real challenge to the designers and makers of boots.

The ideal boot must: (1) have a hard and rigid shell, (2) be soft and resilient inside (foam synthetics or similar padding contoured to foot shape); (3) let the ankle bend forward (hinges, notches, etc.); (4) support the ankle and fit closely—therefore be tight; (5) not be so tight that it cuts off blood circulation; (6) be waterproof; (7) let the foot "breathe" to avoid condensation; (8) have a rigid sole to permit solid and steady fitting in the binding; (9) have a sole that is not *too* rigid. The outcome of these conflicts is that as a design, a ski boot is a compromise between support and comfort. With the added variables of price and highly individual shapes of feet to accommodate, there is room for many solutions to the bootmaking challenge. Because of the

A typical lace ski boot is shown at left, while a typical buckle boot is illustrated at right.

hard, intricate work involved, the bulk of ski boots for many years have been imported from Europe where skilled labor still exists at a lower, although steadily rising, cost. The development of the plastic boot, however, has brought about a renaissance of bootmaking in the United States.

Boot Closure System

The most obvious feature that meets the eye and the mind in considering ski boots, is the system of closure. Lacing is almost obsolete now in ski boots. The laces, originally leather, later cotton or nylon (World War II parachute cords were very popular in the late forties), pull together the right and left section of the boot uppers through eyelets or hooks. These spaced eyelets or hooks spread the tension of the laces evenly around the foot and force the leather to conform to the shape of the foot.

Lacing still is common in the double boot. A soft inner boot may have flat eyelets; lacing is loosened and tightened at every eyelet, a

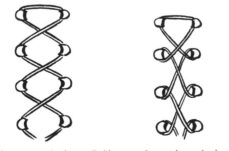

Crisscross lacing (left); nonloosening lacing (right).

time-consuming and frustrating process. An improvement known as speed lacing consists of special eyelets which let the laces slide easily. One pull from the top tightens the lacing.

By far the most common closure for ski boots is the buckle. A Swiss manufacturer (Henke) introduced the buckle to the ski world in the late 1950's. It was actually an adaptation of the old ladder and buckle still widely used in European farmlands on felt house shoes. Although very convenient and quick (buckled tight for skiing, frequently flipped loose to ride the lift or while resting) it took several years for buckles to catch on.

Four to five buckles are attached with rivets to the inside and outside sections of the upper boot. They exert pressure on those localized points of attachment. This necessitates the use of strong, thick, stiff leather or plastic for the rivets to be anchored securely and to protect the foot from the sharp pressure while closing. The buckles must be located precisely to spread the tension as uniformly as possible. Their biggest advantage over the old lacing is that they provide enough leverage to get a really tight fit that even the strongest hands often cannot do. In addition, most of the buckles have screw and tension adjustment features that allow for very fine variations in fit and comfort.

Boot Materials and Construction

Ski boots were known as such with the coming of Alpine skiing, but they did not develop as a species distinct from mountain boots until the development of cable bindings

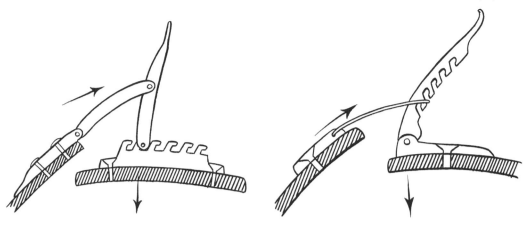

Two popular buckle systems, showing how pressure is applied to the foot as the buckle closes.

in the 1930's. Even the rigid box toe was developed as much for mountaineering as for skiing. The box toe not only helped keep toes warm, but prevented them from being squeezed and chafed by the straps of toe irons and crampons.

One disadvantage of the cable binding was that its tension buckled the soles of existing ski boots. And so, the heavy half-inch sole was developed. But this was only the beginning. With full control over the ski established by the cable bindings, skiers began to demand more support from their ski boots, a demand that developed the high, stiff boots of today. In addition, the rapid increase in the number of lifts made walking an almost incidental adjunct of skiing.

The trend toward the modern boot was sharply accelerated with the introduction of sideslipping as a formal part of skiing technique. This required strong support of wobbly ankles. As boots got higher and stiffer, they also became more uncomfortable and harder to fit. In response to this problem, European bootmakers developed the double boot consisting of a soft inner boot and a stiff outer shell. This helped for a while to solve the problem of comfort and fit, but it raised the problem of lacing; women particularly had difficulty lacing the hard outer boot. This in turn gave rise to the development of the buckle boot.

In its basic parts a so-called "modern" boot was quite simple. It consisted of a heavy sole, usually made of a series of leather layers, and an upper, which included the shaft for ankle support and a closure of the laces. The sole, beyond sustaining the high tensions of cable bindings, had a groove in the heel so that the heel release unit of the binding or the cable could hold the boot in position. The bottom of the sole was usually made of rubber or rubber compound with a ribbed surface to allow easier walking on snow or ice.

In the mid-1960's there were some changes in sole construction. Instead of laminated leather a one-piece wooden sole enclosed in plastic was substituted. This sole was completely moisture-resistant and could be "sealed" instead of stitched to the upper. Another fairly recent development was the canted sole, which counters the tendency of most people to put their weight on the outside of their foot rather than the inside. Raising the inside edge of the sole by about three-sixteenths of an inch neutralized this tendency. This is important in skiing because most ski maneuvers are done on the inside edges. Most ski boots in the 1970's feature canted soles.

The construction of the upper was much more complex in "modern" boots. Because the upper provides the essential ankle support, it had to be stiff and rugged and had to maintain these characteristics over a number of years. This required the best leathers, carefully tanned. Chrome tanning, while expensive, was best for ski boots because the leather stiffens with repeated wettings and dryings. Vegetable tanning, while cheaper,

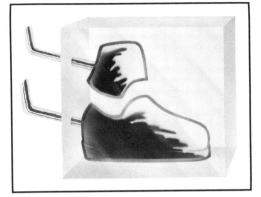

Just five years ago this leather boot was king of the slopes. It was built around a last—a wooden foot-shaped form. The intricate construction required much handwork and stitching, so production was costly—one reason for the trend to synthetics. The boot was reinforced (1) in key stress areas, lined with soft leather (2), padded with foam rubber (3) in the ankle and tongue, and the outer part or shaft (4) was built from thick, top-grade chromed leather. The sole had a stiffener (5), usually made of wood. Then came the buckle revolution and the entry of plastic boots. These are still made on a conventional last, but ⅛ inch of plastic coats the top-grade leather shaft (see peeled-back section) for more durability (bottom left). Also, the sole is injection molded—hot liquid polyvinyl chloride is forced into the mold under pressure and adheres to the plastic-leather upper of the boot. Taking injection molding technology one step further, boot manufacturers hit on the idea of making the entire outer boot from plastic (right). Advantages include great rigidity, strength, and durability. Of course, some bootmakers continue to use traditional techniques to finish the inside of the boot, where comfort and fit are important factors.

was not suitable for ski boots because it turned the leather spongy, allowing it to stretch and lose its support and protective qualities. There are also several methods of combination tanning. While more satisfactory for the occasional skier, the leathers from these processes were not desirable for rugged ski use. One of the drawbacks of chrome-tanned leather, particularly as used in the heavy, stiff outer boot, however, was that it would not readily "break" to the shape of the foot. This is why the double boot was developed.

The inner boot was made of soft leather and was padded. It helped transmit leg and foot action to the skis because it was sewn to the sole, but its main function was to allow comfort and a snug fit. And because it provided another layer of leather, it made the double boot warmer than the single boot.

Then at the end of the 1960's came the plastic revolution in ski boots. As a matter of fact, plastic began at the bottom and worked its way up. First it was the sole. Here plastic made the boot welt watertight because it could actually stick to the leather. Leather soles required stitching which created holes through which water would eventually find its way after extended use. Plastic soles also offered durability. Leather was easily hacked by tough steel bindings, and where notches were required for toe pieces, a leather sole would soon acquire three or four sets—no help in keeping your boot square to the ski.

Plastic also led to the ski-width sole, the idea being that a sole the same width as a ski transmits motion more directly to the ski. It is important to remember that a leather sole would bend slightly at the ball of the foot, but a rigid polyvinyl-chloride sole does

A pair of double boots; note second boot.

not bend, so the pivot point moves to the toe of the boot. This means that the ski bindings must be adjusted to compensate for the stiffer sole when switching to synthetic boots. Simple physics makes it obvious that you have a longer lever now, so your heel piece will open more easily and you will need a higher setting.

In 1969, plastic boots took a giant step up and moved into the main part of the boot, the upper, where its rigidity and durability bring skiers many advantages. Plastic boots offer something like power steering in a car, because their rigidity transfers the skier's slightest whim directly to the ski.

Plastic also gives a boot longer life in the critical ankle area, where leather will break sooner or later under the stress of repeated up-down flexing. Sooner or later depends largely on the weight and agility of the skier. Also, plastic is generally hard enough not to be affected by slashing steel edges or scrapes from sharp binding parts, so the boot will last longer and will not chip or tear like leather. Then there is color. For years, ski boot makers have offered their products in the Henry Ford color range—black or black. While leather can be dyed, the hues are weak and lackluster. Not so with plastic. And although black still dominates the scene, you have a choice of a wide variety of blues, reds, and yellows too.

It seems likely that economics and skier

preference are leading in the 1970's to the abandonment of all-leather ski boots. Ski shops, however, still are offering plastic-leather laminated boots; a layer of plastic bonded to the leather gives the boot some of the lateral rigidity of the all-plastic models. Finally, in the highest price category of all are most of the all-plastic boots, costing as much as $200 a pair.

The revolution in ski boots has been one of price as well as materials. In the mid-1960's, a skier could pay $80 for a pair of boots and get the best quality offered by ski shops. At the same time, he might have paid $150 or almost twice as much for the best quality skis of his choice. In the 1970's, however, skiers often are paying as much for boots as for skis. One expert who has tested dozens of pairs of skis and boots insists that in the case of skis and boots priced above $100 a pair, the additional dollar invested in boots will yield more performance value than a dollar invested in skis.

Molded boots, the exotic branch of the synthetic family, range from ones in which no leather is used, to a two-piece fiberglass shell padded inside with leather sacks of synthetic dough (plastic), to a boot with socklike leather inner boots that can be worn independently as après-ski footwear.

Hinging at the ankle is one of the main problems with molded boots. The whole point of using rigid synthetic materials is to give the skier a stiffer boot with more lateral support so his motions will be transferred directly to the ski. These materials, however, obviously do not bend the way leather does. Thus the bootmaker is faced with a choice— mold the boot in one piece and sacrifice some of the forward movement at the ankle, or mold it in two pieces and use a mechanical hinge. For the skier, choice of hinge will boil down to a matter of personal taste. You may find a particular hinge is too flexible for your liking, or, on the other hand, it may be too stiff. No-hinge boots are used almost solely by racers or very advanced skiers who have the ability to sit way back and who want instant tip pressure when they move forward. The manufacturer mounts an adjustable mechanical lock on the molded boot to freeze the ankle hinge in a forward lean position.

Fit can also be a problem with molded boots. When you have an extremely rigid exterior with absolutely no give, it is difficult to protect the foot from pressure points. The solution is either some sort of malleable material to fill the space between the foot and the exterior, a lining built on a traditional shoe last in various foot sizes, or the injection of plastic foam while the foot is in the boot during the fitting process at the shop.

Selecting Ski Boots

Buying boots that do not fit is not an uncommon mistake, but it is one that can be avoided by acquiring a little knowledge and by devoting a lot of time to the actual task of trying and fitting.

Fitting the Boot. The best-fitting boot of all, of course, is a custom-made boot. No manufacturer has yet developed a mass-produced boot that can comfortably fit the whole spectrum of shape and sizes of the human foot. Probably no one ever will. One manufacturer's boot shape (formed from a last) may follow your foot better than another's. It is definitely worth experimenting to find out who has the boot closest to your type of foot. One skier may find boot models of several manufacturers fit satisfactorily. Another may find that no manufacturer makes a boot that fits him. Fortunately, however, most skiers fall into a broad middle category with feet that can be fitted with a number of brands and price ranges of boots. Also fortunately, boot manufacturers are coming closer all the time to the configuration of the human foot and have developed tools and chemicals for dealing with recalcitrant pressure points and needed bunion bulges. But if you should be one of the unfortunates with a very unusual foot shape or extreme fitting problems, you will be better off ignoring the standard criteria for boot buying—price, appearance, brand name, etc. —and simply buying a boot that fits. This may even mean a very high price for an occasional skier or a lower price for a frequent skier—but the important point is good fit.

The ski boot must surround snugly not only the bottom of the foot but the instep and the ankle, and particularly the back of the

heel. Almost every skier past the most novice level knows the feel of wearing a ski boot and has heard that tried but true cliché about a boot becoming part of your foot. Beyond that, a well-fitted boot feels about like this:

1. It feels tight. It should not hurt, but you should be able to feel the boot on most parts of your foot.
2. The boot should grip the heel, just below the anklebone. This should not be a pinching feeling.
3. You should be conscious of the boot touching your instep, but it should not press on this area. When you bend forward, the boot must not squash your foot.
4. You should be able to wiggle your toes with ease. You may not have much space to the end of the boot, but you must still be able to move those toes to keep them warm and avoid cramps.

Getting the proper fit in a conventional, non-foamed, non-customed boot is no secret, but there is a technique to it. First, tell the ski shop man what boot you have been wearing, to give him some idea of your size. Once you find a brand that fits, walk around for about 10 minutes. Then find a solid structure—a pillar or wall will do—and lean forward against it with your arms stretched out in front of you as if you were skiing, but with your knees unbent. Lift one foot and tap the toe gently on the floor. You should feel your toe just touch the end of the boot. If it hits too hard, the boot is too short; if it does not hit at all, the boot is too long. Then stand sideways to the post or wall, as if it were a slalom flag around which you were making a turn. Lift the inside foot and tilt the outside foot inward, toward the post. If the boot does not fit properly in the arch area, this exercise will probably alert you to a sore spot. Turn around and do it with the other foot, too.

Then plant one foot in front of you. You should feel your foot slide slightly to the front of the boot. When you take another step forward, the heel of the first foot should slide back slightly in the heel of the boot. Tradition has it that the foot should be immobile in the boot, and so it should be—when your knees are bent forward in a ski position. When your knees are in the normal walking position, there should be just enough movement

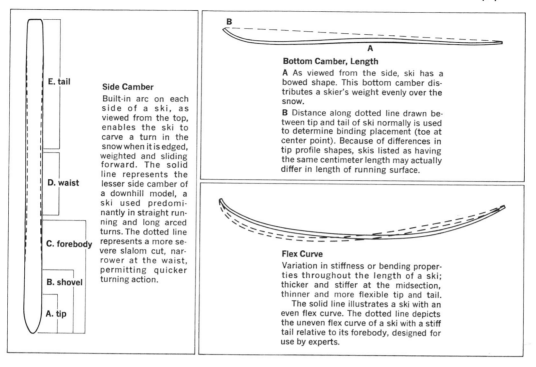

E. tail

D. waist

C. forebody

B. shovel

A. tip

Side Camber

Built-in arc on each side of a ski, as viewed from the top, enables the ski to carve a turn in the snow when it is edged, weighted and sliding forward. The solid line represents the lesser side camber of a downhill model, a ski used predominantly in straight running and long arced turns. The dotted line represents a more severe slalom cut, narrower at the waist, permitting quicker turning action.

B

A

Bottom Camber, Length

A As viewed from the side, ski has a bowed shape. This bottom camber distributes a skier's weight evenly over the snow.

B Distance along dotted line drawn between tip and tail of ski normally is used to determine binding placement (toe at center point). Because of differences in tip profile shapes, skis listed as having the same centimeter length may actually differ in length of running surface.

Flex Curve

Variation in stiffness or bending properties throughout the length of a ski; thicker and stiffer at the midsection, thinner and more flexible tip and tail.

The solid line illustrates a ski with an even flex curve. The dotted line depicts the uneven flex curve of a ski with a stiff tail relative to its forebody, designed for use by experts.

inside the boot to allow for changes in the size of your feet (for instance, your feet might tend to swell in the morning).

The last check is to stand knock-kneed—feet about 14 inches apart, knees together. This will reveal any pressure points at the inside of the ankles. Finally, with feet in the same spot, bow your knees and check for sore spots on the outside of the ankles. The reshaper can quickly solve these problems.

No shop can guarantee a perfect fit with a conventional boot. However, through the use of padding and the boot reshaper, the fitter should be able to make adjustments until you feel totally comfortable. Remember that many boots have a severe forward lean built in. This means that before buckling, your toes may touch the front of the boot, but afterwards when you stand up with your knees relaxed forward, your toes will be sufficiently back in the boot. With buckles, it is easy to vary the amount of tightness over this or that spot. You can also see, as you buckle, that when a boot buckles only in the first notch it is too narrow, or that when it is tight enough only in the fourth notch, it is too wide. A boot is the correct size when it feels comfortable yet tight and when the buckles snap shut in the

middle notches. Keep in mind, too, that the top four buckles are the only really vital ones. The buckle over the toes is mostly to help you get in the boot easily.

Looking into the boot and feeling inside with your hand can tell you a lot about how the boot will fit. Beware of boots that are heavily padded, particularly around the ankle area. This padding will fit fine when the boot is new, but after some wear the thick padding tends to compress, destroying the good fit. Very strong skiers may even find that their feet move within the thickly padded ankle shafts, slowing the transmission of forces to the skis. An arch on the sole is good for people with normal feet, but for flat-footed persons it is pure murder. You may be able to remove the sole if the boot seems to fit in every other way.

A boot should fit comfortably from the first day you wear it, but beware of too much comfort. This can indicate a boot that is too big. The result of using such a boot will be not only loss of control over your skis but faster breakdown of the leather and shorter life of the boot. It is possible to make a narrow boot wider, by stretching it, but you cannot make a large boot smaller. If a boot takes the basic shape of your foot easily, you can make it extremely tight without having any pain (you may even cut off circulation without immediate pain). When you have got this kind of fit, you can be sure the boot will not bite back.

Boot Stiffness. In the process of arriving at the great advances in design, the ski boot of the professional or racing skier has evolved into a massive, unified piece of load-bearing armor—a sort of exoskeleton. As in the evolution of knight's armor during the early Middle Ages, boots have become heavier and less flexible. Within such armor, a proper fit is crucial. If the boot is too tight, loosening it causes the feet to swell and makes later tightening more difficult and painful. A stiff boot must fit absolutely right the first time. This is why, unless a skier is prepared to buy a custom boot or spend a great deal of time finding just the right ready-made boot, he can turn to foam injection to get the right fit.

The pressure points of stiff boots are usually:

1. At the sides of the foot (in the case of buckles, the first and second buckle can pull the boot too tightly at this point).

2. At the instep, since feet arch in varying degrees.
3. At the ankle joint, where anklebones can chafe against the sides of the boots.
4. At the shin, where high, stiff, thick boots can cut into the leg as a skier tries to lean forward to ski.

The first question to ask yourself when buying very stiff boots is: does the amount of forward lean of the boots suit your own stance? To find out, put the boots on, close the buckles and get into your normal ski stance. Take care to put a thick magazine under your heel; this will correspond to the elevation created by most bindings. Execute small up-and-down motions to get the feeling that you are skiing. You may feel comfortable, but find that you are forced to remain in a more bent position than you are accustomed to. If you did not bend forward previously in your skiing, the boots will help you to correct this mistake. If you lack strength in your legs, you may even tire after a few minutes of the forward lean imposed by the boots. On the other hand, if your stance was already too forward, a lot of forward lean in the boots will be a disadvantage if it reinforces your mistake. Also consider whether you are ready to

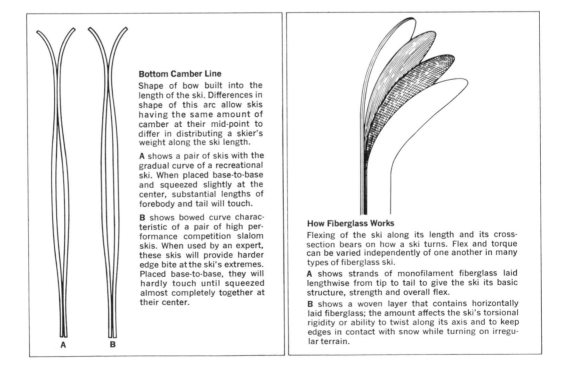

Bottom Camber Line

Shape of bow built into the length of the ski. Differences in shape of this arc allow skis having the same amount of camber at their mid-point to differ in distributing a skier's weight along the ski length.

A shows a pair of skis with the gradual curve of a recreational ski. When placed base-to-base and squeezed slightly at the center, substantial lengths of forebody and tail will touch.

B shows bowed curve characteristic of a pair of high performance competition slalom skis. When used by an expert, these skis will provide harder edge bite at the ski's extremes. Placed base-to-base, they will hardly touch until squeezed almost completely together at their center.

A   B

How Fiberglass Works

Flexing of the ski along its length and its cross-section bears on how a ski turns. Flex and torque can be varied independently of one another in many types of fiberglass ski.

A shows strands of monofilament fiberglass laid lengthwise from tip to tail to give the ski its basic structure, strength and overall flex.

B shows a woven layer that contains horizontally laid fiberglass; the amount affects the ski's torsional rigidity or ability to twist along its axis and to keep edges in contact with snow while turning on irregular terrain.

stand in a permanent flexed position when you are resting on the side of a trail or standing in a gondola. Opening the top buckle often will facilitate a more upright position, but not always.

At first, manufacturers of highback boots tended to believe that the human leg rose from the ankle to a 90-degree vertical when viewed from the front or back. For this reason, when stiff boots and very high backs first appeared several years ago, many skiers whose legs were a little bowlegged found themselves leaning on the outside edges of the boot soles. Boot designers soon discovered this fault, and now they tilt the boot shafts to the outside. Unfortunately, this does not suit every skier. Women especially may feel their boot tops exercising painful pressure on the inside of the tibia.

When you try on boots, to feel whether your feet are comfortable laterally, close the top buckles securely. Place your feet parallel and about eight inches apart. Get into your normal ski stance and do some small up-and-down and edging motions. Any acute discomfort will be felt immediately.

There are two categories of skiers today: those who want their boots to offer immediate and maximum resistance to forward flexing, and those who only want a moderate resistance at first. In either case the boot should limit excessive flexing of the ankle. Too much ankle bend can create real trauma by compressing the bones against one another in the front of the ankle. Some skiers feel this discomfort with a relatively small flex angle of the ankle, others only after the ankle is flexed a lot. The two types of skiers cannot be satisfied with the same boot model, unless the boot itself has a flex regulating system.

To determine the right fit for your ankle flex, put on the boots with the heels elevated an inch or more from the floor. Try to flex completely. Straighten, then flex once more. You will notice that if you cannot flex enough, you will lose your balance backwards. On the other hand, if the boots' forward flex is excessive, your shin will not get enough support from the tongue of the boot when the ankle is flexed sharply. This is the equivalent of not being able to apply enough pressure on the forebody of the ski in carving turns.

Be sensitive to any painful pressure on the inside or outside of your leg after flexing. Any sensation of pain during flexing will encourage you to avoid bending your ankles, a practice which disturbs balance and proper ski technique.

For many years we at *Ski* have been insisting on the importance of sensations in the foot as well as the importance of slight foot movement in refining the movements transmitted to the skis by your body, especially your legs. Does the almost total rigidity of the modern boot top still permit this delicate refinement? Does the initial numbness felt by the skier who has abandoned his old boots for plastic shells really result in a lack of feel for his ski and the snow? Absolutely not! It only means that the foot must adapt to new sensations and discover a new way of acting.

With the old soft boot, each movement of the ski actually corresponded to several movements of the foot-ankle-joint system. Inside a stiff plastic boot, on the other hand, there is no movement, only a variation of pressures exerted on skin and bone surface. The skier must then learn to decipher a new code of information transmitted by his foot and lower leg. Once you have learned to interpret these new sensations, you can direct your skis much more effectively than in the past. Instead of moving around, the arch, the anklebone, and the heelbone act directly on the walls of the boot. Once you have adapted to the new boots, the "intelligence" of the foot can play an even greater role in your skiing.

Since most major boot manufacturers now offer one or more highback models, the fall boot buyer, be he racer or recreational skier, will have several brands and models to choose from. Besides boots with extremely high backs that provide rigid support for racing, there are medium-height highbacks for more recreational skiing and even nonfunctional, soft highbacks for those who just want the racer look. If you are not in the market for a new pair of boots this year, you can try highbacks by purchasing a pair of plastic, foambacked supports which can be attached to most boot sizes.

Highbacks are helpful in maintaining balance, one of the most critical factors in skiing on moguled slopes. On these uneven trails, a skier is pitched both forward and aft. In a pitch forward, a skier uses his foot as a lever to adjust his balance. But in rocking backward, balancing is more difficult, since there is no natural lever, no foot to support the body weight. Highbacks supply the support; the lever behind the leg enables the skier to lean back and rebound forward again. If you have badly misjudged your line in the bumps, you can use the highbacks to avoid an abrupt transition and get back on the course: simply push your feet forward and pull back on the boots to lever ski tips upward. Of course, you should be sure to allow your body to stretch full length to absorb the impact, and land squarely over your feet in a forward position ahead of the boot backs. This is not a graceful maneuver, but thanks to highbacks it is a

great way to get yourself out of trouble. Highbacks also make skiing in deep snow and crud a less tiring experience; you gain tremendous stability, with the highbacks acting as a subtle but constant lever to keep ski tips planing.

Every silver lining has its cloud, and with highbacks it is the temptation of many racers and recreational skiers to develop too great a dependence on highbacks. The most common misuse occurs when a skier sits back at all times, balancing his weight against the highback. If a racer begins his turn from a back position, he will start slowly and fail to accelerate his speed. A recreational skier will complete each turn off-balance, with his weight on the tail of the uphill ski.

SKIS

To a prospective skier unfamiliar with the sport, shopping for skis can be a surprising experience. The number of brand names (as many as 200), the variety of colors and model names (geographical, technical, automotive, zoological, scientific, with a good measure of strange foreign sounds and spellings), and, above all, the range of prices (from $25 to $200 a pair) are bewildering. This diversity reflects the youth, novelty, enthusiasm, and competitive nature of skiing more than almost any other phase of the sport does.

Once the bright colors, resounding names, and superlative claims have been removed, however, the different types of skis become simpler. Let us start by looking at the following necessary features and qualities:

1. A ski must be permanently cambered.
2. It must be flexible and resilient.
3. It must also twist a little (torsion).
4. It must be strong and sustain heavy stresses. A skier weighing 150 pounds and sliding down at a gentle 12 miles an hour can actually release several tons of energy in the case of a sudden stop.
5. The outside surfaces must be moisture-proof and highly resistant to abrasion—by ice, rocks, bare ground, steel edges.
6. A ski should resist exposure to the most varied outdoor and indoor conditions imaginable—from contact with the snow, hot sun, and driving rain to long periods of storage in every type of climate.

When one is standing on a ski, his weight applies pressure in the center. The pressure must be distributed gradually along the entire surface. To achieve this load distribution, a ski is cambered and is tapered very precisely from a thick center to the tip in front, and to the tail in the rear.

Because the terrain on which a skier slides is never perfectly even, but varies constantly, and because the consistency of the snow passes from hard to very soft, the front of the ski must lift over obstacles. Therefore it must be longer and more flexible in front than in the back. In addition, the bottom has a longitudinal groove to help the ski track when sliding straight. Actually, if all skiing were done straight down the hill (down the fall line), the characteristics described thus far would be sufficient for a good ski design. Indeed such a ski could run effectively with straight sides. But because a ski must turn, the sides must be curved. This is known as side camber. Because of side camber a ski, when banked, will rest on the curved edge, helping it to turn.

A slalom ski (top) will flex into an even curve. A downhill ski has stiffer tail in order to provide good tracking despite flexible tip.

Side camber is more exaggerated in front than in back. This gives us the familiar shape of the ski: narrowest in the center, wider at the tail, widest at the tip. These three widths are called the dimensions of the ski

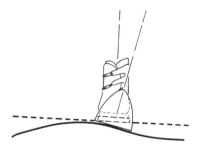

Torsion in ski enables tip to twist as it hits bump while the center of ski and boot are unaffected.

and are usually given in millimeters. Incidentally, it should be noted that one result of side camber is to cause the edges of the skis to skid slightly when they are moving straight forward. For this reason, it is important that the bottoms of skis be flat and smooth, with the edge perfectly flush; otherwise the edges can catch easily and send the ski off its track. Side camber then promotes turning. In a sharper turn, the ski not only skids sideways but also bends lengthwise (flexes) and twists slightly. Thus, what determines the ability of a ski to turn well is the combined result of three elements: side camber, flexibility, and torsion. Combining the three is the central challenge to the ski maker.

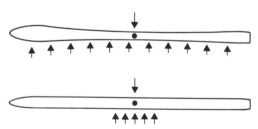

Illustration above shows how curved side of ski enables pressure from skier's weight to be distributed all along the edge of the ski in a turn. If ski had straight sides (lower figure), all the edge pressure would be concentrated directly under the skier's feet.

A medium or standard flexibility spreads the weight over a longer surface and increases stability while retaining fairly sufficient ease of turning. Skis with such a flex

normally are best for all-around recreational skiing in all conditions.

Hard flex will spread the weight well under the tip and tail area, making the bottom groove and edges bite in the snow along the entire length of the ski. Turning requires more power, but stability and holding on hard snow or ice are greatly increased.

Other factors modify the influence of the flex. One, obviously, is the weight of the skier. For example, a woman weighing 100 pounds and a man weighing 200 pounds skiing on the same pair of medium-flex skis will have different feelings. For the light woman the skis may feel too hard to turn, while they may be too soft and unstable under the heavy man.

Another factor is the ability of the skier. A beginner has very little need for stability and tracking, since he skis at very slow speeds on gentle slopes. Turning is the main problem, and a flexible ski is well suited to his needs. A good intermediate, on the other hand, skis faster on steeper slopes. With the speed, centrifugal force or momentum adds to the weight and a medium flex becomes a necessity. Hard flexes with emphasis on the tails of the skis are reserved for heavy people and for racers.

Thickness of a ski is not necessarily a reliable indicator of its stiffness. A thick ski of the fiberglass epoxy type, for instance, can be more flexible than a thin-looking metal ski. Standard, combi, pro-professional (ski instructor), "G.S.," "R.S.," "S.G." (giant slalom in English, German, and French respectively) are generally in the medium flex and medium-to-hard range. Downhill (DH) skis normally come in a soft flex. Deep powder skis have a very soft flex.

While a ski should be flexible throughout its longitudinal axis, it should be quite rigid through its latitudinal axis. The ability to resist the twisting forces imposed on the ski is called *torsional stiffness*.

Owing to the shape of the ski and, quite frequently, the nature of the terrain, a ski has a tendency to twist when put on edge. A complete lack of torsional stiffness would defeat the turning ability built into the ski, since the tip would flatten out and break away every time the ski was put on edge. At the other extreme, too much torsional stiffness would tend to deflect the ski from its true path every time it ran over the side of a bump. The ski should therefore have relatively high torsional stiffness. How high depends on its use. But a little bit of torsion must be present.

When the tip of a ski is deflected, it will vibrate. Vibration is desirable up to a point because it helps break the vacuum between the skis and the snow and therefore allows the ski to run faster. Excessive vibration, however, is highly undesirable, for it breaks the contact with the snow, making the ski chatter in a turn and difficult to control in straight running. The amount of vibration a ski generates depends to a large extent on the material used. In better skis, materials may be added to dampen the vibration rate, or vibrations may be damped by modifications of design.

Wood Skis

The early European Alpine skis were made of solid ash, the best local wood available. Then hickory, which has better natural characteristics of flexibility and resilience, was imported from the southern United States. Still, there were serious problems in finding planks of uniform grain able to resist drying and warpage. As a result, manufacturers began to fabricate laminated skis—following the concept of plywood. This is the current

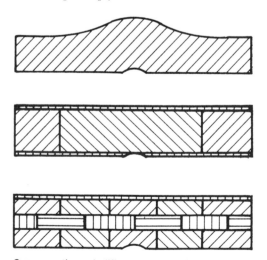

Cross section of different types of wooden ski. Top to bottom: straight wood construction; lower cost lamination; high-grade lamination.

wood construction method used, with much variation in the arrangement and types of wood laminated depending on local supply, costs, and traditions. Generally the harder woods are used on the outer surface; softer and cheaper laminations are inside. Highly laminated wood also forms the cores of some high-priced plastic skis.

All-wood skis are now sold entirely in the low-priced range and are relatively simple and inexpensive to make. Although they are cheap, on the negative side it must be said that wooden skis have to be fairly thick to be strong. And although they can be very flexible, their thickness, low resilience, and high torsion make them difficult to turn in soft snow. They are not very durable and lose camber or springiness.

Metal Skis

Beginning in the 1930's, a number of attempts were made to design and manufacture a ski of metal to solve the deficiencies of the wooden ski, including the need for separately installed metal edges. The problems were many: steel hard enough for edges was too heavy and too stiff for a good running ski. Soft aluminum was light enough but too soft for edges and not resilient enough. Bonding metals together or onto wooden frames was not easy. In addition, the men making these efforts generally had their background in woodworking concepts and procedures.

In the late 1940's an attempt was made to produce skis using the aluminum metal sandwich construction commonly used in aircraft production. Although the engineering was sound, success did not come easily. A multitude of differences between the properties of a ski and an airplane part kept appearing, and solutions, one by one, had to be found. After about five years, most of the major basic problems were solved. A metal ski not only was designed but began to be produced in quantity. Since then new manufacturers have appeared, and the older traditional wood ski makers have added metal skis to their lines.

The metal ski helped to create a new era in skiing because it made possible for thousands of recreational, weekend, and nonathletic skiers the pleasures of advanced skiing, easy

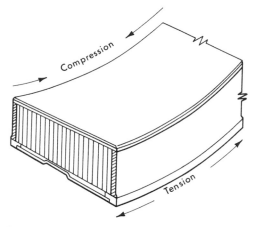

The basic structure of the metal ski consists of two layers of springy aluminum alloy bonded to a lightweight core. When the ski deflects through a bump, the top layer shortens in compression and the bottom layer lengthens in tension. When the strain is relieved, both these metal layers snap back to their original length and the ski regains precisely its original shape, ready for the next maneuver.

turning, a measure of deep snow skill, and a durable product.

A metal ski normally is made of two thin metal sheets or skins, bonded to and separated by a core which can be made of various materials—plywood, particle board, or laminated wood. When the ski bends, one metal ski stretches, the other compresses. Because the metal is highly tempered or springlike, the ski "springs back" to its original shape immediately. This is resilience. The degree to which the ski can bend and still return quickly without taking a permanent set or breaking is a measure of its strength. In a metal ski, strength is very high.

The elasticity of metal is partly in proportion to the length involved. A six- or seven-foot-long ski bends lengthwise easily; but in its width, roughly three inches, it hardly bends at all. In fact, it is practically rigid and has very little torsion. The combination of longitudinal flexibility and latitudinal rigidity is responsible for the skiing characteristics of the metal ski. When the ski is banked to turn, the entire length banks as a unit. Similarly, the pressure along the edge in contact with the snow can be relieved all at once. The ski reacts instantaneously to the slightest ripple on the ground or the slightest impulse or bounce

given by the skier. The result is to facilitate sideslipping and turning on metal skis.

Flexibility in a metal sandwich varies with the square of the distance between the two sheets. As a result of this mathematical relationship the metal ski can be made very thin at the extremities, without loss of strength. Thinness also accounts for the excellent performance in deep snow, where the metal ski can slice sideways through the layers of snow.

Because it is difficult to roll a sharp edged groove in a sheet of metal without breaking it, the metal ski's running surface has a shallow smooth groove, and this also adds to its easy turning characteristic. The hold in a straight line provided by the groove is easily broken to allow motion sideways. On a hardpacked icy surface a metal ski will vibrate. This alternatively breaks the contact of the ski with the ground and makes it slide fast, independently of the sliding qualities of its sole. To these advantageous performance characteristics a metal ski adds the perhaps more important quality of extreme durability. As long as it stays bonded together a metal ski is practically a permanent structure. It cannot warp, or lose its camber or original flexibility, unless accidentally bent. The four corners of its cross section are hard metal and will resist scratching for a long time. Extreme temperature and humidity variations affect it in a minor way, but it will return to normal under normal conditions. Repairs and maintenance are held to a minimum.

Yet each of the performance qualities of the metal ski carries with it a proportion of disadvantages. For the same reasons that it turns easily, it is not very stable in a straight line at high speed and on hard surfaces. Because of its lack of torsion it enters easily into a turn but then does not hold very precisely along a sharp curved line. It springs back so quickly that it is difficult to hold under control when riding hard bumps or when it starts to chatter sideways. Major repairs necessitate factory service.

By the combination of flex curve, dimensions, and torsion factors outlined earlier, improvements in the metal ski have taken place at a slow pace. The flexible ski for the pleasure skier tolerates wide variations in dimensions. But when a ski becomes stiffer—as it must for the racer to track well and to hold on ice—the flex curve must be determined precisely to match dimensions, and some torsion must be present. Tolerances become crucial. Variations of one millimeter in width, a few degrees on an irregular curve, or a few thousandths of an inch in the thickness of metal skins can produce variations in performance from unpleasant to catastrophic. After much trial and error, metal skis were made to meet the requirements of fast skiers. To quiet the vibration and permit some torsion without losing structural strength, a thin film of rubber was introduced, sandwiched between two metal sheets of different thicknesses. The result was to create a "snake effect" which allows the ski to shear and roll over an obstacle. Whenever the ski is deflected in one direction the rubber counteracts in the opposite direction, helping to maintain steadier contact with the snow, thereby increasing stability.

Plastic Skis

While metal skis were making inroads into the wood market in terms of performance, prestige, and price, a few wood ski manufacturers and some independent researchers were looking in a new direction: the ultramodern wonder world of plastics. By 1968 plastic skis were on the slopes in large volume and if the present trend continues, wood and metal skis will be as scarce as dodo birds.

The basic material is fiberglass-reinforced laminated sheets of polyester or epoxy resins, by now very popular in boat hulls, car bodies, fishing rods, and archery bows. The material is produced from millions of tiny glass fibers which are first made into threads. The threads are woven into a loose cloth. The cloth is then dipped in resin which cures under heat and pressure into hard, glasslike material.

The fiberglass threads act very much like the steel bars in reinforced concrete; they supply the strength and elasticity as long as the resin holds them bonded in place. The resins themselves, like cement, have no spectacular mechanical properties. They vary in price, binding power, and hardness—from the polyesters to the best epoxies (which give their name to the most expensive skis).

The manufactured fiberglass-reinforced

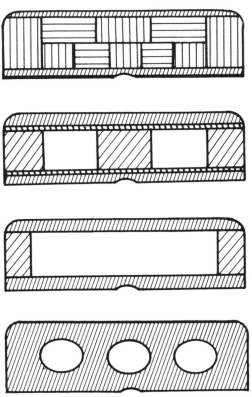

Plastic ski cross sections.

plastic (FRP) sheet for skis compares with aluminum alloy in that it is man-made. It is stable, light, strong, elastic, resilient, highly impact-resistant (bullet-proof vests are made of it), and completely moisture-proof. An interesting feature is that by varying the pressure under which the sheet is cured, the density, and therefore resilience, can be varied. For example, low pressure will produce a sheet that will react somewhat like hickory. High pressure yields a sheet reacting somewhat like metal.

Plastic skis (under varied names: epoxi, fiberglass, glasskis) perform with some of the best characteristics of both the wooden ski and the metal ski. In fact some of the best models come nearer to being the "ideal ski" than any ski ever made before. They turn easily, track extremely well, and hold on ice. With the exception of a very flexible metal ski whose ease for beginners and deep-snow skiers cannot be surpassed, the plastic ski is able to please most skiers under most conditions. The durability of the fiberglass ski, having undergone the test of time, appears to be very good. However, when repairs must be made, they can cause some problems.

Running Surfaces

The days of the bare wooden running surface remain (perhaps with a touch of nostalgia) only in the memory of older skiers, along with the scent of pine tar and secret wax formulas. With few exceptions, today, polyethylene plastic, in an array of bright colors, lines the running surface of the modern ski. The virtue of this inexpensive plastic is that it does not stick to anything; and in particular, not to snow. To attach it to the bottom of skis, it is pressed onto a strip of cloth which, in turn, is bonded to the ski.

Polyethylene is compounded with other additives, paraffin, silicones (and dyes of the desired color), which increase the sliding qualities and hardness. Early compounds were quite soft, scratched easily, and melted at low temperature, necessitating a separate gluing operation for manufacturers who used high-temperature, fast-setting adhesives. Latest improvements are in the direction of high-density compounds which slide even better under all conditions, are much harder to scratch, and can be bonded at high temperature. Teflon also is being tried for ski bottoms.

In repairing polyethylene running surfaces, scratches are easily patched by melting a piece of the same material into the cut, and then sanding. Replacing the entire running surface requires factory equipment.

The *top surfaces* of skis vary from varnishes and paints to plastic layers and anodized metal. These surfaces protect (wooden skis) and hide (bare metal and raw fiberglass) the structural top of the ski. The sides of wooden skis are coated with paint or sprayed plastics. In metal sandwich skis, the sidewall is part of the structure and is usually made of a hard and thick layer of phenolic plastic.

One or more grooves in the bottom of the ski are, as previously stated, essential to make the ski run in a straight line when it is flat on the snow. The groove enables the ski to run straight because the pressure of the ski on the snow forms a small ridge, which keeps the ski in its track until some positive action is taken to change direction. The groove is particularly useful in straight running, but is also helpful in maintaining direction during the first preparatory motions for the turn when the ski is momentarily "light" and relatively free to slip off to the side.

While the extent of the groove's usefulness is often debated, there is no question that it is necessary. One of the reasons why it is so difficult to ski on ice is because the groove is not functioning in its tracking capacity. On anything but ice the groove is undoubtedly effective. A ski whose groove is rounded at the edges is easier to turn than a ski whose groove has a sharp edge. However, the latter tracks better. Groove design usually is governed by the purpose for which the ski is intended. From time to time manufacturers experiment not only with groove shape but also with multiple grooves. The idea behind multiple grooves is that the ski will maintain directional integrity even though it is partially edged. This idea has considerable merit on hard-packed racing trails, but under average conditions it makes the skis harder to turn.

Edges

Steel edges, by giving the bottom edges of the ski a sharp, square profile, enable the skier to control his skis in traverses and turns. The passing years have seen various experiments with serrated or hollow ground edges, edges set at diverse angles, or installed on the side of the ski. But all that is required of the edge basically is that it be a freshly sharpened 90-degree angle made of hard steel. Since steel does not slide very well on snow, one of the notable contributions to edge design has been the L-shaped or hidden edge which exposes a minimum of steel on the sliding surface.

Edges should be sharpened from time to time with a file or grinder. Because frequent sharpening will wear away the steel, the edges normally are made to extend beyond the side of the ski and are referred to as offset edges.

Edges for racing skis are usually made of relatively soft steel so that they can be sharpened easily and often. Edges of pleasure skis, on the other hand, are normally made of highly tempered steel, more difficult to

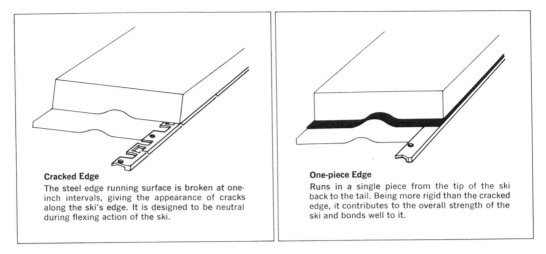

Cracked Edge
The steel edge running surface is broken at one-inch intervals, giving the appearance of cracks along the ski's edge. It is designed to be neutral during flexing action of the ski.

One-piece Edge
Runs in a single piece from the tip of the ski back to the tail. Being more rigid than the cracked edge, it contributes to the overall strength of the ski and bonds well to it.

sharpen, but retaining cutting power for a longer period of time.

There is an important difference between segmented edges and edges installed in a single piece covering the entire length of the ski. Segmented edges, generally used on less expensive skis, are applied with screws or rivets individually, in lengths of about six inches. They are not a part of the main structure of the ski. When the ski bends, the segments separate slightly. On the other hand, "one-piece" edges are usually bonded or welded as an integral part of the bottom surface of the ski. When the ski bends, the edge stretches. Since steel is much less elastic than any of the other materials of which skis are made—be it wood, other metals, or plastic—the result is a stiffer and stronger ski. "One-piece" edges can be supplied with each type of ski. But it is obvious that their action blends better with the action of a metal ski than with that of plastic, and least of all with wood.

In performance, segmented edges may tend to help the ski hold better on ice and steep slopes, probably because they do not increase its torsional rigidity. "One-piece" edges, on the contrary, add to the "life" of the ski, and help make it slide faster. Segmented edges can loosen and break, but can be repaired easily by replacing one or more segments. "One-piece" edges are generally free of maintenance. A "cracked" edge, used on more expensive models of ski, tends to combine the properties of the segmented and the one-piece edge. At the point where

the edge is bonded to the ski it is a continuous strip of metal, and the factor promotes the union of ski and edge. On the outside bottom surface, however, the steel strip is broken at about one-inch intervals, thus permitting the ski to flex as if it had fully segmented edges.

In addition to edges and running surfaces, and beyond the standard coat of paint, all but the cheapest skis have other protective features. Most have some form of tip and tail protection to reduce damage from the chopping action of the edges, which is almost unavoidable. Tail protectors have the additional job of keeping the skis out of their own puddle when they are stood up to dry off after a day of skiing.

To further reduce the damage of the chopping action of the edges, all except metal skis should have a top edge. In wood skis, these top edges are usually made of plastic and can be replaced. In the better synthetic skis, the top edge is usually made of metal or of a separate, replaceable plastic sheeting. The major function of this sheeting, which is easily repaired, is to seal the main body of the ski against moisture.

Models of Skis

Skis are made in different models to meet specific requirements.

Downhill skis are designed to handle high speed. They are long, wide, and heavy and have little side camber. The downhill ski's flex curve shows a long gradual forebody and a firm tail. The binding is usually positioned toward the rear. While the downhill ski is very stable in straight running and in long turns, it does not sideslip easily and resists quick maneuvers. Despite the weight and thickness, the long length, width, and long flexible front make it a fair ski in soft snow. A popular example of a men's downhill racing ski would be 7 feet 3 inches or 220 centimeters in length with millimeter dimensions (side camber) of 90–74–83.

Slalom model is designed to grip on steep, icy slopes, and for quick maneuvers. It is short, light, and narrow and possesses important side camber. The slalom racing ski has relatively stiff flex in the tail. It turns easily and quickly and holds very well underfoot in turns. It is good for skiing on hard snow, but does not hold high speed well. A popular example of a men's slalom ski would be 6 feet 9 inches, or 205 centimeters, with dimensions of 88-67-78. In recent years, there has been a trend by slalom racers to use shorter skis. They claim that these skis are more maneuverable.

Giant slalom is essentially a compromise in skiing, with some of the speed of downhill, and some of the braking and turning of slalom. The skis reflect this by showing a blend of characteristics, varying with manufacturers and schools of thought. The binding is in standard position.

Combination or *Combi* or *Standard* is an all-purpose ski for all skiers. As in the giant slalom model, it is a compromise design. Some manufacturers lean toward downhill characteristics, others toward slalom, with most holding safely to dead center. In all combination models, the more flexible the ski, the easier it is to run, but the less stable it becomes. Special skis for deep snow are very flexible combination models, with occasional wider dimensions.

The models just described comprise those skis used for Alpine skiing. There are, however, skis designed for Nordic skiing to satisfy those whose preference tends toward jumping and cross-country running. The jumping ski is long, wide, and heavy and generally has three grooves in its running surface and no metal edges. The cross-country ski is extremely light and narrow and also has no metal edges. Nordic equipment is fully discussed later in this section.

Of the tens of thousands of skiers who buy new skis, many feel uncomfortable at first with their new equipment. As a rule, they should ignore this initial uneasiness about the feel of a new pair of skis. If you have skied on your previous pair for three or four seasons, you are accustomed to handling skis with dull edges and with much of their early liveliness dissipated by hard use. In effect, you have adjusted your technique to an old pair of skis, and it isn't surprising to experience difficulty in readjusting to new, livelier skis with positive edging. The difference will be even more noticeable if you are switching from metal skis to fiberglass. Much has changed in ski design in the last two or three years. That you must adjust your technique to the new skis should not cause you to find fault with the equipment. Rather, by adapting to the skis, you will eventually improve your technique.

As in many other fields, much progress in ski design has been accomplished in recent years. Yet a pair of skis is only a tool. Many a spill, many a poor turn, and many a DNF (Did Not Finish) at the end of a race results sheet have more to do with skier error than with flex curves, faulty dimensions, or a low Rockwell reading (hardness rating) on the steel edges.

Selecting Proper Ski Length

There is no question today that the problem of the right ski length for the skier has become more and more vexing. There are people who claim that the best ski for beginners is a two-and-a-half-footer, and others who say that the ski should be as tall as the beginner. Still others (this includes a good portion of the experts) stick with the old tried-and-true "hand-high over the head" rule, a philosophy by which every skier, novice to racer, is fitted with a ski that reaches from the floor to the bottom of the palm when the hand is held as high overhead as it can reach.

Experiments and trends of recent years have warmed the air with questions. For one thing, there was the sudden appearance of shorter skis for adults. Some skiers have had great success with expensive five-foot skis designed especially for adults, wider and heavier than juvenile skis of the same length. Evidently a great number of grown-ups felt much more comfortable on a ski radically shorter than that prescribed by the prevailing standard, and thousands of adults on five-foot skis refuted the idea current a few years ago that such skis would be unmanageable. They turned out to be very manageable.

There are signs that the old "hand-high" method is not an iron-clad rule anymore. Today many instructors, and more important, many ski shops, recommend skis that are shorter than "hand-high" for beginners. And skiers of all ages and abilities, regardless of advice, have been buying skis an inch or so shorter than before. The average length of "long" skis sold in the shops has dropped almost two inches. In 1970, for instance, the so-called standard men's slalom racing ski was 6 feet 11 inches, or 210 centimeters. Today the most popular version of this model is 6 feet 9 inches, or 205 centimeters, and the trend seems to be toward even shorter slalom skis.

Top skiers have known for some time that ski length based on height is not the way to select a winning ski. That is, most experts, regardless of their height, purchase skis in a narrow range of sizes from 6 feet 7 inches (200 centimeters) to 7 feet 1 inch (215 centimeters).

Ability plays an important part in the selection of skis, the proper length of ski varying according to your skiing ability. The following chart, compiled from a *Ski Magazine* survey, can serve as a basic guide:

Range of Ski Lengths

Ability of Skier	Length Recommended	
	Men	Women
Expert	205–210	190–195
Advanced	195–200	180–185
Improving Intermediate	185–190	170–175
Casual Intermediate	175–180	160–165
Novice	165–170	150–155
Beginner*	100–150	100–150

* Most beginners outgrow these short-short lengths after three to five days of lessons. For this reason we recommend that you rent rather than purchase such short skis.

The length or size marked or stamped on a ski is only an approximation of length, mainly because there are three different dimensions that manufacturers use: chord length, projected length, and sole length. A manufacturer can call any of these measurements the size of his ski. That is, a pair of skis marked 205, for instance, may actually be up to 5 centimeters (2 inches) longer or shorter than another pair marked 205. While a racer may detect subtle performance changes as he switches from one manufacturer's ski to another within the same size category, a recreational skier probably will not notice any unusual ski behavior unless the differences are more than 5 centimeters.

Purchasable Length

Feet/Inches	Centimeters	Feet/Inches	Centimeters
7' 3"	220	5' 1"	155
7' 1"	215	4'11"	150
6'11"	210	4' 9"	145
6' 9"	205	4' 7"	140
6' 7"	200	4' 5"	135
6' 5"	195	4' 3"	130
6' 3"	190	4' 1"	125
6' 1"	185	3'11"	120
5'11"	180	3' 9"	115
5' 9"	175	3' 7"	110
5' 7"	170	3' 5"	105
5' 5"	165	3' 3"	100
5' 3"	160		

Other Tests

In selecting the proper skis, look for camber and flexibility. Here are some simple tests which will help you to choose the skis that are right for you.

Test for Camber. As was stated earlier, camber is the amount of bow or arch built into your ski. You can see it by putting the ski bottoms together: they will touch at a point where the tips begin to curve up. They also touch where the tail ends meet. In the middle, or waist, however, the skis should measure 1½ inches to 2 inches apart. This is the camber, and too much of it will make turning difficult. Too little camber, on the other hand, will make the skis wander and hard to control. To check your skis for equal camber, lay them down on a perfectly flat surface. The tips should have an equal amount of up-bend, and the height of both skis at the middle section must be identical.

Test for Flexibility. The flexibility of your

skis, as we know, is extremely important. Too many skiers are using skis that are entirely too stiff. Generally speaking, your weight and skiing ability should determine the amount of flexibility in your skis. To check flexibility, grasp the ski tip with one hand, with running surface up, and place the other hand at the waist of the ski. Flex slightly. Then turn the ski upside down and grasp it by the tail end. Flex it again. Examine at least two or more models of the same ski in this manner, and by process of elimination select the ski most suitable for you.

Test for Straightness. Holding the ski by its tip, sight down the running surface. Imagine a line drawn across the ski at the point where the tip begins to turn up, and another line as close to the tail as possible. If these imaginary lines are parallel, the ski is free of lateral warpage. To check for longitudinal twisting or warpage, place the running surfaces of the skis together, carefully matching the sides at the points of contact. Squeeze the skis until they are absolutely flat against each other.

Make all these tests before you buy skis.

SKI BINDINGS

Ski bindings today mean release bindings. And, as with most other items of ski equipment, there are no "absolutes," but only "compromises" to be considered. The binding is supposed to provide a solid, secure, precise link between the boot and the ski, sustain all the stresses and shocks commonly encountered in leaning forward, turning, chattering, riding bumps, edging, etc., without releasing. Yet, we expect it to release and prevent injury when we make a mistake and fall, although the forces applied in such a case may be similar to those outlined above. This presents intricate design problems to manufacturers and has caused the market to be literally swamped with systems, none of which is close to perfection yet.

Up until the early 1950's, the concern of most binding manufacturers was to hold boot

and ski ever more firmly together. The ultimate of this ambition was finally reached some years back in an ingenious device which simply locked the boot sole to the ski with metal plates, thus eliminating, it was claimed, any danger of the ski's coming off one's foot accidentally.

Today, all but a few die-hards (or perhaps die-easys) have been converted to release bindings of one kind or another, and even Olympic racers would not be caught dead in "bear traps." The main argument now is over the kind of release bindings.

Without going into the details of the different mechanical systems, let us review the fundamental requirements of release bindings. Between releases, a binding system must be: reasonable in cost, simple to install on the ski, and easy to step into and out of; as

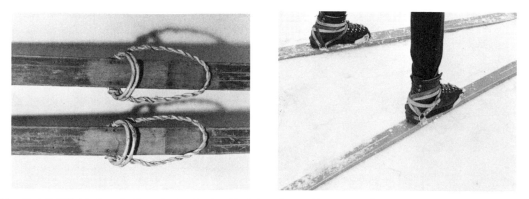

The first "stiff" binding (left) made by Sondre Norheim about 1850, mounted on telemark skis. The popular "bear-trap" binding (right) was abandoned in the early fifties. This binding, of course, had no release.

A

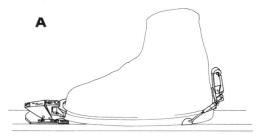

B

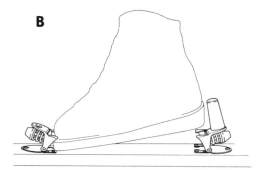

C

D

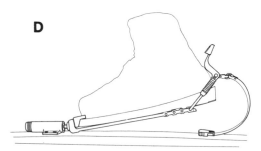

E

F

G

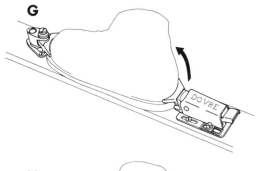

H

I

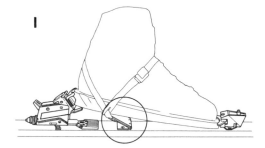

J

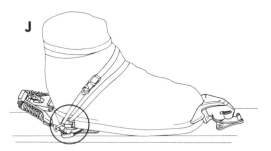

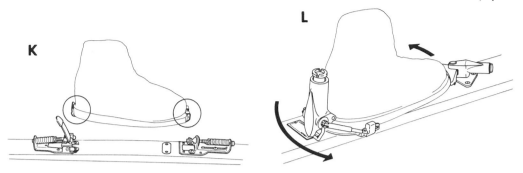

Popular modern bindings and their functional features: (A) vertical flexibility, (B) step-in binding, (C) latch-in binding, (D) integrated binding, (E) toe hold-down, (F) heel hold-down, (G) forward release, (H) lateral release, (I) two-point fixation, (J) D-rings, (K) boot plates, (L) turntable.

much as possible, it must make the boot and the ski an integral unit. The release system must provide: (1) simple, effective, and visible adjustment to accommodate skiers of different size, weight, strength, and ability; (2) precisely calibrated mechanisms operating in as many directions as possible to afford a broad range of protection; (3) adjustment settings that will sustain vibrations and shocks without slipping; (4) a mechanical system designed to operate under standard conditions (i.e., unaffected by moisture and icing).

In very broad terms, when a skier sliding downhill falls, the key force will be exerted forward in the general direction of travel and be applied through the body to the base of the bone structure, the heel. Once the heel is free from the ski, the entire foot and leg can swivel in any direction and the probability of injury is all but eliminated. Thus, a binding that does not include a heel release system should not be thought of as a release binding. Yet, because in the early days of skiing the toe of the ski boot was held in viselike toe irons, years were devoted to perfecting toe releases before the heel was even considered. Subsequently, a system was developed so that the cable would release the heel in a front fall. But regardless of how well engineered it was, the fact remained that the force had to be transmitted from the heel, up to 20 inches behind the release, by a cable sliding through side hitches of various types. The cable, usually of the sheathed type, could and eventually would kink; and the hooks could and eventually would bend and pinch the cable, altering or completely stopping the possibility

of release. Another shortcoming of the cable release system was that it functioned fairly well in a straight forward fall on a vertical plane but did not operate so well when the strain was directed forward and to the side with an uneven pull on the right and left sections of the cable.

A better solution to the heel release problem is provided by the cableless step-in bindings now almost universally in use. The drawbacks in some step-in models are due to the small, complex, enclosed mechanism; in others which have large, exposed parts, to the necessity of having metal plates fastened to the boots. The latter type does, however, offer the best safety factor available with many angles of release.

In principle, the best all-around system includes a toe and heel unit designed and calibrated to work together as a unit. "Step-in" boot-lock bindings are of this type and have the additional convenience that the wearer does not have to bend down to put skis on.

Mounting Bindings

With all bindings, the installation is a very important and often neglected factor. It should be done carefully by a ski repairman who knows his trade. The safety designed in the system depends to a great extent upon proper installation as well as the initial adjustments, which should be made and tested on each ski separately by qualified personnel. The location of the binding on the ski must be accurate, allowing for the individual's physique, ability, and boot size. A binding buyer should expect to pay at least $5 and usually more for such skilled work.

Of course, skiers should face the fact that good physical condition is vital. Even a good, well-adjusted binding system which releases in a fall puts a certain amount of strain on the skier himself. While not much can be done to strengthen the bones and the ligaments in the body, a great deal can be added to the strength and especially the elasticity of muscles and tendons by a simple program of preseason exercises, and a few minutes of warming up before taking off down the slope. "Mental" safety is another factor which should operate at all times: keeping uppermost an awareness of one's ability and reflexes versus the speed, terrain, snow conditions, and visibility. A modern release binding should be considered only an "extra" precaution in case of emergency.

The mounting of the bindings on the skis is *not* a job for the occasional fix-it man. While the location of the bindings on the skis is not as hypercritical as some make it out to be, proper installation is a precision job which should be done with the tools and jigs especially designed for this work. This is particularly true in the case of metal and fiberglass skis, on which mistakes are expensive and difficult to correct.

First-rate installation work is important because of evidence that improper mounting can negate the release mechanisms of even the best binding. For instance, if a toe piece is not mounted correctly it can release with little provocation in one direction, but is unable to release at all in the other direction. This is but one of many possibilities of error, and it will pay in the interests of safety to make use of the check list that follows.

There are a number of systems for binding placement, none of them perfect or inevitably best. Different types of skiing require different binding locations. For average use, the following formula works out just about right: Divide the length of the ski (measured along the running surface from tail to tip) in half. The toe of the boot may be placed at or slightly behind this point, but never in front of this point.

According to more precise systems, particularly those used by the racers, this is the location best suited for hard-snow slalom and beginning skiers. Better skiers may want the binding about half an inch farther back for general skiing, and as much as an inch back for powder skiing and downhill racing.

Keep in mind that if your binding is not mounted straight on your ski, you are in danger either of releasing too easily in one direction or of not releasing at all. To assure that your toe unit is mounted straight, make sure that it lines up with a straight line down the center of the ski. (If you use turntables which must be mounted off-center to fit your boot heel, be sure the toe unit is in line with the heel unit.) In this way you can be sure that when you tighten or loosen the adjustment in your binding, you are making an equal adjustment for each side.

One final tip: be sure to place your boot straight on the ski before closing the binding; and with turntable heels, be sure your boot is in the center of the unit when you latch it. In this way, you will avoid causing premature release in one direction.

Bindings and Safety

A lack of understanding of the differences among various brands of bindings, plus the failure to recognize the extreme importance of correct installation and adjustment, has led to much undeserved criticism of release bindings per se. Of the few accident studies conducted in recent years, none has taken into consideration the specific performance of the bindings in the accidents recorded. In other words, little effort was made to determine whether the binding, through a design flaw or manufacturing error, was responsible for the accident or whether it was a case of using an otherwise adequate piece of equipment improperly, as a result of either poor shop work or adjustment.

The original testing program started in 1960 by Gordon Lipe, a product development engineer from upstate New York, grew out of a search for a simple mechanical device that could be used in shops and by individual skiers to test the releasing characteristics of bindings. "I soon discovered," Lipe said, "that proper installation and adjustment was just as important as, and sometimes more important than, the binding itself."

As a result, the single most important de-velopment since the invention of the release binding itself is the introduction of Lipe's Release Check. This is a mechanical device designed to measure the force required to obtain a lateral release at the toe in either direction. Much of the new understanding of how and why bindings perform as they do has been a valuable by-product of the Release Check development program. The Release Check is available for use by ski shops, and there is even an individual Skier's Release Check for personal or family use. So while there is still considerable mystery surrounding the use of release bindings, it is, nevertheless, becoming obvious that skiers today have better understanding and that they are exert-ing more careful selection and use.

Here is a list of ten steps you can take to make certain that you will be getting maxi-mum service out of your bindings. If you follow this check list carefully, you will also learn more about how your bindings work than you ever knew before.

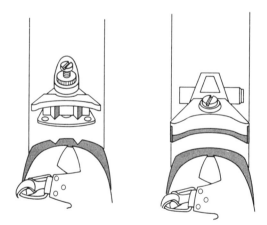

1. Check your boots to see that there is not excessive curl in the sole. All leather boots should be kept in a boot tree. But if your sole is warped, make sure when you step into your bindings that your foot is flat on the skis when you make the adjustment on your toe hold-down. The toe hold-down adjustment should barely touch the top of the sole at the toe. You may be able to slip your toe into the toe unit easily with your heel up, but when you step down, you may build up excessive pres-sure under the ball of the foot and create friction under the sole that makes a release

more difficult. Even if your boot sole is flat, check the toe hold-down adjustment to see that it is not pinching the toe of the boot to the ski. The toe hold-down is simply to keep the boot from coming up away from the ski and should never be used as a clamp. If the toe hold-down is too tight, it will be impos-sible to obtain proper release.

2. Check the notches at the toe of your boots if you use a toe unit that requires boot notching. When forward pressure is applied through the latching of the cable, if one notch is cut deeper than the other, the toe unit notches will "bottom" in the boot notches, forcing the toe unit to begin a partial release. This will cause you to get a release in one di-rection more easily than in the other. If you tighten your bindings to prevent releases on the light side, you may have locked yourself in on the other and made it possible to get a release on one side only. If the toes of your boots have been chewed up by improper notching or placing of boot in binding, have metal plates installed at the toe.

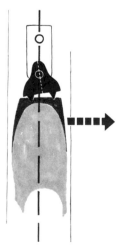

3. Check to see that your bindings have been mounted straight. Sight an imaginary line down the center of your ski. If the toe unit angles off center, you will have a problem similar to that caused by improper boot notching. When the boot is forced up against the toe unit, it will tend to square up with the toe of the boot, beginning a release in one direction. As is the case with boot notching, the boot will release more easily in one direction than the other. To obtain a release in the other direction, the boot must force the toe unit to center before it can swing on through and release.

4. Mark your left and right skis so that you use the same boot in the same ski at all times. Few boots are exactly the same length. If you put a boot in the wrong ski (without readjusting the setting), there can be considerable difference in the force required for release.

5. Check to make certain there are no protruding screw heads. See that there are no protruding nails from your boot sole to interfere with a normal release. Often toe units that can be swiveled by hand cannot be made to work with the boot in place.

7. Check the tension of your cables or forward push of the heel unit to make certain tension is adequate to hold the toe of your boot against the toe unit, *but no more*. Forward tension directly affects the ability of a toe unit to swivel. When it is too strong, the force necessary to obtain a release will always be higher than is necessary for safe skiing.

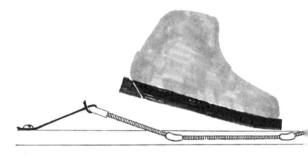

8. Again, if you have cable bindings, fasten the Arlberg or runaway straps to the cable behind the rear side hitches. If the straps are attached in front of the side hitches, they can interfere with the cable and prevent it from sliding to the rear if a forward release is necessary. Such straps should not be used for support as a form of long thong.

6. If you have cable bindings, check side hitches to see that these are no more than two-thirds of the distance from toe to heel. Hitches placed too far back for purposes of holding the heel down often kink and create a point of high friction.

9. If your bindings pass all these checks, you would be wise to take your skis to a shop (with your boots in place) and have your release settings checked mechanically. Or you may wish to buy or borrow a checking device, Lipe's Release Check or other, to do the job at home.

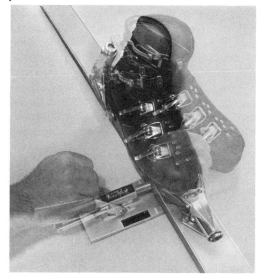

10. To obtain consistent releases, check to see that moving parts are lubricated. Silicone grease, tube or spray, is obtainable at your local hardware store (or at some ski shops). Quite often bindings are "frozen" with friction caused by corrosion from highway chem-

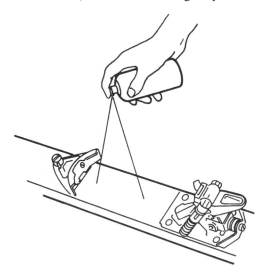

icals. Bindings are seldom made inoperative by frozen snow or ice as is commonly believed. Also check your bindings for wear. Bindings do wear out if subjected to hard use.

In addition, you should be aware of these skiing factors which can affect the operation of your bindings:

1. The "slow twist" is the release action that calls for the maximum performance from your bindings and is responsible for the greatest number of injuries. The "eggbeater" fall is actually far safer, because an "impact" blow rather than a slow twist starts the operation of the binding and overcomes the starting friction. Speed on skis (up to a point) can increase your safety as well as improve your technique.

2. Rough planting of skis, or "flailing" the shovels or tails while climbing, can cause the bindings to release. The impact from such abnormal movements is far greater than you usually experience in ordinary skiing. Do not let such annoying releases tempt you to tighten a binding setting which has been set correctly.

3. You can take many falls without having your bindings release, and if you are in reasonably good physical condition and have learned good falling technique, such tumbles will not injure you. If you think your bindings are too tight, have them carefully checked at a ski shop rather than adjust them to a lighter setting yourself.

4. Rigid-soled boots, such as plastic boots and many sealed-sole boots, require special settings for forward release. Boots with more flexible or bendable soles (like ordinary leather-soled boots) have greater leverage available to release the mechanism (as much as 50 per cent more), because their pivot point is closer to the heel unit; therefore they can use tighter heel settings. Conversely, the rigid-soled boot (which has the advantage of not warping) has its pivot point for a forward release near or at the point where the toe contacts the ski. This farther-forward point of pivot reduces the leverage available for release; hence the mechanism must be adjusted to a lighter setting for a quick, easy forward release.

5. Children's bindings should be of com-

parable or of higher quality than adults', because children have less weight to start a release and therefore need lighter settings. The best bindings for children are those which have the least friction and the most flexibility (ability to absorb shock loads or a slight movement of the binding without a release). This is because, with lighter settings, the friction at the start of a release represents a higher percentage of the pressure holding a child in a binding.

6. Most step-in and latch-in bindings come equipped with a runaway strap that attaches to the binding on the ski at a single point. Upon release, this type of retaining strap can allow the loose ski to windmill and possibly cause injury. A safer arrangement is to use an Arlberg strap, which attaches to the binding or ski at two points, and buckle it very loosely. Ski-stopping devices which do not employ straps are also available.

7. To get maximum performance from step-in or latch-in bindings, your boots should be in good condition. If you have very old or very soft-soled boots, cable bindings may work better.

Adjustments

When selecting a ski binding keep in mind that cold fingers are not the world's most precise instruments. Do not expect them to accurately measure a sixteenth of a turn on a semi-hidden, quarter-inch-diameter knurled knob. Ridiculous? Well, plenty of designers appear to expect it. Tiny adjustments which produce major changes in release pressure are to be avoided where possible. Remember, too, that adjustments can slip. So try to allow some leeway for error.

Having chosen your binding, be sure to keep it properly maintained. Like the engine of a car, it is a mechanism that can wear, corrode, and collect dirt. Keep it clean. If necessary, have it lubricated (with nonfreezing lubricants only). Check it from time to time for wear. If in doubt, take it to a ski shop mechanic. And most important of all, keep it adjusted.

No binding is any more effective than its adjustment, a fact that many skiers appear to forget. Constant checks should be made on the setting. The setting can be altered by vibration of the ski while being carried on a car, set down in the snow, placed against a wall, or even while skiing. Learn the correct setting, check it frequently, and test the release frequently in practice (it should be just possible to force the release while standing). Many injuries have resulted from improperly adjusted bindings and most of these could have been avoided by a simple check.

Check your bindings periodically throughout the day for icing. Actuate the release and see that it still works. This is especially important during snowstorms, in frozen rain, or in very cold conditions. And if you really want to be kind to your bindings, wrap a rag or something around them on your car. Salt from the road can play havoc with almost any binding, for it is many times more corrosive than water.

The only remaining piece of advice is: never rely on your ski's releasing in a fall. Probably it will; possibly it will not. Your best safeguard is to ski as well as you can and use your head. Avoid unnecessary risks and uncontrolled speed. Timid, slow skiing can be just as dangerous as reckless, fast skiing; sometimes more so in the event of a fall. In general, if you are more than a novice, try to stay on your feet. Do not rely on falling as a safe way out of trouble, for it may not be.

It would not be far-fetched to say that if we can land men on the moon, we should be able to engineer the perfect ski binding. Obviously, if the same time, talent, and money were applied to binding design, the answer eventually would be found. As a matter of present reality, however, the perfect binding is still remote. Even worse, some bindings do not function at all in a variety of situations. An orthopedic surgeon from Stanford University's medical school found, in a study of over 600 ski injuries at Squaw Valley, that 55 per cent of the bindings failed to release and 3 per cent released accidentally. The fact that so many accidents were due to the skier's failure to adjust bindings properly is merely a commentary on the public's need for the perfect binding: that is, a boot-to-ski linkage which cannot get out of adjustment once it has been properly set.

Still other accidents occur when the toe

units will not release because of friction buildup between ski and boot sole. Now, however, there are antifriction sole devices that solve this problem.

Bearing in mind the criteria for the ideal binding, here are three factors to keep in mind when shopping for bindings:

Adjustment. Is it easy or do you need a master mechanic? Can you make setting changes easily with skis on without standing on your head? Is there a setting indicator that is easily visible? If you have the binding adjusted correctly at a ski shop, the indicator lets you check that the setting remains constant. Can the toe and heel be adjusted if you buy new boots next year?

Release angles. How many release angles does the toe piece have? The majority open left-to-right, but some release upwards, too. Do you need a heel piece with more than one release angle? Many experts claim that upward release alone is sufficient, since few side releases occur at the heel. Do the heel and toe pieces have elasticity; that is, can they absorb low-level shocks to take the strain off your legs without opening? Should you choose a single- or double-pivot toe piece? Manufacturers claim that the double gives a cleaner release because it allows the boot to move forward and sideways at the same time.

Ease of entry/exit. Will the binding easily be fouled by snow or ice? Do you want a cup-type toe piece or one requiring notched boots? Cups are convenient, but notches cut down friction between boot and toe piece. On the other hand, uneven lateral release can occur if boots are incorrectly notched and the notches can cause boot-sole wear.

Remember, there is no safety binding. There is only safe skiing.

SKI POLES

The purpose of ski poles is to make skiing easier for traveling, both uphill and downhill. Offhand, many beginners may not agree with this idea. It usually takes beginners some time before they learn to use their poles effectively for climbing, and even longer for downhill skiing. Thanks to modern-day lifts, however, skiers no longer need do much climbing. But modern-day techniques place increasing emphasis on the use of poles in downhill skiing.

Until about 1960, ski poles were a relatively simple part of the skier's panoply, with most arguments and fashion trends centered on how long or short they should be. Then Edward Scott of Sun Valley focused his attention on the subject and designed the ultra-ultra-light pole for the slalom racer. Starting at the Olympics at Squaw Valley in 1960, the revolution spread rapidly from the ranks of the international ski racers to the ski public in the United States and then to the rest of the ski world, with the price of a pair of poles almost doubling in the process.

Soon other manufacturers picked up the new design. The question remains, however: If the taper-shafted, slant-gripped, feather-light-ringed, swing-balanced, hollow-pointed pole can make a difference in the rhythm of a slalom racer whose time is measured in hundredths of seconds, can that one and a half gram of extra tip weight also actually affect the making of an ordinary downhill Christie? This, after all, remains the major concern of most ski-pole buyers. Nevertheless, the effect of the pole revolution has benefited the ski public with better design, use of high-quality materials, and, owing to a widespread and fiercely competitive market, reasonable prices. The importance of the pole plant, profusely used in the current ski techniques, has aided in keeping ski poles in the spotlight.

Compared to skis, boots, and bindings, a ski pole is a simple unit composed of a shaft, tip (separate or an integral part of the shaft), handle or grip, strap, and ring (or basket). The higher-quality shafts, which should be as rigid as possible, are made of highly tempered aluminum alloys, high-grade steel, or wound fiberglass bound in epoxy resin. To make them "feel" light and reduce the swing weight, they are tapered with the point of balance as close to the top as possible. To achieve this result, one design has tapered the tube twice, from the middle toward both ends. Fiberglass shafts, although they can be

Correct length of pole (top left) puts the body in a comfortable position from which to unweight the skis. A pole that is too long (top right) makes the body too upright compared to the outline of the correct body position. A pole that is too short (bottom) makes the skier bend over too far compared to the outline. Note that the wrong pole length throws the skier's timing off, forcing him to plant the pole too far forward or too far back.

made very light and are more resistant to breakage than metal shafts, are generally too flexible and are too subject to nicks and scratches near the tip by the steel edges of the skis. These factors thus far have prevented them from being very successful.

For finish, eye appeal, and durable surface wear, aluminum shafts can be anodized (any color), hard-coated (black), or simply polished. Steel shafts have to be protected against rust and are usually chromed or even gold-plated. Glass shafts can be finished in any color. The latest designs have two metals, top half aluminum, lower half steel. Adjustable (telescopic) shafts were very popular in the early fifties, disappeared (the telescoping device added weight), but are now reappearing for practical reasons (rental use). The pole point is made of very hard steel, pressed and glued at the tip of the shaft (only steel poles can be tapered to a hard point) with much fuss to shave fractions of grams in weight. Even titanium is used for points—lighter than steel, harder than aluminum. On very cheap poles, the tips are made by simply spinning the aluminum or steel shaft to a point. These, unfortunately, dull very quickly.

As far as grips are concerned, manufacturing the mold used to form the grip is the costliest part of this item. As for materials, polyethylene plastic, which often looks very nice but tends to crack with age, is used on many cheap poles. The two materials used to make grips on the higher-priced poles are rubber (neoprene) and polyvinyl chloride. Both have good flexibility, but rubber can cause stains on light gloves. The pole should be made in a contour to fit the shape of the handgrip. A refinement originated for slalom use consists of tilting the handle forward, which counterbalances the tendency of the hand to hold the pole at a slightly backward-slanted angle. Finger-fitting ribs on some models help to ensure a firm, nonslip grip. Some handles are shaped with opposed contours to fit the right and left hand.

Leather straps often come from leather goods manufacturers who make them from scraps. It is difficult to maintain a constant quality with this kind of source, so on cheaper poles the straps may be considerably different in thickness. The best pole straps are cut from prime leather and are the same thickness throughout. When polyurethane is used to make pole straps, a standard quality is maintained, but they may stain light gloves. Cheaper pole straps are often made of polyethylene, which tends to break and become rigid in the cold. Straps should be contoured to fit around the wrist, and better ones are adjustable in length, a good feature to accommodate different hands and different gloves. Some straps are designed for right and left hand use with functional efficiency characteristics similar to the ones described for handles.

Baskets are the other major item of cost on a pole. They must be lightweight, yet strong enough to sustain the constant hard shocks of pole planting. The better web-style baskets are made by molding high-quality rubber around a very light, strong tube of aluminum —a complicated process. Cheaper baskets are made with an inferior grade of rubber and ordinary aluminum tubing or solid aluminum, which is even cheaper. Sometimes the rubber webbing on these baskets is merely bonded to the inside surface of the rim, rather than wrapped around and bonded, and can tear loose very easily. Recently polyurethane, which is stronger than rubber but tends to stiffen in the cold, also has been used for basket webbing. The one-piece, all-plastic baskets are molded at a very low cost.

Ski pole lengths seem to run in cycles. Look back at the 1950's when wedeln was introduced: we all had poles that reached almost up to our eyeballs. Just prior to that, during the Arlberg period, poles were very short; knee-high, you might say. Before that, in the early forties, long poles were in style. It is not as arbitrary as it sounds on the surface, however. Pole lengths reflect changes in ski technique, and there are usually sound rea-

sons for moving up or down. Today, following the technique of the racers, with skis staying more in contact with the snow during the unweighting period, a skier needs slightly shorter poles.

To prove this, look how a pole can help you make a good parallel turn. With a short pole, you will naturally bend over quite far at the waist with weight on the balls of your feet, and to allow yourself time to straighten up to a balanced position, you will probably reach out too far in front of your ski tip. A pole that is too long, on the other hand, will cause just the opposite movements: your body will be upright with too much weight on your heels. The pole plant will be too far back, and you will have to bounce up to unweight the skis. You may also tend to plant a long pole sooner than you should.

A pole of the proper length allows you to stay in a balanced position on your skis— slightly crouched and relaxed. It is a comfortable position from which you can unweight with an up or down motion or shoot the skis out in front for a racer's turn. A good rule of thumb on pole length is that a person 5 feet 8 inches should use a pole between 48 and 50 inches. For every two inches in height, add one inch to the pole length. You will notice that we allow a two-inch leeway to accommodate personal preference and individual feel. (Remember poles are usually made in lengths of two-inch intervals.) Before you start cutting your poles off or buying new longer poles, try a friend's different length or rent shorter or longer poles for a day. You may find that your own poles are keeping you up —or down.

The average skier uses heavier poles than he should. This excess weight impedes his dexterity with them. The next time you watch a really good racer, notice how he uses his poles on every turn. The ease with which he uses them is due in large part to their lack of weight. He uses the lightest, strongest poles he can. When you are shopping for a new pair of ski poles, therefore, spend as much time checking their weight as you do their length.

A good way to test the weight of a pole, after deciding on the proper length, is to grip it in the normal manner. Then, raise the tip until the pole is horizontal with the ground. Holding it in this position, shake the pole until you begin to get the "feel" of it. Compare several sets of poles in this manner. Your choice should be that set which feels lightest, particularly at the tip. In addition, check the size of the basket. Find out what material it is made of. Often, an otherwise good pole may have a too heavy or too clumsy basket, in which case the basket can be changed.

Special points are now available for gripping icy surfaces. These points range from those that are simply crosshatching on a flattened point to sharp, jagged edges that really grip, even on mirror-smooth blue ice. Such ice-pick points, of course, can be a hazard and should certainly not be used except where snow conditions specifically require the positive hold these attachments afford.

Another recent innovation in poles is the no-strap grips. While they are considered, by many, to be more comfortable to handle and are possibly safer (doctors blame pole straps for most thumb injuries in skiing), they have the disadvantage of getting away from a skier during a fall.

What should you spend for ski poles? Prices generally range from about $15 to $35, depending upon the material the pole is made of and the workmanship involved.

Children's poles should be light and proportionately short. Seen all too frequently on the slopes are youngsters struggling with ski poles about a foot too long for them. Any ski shop will shorten them to proper length in a few minutes. At the same time, however, a pole too short will also hinder a child in learning how to ski. Since ski poles play such an important part in balance and ski technique, it is unfair to expect a youngster to learn with improper equipment.

SKI ACCESSORIES

In addition to skis, boots, bindings, and poles, the well-equipped skier needs a number of accessories in his equipment kit. Some of these items are essential for safety; others add greatly to the skier's convenience.

Sunglasses and Goggles. These are essential to safe skiing and must be a part of every skier's equipment. At worst, the reflection of the sun's ultraviolet rays off the bright snow can actually burn the eyes, causing snow blindness. Less serious, but more annoying for the skier, is the constant squinting of the eyes which constricts and tires the muscles. By the end of the day your eyes are more fatigued than your knees. The choice between sunglasses and goggles is a matter of individual preference.

In selecting sunglasses or goggles, it is important to look for several points of quality. The lens should be smooth and without any irregularities or distortion around the edges. This is particularly important to watch for in wraparound types. Most optical authorities agree that a gray-colored lens allows the wearer to see colors in their truest value while still reducing glare. A yellow lens is useful for hazy or overcast days to increase contrast, but does not reduce glare. If the lens is plastic, be sure to protect it from scratches. If it is glass, check to be sure that it has been heat-treated to resist shattering. Remember that "summer" sunglasses are not.

Because you wear them all day, the frames for either glasses or goggles should be comfortable over the ears or around the head. Glasses, of course, can be fitted by an optical supplier, but you should try goggles on to be sure they are comfortable. Frames should be durable and made of material that can withstand extreme cold.

Goggles are available for people who must wear eyeglasses while skiing. There also is a shield which flips down over the glasses and does not fog.

With the advent of contact lenses, which can also be made of plastic, the skier who requires the use of a visual aid has an additional safety factor. The number of contact lenses being worn increases each year. The smaller and by far the most numerous approximately 9-millimeter contact lenses are easier to adapt to and are generally worn by most, in spite of the fact that they present a small hazard in loss and somewhat less safety while skiing. Wearers should consider the fact that larger sizes not only remain more securely on the surface of the eye in the case of a fall, but also protect against injury to the eye itself by a striking force, since this force is dissipated over a larger area. For the myopic or highly astigmatic racer, the use of the larger scleral or mold-fitted lenses should be considered.

The most common problem with commercial ski goggles is fogging. Even the best goggle, when fogged, represents an increased accident hazard rather than a protective or safety device. Many of them can be improved with increasing venting so that circulating cool air between the face and the back of the goggle prevents the annoying vaporization. Because of this problem, the shield or hood, some of which have a lever-acting device on the air vent, remains popular.

The antifog chemicals can also help prevent fogging, but they must be reapplied if snow gets on the lens. Actually an antifoggant is a wetting agent that changes the glass or plastic surface from its "natural state of being 'hydrophobic' (water-hating) to a more suitable state of being 'hydrophilic' (water-loving)." When a cold lens surface comes in contact with warm, moist air, the water vapor condenses, forming small droplets of water. An antifoggant destroys the droplets by reducing the surface tension of the water on the lens. The drops spread out until they are no longer thick and round, but rather oval and then finally flat and parallel to the lens surface. Evaporation then takes place quickly, eliminating the fogging-up.

The best known surface tension breaker is detergent. This, used with a silicone or glycerin base, makes up most of the antifog preparations now available.

Safety Straps. Arlberg, or safety, straps are another piece of ski equipment. With the advent of the release binding some years ago, the problem of runaway skis increased greatly. More and more stories were heard of the enormous power and damage attributed to a ski hurtling down a mountain after being released in a fall. The solution was obvious: attach the ski to the skier. This was done, with the first "safety" strap being merely a short length of straplike material, frequently elastic, attached simply to the ski and the boot. However, it soon became obvious that elasticity was detrimental because, upon re-lease, the straps would stretch to their limit and come flying back to bruise or lacerate the skier with a vicious force.

Regardless of the type of runaway straps or safety device you use, be sure that the mounting plates, rings, and screws attached to the skis do not interfere with the lateral release of the boot. Also, avoid attaching the strap to parts of the binding that can come apart from the ski.

Sun Creams and Lotions. Snow is the world's best natural reflector of ultraviolet rays, and a skier who is merrily skiing along over it is in the peculiarly vulnerable position of being attacked with these dangerous rays. Ordinary commercial sun-screen creams and lotions offer protection by absorbing some of the harmful ultraviolet rays while still allowing your skin to tan. Because these creams have varying effectiveness on different skin types, it is best to try some that have been tested for resistance to snow reflection. Most of these come in small unbreakable tubes that fit in a parka pocket. They also have long-lasting qualities, but for maximum protection and moisturizing effectiveness it is best to reapply the cream several times a day or each time after heavy perspiration.

Most seasoned skiers know that wind, cold, and sun can crack and chap lips. Regular use of heavier balms will protect lips. Girls can use the new, small-size medicated lipsticks for lip protection and glamour.

Ski Boot Trees. These are a modest investment for the protection of expensive boots. Even in the best boots there is a tendency for the sole to curl. This curling should be avoided since in its advanced state, it tends to pinch the toes in the vicinity of the ball of the foot and prevents the binding toe release from functioning properly. A ski boot tree will prevent this condition from becoming permanent. It also makes it easy to carry boots when traveling. Ski boot trees come in a variety of designs and prices. Many use a rigid center post made of box metal. Some carrying models are all plastic and even form a protective bag.

Skier's Carrier Case. Some good bags have been developed for skiers who want to carry big or small loads up or down mountains. For a lunch, parka, camera, wax, and sun lotion, a belt pouch or fanny pack is adequate.

While the leather and sealskin ones are expensive, the ones of nylon or canvas are cheaper and stronger. These come in a variety of sizes, some with their own belts, others merely with loops. Make sure, however, that it is sufficiently padded to prevent damage to yourself and the contents if you fall.

Over-the-shoulder bags will do for certain loads and are inexpensive at surplus stores. Be sure they have secure waist straps to keep them from flailing about when you ski.

Rucksacks are big-load carriers. The best ones are those made for mountaineers. You will find them at stores that specialize in climbing gear—not ordinary sporting goods shops that carry only a knapsack or two. Look for a rucksack that is strong and light and will keep the load flat and tenaciously against your back. All but the smallest size need a waist strap. Again, nylon is the strongest, but cotton canvas has a slight stiffness that can be helpful. Always bag things in polyethylene before you put them into a rucksack. This way sandwiches and ragg socks will maintain their uniqueness and you will be able to move containers aside when you have to dig to the bottom.

When using public transportation, it is a good idea to protect the skis from the smashes they are likely to encounter en route. A ski bag which holds both skis and poles is particularly useful when the skis are carried on buses with outside racks and where salt is used to melt snow and ice on the highways. But the skis and poles are only one of the problems that a skier en route to a resort must face. In addition to skis, poles, and everyday clothing, the skier carries boots, bulky ski clothes, goggles, gloves, and often camera equipment. Since you only have two arms, the trick is to consolidate all the gear into as few bags as possible. It is helpful if you can sling some of the stuff across your back. It also helps if the luggage is lightweight.

To solve such problems for the traveling skier luggage makers, ski equipment firms, and a few inventive skiers in the past couple of years have come up with marvelous lightweight soft-sided luggage. The new ski luggage is made of canvas, vinyl, or nylon and travels remarkably well. It comes in some blazing colors like pink, orange, silver, red, and blue, and it stands up well to hard use.

For overseas air travelers who are going economy class or on supplemental airline charter flights where only 44 pounds of luggage are allowed, these new lightweights offer a special advantage. The largest Gerry bag weighs only 2 pounds, while a large conventional suitcase may weigh in at 7 to 10 pounds when empty. Packing these formless shapes however, is a bit like dressing underwater: just when you think an opening is available to be filled, it disappears. But for ski accessories and bulky clothes, the soft bags make for easy packing and hold a lot.

When you are carrying the skis between the hill and the car or lodge, a pair of rubber ski straps is helpful. They hold the skis together for easier carrying and prevent the edges from rubbing against each other.

Ski Wax and Repair Kit. No skier should be without a small wax kit. Although most skis will glide easily under average conditions, waxing not only improves the skis' performance under all conditions, but also makes them track better, and offers a certain amount of protection against wear and minor scratches. The three-pack, consisting of silver (for wet snow), red (for corn snow), and green (for cold, dry snow) waxes is adequate for most ski conditions. For a full discussion of waxing, see page 106.

Other useful accessories are an edge sharpener (there are several on the market which allow touching up of edges without worry about squareness); a small base repair kit consisting of a polyethylene candle and a small soldering iron; and a few hand tools— hammer, Phillips head and regular screwdrivers, pliers, file—and some epoxy glue.

SKI CLOTHING

Only a decade ago ski clothing amounted to little more than a glorified lumberman's outfit. Considering its bulk, it was not very warm. Nostalgia may run rampant over the departure of the baggy pants and parkas of the thirties and forties, but the ski clothing of those earlier eras left much to be desired, both in quality and in variety.

Modern ski clothing is at once warm and fashionable, and can be divided into three basic categories: authentic ski clothing, "ski-look" clothing, and after-ski fashions. What are the differences among authentic, functional skiwear, after-ski, and ski-look clothing?

Nearly everyone has some idea of what is considered the after-ski look. It runs the gamut from the most elegant at-home clothes to offbeat loungewear or sportswear. At smart resorts, it is sometimes a completely authentic ski costume in light, pastel colors. The objective in wearing after-ski clothing is to look pretty and relaxed.

To make the distinction between authentic ski wear and sportswear with a ski-look is not as easy as it would seem. In the past, any one of the following were clues to the authentic for those who took their skiing seriously: quality and weight of fabrics used, simplicity and function of design, an "imported from Europe" label, lack of resemblance to any other type of clothing. Function in design, with much finer definition than ever before, is probably the only one of these distinctions that is still valid.

The quality and weight of fabrics used are still of prime importance, but the finest qualities are sometimes used in ski-look clothing also. Simplicity of design can be a matter of personal taste rather than a distinction. There are some exciting flamboyant fashions, for those who like them, in authentic ski clothes, just as there are simple, quiet styles for the casual spectator.

The idea that an imported label has some magic superiority over a domestic one is as outmoded as baggy pants. Fiber and fabric technology have advanced by leaps and bounds in the United States, with stretch fabrics, insulation materials, and knitting yarns particularly benefiting. In the *Encyclopedia of Skiing* only authentic ski clothing will be covered.

Keeping Warm

Staying warm in cold weather, avoiding frostbite, numbness, and other unpleasantness.

Ski styles have changed since the twenties.

is a science that should be understood by all skiers. One of the most basic of body functions is to maintain body heat. We each possess an exceptionally efficient system of control to ensure that our body heat remains within a few tenths of a degree of 98.6 degrees Fahrenheit despite a tremendous range of outside temperature.

The initial source of our body heat is the food we eat. In cold weather, the conservation of this heat is aided by nature in two primary ways. First, as temperature drops radically, more and more blood vessels, especially those close to the skin, begin to contract. This action is similar to preventing water from running through the cooling radiator of a car so that the "water" in the "engine" itself increases in temperature. Second, we begin to shiver. This is merely the rapid contraction and relaxation of muscles —an activity which in turn increases production of body heat. These same effects can be obtained by running up and down or increasing muscular activity.

Although these factors come into play involuntarily, we can do much to increase their efficiency. One efficient method of maintaining a temperature is to surround it by a vacuum (the famous Thermos bottle). An easier and almost as efficient way is to surround the body with a layer of dead air. The closer we come to so encasing ourselves, shielded from wind and air currents, and without any other body contact, the warmer we will be.

To accomplish this, the following principles should guide us in selecting layers of clothing. The key is the air layer next to the skin—some type of fishnet underwear with large spaces to trap the air. The second layer, which forms the cover for the spaces, can be the traditional single-layer or the quilted or double-layer underwear. The latter two provide still more dead air layers. Finally, the outer layers, a series of lightweight, closely knitted, windbreaking layers such as a "windbreak sandwich"—poplin or comparable shirt covered by a wool sweater or shirt with a nylon outer parka (quilted again or laminated).

In skiing, it is important that you not become overwarm. The excessive perspiration of a run down can be the cause of a chill on the way up. Your clothing should permit you to ventilate, and you should dress in such a way that you can take off one or more layers without difficulty.

Much research is being made on the theory of warmth and thermal comfort. It is now up to the skier to take advantage of the collected knowledge and keep abreast with the changes. Excuses for being cold are fast disappearing.

Selecting Clothes

Fashions change from year to year, but it is safe to say that the streamlined look of the last few years will continue to maintain its popularity. After all, skiers have been trying to reduce their bulk for a long time. The very nature of skiing dictates that fashion follow function, and not the other way around as is the case with so much other clothing.

A kaleidoscope of styles, patterns, colors, fabrics, and prices awaits you when you set out to buy your skiing wardrobe. Because ski wear is in the forefront of the sportswear world, you will encounter a lot of sales talk concerning the merits of an almost bewildering variety of new fabrics, most of which you may have never heard of, and of strange chemical-sounding terms and esoteric brand names. If you feel uneasy, it is best to fall back on established brands, those with a reputation of having served skiers well for many years.

Pants. Fiber content is the principal determinant in ski pants. The standard combination is wool plus nylon plus Spandex, with the higher percentage of wool usually indicating the warmer, costlier, and more durable pants. Spandex puts the stretch into stretch pants and therefore is essential to proper fit. If you plan to own one, and only one, pair of stretch pants, you had best plan on a pair with at least 50 per cent wool since these are most suitable.

Price ranges on pants are determined by weight of fabric (wool content plus stretch nylon) and workmanship. Thirty-dollar pants are not meant to take the beating sixty-dollar pants can absorb, and the value you get is generally in direct relation to what you spend. Average recreational skiers should manage nicely somewhere between the cost extremes. But remember that fabric should be tightly woven for water resistance as well as durability. Many fabrics, of course, are treated for resistance to water, but they are not water-proof. Be suspicious of any label that makes the latter claim.

The lighter-weight pants (less than 30 per cent wool, or rayon/stretch nylon) are most comfortable for warm-weather skiing. This is the place to exercise your whimsy and color cravings, since the cost factor is not that serious a consideration. As a general rule, these fabrics are not as durable, but they will serve you well for both ski and après-ski. There are pants made of other synthetic fabrics which are not only functional but washable.

It goes without saying that no one should buy stretch pants without trying them on and checking the fit under the seat and behind the knees with leg bent, to be sure there is a little but not too much strain. Pants from different manufacturers differ in cut, fullness in the leg, length of rise, type of waistband, and type of foot used—as well as in quality of construc-tion. Watch out for any cuts that are slightly off the straight. Sewing thread used in seams should match the stretchability of the fabric, or ripped seams will result.

The front zipper, standard for men, is also becoming standard for women. Waistband variations are numerous, but regardless of which style you select, make sure that there is a strip of rubber or elastic material at the pants top to anchor your tucked-in turtleneck shirt. Failure of the pants to hold in the shirt can result in a chilled back when you are closing your bindings or when you go through the contortions of a spill.

The most common foot construction for ski pants are the elastic strap, the stretch-fabric strap, and the wraparound heel. The latter two are the smoothest inside the boot. In any foot construction, watch out for bulky seams which could cause chafing. The foot should slide easily over the sock, yet fit snugly.

Width of the conventional stretch ski pants leg should not be so narrow as to resemble a leotard. Such pants are best left to the racers who count time in hundredths of a second. The recreational skier looks and feels better in a slightly wider pant that can accommodate insulated underwear without binding and is properly proportioned from waist to ankles. Waist size should allow room for both turtle-neck and underwear. From the hips down, the pants should flow smoothly into the legs and there should be a straight, unbroken line from the buttocks down the back of the legs.

As for the over-the-boot pants, don't expect them to be like the older stretch pants. This is a totally different look, a totally different fit. The straight-legged style reflects what skiers are demanding in their sportswear pants—a more flattering, easy silhouette. Re-laxed is the word. No more uptight ski pants. Do not let the fact that these ski pants are still made of the traditional stretch fabric deceive you. Since the stirrup-less pants no longer utilize the vertical stretch properties, skin-tight fit is both impossible and unnecessary.

The stirrup-less versions offer two major comfort features: no pull at the instep and no pull at the waist. The waistband is replaced by more comfortable hip-riding construction. The stirrup is replaced by an inner storm cuff which fits snugly over your ski boots or around your ankle, depending on which brand you buy. Racers first spurred development of this kind of pants to eliminate all the pressure points between their feet and boots. The stirrup-less pants are also an excellent choice if you are going to be wearing the bulkier of the plastic boots because the legs are wide enough to cover them. You will also find that since the plastic boots, without the give of leather, fit your feet much more closely, the lack of pressure points from a stirrup under-foot will be welcome.

Another type of over-the-boot pants on the market features an additional elastic stirrup that can be pulled taut under the arch, outside of the boot, and hooked to either side of your pants.

If you want the look of straight-legged pants but are not ready to go the stirrup-less route, the perfect compromise is the over-the-boot pants with the same inside stirrup con-struction as the in-the-boot pants. The wider, stitched-on leg falls neatly over the ski boot while the inside stirrup gives you the smooth fit to which you have been accustomed in tapered pants.

No matter what kind of ski pants you buy, fit is still a matter of your particular figure. Experimentation is the only way to find the brand that fits you best. When buying your over-the-boot pants, find a pair that fits smoothly around your hips and crotch, since these are the critical areas. It is a simple matter to shorten leg length or to take in waist or hip-yoke band.

The first measurement used in selling men's ski pants is the waist size (a 32-inch waist takes a size 32 pants). For the ladies, ski pants are traditionally sold according to dress size and waist measurement, but pants cuts vary according to manufacturer. Instead of relying solely on these gauges, gals should measure their hips. If ski pants sit well, they fit— a waist alteration, if necessary, is then relatively simple. Here is an approximate ratio of women's measurements to pants sizes:

Women

Waist	23	25	27	29	31	33
Hips	34	35½	37	39	41	43
Size	8	10	12	14	16	18

Buying the proper length ski pants is equally important to ensure a taut fit from waist to heel. A guide to porportioned lengths for both men and women follows:

Length	Men's Inseam	Women's Height
Extra short	26–27″	4′10″–5′ 1″
Short	28–29″	5′ 2″–5′ 4″
Regular	30–31″	5′ 5″–5′ 7″
Long	32–33″	5′ 8″–5′10″

When purchasing pants, try several brands and sizes to make sure that you get the right fit. One manufacturer's model may have a slightly different cut that could make a substantial difference in your particular case. Here is a note on fashion: One-piece jumper suits are a pleasure to wear, but the fit must be perfect. The stretch-fabric jackets to match pants look sleek and smart, as long as both come from the same fabric cut for a perfect color match.

Knickers. This type of pants was once the trademark of the hot skier, but today it no longer enjoys overwhelming favor. Knickers are, however, ideal for skiers who do not have stretch-pants figures, for spring skiing, and for those who enjoy wearing colorful socks. Unlike the saggy, baggy bloomers of yesteryear, today's knickers should fit snug to the thigh, blousing at the knee only enough to afford skiability.

Knickers are made of wool/nylon stretch-pant fabrics as well as the traditional wide-wale corduroy. They range in price from $15 up.

Parkas and Jackets. The parka has proved to be one of the most versatile parts of the sportswear wardrobe. To all skiers it is a mystery why it took the nonskiing public so long to discover the virtues of this lightweight, warm, attractive, and practical garment. A well-made parka is extremely light in weight without bulk, keeping the body warmth in at the same time it keeps the cold out. In quilted parkas, some of the newer fiberfill battings, such as Dacron 88 polyester fiberfill, do a reasonable job of keeping the skier warm. This type of material has the added advantage of being non-matting and resilient—having the remarkable ability to "bounce back" and regain its bulk and shape after packing, cleaning, laundering, or rough treatment.

The warmest and most expensive parkas are made of down—the natural feather of waterfowl. The thermal secret of down is threefold: adequate "loft" or volume displacement, sufficient air circulation or breathability, and good resiliency. It is the lofty fill of a parka that retains warm body heat in trapped air. The greater the loft, the lower the heat loss and the greater the thermal efficiency. Down's high loft is unsurpassed. Yet an effective insulator must also be able to breath. Air circulation eliminates excess moisture which could cause chill. Down, as a tridimensional fill, breathes naturally; and the shifting of loose fluff increases air movement. (Note: shifting and settling can mean empty cold spots. A well-made down parka is quilted into small pockets to control the down. The down then ideally shifts only enough to mold and remold itself to the body contours. Air holes and drafts are thus eliminated.) In addition, for lasting effectiveness, an insulator must be able to retain its loft. Taken out of a packed suitcase or a washing machine, a fill must be able to assume its original bulk. Also remember that down will lose its loft when wet. And its feathers, unless enclosed in a tightly woven fabric, will somehow find their way to the outside. To protect its insulating value and to keep the fluff from working out, down must be enclosed in a top-quality fabric.

This means the shell must be unquestionably waterproof, "downproof," and windproof.

Fake fur, fake leather, metallics, velvets, and denim are all part of a group called "novelty fabrics." Frequently these are laminated to foam insulation. They are lightweight, warm, and have maximum fashion as their most persuasive selling point. Since they do not pretend to be a rugged basic, they serve best as a second parka with price tags to coincide with whatever amount you feel like spending.

The new direction in the styling of parkas is toward a more streamlined, less bulky look. Quilted parkas are likely to be smooth on the outside with the quilting on the inside. As a matter of fact, be sure the quilt stitching detail appears on only one surface. Wind can blow through the seams.

Parkas of either down or fiberfill may be worn belted or unbelted. But when the parka is belted at the waist, the wind is prevented from whistling upward. If you plan to wear the parka unbelted, look for an inner construction which creates a close fit to keep out upward breezes. Also look for such wind stoppers as knit inserts at the wrists and collar. A hood, hidden in the collar or stowed away flat inside the back, is useful on snowy and extra-cold days as an extra hat. Also make sure that all pockets have secure closures, either zippers or sturdy buttons. Look, too, for enough pockets and for a device for attaching lift tickets—all are details which indicate a well-made parka.

There are stretch jackets, pullover parkas, wind shirts, and a dozen other fashion variations including exotically printed nylon parkas and stretch quilted nylon parkas. They range in length from waist to midthigh. While parka lengths, like women's skirts, rise and fall for no particular reason, the midthigh is warmest because it is long enough to cover the backside when sitting on a chair lift. When fitting a parka, always try it on over a sweater. Swing your arms to make sure there is enough room across the shoulder and under the armpits. In other words, make sure that it allows your shoulders and arms to move freely.

How much does warmth cost? While there is a large selection of fiberfill parkas available

for $35 and up, a good down parka will cost at least $50. This variance is easy to understand. Synthetic fibers are manufactured domestically and produced economically en masse. The duck and goose down used in ski wear, however, must be largely imported from Europe and Canada. The supply is not unlimited, and the cleaning and grading process is delicate. But do not be misled. There are fiberfill and stretch parkas available which cost a great deal more than down parkas. A high price tag does not automatically imply warmth. You might be paying only for styling.

Ski Suits. These are available in several basic styles: the one-piece suit with long sleeves; the one-piece sleeveless suit to be worn with a sweater or parka or its own matching jacket; and the two-piece suit. The latter is comprised of a parka and pants which match in both fabric and color. It fits close to the body in a slim line from shoulder to heel. Of all the various ski suits, all are designed basically for women, except the two-piece affairs.

With new superstretch materials, suits should present no great fitting problem, but fitting should nevertheless be done with great care. Ski suits are available in a price range anywhere from $60 to $90 and over. Jackets span the style range from knit collars to side-zips. In the long run, these suits can prove a sound investment, with slim good looks an added dividend.

Warm-up Suits and Foul-weather Gear. The warm-up suit was first made for the ski racer. At the starting gate, racers pull on overpants and windbreakers to keep warm until their number comes up. Designers picked up the concept and have translated the bulky racer outfits into the fashionably cut warm-up suit. In its new recreational role, the warm-up suit is either an insulated quilt or a thermal-lined jacket with pants to match. It is roomy enough to be worn over your ski pants and sweaters, yet sleek enough to eliminate that overstuffed pillow shape. In addition to warding off the cold on windswept hills, the warm-up suit extends its boundaries into nighttime as an après-ski suit and into springtime, when it can be worn without underpinnings.

Waterproof "foul-weather" suits are made

for wet conditions. These too are zipped on over your ski clothes, and since they are made of light coated nylon, they fold up neatly into a carryable size. When rain or snow moves in, onto the skier the suit goes. The wet suit has other uses too—for all those nonski sports: snowmobiling, ski-bobbing, sledding, and the like.

For subzero weather there are warm-up pants, also referred to as starting pants or preracers. These insulated pants are made for men, women, and children, and are the best answer to icy chair lifts; they also help to cushion falls on icy slopes. Wet weather versions of the warm-up pants are lighter and noninsulated, but well waterproofed. Called rain pants, they too zip on over your ski pants and often fold up into a small belt bag to wear around your waist. Another suggestion for cold legs is leggings to pull on over your ski pants for extra warmth.

Sweaters and Shirts. These are interchangeable and, to some extent, optional. Many skiers wear a woolen sweater over a thin woolen shirt. Some men prefer to wear a heavy shirt over a sweater. The ski sweater does not replace the parka, of course, for the beginner who needs a water-repellent protection from the snow picked up in tumbles.

Long before styling was focused on the parka, sweaters were considered an outer garment. Skiers began searching for a look of individuality in sweaters, often by snapping up the wonderful, warm handkits from Europe. In recent years, American knitters have also shown a surge of creativity. Ski sweaters made in America and knitted of man-made fibers can be as functional and exciting as the classic handmade designs. The advantages of warmth without weight, easy washability without the need for blocking, quick drying, and moth resistance are all found in the knits of the synthetic fibers. In addition, new means of processing the yarns, such as Orlon, offer the versatility required to step up their styling.

Undoubtedly the most basic sweater style ever invented was the flat-knit turtleneck pullover, worn by the skier under the heavy knit V-neck or crew-neck ski sweater. In the ski wardrobe, this is as standard as warm underwear. Beneath the bulky V-neck sweater, it is

the foundation of the layered principle of keeping warm and looking smart.

A good look in ski sweaters, as of 1970, is long and skinny, in flat knits or ribs or cables. Racing stripes are favored by many; geometric color blocks, by others. In the early 1960's, bulky sweaters were in vogue. Though the pullover is predominant, the zip-front or buttoned cardigan is often preferred by women. After-ski knit fashions are equally varied. There are smart, bulky-knit ponchos and capes to don after the last run down the mountain, and an extensive variety of lighterweight sweaters and knit costumes—such as the doublet, sometimes with its own knit pants —for ski-lodge wear. Lightweight silk and nylon jerseys worn with long skirts are increasing in fashion interest.

When selecting a sweater there should be enough room to maneuver arms and shoulders with no strain or pull across the back. The bottom of the sweater should be firm but not tight around the hips; the cuffs should be snug at the wrist; and the shoulder seams should fall at or slightly below the shoulder. There should be no extra bulk in sweaters employed under parkas.

The turtleneck shirt is fashionable, and the choice in colors, fabrics, patterns, and styles is almost unlimited. In selecting turtlenecks make sure that the collar is not too tight, that both torso and sleeve length are adequate, and that the fabric is not too flimsy. At small extra cost, it is possible to get turtlenecks with zippers, a desirable feature that permits you to ventilate.

Underwear. Long underwear is an essential part of any skier's wardrobe—either male or female. The two-piece sets—tops and tights —are the most popular. Tops may be made of multilayered thermal cotton, soft wool, cotton-lined wool, or a combination of natural and synthetic fibers. The tights can be made of double- or triple-layered thermal cotton, soft wool, or a wool and nylon combination. Although bulky, the quilted insulated undervests and jackets that are sold in underwear sections of most department stores are another means of keeping warm when they are worn under parkas. Other possibilities are downfilled vests for men. Nylon wind shirts, too, will cut down wind and maintain a little more warmth under your parka. It is important to keep in mind that the correct underwear can help raise your temperature several degrees.

Socks. The cold-feet syndrome still has not been totally solved, but help is on its way. Buckle boots assist in one way—they can be easily unfastened for blood circulation. Plastic boots also are warm, although they can cause foot perspiration, so wear absorbent socks.

As far as ski socks are concerned, the layer concept is the best answer. Put a thin cotton, silk, wool, or fishnet sock under your thick thermal ski sock. Wick-dry liner socks became popular a few seasons ago because they pull out or "wick" the moisture from your feet and transfer it to the outer sock, thus keeping feet dry longer. That is, these "wicking" socks are made of specially treated synthetic nylon or Orlon hydrophobic (i.e., lacking an affinity to water) yarns, which do not absorb moisture but rather wick, or pull, it away from the skin. Thin inner socks of hydrophobic yarns are made under various brand names. Wicking outer socks are also available, usually woven in combination with hygroscopic (i.e., readily taking up and retaining moisture) yarn, which holds the moisture that is wicked into it. These socks are made with a wicking yarn knitted into a soft-textured terry for the innermost layer, a middle layer of wool to absorb the moisture, and an outer layer of nylon for durability.

Even with these magic fibers and processes, wool remains the old reliable thermal fiber not only because it feels warmer than other materials, but because it seems to generate heat of its own. For many skiers nothing beats the Norwegian ragg sock of 85 to 100 per cent wool and low price.

More popular today is the insulated sock, which is made with a terry knit to hold heat next to the skin in tiny air pockets and a tightly woven outer layer, reinforced with nylon for durability. Prices vary according to the wool content. Remember that wearing two *heavy* pairs of socks—as is the habit with some skiers—does nothing for keeping the feet warm, and moreover is likely to reduce control of the skis.

Regardless of type used, the socks should be carefully fitted. If they are too small, they will restrict circulation; if they are too large, there will be bulky lumps to rub against the foot. You should be able to move your toes freely inside the sock.

A few additional tips for keeping feet warm: unbuckle boots while riding lifts to get warm blood circulating in your feet, keep active by wiggling toes and stamping feet, and whenever possible, elevate feet to aid blood circulation. If exercise does not warm them up, the best thing is to return to the lodge, take the boots off, and warm the feet in front of a fire—gently. Then, before putting the boots back on, warm the insides of the boots by placing or holding them upside down over a radiator. This is also recommended if the boots are cold first thing in the morning. Incidentally, laughable though it seems, the best device for warming and drying boots is a lady's electric hair dryer.

Mitts and Gloves. Mitts are warmer than gloves, but many skiers will put up with some cold for the improved grip gloves allow them. However, when temperatures plummet to below zero, even the glove-wearing skier will change to mitts. The well-equipped skier will have both.

If you are resigned to perpetually having cold hands, try the two-layer system—silk, wool, or cotton liner gloves or mittens worn under your regular leather layer. And carry a spare pair of liners in your pocket so you will have a dry layer when needed. Even the best gloves or mitts will not keep your hands warm in cold weather unless you keep your arms moving, but they can, if they are good, store the heat that the hands generate. This is not much. For this reason gloves and mitts should be made of the best wind- and water-repellent materials available: lined leather properly treated. They should also be long enough at the wrist to fit snugly under the cuffs of the parka. In addition to keeping your hands warm, ski gloves also serve a protective function. A good ski glove is padded across the knuckles to protect them in a fall on hard snow, ice, or breakable crust.

When buying gloves make sure that they fit easily over the liners, keeping in mind that leather will stretch a little in use. The leather should be pliant and of high quality, and the stitching should be especially sturdy in the area between the thumb and forefinger, where many gloves break down. Another desirable feature in gloves is snap links, which make it possible to hook the gloves together and to a belt loop when they are not in use. And if you ride rope tows frequently, look for gloves which are reinforced across the palm. Remember that whenever your gloves are too tight, your hands are going to be cold. Make it a policy not to let your hands touch cold metal. If you wear mittens with a liner underneath, you can take off the mittens to fix your bindings and still leave on the liner.

Headgear. There are a few hardies who can do without a hat, but for most it is an essential clothing item. Ears are quite vulnerable to the cold, particularly the lobes and edges. A headband provides some protection; a hat does a better job.

A hat should be so designed that it will stay on under all but extreme circumstances. There are hats available which do this job without the use of tie strings, and are still comfortable. Hats also come in a great variety of styles, from the conservative to the zany. For instance, fur hats are warm, luxurious, and can double for street wear. Avoid wearing them in very wet weather, however, as wet fur will flatten and mat. Actually hats that convert from caps to hoods are good insurance for uncertain weather. Knit hats are practical, usually inexpensive, and come in a multitude of styles and colors.

For the head, helmets are the best-looking solution to cold. They snap securely under the chin, yet do not impair your side vision.

Ski masks are another piece of headgear that should be considered in cold weather. The ski mask vogue apparently got started awhile ago when an American couple, Stanley and Leona Selengut, were traveling through Peru. They ran across an Indian riding a burro in the high plateau country between the villages of Cusco and Puno. What particularly caught their attention was the unusual face mask the Indian wore to protect him against the high winds of the treeless terrain. Mrs. Selengut, correctly figuring she had spotted a good thing that would make a hit with skiers back home, bought up as many of the face masks as she could and

brought them back with her to this country. Almost immediately the masks caught on with skiers, and they are now as much a part of a skier's outfit as stretch pants and parkas. Cold-weather masks, covering the skier's nose and lips, are available and allow him to breathe warm air, which conserves energy that in turn helps keep him warm.

In summing up the ski clothing situation, the skier or would-be skier now has available a choice of garments that are not only functional and warm, but at the same time versatile and fashionable.

Clothing Size Conversion—United States and Foreign Equivalents

Men's Sizes

Gloves

Sizes are the same in all countries and come in quarter sizes from 7¼ through 9.

Hats and Gloves

U.S.	6⅝	6¾	6⅞	7	7⅛	7¼	7½
England	6½	6⅝	6¾	6⅞	7	7⅛	7¼
France, Italy, Germany, Switzerland	54	55	56	57	58	59	60
Spain	S	S	M	M	M	L	L

Parkas, Coats, Jackets

	Small	Medium	Large	Extra-large
U.S., England, Spain	36–38	40	42–44	46
France, Germany Switzerland, Italy	44–46	48–50	52–54	56–58

Socks

U.S., England, Spain	9	9½	10		10½	11	11½	12
Switzerland	11	11½	11½	12		12	12½	12½
France, Germany, Italy	37/38	38/39	39/40	40/41	41/42	42/43	43/44

Sweaters

	Small	Medium	Large	Extra-large
U.S., Spain, Germany	36–38	39–40	41–42	44–46
England	34	36–38	40–42	44–46
Italy, Switzerland, France	44	46–48	50	52–54

Shirts

	Small	Medium	Large	Extra-large
U.S., England,				
Italy	36–38	40	42–44	46
France, Germany,				
Switzerland, Spain	44	46	48–50	52–54

Men's Underwear

	Small	Medium	Large	Extra-large
U.S.*				
England	34	36–38	40	42–44
Continent	5	6–7	8	9–10

* Now often sold in the U.S. according to the English (i.e., waist and chest) sizes.

Ladies' and Children's Sizes

Gloves and Hats

Sizes in all countries are the same and come in quarter sizes from 6¼ through 7½. Ladies' hat sizes vary in each country and are usually made to order in Europe.

Blouses and Sweaters

U.S., England	32	34	36	38	40	42
Germany	40	42	44	46	48	50

Blouses and Sweaters

France, Italy,						
Switzerland	38	40	42	44	46	48
Spain	12	14	16	18	20	22

Parkas, Coats, Dresses, Skirts, Long Underwear

U.S.								
(Junior)	7	9	11	13	15	17		
(Misses)	8	10	12	14	16	18	20	
(Women's)			34	36	38	40	42	44
Switzerland	34	36	38	40	42	44	46	48
England								
(Junior)	9	11	13	15	17			
(Misses)		10	12	14	16	18	20	22
(Women's)		32	34	36	38	40	42	44
France		38	40	42	44	46	48	
Italy, Germany		40	42	44	46	48	50	52
Spain		30	32	34	36	38	40	

Socks, Stockings

U.S., England,						
Switzerland,						
Germany, Italy	8	8½	9	9½	10	10½
France	0	1	2	3	4	5
Spain	6	6½	7	7½	8	8½

Note: Children's clothing sizes vary in each country. Clothes are ordered by child's age and height.

TOURING EQUIPMENT

Touring is skiing without the aid of a lift. It can range from a simple walk in the woods to a week-long adventure in the high mountains. In terms of equipment employed, it may be wise to make a distinction between the two basic forms of touring: Alpine and Nordic. The former involves steep mountainous terrain; the latter is a means of hiking over rolling countryside. The equipment required differs for the two forms of touring.

Alpine Touring Equipment

For the Alpine tourer, equipment is essentially the same as for the downhill-only skier. That is, he generally uses the same skis and poles, though he may decide for uphill walking comfort to change to a softer pair of boots. (True Alpine touring boots are usually considered as a compromise between climbing boots and regular downhill ski boots.) There is, however, a difference in touring bindings. In the days when toe irons were universally used, this posed no difficulty in converting binding for touring. The skier simply unhitched the cable from the rear side hitches. This gave him sufficient heel play for walking long distances. But since the advent of release bindings, this is no longer possible.

There are, however, two solutions: a touring attachment made for release bindings or a toe iron with a release feature. The former is a plate with lips that fit on the ski just behind the toe unit. It keeps the boot from slipping off the ski and can be easily removed for the downhill run. Although it works fairly well on relatively easy tours, this type of binding, under stress, frequently permits the toe piece to pivot due to insufficient cable tension. As for toe irons, there are a few styles available with a release feature. They are heavy and not the most reliable of release bindings, but for touring, where safety is of even greater concern than on the lift-served slope, they are the most satisfactory solution to meet the needs of both uphill convenience and downhill safety.

Since the best climbing wax will not prevent backslip on the steeper slopes commonly encountered in Alpine touring, and since the plastic bottoms of Alpine skis do not hold wax too well anyway, Alpine tourers employ "skins" for climbing. Although those made of sealskin are preferred, a number of substitute "skins" are on the market. Skins are fastened to the bottoms of the skis. The hair flattens out on the forward motion, allowing the skis to glide, and stands up if the ski tries to slip back. There are various other devices available for preventing backslip, but the majority of them have the disadvantage of being inoperative in loose or soft snow.

Nordic Touring Equipment

Unlike Alpine skiing, touring's swing toward synthetics and newer construction techniques has been slow. There are three reasons for this: First, because conventional, virtually handmade bamboo poles, laminated wooden skis, and sewn-welt boots were durable and strong enough for general use and were far lighter than comparable products using synthetics. Second, because ski touring gear, with few exceptions, has traditionally been produced by the smaller factories. In Scandinavia, where most of the world's touring gear is still produced, there are more than 30 ski factories, many of them family businesses, each producing 15,000 to 30,000 pairs of skis a year, barely a tenth of the total of a European Alpine ski producer. Finally, cost and pricing have always been a controlling factor in touring equipment production. Synthetic materials are cheap when mass produced but expensive in smaller-scale production using more conventional techniques.

Skis. To those unfamiliar with Nordic equipment, the ski selection can be bewildering. Most major ski brands are offered in eight to twelve models—usually three cross-country racing skis, three light-touring skis, two touring skis, a mountain ski, a children's ski, and one or two waxless and/or fiberglass skis.

Nordic skis may use as many as 36 individual laminations. Spruce is almost universally used for the midsections, while birch, beech, hickory, and ash are used for the side and top laminations. While both birch and hickory are used for running surfaces, birch holds touring wax better and is lighter but less durable than hickory. Hickory and Lignostone, which is wood compressed in an oil-impregnating process to one-seventh its original volume, are used for edges.

Nordic skis are side-cambered to aid tracking and except for mountain varieties have extremely soft tips and hard tails. The combination of tension allows the tip to follow small

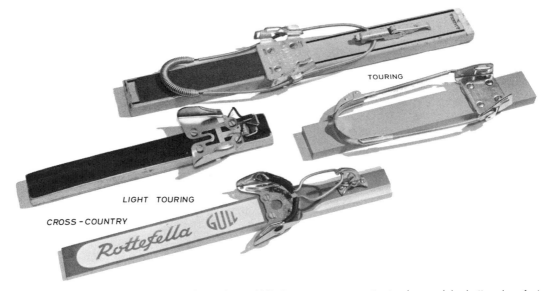

Top binding is for general or mountain touring; middle two are cross-country touring models; bottom is a fast touring or cross-country racing model.

terrain variations while giving the ski a "forward-spring" characteristic.

Because of their relatively narrow cross-section, Nordic skis tend to have a thicker midsection and a higher camber than do Alpine skis. Camber and total ski stiffness should be selected to match a skier's weight and touring style. Generally, the camber and stiffness should be enough to just barely hold the center of a ski off a flat surface when the skier stands on it. Too stiff a ski will not contact the snow over its entire running surface and thus will lose the benefit of any wax used. Too weak a ski will turn up at the tip and tail. The length of most Nordic skis may be chosen in the same way as that of Alpine skis, but in fact the 210-centimeter (6 feet 11 inches) length is used most by racers from 5 feet 9 inches to 6 feet 3 inches in height.

Cross-country Racing Skis. The lightest and most lively of all Nordic skis is the cross-country racing ski, which achieves light weight at the price of only moderate strength and durability. The "special cross-country" ski employs balsa-wood center laminations or vacant channels to further decrease weight by almost one pound. Its decreased strength is compensated for with thin synthetic-fiber sheets laminated in the ski's tip, midsection, and tail. Still, their use should be restricted to prepared tracks.

Fiberglass skis for cross-country are available at weights rivaling those of wooden skis. The simplest glass skis are lightweight laminated-wood skis with fiberglass top skin and bottom plates running their length. Their weight is kept down by using lighter woods in the core than are used in a comparable all-wood ski.

Cross-country ski tips have relatively low torsional rigidity, for they must follow terrain bumps without upsetting the balance at the center of the ski. Because in cross-country technique skis may be flat on a snow surface or lofted to meet angles up to about 45 degrees, cross-country ski tips are turned up more than any other type of ski. The tips are usually extremely soft to achieve maximum forward spring for a given length of ski.

Light-touring Skis. Light-touring skis are made of stronger and heavier woods and are up to 25 per cent broader than cross-country racing skis. They generally are used for touring in wooded and rolling terrain, and, although they are not usually strong enough for trail-breaking through wind-packed snow on high mountain tours, recent construction developments have produced stronger models that are becoming popular among expert mountain-touring skiers in the Scandinavian countries.

Wet-wrap fiberglass construction, simply the wrapping of fiberglass around a core of expanded plastic, wood, or aluminum honeycomb, is also used in several touring lines. Wet-wrap designs are superior in terms of sealing the core against moisture while retaining both strength and light weight.

General-touring Skis. "General-touring equipment" means ski equipment to most Scandinavians and usually resembles the U.S. Army Mountain Division's ski equipment from World War II. The general touring ski is durable and has a shape quite similar to that of a wooden Alpine ski. Although not quite as lively as other cross-country models, general-touring skis are perhaps the best all-around compromise for the Nordic recreational skier. Some skiers who take mountain routes which are predominantly crust or wind-packed snow add two to three feet of steel edge to the midsection of their general-touring skis to achieve a compromise model.

Mountain Skis. A mountain ski has the same profile as a slalom ski, but compressed hardwood or steel edges are used in conjunction with an all-hickory running surface. The forward-spring characteristic is present; however, the tips have a good deal more torsional rigidity than the other Nordic skis. Because of their weight, mountain skis should be used only for high mountain or glacier skiing where breaking trail through wind-pack and crust is necessary. Mountain-ski length should be selected according to use: shorter skis are better for steep mountain ranges which require a considerable amount of downhill skiing, while longer skis are better for glacier and flatter terrain touring.

No-Wax Skis. One of the major developments in Nordic equipment in recent years has been the no-wax ski. And as might be expected, the development has touched off a controversy between the wax and no-wax camps. On one point, ironically, both the wax and no-wax proponents agree: expert touring skiers and cross-country racers must learn to wax, as good waxing is essential to getting optimum kick and glide.

Waxless-bottom skis—there are now seven models on the market—achieve their action either by base serrations or by inlaid mohair strips, which allow the ski to slide forward but not backward.

No-wax bases, of course, have several distinct advantages for the occasional or recreational skier. They need never be waxed, they work best during transition conditions just above freezing (the most troublesome temperature range for waxing), and they need no cleaning. With these obvious advantages, look for no-wax skis to soon become the standard rental ski.

Bindings. Several different models of toe binding for *cross-country racing* and *light-touring* are available, but all are designed to attach the boot only at the very tip of the sole in front of the toe, allowing the heel to be lifted off the ski. Because cross-country and light-touring boots are supple, they may twist horizontally when held only at the toe. To prevent this, a serrated or U-shaped metal plate can be mounted on the boot heel. Bindings should be mounted slightly back of the ski's balance point so that when the ski is picked up by the center of the binding ears, the tip will drop down at an angle of about 20 to 30 degrees. Thus, even when the ski is lofted in the touring stride, its tip will follow and hold to the snow surface, affording a maximum amount of ski control. Aluminum is the most often used material for the binding ears, while the bail (the clamp-down unit that presses the sole down into the binding) is usually made of spring steel. Otherwise, bindings differ only in boot-to-binding attachment.

Boots. Nordic boots and bindings work together and must, therefore, be selected together for a specific use.

Like ordinary shoes, most touring boots are still made of leather. Nordic boots must flex, breathe, and be light in weight, and no satisfactory synthetic has yet been found to do the job as well as leather. Polyurethane soles are now frequently vulcanized onto leather uppers. This construction has the advantage of sealing the boot and fixing the

shape of its sole, a definite advantage in mounting bindings whose side ears must fit the boot and at the same time align properly on the ski. Most Nordic boots now have pre-drilled recesses in the toe to fit standard peg-type Nordic bindings. If there is a disadvantage to vulcanized construction, it is its comparative inflexibility when judged against the more conventional laminated leather-and-rubber sole, still the dominant construction for racing boots.

A *cross-country boot* is cut below the ankle and resembles a track shoe. While some plastic has been used, soft, pliable leathers, such as goatskin, are by far more popular for the uppers, and laminated leathers, designed to be as flexible as possible under the ball of the foot while simultaneously resisting twist to the side, are used for the sole. The boot last is made as narrow as possible so that the sides of the boot will not drag against the snow edges of a cross-country ski track.

Light-touring boots resemble cross-country boots but are made of stronger leather or plastic on the uppers, have thicker laminated leather or composition soles, and are cut higher (slightly above the ankle). Most light-touring boots have a cable groove milled into the heel so they can be used with toe-iron-and-cable general-touring bindings.

General-touring and *mountain boots* are about the same size as hiking or mountain-climbing boots and resemble the single Alpine ski boot. Most models are semipadded and have a double-tongue or double-lacing arrangement to keep them watertight. Like Alpine ski boots, the soles are usually made of laminated leather with a serrated-rubber sheet running from toe to heel. Metal plates are attached to the forward edges of the welt to protect the boot where it fits into binding irons.

Poles. Shafts of Nordic poles have shown a trend away from the traditional bamboo or Tonkin (treated bamboo) toward fiberglass and aluminum or steel. Actually fiberglass, once considered too dead a material for touring poles, is now common. Polemakers, it seems, have taken a tip from the fishing rod manufacturers and are now winding fiberglass around a hollow core. Result: a lighter, livelier pole, competitive in price with aluminum and steel. Remember that good Nordic poles

TOURING

LIGHT TOURING

CROSS - COUNTRY

Typical cross-country and light touring boots.

should have a little whip to help push the skier forward.

Baskets have for many years been made of the same kind of rattan used for wicker furniture, although recently plastic baskets have become popular. The wrist loops should be adjustable so that the pole can be swung easily without the risk of pulling off. The grips have a tapered elliptical cross section which fits the various hand positions used in touring technique. The metal tips of Nordic poles are set at an angle to the pole shaft, so that when the pole is swung forward, pendulum-like, the tips snag on the snow surface.

The proper pole length for cross-country racing and light touring exists when the grip fits snugly under the armpit: a 5-foot 9-inch skier will use poles that are approximately 4 feet 7 inches long. For touring and mountain use, poles should be a little shorter.

Among the serious tourer's equipment should be a rather complete waxing kit containing a cork for spreading the wax evenly on the skis, and preferably also a waxing iron so that the wax can be melted on. Correct waxing is essential in order to climb without slid-

ing back. A selection of cross-country waxes should be carried in order to cope with different snow conditions and to avoid the skis becoming snow-clogged. For ordinary touring, it is not necessary to have many waxes. It is better to concentrate on one brand of cross-country wax and learn how to blend the manufacturer's waxes properly. The waxing charts obtainable from ski wax manufacturers will tell you how to blend. More details can be found later in this section.

In general, Nordic equipment is less costly than Alpine gear. A good set of Nordic equipment comes to about $115 for the complete outfit—$25 to $80 for skis, $20 to $35 for boots, $10 to $25 for bindings, and $7 to $20 for poles. Clothing and accessories, of course, are the same as for the Alpine downhill skier, except that as a rule the cross-country racer's clothing is light and loose. He usually wears a knicker outfit consisting of light flannel and knee socks. This is warm enough during the race; to keep warm before the race, he usually uses a long parka. A good rucksack is essential for Nordic skiers.

Young people are dominating the ski racing scene. At left the three-time winners of the World Cup, Gustavo Thoeni of Italy and Annemarie Proell of Austria. (Photo A.F.P.) At right, U.S. Barbara Cochran after her win in the Olympic games in Japan.

Comparison of Characteristics and Weights of Nordic and Alpine Equipment

	205-centimeter Skis			Men's Size 9 Boots		Bindings		
Type	Edges	Maximum Width	Pair Weight	Features	Pair Weight	Type	Pair Weight	Total Weight of Skis, Bindings, and Boots
Special cross-country racing	Hardwood	2 $\frac{1}{16}$″	3 lb., 9 oz.	Light, flexible, cut below ankle	1 lb., 10 oz.	Cross-country toe clamp	8 oz.	5 lb., 11 oz.
Cross-country	Hardwood or compressed hardwood	2 $\frac{5}{16}$″	4 lb., 14 oz.	Light, flexible, cut below ankle	1 lb., 10 oz.	Cross-country toe clamp	8 oz.	7 lb.
Light touring	Compressed hardwood	2 $\frac{9}{16}$″	5 lb., 9 oz.	Similar to cross-country cut above ankle	2 lb.	Cross-country toe clamp	8 oz.	8 lb., 2 oz.
General touring	Compressed hardwood	2 $\frac{7}{8}$″	6 lb., 3 oz.	Resembles hiking boot or single Alpine ski boot	3 lb., 9 oz.	Toe iron, heel cable	2 lb., 2 oz.	11 lb., 14 oz.
Mountain	Compressed hardwood or steel	3 $\frac{1}{8}$″	8 lb., 7 oz. (steel edges)	Resembles hiking boot or single Alpine ski boot	3 lb., 9 oz.	Toe iron, heel cable	2 lb., 2 oz.	15 lb., 2 oz.
Slalom		3 $\frac{7}{16}$″	9 lb., 13 oz.	Double boot with steel shank in sole	7 lb., 4 oz.	Toe release, heel release	2 lb., 13 oz.	19 lb., 14 oz.

JUMPING EQUIPMENT

Jumping equipment is designed primarily to give high speed on the in-run and stability in the air. Jumping skis, for instance, are usually longer and heavier than Alpine skis. The proper length of a jumping ski, according to an old Norwegian saying, is "as high as you can reach and a little higher." With most adults, this will call for a ski from 8 to 8½ feet long. A pair of skis of this length will weigh between 12 and 16 pounds. Until the technique of "riding the air" became prevalent, jumping skis were heavier than that, but the extra weight for control was found to be unnecessary with the modern technique. However, skis that are too light tend to "swim" and are unstable in the air on longer jumps.

Although jumping skis are often referred to as "planks" in the jargon of jumpers, they are far from that. They are long but not stiff. Flexibility, it has been found, is desirable in taking up the shock of landing. Flexibility and camber, of course, must vary with the weight of the jumper.

Jumping skis are usually made of multiple laminations of hickory and other woods, and a few models are available built on the principle of metal Alpine skis. The better models feature plastic edges (metal edges are dangerous and slow down the skis) and polyethylene running surfaces, To enable them to track in a straight line on both the in-run and the out-run they are made with three grooves on the running surface. The cost of jumping skis runs from $100 to $250; cost is in part determined by the length of the skis and the material used in their construction.

The bindings used in jumping must be freely flexible. The most popular type is the old-fashioned toe iron with a front throw release cable. A jumping binding employs only two side hitches, and these are located roughly under the ball of the foot. When the cable is tightened, it should allow enough freedom of heel motion so that the jumper can touch his knee to his ski. This arrangement also provides for enough freedom to release the skis in the event of a spill. Bindings of the type just described cost up to $30.

Jumping boots need to be both flexible and light. A stiff pair of Alpine boots makes it impossible for the jumper to get a proper lean from the ankles in the air, nor can he make a good take-off or landing. In fact, the better the Alpine boot the worse it will be for jumping. Boots designed specifically for jumping are available at a few highly specialized ski shops.

Youngsters learning to jump can use their Alpine skis and boots. Most children's boots are flexible enough for jumping, and if the top eyelets or buckles are left undone they should have no trouble leaning forward from the ankles. More on jumping can be found in Section IV.

EQUIPMENT RENTAL

Earlier in this section, we said that one way of obtaining equipment was to rent it. While much of the information already given for the purchase of equipment holds true when renting it, there are relatively simple guidelines that the rental customer can follow to make certain he is renting from a quality rental business. They are as follows:

Condition of Shop. Look at the general conditions of the shop. If conditions are messy, the chances are that the shop will have a sloppy rental program. Renting ski equipment is physically awkward, and it requires a well-organized shop to provide adequate service.

Skis. Check the individual items to be rented. First, examine the skis. They should have reasonable camber and they should not be warped. (Tips and tails should rest squarely on the floor or against a flat wall.) Look at the bottoms of the skis to make sure, if the skis have a polyethylene base, that the base is free of excessive gouges. If the base has been repaired, the repaired spots should have been smoothed out. If the skis do not have a polyethylene-type base, make sure there is a good lacquer covering and no bare areas showing. The edges should be intact with no broken section or protruding screws. Skis should be selected by length as described earlier in the section. If you rent at a ski area, remember that the skis will probably be warm if you take them immediately outside. Do not put them down in the snow until they have had a chance to cool off; otherwise they will cake with snow or ice on the running surface.

Poles. Select the proper length and weight that you feel most comfortable with. Do not forget that when skiing, the tip sinks into the snow. Also do not forget to allow for high heels if a girl is wearing them when being fitted for poles. In selecting poles, check to see that the straps at the handle are all right, that the baskets are firmly attached, and that the points have not fallen out of the tips. Check to see that the poles really are a matched pair, are of identical length and weight.

Boots. There is probably no better way to determine the quality of the rental shop than by the boots rented. First, note where and how the boots are stored. The shop should keep them in boot presses to prevent the soles from curling or warping. You can accept as a danger signal any indication that boots in the rental department are of a great number of various makes and styles. Usually this means they are used boots taken as trade-ins or miscellaneous rejects from who knows where.

The boots, even if they have been used a season or two, should be clean and polished. It takes little effort to buff a pair of boots. There is no excuse for renting boots with dirt caked on the soles or with unprotected seams and leather that will sop up water. Next, check to see that there are no missing hooks or buckles. Finally, try on *both boots.* Do not take it for granted that if one fits, they both do. In a rental operation it is easy to mismatch boots. Also, this will give you the opportunity to make certain the laces are long enough and not frayed, or buckles are not broken.

Bindings. The next and probably most important step in renting is to make sure the boots and bindings are compatible. Some toe units have teeth that require matching notches on the sole at the toe of the boot. When the sole is chewed up at the front, it usually means that the shop has never cut proper notches to match the binding it rents. There are also toe units that require metal plates on the boot and "cup"-type toe units that do not require boot notching. Unfortunately, it is too much to expect the beginner skier to be able to recognize whether or not boots and bindings are truly matched. But it is not too much to expect rental personnel to be sufficiently trained to provide compatible boots and bindings for the customer.

There are several obvious points that should be noted about bindings on rental skis. First, bindings do wear out, so beware of equipment that is dirty or shows signs of rusting or corrosion. If the heel is held down by a front-throw type of cable, the cable should be free of twists and kinks. And, of course, there should be no protruding nails or screw heads that might prevent the binding from functioning. Finally, be sure to ask the clerk to explain how the bindings work, how they are adjusted, and ask for a demonstration. Many skiers have accepted second-rate equipment from rental shops because they hesitated to admit ignorance of equipment and its function.

The adjustment of rental bindings can be the weakest area of performance in many rental shops. Many do not use equipment such as the Lipe's Release Check to test bindings. The most common system of testing is to hit the toe of the boot with the fist or heel of the hand. This situation will not do much to build up the confidence of the beginning skier. Fortunately, or unfortunately, few beginning skiers are aware of any problem in renting equipment.

SKI EQUIPMENT MAINTENANCE

When the ski season opens, not only must the skier be in reasonably good physical condition to overcome early-season fatigue, but equipment must also be at its best to deliver the utmost in enjoyment and to provide the maximum in safety precautions. A few well-spent hours working on your equipment can mean untold satisfaction and safety.

Skis

Although skis no longer need the maintenance they did in years gone by, they nevertheless require a quick inspection and minor check-up to assure perfect performance and to protect them from deterioration in the face of winter elements. Generally speaking, the more you paid for your skis initially, the less amount of work you will be compelled to do on them now. The fortunate owners of metal skis can expect to expend the least amount of energy on their equipment. Bottoms should be checked for noticeable gouges, which can be filled by plastic repair kits, available at any good ski shop. Undoubtedly the edges have picked up rust during summer storage; these should be cleaned with an oily cloth or steel wool. While working on edges, it is always advisable to square them up and sharpen them. Sharpening is achieved most easily by the use of an 8- or 10-inch mill file. Work first along the surface of the edge and then at a 90-degree angle to the edge surface. Sharp edges are essential to controlled skiing, as is the elimination of the burrs on edges caused by hitting occasional rocks during the previous season. The chances are that there are no visible edge screws on your metal skis, but if there are, it is advisable to check their firmness with a suitable screwdriver, possibly saving yourself lost edge sections later on.

The tops of skis usually need no vital attention. However, if you are concerned with their appearance, you may wish to take advantage of some of the ski polishes that are available for just this purpose, or you can use a more general-purpose wax to shine them up. For skis that have really been through the mill, many manufacturers offer factory refinishing or rebuilding services.

The tops and sides of your skis should be adequately protected to prevent excessive moisture from penetrating the ski. If the tops are inadequately finished, or if you feel they need a face lifting, there are rugged plastic-based finishes now available which do an admirable job with a minimum of effort on both tops and sides.

Above all, do not neglect the running surface of your skis if you expect to get the greatest satisfaction and service from them. Generally, the more costly models will have a lifetime plastic sole which requires only occasional repairing of scratches or gouges. Some of the less expensive models, however, have thinner and less-permanent plastic coating on the bottoms, which can literally wear out. These may require replacing if exceptional service is expected of them. Varying types of plastic bases are available which can be painted on as a replacement. Although not as durable and lasting as the better factory jobs, they are nevertheless quite satisfactory.

Although ski warpage is considerably less of a problem now than it used to be, thanks to superior laminated wood and metal construction, it is still an item that should be checked. Sometimes only a slight warp can make skiing difficult, and any significant warpage can render a ski practically uncontrollable.

Actually, to give top performance, skis must be honed to perfection by hand, a secret that racers have known for years. Even the slightest imperfection can make a lively, sensitive ski seem "hooky," "grippy," too hard to turn, or too difficult to control. Such flaws are readily noticed while skiing.

The problem is in base and edge finishing. In the factory, most ski bottoms are finished on sanding belts to give them a uniform flatness from tip to tail. Unfortunately, with the pressures of mass production and the variation in the skill of the workmen, human errors produce imperfections. And even on a ski that is perfectly finished, the polyethylene base material can shrink days or weeks later because of changes in temperature or humidity, making the bottoms slightly concave. Such concavity makes for difficult skiing and miserable falls because the ski bottom is really more like two rails than one flat surface. Such skis need to be flat-filed the way the designer intended them to be.

Ski care should not start and stop with new skis, however. The finishing process illustrated on page 104 will improve the performance of any ski, new or old, and will improve your skiing along with it. Periodically you should examine the bottoms of your skis to check for these problems:

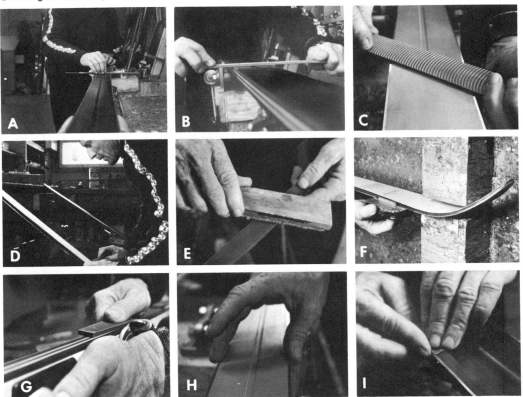

Steps in preparing your skis: (A) To check for burrs and roughness on the steel edges, push a file lightly down the ski's base. The file will grab at rough spots which need extra filing. (B) Flat-file the bottoms with a 12-inch mill Bastard file. Hold the file diagonally across the ski, take long strokes; do not apply too much pressure. (C) If the skis are badly railed or edges are very worn, use a coarser body file. This leaves a rough finish, so you will need to use a finer file. (D) If you must file without a vise, hold the ski with your body and support it against a table. File from one end, then the other. Finish with the midsection. (E) Clean the files after five or six strokes or if you see filings gathering on the ski. Use a wire file brush and sweep in the direction of the file's grain. (F) When side-filing, the surest way to get a true 90-degree angle is to use a holder with a rasp file. Take two or three long strokes; finish with a finer file. (G) When side-filing without a file holder, keep your index finger against the ski's bottom to prevent the file from turning and rounding or burring the edge. (H) After filing, run your fingers lightly down the edges to check for burrs. (Be careful of metal slivers.) Gently refile any burrs or rough spots. (I) As a finishing touch use a small piece of very fine emery paper, folded in half, to smooth the bottom of the edges. Guide the paper with your free hand.

1. Concavity, described above, can happen any time, but particularly if you ski on hard snow.
2. Nicks and scratches occur most often when snow is scarce. They can be repaired with polyethylene sticks or powder.
3. Edges around the shovel area get rough from the skis hitting together. Check this every few days, and keep the edges smoothly filed.
4. Dirt collects on the ski bottoms, especially in the spring, making them slow. Wipe the base with kerosene and a clean cloth until no more dirt comes off.
5. New skis should be waxed to seal the base against dirt and water, and all skis should be waxed periodically to make them faster and easier to turn. Not only will they ski better with wax, they will last longer. Waxing is discussed fully later in this section.

After a day's skiing, do not drag your skis across the driveway and carelessly throw them down. Clean them off first, if necessary, and put them in a safe place. If you have enough room, mount two brackets on the wall and stand the skis up with the running surfaces toward you. If the skis will be standing on a cement floor, put a wooden board under the ski ends. And never store your skis for any period of time near heating installations.

At the end of the season, you should clean your skis, and put a light coat of oil or grease over the steel edges. If you have wood skis, place them face to face, with running surfaces together, strap them at the tip and tail, where the skis touch each other. Then put a square wooden block between them at the point where the toe plate of your binding is mounted. The wooden block should be just wide enough to stay in place by itself, without increasing the normal distance between the skis.

Protecting Skis Against Theft. Many ski area operators and local law enforcement officials have stepped up campaigns to prevent thievery. Many ski areas have established checking services or "ski corrals" where skis can be left during breaks and the lunch hour, either at no charge or for a dime. Other than keeping equipment locked, there are a number of steps skiers can take to reduce the odds of having it taken:

The most important step is to mark skis with distinctive identification. The more unique the ski looks, the safer it is. It would help if ski shops sold their clients larger name plates, insignia, stripes, or other identifying marks. Although engraving the tops of the skis with the owner's name helps (and it helps to add the name of the owner's hometown), it is possible also to mark the polyethelene bases of skis with a Magic Marker or felt pen.

Another way to protect skis is to deposit them separately, rather than leaving them in a pair. The *divide-and-confuse* system is far from foolproof and obviously is not as safe as checking skis or locking them in a rack.

If your skis are stolen, report the loss immediately to the ski area office. Be prepared to provide adequate identification—serial number of the skis, brand name, length, color, type of bindings, and any descriptive markings or identifiable defects. Write this information down on the back of a business card now and keep it in your wallet.

Some ski areas announce the loss of skis over their public address system. Most areas also provide a form to fill out, on which the skier can describe the equipment in detail. The ski area should be able to tell you how to go about notifying the proper law enforcement agency. Once the ski area has been notified, the area is in a position to alert its security people. In some areas, local police will cooperate to stop cars leaving the parking area.

Bindings

Since nearly all skiers now use some form of release binding, it is imperative that these be checked, if for no other reason than safety alone. Many of the release-type bindings have moving parts which should be inspected for corrosion and wear, and which should be cleaned and properly greased or oiled periodically. If you are contemplating buying new boots this winter, do not forget that your bindings will probably need readjusting to accommodate the new boots. Even if you are resigned to your old boots for another year, it is a good idea to check the binding adjustment. The top of a lonely mountain on a sub-zero December day can be a highly frustrating place to readjust a release binding!

Full information on checking your bindings can be found earlier in this section.

Boots

Plastic boots require little care, except for cleaning them after use. This should be done as directed by the bootmaker.

Leather boots, on the other hand, require considerable care. When in use, leather boots should be polished frequently with a good wax-based shoe polish. This will preserve the leather and, at the same time, prevent the boot from getting too hard or too soft. Never use any type of oil or softener on your boots because you will oversoften them and so lose the natural support of the leather.

The seams of leather boots should be waterproofed with a commercial waterproof sealer, ski lacquer, or any melted cold-snow wax. Boots should be kept in a press—both after a day's skiing and at the end of the season. If dampness occurs in your inner boots, do not put them near a fire or a radiator to dry. Rather, stuff them full of newspapers which act as blotters to soak up the moisture. At the end of the season, store leather boots in a dry closet. Put them away clean and polished, stuffed with newspapers, in a press. A plastic bag will keep off the dust.

Ski Poles

These need little maintenance. Most of what goes wrong with poles cannot be prevented or even repaired, although the difficulty can sometimes be anticipated.

With poles, corrosion is merely unsightly. If they have been exposed to salted roads, corrosion can be prevented by washing the metal. In the off-season in humid climates, a light coat of oil on the shaft only (not on the rubber grips or webbing) will prevent corrosion. The life of the leather straps can be extended with an occasional treatment of saddle soap.

The loss of strap or grip can frequently be prevented by checking on the screw holding the grip and strap to the shaft. Occasionally, this loosens. If the assembly should come apart on a lift or in deep snow, it may be impossible to find it again, so it pays to check this point.

A more frequent source of trouble is the loss of a basket, usually in deep or heavy snow. This trouble can be anticipated by ex-amining the cotter pin holding the basket to the shaft or the condition of the ring around the grommet. If the pin is loose or if there are cracks or tears where the ring is fastened to the grommet, a lost basket is not too many runs away.

Even the best poles can be broken, either by falling on them or by cutting them with the edges of the skis. The latter is far more frequently the case, particularly with aluminum poles. When the edge of the ski rubs against an aluminum pole, it leaves a small nick. If this happens often enough, the pole is weakened at that point and eventually snaps. One way to reduce edge damage on poles is to wrap two or three layers of cellophane tape around the pole for about six inches up from the basket. The tape does not last long and will not prevent the heavier cuts from penetrating to the metal, but it avoids a great deal of the wear and tear.

Poles will occasionally bend. It is possible to straighten a pole out, although there will always be evidence of the bend. If the bend is not too severe it is best to leave it, since straightening the pole only helps weaken it. The life of a straightened shaft is limited, and it is a good idea to have a replacement close at hand.

WAXING SKIS

More and more skis are being made with plastic soles which run fairly well with little or no waxing on most kinds of snow. But the inexperienced skier should learn to wax his skis not so much for added speed (the reason many naïve beginners do *not* wax) as for increased control, safety, and ease of handling. Usually all it takes to convert a non-waxer is an attempted run down a slope in wet snow. Unwaxed skis will not slide. Instead, they will stick and throw the skier off balance, or pick up so much snow that he can walk down the slope as though he were wearing snowshoes.

Basically, wax is needed on the bottom of skis to keep them dry and to offset the friction and vacuum snow creates. Sverre Østbye is credited with making the first popular ski wax, in the early 1900's, by adding resin and pine tar to candle wax, thus enabling the skis not only to slide downhill easily but also to grip the snow in climbing so that the skis do not tend to slide backward. Even in ideal snow conditions there is nothing so frustrating as to have your skis tending to slide backward as you are trying to make your way uphill. Actually, one of the most controversial of all subjects in skiing is the proper method of waxing. No two skiers will agree on the kind of wax to use under every condition; however, there are some pointers that you should consider.

First, waxing is essentially a matter of matching the running surface of the ski with the texture of the snow. This is determined by the air temperature, the amount of moisture in the snow, and the character of the snow (new, old, coarse, or fine). A good rule of thumb for selecting a wax is "the harder the snow, the harder the wax; the softer the snow, the softer the wax." This is satisfactory for the majority of conditions the skier is likely to encounter. However, in the spring or on large mountains, conditions are likely to fluctuate, and some sort of compromise will have to be made, usually by adding some paraffin to the running wax dictated by the temperature. Most waxes today are compounded for temperatures below freezing (usually green), around freezing (blue or violet), and above freezing (red). To these is usually added silver (a combination of graphite and paraffin), depending on the moisture. The degree of moisture is determined by squeezing the snow in the hand. Dry snow will fall apart when the hand is opened; moist snow will ball up, and wet snow will show a distinctly wet surface. The wetter the snow, the more paraffin should be added.

Waxing Guide to Snow Conditions

Numbers in parentheses in the table on page 109 refer to the waxes listed in numerical guide to waxes, page 110. The temperatures given are approximately those corresponding to the still-air temperature immediately above the snow surface.

Wax should be applied to dry skis only. It comes in three forms: stick, paste, and spray. It can be applied directly (paste and sprays are convenient but wear quickly) by rubbing it on the ski. A more lasting and satisfactory way, however, is to melt sticks or cakes of wax and paint it on. If two or more waxes have to be blended, melting them together will assure that neither wax predominates.

When racing and jumping, a great deal of care must go into the selection of waxes. Usually a racer will start off with a basic mixture of about 80 per cent medium-temperature wax and 20 per cent high-temperature wax and begin his experimenting from there. He must attempt to predict the temperature at the time of the race. If ski conditions are extremely variable, he must wax in very thin layers so that the wax wears off by the time he encounters the changed condition.

Cross-country and touring waxes provide both gliding and gripping properties. Actually, the difference between a happy and a miserable day of touring and cross-country skiing is the difference between using the right and the wrong waxes. The reason is that snow has as many strange characteristics as silly putty. Under the weight of a ski it may give like rubber, flow like grease, shatter like a lump of sugar, or act in a combination of these ways.

If a ski is correctly waxed for touring, the small microscopic irregularities and loose particles of the snow surface will penetrate the wax just enough to allow a good grip (for climbing and pushing) with the motionless weighted ski, yet allow the moving ski to glide. A properly waxed ski will glide as long as it is in motion. Once gliding stops, the ski must be unweighted to start it gliding again.

A ski may be improperly waxed in two ways: *too hard* and *too soft*. If the wax is too hard, the snow will hardly penetrate the wax, and the ski will glide but will not stand firm when weighted. On the other hand, if the wax used is too soft, then snow particles will penetrate the wax, ice up, and collect snow. The technique of waxing can be divided into three parts: base preparation, wax selection, and wax application. Base preparation assures a good wax-to-ski bond so that wax will not rub off easily; wax selection and wax application produce the desired surface. The smooth plastic base of a modern slalom ski is designed to shed anything wet. The base of a touring ski, on the other hand, must be semiporous and soft to hold the tacky touring waxes. As yet, no synthetic material has been found that will hold touring waxes as well as treated wood. Birch and hickory are the most commonly used base wood. Birch holds wax better and is lighter, but is less durable than hickory.

Touring ski bases must be treated with compounds that seal out water and provide a good surface for waxing. Wear depends on how much and on what type of snow the skis are used. For average snow conditions, normal touring skiers will treat their ski bases once or twice a season while active cross-country racers may treat their ski bases once a week.

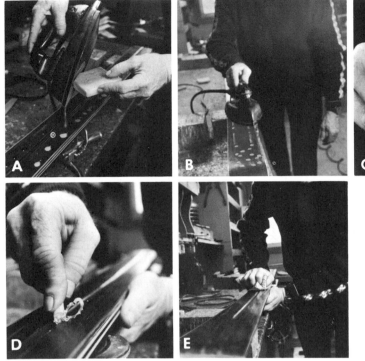

How to Wax Skis. (A) With a hot iron, drip wax onto the skis, but do not touch the point of the iron to the ski, because it can dent the base material. Excessive smoke means the iron is too hot. (B) Spread the wax with the iron. If film appears on the wax as you are ironing, it means that the iron is too hot and may burn or blister the base material. (C) Using a carpenter's scraping tool, scrape the wax off until all of it seems to be removed. Actually a thin protective film remains to seal the ski's base material. (D) To scrape the wax out of a round groove, use a P-Tex stick; for a square groove, use a screw driver that fits properly. Finish by running your fingernail down the groove. (E) Finally, polish the bottoms with a clean cloth until they shine. The entire job of preparing ski bottoms may take an hour or more, but it is well worth the time.

There are two commonly used methods of base treatment: burn-in and brush-on and air-dry. The burn-in treatment provides the best base. However, it is messy and requires great care in application. Both methods require the ski bottoms to be clean, dry, and fairly smooth before treatment. To remove old wax, use a small blowtorch and a ski scraper or greaseless cleaning solvents such as cleaning fluids containing trichloroethylene, gasoline, or lacquer thinner. Some special wax removers are available in the form of a nontoxic, nonflammable paste in a squeeze-type tube. Steel wool can be used to polish the final smooth surface.

The burn-in treatment consists of using a blowtorch to heat-impregnate clean skis with a tar compound. The compound is brushed evenly over the entire ski bottom including the tip, and then a blowtorch is run over the surface until the compound bubbles and dries. The blowtorch should be moved continually and not be allowed to play on any one section of the ski long enough to singe or burn the wood. The result is a completely dry base.

The brush-on and air-dry process consists of single or successive applications of base compounds. Some wax manufacturers offer a two-application method that consists of successive brush-on applications, with an intervening 24-hour drying period.

The major job in selecting the right wax for touring is to judge the existing snow conditions. There are relatively few waxes for dry snow, a few more for wet snow, and a large number for transition conditions. Waxing for dry and wet conditions is almost a negligible problem. Because of the critical balance of wax and snow at temperatures around freezing, the transition range of conditions presents the greatest problem.

Touring wax should be applied to a clean, dry, base-waxed surface or over the dry surface of a "harder" wax so that it binds or sticks to the ski and does not rub off too rapidly in use. Wax applied to a wet surface

Range	Usual Temperature (F.)	New Snow	Settled Snow	Metamorphic Snow: Heavier Corn, Pack, Ice
Very dry	Below 18	Powder: blows easily from hand (1)	Small crystals will blow (6)	Pack—cut with sharp instrument (11)
Dry	18–27		Small crystals will form snowballs (7)	Corn or crust varying from hard to damp—will clump in hand (12)
Transition	27–31	Barely clumps in hand (2)		
	32	Clumps in hand (3)	Large clumps (8)	
Mushy	32–36	Rolling snow-balls "dig in" (4)	Hand wet after squeezing (9)	
Wet	Up to 41	Soaking wet (5)	Slush (10)	Slushy corn (13)

or over softer wax will not last for more than a few hundred yards of a tour.

Hard waxes are best applied when the wax itself is cold, and they should be smoothed out with a waxing cork or waxing iron. Some people prefer to use the heel of their hand for smoothing: this is not only messy but can result in frost-bitten hands. The waxing cork is simplest to use, but the waxing iron does the smoothest job.

Soft waxes comprising mixtures of hard waxes and tacky "klister" are best applied when the wax itself is slightly warm, and they should be spread out using a scraper

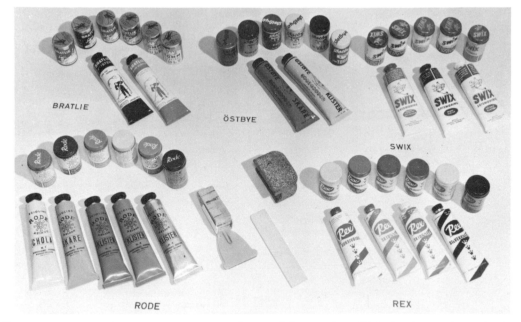

BRATLIE

ÖSTBYE

SWIX

RODE

REX

Touring waxes are made by five manufacturers. The round tins are about 2¼ inches long and contain either hard or soft solid wax. The tubes contain fluid klister. A waxing cork, a fluid-klister spreader, and a combination scraper-cork are shown for size comparison.

followed by smoothing with a waxing cork. A small blowtorch can be used for "warming-on."

Fluid waxes should be applied warm and should be spread out using a small spreader or a scraper. They will hardly flow when cold, so it is necessary to warm a tube in the inner pocket of a shirt before waxing.

Many thin layers of wax work far better than a single thick layer. A rule of thumb for the thickness of a layer is that it should be semitransparent when smoothed out. The number of thin layers applied depends on snow conditions. For a given wax and set of snow conditions, a thick layer will give a ski more "bite," and a thin layer will give a ski more "glide." A tour with many uphill stretches requires more "bite" and thus a thicker total wax layer than a tour on flat terrain, which requires more "glide."

The entire running surface should be waxed, with the greatest care being given to the bow of the ski's camber. It makes absolutely no difference in which direction wax

Number in Table	Bratlie	Østbye	Rex	Rode	Swix
1	"Silk" (h)	"Mix" (h)	Green (h)	Green (h)	Green (h)
2	"Blend" (h)	"Medium" (h)	Blue (h)	Blue (h)	Blue (h)
3	"Blend" (h)	"Medium" (h)	Violet (h)	Violet (h)	Blue-red (h)
4	"Klistervoks" (s)	"Klistervoks" (s)	Yellow (s)	Yellow (s)	Klister (s)
5	"Wet Snow Klister" (f)	"Klister" (f)	Red (f)	Red (f)	Red (f)
6	"Silk" (h)	"Skare" (f)	Green (h)	Green (h)	Green (h)
7	"Skarevoks" (h)	"Skarevoks" (h)	Blue (h)	Blue (h)	Blue (h)
8	"Wet Klister" (f)	"Klister" (f)	Violet (h)	Violet (h)	Violet (h)
9	"Wet Klister" (f)	"Klister" (f)	Red (s)	Red (s)	Red (s)
10	"Wet Klister" (f)	"Klister" (f)	Violet (f)	Violet (f)	Violet (f)
11	"Green Klister" (f)	"Skare" (f)	Blue (f)	Blue (f)	Blue (f)
12	"Skare-Klister" (f)	"Mixoln" (f)	Violet (f)	Violet (f)	Violet (f)
13			Silver (f)	Silver (f)	
Wax binder for cross-country and touring			Orange for all waxes (h)	Base wax for dry (h) "Chola" for wet (f)	Base wax for dry (h)

is applied or smoothed out because it is its microscopic surface and not roughness that determines behavior in relation to a snow surface.

Waxed skis should always be the same temperature as the outdoors before they are used. This should not be done by placing them base down on the snow. If waxing was done at room temperature and the outside temperature is several degrees below freezing, then the skis should not be set directly outdoors but should first be cooled down in an anteroom or entrance. The reason is that wax is porous, and warm wax placed in a cold environment or in contact with snow will absorb moisture and freeze.

The effort required to do a neat job of waxing can be considerably reduced by first waxing the sides of the skis with downhill paraffin wax. This not only prevents moisture from seeping in and undermining the waxed running surfaces but also prevents the tacky touring wax from adhering to the ski edges where it can easily rub off on hands or clothing.

Newly waxed skis must be given a little time to adjust to snow conditions. Generally, newly waxed skis will begin to "hold" and "glide" properly after the first 300 to 600 yards of a tour.

Changing snow conditions present the greatest waxing problem. The simplest solution is to stop and re-wax for any significant change in snow conditions that makes skiing on the old wax difficult. The ability to wax for all but the simplest of changing conditions in racing seems to involve a bit of black magic; very few who succeed at this game ever divulge their secrets. Fortunately for touring skiers, the most commonly encountered condition change is from wetter to more settled snow to dryer snow as one gains elevation. For this change one should wax with a few thin layers of a hard wax followed by just enough layers of a softer wax to last until the dryer snow is reached.

The secret of successfully applying touring waxes is experience with the waxes one uses; pick one manufacturer's series of waxes and learn their characteristics under use. After some experience you will be able to look at a snowy mountainside, squeeze a bit of the stuff in your hand, and exclaim something like: "Ah-hah! today is lemon-spotted wasp-wax!"

Numerical Guide to Waxes

Wax list—(h) denotes a hard, solid wax in a tin; (s) denotes a soft, solid wax in a tin; (f) denotes a fluid wax in a tube. The listing of the different brands of wax opposite each other does not necessarily mean that they are equal.

When doing *any* ski-waxing job, keep these three rules in mind:

1. Careful measuring by the skier of those factors that will influence his mixture (temperature, moisture, and probable changes therein).
2. Care and patience in application, carried out according to instructions.
3. The determination of an ideal wax blend by each skier for each condition through experience.

SECTION III

Principles of Skiing

Ski technique is constantly changing, evolving. In the 1950's rotation (exaggerated turning of the upper body in the direction of the turn) was dropped. By the sixties angulation (exaggerated sideways tipping of the upper body) and counterrotation were the accepted way of skiing. We are now in the throes of yet another change, which will surely be the style of the seventies. The key difference in this new trend is the abandonment of extreme angulation and counterrotation in favor of more natural, square body movements in the direction of the turn.

AMERICAN SKI TECHNIQUE

Contrary to some opinion, these changes are not merely whims of ski instructors. Recent improvements in boots and skis have dictated the need for technique modifications. And there has been a growing desire among instructors to make learning easier and skiing more enjoyable. To this end, ski instruction is now divided into three stages: Basic, Advanced, and Racing. The Basic Technique is instruction from the beginning stages through parallel and short-swing turns. The Advanced Technique teaches better parallel skiers to ski all snow conditions and types of slopes with finesse and control. The Racing Technique is intended for those few who are in prime physical condition and can apply the refinements necessary for competition skiing.

The majority of skiers use only the Basic Technique and move up within that category. The steps of the ladder of skills (called *final*, or *demonstration, forms*) are those of the American Ski Technique in its revised form. The technique is based on seven principles which are present in some or all of the final forms. These basic principles are:

Natural Positions. The relationship of the anatomy to balance on skis. Under normal conditions the skeleton, rather than the leg muscles, carries the body weight. The skier should maintain a relaxed stance.

Total Motion. This is intended to imply that muscle action is a product of the entire body. Body motion should be continuous throughout the maneuver.

Unweighting. The reduction or elimination of the skier's weight on the snow. This can result from traditional up-unweighting or from down-unweighting.

Axial Motion. Motion about the body's axis. This includes both rotation and counterrotation.

Edge Control. The adjusting of the angle

between the ski's running surface and the snow.

Weight Transfer. The movement of the body weight toward one ski.

Leverage. The effect produced in ski turns by a skier's moving his weight forward or back in relation to the centers of the skis. This principle applies primarily at advanced levels of skiing.

While there are many other "techniques" now employed by ski schools—they are explained later in this section—let us first take a look at the so-called American Ski Technique.

The American Ski Technique, which is taught in *most* ski schools in the United States, was created by the Professional Ski Instructors of America (PSIA) in 1958 to answer an obvious need for a unified system of teaching. The idea was, and is, that a skier can move from one ski school to another without missing a step in his progress up the ski-learning ladder. There are six class levels from A to F, and each one has an objective "final form," or as it is now called, "demonstration form." In Class A, a student learns straight running and straight snowplowing. When that is mastered adequately, he moves on to Class B for snowplow turns and traversing, and so forth up to short swing and wedeln in Class F.

Final Forms of the American Technique

	Level of Skiing
Class A	
Straight running	
Straight snowplow	Novice
Class B	
Snowplow turn	
Traverse	Beginner
Class C	
Stem turn	
Sideslip	Intermediate
Uphill Christie	
Class D	
Stem Christie	Advanced Intermediate
Class E	
Parallel turns	Advanced
Class F	
Wedeln	Expert

Each form belongs, as you can see, to a

class, each class to a certain level of proficiency. Each is a logical step beyond the last. For instance, the final form of the stem Christie is a logical next step after the uphill Christie. However, there is no restriction on the *manner* in which the final form is to be reached. This is made clear in the second part of PSIA's technique, the methodical or teaching sequence. The PSIA manual makes it clear that the individual ski school is free to choose the all-important *approach* to the final form; that is, if a ski school wants to approach the final form of the parallel turn by a hop-turn exercise, that is fine with PSIA. On the other hand, if it wishes to approach the parallel turn via a gradual elimination of the stem motion in the stem Christie, that is O.K., too.

The last part of PSIA's system is concerned with the physics involved in the various ski turns and maneuvers and is pertinent only to the instructors within their profession. The technique was based on the Austrian system as developed by Stefan Kruckenhauser in 1954. The United States national PSIA demonstration team completed a successful tour to the International Congress of Ski Teachers at Bad Gastein, Germany, in 1965, where the American system was recognized as unique and on a par with Europe's best.

Originally, the principles of the American technique are: *counterrotation,* the turning of the upper body in a direction opposite the skis; *weight transfer,* the moving of the weight to the turning (outside) ski; *total motion,* the continuation of motion throughout the turn, once body motion has started; *up-unweighting,* the decreasing of resistance under the skis by an up motion; *natural position,* the feeling and appearance of naturalness and lack of exaggerated leaning or counterrotation; *angulation* (sometimes called the comma position), the control of the edges by the leaning-out of the upper body and leaning-in of the lower; *forward lean,* the position of the skier at right angles to the skis or forward of that.

Like other systems, the American system begins with an exercise: walking across level ground. This is an optional method of reaching the first form: straight running.

Basic Technique, Class A

Before you venture onto the slopes for the

Carry skis over shoulder, bottoms together, tips forward and down, supported by one hand.

first time, we suggest that you spend a few moments familiarizing yourself with your skis and poles. Put them on and take them off a few times indoors or on your lawn. In this way, you will find it easier to practice and get the feel of the basic positions without slipping around on the snow.

To carry your skis, place them bottom to bottom. With the tails pointing away from you, hold the tips with one hand, and with the other hand swing the middles and the tails over in an arc to rest on the nearer shoulder. The hand that was at the middle of the skis moves to the front. Now the other hand is free to lift your poles to the other shoulder under the skis.

When you are ready to go skiing, it is important to get the skis accustomed to the outside temperature. Many skiers take their skis out of warm cars, heated lodges, or rental shops, and lay them directly on the snow. The result is that the snow, contacting the warm skis, melts into water or moisture which then freezes again to ice on the running surfaces of the skis. This condensation and freezing process will occur even if your skis are lacquered and waxed. Then you will have the hard task of scraping ice from the bottoms of the skis. Beginners, especially, are never aware of this condition, and it makes their first try on skis almost impossible. The skis will not move, since the ice under the ski acts as a brake. To remedy this condition it is not necessary to bury your skis in the snow overnight. If you stand the skis up against an outside ski rack or wall for at least 15 minutes before putting them on in the morning, you will condition the running surfaces of the skis to the outside temperature and keep them from icing up. Also be sure to remove snow and ice from boot bottom. An ordinary plastic ice scraper, the type given away at most gasoline filling stations, becomes a very handy item to carry in your parka pocket for this purpose. The scraper is also very handy when the snow conditions change rapidly, causing unwaxed ski bottoms to ice up. One swipe of the blade is usually all it takes to clean them.

Get used to putting on your skis and bindings properly. With most modern bindings, there is no left or right ski (unless you use toe irons that fit against the sides of your boots; in this case, you can tell which ski is which by the angle of the irons). Generally, you can judge by the location of your Arlberg straps. These should be attached to your bindings so that the buckles or fasteners remain on the outside of each foot, preventing them from catching on each other. These straps, which prevent the loss of a ski if one of your bindings releases, and which also give you added support, are generally preferable to the ordinary retaining strap or leash, since they are secured at both ends to your bindings, thus preventing a free ski from thrashing about in the air during a fall. After you get your skis on, try moving around with them. Notice how the toe has a tendency to drop whenever you pick up a ski. You will have to compensate for this by picking up the toe when you lift a ski.

Hold your ski poles correctly. Place your poles in the snow, a bit in front of and to the sides of your boots. Open the straps so that they lie smoothly, without any kinks in the leather. Usually, the rough side of the strap will face toward your hand. You will note that, at the point at which the strap joins the pole, one end of the strap usually overlaps the other. Always keep the overlapping strap to the outside as you face your poles. In this way, you can tell which pole fits your left hand and which the right. Using them in this manner will prevent chafing and give you a comfortable grip. Now slip your hand up

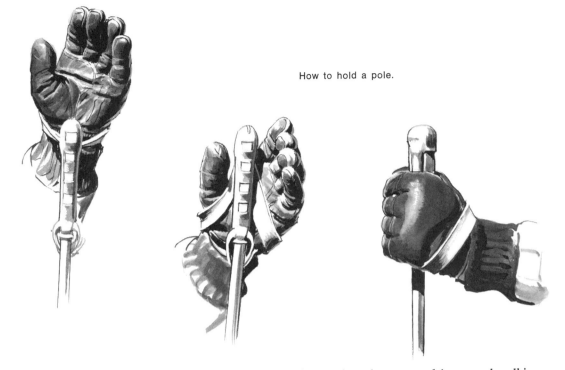

How to hold a pole.

through the open loop from the underside. Spread your thumb from your fingers and bring the whole hand down over the straps, grasping both straps and the pole handle at the same time with a firm grip. The strap should fit smoothly and comfortably over the back of your hand near your wrist without twisting, and lie evenly between your thumb and fingers. Tap the pole in the snow and, at the same time, open your hand. To make sure that the strap is firm and snug on your wrist, close the hand as the pole is stopped by the snow. Holding your poles in this manner will give you full control over them at all times. If your hand should slip off the pole handle while skiing or in a fall, the strap will remain on your wrist, preventing loss of the pole. You can then regain control of the pole by tapping it lightly on the snow and grasping it once again as you did when putting it on.

Walking and Gliding. Walking on skis is really no more difficult than walking without skis. The difficulty the beginner encounters is that the skis are intentionally slippery. To overcome this slipperiness on the level, the skier makes use of his poles and edges.

Walking on skis involves a step somewhat shorter than the one used in normal walking. There is also a pronounced shift of weight, from the ski to be moved forward to the ski remaining in place. This weight shift momentarily "sets" the ski, enabling you to push off on your step. Also make use of your poles. The pole and arm opposite the forward-moving leg move forward as the leg is moved forward and the pole planted in the snow. This enables you to pull against the pole in the first part of the stride and to brace against it when you bring the other leg forward. Practice following an imaginary straight line and walk relaxed. Practice on flat or almost flat terrain. When walking up a slight incline, you can prevent backslip by more bracing against the pole and by slightly edging your skis. By "edging," we mean the controlling of the sideward slippage of the skis by setting the skis at an angle to the snow so that they "bite" the surface.

A more vigorous form of walking is gliding. Each gliding step is preceded by your going into a slight crouch. As you take your forward step, you rise out of your crouch and propel yourself forward and upward, using the pole as an aid. The skis are then allowed to glide for a distance before the next step

Walking consists of short rhythmic steps accompanied by a forward swing of the pole and arm opposite the forward-moving leg. The weight goes from the stationary ski to the advancing ski to effect the skier's first weight transfer in motion.

When stepping around, lift only the tips of your skis, letting the tails pivot on the snow. Move the tip of one ski, shift your weight to it, and bring the other ski parallel.

is taken. Actually, gliding emphasizes swift movement and introduces up-unweighting. The body is propelled forward and at the same time up-unweighted by the springing action of the propelling leg and by a simultaneous sharp stroke of the opposite pole.

Step Around. Skiing in the modern sense means turning. And the simplest way to turn around or change direction from a stationary position is to step around. You should practice this first on level ground where there is no danger of your skis slipping away from you in either direction. Starting with your skis parallel, place all your weight on one ski. Lift the tip of the other ski and, using the tail of the ski as a pivot, swing the tip a foot or two to the side. Then place it back on the snow, shift your weight to it, and bring the other ski parallel again, lifting the tip and pivoting on the tail. Keep your poles in the snow for balance and move them only when necessary. Note that the tails always remain on the snow and that the movement of your skis resembles the motion of the hands of a clock. If the snow is soft, you will leave a pattern resembling a large fan.

Another variation of this turn is to move the tails of your skis and pivot around the ski tips. You will find that you will be able to use this turn on gentle grades, opening the tips if you are facing uphill and opening the tails if facing downhill. By edging your skis inward and using your poles for support, you will be able to turn without slipping.

The important aspect of practicing the step-around turn is the weight shift. In order to

move a ski, weight must be removed from it and transferred to the other ski. This is an almost automatic reaction, but it must be emphasized in skiing. In the step-around there should be a conscious transfer of weight to the stationary ski before the other ski is moved.

The Kick Turn. The kick turn is another method of turning around from a stationary position. It is usually taught only after a skier has gained more experience, since it requires a close coordination of skis and body and a conditioning of the skier's muscles and sense of balance. However, on steeper slopes, it is often the only practical method of changing direction from a stationary position. For the sake of keeping the climbing turns together, we will consider it here. Again, this turn should be practiced first on the level where you can stand firmly without slipping. Stand with your skis planted solidly on the snow. Place both poles in the snow, one near your ski tip, the other near the tail, on the outside of the same ski. (It makes no difference which. You can kick either the uphill or the downhill ski. On a steep slope, most skiers seem to prefer to kick the downhill ski.) Now put all your weight on that ski and kick the other one forward—up into the air so that it is perpendicular to the snow surface. Place the tail into the snow near the tip of the weighted ski and, using the tail as a pivot, let the ski swing around to the outside until it faces in the opposite direction, parallel to the

The kick turn is a complete change of direction from a standstill. One ski is kicked up and swung around to face the tail of the other ski. Then, in one motion, the other ski and pole are brought around next to the moved ski and pole.

weighted ski. Now shift your weight to this ski, pick up the other one, and bring it around too, parallel to the one you moved first. You will have to pick up your pole too as you complete the maneuver. If all goes well, you will be facing in the opposite direction, ready to traverse. A word of caution, though—be sure that each ski is securely placed directly across the hill before you weight it completely. Otherwise, you will find it sliding

Sidestepping requires horizontal skis and small steps for easy transfer of weight. The upper ski moves up first.

out from under you as it is weighted.

The secret of completing the kick turn from the ski's vertical position is to follow the moving ski tip with your shoulders. As soon as your ski rests in the snow you can easily transfer your weight to it and finish the turn by lifting the other ski around. Timidity and lack of vigor are the major problems in executing the kick turn. To get the ski on its tail, the leg should be swung up briskly and the rest of the action should follow quickly.

Another problem is that skiers often tense leg muscles during the kick turn. This makes it impossible to complete the turn easily. So, in order to relax, make sure of your balance by doing this: Kick the ski up to the vertical position, then bring it back to the starting position. If you can do this well in balance, then you will have no trouble with the turn. If you find the exercise uncomfortable, then check the position of your poles (wide enough apart?) and the point at which you rested the tail (close to the first ski is correct). Try it again, several times, until you find you can do it easily. Then do the kick turn from start to finish.

The Climbing Steps. In the early days of skiing, before the advent of ski lifts, climbing was a necessity. Today, it seems impossible for the modern skier to visualize himself climbing to the top of a mountain two or three times a day just for the trips down.

However, the satisfaction gained was well worth the labor, although it probably deterred quite a few people from taking up the sport. But even with modern lifts, a little climbing is not only necessary but advisable, especially for the beginner. It is still one of the best ways we know to warm up the skiing muscles and condition the body to the demands of the sport.

Begin by walking up the hill, using your poles for support, just as you would when walking on the level. As the hill gradually becomes steeper, you may have to keep your poles more to the rear to support you from behind. When the slope becomes too steep for this, you must resort to one of the following climbing methods:

1. The Sidestep. Stand with your skis across the hill so that they will not slip either forward or backward. Place your poles in the snow, well to each side, and then step sideways up the hill. Put your weight on the downhill ski, edging it slightly into the hill if necessary to prevent slipping. Lift the entire uphill ski off the snow and place it up the slope a bit. Then shift your weight to the uphill ski, edging again if necessary, and bring the downhill ski up to it. Now move your poles back into position again and repeat the entire process. If you find that you are slipping sideways down the hill, edge your skis a bit more. By "edging," as was previously stated, we mean placing the skis on their uphill corners so that the steel edges on the bottoms of your skis will bite into the snow and give you a grip. This is most easily done by pushing your knees sideways toward the hill. The more you edge, the more you will grip. Do not try to edge too much by rolling your ankles into the hill. Most ski boots are purposely constructed to prevent lateral movement of the ankles for better support when the skis are edged. If the slope is very steep, the skier can support himself with his poles. However, care should be taken not to rely on the poles to the point where they substitute for positive weight shift. The weight-shift rule applies in sidestepping particularly. There must be no weight on the ski to be moved.

A frequent error in sidestepping is to be ambitious. Too large steps result in an awkward position; this makes sidestepping more tiring than it already is and may lead to a fall.

2. The Traverse Sidestep. The traverse sidestep is the most practical method of climbing. It differs from the sidestep in that you climb not only sideways but forward as well, moving your skis up and forward whenever you lift them off the snow. You climb, therefore, in a zigzag manner, "tacking" first in one direction, then in the other as the edge of the slope is reached. This means that you must also turn around on the hill as you complete each "traverse" and switch to the other direction. Until you have perfected your kick turns, you can change direction by stepping around, using both poles set firmly in the snow behind you for support and to prevent slipping. Normally the kick turn is used in this method to link your traverses on steep slopes.

A frequent error in this approach to climbing is to move the ski up the hill too much for comfortable walking. The uphill motion of the ski is usually less than in the straight uphill sidestep. If the slope is very steep it may be necessary to make several traverses before the destination is reached.

3. The Herringbone. Another climbing method is the herringbone, which is quicker than sidestepping but quite tiring, especially on steeper slopes. Face straight up the hill and spread your ski tips into a wide V position, making sure that your skis are on their inside edges to prevent slipping backward. Keep your poles behind you and to the sides so that they can give you necessary support. It helps to slip your palms up onto the tops

The traverse sidestep combines walking and sidestep. Start to sidestep, but lift ski forward as well as up the slope. Stay on uphill edge of each ski to prevent sliding. At end of traverse, do a kick turn or step turn and continue.

of your pole grips instead of grasping them in the usual manner. Maintaining the V position, lift one ski and step it forward and outward, far enough to clear the tail of the other ski, and set it down firmly on its inside edge. Shift your weight to it and repeat the process with the other ski. The steeper the hill, the wider your V must be. Be sure that the tails of your skis clear each other as you lift them alternately up the hill, creating the herringbone pattern for which this maneuver is named. As in most skiing motions, keep your knees flexed and try not to let them stiffen. You may wish to alternate side-stepping with the herringbone, since the latter is tiring. It is best to learn the other climbing steps first until your skiing muscles develop.

Straight Running. Straight running means sliding downhill without turning. Though it is the simplest form of skiing, it can become difficult at high speeds on rough terrain. It is the first thing a beginner should try after walking and climbing but, of course, only on the slightest hill. That is, straight running should be practiced on a very gentle slope with a level runout at the bottom so that you can come to a natural stop without falling

When running straight down the fall line, keep your skis even, parallel, close together, and flat on the snow. Your weight is equally distributed on both skis; ankles, knees, and hips are slightly and equally flexed. Hands and arms are held slightly in front of your body with elbows bent and poles pointed backward. Keep your head up and your eyes forward.

To climb by the herringbone technique, start with both skis firmly planted in the snow. The weight transfer frees one ski for the step up the slope. The pole opposite the ski being lifted supports the skier.

or turning. Learn the proper downhill position thoroughly because it is basic to all subsequent maneuvers that you will perform. It is important that you learn to stand on your skis properly now in an easy, relaxed manner. It is always easier to learn to do something correctly from the beginning than to have to unlearn a bad habit later on.

Straight running should be done with your feet close together and the skis parallel to each other. Keep your knees and ankles bent forward enough to absorb irregularities in the snow. Bend slightly at the waist, but be careful not to overdo it or you will have difficulty maintaining balance and control. Keep your weight equally distributed on both feet, and try to keep your feet and skis as close together as possible, actually touching as much as you can. At first, your stability will seem shaky with your feet so close to each other, but you will find this stance both necessary and preferable in advanced skiing. Make a habit of it now so that it will seem natural later on.

Keep your poles off the snow with your hands slightly forward of your body and the rings trailing to the rear. Let your arms hang naturally with the forearms held in a "ready" position, almost parallel to the snow surface. In this way, your poles are out of the way but still available should you wish to touch them to the snow for balance. One thing you should be sure to avoid is trying to stop yourself with the poles. This is a common mistake which can be dangerous.

Keep your body relaxed and flex your knees as you descend so that they absorb the shocks going over bumps and hollows. Keep your head up—look where you are going, not down at your feet or ski tips. The faster you move, the farther ahead you should look so that you are prepared for any terrain changes that you might encounter. To help overcome the tension that most beginners feel, start pushing with both poles as you start to slow down at the bottom of the slope. Most people are literally "scared stiff" their first time on skis. Any movement to prevent freezing in one position is helpful. If you feel tense, try flexing your knees as you descend.

Another good exercise to familiarize yourself with your skis and to develop your balance while running is to ski alternately on one foot and the other, getting used to the reaction of your skis as weight is applied or released. Or occasionally try reaching down with both hands and touching the sides of your boots. These are good tricks for improving balance and promoting relaxation. You should be skiing only on gentle slopes at this time, but when you graduate to steeper hills you must always keep your body perpendicular to the slope, not "plumb" as you would when walking down a flight of stairs. Proper indoctrination now, concentrating on balance, relaxation of tension, and proper flexing of the knees and ankles, will help you to achieve a natural and correct position. In other words, the sole major principle of straight running is one of Natural Positions. The skier is in a comfortable, balanced, relaxed stance over the skis.

The Snowplow. The snowplow, while mainly a beginner's tool, is often used by even

In the straight snowplow, the tips of your skis should be close together, while the tails are separated and held at equal angles from the fall line. Weight is even on both skis, and the skis are on their inside edges. Your ankles, knees, and hips are slightly flexed; arms, head, and eyes are the same as in straight running.

expert skiers because it is the only way to slow down on skis without changing directions. However, it should be considered more than a brake. Through it the beginner learns the basic elements of edge control, which are so vital to advanced skiing.

In the straight snowplow position, the tips of your skis should be close together, while the tails are separated and held at equal angles from the fall line. (The fall line is an imaginary line marking the shortest route down a slope.) Weight is even on both skis, and the skis are on their inside edges. Your ankles, knees, and hips are slightly flexed; arms, head, and eyes are the same as in straight running.

Practice the snowplow position on level ground. Then, when you have the feel of it, climb up the slope and step around into the downhill running position, placing both poles solidly in front of you to arrest your forward motion until you are ready to move. Slide both heels out into a wide, inverted V position, keeping the ski tips together. Edge both skis slightly inward. Then push off with your poles. Concentrate on maintaining an even plow with both skis at the same angle, weight equally distributed on both feet. Keep the tips together and push your heels outward to maintain the wide V. Bend your knees more than in straight running. The universal mistake is to stand too straight. Your skis should be on their inside edges because they will not slow down if they remain flat on the snow, but be careful not to edge too much or your skis will cross in front. Govern the amount of edging by the position of your knees. To edge more, move the knees toward each other; to flatten your skis, move the knees apart. Avoid extreme bowlegged or knock-kneed positions.

Stay loose and try not to freeze up. You can maintain an even speed down the hill, controlling your skis by the width of the plow and the amount of edging. To stop, increase the bend in your knees and apply more edging. To start again, straighten the knees slightly and release the edges. Practice this until you can control your speed and your ability to stop at will on a gentle slope. But remember that the slowing action from a snowplow does not come immediately and it will take a few yards for the braking action to take effect. So anticipate your speed to slow down.

Basic Problems with the Snowplow

Problems	Causes	Cures
Too fast, cannot slow down or stop	Insufficient edging	Press knees forward and in; roll ankles in.
	Insufficient snowplow	Increase angle of snowplow.
Skis wander or cross	Unequal edging	Press knees forward and in equally; roll ankles in equally.
	Unequal weighting	Center weight squarely over each ski with equal knee bend.
Skis separate, cannot maintain snowplow	Improper weighting, sitting back, stiff knees, or standing up	Center weight equally over each ski, bend knees, and press forward and in. Push heels out; keep tips together.
Inside edges catch	Overedging or knock-kneed position	Roll ankles out; press knees forward.
Outside edges catch	Insufficient edging or bowlegged position	Press knees forward and in; roll ankles in.
	Loose boots	Tighten boots, or inquire at ski shop about need for new boots.
Cannot control edges	Stiff knees	Bounce to loosen up. Press knees forward and in.
	Loose boots	Tighten boots, or inquire at ski shop about need for new boots.
Cannot hold direction	Unequal weighting	Center weight equally over each ski with equal knee bend.
	Rotation of upper body	Keep hips and shoulders facing in direction of snowplow.
	Unequal edging	Press knees forward and in equally; roll ankles in equally.
Forward fall	Extreme bending at waist	Straighten upper body; press knees forward.
	Extreme forward lean	Keep weight on balls of feet.
	Loose bindings	Have bindings adjusted by ski shop.

Problems	Causes	Cures
Backward fall; skis slip forward	Standing up, stiff knees	Flex knees and press them forward.
	Bending at waist	Straighten upper body; press knees forward.
	Sitting back on skis	Flex knees and press them forward.
Instability, poor balance	Standing up, stiff knees	Flex knees and press them forward.
	Upper body or arms tense	Relax. Keep hands low.

After you have mastered the basic plow, try starting in a downhill running position, sliding your skis out into a snowplow while in motion and slowing down to a near stop. Then flatten your edges, rise slightly from the knees, and let your skis run parallel again to resume speed. Repeat this several times during your descent, finally snowplowing to a complete stop at the end of your run. Practice this until you have complete control of your skis at all times during the descent. Remember to keep an even plow with both body and knees forward; never let your speed get beyond your ability to control it, and maintain a straight line down the hill. Natural Positions again apply to the snowplow. Edge control is present too as the skis are placed slightly on their inside edges.

Falling and Getting Up. Everyone falls sooner or later. Actually only when a skier resigns himself to the idea that falling is as much a part of skiing as downhill running—and learns the proper way to fall—will he truly become a good, safe, and confident skier, who is equipped to tackle any slope under any conditions.

To ski well, you must stay alert, with your eyes open, and be able to size up quickly the conditions of the snow and slope ahead of you. You cannot do this if you are the least bit preoccupied with fear, or even concerned about falling. What is more, when you are afraid or concerned, it is likely that your muscles will be tense, your limbs less mobile. When that is the case, you cannot possibly expect to be able to ski with the quick responses necessary for today's tricky slopes, dotted with people. To become a good skier, then, you must lose your fear of falling. And to do this you must learn to fall without getting hurt. Here are some of the ways that can be used to teach the rules of safe falling.

The basic beginner's fall is first. While traveling slowly across a gentle slope covered with soft-packed snow, prepare for the fall by holding the ski poles about parallel to the snow, with the points away from your body. This position of the poles is important and basic to all controlled falls. It ensures that you will neither stab yourself nor catch a pole in the snow which could cause a wrenched shoulder. As you move your poles to the safe position, begin to sit back, as if you were going to sit on a low chair. As you sit back, twist your hips and shoulders so that your upper body will face downhill. Your hands should remain about the same distance from the snow at all times. There is a good reason for this. You should avoid all uncontrolled movements of the arms, since a jerky arm movement will throw you off balance. Your hips should be just a few inches away from the snow and well to the uphill side of the skis. Now, prepare to land.

As you sit all the way down, lean back. At the moment of impact lie flat on the snow keeping your chin close to your chest to prevent your head from receiving a possible hard knock. Slam your forearms against the snow just as your back is about to hit. Such a slam takes up any undue stress which your back might receive. This basic beginner's fall is painless and easy. Therefore, it is ideal for learning some of the characteristics common to all falls. For example, after a few preliminary warm-up falls, never let your muscles go limp. You must not overrelax, nor should you cause your muscles to stiffen. To fall safely, your muscles must be in good tone; they must be supple and relaxed. Gymnasts use the phrase "stay pulled together with your muscles ready for immediate action." This takes practice.

Another common rule for a safe tumble is

this: Keep your eyes open when you fall. You will always have better balance and react faster if you can see. When you "know where you are" (to borrow another phrase of the gymnasts), you can usually make the right movements to come back right side up. Perhaps you have read of the psychological experiment in which a cat is dropped upside down from a few feet above ground and always manages to land feet first. Yet, when the cat is blindfolded and again dropped, it is as helpless as a bird in a blizzard. So it is important always to keep your eyes open when you fall. Actually, there is a good deal of truth in the statement that if you do not fall, you will not get hurt. But it is also just as true that if you do not fall, you are not learning a hard fact of skiing. It is one thing not to fall because you are a great skier, but it is quite another thing if you never fall because you avoid all challenges. You will never become a really good skier, or good at anything for that matter, if you constantly avoid challenges. To become a good skier, accept challenges, and as you gain confidence and skill in overcoming them, you will become an expert. You may lose your footing along the way, but you will pick up many tricks to regain your balance before a fall actually occurs. Let us look at a few of these.

Suppose you catch an uphill edge and it looks as if you are going to fall into the hill. There are at least two things that you can do to prevent a tumble. If you have control of your arms, you can quickly stab your uphill pole into the snow to prop yourself back to a balance position. Or you can make a quick, forceful push-off from the leg on which you are standing. Then, while your skis are free of the snow, you can swing your legs back under your hips to land in a balanced stance.

If you caught a downhill edge, you could use a ski pole, outrigger fashion, to prop yourself back up. Or, you could quickly push off from your standing leg, swing your skis and feet under you, and land in a good, balanced position. The next time you are on the slopes, try these exercises. You will be well rewarded for your efforts in terms of new confidence.

The trickiest of all falls to cope with are those in which you cross your skis in front, dig a tip, or somehow get your skis caught on a twig or rock. These clobbers pitch you forward and happen so fast that you have seldom much chance to try to regain balance. When you feel you are about to be thrown forward in an ungraceful dive, the safest thing to do is to go with the momentum of the fall. Do not fight it. When you get thrown violently forward into the eggbeater type of

To get up from a fall, simply swing your skis across the slope so that they are at a 90-degree angle to the fall line. Then tuck your legs under your hips and get up. If this is too difficult, use both poles, pushing them into the snow near your hips. Then, with one hand around the handles and the other around the poles near the basket, push down hard and get on your feet.

tumble, just strive to keep your legs together and your skis parallel. Try to attain a compact, pulled-together feeling. With a little practice, you will soon become an expert at recovering from a forward fall. And once you completely lose your fear of falling, you will find skiing any slope easier and much more fun.

Getting up from a fall sometimes requires a little special technique. If you find that you can rise from a fall without difficulty, then perhaps this paragraph is not necessary for you. If you do have trouble, try this method: First, arrange your skis so that they are parallel to each other on your downhill side, pointing directly across the slope so that they will not slide away when you put your weight on them. Now, draw your legs up underneath your hips and, if the snow is well packed, push up from the uphill side with your hand. Edge your skis into the hill to prevent slipping. If the snow is soft, lay your poles on the snow and push from them. When the snow is really soft and deep, leave the poles on your wrists and place the downhill pole across your chest with the basket in the snow on your uphill side. Place your uphill hand over the basket and push down, at the same time pulling up on the pole with your other hand. It also helps to throw your knees downhill to help support your weight. Beginners often make the mistake of trying to rise with their skis on the uphill side or in a position where they can slide forward or backward. It is much easier to spend a few seconds more and make proper preparations.

When you fall, try to get up as soon as possible so that you will not endanger yourself or others coming down the slope. Do not lie motionless any longer than is necessary. Others may think you need assistance and summon the ski patrol on a false alarm.

After a fall when your ski has come off, it is sometimes difficult to get the ski back on. It may be that you are on a steep slope, or that the snow is boiler-plate hard. In either case it is easier to put on an uphill ski than a downhill ski, so, if it is possible to do so, turn yourself so the foot that lost the ski is uphill. Then start putting on the ski. From this position, if the ski should start to slide sideways, you can stop it. Jam your poles in the snow to act as an obstacle. Once you are

in position to replace the ski, put your mittens on the snow under your loose ski. Then the ski will stay in one place while you are scraping the snow off your boot sole (this should always be done) and putting the boot back into the binding. It is always a good idea to stamp the newly refastened ski on the snow a couple of times to make sure your heel and toe fastenings are well seated on the boot. Then press the leg forward; this is a final test of the security of the binding. Lastly, do not tear off in a hurry as if to make up for lost time. The fall may have been a warning you are getting tired. Make one or two nice rounded school turns in perfect control before you decide to open up again.

Basic Technique, Class B

In the beginning class we deal with the snowplow turn, the traverse, and skating. The snowplow turn is a devoutly-to-be-wished-for consummation of the first day on skis, because it means that not only downhill speed but downhill direction can be controlled by the skier, enabling him to negotiate trails and slopes rather than shooting down them in an uncontrolled fashion.

Snowplow Turn. From a snowplow position, all you need do to turn is to place your body weight over whichever is to be the outside ski of the turn. Very shortly you will find yourself turning in a broad arc. The important thing is to wait for the turn to occur; do not try to force it. To place your weight properly over the ski, pull back the shoulder slightly on that side and lower it toward the heel of the foot, at the same time bending the same side knee a little more to keep the ski on edge and fully assure the weight transfer. To return to the fall line after you have turned enough, simply return your body to its normal snowplow position directly between the skis. With both skis equally weighted, you will find that you drift naturally into the fall line again. As long as you wish to turn away from the fall line, keep your weight over the outside ski—and do not lean forward at the waist.

If you wish to turn left, lean over the right ski, accentuating the bend in the right knee. Turn right by leaning left and bending the left knee. Do not lose the correct plow position

Snowplow Turn. Starting from a straight snow-plow, you can turn by gradually shifting more weight to one ski. This ski will be on the outside of the arc of the turn.

ing. Edge the ski by moving the weighted knee inward until the ski bites into the snow and holds.

Snowplow turns can be linked very easily by placing your weight alternately over one ski, then the other. It is necessary, however, to move through the normal snowplow stance en route if the maneuver is to be carried out smoothly. This will permit you to drift gently toward the fall line for the start of each new turn. Do not hold yourself in the straight snowplow—simply pass through it with a gentle up-and-straighten motion of the shoulders. The whole motion should be slow and rhythmic, first to one side, then the other.

Remember to concentrate on putting nearly all your weight on one ski when you turn. The instinct of self-preservation is strong and it usually works against you in skiing. Your normal reaction will be to lean into the hill. If you obey this impulse, it is quite likely that you will fall without turning. Therefore, you must concentrate on leaning out—away from the hill. We think your ability to learn quickly is based largely on how well you can overcome your natural instincts.

It is neither necessary nor advisable to master snowplow turns before going ahead with the traverse, the next basic position that must be learned. As you advance and acquire more proficiency, it will prove beneficial to your skiing technique to go back and perfect your snowplow turns. In fact, practicing them is still one of the best cures we know for those who continually place too much weight on their uphill ski. For the beginner, the snowplow and snowplow turns offer a quick method of learning to control speed, change direction, and come to a stop at slow speeds. There are better and easier ways of skiing at higher speeds on steeper slopes. They should be learned now without delay.

while turning. Keep your ski tips even and close together, the tails wide apart.

Hold your poles in a ready position, as in downhill running, but be careful that you do not rotate your arms or shoulders in the direction of the turn. In fact, do just the opposite: keep the outside shoulder slightly back during the turn. This is a good habit to acquire early in your skiing, since it is important in the advanced turns that you will learn later. Right now, however, the important thing is to get all your weight over one ski at a time. It is also important that you edge the ski that you are weighting. If it remains flat on the snow, you will slide without turn-

Basic Problems with the Snowplow Turn

Problems	Causes	Cures
Cannot turn	Weight on inside ski	Line up outside knee, hip, and shoulder over outside foot. Press outside knee forward.
	Outside ski overedged	Roll outside ankle out.
	Stiff knees	Flex knees, press them forward.
Cannot start turn (See "Cannot turn," above)	Outside ski too flat	Roll outside ankle in.

Problems	Causes	Cures
Cannot start turn, *cont.* (See also "Cannot turn")	Upper body leading turn	Keep hips and shoulders perpendicular to skis; do not rotate, but let waist break slightly.
Uneven turn	Incomplete weight shift	(See cures for "Cannot turn," above.)
	Outside ski too far ahead	Inside ski is overedged. Flatten it and unweight it.
	Overrotation	Keep hips and shoulders perpendicular to skis. Do not let hands lead turn.
Cannot complete turn	Faulty weight shift	Keep weight on outside ski. Press knee forward.
	Stiff knees, standing up	Flex knees and press them forward.
	Overrotation	Keep hips and shoulders perpendicular to skis. Do not let hands lead turn.
Turn in wrong direction	Weight on wrong ski	Line up outside knee, hip, and shoulder over outside foot. Press outside knee forward.
Skis cross or wander	Sitting back	Move weight forward, press knees forward.
	Faulty or incomplete weight shift	Keep weight on outside ski. Press knee forward.
	Overedging, faulty edging	Flatten skis by rolling ankles out.
	Lead ski too far forward	Inside ski overedged—flatten it.
One ski runs straight	Stiff knee	Flex knee and press it forward.
	Ski overedged	Flatten ski by rolling ankle out.
	Faulty weighting	Weight the outside ski (see above).
Inside edges catch	Skis overedged	Flatten skis by rolling ankles out.
Downhill fall	Faulty edging	Roll both ankles in, toward each other. Do not roll outside ankle out.
Uphill fall	Weight on wrong ski	Keep outside hip and shoulder directly over outside ski.
	Sitting back	Press knees forward.

The principles of Natural Positions and Edge Control apply in the same manner as in the snowplow. Weight Transfer is also present as the turning force. With Total Motion the entire body is involved, and all movements are smooth and uninterrupted.

Traversing. In skiing, the word "traverse" means to ski across the hill. This is always done with the skis parallel to each other, much the same as in straight running. Now, however, the skis are not equally weighted. The lower ski should carry most of the weight. The uphill ski should lead the lower ski by about 4 inches (or approximately half the length of your boot). These are fundamentals that must be kept in mind, for a violation of these rules will literally start you off on the wrong foot.

The knees and skis must stay close together as in straight running. If you can keep your skis and knees actually touching each other, so much the better. With the uphill ski advanced and unweighted, and with skis together, the possibility of crossing them is remote, since the upturned tip of the downhill ski acts as a barrier. The lower knee will

Traverse. While moving across the hill, your lower body (ankles, knees, and hips) leans toward the hill, causing your skis to turn on edge. At the same time your upper body (chest, shoulders, and head) leans out over the downhill ski, causing most of your weight to be on that ski. In this position your ankles, knees, and hips are slightly flexed, and your hands and arms are held comfortably in front of your body with the poles pointing backward. Your head is up, and eyes are forward.

necessarily be slightly behind the upper one. Knees should be flexed, but do not bend them too much. You will need some reserve for use in turning and absorbing bumps.

If the snow is hard packed, you will have to edge both skis into the hill to prevent them from slipping sideways. To do this, press the knees tightly together and into the hill. This will make your skis act as a unit, rather than as two separate skis, with an equal amount of edging on each ski. This is what you should strive for. It is the correct approach to modern ski technique. Move only the *knees* toward the hill. Keep your weight out over the lower ski by facing the upper body slightly downhill with a slight bend at the waist. A common mistake is to lean the entire body

into the hill instead of just the knees. This only puts weight on your uphill ski and results in loss of control of the skis. You must get your weight out over the downhill ski by leaning the body downhill in opposition to your knees. This will also automatically place your shoulders and hips at a slight angle toward the downhill side, away from your line of direction, so that the uphill ski, arm, hip, and shoulder will always be leading. This double bend of the body is known as angulation, and it is best achieved by twisting the chest and hips toward the valley. This twisting has the further advantage of pushing the upper ski slightly ahead, the position it must ride in a traverse to prevent the tips from crossing. In all but powder snow, it is necessary to carry most of the weight on the downhill ski, and this is done by increasing the angulation of the upper body. Despite the apparent awkwardness of the stance, it can be adopted in a relaxed manner with practice. Think of a corkscrew in action, avoid forward or backward lean, and keep the legs flexed loosely.

Practice the traverse on a wide slope that will allow a long running distance. Be sure to ski in both directions, not only in this but in all maneuvers, since all skiers have a "preferred" side that they constantly favor. Remember to keep your weight rather forward on your feet by pressing the knees forward from the ankles. This is true when you are pressing them inward to edge at the same time. If you can, make your track straight and narrow by keeping your feet and knees close together. But the main thing is to feel comfortable, and if this means your feet are slightly apart to create a wider track, so be it. Should your downhill ski start to slide away, tip your upper body laterally downhill and press the knees into the hill.

To prevent the common fault of leaning the whole body into the hill, practice lifting your uphill ski off the snow as you traverse on your downhill ski, or reaching down and touching the calf of your lower leg. Looking at the heel of your downhill boot will help you to find the proper body position too. These exercises will give you the correct feel, but the only real cure is confidence, gained through experience and practice.

You may use your poles to help you

traverse by pushing on them lightly. This will keep you from stiffening your arms and is most helpful in aiding your balance.

Most beginners tend to end their traverse by making a crude sort of snowplow. The usual result is a fall caused by the skis crossing in front. A much better way is to step up the hill in a skating step—the same step you would use on ice or roller skates. A couple of steps up the hill will usually be enough to bring you to a stop. And when you have finished a traverse, go back and practice it again. It is most important in learning modern ski technique.

Basic Problems When Traversing

Problems	Causes	Cures
Cannot run straight	Weight on uphill ski	Center weight over downhill ski. Try to pick up tail of uphill ski.
	Sitting back	Move weight forward by pressing downhill knee forward.
Skis wander	Sitting too far forward or back	Move weight forward or back as indicated.
Skis cross	Sitting back	(See above.)
	Wrong ski leading	Move uphill ski half boot length ahead of downhill ski.
Skis separate	Weight on uphill ski	Center weight over downhill ski.
	Sitting back	Move weight forward by bending knees and pressing forward.
Skis slip downhill	Insufficient edging	Roll knees and ankles into hill.
	Weight on uphill ski	Center weight over downhill ski.
Downhill edges catch	Overexaggerated angulation or comma	Modify position; downhill shoulder never beyond downhill ski.
	Stiff lower leg; downhill ski too flat	Flex downhill knee and bend it forward and in.
Uphill edges catch	Overedging	Roll knees and ankles out.
	Leaning into hill; weight on wrong ski	Shift weight from uphill to downhill ski.
Fall into hill	Wrong ski, shoulder, or hip forward	Advance uphill ski, shoulder, and hip
	Weight on uphill ski	Center weight over downhill ski.
Fall downhill	Overexaggerated angulation or comma	(See above.)
	Faulty edging; outside ski too flat	Roll knees and ankles equally into hill.
Instability	Stiff knees, stiff downhill leg; standing up	Flex knees, press them forward.
	Sitting back	Move weight forward.

When traversing, the Natural Positions principle applies, as before. Edge Control is involved in that the skier turns the uphill edges of his skis (by moving his ankles, knees, and, to a lesser extent, his hips) toward the hill. This holds him in the traverse.

Skating. One maneuver for every level of ski ability is skating. (1) It offers inherent

Three-part rolling motion of the skating step is: one, in the first split second as the ski hits the snow (in this illustration, the left ski), it is tilted on its outside edge; two, as soon as direction is established, the skier moves his weight onto that ski and flattens it for a glide; three, as the skier bends his knee and assumes a crouch position, the ski is tilted on its inside edge to produce a platform for the powerful push-off to the other ski.

value as a way to move and to change direction on skis. (2) It is a fine balance exercise. (3) It is one of the best possible aids in learning weight shifting and the feeling of edge control. In fact, beginning skiers might consider skating a further development of the step turn in which the ski tips are moved around ahead of the tails.

The real secret of learning how to skate on skis is to analyze the way the ski edges work. In slow-motion photography, for instance, you would see that the ski touches the snow first on its outside edge, rolls to a flattened position, and then to its inside edge, from which the skier pushes off. You can begin to learn skating by practicing these simple edge changes on level ground without moving forward. Then gradually combine edge changes with forward motion.

It is at this point that you should analyze the other components of skating. One leg is your power leg, the other your gliding leg, alternating back and forth. Bend the power leg, put all your weight on it, and push off from the inside edge of the ski. At the same time, step the gliding ski forward with the tip pointing outward. Move your arm and shoulder forward as body weight is transferred onto the gliding ski.

If this seems confusing, think of how a fencer lunges forward from his rear foot with his arm and shoulder moving in unison with his forward foot. Once you have made forward progress on flat terrain, you can try skating on a *very* gentle slope. Moving downhill, your skating steps need not be as precise as those on flat terrain because the slope provides forward momentum. However, your glide on one ski will have to be longer, re-

quiring more accurate balance. Naturally, at first your balance may be precarious, but a little courage will keep you going.

When you want to stop skating downhill, make several steps to one side. This maneuver introduces "skating into the hill": that is, repeated push-offs from one foot with repeated shifting of your weight—from the downhill ski, which acts like an exploding spring, onto the uphill ski, skis together in an edged traverse, then another push with the downhill ski. As your skill develops, you should be able to handle steeper slopes. Finally, you will be able to skate in one traverse, go down the fall line, skate in a traverse in the opposite direction, and finish skating into the hill. Exercises like these will eliminate any leftover fear of the fall line.

A final skating achievement is to do figure eights, either on level terrain for intermediates or on a fairly steep slope for experts. To do a figure eight on a steep slope without losing altitude, take several short, strong parallel steps uphill at the crossover point before making a tight turn downhill.

A final word of advice: Do not try to reach perfection during your first attempt to skate. But, whenever you find the right terrain, try it again and think consciously about your movements until you are able to do them with ease. You will find skating games add to your confidence and control and to your ski fun.

Basic Technique, Class C

The skier in the intermediate class is ready for more sophisticated maneuvers. The stem turn, sideslipping, and the uphill Christie will concern us here. The basic form of each is to

In action, down the fall line of a gentle slope, the component parts of skating are smooth and rhythmic as the skier moves his upper body, arms, and shoulders with the stepping ski. The weight shift is definite, as indicated by the pattern of the skis in the snow. Starting with skis in a V shape, the skier pushes off from one ski to another, gliding between.

be learned in order that the logical progression to the more advanced movements of the American Technique may be made.

Stem Turn. This first final form of the American system Class C marks a milestone in the skier's progress. It combines the snowplow turn with the traverse, allowing for travel across the trail in a much more rapid manner than with the snowplow turn alone. In the snowplow turn, you are always braking. In the stem turn, you stop braking as you come into the traverse position and glide easily across the slope to the point where the next turn begins. The stem turn is used primarily to link traverses together into a continuous run at slow speeds. It should be practiced on a fairly gentle slope.

Start with a shallow traverse, making sure that your position is correct and that you have complete control of your skis. To make the turn, "stem" the uphill ski by pushing its tail into a V position. This will put you into a snowplow position from which you can accomplish the actual turn. Follow the same procedure you learned in snowplow turns but, as the turn is concluded, bring your inside (uphill) ski back to the parallel position so that you finish the turn in the traverse position facing the opposite direction.

If you are traversing to your left and wish to turn downhill to your right, the procedure is as follows: stem the uphill (left) ski into a V position, keeping it flat on the snow and unweighted. The weight must still be on the downhill ski in order to permit proper stemming of the uphill ski. At the same time, draw the uphill shoulder and upper body slightly back in a counterrotational movement. In a proper traverse position, your upper body should be facing slightly downhill. As you stem, this position is reversed until your upper body faces slightly up the hill. Then, as you make the turn, your body will assume a slight "reverse shoulder" position, permitting you to finish in the proper traverse position again. The stem and the counterrotational movement should be done simultaneously. You may have some trouble coordinating them at first, but a little practice when standing still will help you to master it. Now, with your uphill ski stemmed, your body facing slightly uphill, and the downhill ski still edged and carrying your weight,

Stem Turn. Start with a traverse. Then stem your uphill ski while bringing your upper body "square" (i.e., at a right angle) to the direction of travel. Gradually shift your weight to the stemmed ski. When the turn is completed, bring your inside ski next to the new downhill ski.

start your turning movement. Flatten the downhill ski until it begins to slide down the hill. Shift the weight to the stemmed uphill ski, just as you would in a regular snowplow turn. Remember that once established in the reverse position, your shoulder position does not change throughout the turn. Stay in the snowplow until you have made a complete turn, then bring your uphill ski in to the parallel position, a few inches ahead of the downhill ski. If you have executed the turn properly, you should end up in the traverse position with your shoulders and upper body facing downhill again.

You will find it helpful to bend the knees more during the turn. Then, as you bring your skis together at the conclusion, straighten up a little before settling down again into your traverse. This "up-and-down" motion is extremely important in more advanced skiing and should not be neglected at this stage. The advanced snowplow turn is used to develop correct habit patterns of body position and weight distribution. The two are inseparable and important. Do not fight your way around on skis—let the weight of your body do the work for you. You will make smoother turns, not just in these preliminary stages but in advanced skiing as well.

All skiing pupils make the same mistakes—

using protective motions for self-preservation which are contrary to good skiing technique. They forget that people who are not afraid learn to ski quickly. This has nothing to do with natural ability or coordination, for often an otherwise good athlete finds skiing difficult. These people will become good skiers when they gain more confidence. For instance, the basic fear is of falling downhill, so beginners automatically lean back and toward the uphill side. The next false move is to edge the skis in an attempt to stop. Done while trying a stem turn, this results in either a fall toward the hill or a clumsy stop with the skis crossed in front. If this happens frequently, practice skating steps on the near-flat, using both poles simultaneously. The skating makes you shift weight, and the poling gives support and tends to bring your weight forward. Using the combination of poling and lifting your skis, you develop relaxation, a better knowledge of edging, and a neat way of uncrossing skis and correcting other mistakes.

In the stem turn, all the basic principles involved in the traverse and the snowplow turn also apply here, in exactly the same manner.

The Sideslip. The sideslip is the second final form in Class C. It is the transition from a steered or stemmed turn to the fine feeling of a sliding or slipped turn. (The sliding turn is referred to in skiing as the Christie turn.) Learning the sideslip is to unlearn the hard bite of the edging that the good traverse position requires. Sideslip edging is relaxed. The ski must slip sideways down the hill. Sideslipping is also a useful maneuver, since it often affords the easiest descent over a given spot. The skier who spends some time getting his ankle muscles accustomed to the feeling of letting go has made the best possible investment in his future on skis.

The sideslip and the traverse are almost identical. The body and ski positions are the same in both. The difference between the two maneuvers is that the skis slip sideways down the hill in the sideslip, whereas they slide only forward in the traverse. The amount of sideslip is controlled by the edges of the skis and determined by the steepness of the hill and the condition of the snow surface.

There are three kinds of sideslips: the vertical slip, the forward slip, and the backward slip. The vertical slip is a complete broadside skidding of the skis down the hill. The other two are similar but include a simultaneous forward or backward slip with the sideslip. All three are performed with skis parallel and together, the upper body in the traverse position. They should be practiced on a fairly steep slope and on well-packed snow.

Start the sideslip from the traverse position Although there are several ways to initiate the slip, many skiers prefer to use an up motion, creating a momentary unweighting of the skis by the rising movement from the knees. During the unweighting, the skis will start to slip sideways, provided they are not edged. Sideslipping always feels insecure at first, and it is only natural to edge the skis for security. However, you must learn to keep them flat on the snow during the slip. Keep your knees and feet as close together as you can so that both skis work as a unit. Control the edges of your skis by moving your knees either toward the hill to apply the edges or away from the hill to release them. The flatter the skis lie on the snow, the easier they will slip. To slow the slip down or to stop the slip, simply apply your edges by pressing the knees into the hill. Be careful, however, that you do not flatten your skis so much that your outside (downhill) edges catch the snow and cause you to fall.

Be sure to keep your knees bent at all times, just as you would in a traverse. Try to stand more on the lower ski than on the upper one, and keep your weight evenly distributed over your foot, neither completely on your toes nor on your heels. You will find that nothing remains static in a sideslip and that you will have to make minor adjustments in your weight distribution constantly. A little more weight forward will cause the skis to slip forward and down in a forward slip. Shifting your weight slightly to the rear will cause a backward slip in a similar manner. Both maneuvers have definite usefulness in skiing, but you should also know how to control them when you desire to do a vertical sideslip. You will also find yourself varying your edging as the slope and snow surface change, and you might even find it desirable to shift a little weight to the other foot occasionally as you slip down the hill.

Forward Sideslip. Starting from a traverse, sink down in your ankles and hips, and then come up to unweight your skis. At the same time, release (flatten) the ski edges. The result will be a slipping movement forward and downhill. With another sinking motion, reset your ski edges and return to a traverse.

As in the traverse, you will find it easier to slip in one direction than in the other. Do not neglect your weak side; all the more reason to practice it. Spend more time perfecting your sideslip than on any of the other exercises you have learned to this point. It is not as easy to do, but it is of more value in learning the advanced maneuvers.

Practice sideslipping only on a hard-packed surface on a relatively steep hill. Start it from a traverse, by making the skis flat on the snow. This is best done by a slight straightening of the knees in what is called an "up motion." Do not set the skis too flat, or you may catch an outside edge and fall. Good fitting boots will promote correct sideslipping. The inevitable mistake is to allow the downhill ski to advance ahead of the upper one. It does not work, because the skis may cross and you will stand on the uphill ski. Instinct will tell you to do this because it seems the safest thing to do. It is not.

The following suggestions may help: Though the uphill ski should properly be advanced only about half a boot length, try to keep it a foot ahead. This way it will not cross the lower one and it will make you stand more on the lower one. You can correct this exaggeration later. Facing the whole body more downhill, and looking downhill, will help too. An occasional push with the upper pole can be useful in starting a skid, but do not lean on the pole. Once you can sideslip consistently, try stopping quickly by edging the skis. You must be skidding nearly broadside to the hill, or you will continue forward. Move both knees toward the hill to edge, but remain dominantly on the lower ski, with your weight mostly on your heel. A good skier will plant his downhill pole at the same moment he edges his skis. Later you will notice that edging (or checking, as it may be called) with simultaneous planting of the downhill pole is standard procedure.

Basic Problems with the Sideslip

Problems	Causes	Cures
Skis separated	Faulty body position	Uphill shoulder and hip slightly ahead, knees bent; do not sit back.
	Too much weight on uphill ski	More weight on downhill ski; bend downhill knee.
Skis cross or wander	Weight on uphill ski or too far back	More weight on downhill ski; bend downhill knee; press knees forward.
	Wrong ski leading	Advance uphill ski half a boot length ahead.
	Faulty edging	Roll knees and ankles into hill.
Skis slip separately	Faulty body position	Uphill shoulder and hip slightly ahead, knees bent; do not sit back.
	Unequal edging	Edge both skis together.
	Weight on uphill ski or too far back	More weight on downhill ski; bend downhill knee; press knees forward.
Downhill edges catch	Overexaggerated angulation or comma	Modify position; uphill hip and shoulder slightly ahead, knees and ankles in.
	Faulty coordination of arms, body, and legs	Arms, body, and legs move as a unit in normal comma position.
Uphill edges catch, cannot start sideslip	Faulty coordination	Arms, body, and legs move as a unit in normal comma position.
	Overedging	Flatten skis by rolling knees and ankles out a bit.
	Weight on uphill ski	Bend downhill knee and press forward. Try to pick up uphill ski.
Skis slip too far backward	Weight too far back	Bend knees, press them forward. Lean body forward.
Skis slip too far forward	Weight too far forward	Shift weight slightly to rear. Relax forward pressure in knees.
Loss of speed control	Faulty edging	Roll knees and ankles into hill.
Loss of slip control	Skis not parallel	Keep knees and skis together, weight on downhill ski.
	Faulty weighting	(See "Skis slip too far forward or backward.")
Instability	Stiff body, arms, or legs; faulty coordination	Arms, body, and legs move as a unit in normal comma position.
	Faulty weighting	(See above.)
	Skis not parallel	Keep knees and skis together, weight on downhill ski.

In sideslipping, Natural Positions and Total Motion apply, as in the previous maneuvers. Sideslipping is an exercise in Edge Control as the skier releases and sets his edges. For the first time the principle of Unweighting is present when the skier unweights his skis with an up motion. The skier may also release edge pressure by a simple down motion, which will unweight the skis for a split second.

The Uphill Christie. The last of the Class C forms is the very first taste of "Christie skiing." The uphill Christie is actually an application of the forward sideslip and is a parallel turn executed from a traverse which brings you up into the hill instead of around and down the hill. When completed, your skis will face somewhat up the hill, which will bring you to a stop. It is generally used for stopping and as a training exercise for more advanced skiing, since it is actually the last part of both the stem and parallel Christies. It can be performed from various angles of traverse, from across the fall line or from down the fall line. When used from a steep traverse down the fall line, it is often referred to as a "Christie into the hill" or "Christie off the fall line." The execution is the same in all cases.

Start with a traverse, rise into a sideslip, then, on sinking again, thrust the heels downward and outward. Power rather than speed is what you need. Just sink, slowly but purposefully, holding your chest slightly facing downhill and pushing down on your heels as though you were grinding a pair of cigarette butts into the ground. Be careful, however, not to let the hips move outward from the hill. Although they will rotate slightly in the direction of the turn, the hips, together with the knees, must always be held farther into the hill than the upper body. Otherwise, your weight will go onto the uphill ski and your control will be lost immediately.

There is some delicate coordination involved here that takes a considerable amount of practice. Most people forget to maintain their traverse position and almost invariably allow the uphill ski to lag behind the lower one. This puts their weight on the uphill ski, resulting in crossing the skis or falling in a spread-eagle position. Remember to keep your knees and feet as close together as possible, preferably with the lower knee actually touching the side of the upper knee. This will keep the uphill ski ahead, where it should be at all times. Never allow it to lag behind the lower ski. Remember, too, to keep your upper body in the proper traverse position: downhill hip, shoulder, and arm held slightly back so that you are facing slightly down the hill. Maintain this position throughout the maneuver.

Uphill Christie. Start moving in a steep traverse, or straight down the fall line, and prepare by sinking down. You may plant your pole at this time. With an up motion, unweight your skis and displace them to one side to start the turn. Increase edging to control and encourage the turn. Reset the edges at the end of the down motion to complete the turn.

The only change or movement necessary is in the knees and ankles. And make doubly sure that almost your entire weight remains on the lower ski throughout the turn.

At this point, begin using your ski poles as aids in making the turn. This should be done without effecting any change in body position. When turning left, touch the left pole lightly to the snow just before the up motion. Do just the opposite in a turn to the right. Remember, left turn—left pole; right turn—right pole. If you use a pole when you turn, do not lean on it. Merely touch it lightly to the snow to act as a sort of pivot around which to turn.

If you are making an uphill turn to your

The fan exercise demonstrates to skier that the uphill Christie can be done at a steeper and steeper angle to get more and more sideslip during the turn. Sideslip is increased in duration to prepare skier for the side-slipping involved in the stem Christie final forms.

right, you would start it by touching the right pole, but would stop by facing to your left and planting the left pole.

Usually, people who are right-handed have more difficulty with the left turn than do left-handed people. So be sure, when practicing a left turn, that you are weighting the right ski and keeping the left one forward, with the upper body facing toward the right, or downhill, side. In other words, do not neglect practicing turns to your weak side. You cannot ski by turning in one direction. To do so would require either a lot of kick turns to reach the bottom or a hill built like an ice cream cone. Learn your uphill Christies in both directions and vary the steepness of your traverse until you can even do them off the fall line. Once you can make good uphill Christies to a complete stop under full control, you have conquered many of the problems in your progress to advanced skiing.

Basic Problems with the Uphill Christie

Problems	Causes	Cures
Cannot start turn	No unweighting	Keep skis together; sink into downhill knee.
	Skis not parallel	Keep skis together, weight on downhill ski.
	Failure to release edges	Flatten edges as skis are unweighted.
Cannot turn	Skis not parallel	Keep skis together, weight on downhill ski.

Problems	Causes	Cures
Cannot turn, *cont.*	Weight on inside ski	Bend outside knee and press forward.
	Overedging	Release edges at start of turn.
Jerky turn	Overexaggerated angulation or comma; too much windup at start of turn	Modify position. Inside shoulders and hip lead. Do not lean out too far.
	Rotation	Maintain comma position.
Cannot stop	Edging too slowly	Edge set should be completed by end of turn. Roll knees and ankles into hill.
	Faulty weighting	Weight forward over downhill ski.
	Body stiff and not centered over skis	Sink down into knees. Do not over-rotate.
Overturning	Rotation	Maintain comma position.
	Edging too quickly	Set edges gradually as turn is completed.
No heel slip	Faulty weighting; overedging; skis not parallel	Weight forward over downhill ski. Keep skis together. Flatten skis in turn.
	Insufficient knee action	Push knees into hill, heels downhill.
Skis cross	Wrong ski leading	Advance inside ski half a boot length.
	Faulty edging or weighting	Weight forward over downhill ski. Release edges at start of turn.
Downhill fall	Edging too quickly; overexaggerated angulation or comma	Set edges gradually. Modify position. Inside shoulders and hip lead. Do not lean out too far.
Uphill fall	Faulty weighting; weight on inside ski	Weight forward over downhill ski.
Instability	Faulty weighting	Weight forward over downhill ski.
	Stiff body, arms, or legs	Flex knees; bounce if necessary. Keep arms and hands down. Stand solidly over skis.

In the uphill Christie, Natural Positions, Total Motion, Edge Control, and Unweighting principles all apply. Axial Motion now comes into play in the form of a slight counterrotation, which displaces the skis and starts the turn. The Leverage principle will often be involved in the execution of an uphill Christie as the skier moves his weight forward over the edged, carving ski to encourage the turn and control its arc.

Basic Technique, Class D

The only final form for Class D (Advanced Intermediate Class) of the American system is the stem Christie. This maneuver is a combination of the stem turn and the pure Christie.

The Stem Christie. The stem is actually similar to the advanced snowplow turn. The basic difference is that the stem Christie is a quicker turn, performed at higher speeds, in which the V or stem configuration (tips together, tails apart) is abandoned as the skier crosses the fall line of the hill, and the skis are made parallel again. The skis are then allowed to skid sideways to some extent after they become parallel.

Begin your stem Christie from a traverse. Stem the uphill ski, dropping slightly with

Stem Christie. From the traverse position, prepare to turn by stemming your uphill ski, turning your body to a position square to the direction of travel, and sinking down. At this time you may also plant your inside pole. The actual turn is initiated with an up motion to unweight the skis and a transferal of your weight onto the outside ski. Immediately bring your inside ski alongside this turning (outside) ski. Control and encourage the turn by increasing the amount of edging as you gradually sink down. Set your edges at the end of the turn to complete the maneuver and to start a new traverse.

your knees and counterswinging your upper body as you did in the stem turn. However, after you have started the turn with a stem, you must bring the inside ski parallel to the outside ski and thrust out with the heels as for an uphill Christie. In order to make the down motion to thrust the heels, it is necessary to come up somewhat at the beginning of the turn. The up motion should be made at the moment you start the stem. To do it properly, you must get the feeling of stepping up from your downhill ski onto the stemmed one. This will also give you valuable experience in the up-unweighting and weight-change method needed for the more advanced turns that you will meet with later. To work yourself easily from stem turn to stem Christie, start out by going into the heel-thrust phase only

when the turn is almost complete. When you have mastered the combination of stem and thrust, start the heel thrust a little earlier. Work it in by stages until you can bring your skis together as soon as your weight is over the stemmed one. As you become more and more proficient, reduce the angle of the stem and emphasize more the stepping of the weight from one ski to the other.

It is a good idea to use your poles in this maneuver. On the first down motion, as you stem the uphill ski touch your downhill pole lightly to the snow about midway between your ski tip and boot. Then, as you transfer the weight and come up again, the pole is removed from the snow. Using your pole does three things for you. First, it gives you more stability during the critical phase of the turn as the weight is shifted, providing a point about which your turn can pivot. Second, it helps coordinate the timing of your unweighting and turning actions. Finally, it helps to keep your weight forward, particularly if the pole is placed well ahead of your feet. Be careful, however, that you do not place the pole too much to the side and that you do not permit it to lag behind your body as you accomplish the turn. Either of these mistakes will upset your timing and throw you off balance.

The most common fault in performing the stem Christie is permitting your weight to get too far back or onto the uphill ski. Your weight, as always, should remain on the downhill ski. After the weight is shifted, the new uphill ski (the inside ski) should be completely unweighted so that you can actually lift it off the snow during the turn. In all your practice exercises, strive to ski with your weight almost entirely on the lower ski.

Without question, stemming can become a habit that is not only unnecessary but a positive drawback to advancement. Yet very few beginners are capable of making a turn across the fall line with parallel skis. The only alternatives to stemming are to jump the skis around or to ski quite fast. For the beginner, the former is almost impossible, the latter is dangerous, so the stem lingers. Actually you should use the stem only long enough to get you "over the hump" into the fall line. Then make your skis parallel as soon as you can. As you become more familiar with the stem Christie, try to reduce the amount of stem you use and your dependency on it.

Basic Problems with the Stem Christie

Problems	Causes	Cures
Cannot start turn; cannot stem	Weight on uphill ski; leaning into hill; sitting back	Bend both knees and press downhill knee forward. Do not shift weight until stem is completed.
	Overedging	Flatten skis before stemming.
	Too much weight on heel of stemmed ski	Bend uphill knee.
Cannot turn	No weight shift	Transfer weight to stemmed ski and keep it there. Press outside knee forward.
	Rushing turn	Stay in "up" position until fall line is crossed. Do not drop down until then.
	Overedging	Release edges until fall line is crossed.
Cannot complete turn; jerky finish	Overrotation	Inside hip and shoulder lead throughout turn.
	No heel slip	Keep weight on outside ski; do not overedge.
	Faulty weighting	Sink down into downhill knee; press knee forward.
Poor rhythm; jerky turn	Faulty weighting; standing up in turn; no "down-up-down" motion	"Down" at start of turn, "up" during turn across fall line, "down" at end. Keep weight on outside ski after stemming. Knees always bent and forward.
	Rushing turn or overrotating	Inside hip and shoulder lead throughout turn. Do not drop down until fall line is crossed.
	Faulty pole plant	Plant inside pole midway between boot and ski tip when ski is stemmed at start of turn. Pivot around it when coming up.

Problems	Causes	Cures
Cannot unweight	Standing up	Keep knees bent and forward.
	Weight on inside ski	Keep outside knee bent and forward.
	Faulty rhythm; poor "down-up-down" motion	(See "Poor rhythm" problem, above.)
Skis run straight	No weight shift	Transfer weight to outside ski after it is stemmed.
	Overedging in turn	Flatten skis during turn.
Cannot keep skis parallel in turn	No weight shift	Transfer weight to outside ski after it is stemmed.
	Faulty unweighting	(See "Cannot unweight" problem, above.)
	Faulty weighting	Keep weight on outside ski.
Inside ski drags	No weight shift; overedging; skis not parallel in turn	Transfer weight to outside ski after stemming. Flatten skis and keep them together.
Edges catch	Faulty unweighting; overedging	(See "Cannot unweight" problem, above.)
	No lead change	Advance inside ski half a boot length while coming up during turn.
Skis wander or cross	No lead change	(See above.)
	Sitting back	Keep weight forward, knees bent, proper comma.
	Unequal edging	Edge both skis equally.
	Overedging	Flatten skis during turn.
	Excessive stem of downhill ski at start of turn	Stem the uphill ski.

In the stem Christie, Natural Positions and Total Motion basic principles are involved, as before. As the skier accelerates in the turn, he moves his center of gravity forward to keep his balance and to encourage the turn, thus applying Leverage. The skier unweights with an up motion while he applies Weight Transfer, the force that initiates the turn. Edge Control and Leverage determine the radius of the turn and finish it.

Basic Technique, Class E

Here we are at the step in which the skier learns to minimize the stem—the parallel turn. The goal is to make sure that the "residual stem" is completely removed, and that the skier's mind does not even think stem, but substitutes unweighting. Instead of stemming,

unweighting becomes the key to bringing the skis around. Unweighting reduces friction, or the resistance of the skis to moving in a new direction. The lower body turn is accelerated by an opposite counterturn in the upper body. This "countering" supplies the force with which it is possible to start the skis turning. One of the easiest ways of approaching the parallel Christie is by the sideslip garland exercise.

Sideslip Garlands. Sideslip garlands derive their name from the track they leave in the snow. These exercises are most helpful in learning how to "set" the edges before a turn. This is an important part of modern ski technique because setting the edges will eventually take the place of your stem as you prepare for each turn.

Sideslip garlands are nothing more than a

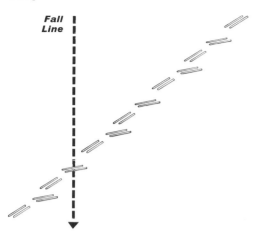

Fall Line

Garland Pattern. This stem garland exercise consists of a combination of traverses and forward sideslips. From traverse, unweight skis with slight up motion, causing forward slip. To end slip, sink down again and set the edges. Note pattern of traverses and sideslips.

continuous series of traverses and forward slips repeated in sequence; traverse, slip, traverse, slip. Start in a traverse, maintaining proper traverse position. With a very slight up motion, unweight the skis, release the edges, and go into a forward slip. Then stop the slip immediately and definitely by sinking down with the knees and edging sharply into the hill. This will "set" the edges (make them bite positively) and place you in the correct traverse position again. Resume your traverse, repeating this sequence as long as the terrain will permit—traverse, up, and slip—down and set the edges—traverse, up, and slip—down and set again.

Once you start in the correct traverse position, do not lose it. Try to make your garlands with rhythm and accuracy, neither too fast nor too slow, always correctly and with precision. Be sure that you get the feel of your edges and that you become accustomed to the amount of pressure you need to set and release them. This is not the easiest thing to do at first, but this exercise is a basic movement which must be learned. The more you practice it, the more natural it will become—and do not forget to practice it in both directions.

The Parallel Christie. As we mentioned before, the parallel Christie is the goal of all modern skiers. To be able to perform smooth, controlled turns with precision on all types of terrain in all snow conditions, keeping the skis together—this is what we are striving toward.

The best way to learn to make parallel Christies down the hill is to sneak up on them gradually. So, we start on a well-packed slope of medium grade. Traverse across, stopping with an uphill Christie. Starting again from the same point, make another traverse, and stop again with an uphill Christie—but this time make the traverse a bit steeper. Repeat this several times, making your traverse steeper and steeper, each one closer to the fall line. Soon, you will be starting straight down the hill and turning to a stop. Continue in this manner, making all your turns in the same direction. Eventually, you will traverse across the fall line and have to make a *downhill* turn that crosses back over the fall line again.

The flatter the traverse, the more difficult it will be to make a downhill turn with parallel skis. There are several aids to overcome this: one is to ski faster, another to use your pole, and a third to use plenty of "lift," which is just another word for up motion or unweighting. Since speed will always facilitate turning, ski a bit faster if you have trouble with parallel skiing, but make sure your basic technique is up to it. Using your pole, just as you did in the stem Christie, will help you to stay forward on your skis and will aid your balance. All advanced skiers use their poles in turning, particularly at slow or medium speeds and on steep hills.

To ski faster, you must head down the hill. This automatically puts the tails of the skis behind you, or up the hill. From this position, the fall line, it is quite simple to make a parallel turn, for the tails of the skis will slip off to either side with little effort. Those who hesitate to ski faster will find parallel turns difficult. If they have speed enough to make a parallel turn, they frequently lack the courage to shift the weight sufficiently to the outside ski to make the turn. For such people, rather short skis may help, for these turn in a shorter arc with less effort and this helps to give confidence.

Lift, or unweighting the skis, is of great help in starting turns too. Before you can unweight your skis, you must have a "platform"

Parallel Christie. As you move across the hill in a traverse, prepare for the turn by sinking down while you square your upper body. The downhill pole may now be planted, if you use it. Immediately follow this with an up-forward motion, a change of your ski edges, and a transfer of your weight to the outside ski. During this unweighting phase, the turn is begun by displacing your skis to the outside. Gradually sink down throughout the turn, and complete it by resetting your edges into a new traverse.

from which to push off. This acts as a springboard from which to launch the turn. Previous to this, we used the stem position, which offered a good base. But since a stem precludes the making of a parallel Christie, it is necessary to use some other platform from which to start the turn. So, we set the edges instead. This is, of course, done with parallel skis and is accomplished by a down motion (lowering the body and flexing the knees) and then edging the skis into the hill. As you sink with your knees, reach forward and touch

the downhill pole to the snow. This is a very brief movement, followed almost immediately by the up motion, springing up off the platform, and a lateral displacement of the tails of the skis. More specifically, if you are making a left turn, drop down and touch the left pole simultaneously, then come up with the knees and push the heels of both skis to the right while unweighted. This will start the turn on its way. You then complete it on the newly weighted, outside ski of the turn.

Setting the edges in this manner prevents

the skis from slipping away when you start to come up for the turn. Pushing both skis to the side replaces stemming and allows you to keep both knees and skis close together and parallel. Touching the pole to the snow gives you added stability and timing when most needed.

It is not necessary to lift the skis high off the snow when displacing them to the side after unweighting. Ideally, the skis should be unweighted only enough to permit easy movement. If they are "lifted" completely off the snow, conditions must be unusually rough. The amount of lift required cannot be specifically determined, since it will always vary with your speed, angle of turn, terrain, snow conditions, and even with the flexibility of your skis.

Once your skis have started in the turn, place your weight hard over the outside turning ski. This is the key to good skiing, and there is nothing more important, regardless of the technique used. It often works well to remember to draw the downhill hip back throughout the turn.

One easy way to make parallel turns is to turn over a bump. At the crest of the bump there is very little ski touching the snow, and, therefore, the ski turns easily. This can be done with little speed, so it is a good way for a beginner to learn. A parallel turn can also be done from a traverse by displacing the tails of the skis up the hill in a series of hopping motions—2, 3, 4 times—until the skis finally cross the hill and head in a new direction. This exercise promotes but it is not the best way to do, parallel turns.

Basic Problems with the Parallel Christie

Problems	Causes	Cures
Cannot turn	Faulty unweighting; faulty rhythm	Emphasize "down-up-down" sequence. Try lifting heels off snow on up motion.
	Faulty weight shift and lead change	Weight the downhill ski. Lead change as weight changes.
	Faulty edging	Set edges on down motion, release on up.
	Skis not parallel	Keep knees and skis together. Maintain proper weighting, unweighting, and edging.
Turn too early (too much check)	Edging too quickly	Set edges after assuming down position.
	Overrotation	Inside hip and shoulder lead throughout turn.
Turn too late (too much float)	Edging too slowly	Set edges in down position before rising to up position.
Inside edges catch	Faulty weight shift	Shift weight in up position to new downhill ski.
	No heel thrust	Let heels slip throughout up motion.
	Faulty pole action	Plant inside pole earlier.
Outside edges catch	Faulty weight shift	Do not shift weight too early. Slow it down a split second.
Cannot keep skis parallel	Faulty weight shift, unweighting, or edging	(See cures for "Cannot turn.")
Poor rhythm, jerky arm movement	Pole action too early	Slow down pole action.
	Insufficient "down-up-down" motion in knees	Sink down and forward into knees before coming up.

Problems	Causes	Cures
Uphill shoulder drags or rotates	Pole action too late	Plant pole earlier.
Cannot link turns	Skis not parallel, faulty weighting, unweighting, lead change, pole action, or rhythm	(See cures for "Cannot turn.")
Instability, poor balance	Faulty weighting, unweighting, lead change, or edging	(See above.)

The Parallel Fan

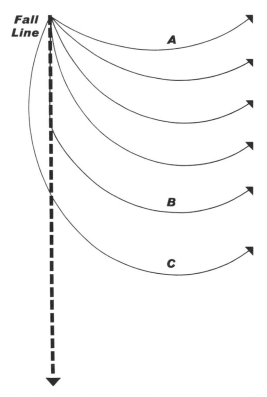

Fall Line

A

B

C

"Parallel fan" exercise develops parallel Christie gradually. It consists of a series of uphill Christies, each performed from a successively steeper traverse until you finally complete a Christie across the fall line. Start from a shallow traverse (A), increasing angle of descent until you make a Christie off the fall line (B). Now increase angle even more and make your parallel Christie across the fall line (C). Do not neglect unweighting and weight shift as you enter the fall line.

The parallel Christie employs all seven basic principles (see pages 113–114).

Linked Parallel Turns. Neatly linking one parallel turn to another is just a matter of experience and practice. It involves nothing new in technique. The common trouble is that your thought processes cannot keep up with your skis, so to speak. This is especially true when you are required to make several turns in a confined area. Try following your instructor or any good skier, making each turn that he does. Seeing the turn in front of you helps develop your rhythm and timing. A few properly spaced control flags can force you into making good linked turns, too. If you plant your pole on every turn, your chances of maintaining good rhythm are better. The old axiom "down-up-down" is still true. It is *down* before the turn, *up* during the turn, and *down* at the end of the turn. If you make a long traverse between turns, stand fairly high again so you will have some knee bend left for the next down motion.

Do not forget that down motions are done simultaneously with the planting of the lower pole and that your weight is always on the lower leg. The skis are edged on down motions, too. The up motion is used when you turn and helps you transfer weight from one leg to the other. Never forget that shifting the weight from the inside ski to outside or turning ski is most important. This is done by angulation–deangulation–angulation. Except when the turn is being initiated, knees are toward the hill and upper body away from the hill.

If you have trouble getting an up motion at the right time, then maybe a little practice with the following hop turns will help.

Hop Turn Exercise. The unweighting of both skis normally is used in making parallel turns. Without unweighting, it is difficult to turn without stemming. It is reasonable, therefore, to assume that if you are stemming too much you are probably not unweighting enough. Hop turn exercises will help you to correct this.

Stand on a level spot, both poles in the snow somewhat ahead of your feet. Now, hop up and down, raising only the tails of your skis, keeping the tips in place on the snow. As you do this, press the knees together tightly and keep them touching at all times as they bend and straighten. Next, do the same thing but hop your skis alternately to one side, then the other, with knees pressed together but flexed. When you have the feel of these two simple exercises, try them while in motion on a gentle slope. While practicing these exercises, touch only one pole at a time to the snow, just as you would when making regular turns. Try to develop a rhythm as you hop down the slope, reaching forward and touching both poles simultaneously into the snow. This also helps you to become accustomed to making parallel turns in steep

Hop in Fall Line. This exercise provides practice in making the quick up-and-down motions needed in wedeln and short swing, and improves balance through rhythm. Tails are hopped across the fall line.

terrain without gaining too much speed. These two-pole turns, as they are commonly called, work well on steep, rough slopes and are useful as part of your regular skiing repertoire.

Be careful that you do not start to hop habitually like a rabbit just because you have learned to do these exercises well. Hopping is merely an exercise and not a technique in itself. The good skier moves smoothly on the snow and hops his skis around only when it becomes necessary because of variations in snow conditions or terrain.

Parallel Christie with Check. On steeper terrain and in difficult snow conditions, the speed of the skis will be such that the skier will experience some difficulty in setting his edges. In these instances, a check prior to the turn is the proper remedy.

The parallel Christie with check is the same as a parallel Christie except in its initiation. Instead of using a simple down motion to provide himself with a position from which to unweight, the skier uses a more forceful method. From the traverse, he begins a sideslip as though for an uphill Christie. Then, as the tails of his skis begin to slide out, he drops his body, increases angulation, and plants his pole. This sharp drop sets the edges of the skis very firmly into the snow, giving the skier a strong platform from which to push off vigorously into the unweighting phase of the turn.

By far the most important point to remember in the parallel turn with a check is: Do not try to compensate for the braking effect on the skis during the check by sitting back. The more forward your body is, the more quickly you can move the skis under it.

In this parallel Christie maneuver, all seven principles are still involved, with more emphasis on Edge Control during the preparatory part of the turn.

Basic Technique, Class F

The American Technique no longer makes a distinction between short swing and wedeln, since the two are so closely related. Actually, they are not really different turns from parallel Christies, but rather refined applications. However, for reasons of

Parallel Christie with Check. From the traverse, the skier begins a sideslip as though for an uphill Christie. Then, as the tails of his skis begin to slide out, he drops his body, increases angulation, and plants his pole. This sharp drop sets the edges of the skis very firmly into the snow, giving the skier a strong platform from which he can push off vigorously into the unweighting phase of the turn.

tradition and to demonstrate some aspects of edge application, they are treated separately here.

Short Swing. The definition of the short swing is: "Consecutive parallel Christies without traverse, using the setting of the edges and pole plant." In essence, it is a series of parallel Christies with check, the heel thrust and finishing edge set of one turn being used as the platform for initiating the next. For the first time, the use of the pole becomes a stated requirement, for it acts as a means of bringing each heel thrust to a sharp end, leading to a quicker setting of the edges than would be possible without it. The term "short swing" implies a series of tight rather than long, drawn-out turns. The pronounced and rapidly repeated check between turns permits much slower speeds to be maintained than would be possible in linked traverses or long linked parallel Christies. It is, therefore, used mostly for control on steep slopes. The upper body is kept facing down the fall line, the counter-rotation being only sufficient to balance out the twisting of the lower body. In point of fact, there is no sensation of counterrotation but only of a lower body rotation and resulting torsion at the waist. The mass of the upper body is used as a stabilizing factor, and

the action is like that of a coil spring held fast at the top but coiling and uncoiling at the bottom.

In its extreme form, short swing leads to an actual hopping of the ski tails from side to side, with the skier's body continuing in a straight line down the slope. In this case, the ski displacement is used purely as a braking mechanism and not as a means of turning. At the other end of the scale, short swing merges into wedeln.

Wedeln. The American definition here is: "Consecutive parallel Christies without traverse or appreciable setting of the edges." In fact, the main difference between wedeln and short swing is in the edge set. Wedeln is a smooth, snakelike motion in which the skis are kept almost flat on the snow. The tails are brushed from side to side by leg action, the body being kept almost motionless and used as a stabilizing mass for the leg movements. During wedeln, the legs are gently contracted and extended just sufficiently to permit the skis to travel beneath the skier's body in a side-to-side motion. Almost all of this action takes places in the knees and ankles. The upper body always faces down the fall line, and the poles are planted with the minimum amount of hand and arm movement. As a cat

Analysis of Wedeln. Elimination of traverse between turns makes for serpentine track down the fall line. Edge set and pole plant are easily seen in second figure (from top), together with the rapid down motion with which the edges are set, as in parallel, with check. Up-unweighting is shown by third figure. In fourth figure, the skier has already started down motion and begun to set the edges. In fifth figure, he has made pole plant for the turn. Up motion in sixth figure is followed by down motion of seventh; and up motion of eighth by down motion and edge-setting of the last figure.

Short Swing. Starting almost directly down the fall line, do short, rhythmic parallel Christies, linking each turn without a traverse in between. These turns are done like the parallel Christies, and checks may be added on steeper slopes.

stalks its prey, so does a skier execute wedeln, perhaps the most graceful maneuver in skiing.

Wedeln is performed in the fall line and is most easily done on a medium-grade slope. If the hill is too steep, you will probably lose control unless you have mastered the maneuver well enough to maintain a firm check throughout your descent. It is most important

that your knees remain pressed together tightly so that both skis act as a single unit at all times. Start in the fall line and never turn far away from it. Touch your pole to the snow in each turn, but use no shoulder rotation. The upper body must face squarely down the slope at all times. Only the legs, hips, and skis change direction.

Rhythm and timing are important. You must use an up-and-down motion to unweight your skis, but it is not necessary to jump or hop. Bring your poles straight forward and place them about a foot behind your ski tips. Always do this on the down motion, which will be the end of one turn and the start of the next. Knees are together, flexed at all times, and stemming is taboo. Set the edges of your skis on each down motion, and change the lead of your skis as the weight is shifted on the up motion. Keep your arms and poles forward, close to the body, and do not raise your poles higher than necessary to clear the snow. Never let your hands or poles lag behind the body. Your weight must be mostly on one ski at a time. Be sure that you make a definite shift in weight for each turn. This will help your turns to follow one another without a pause or break in rhythm. If necessary, control your speed with a little slip at the end of your turn, then set the edges, plant your pole, and unweight again for the next turn. Your edge control must be precise and subtle, changing on the up motion as you shift your weight and change your lead ski. Be careful not to overedge, or you will catch your outside edge and lose balance.

Wedeln can be done in almost any type of snow condition except breakable crust. Make use of bumps in the surface to aid your turning. Above all, keep your knees and skis together and do not stem. If you find that you are still troubled by a stem that upsets your rhythm and prevents you from doing a sustained wedeln, go back and check your basics: more up-and-down motion, correct edge set and change of edges, proper weight shift and distribution, timing of pole plant, change of lead ski, and sufficient unweighting to permit your tails to sweep around in each turn. Check to be sure you have enough speed to permit a natural flow of these basics without upsetting your rhythm.

Wedeln is difficult to analyze on paper. Even when seen, it is hard to distinguish the many subtle factors that appear to be happening at the same time. We have found these five points to be all-important in developing a good wedeln technique, and we suggest that you keep them in mind constantly:

1. Keep your knees and skis together at all times. Do not stem.
2. Use your pole on every turn.
3. Use unweighting (up-and-down motion).
4. Control your speed and length of turns with your edges.
5. Keep the upper body facing down the hill at all times. Use no shoulder rotation.

Basic Problems with the Weldeln and Short Swing

Problems	Causes	Cures
Cannot link turns	Faulty rhythm	Check coordination of "down, edge, up, slip" sequence and of lead change.
	Insufficient pole action	Check timing of pole plant.
	Too much pole action	Check for too much arm motion, which delays pole plant and upsets rhythm.
	Traversing between turns	Shorten turn. Use quicker edge set at end of turn.
Too much acceleration in turn	Insufficient pole and edge action	Check timing of pole plant; do not let upper body lag. Use stronger edge action.
Faulty rhythm	Faulty pole action	Check for too much pole action.
	Faulty edging	Check timing and sufficiency of edge action.
	Faulty unweighting	Check "down-up-down" motion for timing and sufficiency.
	Poor coordination	Check coordination of "down, edge, up, slip" sequence and of lead change.

Problems	Causes	Cures
Cannot check	Faulty rhythm	(See above.)
	Faulty pole or edge action	Check for too much pole action. Check timing and sufficiency of edge action.
	Faulty lead change	Check timing and point of lead change—in the up motion as weight is shifted.
	Sitting back	Press knees forward.
Faulty weight shift	Faulty rhythm	Check coordination of "down, edge, up, slip" sequence and of lead change.
	Faulty body position	Check for overexaggeration and overuse of comma.
	Faulty weight change	Check timing of weight shift—in the up motion as lead is changed. Unweighting follows down motion as the up motion starts.
	Sitting back	Press knees forward.
Cannot keep skis together; stemming	Faulty weight shift	Check timing of weight shift—in the up motion as lead is changed. Unweighting follows down motion as the up motion starts.
	Faulty edging	Check timing and sufficiency of edge action.
	Faulty body position	Check for overexaggeration and overuse of comma.
	Faulty rhythm	Check coordination of "down, edge, up, slip" sequence and of lead change.
Inside edge catches	Edge change too late	Change edges earlier.
Outside edge catches	Edge change too early	Change edges later. Keep edges flat in turn.
	Faulty weight shift	Check timing of weight shift—in the up motion as lead is changed. Unweighting follows down motion as the up motion starts.
Skis cross	Faulty lead change or edging	Check timing and point of lead change—in the up motion as weight is shifted. Check timing and sufficiency of edge action.
	Sitting back	Move weight forward.
Instability, poor balance	Faulty body position, weight shift, rhythm, late edge change	(See above.)

When doing the short swing and wedeln, all seven basic principles are employed. There is, however, great emphasis on Total Motion, so that rhythm is maintained. In fact, rhythm, as previously stated, is the key to both the short swing and the wedeln.

Emphasis on Ski Poles

Through the various steps of learning how to ski, we have made mention of the use of ski poles. Actually ever since man first began to ski, his basic equipment has always in-

Pole Use. This exercise is designed for teaching quick pole motion, a vital part of short-swing technique. Pole goes in one side (top) and then is pulled out as skier passes it (middle) and the other pole is thrust into the snow (bottom). Skier makes no turns while doing exercise, but simply runs down the fall line, planting first one pole and then the other in light, fluid thrusts, accompanied by up-and-down motions.

cluded skis and poles. As his knowledge of their use increased through the years, other items were developed that have become essential too. The emergence of various ski techniques necessitated advances in boots and bindings, and as these became modified, the importance of ski poles was often minimized. At one point, some people even advocated skiing without poles. Today, however, as we learn more and more about technique, the emphasis is again on poles. As in the early days of skiing, they are again considered essential. Modern skiing methods demand that the pole be used as an integral part of a skier's technique—not merely as an aid to balance, as they were first conceived, or as a "crutch" for the beginner to lean on as he learns to ski, but as a dependable aid to help him ski with greater ease and more proficiency.

In those early days, a ski pole was a necessary evil. The first skiers used a single pole hewn from a convenient branch or sapling. Long and heavy, its blunted tip was manipulated partially as a brake, partially as a steering rudder, partially as a balance rod. Then someone discovered that *two* poles, shorter and lighter, with snow rings attached near the tips, not only aided in pushing forward on level ground, but also helped in climbing and provided more flexibility and balance while in motion.

As techniques made more use of the poles, they gradually evolved to their present size and appearance. First they became shorter, then longer; rings diminished in size; new materials, stronger and lighter, were developed. Today's ski pole represents the product of many decades of experimentation and enlightened knowledge (see Section II).

In modern technique, pole work is an integral part of the learning process. The beginner first learns to use his poles in walking on skis. Here he learns the proper way to plant his pole into the snow and how to remove it. Only when he learns the proper cooperation of pole and ski action in walking is he ready to move on. Then he learns how to use his poles as an aid to the climbing movements and standing turns. During the snowplow and stem turns and the traverse, the pole is used primarily for balance. But in snowplow Christies and stem Christies, the

Pole turn.

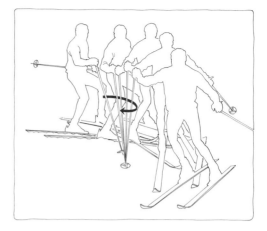

application of the pole as an aid to turning becomes evident. Used as a point on which to pivot, it helps the skier to shift weight, to develop timing, and to master the all-important sideslipping movements necessary for advanced skiing.

In this stage, too, the skier learns to use his poles in a playful, relaxed manner rather than in stiff, tense jabs. He plants the pole with his upper arm relaxed. During the plant, the palm is slightly outward. As the skier comes up on his pole and shifts his weight, he brings the palm inward in front of the body. Otherwise, the hand would lag behind the body and pull him off balance.

The intermediate skier soon learns to rely less on his poles and more on weight shift and edge control for smooth execution of turns. But now the poles assume another role. Hop turn exercises, at first using both poles, then each pole alternately, substitute unweighting for the stem as the skier approaches parallel turns. The less stem he uses, the more Christie he gets. Substituting the hop for the stem helps to eliminate the "stem hangover" that plagues many skiers, since it gets the tails of both skis off the snow and across the fall line without dependence on the stem.

In the advanced stages of skiing, the pole becomes a somewhat secondary but nevertheless important factor, since it helps the skier to establish the necessary rhythm and timing required for short-swing turns and wedeln. Used properly, poles add the coordination demanded for smooth, effortless skiing. They also become indispensable in the execution of the various aerial maneuvers that are a part of any advanced skier's repertoire.

ADVANCED SKIING TECHNIQUES

What sets the expert skier apart? He is one who can formfully handle any terrain under any conditions. While few skiers reach this ultimate plateau, the refinements discussed here will not only increase your ability but will add a further measure of enjoyment of the sport.

In the past several years, there has been so much talk throughout the skiing world about wedeln that people have almost forgotten that there are other ways, just as pleasurable and sometimes even more practical, to ski. Skiers do not seem to realize that every top racer or expert uses three or four different techniques in making one single run down the mountain. The *expert* varies these different methods according to the different types of snow conditions and terrain. Let us look at two of the older methods of turning.

Arlberg and Ruade Turns

The first method, Arlberg, is still in evidence in the technique used by many of the

The progress of ski technique in the past twenty years has been marked by a changing emphasis on different parts of the body. In the rotation era, emphasis was placed on rotating the shoulders and upper torso (left). With the arrival of wedeln, emphasis switched to angulation of the body at the hips, the comma position (center). Today, many top skiers are starting to talk of knee comma or angulation (right).

world's top skiers today. Through slow-motion photography, it has been shown that some of these top skiers are using a slight stem at times, when it is advantageous. They are also using a certain amount of rotation, which is, of course, the basis of the Arlberg technique. As previously stated, the Arlberg technique was originated by the late Hannes Schneider, and it has probably been the most influential technique used throughout the ski schools of the world. When people think of Arlberg, they automatically think of skiing with a stem, and it is true that in this method of teaching the skier learns by using a stem in the early stages. Later on, however, this stem is modified to a point where the skier turns with skis parallel or stemmed very slightly.

As skiing became more popular in Europe and North America, Émile Allais and others of the French school developed a more parallel turn done at slower speeds, which they called the ruade. In this French system (see page 193), body rotation is still very similar to the rotation method used in the Arlberg, the main difference being that in the ruade turn there is more blockage in the hips.

The real difference between these two methods of skiing is that the Arlberg is always started with a countermotion and a stemming of the uphill or downhill ski. (The uphill stem gives a more positive quick change of weight to the outside ski, thus eliminating some of the powerful rotation otherwise necessary at the beginning of a turn. Many

schools feel that this is advantageous, since it cuts down on overswinging, a common fault of many skiers. When the downhill stem is used, the turn is begun by a springboard effect of the downhill ski, followed by a powerful swing or rotation of the body, which causes the skis to turn.) In the ruade, however, a change of direction is begun not by stemming one ski, as in the Arlberg technique, but by lifting or retracting the tails of both skis together and placing them down again close to the fall line. The countermotion is not as exaggerated as in Arlberg, and the body is lowered more in preparation for the lifting of the skis. Upon landing, the upper body follows through to complete the rotation, but, again, with more blockage of the hips.

When it first was introduced, the ruade started a trend, since people became more conscious of parallel skiing because of it. But widespread use of the ruade seemed to fade as the years went on and ski technique progressed. Still a very useful turn to know, the ruade has advantages in skiing on steep slopes and particularly in wet cement-like snow or in slab. It is also a great aid in carving a sharp enough arc to keep speed at a minimum. As a learning exercise, it will help you turn with your skis together as a unit.

Mambo

Another type of skiing, the mambo, is more of a fad than a technique. It seems to have been started by the top racers, and it is not a part of any formal teaching sequence. Rather, it is often demonstrated to advanced classes in ski schools for added enjoyment and variety. Even today, you will see several good skiers using it just for fun.

In theoretical terms, the mambo starts with overrotation. You simply swing one hand vigorously forward across the skis in the direction you are going to turn. Up to that point your skis are not affected. They keep moving in the direction they were going when you started. However, when that hand has been swung across the skis as far as it will go and then stops, the arm behind the hand stops and the shoulder behind the arm stops. Stopping all this weight transmits a pull in the direction of the turn to your lower body and thence to the skis. This completes the rotation part of the turn.

As soon as the skis start to turn, the reverse phase begins. Hand number one, which has been swung forward, is pulled back until it is well behind the shoulder. Since this hand (and the upper body with it) is now turning in the direction opposite that in which the skis are turning, this is easily recognized as the reverse phase of the mambo. While hand number one has been swinging back, of course, hand number two has been swinging forward. When number two hand can swing no further, then it has to stop, and as it stops, it starts to pull the body into the next turn. Hand number two then pulls back to start the reverse phase, as hand number one comes up again.

This is the technical outline. Now let us break it down into the following sequence of steps:

1. *Run.* It is best to get up a little speed because the skis will handle better. Assume a running position, and start the skis down the fall line.

2. *Sink.* Go into a half-crouch; let the skis keep running flat in the fall line.

3. *Rise.* Come up from the crouch with a quick movement to help take the weight off the skis.

4. *Swing.* At the same time, start swinging the arm that will lead the turn; swing it up and across vigorously, turning the upper body with it.

5. *Twist.* Start twisting the hips in the same direction as the upper body. Skis are still flat and in the fall line.

6. *Stop.* As you rise to an erect position, the hips and upper body have twisted as far as they can, and they will stop automatically— the body will not twist any further. This is what some call "blocking," the movement which transmits the twisting movement of arms, torso, and hips to the skis. All you have to do is keep the skis flat so that they will start to swing quickly and easily out of the fall line in response to the twist from the body.

7. *Reverse.* As soon as the skis start to swing, edge them and start reversing the direction of your upper body twist. The outside hand (hand number one) comes back, the torso and hips twist to follow. The hand on the inside of the turn (hand number two) comes forward as a natural consequence.

At this point, you should sink and then rise, continuing to swing hand number two. Repeat the sequence for the second turn. In your next turn remember to flatten your skis at the moment you rise to the top of your erect position, and not before. You will be turning from a traverse line rather than the fall line—something that will not bother you if you keep your skis edged until your weight is off them. At that instant, you have hit the top of your rising movement, and it is natural to let the skis go flat as the body twist comes to a stop and the turning force is transmitted to your skis.

Mambo should never be confused with wedeln. Many people who see a skier mamboing down a slope think that he is skiing wedeln because of the popular misconception that wedeln entails this exaggerated, snaky look. Wedeln is completely different. In wedeln, the body never overswings and the turn is started by a powerful down-and-up motion of the knees, which unweights the skis. The inside ski pole is placed halfway between the boot and the tip of the ski, helping the skis to pivot into the turn. A steering action of the feet and knees starts the skis turning. It is true that this steering action will force the upper body to lean to the outside of the turn, causing a slight comma position. Some people have seen photographs of this wedeln position and have confused it

Pepi Stiegler (left) displays classic form of the pure carved turn. At right, he demonstrates the difference between a carved and a skidded turn. His skidded, "windshield-wiping" turn cuts a wide swath on the snow. Inside the skidded turn is the narrow track of Stiegler's carved turn.

with the exaggerated mambo swing. In wedeln, however, this comma position lasts for only a split second, until the upper part of the body catches up to the lower body and is again square to the skis.

Carved Turn

The carved turn is the ultimate in effortless, efficient, parallel turning. It is the most difficult of all turns to do. A *pure* carved turn is a lazy, accelerating turn that makes maximum use of the design of the ski and a minimum of body motion. There is no lift or up motion, and the skis carve a lovely, narrow track a foot or so wide down the slope, while the skier seems to come out of the turn with more speed than when he started. It is a turn that will give speed and grace to the person who masters it.

A carved turn is easier to make in soft or packed snow because only a light use of the edges is necessary. The harder the snow, the more difficult it becomes to carve turns. At the same time, you will know of no more thrilling feeling than when you are able to make a faultless carved turn on an icy slope. To ski on ice without skidding is one of the highest goals of skiing.

The ideal position for the carved turn is: relatively upright upper body and a deep bend in the knees so that the weight of the body is over the front of the skis. So exaggerated is the knee action that we can actually refer to the knees being angled into the hill, a sort of knee comma. This is as much psychological as it is physiological. The skier has the feeling that the knees are locked and that his weight is bearing at one point on the ball of the foot of the outside ski that is carving the turn.

The carved turn is perhaps best made with a slightly counterrotated position, but there is no need to be doctrinaire about this. The turns can be equally well made with the upper body more or less square over the skis.

The change of direction is started with very little up-unweighting accompanied by a quick changing of the edges. It can also be accomplished by a step. This is a favorite with racers who often step into the carved turn.

In the carved turn, the skier and his skis are deflected by applying and weighting the edges. The more resistance to sideslipping by this edging, the more the skis are deflected in the direction of the turn. The skier is aided by the shape of his skis—narrower in the middle, wider at the tip and tail. The curved side of the ski promotes the carving of the ski in the turn. The ultimate carved turn is one which uses an absolute minimum of muscle power, and almost entirely employs external forces—ski side camber, speed, gravity, terrain, and snow resistance—to create the turn.

To do pure carved turns, here are some useful things to remember:

1. To initiate the turn, think in terms of shifting weight forward onto the uphill ski and moving the tip of the inside unweighted ski ahead.

The Pure Carved Turn. In the pure carved turn, shoulder position is almost incidental, since the twist is at the knee. For best balance, the shoulders are naturally at right angles to the skis, or close to it. Start by making a good, fast traverse, as in the first figures above, and plant the pole; shift the weight to the uphill ski, rock forward, and change lead without lifting the downhill ski from the snow. Twist the uphill ski with the knee to start the turn (third figure from the top). Increase the bite of the edge by reaching to the outside. (Note that the turn has been started without unweighting.) Control the carve of the turn by increasing the edge, and move the knee more to the inside of the turn (the fourth through the sixth figure from the top). To begin the second turn, plant the pole while still carving the first turn (sixth figure) and simply interrupt it without any preparation, edge set, or unweighting. Just change weight to the outside ski and rock forward (seventh figure), twisting the weighted ski into the turn (eighth figure). Finish this carve, and feel the smooth acceleration as the skis bite in around the turn.

2. Do not consciously try to up-unweight. Too much unweighting will prevent you from applying early edge pressure to the outside ski which will carve the oncoming turn. The forward rock onto the outside ski should provide all the unweighting you need.
3. Change edges rapidly by lateral knee action (knee comma).
4. Carve a perfect turn into the fall line. Do not rush the turn. Its radius is determined by the amount of edge pressure in the carve.
5. At no point should the skis leave a track much more than a foot wide.
6. Remember that on a steep slope, this is a high-speed turn that can throw you like a wild bronco. Speed is controlled by continuing to carve the turn up the hill. To check by conventional edge-setting is just not a part of this technique.

It is probably no exaggeration to say that for the recreational skier, the pure carved turn would have been impossible a few years ago without the tremendous improvements that have since been made in ski equipment. Skis are important. Here the carved turn is aided by the increasing sophistication of the side camber and torsional properties being built into the newer skis today. Edges must also be superior. And for carving turns, boots should be stiff at the sides to increase the edging power from the knee action, while giving forward action at the ankle. It is literally impossible to perform a pure carved turn with soft boots.

Acrobatics

The essence of acrobatics for the ordinary skier (as opposed to someone who does them professionally at ski shows and exhibitions) is to vary the routine of skiing. It is a well-known fact that intermittent practice of a given skill is more efficient than massive doses of practice. In other words, it is practical to introduce a few acrobatic maneuvers to the skier who is classed as intermediate and better. The experience of the teachers who have tried it, and the skiers who have tried it, is that the introduction of the element of "having a ball" pays off.

For one thing, most American skiers are quite technique-conscious. They have, whether they realize it or not, considerable concentration on doing things *right*. This is fine. But it can also lead to stiff and unrelaxed skiing. This is where acrobatics comes in. The simple introduction of something different, something quite useless in itself, something on which nothing depends and which means little if not successful—this is the ideal "relaxation."

The skier who tries something, even a royal (turning with one ski lifted to the side), is likely to find that after a few successful or unsuccessful turns, it does not matter which, he will suddenly start skiing better when he returns to his "standard" turns. This is, of course, a well-known gambit: one "just for fun" interlude is used in many kinds of teaching, particularly in the teaching of physical skills. Something about the complete lack of pressure in attempting an acrobatic turn—you have never tried it, so do not worry about not making it—is carried over into your next turn.

This is not to say that more specific results cannot be had from acrobatics. The very act of attempting to do something a bit out of the ordinary will call forth additional skill at balancing, timing, and edge control—the skills which are the "secret" of expert skiers.

The skier could start with something as simple as a mild jump off a bump, or a jump turn of 180 degress in place or a half tip roll. Or simple skating steps. Beyond that, some rhythmical acrobatics, like the "Charleston step" or consecutive royal Christie turns, are even better for the skier's frame of mind and for his ski skill. Today ski acrobatics also forms part of the equipment of every top racer. Acrobatic skiing cultivates balance, agility, and lightning reactions. Anyone who sees international races such as those shown on television will agree that only a truly acrobatic control over skiing technique can give the power to master downhill courses at full speed, to deal with the forest of slalom poles, or to prolong the flight off a ski jump by means of tiny corrections of posture.

In fact, the theory of play as a way of learning is becoming more popular even as related to standard learning routines in ski classes. The attempt is being made, particularly by those interested in the value of acrobatics, to make the movements of the turns light and playful, rather than forceful and rigid. This has been the implication of the wide acceptance of the wedeln turn as a goal of skiers. The wedeln turn is extremely useful in racing and on steep slopes (in the form of "jump wedeln"), but most skiers who wedeln are doing the lazy, light, and fun-creating dance down a ballroom slope just for the heck of it. This is perhaps, more than any other facet, the indication that skiers are looking for fun turns just as much as control and direction turns. Acrobatics just makes this wide implication into an explicit goal. The whole theory of the acrobatic turn is based on the fact that skiers are out to enjoy their own movements on skis as much as enjoying mastering the slope.

Here is how a few of the more popular and useful acrobatic maneuvers are accomplished:

Inside Christie. This is a "backward" turn in that the weight is on the inside ski. The inside Christie first will help you to know when your weight is on the inside ski. This means you will be more sensitive to this feeling and be able to eliminate having your weight inside when you do not want it, as in most normal turns. Second, the inside Christie will make your "skate up" an effective ma-

The inside ski Christie.

neuver. Third, like all acrobatic pointers, it will improve your balance.

To start the inside Christie, make your first turn from the fall line into the hill. Start down the hill in a straight run on both skis at fair speed; then lift one ski and edge the other. As you edge, lean and turn to the side you are leaning toward. Swing the weightless ski so that it makes a right angle with the turning ski. You will find you have to sit back a bit more in the turn than you usually do. Hold the lean and the edging until you have completed the turn to a stop.

Now, when you have learned the single turn, you connect the inside Christies: instead of coming to a stop, you "change edges," that is, forcefully rock your weight to the other side of the ski as you come to the traverse line. Then skate your weight onto the other ski with a pronounced forward thrust. Make your next inside Christie on this ski. Connected inside Christies are like long skating steps down the hill, an extremely valuable exercise for balance, strength, and for getting you out of a rut to have a few minutes of wild fun.

Knee Wiggles. Acrobatic skiing has many things to teach the average and above-average skier. One of the simplest acrobatic trick maneuvers, the knee wiggle, contains a very basic lesson for every skier. In order to get into the proper edging position so the skis will hold when going across the hill, the skier must bend his knees "into the hill." This puts the skis on edge, so they will hold. But many people do not make this "bending-in motion" often enough. They should, because it is a fundamental reflex action necessary to stop the skis when they are sideslipping. In order to make the bending-in motion, the knees first have to be bent forward in a "half-kneeling" position. Otherwise, the knees cannot be turned toward the hill at all!

The knee wiggle, which builds up this bending-in reflex is done as follows: first traverse slowly across the hill. Push the knees forward (half-kneeling), and push them toward the uphill side or "into the hill." Then, with knees still bent, move them out until they do not bend in toward the hill at all. Repeat this, slowly at first as you ski, and then faster and faster until you have a true knee wiggle. Keep the upper body bent over

the lower ski a bit, but keep it as quiet as possible. Let the knees do all the moving. Lastly, do the knee wiggle on steeper slopes. It will give you "instant edging" when you need it for traversing. Better skiers will use it to carve a nice controlled arc in the last part of a turn.

Javelin Traverse. The all-important traversing position is composed of two bends—first, the bending in of the knee (as in the knee wiggles), and second, the bending in of the hips. Here is an acrobatic trick which will help you develop proper hip bend (or "hips into the hill"). Called a javelin traverse, it consists of picking the uphill ski off the snow and pointing the ski down the hill as if it were a javelin or spear. The total result of knee and hip bend is the perfect comma position when traversing.

To do the javelin traverse, start with a traverse and pick up the upper ski without changing the upper body position. Keep doing this until you can do it comfortably. Then, when you have your balance, pick up the ski and point the tip downhill until it is at right angles to the ski on the snow. The hip is now

The javelin traverse.

bent properly, and is in the proper "into the hill" position. Try to keep the hip in this position as you return the ski to the snow. Keep working on the javelin traverse on steeper slopes and at faster speed. You will soon be traversing in expert form. This same hips-into-the-hill position is the one to use to carve the last part of an expert parallel turn.

Hinge Hop. The skier with the "trained ankle" is the skier who is going to be able to do what he wants to do on skis. One very fine way to train the ankle—both in terms of speeding up reflexes and in terms of strength-building—is to do the simple acrobatic "hinge hop." It is also a great way to warm up before taking a run, or to restore confidence after a bad run or a fall. Hinge hopping helps in timing and in getting that loose, relaxed feeling which is essential to any kind of skiing.

To do the hinge hop, first go straight down a gentle slope at a slow speed. Lift the tail of one ski but press the tip onto the snow. The weight is now entirely on the other ski. Then jump the weighted ski up so that, for an instant, both skis are up and both tips are pressed into the snow. Land on the first ski, leaving the second ski in the air. For the next move, hop the first ski again, and so on. Keep doing this in a very relaxed, lazy

manner for four or five hops to begin with. To use it as a real strength-builder, work up to ten or fifteen hinge hops. There is an extra great dividend to this hinge hop. The hinging action, whereby the ski tip is pressed into the snow, is the very same action used to "unweight" to take the weight off the skis in a parallel turn. (Of course, then it is done with both skis at once.) If you already know how to hop and keep the ski tips pressed into the snow, you have a head start on parallel skiing; or if you already ski parallel, you have a good exercise for improving the speed of your unweighting. The hinge hop also teaches you to ride one ski at a time. The best way to get across a small, particularly sharp dip or series of ruts is to ride over on one ski. You will have developed the proper reflex for it by training in the hinge hop.

Javelin Turn. You need balance, courage, and most of all proper angulation for a good sharp parallel turn. All these qualities can be built up by a little acrobatic exercise which we call the javelin turn, but which is really an exaggerated, intentional crossing of the fronts of the skis. There is no other exercise that illustrates so clearly how the hip must be placed for angulation in the parallel turn. In normal parallel skiing, the inside ski, boot, leg, and hip must lead the turn. In the javelin, or tip-cross turn, the inside of the body *has* to lead or you will fall.

To practice the javelin turn, start off as in any parallel turn, and then pick up the inside ski of the turn. As the turn progresses, keep pointing the tip of the lifted ski farther and farther to the outside of the turn so that by the end of the turn the lifted ski is at right angles to the tracking ski. Make sure to keep

Hinge hop.

Javelin turn.

The sit-back.

the tip of the lifted ski well off the snow.

Two or three javelin turns early in the day will get you set in the correct, powerful "lead with the inside" that is the secret of a really good carved parallel turn.

The Sit-back. The thing that every skier has to do to make long successful runs on a mountain (rather than stopping after every two turns) is to build up the thigh and leg muscles so that he can put strain on them without feeling uncomfortable. The sit-back acrobatic trick is the best and quickest way to condition the legs. You can also measure your condition with it. If you are able to get all the way down on the skis and back up you are in excellent shape.

To perform this trick, pick an easy slope, hold the poles out from your body, bend your knees slightly, and start to sit down slowly. Keep your upper body relaxed and sit back until you feel uncomfortable.

Then come back slowly to the standing position. Try it again. Try to sit back a bit farther. Do this acrobatic trick several times a day, and by the end of the season you will

be able to sit right down on the skis and come back up. And you will also be able to make good long runs with good skiers on the slopes.

The Butterfly Turn. The skier must swing the ski up behind him in a skating motion. In the final position the ski is cocked with the tip pointing back. The timing of the quick swing from the snow to a position behind and above the skier is crucial.

The Single Ski Christie. In this maneuver, the skier goes down the fall line of a gentle slope. The skier lifts one ski and thrusts it out behind him as far as he can. This straight run can be changed into a Single Ski Christie by leaning to inside while extending the tip of the lifted ski to the outside to maintain balance.

The Crossed Ski Turn. In this acrobatic, the ski on the inside of the turn is moved out over the weighted outside ski as the turn progresses. The final right or left turn should be completed with the lifted ski at right angles to the running ski. The upper body stays in a reverse throughout the turn. This exercise puts

The butterfly turn.

The royal Christie.

a skier's flexibility to the final test. If you can make a turn on a single inside ski and on a single outside ski, your flexibility and timing are such that you can go on to the butterfly turn.

Single Swing. The large percentage of skiers, who find that their first run is a tough one and that they need two or three runs to get in the groove, ought to consider the single swing as a way of making the early runs count. This is a sure-fire way of getting your important muscles limbered, of sharpening your timing sense, and of making you ready to go out and really knock that first run dead.

To do the single swing, you start by going straight down an easy slope. Then you lift one ski and swing the ski tip out to the side until it is almost at a right angle to the ski on the snow. In order to do this properly you have to swing your upper body and hands in the opposite direction.

Next, swing the tip in and across the other ski until it points in exactly the opposite direction. At the same time, to balance correctly, the upper body and arms swing in the opposite direction. Do this swing first with one ski, and then with the other. Then start doing it at a higher speed, so that the ski swings

The crossed-ski turn.

The single swing.

in and out like a windshield wiper. Two or three minutes of this and you are ready, relaxed, and willing for that first run.

Royal Christie. If you are able to "skate" on skis and to maintain your balance well while on one ski, you also can do a royal—one-legged—Christie. First, be sure to pick the right terrain—a concave surface (a shallow gully is perfect) with a gentle slope. Skate off in either direction at a fairly slow and comfortable speed, pushing off with the outside ski and then shifting *all* your weight to the inside ski. Do not ski too fast. Now try rotating your body as you would in a regular Arlberg turn. The first few times you try the turn, lift only the tip of the outside ski and let the tail ride on the snow for balance. Later, as you get the feel of the turn, you will find it more comfortable to bend your body sharply forward at the waist. The outside ski then can be lifted high above the snow. However, the general position of the ski will remain the same—the tip must be higher than the tail.

The best way to learn edge control for a royal Christie is to practice uphill Christies on one ski. Using the right ski, practice turning to the right, and vice versa. From a traverse, lean your upper body slightly uphill in the direction of the turn, pressing your knee downhill to release the ski's edge in a forward sideslip. Use your leg muscles and foot

The single-ski Christie (left) and revel Christie (right).

to steer the ski uphill. To improve your balance, spread your arms wide to either side. When you gain confidence, increase the steepness of your traverses.

Naturally, linking royal Christies is much harder to accomplish. When you have completed one turn, you will find it helpful to plant one pole, or both poles, in the snow as you go into the next turn. Using the poles for balance, skate off at about a 45-degree angle, trying to shift your weight *forward* onto the new turning ski. Again, the same policy holds: the tip of the outside ski should be held well above the tail.

The Charleston. The Charleston is a medium-difficult acrobatic maneuver, yet it

The Charleston.

is great and it *looks* hard. In fact, this acrobatic will give you a few minutes of good training in rhythm, coordination, and balance to enliven the next dull runout.

Practice first on the flat without moving down the hill. Stand in place, and jump rhythmically from one ski to the other; the tail of the unweighted ski is kicked out to the side, while the shovel stays on the snow. As soon as you have that rhythm down pat, try doing it while moving down a gentle incline. Shift from one ski to the other, kicking the tails out. Keep the upper body moving straight downhill while the legs dance. There is an almost automatic little turn that occurs, "wedeln on the inside ski," when the Charleston is really done right. You lean uphill a bit on the weighted ski to make the turn come quickly—and it has to come quickly or you lose the rhythm. Next try it on steep slopes. On the steep slopes it is difficult. You will find you have to kick the tail of the ski over the fall line to keep your speed down. But once you have it, you will find your ability to control the edges has improved tremendously and the fun has increased your enjoyment of each run by 100 per cent.

The Tip Roll. This maneuver is a medium-hard acrobatic routine which a good skier can master without too much risk if he wants to put in a bit of time at it. It is a great tuner-up before you start down a hard trail: a couple of tip rolls and you are psychologically ready to tackle anything.

The tip roll should be performed on an almost flat slope. It should be done with very little speed and can be made to either direction, left or right. To execute a tip roll changing direction to the right, start forward slowly and plant both poles to the right side of your ski, about a foot behind the tip. Sink down immediately into a comfortable crouch. At the moment the toe of your right boot is close to your poles, spring up, pulling your knees up and, at the same time, keeping your tips close together on the snow. Now shift all of your weight completely onto your poles. Keep your arms in a half-bent position and your knees together. Your slight downhill motion, with which you started, will automatically cause your tails to swing out to the left as you roll around on your tips to change direction to the right. Sink down into your knees to

The tip roll.

absorb the shock as you land. For a tip roll to the left, plant your poles on the left side and proceed in the same manner.

When first attempting this turn, in order to build your confidence, stand in one place in a stationary position. Plant your poles in the manner described above and have someone pick up the tails of your skis and roll you around. This will give you the proper feel of the motion involved and help you to become accustomed to the unusual sensation of the tip roll.

There are several methods of turning, and the major ones are discussed in this section. The racing technique turns are described in Section IV. The type of turns employed by an expert skier generally depends on snow conditions and types of terrain.

SPECIAL SNOW AND TERRAIN CONDITIONS

According to the Meteorological Glossary of the British Air Ministry, "Snow is precipitation in the form of ice crystals of feathery or needle-like structure. The crystals may form singly or a large number of them may be matted together in the form of large flakes."

The characteristic shape of the simplest crystals is a hexagonal (six-sided) plate, but most are much more complex in structure, ranging from needles to many-branched stars. At least 5,000 different forms have been recorded. Furthermore, the different shapes of snowflakes give rise to different snow conditions. When snowflakes fall, their activity just begins. Settling and shifting, melting and freezing, they produce the infinitely varied surfaces on which we ski.

All snowfields go through basic changes, whether they melt away into mountain streams or become immense glaciers. The process of converting a snowflake into a glacier is *firnification*—a process that never ends. *Wild snow* is the fine feathery froth that falls in the coldest weather. Loose and downy, 98 per cent air, it rests lightly, with just the ends of its crystals touching. *Powder* refers to all early, loose-lying stages of fallen snow; wild snow refers to settling and settled snow. Then the wind takes effect, and the sun beats down. Warm, dry breezes—the *chinook* —may soar along the snow's surface, melting it during the strange, warm nights of the dead of winter.

The snow consolidates—partly due to its own weight. Tiny plumes of the snowflakes are crushed; minute projections break off, and the snow settles closer. The air between the particles diminishes. The powder develops a crust—a *sun crust* or a *rain crust*. Crisp and crunchy in the morning, soft and heavy at noon, the watery substance freezes hard at night. The transition point is breakable crust —the skier's nightmare.

When a snowfield is *befirned*, hard, dense snow is all that remains except for a softened surface at noon (spring snow). This snow, hard as it is, should not be called ice. *Ice* is a term reserved for green, black, or bluish vitreous substance.

Some mountains now lose their snow to the gurgling brooks, and the greenery breaks through the last patches of snow. But on others, high and forever cold, there is one more stage for the snow (as snow) to go— glacier ice. Here, there is no air between crystals. There is nothing between the crystals but a thin amorphous cement of water. Ultimately the glacier melts to water, and the water vapor rises. The atmosphere absorbs it, and so the snowflakes fall again.

Fortunately for the skier, these various snow conditions do not call so much for special practices as for adapting the technique you already employ to the conditions. Although you may not always be 100 per cent happy with all snow conditions, you probably won't do much skiing if you wait for the day when everything is perfect. By being able to ski in special snow conditions you can improve your technique for those days that could be considered ideal, and after a while you may find that the conditions you considered the worst are more than bearable after all.

Skiing Ice

There is something about the *sound* of skis on ice—the spine-tingling clackity-clack, the high-pitched screech, the death rattle—that completely takes the zest out of skiing for most people. They get nervous, insecure, forget ski fundamentals or panic, exaggerate and apply brute power to hold on. In any case, the effect is usually disastrous, and a hard fall on ice is very hard indeed.

Hardpack or ice is all too often the condition you might find at your favorite ski slope on frigid winter days. Even where the base is 50 feet deep, if enough skiers travel the slope without further snowfall, the surface can become as hard as the cement in your basement. Ice may also form when temperatures drop below freezing following a day of warm temperatures (a frequent condition in spring). Ice may affect an entire slope; it may also be found in patches where shadows prevent the sun from thawing the snow.

Of the two conditions, patch ice is the more disconcerting simply because it may be unexpected. However, patch ice should not catch you completely by surprise. By looking ahead you can usually predict when you are likely to encounter a patch of ice: shadows on the slope, a spot where there has been a lot of turning, and the downhill side of moguls where the snow has been badly scraped.

Skiing ice demands two considerations. The first is equipment. Most important is a flat bottom surface on the ski. Skis may wear more or less in the middle than they do on and along the steel edges, so that a slight bulge or hollow forms in the middle of the ski as you go from edge to edge. Such a ski will hook or behave erratically, especially on ice. Get out a file and "flat-file" the ski edges and the ski so that the bottom surface is perfectly flat. A good 12-inch, No. 2 file will do it; it takes about 20 minutes to do a ski.

It is also important to have the edge "square." That is, the side of the edge should form a sharp right-angle corner with the bottom, not a rounded corner. This means touching up the sides of the edges once or twice a day when skiing on ice. With careful filing you can keep an edge really square so it will bite in.

Boots are another important equipment consideration. They must have good stiff sides to transmit the nuances of edge control from the ankles to the skis. Skiing ice is a delicate matter. Precision counts. A soft-sided boot which transmits movement of the ankle badly is out.

The second consideration is technique. The best generalization is that ice and boiler plate force you to ski correctly, only more so, at pain of losing control. There are some subtle changes to be made from the normal ski positions, but most people get into trouble because they do not ski correctly in the first place. On softer snow, you can get away with cheating. On ice, no.

Another secret of skiing technique on ice, at any ability level, is economy of movement: neither too much nor too little, neither too fast nor too slow. Just smooth, flowing, effortless, calm, icy elegance.

For most beginners and intermediates, who are doing snowplow or stem turns, this majestic calm must be applied during traverses across icy patches. Turns should be made on snow or rough, granular ice at the sides of the trails. More advanced skiers, to whom angulation has become instinctive, can carve or do short turns on ice as long as they keep their motions subtle and their skis in contact with the snow—or ice.

Here are some "do's and don'ts" to remember when skiing on ice:

1. Do not overreverse. The skier who twists his upper body too far into the "reverse" position when he's in a traverse forces himself to stand up straight. He can no longer make the bend from the waist and knee which is the necessary "angulation" (crucial on ice) for getting enough weight on the downhill ski. Furthermore, overreversing tends to straighten the legs and throw the skis on their downhill edges. This means "catching an edge" in short order. However, you should not overedge; just keep the skis slightly on edge or they will tend to lose their hold on ice.

2. Do not drop your hips back. The hips should be well over the boots. The bend at the ankle is what is supposed to bring the upper body far enough forward; do not bend forward at the hips or waist. When someone in the "hip back" position hits ice, he will sit farther back; his skis will speed up and he will sit down. But, with hips properly over the boots, he will have time to recover if the skis speed up.

3. A similar line of thought is that when you ski boiler plate or ice, you should be neither too far forward nor too far back. Try

to stay in a "neutral" position, *directly over the boots.* As the ice speeds you up and as the softer snow slows you, you will be in a better position to recover. Stay relaxed; stay neutral.

4. In the traverse, exaggerate the weight on the downhill ski by exaggerating the normal comma. The comma position has two elements: angulation, the outward bend at the knee and waist, and reverse, the slightly sideways twist (so you face downhill) of the upper body. You have to have a good comma to get enough weight on the downhill ski to keep it biting in the ice.

5. Conversely, get the weight *off* the uphill ski. One of the best ways of doing this is to lift the knee of the uphill leg and squeeze it against the knee of the leg that is taking the weight. This puts the weight on the "turning ice." To remind you to do this, you can practice holding your hat between your knees in traverses and gentle parallel turns.

6. Do not try to turn with the upper body. The skier who tries to twist his shoulder in the direction of the turn will get tense, his poles will come up in the air, his arms will ache. Remember to take your turning stance with the proper angulation and reverse, and keep your upper body relaxed. This puts the weight on the turning ski, and you turn. Feet do it, not your shoulders.

7. When you plant the poles for a parallel turn, *sink* straight down toward the boots. Do not dive forward as you would for softer snow. The forward dive kicks your skis back when you are on ice, and then you are in trouble. However, a hard straight-down *sinking* motion, with solid pole plant and a good setting of the edges, in balance, will control you nicely.

8. In stem turns on ice, exaggerate the shift of weight to the turning ski as you change direction down the hill. Make sure that the inside edge of the turning ski bites in *hard.*

9. In the parallel turn, the weight shift is also exaggerated. Assume a very pronounced comma with skis just slightly on edge, so that as much weight as possible goes onto the outside or turning ski. This will make the edge drive into the ice and hold you smoothly in the turn without "overedging"—an exaggerated edging that makes skis chatter.

10. When turning on hardpack or ice, accept the fact that your turns will have a longer radius and a larger curve. Allow for this by giving yourself plenty of room to turn in. Stay on the wide-open slopes where you can traverse between each turn. Remember that if there is one consolation on ice, it is that the skis are easy to turn—perhaps too easy. An icy period is a good time to stay on the easier slopes and to practice turning by pressure of the knees in the direction of the turn. It is one of the better ways to get the feel of wedeln.

Skiing Powder Snow

Deep powder! These words have probably done more to generate interest in skiing than any other term. Deep powder whets the appetite; it is at once the average skier's dilemma and the photographer's delight.

What is deep powder? To skiers in certain parts of the country, it is a foot of any kind of new snow. To the more fortunate skiers who live in areas boasting high altitudes and heavy snowfalls, deep powder is several feet of dry, cold snow that has settled and compressed itself sufficiently to make a feathery carpet with a spongy firmness. The spongy quality of the snow affords a fairly solid platform under the skis and allows the skier, exercising proper technique, the greatest amount of deep-snow control. But these varieties of snow are only the beginning. Also to be encountered is the season's first snowfall which produces a dry, cold, feather-light powder and falls to great depths over a snowless base of rocks, stumps, logs, and sagebrush. It is a beautiful white carpet, but treacherous, because of its many hidden air pockets. Even an expert will flounder waist deep in this type of snow, providing he is still upright.

The varieties of powder already discussed may be complicated by a thinly crusted topping, created by wind or snow. This truly provides a challenge for the powder-snow skier. But to simplify matters, we will concern ourselves here with those varieties of powder whose solid snow base lies more than a few inches under the surface and that are defined by the word "deep."

Choice of equipment is not as complicated as determining the texture of the powder. Skis

When making uphill Christie, substitute the sideslip for the carve to end the turn. Notice figures at left: the upper body leans out, the weight shift is pronounced, and the turn is carved. The same maneuver in powder shows the upper body over both skis, unweighting (right) from both skis, and the turn is skidded at the end.

of medium length should be used. A soft, overall flex is most desirable. Thick skis are a definite disadvantage. Thin skis, such as metal skis, act much like a cheese cutter under snow. They may mean the difference between a fall or a recovery.

It is interesting to note that modern skis offer two distinct advantages for powder skiing: they have less bottom camber, and they are softer and more flexible in front. This, combined with relatively stiff tails, make these skis suitable for hardpack as well as for almost all powder snow. However, if you do a lot of deep-snow skiing, nothing beats a good ski specially designed for powder. This kind of ski is particularly advantageous for heavy, wet snow or wind-blown, crusted snow. The next best thing to real powder skis is an old pair of soft skis with the bindings mounted 1 to 1½ inches back from the normal position; if they are in fairly good condition, they make powder skiing a new thrill.

Goggles are almost as important as skis for powder skiing. Most skiers come out of the lodge and instinctively turn their backs to the wind to put skis on. From body heat, warm breath, and drifting snow their goggles are fogged over by the time they stand up. It is better to face the cold wind during your first minutes out of the lodge and while putting on your skis. Another good idea is to carry two pairs of goggles or sunglasses. Then if you

fall or the goggles get fogged, you can clean them and put them under your parka to dry while using the extra pair.

For very deep powder, the greatest clothing advance is the warm-up pant. Not only do these pants keep you warm while skiing, but they keep you dry while riding snow-covered chair lifts. A warm hat and parka are also important, but do not overdress; if you perspire, you will eventually get cold. Allow air to escape around the neck of your parka, and remove your hat if you get too warm.

The teaching technique for deep powder starts at the snow line and is taught from the feet up. The effect of the snow upon the skis is determined by speed and resistance to slipping and by the depth to which the skis sink in. So, the first hard and fast rule should be: *Ski on equally weighted parallel skis.* In straight running or traversing, the skis run on a step which they cut in the snow. Therefore, the two skis, weighted alike, offer the most efficient support to the skier. It is advantageous to have the knees as close together as possible.

Rule 2 takes the form of a practice exercise. *Traverse, make forward sideslips, traverse, and repeat.* This exercise cannot be overdone. It is the only way to feel the snow and the skis. Every new snowfall has slightly different characteristics. Feel the effect of the snow on the skis and then use your legs and

After some experience with uphill Christies in both directions, an intermediate skier can start doing stem Christies in deep snow. One of the main points to remember is to hold the stemmed ski out until the body faces down the fall line. This delay allows the outside ski to cross the fall line and point in the new traverse direction, at which point the skis are brought together still evenly weighted. This is done with a down-and-up movement, with even unweighting from both sides. The skier then lowers his body over the skis and lets them slide sideways.

upper body accordingly. The deep snow of perfect density must be compressed. The thin, breakable-crust variety must be forcefully broken and pushed aside. The hollow, very light early-season snow must be gently caressed by the skis.

The weight of your body on the skis must be such that the tips will plane up. This is true even in crusted powder, for there is deep powder underneath. In order to maintain the very sensitive balance that causes the tips to plane and still does not immobilize you too far back on your heels, the ankles and knees are bent a little more deeply than normal and never are straightened completely. This rule holds true even in the event of a forceful rising motion of the body.

When traversing deep snow, there is no severe edging as there would be on packed snow. Thus the knees and hips do not angle into the hill as sharply as they do on packed snow, nor does the upper body angle downhill as much. It naturally follows that your uphill hip and shoulder lead only slightly. In all senses of the word, the body is kept more squarely over both skis.

Your upper body is fairly erect under powder-snow conditions. Your arms are extended more than normally for balance, but not to the extent of hindering pole use in preparation for each turn. When making forward sideslips or uphill turns from a traverse, the turns are effected the same as on packed snow—with a slight sinking action in the ankles and knees and with the unweighting and turning of the skis on the rising motion. Your upper body helps the lower body counteract the resistance of the skis. It is used, with the planting of the pole, to supply a balanced preparation for the turn. In this

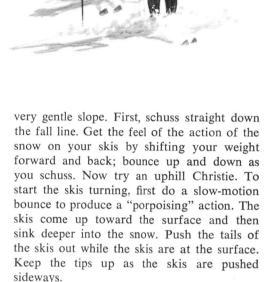

How "porpoising" helps the parallel skier.

stage, your upper body may actually turn in the opposite direction of the intended turn in the so-called "countermotion." But in no event should you be twisted to an extreme in one way or another. It is obvious that this would cause loss of balance.

At this point, we would like to caution skiers who want to wedeln or "short-swing" that this method of skiing will work only in the perfect, desirable variety of deep snow described earlier. This is when the snow can be compressed efficiently under the skis and when the snow surface offers no resistance. With consistent terrain and speed facilitating rhythmical linked turns, this can be the acme of deep-powder skiing. However, except in perfect snow, it is much sounder technique not to let the upper body wind or "reverse" against the lower body in the so-called motion of angulation. Instead, the upper body is more square to the skis. The upper body should follow the lower body in the turn, in the same direction, with a motion of partial or complete rotation, according to snow resistance, speed, and turning radius. Traverse, make a slight uphill turn, then traverse more steeply and make a sharper uphill turn. Make linked traverses and uphill turns. Feel the snow.

When skiing parallel in powder, remember four things: Maintain even weight on both feet, keep the body low for stability, make slow-motion movements in unweighting and in the turn (to give the skis time to react and make rhythmic linked turns), and do not stop turning. Build confidence by practicing on a

very gentle slope. First, schuss straight down the fall line. Get the feel of the action of the snow on your skis by shifting your weight forward and back; bounce up and down as you schuss. Now try an uphill Christie. To start the skis turning, first do a slow-motion bounce to produce a "porpoising" action. The skis come up toward the surface and then sink deeper into the snow. Push the tails of the skis out while the skis are at the surface. Keep the tips up as the skis are pushed sideways.

Keep your hips low over the skis. Figures on the left show the conventional high position for down-up-down unweighting on packed snow. Figures at right show how low you start in powder, even while unweighting. If you have enough speed, you will feel the skis porpoising even in the uphill Christies, as you stay low. Practice some stop Christies in the same way (i.e., with the porpoising bounce), but pick your stopping places carefully so they are not too steep. Remember to keep your weight even on both skis during the stop.

By surfing in powder, you link parallel turns in powder. Apply all of the new principles: equal weighting, lower hip position, slow motion movements. As you get better, the unweighting increasingly becomes a sideways push movement of the feet, like a surfer sliding his board sideways to catch a wave. The upward bounce diminishes and the skis stay down in the snow. Keep the ankles bent and knees pushed forward. This low stance gives you a very stable position from which to control your skis in powder and permits more forcefulness in moving the skis sideways.

One of the more popular powder turns is the "hop wedeln," in which the skier performs a series of short turns and keeps the skis more on edge. This necessitates up-unweighting, or lifting the skis between turns, to avoid the steering effect of the snow on the edged skis. Hop wedeln turns must be short, quick, and made close to the fall line at fairly high speeds. For all practical purposes, it is impossible to practice this powder hop profitably at slow speeds or on packed snow. The would-be powder skier must wait for powder and then plunge precariously into it at high speed, sustaining lots of hard knocks.

The Submarine. The, submarine technique for deep snow is one in which the skier keeps his skis almost continually submerged in the powder. The technique essentially is a series of connected sideslips. The skier goes from one turn to the next without bobbing up and down. There is no lifting of the skis from the snow. The skis stay down *in* the snow (hence the name submarine).

With the submarine technique in deep snow, the turns are short, rounded, and quickly linked. Like the French Serpent (see page 197), the submarine places extreme importance on leg action, quick edge change, and little up-and-down motion. The two important points are: (1) keep the skis in the snow and (2) keep them turning. There is almost no interval between turns.

A third important point is: Make the turns with very little unweighting. The skier keeps his knees forward and moves them literally across the skis to go from one turn to the next. He does not "come up" and straighten the knees. These lower leg movements are supported by angulation and by facing the upper body downhill. Such minimal unweighting as there is occurs when the skis flatten to go from one turn to the next. The ski tails are thrust quite far out to each side, with the skier's upper body remaining in the middle, as it were. The thrusting is accomplished very quickly, so there is little chance for the skis to pick up speed. To initiate the change in direction, your knees are moved across the skis to flatten them in relation to the snow. Then you literally turn your skis

where you want to go, angulate for just a few feet, and then bring your knees over the skis again to start the next turn.

In conclusion, a few words of caution about powder skiing: stick to the main trails when there is little snow covering the ground or when you are in an unknown area, because you could hit a rock or tree stump hidden under the snow. During storms or in flat light conditions, avoid open slopes where you will have difficulty seeing the degree of pitch. Choose narrower, tree-lined runs, where the trees can give you some idea of the contour of the hill.

One of the great worries of deep powder is the mess that results from a fall. A fall in powder is not physically dangerous, but the problems of disentangling yourself from your equipment and the snow (which, being light and loose, will have penetrated into every opening in your clothing) can be formidable.

No matter what your level of ability, the best way to learn powder skiing is to start in snow that is not really deep and on trails that are less steep than you might normally ski. You will find that with good balance and body position and sound basic ski technique, the snow depth has little effect on the maneuverability of your skis. Once you have established some confidence, you can move on to deeper snow and try for that dream ski sequence: dashing down an open white space, seeking out the hollows and steep pitches for deep snow, floating on skis in the quiet noplace that is powder skiing.

When Snow Turns Extra-Heavy

Skiing in the "spring" months of March, April, and May can be the most delightful—indeed hedonistic—pleasure offered any sportsman. The air is crisp but the sun is warm. Light stays good into late afternoon. The skin glows with a deep tan. And corn snow—soft at the surface, firm underneath—makes turning easy, even on steep slopes.

There are occasions in spring, however, when skiers are confronted with unusually wet, heavy, and sticky snow. In ski slang, these conditions are often called "crud" or "junk." They are difficult to ski and can be dangerous. The instructor or expert skier may be able to ski under all snow conditions be-

The "hop" wedeln.

Such snow conditions arise when evaporation, humidity, wind, sun, and the heavy water content of the snow itself cause the snow crystals to adhere to each other. Eventually, this process results in the crystals forming a firmly packed, wet, heavy snow. It is because of this wet, solid pack that a skier meets increased resistance. Skis will not slide. Tips will not plane on the top of the snow, and turning the tips and tails through the snow seems impossible. Obviously, it becomes necessary to alter the ski technique.

Starting with the proper equipment, skis used for heavy snow should be of soft flexibility—especially in the tail. Stiff skis are very difficult to turn in wet, heavy snow. Metal skis are best for such conditions because of their torsional rigidity (the small amount of twisting in the tip of the ski). The type of running surface and wax is important, too. A medium-to-soft wax should be applied with

cause of his experience and excellent physical conditioning, but the inexperienced novice or intermediate weekend skier may find the heavy snow a nightmare.

iron or cork. This will bind the top layer of silver or paraffin running wax to the skis. Wax combinations are many for spring skiing (see Section II), but in general, soft, wet snow requires a soft type of wax. Consult the shop at the area where you are skiing for the best wax to use on a particular spring day.

A last requisite is a good release binding. Be certain that it is properly adjusted. You can ski out of your bindings in crud snow if the bindings are too loose, while at the same time, the heavy crud can create extreme leverage that could cause you to break a leg. Be sure to clean your bindings from time to time while skiing, since the snow will have a tendency to "pack" in the binding and disturb the release adjustment.

Skiing in extra-heavy snow requires excellent physical conditioning, and coordination. This means work. Lazy habits will cause trouble in rough snow. Then, too, the mental attitude of the skier is important. Heavy snow naturally causes a skier to be afraid. And since such snow should be skied in the fall line, a skier can develop a mental block. As long as the skier is afraid of the snow and the hill, there is little hope of skiing effectively. These fears must be overcome by building up confidence and ability.

Developing a heavy snow technique is similar to learning how to ski again. You review many fundamental maneuvers and practice them in logical steps. In essence, these are the important rules:

1. Whenever possible, the skis should be equally weighted and parallel. Snow resistance can cause a single unweighted ski to wander, resulting in a dangerous position. And since it is unnatural to maintain equally weighted skis in a traverse, weight must be forced upon the uphill ski by use of muscular pressure.

2. In heavy snow, the skier's center of gravity should be placed in a position that will cause the tips of the skis to plane out of the snow. Edge control is not as critical as on packed slopes. Edges are applied in crud snow to effect a banking of the skis, rather than a gripping action.

3. The most drastic change in crud snow technique is the unweighting of the skis. The down-up-down movement in the knees must be exaggerated, and the unweighting must be limited to the legs, not the upper torso. Bending forward from the waist will only cause the ski tips to dive under the snow.

4. Learn to ski in the fall line because there is less resistance and increased momentum there.

Observe how these fundamentals are applied in practice. First, choose a shallow slope with a runout. Try running this slope straight a few times until you have the feel of skiing on parallel, equally weighted skis. Now try the same position in a traverse. Be sure you apply enough pressure to the uphill ski so that it will not wander. Do not turn—use a kick turn to link traverses. Steepen the angle of traverse while practicing the unweighting exercises. Drop down, rise up—hold the up position—and drop down again.

The next maneuver requires good timing and coordination—the pole plant with the down-up-down movement. The ski pole is planted in the snow at a point approximately halfway between the boot and ski tip, out to the side of the ski. Plant your pole at the end of the down motion, as you start the up movement. With a slight push on the pole, you can help diminish your weight on the snow, and this will greatly assist you in unweighting the skis. Pole plant has other advantages—helping to coordinate timing and providing a pivot for the turn. Practice this pole exercise while traversing, being careful not to gain too much speed in the traverse.

Next, try a Christie-into-the-hill from a traverse position. This maneuver is done by planting the pole and unweighting the skis with a down-up-down motion. Turn the skis by initiating a hip rotation, causing the heels of the skis to slide downhill and the tips to head up the hill.

Because heavy-snow conditions offer extreme resistance, you will often need upper body rotation (shoulder follow-through) to aid in the final turning of the skis. In this manner, the competent skier is able to utilize many sources of turning power to change the direction of the skis. Remember to start the turn of the skis at the top of the up motion in your unweighting movement. When the skis are lightest on the snow, they are most easily turned.

Practice Christies-into-the-hill until they can be executed from the fall line. This is

The submarine technique.

similar to a stop Christie. Now try turning the skis into the fall line from a traverse position. Sink down to start the turn, rise up to unweight the skis, and sink down again with most of your weight on the new downhill ski. Since the critical problem of any turn is to start the skis turning downhill, this exercise will build up fall-line confidence. Now it becomes a simple maneuver to make a complete downhill turn.

If you have difficulty with the parallel approach, try using a limited uphill stem. This is called stemming-to-the-fall-line and is finished with a Christie-into-the-hill. Be careful, though—stemming can be dangerous in crud. Thus, the stem maneuver is done very quickly. From a traverse, with skis equally weighted and parallel, shift your weight to the lower ski and push out the tail of the upper ski. Now quickly place your weight on the stemmed upper ski and bring the downhill ski parallel to the uphill ski. Both skis are equally weighted again, in the fall line, and the turn is finished by a Christie-into-the-hill. The transition from parallel skis to stemmed uphill ski

The submarine technique in crud.

and back to parallel skis again should be done rapidly. Practice this exercise, as all the exercises, from both directions. Link maneuvers and turns with as little traversing as possible. The finish of one turn should be the beginning of the next turn. Thus, you are able to utilize the momentum from one turn as the springboard for the next.

A parallel turn on crud snow is a combination of all the aforementioned maneuvers, executed down the fall line with more equally weighted and parallel skis. The skis are turned on the up movement, with the pole to aid this lifting action. Turning power will come from the hips, feet, and shoulders. Unweight the skis, using the hips to push the tails outward at the end of the turn, and follow through with the arm and shoulder. Do not overrotate or swing. When skiing crud, you should learn to delay your shoulder fol-

low-through so that you will always have a reserve turning power to finish the turn.

The submarine technique, popular with deep-powder skiers, can be employed to ski crud. This style, of course, keeps the skis *in* the crud between turns; it takes advantage of the resistance of the snow to keep your speed down and therefore to keep you from going out of control. This is the danger of the exaggerated unweighting technique, when the skis are virtually in the air between turns.

In the submarine, the trick is to *change edges* with the skis still pressed into the snow. To change the edges is to move the skis from a tilt on one edge in a turn to the necessary tilt on the other edge in the new turn. In the submarine, you change edges by moving the knees across the skis in the transition between turns, instead of lifting them out of the snow. The continual pressure of the skis on the snow bows them into an arc necessary to make hard, tight turns. A soft, flexible metal ski that bows will hold the turn, and will slice more easily through the crud.

Crud snow is not easy skiing. Attempt to understand what you are trying to accomplish, and seek the help of a professional instructor. Shy away from well-meaning friends who offer free advice. Incompetent instruction can be disastrous in heavy spring snow. Above all, do not be discouraged. Learning to ski spring snow will require time and practice, just as skiing in deep snow or on icy slopes—but once mastered, it can be immensely satisfying.

Skiing Moguls

Few conditions seem more hazardous to skiers than big bumps or moguls. Many intermediate and some advanced skiers flounder when confronted with an entire slope of high moguls and deep ruts. Actually, they are easy and fun to ski—if you use the proper technique.

Good knee action is the most important factor in skiing moguls. Many skiers keep the downhill knee stiff, trying to use it as a brake to control their skis when sideslipping down the side of a mogul. This is completely wrong. Good down-and-up knee action is the best form of control. It provides a basis for turns, gives edge control in traverses and sideslips, and puts rhythm into your skiing.

If you are a beginner, the first rule you should remember is to avoid moguls, or bumps. Stay on fairly flat terrain, increasing the grade as your ability and confidence increase. Experience shows, however, that beginners often do wind up in mogul fields, either because they turn on to the wrong trail or because they possess more derring-do than ability.

Basically, there are two ways you, as a beginner, can ski your way through a mogul field, providing you can sideslip your skis. If you cannot sideslip, the recommended escape is to remove your skis and walk down the side of the trail. (Stay on the side, not in the middle where your boots would make holes and where you would be in the way of other skiers.) When the moguls are of fairly good size—that is, wide enough so that you can sideslip down the fall line without the ski tips or tails hanging in the air—assume the beginning sideslip position taught in most ski schools. Keep your weight on the downhill ski and find a comfortable position over your skis so that your tips or tails do not slide too far ahead of you down the hill. Keep both poles on the uphill side of your body, flatten your skis by sinking down over your downhill ski, and push with your poles.

If you pick up speed and want to slow down, edge your skis slightly, and they will brake your forward motion. Never put your poles in front of you to brake your speed. It will not work, and it could be extremely dangerous if you slip.

If the terrain is not very steep, or if the moguls are jagged and not wide enough to fit your skis across them horizontally, then try the second defensive maneuver: the forward sideslip. Before you begin this maneuver, study the terrain you are about to ski. Pick what looks like an easy line, where you will make the most progress down the hill and avoid the most difficult parts, such as ice, steepness, or a particularly high mogul. Then stick to your line.

Edge control is very important when crossing a mogul field in a forward sideslip. You can control how far down the hill you slide by edging your skis. To avoid a mogul, edge your skis for a few feet, thereby passing above the mogul. If you flatten your skis, you may slip below it.

If you cannot avoid a big mogul, then ski across and over the top of it. When you reach the top of the mogul, just as your skis begin to slip on its steep, downhill side, let your knees sink. This will push the tips of your skis slightly into the hill, slow you down, and help you maintain your balance. When you reach the opposite side of the trail, turn around and repeat the procedure until you are out of the moguls and back on more even terrain, where you can ski with more confidence.

If you are an intermediate skier, still stay away from steep trails with moguls. These are only for very good skiers, and they could undercut your confidence. Pick a slope with a fairly even grade, no surprise precipices, and medium-sized moguls.

The first thing to do before you start to ski a moguled trail is to pick a line. Most mogul

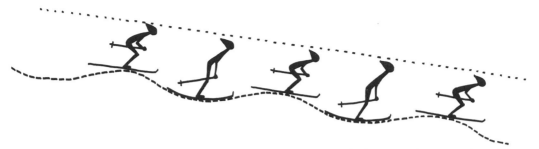

Learn to ride bumps without leaving the snow. Start your run close to the bumps, and as you gain confidence gradually start runs farther up the hill to increase speed. Another diversion in this exercise is to try to keep your head on a fairly even plane (broken line). At the top of the bumps, your ankles, knees, and hips are bent; in depressions, stand up.

fields have a rhythm. Look ahead and try to pick a series of moguls which are far enough apart so that you can prepare for each one; yet close enough to the fall line that you do not have a long traverse from one to the next. Approach the mogul from the uphill side with your weight on the downhill ski and your body in its normal ski position, but be ready to absorb the first impact of the bump. Timing is crucial to making the turn correctly. Just as you reach the top of the mogul, change your weight and, of course, switch your lead ski to become the new uphill ski at the same time. Just after you change your weight, let your knees sink down. The combination of down motion and weight change will give you heel thrust, and your skis will slide easily down the lower part of the mogul. You arc your turn according to how long you stay down. If you have picked a line in which the next mogul is coming upon you soon, you must rise more quickly. Actually, you are using the top of the mogul to help you turn. The skis meet less friction, because they are turning on less snow, and the contour of the steep side of the mogul is easier to slide your skis on.

It is most important to choose your moguls so that they are equidistant. This will enable you to keep a rhythm, and soon you will be humming down through the mogul field. If you encounter some trouble skiing moguls in this way, try the two-pole approach. Using two poles helps bring your weight forward and makes turning easier.

A series of moguls can be a great challenge to an expert skier. It tests your reactions and your ability to pick a good line. You should be able to wend your way through a series of moguls almost the way you would ski a slalom course. You should not be afraid of going fast. Pick a line so that you bypass the tops of the moguls and ski in the troughs, or between the moguls.

Ski into the first depression and then jump off the top of the second bump to clear the second depression and land on the far side of the third bump. Repeat until your timing is perfect and you are gaining more and more distance. Notice the figure, when landing, is bent farther forward than when he was riding bumps in the previous exercise.

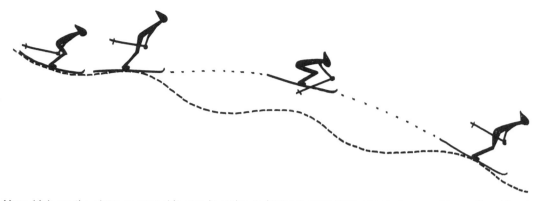

Move high on the slope to start this one in order to increase your inrun speed. As you ride up the side of the first bump, bend sharply; at the top press off hard by springing up and forward. This should give you the momentum to clear the second bump and land on the back side of the third (16 to 20 feet). If you have enough distance, bend more and press off harder. On first attempts, concentrate on distance; later, try to perfect tuck body position.

The most common error good skiers make when skiing moguls is to ski them the way an intermediate does. As a better skier, however, you can have more fun dodging the tops of the moguls, skiing around each mogul and using a quick check to control your speed. That is, a turn over moguls is begun with the same down-and-up motion, but it is not made as sharply. It is easier for the more advanced skier to lengthen each turn, so that the skis slide against and over the top of the next mogul, especially if there are long grooves or ruts between bumps. If you are skiing on a slope consisting mainly of moguls, the turns can be done like wedeln, your body keeping a center balance while the heels of your skis slide from side to side. Use your ski pole as a windup and the top or upper part of the mogul as pivot point for your turn, keeping all the turning motion in your knees and ankles.

Practice a turn to the left and a turn to the right separately, then start linking turns. By linking turns over moguls, you will begin to develop a rhythm which makes skiing both easy and pleasurable.

Jumping and Prejumping

As previously stated, the advanced skier is often presented with problems of terrain. With the ever increasing number of skiers, all using the same runs, the natural snow surface is worn to a point where it is cut up into thousands of holes, ruts, bumps, ditches, and moguls. Expert skiers traveling downhill at high speeds often avoid these terrain obstacles by jumping over them.

Jumping is a maneuver used to clear an obstacle such as an abrupt hole or rut. You lift off the snow at the top of one bump and land on the downhill side of the second bump, avoiding contact with the rut in between. The lifting action is accomplished by a slight sinking motion of the knees before the takeoff, and by quickly straightening your legs again as you reach the crest of the bump. Flexible, bent knees and a slight downward pressure of your heels will help to keep the ski tips from digging into the snow upon landing.

When jumping, remember to use the mogul just in front of the mogul you want to skip, or use the mogul that is in your way. Look ahead to see how far you want your jump to carry you. Before you reach the mogul, get both of your poles set and let your knees sink. Then extend both poles a little in front of you, and when you reach the lip of the mogul, come up out of your crouch and use the poles to give you a lift. While in the air tuck your skis under you. Time your jump so that you land on the upper side of the trough which goes around the mogul you are aiming for, so that your skis will travel downhill and you can continue skiing in the troughs.

Do not land on the top of the mogul unless you are good enough to go up into the air

The technique for crossing moguls for an intermediate skier, which means you can do a secure parallel turn most of the time and have skied long enough not to be scared by a long stretch of moguls.

right away for a second jump. Otherwise you will not have a smooth landing and will probably fall. If you are in very good shape, you can jump whenever you want to while skiing moguls. After you land from the first jump, get set for the second. Keep going down the slope like a jack-in-the-box.

Another method of jumping bumps is the so-called bunnyhop, a maneuver for skiers who really want to become airborne. Instead of approaching the bump in a crouch, remain relatively upright with your legs firm, but not stiff. At the point of the takeoff bounce down with your legs firm and unyielding. Then, push down and then up on the takeoff, rather than try to jump directly upward. The down-and-up movement will almost literally bounce or kick you into the air and will almost automatically force your legs into the desirable tucking position.

Try this exercise without skis in your home. Jump and try to touch the ceiling. You will note that you will not get nearly the same spring by starting from a crouch as you would by standing from a relatively erect position, then sinking or springing down hard toward the floor. Try to drive your legs right through the floor as you spring upward. This provides you with momentum, a kick, and

extra power for the upward spring. Now try riding over a small bump a few times with your legs firm, rather than letting your legs go soft and thereby absorbing the bump. This maneuver will result in a small hop without any further effort on your part. One word of caution, however. Start with small bumps and jumps, and build up height as your feeling for the snow, the bumps, and the air sharpens. Do not lunge or dive forward as you take off, or you will land tips first. Just try to maintain your basic body position directly over your bindings with your legs in a tucked position. After a bit of practice, bunnyhops will become second nature to you, and the result will be increased skiing pleasure as well as increased agility and ability to control your skis under varied conditions.

For those who wish to take a bump at full speed but without becoming airborne for excessive periods of time, prejumping is the correct procedure. Prejumping is done by starting the jump before the crest of the jump is reached. This can be done with the aid of the poles, or by quickly tucking the knees under the chest once the arc of the bump has been reached. If the prejump is timed correctly the path of flight will closely approximate the contour of the bump. The trick in

Proper technique for jumping over a mogul.

timing the prejump is to go sufficiently high on the bump to produce enough lift to clear the crest. If the jump is too late, the skier will be thrown into the air; if too soon, he will be descending before he clears the crest.

Both jumping and prejumping maneuvers should be practiced first separately, and then alternately. Start in a slow run across the slope and then practice these maneuvers closer to the fall line.

In addition to the "simple" jumps and prejumps just described, here are several jump maneuvers that are generally classified as "advanced."

Jump Turn. This is a slow-speed turn in which the skier leaps into the air on his poles, changes direction while in mid-air, and finishes in a stationary position. It is called the "jump turn" and consists of three basic steps:

1. While you are traversing in a line that is more across than down the slope, lower your body into a deep crouch, placing both ski poles into the snow just below the tip of your downhill ski. Be sure to firmly wrap the palms of your hands over the top of the handles, and increase edge bite of your skis slightly to give yourself a firm springboard.

2. Then jump into the air, leaping up from the balls of your feet, using both poles for support. As you rise into the air, turn your head and shoulders to the new desired direction and at the same time bring your feet up toward your hips. Continue the turn by rotating the entire body and the skis around the

poles and into the new direction.

3. As you start to land, straighten out your legs. Once contact is made with the snow, allow your body to continue moving downward. Your ankles, knees, and waist will absorb the shock, with the knees taking up the major portion.

If you wish to make a complete about-face turn (180 degrees), plant your poles so that the uphill pole crosses over the downhill pole. The turning movement of your body will automatically uncross them, and when you land they will be in a normal position.

Airplane Turn. An airplane turn—also known as the jump Christie—is a jump from a medium or large bump with a change of direction while in the air. This is often used when jumping from one mogul to the downhill side of another. The approach to the bump is the same as in the preceding sequences. On a hill with lots of moguls it is possible to make a series of these airplane turns.

To see how the turn is made, let us assume you have chosen the bump from which you will take off and you are approaching it in good traverse position, at considerable speed, looking well ahead, weight nicely distributed on both skis, knees elastic. From the normal crouch position as you come up the bump, you prepare to plant your pole at the very top of the bump, where you will lift up strongly and with full extension of the legs, and the combination of the terrain and the vigorous lift sends you into the air. Once you are

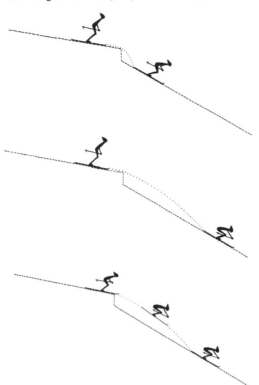

(Top) Find a little bump, about 2 to 4 feet high, with an inrun of from 4 to 10 per cent and a landing of about 30 to 40 per cent steepness. Start with a very little speed, and at a point 2 to 3 feet before the lip of the bump, press off for the jump. However, instead of riding for distance, pump down with your upper body and arms so you will land immediately after takeoff. Try not to be airborne any longer than necessary after jumping. (Center) When you have tried the previous exercise several times and you have a mental picture of where the ground is under you, try jumping for distance. Gain speed by using a longer inrun and increase this as necessary until you can jump 10 feet and then 20 feet from the bump. Land in a low crouch by bending your ankles, knees, and hips. Walking through air is another exercise to develop air coordination. Move one leg in front of the other leg in quick "walking steps" until just before your landing. (Bottom) When you consistently jump long distances without fear, try a split jump. Just as your body uncoils from the jump, split. This requires concentration and coordination. Repeat your longest jump off a bump, but pull your body up into a tuck position as you become airborne. In racing aerodynamics this egg position is for maximum speed. Now use the egg position with a prejump (as in the first exercise) in order to get minimum airborne distance using maximum speed. If you can stay in a low tuck position during the jump, you will have perfect form.

Most skiers enjoy jumping off bumps and moguls and experiencing the thrill of being airborne for brief periods of time. The average skier, however, performs these jumps with complete disregard for form, usually elongating the body, with the ski tails low and the tips high. Not only is this form incorrect, but it causes the tails to land first, and allows no knee bend to absorb the landing shock. Instead of stretching your body when coming off a bump, try to retract your legs into a tuck position. It should feel as though you are drawing your heels up to your body and letting your ski tips drop so that the angle of the skis will be parallel to the slope on which you will land. Not only is this tuck attractive, it also allows a smooth and comfortable landing.

airborne, your outside hand and arm come around exactly as in the parallel turns on the ground, an arcing motion accompanying the turning of the skis, which is accomplished in the air. While executing the turn you will also be drawing up your knees so that the parallel skis are close to the body and as far from the surface of the snow as you can get them. Below you now is the top of the bump you are jumping over; the drawing up of the feet close to the body is important to make sure that you clear this crest, since it is your purpose to land in the groove on the other side of it. Now you prepare for the landing, which will not be difficult if your body has turned to the correct angle for skiing in the

Types of jumps required to cross a mogul field.

landing groove. But before you land, you straighten your legs somewhat (although you must not straighten them all the way and lock the knees, which would make your landing an upsetting jolt). Your purpose is to extend your legs so that as the skis come down onto the snow you will have ample reserve spring in your knees and legs to absorb the shock. Be sure to let your knees flex so that you settle onto the snow instead of pounding down onto it. If the knees are locked, you cannot do this. Similarly, if the knees are still tucked up when you land you will not have any elasticity to absorb the shock.

Geländesprung. Geländesprung, the German word for "terrain jump," is a quick means of turning around that can be fun to do on the edge of a bump or the top of a steep hill. It takes a fair amount of strength in the arms.

When geländesprunging, use the terrain to aid you by jumping from the crest of a small mogular bump. Ski straight down the fall line toward the mogul. Prepare for the jump by bringing both your hands up, ready to plant your ski poles at the crest. But keep your body position high. Do not crouch as yet. When you arrive at the crest, plant both poles near the shovel of your skis and with legs firm, quickly push down hard against the mogul and spring up into the air. That is, push your legs forcefully against the snow. At the same time rise onto your poles by thrusting down hard against them and straightening your arms. Tuck your feet up underneath your hips. Float for a moment. Then extend your legs down, make contact with the snow again, and absorb the landing by slightly bending your ankles and knees, which permits your body to sink softly onto your legs.

Be sure to keep your skis close together, particularly as you approach the mogul. It is also important that you push off both legs at the same time. Do not crouch until the very last moment. Then make your bouncing down and springing up one rapid, continuous action. You will obtain the most support from your poles if you hold them at the very end. But it is also a good idea to practice geländesprungs when holding the poles in the position you normally do use. There will be occasions making this jump when you will not have time to reposition your grip on the handle.

Gazelle Turn. This turn might be considered a combination of an airplane turn and a geländesprung, an airplane turn in which

Steps in making a jump Christie.

the knees are retracted. The gazelle turn is performed on a mogul with the use of either one or two poles. With considerable speed, the use of one pole is sufficient. However, at a slower speed, or to gain more height, both poles are used. While practicing or learning, it is advisable to select a single bump on the hill so that you will not get tangled with other moguls on your landing.

Approach the bump from a traverse and set your edges just before the takeoff to get an even, springlike action with both legs. The best way to set the edges is by a simultaneous sinking motion and heel thrust. This will put you in a good down position and, at the same time, give you a good platform for the up motion or the takeoff. The downhill pole is placed at the top of the bump during the down motion and is immediately followed by an upspringing motion in which the knees are tucked up. At the same time, bank over the pole on the downhill side.

The banking movement will start the turn in the air. Before landing, straighten your legs, enabling the knees to absorb the shock and ensure a smooth landing. Finish as in a parallel Christie by sinking into the knees and ankles, thrusting the heels.

Cornice Jump. As in jumping moguls in the trail, you must bear down hard with the hands, pull up the feet, and relax. Just before you land, drop your feet to absorb the shock.

In deep powder, land with your center of gravity well back.

Steep Terrain and Headwalls

Short, steep places along the trail—sometimes called headwalls—are to be considered not so much special terrain conditions as a state of mind. The skier with some experience should seek them out rather than avoid them. In easy terrain he can get away with sloppy technique. Steep terrain, which reveals every flaw, will help him to perfect his technique.

There are three important things to consider in handling yourself on a steep hill:

1. The planting of your downhill pole to prepare for the turn is extremely important because a firm pole plant acts as a pivot around which you make the turn. Your pole should be planted at the moment you flex your knees (see point 2). The way in which you plant your pole is important: do it by

Geländesprung, or double-pole jump (left), while the gazelle turn is seen at the right.

Making a cornice jump.

For extra steep terrain, you may wish to plant both poles at once; swinging the tails of the skis quickly across the fall line to a wide-angle position where the edges are set. The quick fanning motion of the skis and the hard edge-set means the skis will not gain speed. Both poles are used to aid the unweighting. This helps bring the weight forward at unweighting so the tails of the skis stay in the air for a longer period of time. The tails of the skis travel 45 to 50 degrees in the air. Then they land and continue to slide around to a wide angle with the fall line before they are set. The total amount of displacement is determined by the amount of braking you want. The slower you want to go, the wider the angle from the fall line before each edge set. Step by step:

1. Arms are extended forward in position for planting both poles.
2. Both poles are planted as ski edges are set ready for the unweighting. Knees and ankles are well bent into a position from which to spring up.
3. The poles are carrying some of the weight as the legs have straightened to spring from the snow. The skis are pulled up with bent knees.
4. The skis are back on the snow. The outside pole comes free of the snow before the inside one. The body moves in a down motion.
5. Fanning motion is complete. The arms and poles are again started forward, edge-setting starts.

Practice this procedure on a medium-grade slope with good snow conditions before you try a complete turn with edge set. Then, when you can make edge-set turns in both directions, set slalom poles in a corridor about

throwing your arm forward and laterally down the hill.

2. The flexing of your knees and ankles should be much more exaggerated than on flatter slopes. Only in this way can you set your edges into the hill to make the platform from which to bounce into the coming turn. Skiing on steep slopes is a highly athletic activity: you feel it in the vigorous flexing and unflexing of your legs.

3. Your body angulation—hips pushed uphill, shoulders tipped and facing downhill—is more pronounced on a steep hill. This is because angulation creates edging power and you need more edging power on a steeper hill. Keep your shoulders facing down the hill as you swivel your skis underneath you in the turn.

Headwall skiing.

nine feet wide and try turns within this artificial barrier. When you have mastered this, try tackling a 20-degree slope.

Catwalk Skiing

For most skiers a catwalk results in some embarrassingly awkward maneuvers on skis—muscular holding actions to prevent runaway skis and panic stops in the woods. For a few skiers, a steep, narrow trail or a catwalk is a real "psych-out" situation, causing terror and inability to coordinate. Actually, a catwalk (which is a narrow trail shaped like a gunbarrel cut in half lengthwise) can be mastered to the point where it is swinging fun, if not a groovy ride. Because catwalks can be tricky, however, we advise anyone who has trouble with them to start learning to handle them as a beginner would and work up to the smoother, more elegant turns at your own pace. In any case, since catwalks can vary in shape, width, and snow conditions, it is good to know several methods of skiing them.

A catwalk can be an effective aid to snow-plowing: running up and down the banks, the skis turn practically without effort. Let your skis run in a snowplow across the catwalk toward a high bank. As the tips start to go up the side of the bank, shift your weight to the outside ski. Almost immediately the skis will start to turn and run across the catwalk to go up the other bank. Do not be afraid to let the skis get well up the bank before starting your turn; a positive weight shift will bring a fast change of direction.

Often, attemping to snowplow down the middle of a catwalk makes you feel as if you are doing a spreadeagle on a tightrope. The high banks on each side push back at your skis, restricting your ability to push the tails out to slow your speed. If you lose your braking power, the skis run away from you. To avoid this, let one ski run straight along the crest of the catwalk's bank while the other ski does the plowing in the trough. Because of the shape of the bank, this plowing ski actually runs uphill, adding braking power.

One easy way to get through a catwalk is to sideslip along the bank. Let the tips of

Making a kick turn on a steep slope.

your skis run up the bank until they practically go over the edge. Then sit back slightly to maintain your angle to the slope and put weight on the tails of your skis. From this position you can direct your sideslip and control your speed. Sometimes, however, you cannot slide along the bank because snow snags your ski tips, the bank is the wrong shape, or you simply become tired of sliding. Then you can use stem garlands to negotiate the catwalk. Let your skis slide up the side of the bank, and just before the tips reach the edge, open the skis in a snowplow. As they slide back down into the saucer, bring the skis together and thrust the tails downhill by bending your knees and ankles abruptly. This thrust will slow your speed and send you up the bank again. Repeat these garlands all the way down the catwalk.

Catwalks crowded with skiers are difficult even for experts. One way around this situation is to aim for the side of the catwalk and use the bank to make wedeln garlands. Let your skis slide up the side of the bank, and when the tips reach the edge, sit back slightly and push the tips down toward the fall line. Let them run down for an instant and then bend forward again as you thrust the tails down to turn the skis back up the bank. If

you need to slow your speed even more, use a pronounced edge set at the end of the tail thrust.

The mark of a catwalk master is the ability to wedeln down the middle of it in perfect control. On most catwalks the line down the center is fairly level and even. Use this to make very quick, very tight, linked parallel turns, controlling your speed with strong edge sets after each short turn. The trick of catwalk wedelning is to keep the skis close to the fall line. If they cut across the slope too much, the banked sides will grab the tips and pull you off line. Once you gain rhythm and momentum, you will have it made.

In dealing with unusual ski conditions, it is important not to be discouraged if the first few attempts go haywire. When you consider the amount of practice it took to perfect your turns, you will realize that your adaptation to unusual conditions is not really taking so long. Part of your discouragement and impatience may be the result of thinking that you have mastered ski technique. The grizzled "skimeisters," the true experts, know better. Learning to handle new kinds of snow and terrain conditions is one of the fascinations of the sport. There is always something new to learn.

Four ways to ski a catwalk.

OTHER SKI TEACHING TECHNIQUES

As your skiing time increases and you attend various ski schools, it will soon become apparent that there are techniques and approaches to skiing other than the one to which you have become accustomed or the one just described in this section.

It is important to remember, however, that whatever techniques are labeled—American,

Austrian, French, or Swiss—there is very little difference between them. True they may vary in emphasis on certain aspects of execution, but basically they are similar both in sequence of development (snowplow, snowplow turn, stem turn, etc.) and execution. In fact, the number of truly different ways to ski is extremely limited. This does not invalidate

The skier demonstrates the Austrian technique based on counterrotation.

the many modifications possible. A good instructor is capable of devising an almost unlimited number of ways of getting across to
his skier-student the various maneuvers essential to good skiing in all kinds of snow
conditions and over all types of terrain. But
different approaches do not necessarily mean
different techniques.

Just as a rose by any other name is still a
rose, so in many instances in skiing several
esoteric terms still mean the same thing. Thus
"fersenschub," "heel push," and "heel thrust"
stand for exactly the same type of action,
although in the last few years each, at one
time or another, had a slightly different definition. This "terminology gap" accounts for
many of the arguments among skiers.

There is also confusion between technique
and style. It is a rare discussion of technique
which does not result in someone's citing a
certain picture or movie in which Jean-
Claude Killy or Stein Eriksen "does thus and
so, just like I've been telling you." But style is
individual, much as handwriting is individual.
In many cases the differences between styles
are barely discernible, in others so distinct
that at first glance the writer seems to be
using a different alphabet, or the skier a
"different" or "new" technique.

Technique, on the other hand, can be described either as a distillation of many styles
or as the underlying principles governing
styles. Technique is the field of the scientists
of skiing—physicists, anatomists, and econ-

The skier demonstrates the French system, which uses a modern version of Émile Allais' rotation technique of twenty years ago.

The skier demonstrates the Canadian system that starts with a square stance, reverses at finish.

Unweighting technique of Americans (above), compared to French (below), shows extent to which French move center of gravity when starting to make a parallel turn.

omists of motion—who take into account gravity, incline, resistance of the snow, the momentum and inertia of moving bodies, and the action of skis and poles and then say, "This is what you must do to ski effectively." This does not mean that an unusual stylist cannot make a new contribution to technique. Up to now, the number of true scientists deeply concerned with skiing has been exceedingly small. Much of our present technique has been evolved by trial and error and has reached its current level because of the racers, who are always seeking greater control and precision of turning without sacrificing speed. Today, should a racer win consistently by more than two seconds, movies of his performance would be analyzed down to the twitch of his little finger. But this has risks, too. Is he really doing something different, or is he merely a superior athlete? This the scientists and the coaches of international racers must decide. Appearances can be deceiving, since they are governed by body structure, coordination, and psychological makeup.

Finally, there is the ski school instructor and his problems. The skier cannot afford private lessons from the time he first puts on skis until the time he has mastered every phase of parallel skiing. And even if he could, he does not particularly want to ski at the same place until he has reached this stage.

Hence there is the need for a relatively uniform teaching method based on sound technique. The limitations of the instructor are that he can explain the principles behind certain maneuvers and by example demonstrate their application (usually by exaggeration), but he cannot with complete assurance tell you how to adapt your body to each particular situation, since he cannot feel exactly as you feel. He can help you with exercises, hints, and teaching gimmicks, but in the last analysis, only you can make the adaptation. In other words, you must determine your own style within the limits set by your own anatomy and nervous system and the laws of physics as they apply to skiing.

As was discussed in Section I, ski technique has evolved from the cross-country touring of the Scandinavians and the telemark system of the early Alpinists. Considering their equipment, these old-timers were remarkably skilled sportsmen. Then came Zdarsky, Bilgeri, and Schneider, who brought skiing to the stem Christie stage. In the middle thirties, Toni Seelos's and Émile Allais's French method popularized parallel skiing stressing unweighting, rotation, blocking, and then waiting until another change of direction was desirable. This was perfectly adequate, since most of the skiing of this era was done on open and, by today's standards, relatively uncrowded slopes.

Even as the full implications of the Schneider vs. Allais debate began to reach the public, a few racers were beginning to win slaloms by scratching their backs on the poles. There was talk of *gegenschulter* (reverse shoulder), which meant that the skis turned in one direction while the shoulders turned in the other. World War II slowed this development, but soon after it systematic investigations of this phenomena were made by Professor Stefan Kruckenhauser. The so-called reverse shoulder turn made sense, but not within the framework of the technique then widely in use. Kruckenhauser's contribution was not only in isolating the various aspects of this turn, but in devising a teaching system which would lead up to it in a logical fashion.

After the system was officially introduced at the International Ski Congress in 1955, it swept around the world in prairie-fire fashion, despite criticism that wedeln was fine on billiard-table slopes but would never do on more rugged terrain. What the critics ignored was that wedeln was only one part of the system and that the system as a whole met several needs unvoiced up to that point.

Most important, there was a small but nevertheless sufficient number of recreational skiers with enough skill to be ready for the more sophisticated aspects of the new technique (wedeln); there was a corresponding advance in the development of equipment; and instructors, after a little experience, soon found ways of short-cutting Professor Kruckenhauser's original syllabus. But perhaps more decisive was a reason not originally considered by the New Official Austrian System. Ski resorts were being built on heavily wooded terrain. The trail rather than the open slope was the usual environment of the average skier. Add to this the increase in the number of skiers and the resulting overcrowding, and it becomes clear why short, quick swings down the fall line, the crowning achievement of the system, became not only the prettiest way to ski, but also one of the safest. And since trails rather than open slopes were the usual feature of most American ski areas, it followed logically that the American skier, particularly the eastern American skier, saw the necessity for and the advantages of the Austrian system quicker than his counterparts in the rest of the world.

Actually, the American Ski Technique was based on the Austrian system as developed by Professor Kruckenhauser. At the lower levels of American Technique, as we already know, turns are made by stemming the skis (i.e., pushing the tail of one or both skis out) in order to steer or guide the turn. At the upper levels parallel turns are taught by hopping and skidding.

In the mid-1960's, there were three principal ski teaching systems—Austrian, American, and Canadian—employed in most schools in the United States. In the latter portion of the sixties, however, under pressure from pupils to get them quickly or at least relatively quickly to the beautiful, useful, and desirable (as a status symbol) wedeln turns, new systems have been organized, among them Walter Foeger's *Natur Teknik,* Karl Koller's direct-to-parallel, Ernie Blake's wide-track method, and variations of these at a dozen other areas. Even more impressive is the system of progressing from parallel on short skis to parallel on long skis while learning. This is called the Graduated Length Method (GLM), and was first brought to fruition by Karl Pfeiffer under a research program sponsored by *Ski Magazine.* Let us take a look at some of the more popular systems now in use in North American ski schools, in addition to the most commonly employed American Ski Technique.

Canadian Ski Instructors' Alliance

The Canadian Ski Instructors' Alliance, which was formed in the late 1930's, has a national ski teaching system that is centrally regulated. Because it is not significantly different from the American system, it blends in with the stem and hop-ski approach taught in the United States, and in fact it is used at several ski schools in the eastern United States.

Even with the similarities there have been suggestions of friction between the two North American ski instructors' organizations—until 1969. At that time they held joint annual meetings in Toronto and some headway was made solidifying a *North American Ski Technique.*

The Modern French Method

The French are rugged individualists, and although they have prominent counterrotation advocates in their midst, their national ski school rejects the counterrotational thesis, at least in its fundamental approach to skiing.

The following is a discussion of the "old" French method presented to show how the so-called "new" method evolved from it. This is a compilation of several articles that appeared in the early 1960's.

The French equivalent to the American version of the parallel Christie of the American technique is *Christiania léger,* which translates approximately to "light Christie," "buoyant Christie," or "quiet Christie." It is not a technique in itself. It is a part of the Official Method of the French National Ski School syllabus, a particular form of turn upon which the French method is now based. It is characterized by *projection circulaire,* a distinctive sequence of motion which is used to accomplish the turn. And, as the French are quick to admit, it is not a revolution in ski technique but rather an evolution in instructional method. The astute skier will be quick to recognize certain elements of the *Christiania léger* that are rooted in the earlier concepts of both the classic French and Austrian instructional systems. It is, in a sense, a marriage of these older elements with more recent modifications developed through increased knowledge of the mechanics of skiing, experimentation, and improved modern equipment.

When compared to the Austrian system, the French method is a looser technique, both in organization and in execution. Whereas the Austrians propound a systematic and detailed syllabus, the French pass lightly over the beginning steps, moving their pupils as rapidly as possible to the *Christiania léger* and basing their system almost entirely on its mastery. After a brief introduction to the snowplow as an elementary braking method, the French skip directly to sideslipping, uphill Christies, and the parallel *Christiania léger,* omitting stem turns and stem Christies unless the student's physical makeup absolutely demands it. With mastery of the *Christiania léger* comes a graceful, effortless style of skiing which utilizes the power of the entire body in more natural but equally effective positions. French stance differs radically; hips and shoulders are square across the skis at all times. The comma position and body angulation are conspicuously absent. Movement of the body as a whole unit replaces the static positioning of various parts of the body. Reverse shoulder, perhaps the outstanding characteristic of the Austrian method, has given way to *projection circulaire* with its distinctive rotation-like movement.

The French hasten to point out, however, that *projection circulaire* is not a return to rotation, nor is it rotation in any sense. It is a powerful and almost explosive steering of the entire body with arms and shoulders leading the hips naturally, squarely over the skis, in a single motion preceded by a flexing and extending movement (down-up motion), an unweighting, and a change of edges and lead ski which result in turning of the skis as an automatic consequence. Contrary to appearance, it is not a true rotation, nor is it accompanied by the usual *blocage* necessary to rotational skiing.

The characteristic arm motion of *projection circulaire* already popularized by French racers serves the particular function of aiding the unweighting and triggering the powerful projection of the turn. In the *Christiania léger,* the arm is bent, lifted, and extended forward during the projection phase. The shoulders, hips, and skis move with it, resulting in a rounded carved turn noticeably lacking in the heel thrust and skidding motion common to Austrian turns.

In its entirety, the *Christiania léger* consists of the following phases, performed in sequence:

1. *Flexion.* From a traverse position, squarely over the skis, the knees, hips, and upper body are lowered in a normal down motion and the pole is planted.
2. *Extension.* The body rises to an almost erect position but back remains slightly bent.
3. *Projection circulaire.* The outside arm is bent, lifted, and extended to power the turning of the body and skis as a unit. Weight shifts as lead ski and edges change. Back straightens.
4. *Flexion.* The body is lowered again to finish the turn and to resume the traverse or begin the next turn.

In appearance, the *Christiania léger* is unspectacular and simple. It is, in fact, deceptively simple, for the whole turn must flow smoothly to be most effective. The French warn us that any attempt to rotate the arms in the older sense of the term will result in overrotation and incorrect placement of the weight. Faulty timing or lead change can result in catching the edges. They warn us, too, that contrary to the Austrian dictum, the knees and skis do not remain absolutely together. A slight separation of from 5 to 10 centimeters (2 to 4 inches), depending on terrain and snow conditions, is necessary. The deeper the snow or the more difficult the terrain, the wider the separation.

The French also call our attention to the role played by edge change, weight shift, and change of the lead ski. These all occur in an almost simultaneous action at the start of the projection phase, immediately following the height of the extension. At this point, the outside ski is advanced from 5 to 10 centimeters (approximately 2 to 4 inches), again depending on terrain, conditions, and the speed and radius of the turn. A faster, sharper turn requires slightly more lead than a gentler turn of longer radius. The amount of edging and weight shift required is also affected by these same factors, but the French hold that it will be governed normally as a natural consequence of the other actions.

In explaining the flexion and extension phases, the French stress the point that they can be performed in three varying degrees. The *demi-flexion* and *demi-extension,* most frequently used, produce a moderate amount of body motion (up and down) with an equally moderate turning radius. Less body motion results in a shallower turn, while an accentuated flexion and extension permits a faster, more powerful, and tighter turn. The demi positions, recommended for normal speeds, conditions, and terrain, provide the advantage of holding a degree of power and control in reserve that can be brought into play if needed.

Another interesting factor of the French technique is its recognition of the relationship of weight distribution on the skis to the variations of terrain and conditions. The French designate three running positions. The *position avancée* (advanced), in which the weight is carried ahead of the feet, permits a freedom of the lower body and legs particularly adaptable for quick, tight turns and slalom and for use on steep slopes and good snow. It is recommended for use by better skiers only. For the average skier, the *position intermédiaire* (intermediate), in which the weight rests directly on the feet, is best suited, since it permits use of both the upper and the lower body and can be used in all circumstances. This is the position in which the *Christiania léger* is taught. The *position recul* (backward) rests the weight back on the heels and requires upper body motion for effective maneuvering. Action of the lower body is restricted to stemming motions, and it is therefore used primarily by beginning skiers or in bad snow or unfamiliar terrain. A refinement of this position has been used by French racers in the downhill events, but it is not advised for normal recreational skiing. As a skier's technique advances, he can eventually incorporate these three positions into his repertoire, using them to prepare for changes in conditions or terrain in the same manner in which an automobile driver shifts gears as varied terrain and surfaces require him to alter his speed and caution. The French recommend the intermediate position for normal skiing since, like *demi-flexion* and *demi-extension,* it permits the skier to maintain a reserve for additional control when required.

The French do not claim that theirs is the "only way to ski." In fact, as a skier's skill increases, he frequently incorporates features of the more established techniques into his own style. One of the beauties of the *Christiania léger* is that reverse shoulder can be combined with it at the close of the turn as an aid to faster skiing, sharper turning, and quicker stopping if so desired. French racers, it has been noted, have successfully adopted a combination of several techniques for slalom.

The *Christiania léger,* however, does provide a simple and effective means of skiing for the recreational skier—a natural style, easy to learn, both from its very start or from the current Austrian technique. It is effective in deep snow and can be modified for slalom racing. With the *Christiania léger,* a skier can perform a tight, linked fall-line turn which is what the French term *la godille,* and is the

Unweighting of Austrian technique is a quick light "kick" which leaves some weight on skis as they start to carve.

Gallic version of the Austrian wedeln performed at maximum speed. The French claim that *la godille* is more easily performed by the recreational skier than wedeln.

In 1968, Georges Joubert and Jean Vuarnet published, in France, an updating of the "new" French method in their publication of *Comment se perfectionner à ski*. This book has been translated into English under the title *How to Ski the New French Way*. While rather controversial, this book states flatly that if you want to learn to ski better, you should learn to imitate and master the movements on skis performed by today's top world racers. As previously stated, this is an opinion not necessarily shared by many Austrian and American ski instructors. Joubert and Vuarnet have long held this, however. What gives it new force in the late sixties and early seventies is dominance of world skiing by the French.

Here are some basic concepts, in addition to those already covered, of French *thinking:*

Introduction. An effective movement on ice is not effective in powder, nor is ski technique for a steep slope the same as for a flat slope. It is absurd to learn a single motion on skis and try to apply it to all varying conditions.

Among good skiers emerging from today's ski schools who try racing, three out of four are bothered by the fact that they ski as if their two feet were attached to a single ski. But man is a biped, and he establishes his balance by reacting from one foot to another. Very good skiers and racers maintain a great independence of each leg.

To initiate a turn, the skier can use up-unweighting bounce or down-unweighting.

The essential element is the unweighting of the skis and not the movement which results in the unweighting. In a turn over a bump, unweighting is produced automatically; on some kinds of snow and ice it is altogether unnecessary. The real skier acts according to the friction which he feels between his skis and the snow. Real skiers have a sixth sense, the snow sense.

Feet, legs, and hips are the most important parts of the body in controlling your skis. These are the muscles which generate turning power, rather than any upper body movements. The upper body plays its most essential role in balance. By not using . . . the shoulders and arms . . . in the motor movements of the turn, the skier guarantees maximum balance.

Anticipation . . . is the new essential element of today's ski technique. It is a natural body movement similar to many everyday motions where we precede them by an unconscious anticipatory body movement. To make an ordinary step forward, for example, the body tilts forward first. In skiing the upper body pivots in the direction of the turn about to be initiated.

The Natural Stop. Before ski schools created the idea that formal instruction is indispensable for learning to ski, nine out of ten skiers began by running straight downhill. After a couple of good falls, they learned to stop at the bottom of the hill by turning their skis at right angles across the hill . . . in a natural . . . violent body motion. To do this natural stop turn, your skis should be fairly wide apart, your arms out in front. Pick up a certain amount of speed, then thrust your legs across the hill in a single movement. Then drop down and weight the tails of your skis by lowering your seat.

Steering. Begin by traversing in the natural stop position, ankles, knees and upper body well-flexed, skis apart, full surface of both feet glued to the soles of your boots. In a turn to the right, apply twisting pressure to your left foot. Feel your left knee press to the inside of the turn to control the change of direction. At the same time release pressure from your right foot. The light change of balance makes you tip to the right and helps the left ski to turn, reinforcing the action of your knee. Steering is aided by the shape of the ski: wide at the shovel, narrower under

your foot, flexing in an arc. This type of steered turn in which movement is localized in the legs is very common in skiing. Hidden under ineffective upper body and arm gestures that are often learned with great difficulty, it is a turn commonly used by good skiers and racers.

Anticipation. Supporters of the French method point out that if you have learned to ski under the various other techniques given in ski schools, you will have been taught to initiate a turn by drawing the downhill hand and shoulder ahead to plant the pole so that you start with your upper body facing the tips of your skis. On the contrary, anticipation consists of facing the upper body downhill. This is the position of hundreds of slalom and giant slalom champions photographed at the end of their turns: eyes, heads, and upper bodies already turned in the direction of the next turn, anticipating it.

Anticipation.

Start on top of a mogul. As a result of twisting your upper body downhill in a lowered or flexed stance, your angulation is accentuated (to set the edges). This movement stretches certain lower back muscles. Now, on the rebound (from the edge set), your upper body is supported by your planted pole. You straighten up and these prestretched muscles cause your legs to return into the axis of your upper body: that is to say, they cause your legs and skis to twist in the direction of the turn.

The Jet Turn. You are traversing. Let your skis begin sideslipping and bend your knees lightly to set your edges, planting your downhill pole. You will be thrown into an up-

Turn with anticipation and steering.

motion, and your skis begin turning by themselves without any particular effort on your part as explained above in anticipation. Simply allow your legs to relax supplely into an up-motion and feel your skis lighten. At the end of the up-motion, still supported by your pole plant, feel your legs tend to twist back into the axis of your upper body, drawing your skis into the turn. You can intensify this turning action by steering the outside foot and knee.

The Serpent (Snake) Turn. You have already learned how to do a turn from the top of a mogul by bending the knees and twisting the upper body downhill (anticipation). When you use this method, however, your skis may tend to be unweighted at the beginning of each turn, resulting in sideslipping and insufficient ski-snow contact. A really great skier, in contrast, remains in continual contact with the snow—almost without side-

Jet turn.

slipping. This special ski-snow contact is the result of the Serpent.

Do not attempt to learn the Serpent on anything but an intermediate, bumpy slope. If you already know how to initiate a turn by bending your knees, planting your pole and facing your upper body downhill in the anticipation position, just a few words will introduce you to the Serpent. First, plant the pole earlier in the turn off the mogul.

When your tips are at the top of the bump, get set to perform three movements in harmonious sequence:

1. Plant your pole in the direction in which your upper body is facing, but in doing so, avoid bending forward at the waist.
2. Now, balancing yourself with your planted pole, relax your back muscles and let your upper body bend forward and downhill smoothly in a line passing between your planted pole and your skis.
3. As soon as your body begins to tip forward, bend your knees. Your skis will begin turning very gradually while you continue supporting yourself with your pole.

Once you have learned the Serpent on moguls, you should be able to put it to use on smooth slopes to replace the rebound with its time-consuming up-unweighting. First, link a few tight turns together, each one punctuated by a sharp edge set. Now, instead, try to start one of these turns with the Serpent. Your upper body should be facing downhill and your pole planted as if you were ready to rebound upward from the edge set. Instead, suddenly relax your back muscles and bend your knees. Your upper body will drop forward and you will feel your skis pull progressively into the turn without losing contact with the snow. With practice, the edge set should be reduced almost to zero. At the completion of the turn, stand upright and well balanced. To link up Serpent Turns, plant your pole again, let your upper body drop, bend your knees, and the next turn begins without the slightest bounce as your skis roll smoothly and briefly onto—then off—their edges without an edge setting.

On bumps or ruts, the Serpent Technique enables you to remain in permanent contact with the snow. Legs flexed at the top of the mogul, upright in the dip, you hardly feel the

Classic serpent turn.

unweighting or compression caused by the bumpy terrain. Your legs fold up under you, while the relaxation of your upper body absorbs any shock. At high speeds, you will feel something new happening on bumps or ruts: you are on your way to discovering *Avalement.*

Avalement. Avalement contradicts one of the most sacred tenets of skiing that dates back to the earliest days of the sport. This is the belief that the skier should concentrate on getting his weight forward almost all of the time. But in avalement, a technique designed for skiing and turning at high speed on bumpy terrain, the skier actually sits back for a split second. That is, the skier absorbs or "erases" the bump by retracting his legs under himself. His upper body is relaxed and anticipates the coming turn by inclining down the hill on a line between his skis and his pole, which is planted far out to the side. Having absorbed the top of the bump, his legs then unfold to keep the skis in contact with the snow on the down-side of the bump. Instead

of exerting a vertical thrust on the edges to make the skis turn, he makes them bite with a forward thrust of the feet. This technique makes use of the flex and curved side of the ski to carve the turn and minimize sideslip. In absorbing the bump, the skier's body follows the straightest, most economical path through the turn. Used in slalom racing, this means valuable split seconds cut from the racer's time.

The French word *avalement* literally means "swallowing" and refers to the folding action of the skier's legs as they swallow up irregularities in the terrain. Avalement, however, is not really translatable, and like the German ski terms—*wedeln* and *geländesprung*—it seems destined to become incorporated in the American skier's lexicon in its original French form.

The S-turn. This turn is a refinement of the avalement and is the accepted final form by ski school classicists. To make the S-turn, start a descending traverse on an average slope. Build up some speed. Now cut straight

The French avalement.

across the hill at right angles to the fall line. When you feel your skis, especially your downhill ski, cutting into the snow, bend your knees slightly, then straighten up. Now, pull your legs up and your skis forward with your abdominal muscles. This straightening movement is what makes it possible to unweight your skis by avalement.

In order to understand the true movement, think of jumping an obstacle while holding both feet together. First, you must straighten your body from a slightly low position. Then, you tuck your knees up in order to clear the obstacle. Your upper body and head go forward, and your hips go back. You then straighten up in order to land without shock by compressing your body once again. This movement is analogous to a prejump, or *optraken,* and it also applies in unweighting by avalement. In each case, it is necessary to straighten up from a low position, thus weighting the skis, in order subsequently to

unweight them by pulling your thighs upward and pushing your feet forward.

As you weight the skis again in order to start the turn, you must settle onto the tails. You will find it very easy to start the turn by making your skis carve with the tails. Later, when you are fully familiar with the S-turn, you will no longer have to *make* the skis turn.

What happens, in effect, is a dynamic unfolding of upper- and lower-body tensions that create the pivot or start of the turn. The upper body twists in the direction of the oncoming turn (anticipation). This twisting action builds a tension, or desire to turn, in the legs. The unweighting of avalement releases the pressure of the skis on the snow and permits the legs to start the skis turning. The actual unweighting of avalement is accounted for by the drop of the upper body and a pulling-up of the thigh muscles when the skier goes from a straightened position to the characteristic sitting position of avale-

Here the skier is seen executing turns by avalement from two perspectives.

ment. In effect, the dropping of the body mass momentarily suspends the weight or pressure of the skis on the snow.

When settling with the hips over the tails of your skis at the beginning of the turn, use strong angulation and bend forward from the waist. This will give you stability and the correct amount of weight distributed to the tails of the skis, particularly on your outside ski, which is used as a rudder to describe a perfectly carved turn. However, do not sit back throughout the turn. In the middle, when you reach the fall line, your knees should press forward and your ankles should bend, though not excessively.

In order to return to a traverse and start another S-turn, push your feet forward under your body and remain in an angulated position. Here again you will feel the pressure shift to the tails of your skis, which will finish the turn without sideslipping.

The originality of the S-turn derives from the track it leaves on the snow, traced by an uphill climb of the skis just before the initiation of the turn. Actually, the very advanced skier performs the "pure" S-turn without sideslipping. Through the traverse, as well as at the beginning, middle, and end phases of the turn, he cuts a track no wider than his two closely parallel skis. On hard snow and ice only the edges of the carving skis leave two thin carving tracks. On soft snow, by using his edges as little as possible, the skier can keep his skis almost flat on the snow. In powder he can use the same movement while preventing any sideslipping of the skis; the result is a smooth, narrow track.

The S-turn's essential advantages to the skier are greatly enhanced beauty and efficiency in turning. It introduces the skier to the advantages of starting a turn by avalement: (1) the edges hold better from the very start of the turn; (2) the weight shifts onto the tail of the outside ski, which is applied quickly and very early in the turn; (3) the end of the turn is easily rounded, minimizing sideslipping.

Another advantage of the S-turn is to prevent development of a false avalement, which you have probably seen in skiers trying to imitate racing stars. These racing skiers take the bumps in a kind of permanent crouch. Their imitators constantly pull their thighs upward and push their feet forward, hardly ever straightening up. In fact, they seem unable to straighten. They do not understand that straightening to weight the skis is necessary if the skier subsequently is to unweight them with avalement. The advantage of the S-turn is that it leads to a true avalement.

Of course, the stiff tails and somewhat softer forebodies of the new skis go hand in hand with the new French ski method. Because of this flex pattern, the skier can use avalement to apply pressure to the tails of the skis. Using the skis in this way allows the racer greater speed, the good skier greater ability to arc and carve the turn, and the power buff greater ease of turning.

The Austrian System

As previously stated, the present Austrian and American methods of learning to ski are very much alike. Thus, in comparison with the French method, we will use the parent technique—the Austrian System. As indicated with the French method, we now show how the "new" Austrian system evolved.

It is possible to show the basic differences between these techniques without going into the detailed refinements and scientific rationalizations which have been made, primarily in camera studies, of both techniques. But to begin with, let us be sure of our terms. In the profusion and confusion of names— "Austrian," "wedeln," "short-swing," "modern," etc.—the simplest way to distinguish these schools in the Alps is this: by "Austrian system" one means reverse shoulder, the skiing characterized by the torso turned toward the outside of the turn and by heavy "body English." This is the only method used in Austria or anywhere in the Alps except in France.

The difference is primarily one of upper body position and kinetics. It is a fundamental difference, but there are many points of concurrence between the two systems. An Austrian can learn the French system in a few hours and thereafter switch back and forth at will. Oddly, when the French "wedeln," they combine the two systems, some body English, some shoulder lead, some bend at the waist, and a wide-open and high arm position. It is a highly interesting movement and one from which a new direction of technique growth could well appear.

The Austrian system is a muscular system. The body is coiled, tightly controlled, tensed. A certain amount of strength is required to hold this position and to drive over the skis, to charge into turns and through them. Some of the merits of the technique rest in this coiled stance, however, for a tensed, rigidly controlled body often reacts more quickly and more precisely than a relaxed, fully extended body. There is a great power in this position, and coupled with good legs, it is fast and sure. On the other hand, one of the obstacles encountered in learning to ski is the insufficient leg strength of beginners who lack the necessary muscle power and coordination. A system which places unnecessary demands on muscular strength will necessarily be less suitable for the occasional skier and the beginner than one in which strength is secondary.

The French system might be termed, for lack of a better term, "dynamic," balanced. Its more erect stance is easier to hold, and its substitution of mechanical techniques to throw the weight forward and hold the skis together for the Austrian muscular techniques further diminishes the demands for strength in this system. Both techniques work perfectly, of course.

The differences between the methods can be illustrated by considering four of the basic elements of a skiing turn: the weighting of the outside ski, the movement of the weight forward on the ski, the "slip" of the turn, and the holding of the skis parallel.

Both systems weight the outside ski of a turn by body position. In the Austrian turn the weight is leaned out over the ski. Stand with your feet together, rotate your body until your shoulders face to one side, and lean to that side. Your weight will ride to your outside foot. It works, of course, and the excellence of Austrian racers is a testimony to how well it works. In the motion of a turn there is a certain naturalness about this position, too, for as one reaches forward to "pike" into a turn, the body moves at least partly into this Austrian "windup." The Austrian freezes into this position, accents it, and rides it through the turn. It forces his weight onto his outside ski.

There are important advantages to this

position, apart from the general one of being coiled. The position does not change through the turn. One rides the turn through with the knees and the pelvis and ends in the traversing position without further body motions. It is a simple technique, with the merit of simple things, ease of accomplishment, and small chance for error. Another advantage is that angulation forces the knees to bend, and that deeper knee bend together with the coiled body provide the surest possible footing to handle unexpected patches of ice or heavy snow. Good skiers of all systems tend to move onto this "open" stance, with the downhill shoulder pulled back, for long, difficult traverses, and the French ski schools teach the position unblushingly for that situation.

The "slip" in the Austrian turn is introduced by leaning the body over the outside ski and pushing downhill with the heel. It is an efficient method, and control is exact if performed properly.

A weakness of the Austrian system is that the "wind up" for the turn tends to pull the weight back on the heel. To keep forward at this point, the Austrian-taught skier must exert real effort. As one approaches a turn in the coiled Austrian traverse, one must "unwind" and "wind up" the other direction. With advance skiers this "rewind" does not really occur until the turn is half made, until the skis turn out from under the skier's shoulders. But this approach to a turn is a point of serious difficulty for beginners. It is a question of kinetics and coordination, of judging when to begin "unwinding," how far to swing, where to move the weight, and how much to "rewind." The whole process strongly encourages the skier to stem. In sorting out the motion, shifting the weight, reversing the shoulder, his weight will ride on the heel of his outside ski, pushing it away from the other in an involuntary stem. At the most delicate point of a parallel turn, the shift of edges, he is in motion and out of balance. Because of this complication, the transition from stem turns to pure parallel turns is invariably a difficult state for skiers learning Austrian technique.

How about the French technique, then? How does it meet the demands for ski weighting, forward weight, "slip," and holding the skis parallel?

In the French turn the skis are not allowed to turn out from beneath the shoulders. The outside arm and shoulder are carried through the turn to lead the rest of the body, and the skier's torso is aimed in the direction of his travel all the time. In effect, the French skier throws his outside arm forward as he goes through a turn. He stands considerably more erect, and his body English is only slight if at all. The movement completely alters the dynamics of the turn.

When one throws anything—a rock, a baseball, a fist—the body weight is carried forward onto the foot underneath the throwing arm. It is almost impossible to prevent this from happening. When the skier throws his arm forward through his turn, his weight falls on his outside ski. Furthermore, such are the mechanics of throwing, his weight rides forward onto the toe of that foot. What the Austrian accomplishes by leaning out over his ski and by consciously forcing his weight forward the French accomplish with a single movement of the shoulder and the arm. The arm moves the weight not just to the proper leg, but forward on the ski. The whole body of the Frenchman rides behind that motion, and he is placed up over his skis effortlessly, balanced and relaxed.

The same movement provides him his "slip," and again with automatic ease. Because his weight is thrown forward there is no skid out at the end of his turn. Because the arm throw is a kind of semi-side-arm motion, the leg is swung naturally into the slide. Throw side-armed and your foot pivots out at the heel. It works on skis as well as off of them.

Finally the motion of the arm and shoulder in the French turn throws the skier into an automatic bank. That bank, coupled with the forward weight derived from the arm throw, pulls the legs together. One cannot bank with the legs apart, and one cannot evade the automatic bank that develops in the French turn. Once again the system has substituted natural body coordination for what the Austrians achieve by muscles and somewhat against body inclinations. In the French turn the skis ride automatically together, and learning skiers in France fall into parallel turns with ease.

Both the Austrian and French schools have their own merits. Elements of the Austrian position with its precision and control are unavoidable for slalom, but on the other hand the use of arms and shoulders by current slalom stars is far from the extreme wedeln school. For that matter, one might note that the styles of competition skiers have about as much relation to those of pleasure skiers as driving a Maserati has to driving a Volkswagen.

Professor Kruckenhauser of Austria introduced the wide track at the International Congress of Ski Instructors, Interski, at

A snowplow turn in new Austrian wide-track learning sequence.

In the wide-track system, as soon as the pupil has learned to make a small snowplow turn, he is taught to step the inside ski alongside the outside ski in a quick turn out of the fall line, as seen above.

Aspen in the spring of 1968. In wide track the skis are held apart for better balance and the beginning turns are stepped instead of steered as in the American technique. The student thinks more about what his legs and feet are doing than about how the upper body is angled or moves.

This so-called new Austrian wide-track ski system bypasses, alters, or telescopes several of the snowplow and stem phases of progression that have characterized traditional Austrian and American ski instruction in the past. Most exciting of all, it changes wedeln —hitherto the final, advanced goal of the recreational skier to be reached after parallel—into a simple, stepped, fall-line exercise which the intermediate can learn long before he masters the long curve of the standard parallel turn.

In modern physics, new observations of the world around us cry out for new concepts to explain them. The changed world of skiing, too, in recent years had cried out for new explanations. Skis have been changed to start turning earlier in the turn. Higher, stiffer boots multiply the skier's power to edge his skis. Ski hills now are riven with deep moguls that leave little room for turning. On other hills, there is such heavy skier traffic or so little width as to make it impossible to do long parallel turns. Thus, the new ski equipment makes possible, and the terrain itself demands, a quick, short turn that the relatively new skiers can master right away.

Hitherto, the prime obstacle to early learning of short-swing turns has been the preoccupation of many skiers and ski schools with the beauty of skiing with feet held tightly together. Short swing, or wedeln with skis held tightly together, however, is a turn

In a totally new version of the traditional stem Christie, the skier crosses the hill in a wide-track position in readiness for the turn. The lower ski is pushed downhill. This creates a platform from which the skier can step off quickly and place the ski alongside the outside ski as he enters the fall line. (In figure 2, note the anticipation of the upper body in the direction of the oncoming turn.) Momentum carries the skier around the turn in a wide-track, skidding action. As soon as this is completed, the next turn is started. Linking of the turns is important because it introduces the pupil to rhythm, which is so essential to the ensuing wedeln.

for the expert. As a result, wedeln has been taught as the ultimate stage of ski school progress—after ordinary parallel.

Wedeln executed with wide track is another story. Kruckenhauser has found that a rough, open stance turn of this kind can be performed after only a few days on skis—possibly less time, depending on athletic ability. It is, he believes, a useful turn. It enables the skier, at an early stage, to get out onto terrain and lifts which previously he could not master. Therefore, because it is a useful turn, it deserves to be learned before some of the more polished turns. The result: with wide track, skiers are taught to wedeln before they parallel.

A system that sounds like GLM, while employing the feet-apart stance of the new Austrian teaching, is being used by Ernie Blake at Taos, New Mexico. This system, in "Blakese," is a "desanctification of the ski instructor. Instructors like to show off, but we

In simple wide-track garland exercise here, the pupil learns to push the downhill ski out while traversing across the hill. The aim here is to accustom the skier to the action of stepping off from the downhill or inside ski to initiate the turn. It should be repeated across a wide slope in both directions.

Here it is—a skis-apart, wide-track step wedeln performed down the fall line after only a few days of skiing, sooner if the pupil is on five-foot skis.

know they do not need to hang out there like so many Polynesian outriggers."

Blake's students use four-foot skis for the first day, then five-footers for three days, and their own longer skis on the fifth day, when they also learn stem turns. During the early phases they keep feet wide apart, step around to turn, and generally stand on skis in a relaxed way, according to Blake. He says the wide stance is so secure that it overcomes the fear that many students have, and the stepping produces an emphatic weight transfer which is valuable later on.

Graduated-length Method (GLM)

The most widespread and uniform of the new teaching systems is the Graduated-length Method, in which skiers start on two-and-a-half- or three-foot skis, move on to four-footers, five-footers, and finally to their own longer skis, all within one week of ski instruction.

GLM got its start in 1966 as a cooperative experiment between *Ski Magazine* and Vermont's Killington ski area, where former ski school director Karl Pfeiffer became so convinced after the one-year trial that he incorporated GLM as part of his regular teaching program. He bought more and better short skis, and today GLM constitutes a major portion of ski week business for Killington and several other ski resorts who offer it. In fact, during the high season reservations are necessary to join GLM classes. As a rule, however, there is no weekend GLM program because people cannot learn enough in one or two days of class lessons to ski without an instructor's supervision.

Clif Taylor of Squaw Valley, California, developed and refined the short ski technique in 1960. The following year he wrote his book *Ski in a Day,* and his program was under way. Skiers found that in Taylor's school the first thing you learn is to *slow down by making turns.* (In the standard school, you are taught to slow down by making the snowplow.) They learned to make turns the easy way, standing in place, on the flat. There was no hill to contend with until they learned how to swivel the skis, using the modern (Austrian) body movement. With Taylor and his instructors out front showing how, the beginners were soon *twisting* their little two-and-a-half-foot skis left, and then right, in a rhythm: left-right-left. From there, the novice skier, within an hour of first putting on the skis, actually skied down the hill turning left-right-left in short turns.

In the next two days under GLM, skiers abandon their two-and-a-half-footers for rented four-footers and then go on to five-foot skis. They may still use the "twist-turn" they learned the first day. In a three-day weekend, they can "graduate" to near-normal-length skis and can ski with more control than if they had started out on long skis.

Actually, the present-day Graduated-length Method is based on swiveling (twisting) the skis, rather than stemming, stepping, or hopping. Most ski school directors say they want their graduates to learn to stem the skis *after* they finish the week on short skis, and then as a safety measure for handling uneven terrain and difficult situations. The key is that GLM students are not learning from the beginning a stemming movement, which later they will consciously have to unlearn. They have no difficulty learning to stem after a GLM week, however.

There are some who claim a lower accident rate among GLM skiers, but this has not been proved. Certainly there seems to be less chance for skis to cross if they are shorter and are kept parallel. And people who are not in top physical condition have a chance to develop muscles by working up from smaller, lighter skis to longer, heavier ones.

Comparison of Ski Systems

The trend-setting programs that are most popular at ski schools throughout North America are (1) the modified American technique; (2) the Austrian schwups method; and (3) the graduated-length method (GLM). Actually, all three systems are based on the American technique—that is, they use the maneuvers and sequences of the American technique when they fit into the learning progressions. The difference is in emphasis: the old American system stresses the idea of perfecting maneuvers such as snowplow and stem turns, while the newer systems simply touch on these and move quickly on to the real goal —parallel skiing.

The most widespread and uniform of the new teaching systems is the graduated-length method, in which skiers start on two-and-a-half or three-foot skis, move on to four-footers, five-footers, and finally their own skis, all generally within one week of ski instruction. As a rule there are few weekend GLM programs, because people cannot learn enough in one or two days of class lessons to ski without an instructor's supervision. As previously stated, the new Austrian and American methods of learning to ski are very much alike. The former, frequently called the Austrian wide-track system, bypasses, alters, or telescopes several of the snowplow and stem phases of progression of the American technique into a class of turns called *schwups*. But as shown in the following table, all three widely used teaching systems cover all the basic skills of skiing in about the same length of time.

Ski Learning Programs

Modified American	Austrian Schwups	GLM
First 2-Hour Lesson (3-foot skis)		
Straight running Snowplow	Straight running Snowplow	Straight running Skate from straight run
Basic snowplow turns	Basic snowplow turns	Turns out of fall line
		Short and long turns
		Wide-track turns with hop
		Use of lift
Second 2-Hour Lesson (3-Foot Skis)		
Linked snow- plow turns	Linked snow- plow turns	Repeat and re- fine first les- son work
Traverse	Wide-track schwups turns out of the fall line	
	Use of the lift	
Third 2-Hour Lesson (5-Foot Skis)		
Stem turns	Linked schwups turns	Traverse
Sideslip		Uphill christies
Uphill christies		Turns out of the fall line

Proper stance for twisting in place as shown by Cliff Taylor. In step one, knees and hips are slightly bent; weight centered over the boots no farther forward than ball of foot. Bindings on short skis should be placed so that the ball of the foot falls over the center of the running surface of the skis. With your weight centered over the skis (do not lean forward over the tips), twist the skis clockwise, as in the pictures above. At the same time, twist your arms and shoulders in the opposite direction. The skis should move about a quarter of a full turn in the snow, then are reversed and twisted back in the direction from which they came. Arms and shoulders compensate with an opposite twist, clockwise this time. The pattern is left-right-left and should be done in a continuous movement, until you have worked up a smooth rhythm, as in the well-known dance step.

Modified American	Austrian Schwups	GLM	Modified American	Austrian Schwups	GLM
Third 2-Hour Lesson (5-Foot Skis)			**Fifth 2-Hour Lesson (Regular-Length Skis)**		
Stem turns with some sliding at the end		Wide-track linked turns holding poles	Stem christies with poles	Stem wedeln with poles	Traverse
Use of the lift			Elementary wide-track parallel turns	Wide-track parallel turns	Uphill christies
					Parallel turns out of the fall line with poles
Fourth 2-Hour Lesson (5-Foot Skis)					Wide-track parallel turns
Snowplow christies	Schwups turn garlands	Repeat and review previous lesson			
Stem christie garland	Stem wedeln	How to use poles			
Beginning stem christies					
Stem christies					

Skiers taking ski weeks are taught maneuvers in approximately this order. An advantage of the American system is that students can readily transfer from one ski school to

After you are able to twist in place in an even rhythm, without losing your beat, so to speak, then you are ready to try the same thing going down the hill. Step two involves almost exactly the same movements as step one. The skier moves down the slope, twisting his skis from side to side, and the result is a series of smooth S-turns. In the picture at top left, Taylor is twisting his ski tips counterclockwise and his shoulders and arms are moving slightly clockwise to compensate. In the next photograph, Taylor has completed this swivel, and in the third photograph, the momentum of the arms and shoulders is being transferred to the skis to help pull them into the next turn. Taylor reverses the swing of the skis by twisting them clockwise while he swings his arms and shoulders counterclockwise to compensate, bottom picture, as he makes the second turn. The twist motion causes the skis to edge, the weight to shift, and the lead of the skis to change almost automatically.

another, but proponents of GLM claim that students almost instinctively learn to stem skis for safety during their practice time, which should permit them to attend other ski schools. Those students who practice regularly between lessons and have good coordination should be able to do rudimentary parallel turns with feet apart on an easy slope by the end of the fifth lesson. From this point it is up to the individual to practice and take lessons at regular intervals.

This is where the student who has been following one system can switch to another method for additional help and new ideas. Most students should be doing stem christies with pole action by the fifth lesson in the American system, but much depends on such

factors as snow conditions. Many instructors feel that skiers in the East and Midwest are more intense about learning to ski and prefer a systematic, structured approach. Class attitude, they say, is also a factor; enthusiastic groups advance faster in any system.

Controversy, however, has not ended in the world of ski instruction. Future disputes, while apparently ended on the subject of final forms, more likely will center on the best and quickest teaching methods to bring learning skiers up to the level of parallel and wedeln. Such controversies are critical in tourist-oriented nations like Austria, where the method of ski teaching can be a factor in attracting vacationing foreign skiers. What a ski school teaches is a factor in affecting

American and Canadian skiers' choices of ski areas to patronize.

Ski Schools

What motivates a skier's desire to learn? It is obvious what brings the beginner to ski school. To begin skiing without instruction is dangerous because of lack of knowledge as to where and what to practice. It is common on weekends to see a beginner struggling for a couple of hours trying to get down a hill that he got up in ten minutes by chairlift. Such beginners often are misled by a friend or a ski movie, or they are just trying to do what the others skiers seem to be doing. When this happens two dangers arise: first, there is a possibility of injury from falling, and second, the person is discouraged from continuing to ski.

In early days it was necessary for a beginner to hike to the top of a hill to ski down. This gave him a chance to improve his skiing ability as his climbing ability improved. Today, with gondolas, a person can carry his skis to the top, put them on, and try to ski down.

Because of the obvious hazards, one would tend to think that ski schools primarily teach beginners. In some areas this is true, but the average student in ski schools is in the advanced stem Christie and parallel classes. One of the reasons for this is that it requires very few lessons to reach the stem Christie levels, but practice and instruction are essential to meet the challenge of skiing parallel on changing snow conditions and on steeper terrain. The skiers developing toward this challenge are the ones who come to ski schools.

There are other reasons for taking ski lessons. One important one is for the sociability. It is fun and stimulating to ski with people of the same ability or just slightly better. You can improve your skill by trying to do the maneuvers which a better skier is doing. In learn-to-ski weeks you are placed with the class of skiers nearest your ability for five to seven days. With this concentrated skiing time you can make considerable progress and gain friends of similar abilities.

Lessons also provide the safest and fastest way to explore an area which you may be skiing for the first time. The instructor can give you tips on the snow conditions and can tell you which runs are best for your level of skiing.

One very important lesson for a skier of any level is to warm up to start a new season. We find at the beginning of each season it is necessary to review the basic principles and renew the feeling of leaning forward. Each year it takes a couple of days of skiing to get back to the stride of the previous year. Again, the advise of the instructor will shorten the time necessary for review.

Ultimately, every experienced skier asks: How much instruction is enough? First, you must understand that the rate of learning varies not only with the individual but also in the individual. Progress in the first levels tend to be uniform, but it becomes uneven as the student advances. One tends to level off for a period of time, showing very little progress. Then there may be a sharp jump to a higher level, followed by a leveling off for a period of time. During the stages of the level period one may have good and bad days. These are caused by snow conditions, visibility, even your temperament for that day.

Again, the role of the instructor helps in shortening the time on these plateaus. Seldom is there a student on a level whom the instructor cannot help to move upward. The advancements tend to get harder and require more time as the skier improves. It is like trying to lower your golf score when you already play in the 80's. As in golf, progress in skiing is faster in the beginning stages. To get into the class of the top 10 or 15 per cent requires time. Sometimes the individual's goal may be too high for his circumstances. Never forget that skiing can and should be enjoyed at all levels. You may have perfection in mind, but more important are safety, stability, and maneuverability—then work on progress.

A typical ski school operation offers both group and private lessons. Group lessons last about two hours and usually begin at 10 A.M. and 2 P.M. Costs range around $4 for a lesson, although discounts can be obtained by buying ticket books—eight lessons for $24, for example. Learn-to-ski weeks also lower lesson costs through package instruction plans. The size of a group can vary according to the number of customers and instructors.

Half a dozen pupils is considered ideal. A dozen is a maximum. Any more create problems in learning. Private lessons are usually priced on the basis of one instructor and one pupil for one hour: $10 and up. Each additional pupil, to the limit of three, may cost $5 more. A private lesson for a half-day can cost $20, a full day $40. Although expensive, private instruction has its values because the teaching is direct and concentrated and a better safeguard against the learning of bad habits. On the other hand, however, the organization of ski instruction into ski schools and ski classes is a reflection of a single psychological fact: that at least seven out of ten of us will learn better in a group than alone. A ski school class harnesses the competitive spirit of individuals. It permits you to observe others making the same mistakes that you are. This helps both to soothe your ego and to solve your problems because you can *see* what you are doing wrong, by watching others make the same mistake.

If you want to take a lesson, the ski school desk or the ski school house can easily be located at the ski area. Do not make the mistake of buying an all-day lift ticket before signing up for class. You may not need to use the lift for your lessons, or you may find out that the lift charges are included in the ski lesson. So, go to the ski school desk first.

Do not try to bluff your way into a more advanced class than you belong to. Answer the questions of the ski school honestly. If you do not understand the technical terms, simply say so. The ski school meeting place is usually well marked. Each spot in the meeting place is assigned to a different class. The international class system usage marks spots with letters:

A—*Beginner:* walking, straight running, climbing, straight snowplow.
B—*Snowplow:* snowplow turns, traversing.
C—*Stem turn:* sideslipping, Christie uphill.
D—*Stem Christie:* snowplow Christie, beginning stem Christie, advanced stem Christie.
E—*Parallel:* Christie from fall line, hop Christie, parallel Christie, parallel with check.
F—*Wedeln*

On busy days, many ski schools have to run several classes under the same letter. The school will then use figures to identify different levels within the class. So if you find yourself in B-1, you probably have yet to learn the snowplow. If you are in B-2, you are in the second level of class B, and you very likely know how to make a snowplow turn and have begun to manage a traverse.

On behavior: make sure you are on time. Nobody is going to wait for you. It is no fun to chase your class over half a mountain. The instructor will make sure that the group stays together on the slope. As long as you are with your teacher, you will not have to wait in the lift line.

To get your money's worth, pay attention to the demonstration and explanation of the instructor. Concentrate, but do not get all tied up in a knot. Free, relaxed movements are more important than sheer muscle power. You will find your teacher patient and understanding; he knows what you are trying to do. You may have heard or read about the so-called "natural" way to ski. In the beginning there simply is no "natural way." How can you make a natural movement when you are standing on an incline with the floor going out from under you? As in every other sport, it takes time, practice, and good solid instruction.

The ski instructor also knows the conditions in the area, and he will try to provide you with the best skiing available. You simply cannot struggle against bad snow conditions and still learn much. For the very same reason, you should ski on easy slopes after the lesson is over. While skiing easy slopes, try to work on the maneuvers you learned. Then move on to steeper trails or more difficult snow.

Skiing in class means skiing at slow speeds, under control. The ski instructor will not ask you to attempt exercises that you are not ready for. Since every major maneuver or "final form" can be divided into parts, and since any known exercise may be used to teach you these parts, ski lessons will be varied.

No two teachers will use exactly the same method. The ski instructor is free to use whichever path to "technique" he feels is needed, according to the individual student and to the snow conditions. This keeps ski instruction challenging not only for the pupil but also for the instructor. Also remember that different personalities do exist. One instructor may be fine for a pupil, while the pupil's wife would just as soon take lessons from another. This is usually no problem. Most ski school directors are quick to recognize this fact. Instructor A "gets through" to Pupil B, but not to Mrs. B. "I do not know what he is saying," she may comment. She should by all means try Instructor C.

Because of an association known as the Professional Ski Instructors of America, a skier can be assured of receiving *fairly* uniform instruction no matter where he goes in the United States—that is, if he takes his lessons from one of the more than 2,000 instructors who have passed the rigorous certification course of their regional instructor association and are *certified*.

What does "certified" mean? It signifies that the instructor is approved or qualified. He has taken an examination and met a high standard of ability. However, it has not always been that way. The movement toward certification took a long time (see Section I). Before World War II, there were many self-styled instructors. Ski instruction in some areas earned a bad reputation. But this changed to a degree when the U.S. Eastern Amateur Association established examination standards for would-be instructors in 1938. After the war, with the U.S. Forest Service in the ski business because of their leasing of lands in many areas, USFS encouraged some type of certification procedure. Finally, in the 1950's a Utah instructor named William Lash and several others advocated a high national standard which led to the establishment of the Professional Ski Instructors of America, Inc., in 1960.

To be certified, a would-be instructor must pass a certification examination in which he must demonstrate his form, run a slalom, and show how to teach a class. There is also a written test in this day-long exam. To take this certification examination, a would-be instructor must also have an advanced first aid card and have a knowledge of ski history, map reading, race-course setting, and—in some areas—even avalanche control and ski mountaineering. Actually, there are slightly different conditions and exams in the eight divisions across the United States. The reason is quite obvious: You would not expect the same approach to teaching from an Eastern instructor who copes with a 600-foot-long hill, as from one in, say, Colorado, who teaches in a steep, rock-bordered, 3-mile-long canyon.

How are would-be instructors graded? In one typical region, a student-teacher who wishes to become an associate instructor must have 12 to 15 points out of a possible 20. (An associate is allowed to teach, but he also is expected to try to become fully certified. Not all regions have associate instructors.) A certified instructor needs from 16 to 20 points. The exam is not easy, and a high percentage of would-be instructors fail each year. In addition, to remain an instructor, he must attend a clinic every two years.

TEACHING CHILDREN TO SKI

Each season, more and more families are flocking to the slopes. Children can be taught to ski and enjoy it as much as any adult. Over the past few years, the need to keep children of all ages happily occupied at ski centers has become very acute. Major areas have replied to this demand by installing nurseries for the "wee ones" and children's classes for youngsters aged four and over. These children's classes should not be identified with regular ski school, but thought of, rather, as "play school on skis," where the instructor uses his ingenuity and colorful props to capture the imagination of the children. The youngsters respond quickly, following their leader around and thus learning to handle their skis in a playful and enjoyable way.

Skiing has much to offer a child. To be out of doors, playing in the snow, being warm and dry despite the cold, and going faster than he ever thought possible—no amusement park, television, or other game can offer such a thrill. The child's motive is simply *it is fun*. Take away the fun, and the most determined parent or the best teacher cannot make him learn. He will ski only if he enjoys it.

Parents who want their children to ski should put aside dreams of eventual Olympic glory, and if possible, put them in a ski class before they lose patience. (Losing patience seems to be the inevitable result of trying to be both parent and teacher.)

The child should always be warm and dry, and on skis he can manage—usually no taller than the child. A good age to start is before he is two, for as soon as a child can walk, he can walk on skis. Faced with snow up to his knees—say five or six inches—he finds that skis are easier than feet. For this reason a child of two is apt to be a more persistent skier than he will be two or three years hence.

When he is ready for ski school (or parents are running out of patience), he should know how to cope with bathroom problems, or if he does not, one of the parents should watch from a discreet distance, ready to take him. A preschooler's mother who is not sure if her offspring will last should wait, too, just as she would at nursery school.

Children exposed to bad weather and snow conditions become quickly discouraged. Ski lessons, therefore, though intent on keeping to a two-hour schedule, are sometimes cut after one hour for a short trip to the restaurant. Hot chocolate or ice cream puts new enthusiasm into children, and the outdoor activities can then be continued for the second hour, unless the children show signs of weariness. Remember that children are different from adults in their reactions to the ski environment. When a child says he is cold, believe him. A small child's skin area is more than twice as great as an adult's, relative to body weight and volume. His heat loss is tremendous. He makes up for it, partly, by a higher rate of metabolism, but this also means that when he feels tired, he is on the brink of exhaustion. A child cannot warm up by more activity as an adult can. He should go indoors promptly, preferably in front of a fire with something hot to drink, for he is sensitive to cold in a special way. For him, cold registers as pain, sometimes quite intense.

Compared with an adult, a child's arms and legs are proportionately shorter, his center of gravity is lower, and his muscles are thicker relative to the bone structure. He also has better padding, his joints contain more

cartilage, and his tendons are more flexible. All this works to his advantage when he gets on skis. He has not far to fall, and when he does he has not much momentum. His legs are not long enough or thin enough to get tangled up. Skis of the proper length produce almost no leverage in any direction, and his flexible joints will give, even at extreme angles, with no discomfort. With a class of children, the instructor almost never has to say, "Don't do that, you will hurt yourself." It just would not be true. It takes a freak fall for a child even to bruise. In fact, falling is apt to be such a lark that he may have trouble progressing to anything else. For some, the merry thump in the snow is the most delicious part of the lessons. The rare youngster who is afraid of falling can be brought in line with a ski lesson that resembles a tumbling class in which the instructor falls "accidentally on purpose."

The major cause of anxiety is the ski pole. Not only can poles be used as lances on others and self, they cause most of the black eyes, bruises, and tangles that can result in injury. Children have little use for them except in climbing. It is a good idea to take them away for downhill, lending them for slaloms, underpasses, marking fox and geese circles, or race courses on the flat. A well-coordinated child without poles uses his arms to aid his balance and doesn't think about it.

A child has a different approach to balance anyway because of his proportions. The familiar wide-open stance of the five-year-old is something that should not be interfered with too soon. It is probably the only way he can learn to turn.

Some children go up and down a rope tow hill all day long and never get their feet closer than 18 inches. Awkward as they may look, they are in good shape. All you want to do is to get them turning faster, tighter. On a steeper slope, when skiing with some speed, feet will drift closer together naturally. The child may use that weighty tail of his like a kangaroo's—stuck way out behind to steer with. The weight is not really in his fanny. His trunk is weighty and compact. With knees bent in a squat, or legs so straight that they seem to be bent backward, or at any angle in between, he can steer by shifting his rump behind him. You can give him good reason not to by clowning a little, showing him how he looks, and then showing him how he should look.

Although most children come to ski class because they want to, progress rapidly within the limits of age and coordination, and love every minute of it, there are occasional problems. Attitude is important. Some do not really want to be in class. Although they should get as much encouragement and comfort as seems to be called for, never insist that they stay. They may go to the bathroom, get warm, and come back. Sometimes they stay close enough to watch and when convinced of the fun they are missing, rejoin the class. On the other hand, some competitive-minded children become discouraged when their friends pass into higher classes, leaving them behind. Children do reach plateaus in skiing. If nothing much seems to happen for a few lessons, parents and teachers can help by taking them to a race, a jump, or anything that will put new spark into their desire to learn. A little boy of seven, who could not seem to give up stemming for parallel Christies found new inspiration when he acquired his very own race card.

Poor equipment probably discourages more children than anything else. No adult can learn to turn in boots two sizes too big, nor on skis without edges, or skis that will not slide in the first place. We should not expect miracles from children under these conditions, even though it does seem unreasonably hard to find good equipment for children, even in some reputable ski shops. Full details on children's equipment can be found in Section II.

Let the child experience putting on skis and taking them off at home, and let him walk around indoors or in the yard on skis. This eases the new experience when he first reaches the snow. Give him poles long enough to permit walking without bending at the waist. Now, when he is ready to try his skis on snow, choose a sunny day. Help him get started walking, but do not encourage downhill running until he wishes it himself. And when he is wet and cold, bring him indoors. Do not force instruction on youngsters. They just are not as coordinated as we bigger folk. At these early ages, children learn by seeing and doing, not by being told what

to do. Above all, do not force children to enjoy skiing. They will anyway, soon enough.

To get them in the spirit of things, children love chants, songs, and rhymed teases, and willingly help an instructor to invent new ones. Variations on the theme of "slippery side, slippery side" may forestall the common four-year-old complaint that "my skis are too-o-o slippery."

You may decide to undertake the early stages of getting your child started on skis. Sliding the skis back and forth in place is a good beginning for the first lesson. A little push will get them moving down a barely perceptible slope. Soon they are walking on the flat, taking turns being engine and caboose, busily making train noises. They learn to run by playing fox and geese. In this first lesson, time can always be taken out for digging an important hole, for making "angels" in the snow, and for throwing snowballs.

For downhill running and then snowplows, use a slope of 10 to 15 degrees, about 15 feet long, flat at the top, and with a long, barely concave runout. Very little ones can be caught in your waiting arms the first few times. Older ones are encouraged to bounce in the knees. "Making a jet" mark is then followed by making a series of snowplows.

Climbing is something of a problem. Sidestepping is difficult and unproductive. Herringboning works a little better for some reason, and some children take to it naturally. Others simply have to live with the difficulty of sidestepping. By the end of their first lesson, children are ready for the long walk to the rope tow. This walk includes long traverses up and down, perhaps a little sideslipping and sidestepping, much waving to the people on the chair lift, and a great deal of conversation.

During the second lesson, most children of four and older will begin turning, at least a little, strictly by imitation and correction. Some need more help. The instructor who can ski backward while holding a child in the proper position has a strong advantage. Sometimes it is helpful to put the child between your skis and urge him to push his skis against yours as they turn, open, and close. By the second lesson, they are all sick of sidestepping, eager for the tow, and ready to go up. After you have taken up ten or more four-year-olds, you will have learned thirty-six ways in which children can get entangled. You will also have learned to support them at every point—skis, hips, shoulders, hands, and ankles. There are also those who do not wait for help, who delightedly take hold and zoom up the first time. And there are those who must be chest-carried. Your biceps develop alarmingly, but children love it. An early tow ride gives them a goal to shoot for.

When they can take a slalom set with their poles, it is time to teach them real sideslipping, preferably on a steep, icy bump. After that there is a great deal of follow-the-leader and free-for-all down the hill.

Children who must attend many classes before they can move into intermediate groups should get a real break from time to time. A hike through the woods looking for tracks and birds can be a tremendous adventure. Watching a junior race will sometimes open junior novice eyes to saucer dimensions. In this respect, activities designed expressly for children can be of great help. Before any such event, class time is spent boning up on the fine points of egg racing or the problems of the obstacle course. For children it is a great deal of fun.

Children of three and older believe in their hearts that they can fly—they have done so in their dreams. On skis they have a good chance to prove it.

Ten Positive Rules to Follow with Children

1. Enjoy yourself, your child, and the snow. This is a recreation, remember?
2. Buy good equipment (not necessarily the most expensive).
3. Dress him sensibly, for ease of movement as well as warmth.
4. Show him how. Do not tell him how to ski. Demonstrate it.
5. Listen. You would be advised to believe it when he says he is cold, tired, hungry.
6. Do it yourself. Parents are the best teachers, competence permitting.
7. But quit while you are ahead. Put him in ski school when you lose patience or he loses faith in you.
8. Help him when he falters. You are a parent, not a drill sergeant.
9. Let him take a chance. Most of us are woefully short on opportunities to dare, to take a calculated risk, and to fall on our own faces without being tripped. Let him try the hill, the tow, the competition he yearns for.
10. *Have fun!* That is what skiing is for.

LIFT AND TOW TECHNIQUE

Ski lifts and tows are transportation devices that enable skiers to travel from the bottom of the slopes to the top with varying degrees of comfort and ease. The first lifts were simply animal "skins" attached to the bottom of the skis, and used to "walk" uphill. The next step in the evolution of lifts was the rope tow, which is still very much in evidence today; but it is gradually going out of existence in most areas, except where economy or rapid beginner transportation are necessary for operation.

Rope Tows

The rope tow is a system of pulleys over which a rope travels in a long loop, the lower part of which is used by skiers to travel uphill. At each end of this type of lift, a protective shack is normally located to keep skiers

away from the dangerous "end" pulleys.

When riding a rope tow, slip your ski pole straps over the wrist of your outside hand—the hand that is away from the rope. Sidestep into position at the tow rope, and be sure both skis are in the proper tracks and pointed straight up the hill. Using the "inside" hand, grasp the rope, gently allowing it to slip through fingers of *gloved* hand. Gradually tighten grip. It helps to walk the skis forward as you tighten grip on the rope. As you move forward, bring outside hand around back and grasp the rope with that hand for additional support. Keep skis running straight in tracks and keep knees flexible.

While riding the tow, keep the skis in the track and the knees relaxed and bent. As bumps are encountered, let the bend of your knees absorb the rising action of skis. The outside hand behind your back will give added support. Keep weight forward to prevent the crossing of skis. When dips or hollows occur in tow track, let the legs straighten into depression but avoid stiffening them. Keep your weight forward on the tips to prevent the skis from wandering, and resume your knee bend on upward side of hollow. Resume the normal stance on flat. To slow down, should someone ahead stop, relax your grip on the rope but do not let go. Hold the rope loosely; gradually tighten grasp when the rope resumes motion. For an alternate riding position, grasp the rope with both hands in front or with the inside hand behind and outside hand forward, holding the rope at side. That is, often, by midday, you will find your hands and fingers tiring from using the same position. If you continually change the positioning of your hands during the day, no one hand or arm will become overtired. For instance, if you use a one-hand-forward-and-one-hand-behind-the-back position, you should alternately rest the hand behind your back, then move both hands to the front grip, taking the strain off the arm that is usually forward on the rope. Occasionally, however, when on a steeper incline, you might find the rope sliding through your hand and your forward motion slowing to a stop. The rem-

edy: first, unweight your skis with a sudden drop of the knees. This momentarily takes your body weight off your hands, enabling you to get a new and firmer grasp. As you feel your forward progress resuming, drop your knees even more and keep them well bent until you are under way again.

As you approach the top of the hill, release back hand (the one with the poles). Then at the top of the hill release the forward hand, being careful to avoid snapping the rope. As you do this, place your outside ski across the fall line, edging it. Then bring your other ski parallel and ski away from the track. Always move away immediately from the top of the tow to make room for other skiers following.

The T-Bar or J-Bar Lifts

The T-bar or J-bar lifts are systems using a cable and a series of poles with T- or J-shaped attachments at the end to tow skiers uphill. T-bars normally accommodate two skiers each, J-bars one.

When riding a bar lift, hold the poles in the outside, away from the bar. While waiting for the T-bar, wait until the people ahead have left, and then quickly get into position for the next T-bar unit. As it approaches, the lift

How to ride a rope tow (left) and T-bar (right).

operator will grab the unit and bring it forward to a position under the buttocks and in back of the thighs of you and your partner. You *must not sit down* or attempt to take any weight off your skis. The T-bars and J-bars serve to pull skiers uphill, and not carry them or otherwise support them. You should also grab the central pole of the T-bar (or the inside pole of the J-bar) with your inside hand as the bar is brought into place by the lift operator.

While riding, lean against the bar but do *not* sit. Keep your knees flexed to absorb terrain variations and let the skis run in the track with inside ski next to partner's inside ski. Relax; avoid pushing against your partner's ski. Remain relaxed as terrain changes are encountered and let your flexed knees absorb variations naturally. When the track is higher or lower on one side, partners can adjust the balance by one riding slightly behind or ahead.

When partners are of unequal height or weight, the bar can be tipped to one side to afford better balance for both riders. Further adjustments can be made by one partner riding slightly ahead of the other or by repositioning placement of crossbar.

When the unloading station is reached, one partner "tends bar," holding the bar and pulling it down slightly to allow the other to ski away from the lift line. Then the first partner disengages the crossbar by twisting it to a vertical position and gently releasing it. Let the spring carry bar back to hanging position, but do not snap it. Swinging bars can be dangerous and can foul in the cable. Ski away from lift line as soon as possible when unloaded, *then* replace pole straps on wrists, not before. Others will be unloading right behind you.

Pomalifts

The pomalift, or platter pull as it is sometimes called, is a system of poles and a cable with a dishlike disk attached to the base of each pole, and used as a brace (not a seat), by which to pull a skier.

You should approach the pomalift with poles held in the hand away from the lift operator. The operator will hand you a lift unit. Relax and be prepared to hold to the pole of the poma as it accelerates. The lift operator will ask if you are ready, and upon receiving an affirmative reply, will pull a release cable sending your individual unit and you along your way. Your initial reaction should be much like that on the rope tow, with arms straight, knees slightly bent, and general body position relaxed. Shortly after the lift begins to move, the spring and sleeve of the unit will extend and there will be a few seconds' lapse in speed (usually almost a standstill). At this time, you should push the bar between your legs, so that the disk hits you squarely in the back of the thighs and behind your buttocks. You must *not* sit down or try to take any weight off your feet. The pomalift is designed to pull, not to lift or carry you. Let it pull you uphill.

Once you are comfortably under way, the bar can be held with one hand. Relax and, keeping your knees flexed to absorb minor terrain changes, look ahead for bumps or hollows which may occur in the path. Keep the skis parallel. When variations in the terrain do occur, let your knees absorb them as your legs extend and contract over changes.

When preparing to unload, bend your knees and pull down on the bar with both hands. Spread your legs slightly and disengage the disk from between your legs. Hold on to the bar with both hands until the unloading station is reached. When unloading, gently release the bar with one hand, letting the spring recoil it toward the cable. Do not snap the bar or let it swing excessively as it is released. Then ski away from the lift line quickly to clear the unloading area for those following behind.

Chair Lifts

A chair lift (single, double, triple, or even quadruple) is a chairlike device supported at the end of a pole and attached by either a single or a double bar to a cable used for transporting skiers uphill. The chair may be capable of carrying one, two, three, or four people, with the double chair being the most popular.

When loading a *double-bar chair lift,* step quickly into the position indicated by markers or by the attendant. Hold the poles in your inside hand and watch for the oncoming chair over your outside shoulder. As the chair approaches, grasp the bar with the outside hand and sit down gently.

When loading a *single-bar* chair lift, step quickly into the indicated position as above. Hold the poles in the outside hand and watch for the chair over your inside shoulder. As the chair approaches, grasp the bar with your inside hand, and sit down gently as the chair catches you behind your knees.

When comfortably settled on the chair lift, close the safety gate, if there is one, by pulling it in or down. If hooks are provided, hang up your poles. Then relax and enjoy the ride. When approaching points where the chair is close to the ground, keep your ski tips up to prevent catching in snow. Approaching the unloading station, open safety gate, hold the poles in your outside hand, and keep the ski tips up until clear of the ramp. If the unloading station is on level ground, stand up at the designated point and, with a sliding motion, ski quickly away from the chair, following the prepared track. Chair partners should depart in opposite directions, away from the chair. Clear unloading track quickly.

If the unloading station is on an inclined ramp, ski down the ramp, turning in the opposite direction from your partner. Use a snowplow or stop-Christie to stop. Duck down as you ski away to avoid the chair overhead.

Other Lifts

There are even more complex lifts which are used in the operation of various ski areas in and out of this country. For instance, cable cars and gondolas provide "mass transportation" by carrying from three to three-score to the top. Although cable cars can become as crowded as sardine cans, especially in Eu-

rope, this is luxury transportation. The skis come off and one stands or sits inside, protected from the elements. The small gondola cabins, seating two or three persons, detach from the cable, permitting loading or unloading inside barn-size buildings. Actually, these more sophisticated uphill transportation methods are quite easy to use and require no special training other than ability to follow the directions of the operators and the safety rules as posted.

Lift lines should be avoided if possible since they mean spending hours standing and waiting. Try to learn the heavy-traffic habits of the area you are skiing and arrange your time during the off hours or on the lesser-used lifts at peak hours. (Peak hours at most areas are in the morning when skiers are getting on the mountain.) If one must stand in lift lines, observe good manners. Keep off other people's skis, and do not try to sneak ahead. Also keep in mind these five simple rules, which apply to every lift:

1. Carry both ski poles in one hand—the hand away from the lift support, the loading platform, your left partner, or the operator.
2. Stay alert and make sure that no part of your equipment or clothing will come in contact with any obstacle.
3. Read carefully any and all instructions posted at the lift loading platform or along the route of the lift.
4. When unloading, be sure to get out of the lift track as quickly as possible, and watch out for returning chairs, poles, etc.
5. If you fall off the lift as it starts, fall! Never attempt to hang on if you are in anything but the proper riding position. Do not let yourself be dragged; rather let go.

SKI TOURING

A skier who worships the sight of the mountains and yearns to put his tracks on the untracked snow, is missing something if he does not take up ski touring. The few who do—a select, but surprisingly fast-growing band despite the ever increasing number of lifts—are discovering, or rather, rediscover-

ing, the satisfactions and pleasures which drove the sport's pioneers to bear the burden of pioneering. To be about in winter, to be at liberty to glide across the snow in any direction, is an exhilarating freedom. True, the day's vertical will be reduced, and you are inclined to carefully prolong the downhill

Touring is the way to see beautiful country during the winter months.

runs. What you will get out of it, in the words of a skier who enjoys the best of both worlds, is "fun out of the downhilling and pleasure out of the touring."

Cross-country ski touring has not met with a completely encouraging reaction in the past from recreational skiers in the United States. Essentially it is hiking on skis, and Americans are not a nation of hikers. In the Scandinavian countries, on the other hand, literally thousands of Norwegians and Swedes pack their rucksacks each weekend and take their touring skis northward. Every tour offers its own particular challenge—woods, fields, trails, frozen ponds—the touring skier is never snowbound. Cross-country touring does not mean that you need to give up the more popular sport of running downhill. Rather, it should be viewed as complementary to downhill, adding variety and expanding your skiing horizons. Downhill running, after all, is not always ideal. There are times when you may be grateful for another way to enjoy yourself on skis. For instance:

1. At the height of the day, the waiting period in lift line may be aggravatingly long. With a pair of touring skis handy, you can eliminate your dependence on the lift line and take off for an enjoyable tour with friends through the woods, seeing countryside that others will never see.

2. Consistent running up and down the same hill can actually become uninteresting. Working in a couple of hours of touring can change the whole character of your skiing day.

3. Many people on a week or two-week skiing holiday actually experience a certain boredom in a steady, unrelieved diet of running the lifts and trails. You can add fun and variety to a long skiing vacation by taking along touring equipment. And you will see more of the surrounding country.

4. Occasionally high winds or extreme cold or certain snow conditions can make downhill running unattractive. At these times, conditions in the sheltered woods often can be quite pleasant and you will never get cold running cross-country.

One should, incidentally, carefully distin-

guish between touring and cross-country racing. Cross-country is a fairly specialized sport
with very light skis and minimum bindings.
The racers move along at a speed of around 6
miles in 33 minutes, up and down hill. They
do a 30-mile marathon in 2 hours and 45
minutes. Cross-country is for hot-blooded
racers. Touring is for the skier who wants to
enjoy the healthy feeling of increased circulation and invigoration.

Touring Techniques

The mark of a skilled touring skier is a
relaxed, easy stride with rapid pushing movements plus long glides with the weight balanced entirely on one ski or the other. As in
all skiing, relaxed movements are the crux of
the technique; you should be able to tour
using far less energy than for a trot on foot
over the same terrain. One of the best tricks is
to relax the head and shoulders by focusing
your eyes about 40 feet ahead of you; continual watching of your ski tips, on the other
hand, will result in a cramped and tiring
position.

Ski touring technique differs little from that
used in downhill skiing. Leg, arm, and shoulder movements and breathing should work
together to achieve a smooth, gliding pace.
Poles are used to provide added thrust to help
with your balance and, most important, to
promote that overall body rhythm and timing
which is so typical of a practiced cross-
country runner. As you begin your kick off
on one ski, your *opposite* pole should be so
situated that you can use it for added push or
thrust at the same time you kick. The skier,
having completed the kick off his right ski,
has his weight well over the ball of his left
foot as he gets into his left kick. And to help
push himself along, he places his right pole in
the snow. His right arm is forward, with
elbow sharply bent and the hand nearly in
front of his nose, and he puts the pole tip and
basket in the snow at a point even with his
left foot. His right pole slants forward of the
perpendicular drawn from the snow up
through the basket, thus enabling him to push
effectively and help move himself along. This
angle of the pole, almost parallel to the angle
of his lower leg, is as necessary to proper
poling as it is to a good kick, and for the

same reason. Try it for yourself. If you do,
imagine what would happen if you stuck your
pole tip in the snow ahead of your hand
instead of behind it; if you pushed with your
pole, you would break your pole, stop, or
start going back where you came from. Now
as you combine kick and poling to increase
your glide on your left ski, you are already
thinking of your next stride—and you should
be swinging your left pole forward into action. Place it even with your right foot,
handle ahead of tip, and initiate your stride
with a right-foot kick and left-arm push
simultaneously.

This single-pole stride is often called the
diagonal. Actually the basic term in touring
technique is the "diagonal stride." It means
that you employ the diagonally opposite arm
and leg at any one time. The arm plants the
pole while the leg on the opposite side starts
the *avspark,* as the Norwegians call it. This
is a sort of graceful, almost slow-motion "mule
kick." In form, the touring skier thinks of it
as kicking his weighted ski out in back of
him, at the same time transferring his weight
off that ski onto the other ski which is moving
forward on the gliding stroke. The effect of
the kick is to propel the skier forward just as
surely and smoothly as a blast of burning fuel
from a rocket exhaust kicks the rocket forward. The pole is merely a help in this
maneuver. The main force is in the kick. In
fact, Scandinavians practice *without* poles to
make sure they get the kick motion down
cold first. Then, and only then, do they add
the pole movement.

The movements of the diagonal stride resemble an exaggerated march step as oppos-
ing arm and leg work together, swinging back
and forth in a relaxed, rhythmical manner.
This simple walklike stride is the basis of all
touring and cross-country technique; its use is
the difference between true touring and
simple plodding.

The diagonal stride uses the principles of
ice and roller skating. In ice skating you glide
on alternate skates and obtain the force to
drive you forward from kicking off a
weighted blade that is slightly angled to your
direction of motion. In skating, the "kicking
leg" swings up in back after the push-off. The
other leg gets the weight and gives a push in
its turn. The skating stride is then a kick-

Diagonal stride.

glide, kick-glide stride. To pick up speed in skating, side-to-side arm movements are added to counterbalance the kicking leg. It is exactly analogous to the touring stride.

The illustration on this page shows two complete paces of the "diagonal stride," the foundation of the whole art of touring. In the first four figures, the skier swings his left arm and right leg forward. In the last four figures, the right leg and left arm swing forward. This is what is meant by "diagonal"—the diagonally opposite limbs are swung forward at any one time. Let us look at the movement sequence of the leg and arm movements separately. *Legs:* In figure (1) the left leg has come even with the right, is still almost unweighted. The right starts its backward kick movement. To get the most out of the thrust, nearly all the weight must be on the right at this point. (2) The right leg has three-quarters completed its kick. A gradual shift of weight to the left (gliding) ski has begun. (3) The right leg has completed its kick. Its thrust is over. The left knee is now fully bent. (4) The force of the kick carries the completely relaxed right leg back. This is the gliding phase: the left leg is now carrying all the body weight. The left knee straightens. The glide should be cut off before speed drops too much. The whole secret in going long distances without getting tired lies in a relatively long glide with a relaxed body. (5) The right leg now swings forward again. Weight is still completely on the left ski, even after the right ski comes completely back on the snow. (6) The right leg has come even with the left but still is almost unweighted. The left leg starts its backward kick. (7) The backward kick of the leg is three-quarters complete. A gradual shift of weight to the right (gliding) ski has begun. (8) The left leg is relaxed and is swinging up. Weight is completely on the right (gliding) ski with the right knee at full bend. This alternating kick-and-glide should be practiced at first without poles to gain balance and rhythm. The great part of the driving force comes from leg thrusts. Arms should slide by close to the body almost touching the hips. The hand grip on the poles starts from a firm grip during the "pulling" phase and finishes with the pole lightly held when the arm is completely in back of the body. (1) The left arm begins the push phase simultaneously with the kick of the right leg. (2) The left pole push is complete. The right arm continues its relaxed forward swing. (3 and 4) The left arm, relaxed, swings back and the pole is free to pendulum. The right arm continues its relaxed forward swing. Neither pole is touching the snow. The grip on both poles is relaxed and loose. (5) The right arm pulls down and in on the right pole, planted in line with the toe of the left boot. (6) The right arm completes its pulling movement and the left arm swings forward. (7) The right arm is now pushing. (8) The

Double-poling.

Double-pole stride.

right arm push is now finished, and the left arm is preparing to plant its pole, at the end of the glide.

There are many variations of the diagonal stride. The most important of these is the double-pole stride, in which the skier plants both poles instead of only one. The use of both poles provides variation in movement or to increase speed under good conditions and on slightly downhill stretches. Double-poling can be used with or without strides between successive double-poles. Double-poling takes a good deal more energy than does the diagonal stride; thus it cannot be maintained for a long period. In double-poling, the upper body goes forward to throw weight onto the poles after they are planted. Because the speed in double-poling is greater, the poles are set with baskets further forward and shafts almost vertical. The sequence figures show one complete double-pole maneuver: (1 and 2) The poles are set with arms almost completely stretched. The arms begin to pull. Grip on the poles is firm. (3) The upper body sinks over the poles to add force to the movement as the knees bend. The movement should be continuous and smooth. (4) The arms should push past the knees with hands almost touching and level with or a little below the knees. (5) Push movement ends. The poles are still set in the snow. Knees are now bent to their maximum. (6) The arms are relaxed and swing back as the body begins to straighten. The hands are relaxed. (7) The arms swing forward to prepare the next pole set. The body straightens during gliding.

When going uphill, use the same strides as on the level. The wax (see Section II) inhibits backslip. As the hill grows steeper, first stamp the ski on the snow for better wax adherence, then use a zigzag traverse, herringboning while changing directions.

When starting down a hill, the tourer's technique is different from the downhill skier. That is, be sure your weight is not on the balls of your feet; instead, keep some weight on your heels, which are flat on the skis. In other words, forget about techniques requiring firm downhold of the heel. Body weight should be slightly back of the conventional downhill position. This is necessary in order to plane the tips in soft and deep snow. Toes, knees, and chin should be in an approximately straight line. Your position should be comfortable.

In deep or partially tracked snow it is easiest to turn or check speed with a stem, rotating the upper body in the direction of the turn. Use a hopping motion to turn, too. If you ever get going too fast or get in a tight spot and want to stop and cannot turn, just sit back on your skis and begin dragging your hands. This is a marvelously simple way to stop.

The step turn is an important maneuver that a tourer must know. In making it, you proceed from your regular straight downhill running position, remembering that your weight is evenly distributed on your skis; you are not leaning forward, but your knees are slightly flexed. If you want to turn right, just lift your right ski out of the track, point it toward the right, step forward on it, and then bring your left ski alongside. The weight is definitely back—this makes it easier to lift the ski tips. It may require two or three or four quick little step turns to negotiate a given corner. This is fine. You will learn to speed them up. Two small quickies are better than one big step turn.

While turning is not a major problem when touring, thanks to cross-country bindings which are used on touring skis, it is possible to make one of the oldest and most elegant turns, the telemark (see page 6). This turn is used primarily for deep or heavy snow skiing. The right ski is advanced, turned left, edged, and then brought forward until the right foot touches the tip of the left ski. The right ski is then weighted and edged inward with the knees bent. The left ski stays flat and is guided around by its tip, which remains in contact with the right foot throughout the turn. At the end of the turn, the left foot is brought forward and the body raised. When advancing the outside ski, do not simply poke the foot forward, but keep the knee well over it. Otherwise the needed weight will be taken off the ski and the balance disturbed.

The more you ski, the more natural many of these movements will be for you. Soon you will not have to think about keeping a flat ski or timing your poling. You can get on the snow, go where you want to go at the pace you set yourself.

Ski Mountaineering

Ski mountaineering—exploring high mountains and glaciers in winter and early spring—is a cross between touring and mountain climbing. It takes a great deal of technical ability and knowledge about both sports, plus proper physical conditioning and high altitude training. Since it is such a specialized phase of the sport of skiing, we have not included it in detail in this book, but the interested reader would be well advised to consult a standard text such as the *Manual of Ski Mountaineering,* published by the Sierra Club of California.

SKI SAFETY AND COURTESY

It is immoral to ski unsafely, and unmannerly to ski impolitely. These two ideas shade into each other. The unmannerly skier is also likely to be the immoral skier who skis out of control. The first concern of the skier coming down the hill should be for those below him. Whether they are skiing or stationary, he has a duty to keep from running into them.

The rule makes sense. A skier should be able to start out onto a trail with the expectation that skiers coming down the trail will avoid him. Otherwise, each skier on every trail would have to wait until the last skier on the trail above had stopped before he could take off. This would cause a dangerous pileup.

To keep the trails clear, do not be timid about taking off. According to the rules of the National Ski Areas Association, you, the standing skier, have the right of way. Assume that the skiers above you will steer clear. On the other hand, too many skiers do not take seriously the duty of staying clear of skiers below. They feel they have the right to yell "Track!" and to whiz by. They do not have that right. We would like to see more skiers get into the act and enforce the "stay clear of the skier below" rule among themselves. Everyone would benefit. As a matter of Ski Patrol policy, we like to see the Ski Patrol rescind the ticket of every skier who fails to stay clear or who skis so as to endanger the skier below him.

There is a companion rule: skiers who are standing still should stay off to the sides of the trail. Even if the skier is standing in the middle of a trail, however, the oncoming skier has the duty of steering around him. Again, this makes sense, because the skier standing in the middle of the trail may have come out of his bindings or may be in some other kind of trouble.

The rules apply particularly to blind corners. No skier has the right to come around a blind corner or over a blind drop-off so fast that he cannot avoid someone standing on the trail. Otherwise an injured skier would be at the mercy of skiers coming down behind him. If you ski out of control, you might be the one who runs into an injured skier.

There is a good little trick to passing another skier on a narrow trail without disturbing him. (We find that saying "Track" or "On your right" or "On your left" is fine, but only when you are just at the moment of passing. Hollering it from way up the hill is likely to confuse the skier below.) The best way to pass is to get in the track of the skier below, make one or two turns exactly when he does, and then, when he makes the next turn, keep going straight. In this way the skier gets himself out of the way and whichever way he turns, you clear him.

When you are on a collision course with another skier, pull up. Theoretically the skier on the right has the right of way, but it is wise to take the burden of avoiding collision upon yourself. Do not risk running another skier down just to assert your rights. Never go launching yourself into the path of an oncoming skier when he is going to have difficulty stopping.

Do not take your skis off and walk up or down a trail unless you cannot ski it. The correct way to climb or descend a trail is on your skis. Walking on snow leaves little foot holes that can trip up other skiers.

A rule similar to the "replace your divots" in golf is to "pack out your own bathtub." A bathtub, or siztmark, is a big body-hole made in soft snow by the fall of a skier. You are not expected to fill the hole completely, but you should sidestep up and down the hole a couple of times to make a smooth dip rather than a ragged hole.

The most elementary safety rule is to wear safety straps. If the skis release, it is up to you to keep them with you. A flying ski, running down the hill on its own, is a nasty projectile. If you see a ski running loose, be sure to set up the cry "Ski! Ski!" This will alert everyone down the hill to get out of the way.

Unless it is moving very slowly, do not try to trap a runaway ski: this is very dangerous. The tip of even a slow-traveling ski will do all kinds of damage to an ankle or shin bone. In the case of a lost ski, you can afford to be callous; the skier who lost the ski is in the wrong. Ninety-nine times out of a hundred, a loose ski simply sails harmlessly off the trail.

One firm rule, often ignored, is the duty to come to a stop *below* a standing skier. If you come to a stop just above him, you may skid into him. At best, you spray him with snow; at worst, you catch an edge and hit him. Do not put yourself in the position of endangering another; it is not part of the sport to scare others.

The exception to the stopping rule is at the lift line; you usually have to stop above the line, since you often cannot go below it. Stop and walk to the lift line. Do not come to a stop right at it, as you may catch an edge and fall into the line. This is probably the most widely ignored rule in skiing. We are amazed at the good humor that usually prevails when someone skis right to the lift line, because it is certainly an avoidable offense.

One of the best ways to continue skiing

well is to take plenty of rest stops. Most of all, take an hour for lunch, particularly on the first day of a weekend or ski week, when you may initially be full of energy yet become much more tired than you realize. A tired skier does not ski well. In this connection, avoid taking "one last run." It is a superstition among skiers never to say, "Let us take a last run." (It may really become your last run for a while.) The superstition has a good basis in fact. If you are tired and yet tempted to take just one more run, you are stretching it; this is when you get hurt.

On a cold morning, if you warm up a bit before you make your first turn, you will have a better first run. The first run, traditionally, is a bad one. The reason is that the skier's muscles and his sense of timing have not warmed up yet. The best way to warm up is to quickly climb up the trail about 20 feet —sidestep or herringbone. This gets your body ready for the run and starts you breathing deeply and properly. One of the big faults of skiers is that they generally stop breathing deeply when the skiing gets tough. Lack of oxygen in itself is a mental and physical depressant; if you have had a scare or are skiing badly, stop and take about six good, deep breaths.

These suggestions make skiing sound a bit grim, but it is overcoming the scare and transforming such feelings into a sense of satisfaction at a good run that makes skiing a completely captivating sport.

The International Ski Federation (FIS) has issued some safety rules which it recommends for adoption by its affiliated national associations, of which the USSA is one:

1. *Consideration for others.* Every skier should take care not to endanger or harm others.

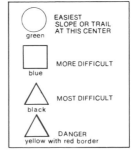

Standard trail-marking system designates relative difficulty of slopes and trails within a particular ski area.

2. *Control of speed and mode of skiing.* Every skier must adapt his speed and mode of skiing to his ability, the terrain, and weather conditions.

3. *Choice of path.* The skier approaching from behind must take a course which does not endanger those ahead.

4. *Overtaking.* This can be performed from above or below, from right or left, but always at a distance allowing the overtaken skier sufficient space for all his movements.

5. *Responsibilities of the lower and the traversing skier.* Every skier intending to join a downhill run or to cross a trail must ensure that he can do this without endangering himself or others higher up or lower down. This also applies after every stop.

6. *Loitering on the trail.* No skier must stop at narrow or concealed points on the trail other than for emergencies. Skiers who fall should get out of the way as quickly as possible.

7. *Walking uphill.* Skiers going uphill on skis may use only the edge of the trail and then only in good weather conditions. The same applies to skiers carrying their skis.

8. *Observance of warning signs.* Every skier must observe the signs on the trail.

9. *Procedure in case of accident.* Everyone must render all assistance possible.

10. *Details of identity.* Everyone, whether witness or directly concerned, whether responsible or otherwise, must give details of identity in the event of an accident.

The Ski Patrol

Most injuries are self-induced. The few impolite and even foolhardy skiers usually wind up hurting themselves, in the long run. The Ski Patrol is a remarkable outfit composed partly of amateur ski patrolmen, who volunteer their time, and partly of paid patrolmen, who spend all winter at a ski area. (Any given area may have all volunteers, all professionals, or both.)

Ski patrolmen are trained to give first aid to injured skiers on the slope and to get them down to the bottom, where they can be treated further. Most patrolmen are attached to specific areas. There is a National Patrol, whose members in rust-red parkas are eligible to patrol any ski area. (Membership is an honor conferred for outstanding service in a local patrol.) The trickiest duty of a patrolman is to get an injured skier onto a toboggan and to ski down, holding the toboggan handles (sometimes there is a second patrolman behind) while guiding the toboggan to the bottom. There are four classes of patrolmen, not counting the professional ski patrol which you will find in some resorts. (Professionals are hired by the area management.) The classifications are:

1. Junior Ski Patrolman (fifteen, sixteen, or seventeen years of age).
2. Local Ski Patrolman (eighteen years of age and over).
3. Senior Ski Patrolman (eighteen years of age and over).
4. National Ski Patrolman (a special appointment awarded to senior patrolmen at least twenty-one years old who have demonstrated ability and leadership and who have been registered for at least three seasons).

For further information on National Ski Patrol Service and its membership, write to the headquarters at 828 17th Street, Denver, Colorado, 80202.

The first thing to do if a skier is hurt is to summon the patrol. If you are observant, you will have spotted the location of the patrol phones on the various trails. Most of the little shacks at the top of the lifts have phones that connect to the patrol. All patrols have a patrol shack at the bottom of the area, often a room in the base building, and there is usually a patrolman there ready to go.

This brings up a safety point. The skier should have an area map with him when he goes up the lift. Coming down a trail, he should know what trail he is on and approximately how far down the trail he is. This precaution makes skiing more fun (what fun is there in skiing a whole succession of trails when you do not know where you have been?), and it can be extremely helpful in an accident, so you can tell the patrol just where the victim is.

Carrying a map will also keep you off trails that are either too hard for you or too much of a hike from the lift. (Some trails end as far as a half-mile from any lift.) It will keep you from getting lost, which can happen. Most ski-area maps, unfortunately, are poor ones. Areas will not spend enough money to make accurate, legible maps, and they seem to refuse to mark the trails adequately. Every trail intersection should be marked, but many are not. Most trail maps at least do show where expert, intermediate, etc., trails are. And trails have signs at the top to indicate whether the trail is "easy," "difficult," or "most difficult."

Ten Tips for Safer Skiing

Here are ten tips that you should keep in mind:

1. Beginners should go to ski school and should stay there until past the snowplow stage. They should avoid "free" lessons from well-meaning but otherwise unqualified persons.

2. Do not overestimate your ability.

3. Do not underestimate the danger of moguls and all "heavy" snow conditions.

4. Stay in condition.

5. Be alert at all times, particularly on lower slopes where traffic is heavy and collision danger is high.

6. Use release bindings. If renting skis, insist on release bindings, preferably the nonadjustable type. When buying release bindings make sure you get the right model for you. Some manufacturers have women's and children's models.

7. Check release bindings frequently and preferably daily, and whenever you suspect tampering.

8. Once bindings are adjusted, do not switch skis. Skis should be marked left and right so that the same boot goes on the same ski every time.

9. Avoid use of runaway straps which allow skis to snap back or too much freedom to whirl around. They are the major cause of lacerations.

10. When giving old equipment to new skiers, take off nonrelease bindings and throw them away.

Injured Skiers

If a skier is injured, the first skier on the scene should attempt to stay with him and send the next skier down for help, even if it means waiting. The injured skier may become cold and need whatever clothes can be spared.

The cardinal rule is: Do not move the injured skier. Assume that something is fractured, even if there is only a sprain. Leave the skier's boots on. If an ankle is fractured, the boot will serve as a cast. (Ankle sprains and fractures are the most common injuries.) Detach the skis from the boots, but do not pull the boots into a different position. If something is twisted, leave it twisted unless the skier himself, free of the ski, can rearrange his own position. Try to keep the skier warm and quiet, and reassure him that help is on the way. The psychological benefit of having someone to talk to is important. Again, to be not quite so negative, we must point out that the risk of injury is small if the skier knows something about ski technique and stays within terrain he can handle. An outstanding example of not doing this is the beginning stem skier who insists on going down expert slopes. The stem turn in the hands of a beginner simply cannot be shortened enough to make it a safe turn on a difficult slope.

If the skier tries to work on his technique and knows what it can do, and if he maintains proper release bindings, his chance of injury will be no more than when walking down the sidewalk in a small town.

Avalanches

One of the major causes of fatalities, however, is avalanches. If you are planning to do any touring, or may be in an area where slides happen, it is advisable to be informed about them.

There are many facts about the lethal avalanche, however, which can be predicted. They have been well cataloged by the United States Forest Service, which has been concerned with the problem over a period of many years. For skiers who may stray into avalanche terrain and for ski touring parties, the facts and necessary precautions are worth recording.

There are two principal types of avalanches: loose snow and slab. Loose snow has little internal cohesion and tends to move as a formless mass, the slide growing in size as it descends. Slab avalanches, on the other hand, are characterized by internal cohesion—a large area of hard snow begins to slide at once from a well-defined fracture line across the slope. Frequently caused by wind drifting, which often gives the snow a dull chalky color, the slab avalanche constitutes a great winter slide hazard because of its unpredictability.

Elaborate avalanche prevention techniques are common at major ski resorts. Artillery mortars and explosives are often used deliberately to trigger avalanches, clearing the terrain and subsequently making it safe for skiers.

Steep gullies and open, untrod slopes are natural avalanche paths; ridges, outcrops, and terraces are natural barriers. Other things being equal, a convex-shaped slope is more dangerous than a concave profile. But both can avalanche.

Avalanche danger is high during and after heavy winter storms. It usually declines as snow settles and stabilizes. But cold weather does not readily allow stabilization.

Underlying snow conditions have an important bearing on avalanche danger. Deep snow smoothes out irregularities and promotes sliding. Smooth surfaces, such as rain or sun crust, also make good sliding bases. Rough, firm snow, on the other hand, offers a good anchorage for subsequent layers. Wet snow avalanches occur when rain or melting water lubricates and weakens snow layers which already are somewhat unstable. Here are tips from *Snow Avalanches* (U.S. Department of Agriculture No. 64) that you should keep in mind:

When avalanche conditions exist, the following should be kept in mind:

1. Never travel alone.

2. Pick the route carefully. The safest route is along the top by way of the ridge. The next safest route is along the valley floor *under* the avalanche. Most avalanches occur on slopes of 30 to 45 degrees.

3. Beware of lee areas, especially convex profiles beneath a cornice.

4. Never expose more than one member of the party to avalanche danger at once. The other members should watch the person crossing so they can plot his probable course in case a slide is started.

5. Do not assume a slope is safe just because the first few crossed safely.

6. Do not camp or stop under an avalanche path. Prolonged exposure is always risky.

7. If you must cross an avalanche slope: remove wrist loops of your ski poles. Unhitch Arlberg or safety straps from your skis so you will not be tied to them in a slide.

Close up your clothing, don hat and mittens, and raise your parka hood. If you are buried in the snow, your chances of survival are much better if snow does not get inside your clothes to cause chill.

Wear a brightly colored avalanche cord if one is available. Tie one end to your belt and let it trail out behind you. If you bring down a slide, the cord has a good chance of floating to the surface.

If you are caught in an avalanche, do the following:

1. Call out so other members of your party can observe your course in case you are buried.

2. Discard skis, poles, rucksack.

3. Try to stay on the surface by swimming. Attempt to work to one side of the moving snow. In a large or fast-moving avalanche, such efforts will probably be of little avail, but they may save your life in a smaller one.

4. If swimming does not help, cover your face with your hands. This will keep snow out of your nose and mouth and you will have a chance to clear a breathing space if you are buried. Avalanche snow often becomes very hard as soon as it stops moving, and your arms may be pinned when the snow halts.

5. If you are buried, try to avoid panic. Many avalanche victims have been recovered dead, apparently uninjured and after only a few minutes of burial. The only explanation doctors can offer is that they were actually frightened to death.

6. In soft snow you may be able to dig yourself out, or at least make room to breathe. Try to keep your sense of direction; actually you might be digging *down* under the impression that it is the way out.

Here is *what to do if your companions are caught.*

1. Do not panic. The lives of your buried companions may depend on what you do in the next hour. Check for further slide danger. Pick a safe escape route in case of a retreat.

2. Mark the point on the avalanche path where the victim was last seen as he was

carried down by the snow. This will narrow the area of search.

3. Search quickly. If there are only two or three survivors, they must make a quick but careful search of the avalanche before going for help. One man should then be left at the accident scene to continue the search and guide the rescue party. The chances of a buried victim being recovered alive diminish rapidly after two hours.

4. Search the surface *below* the last-seen point for evidence of the victim or clues to his location. Mark the location of any pieces of his equipment you find—these may provide additional indicators of the path taken by the flowing snow.

5. Begin probing. If the initial search fails, probe with the heel of your ski, an inverted ski pole, or a collapsible probe *below* the last-seen point. Trees, ledges, benches, or other terrain features which have caught the snow are likely places.

6. Send for help. If there are several survivors, send only two. The remaining survivors may search for the victim in the meantime. If you must go for help, travel carefully, trying to avoid further avalanches or injuries from skiing too fast. The victims' chance of survival depends on your getting through. Mark your route, especially if fresh snow is falling, so you can find your way back. Try to avoid complete exhaustion. The rescue party normally will expect you to guide them back to the accident scene.

7. If the victim is found, apply first aid treatment immediately for suffocation and shock. Free nose and mouth of snow, and administer mouth-to-mouth artificial respiration if necessary. Clean snow from inside clothing and place victim in sleeping bag with head downhill.

It cannot be overstressed that safety in skiing is not a matter of timidity, but calm common sense. The skier who is oblivious to danger is not courageous; he is stupid.

Etiquette

You will not become a ski champion by observing a few simple rules of ski etiquette, but you will increase your pleasure, and everyone else's. What is more, manners among skiers contribute to safety on the hills as well as a rating with Emily Post.

Keep your place in the lift line. Ski area managers try to keep chiselers in place, but somehow there is always one around when it gets crowded.

Avoid stepping on the back of the skis of the fellow in front of you as you would avoid stepping on his feet. You may not hurt him physically, but you will not do his skis any good.

If you are alone in a busy line, double up with someone. When sharing a chair with a safety bar that lowers, make sure that you each know when the bar is coming down, or you may mash fingers. On the T-bar, do not insist on riding with someone a great deal taller or shorter than you, or the ride will be uneven.

Treat a lift as you would your own equipment. Horsing around on a chair lift puts undue stress on the cables and endangers other riders. On T-bars or pomalifts, keep your skis in the tracks and avoid the temptation to run some kind of uphill slalom. On rope tows, try to avoid jerking the rope when you get off at the top.

Move out of the way the minute you step off a lift. Sure, the view is breathtaking, but you can see it just as well a bit farther away. Mitten, goggle, and binding adjustments should be performed at a distance from the debarkation point.

Ski where you belong, and ski in control. There is nothing more irritating or more dangerous than the basher who, unable to turn or stop, knocks down skiers along his way like bowling pins.

Ski defensively. If you feel a skier in front of you might make a sudden turn, warn of your own approach by calling "Track right" or "Track left" to avoid collision. This is like giving directional signals while driving, only in skiing it is done in reverse order, with the one in back signaling to the one in front. If you are the front skier, take the warning and get out of the way.

Cover your sitzmarks. Leaving a hole in the snow from your fall is like preparing a trap for the next skier to catch his ski tips in.

If you stop along the way down, do so only at the side of the hill, where you will be out of the way of other skiers. And if for some reason you decide to walk instead of ski down the rest of the way, walk at the side.

Respect slalom flags set up by clubs and ski

schools. If you knock down flags on a practice course, set them up again; there are others who want to run the course after you. If you are with a ski group and want to set up your own slalom flags, obtain permission from the area manager.

Put your ski gear in a rack near the slope or the lodge. Do not leave it around for others to trip on. If a pole or a ski falls down, pick it up and replace it.

If you bring box lunches be sure to check if you are allowed to eat in the general dining room or if there is a special section for picnickers. When you are finished, dispose of your refuse.

Do not spread out over more chairs than you actually need during the busy lunch hour. Other skiers want to relax, too. Sharing your table with a stranger is part of the spirit of ski camaraderie.

Look out for your own equipment. Even the smallest child should be taught to carry and put on his own ski gear.

Do not keep others waiting. A late riser has no business holding up a group of early risers. That last run before going home—the one that keeps the rest of your group waiting—is likely to be the last one you will ever take as part of their car pool or bus.

If you are with a group occupying most of the rooms in a lodge, make the outsiders feel welcome.

If you want to have a private cocktail party, ask your ski host if it is all right with him. Some farm hosts, especially, do not like drinking on their premises, and since it is their house, their wishes should be respected.

At night, remember that some of the best skiing is early in the morning and that many skiers do not like to burn the candle at both ends. Keep the fun as quiet as possible.

Park your car where the lot attendant at the mountain or the lodge asks you to park. Do not block access roads. They have to be plowed.

CONDITIONING

Proper conditioning is one of the most important and most neglected aspects of skiing. The exercises that follow were chosen by top coaches and experts for their special emphasis on strengthening muscles most subject to the rigors of the sport. As a matter of fact, maximum enjoyment and health may be derived from skiing at any age—but only if you have an adequate level of physical condition. To help skiers of any age achieve proper conditioning, here are several exercises that you should perform.

Warm-ups

It is silly to expect your body to function properly at 15 degrees below zero upon your arrival at the top of a mountain after a bitterly cold lift ride . . . then without any further activity you head straight down on your next run. Or, if you are a competitor, it is wrong to go directly into the start of your Alpine competition. Your muscles, ligaments, and tendons can assist your body and try for perfection only if they are loose, relaxed, and, most of all, warm. When you start your car in the dead of winter, it takes quite a while

A skier without spring in his knees might as well stay home! Here is a good limbering exercise. First, place hands on hips. Now squat, flat-footed, going down low, then up, then down, increasing the tempo. Brace yourself against a wall if extra support is necessary.

(A) Lie on back, hands together behind neck. Rise to sitting position with left elbow touching right knee, then lie back and reverse exercise 10 times. (B) Lie flat on stomach and extend left leg high to rear without bending. Repeat 10 times, then alternate.

before it performs as you expect it to. So, when you push your body's starter button, you must do warm-ups before going into high gear. Besides exercises, there are other factors to consider. If you ride a chair without a foot rest, be sure to lift your legs and move them constantly so the edge of the chair does not cut off the blood circulation. Otherwise your lower legs become stiff and your feet get numb.

If you are very cold, it is rather difficult to warm up thoroughly with your skis on. We have found it much more helpful to start the exercises that follow with skis off and boots loosened. Try to memorize these exercises. They may come in handy on a bitterly cold day anywhere in the country, which generally boils down to the same old story: you enjoy skiing more if you are properly prepared. You will find, too, that you will be able to

Lie on your stomach with hands out to the sides. Knock on the floor with your hands twice. Now swing your arms up over your head and forward, at the same time lifting your chest from the floor. Knock twice again, then return by the same movement to the starting position.

(A) Hold your knees stiff, right arm in air, left arm down at your side. Twisting your body at waist, touch left toe with left hand. Now alternate, rotating body to make blood circulate. (B) For a balance builder, extend left leg, then hop across the room on the right leg. Repeat, reversing legs. You may lose your balance at first, but after a while it will go smoothly.

endure skiing on a cold day much longer without having to take too many "warming house breaks."

Running Uphill in Deep Snow. Since you should never perform stretching and pulling exercises with a cold body, it is best to start with running, either on the level or uphill. Do this with or without poles. Running uphill, particularly in deep snow, moves every part of your body and rapidly speeds up your circulation. Running for just four minutes can easily work up a perspiration even in subzero temperatures.

Warm-ups Without Skis. Here are several warm-up tricks you may perform without skis:

Touching Under Boot, Knees Stiff. Stand on the side of a hill or on the flat and bend forward, keeping your knees stiff, and touch the sole of your ski boot under your toes. (Do this eight to ten times.) This helps loosen the ligaments and tendons in your lower back as well as the backs of your legs.

Pulling Knee Up to Chin. Pull your knee up to your shoulder and chin. (Alternate right and left eight to ten times.) This loosens your knee and hip joints and exercises the abdominal section of your body.

Leg-swinging, Pendulum Style. Put your

(A) Simply walk up and down stairs whenever possible. However, walk *backwards* when descending stairs. This can be done throughout the walking day and will strengthen leg tendons. (B) Assume a sitting position with arms touching the floor behind your derrière. Do fast leg-lifting, up and down, without touching the floor with your heels.

ski poles on either side of you in the snow and, using them as outriggers, swing one leg as high as possible backward and forward like a pendulum. (Alternate left and right ten times each.) This forces the blood down into your toes and gets them warm in a hurry, as well as limbering up the whole leg and hip joints.

In addition to these four exercises, jumping in place and to the right and left will keep you pretty warm and ready to go for recreation or competition.

Warm-ups with Skis. Here are several warm-up exercises you may perform with skis:

Ski Slalom, in Place. Place your poles to the right and left of your skis at arm's length. Jump with your legs together and, lifting only the backs of your skis, land as far to one side or the other as the width of your poles allow. Your ski tips should remain in the snow during this exercise.

Leg-stretching, Sideways. This should be executed on level ground. With legs far apart, bend sideways with an erect upper body, trying to reach the top of your boot. This gets all the tendons, muscles, and ligaments on the inside of your legs ready to perform, as well as loosening your midsection. (Five times each side, alternating.)

Ski Dance, in Place. With the same arm and pole position as in the "ski slalom," jump as you would in a dance, shifting your weight from one leg to the other. At the same time jump from right to left as far as your pole placement will allow. (Do this ten times.) These two exercises require arm as well as leg action, and are quite warming.

Jumping in Place, Without Poles. Take small jumps in place with legs together, and without the assistance of poles. This is rather strenuous and warms not only your feet but your whole body—in a hurry. (Do this ten times.) This same exercise can be done on one leg. (Five times for each leg.)

Body-stretching, Sideways. With your ski tips far apart, shift your upper body over one knee, and bend forward so your chest touches your knee. (Alternate sides, five times each.) This is a good exercise for stretching, and is most effective when done quickly.

Knee to Chin, with Skis On. From a standing position, pull and force your knee up as close as possible to your shoulder and chin. This improves your balance as well as the flexibility of your knee and hip joints. (Alternate, ten times for each leg.)

Do these exercises with skis on when you are fairly well warmed up. This will prevent damage to muscles in your legs and lower back. Be sure to stand up after the completion of each exercise.

SECTION IV

Ski Competition

Thanks to television, watching ski competitions has become a popular spectator sport which, prior to 1960, was relatively unknown in the United States. The high point of ski race spectating was probably the 1950 FIS Alpine World Championships in Aspen, Colorado, and the 1960 Olympics at Squaw Valley, California, where the courses were lined with reasonably knowledgeable aficionados. Television, of course, has created a great deal of interest in ski racing and jumping. But even at their best in the United States, the crowds are nothing like those in Europe, nor are the spectators nearly as knowledgeable.

Ski races and other ski competition can be as dull or as interesting as the spectator makes them. But if the events are really to be interesting you must know all you can about them.

ALPINE SKI COMPETITION

There are three forms of Alpine races: the slalom, the giant slalom, and the downhill. The Fédération Internationale de Ski (FIS) is the governing body of all international ski events—both Alpine and Nordic.

Slalom

When racing first started before the turn of the century, a group of competitors would get together on top of the mountain and at a signal all took off at once and headed for the designated finish line. There were no prepared tracks, no flags to mark the course, and, for all practical purposes, no rules. The first man to arrive at the bottom of the slope was the winner. These mass starts were known as "geschmozzle" starts because of the wild scramble after the starting signals. This type of racing was colorful, exciting, but, as speeds increased, dangerous. To decrease the danger, racers were started individually and each racer's run was timed. This is the method for competition today.

The original races were pure tests of speed over open Alpine terrain. It was very daredevilish (the British were remarkably good at it), but it did little for skiing skill as such. To emphasize the necessity for skill and judgment in maneuvering, Sir Arnold Lunn started slalom competition, which was originally designed to simulate skiing through the woods and around obstacles. Sir Arnold utilized the two-pole gate, a series of which were

A few of the 100,000 people who regularly watch the jumping at Holmenkollen, Norway.

set in various combinations on a hill. Skiing around poles was not new in itself, but the two-pole gates were a distinct innovation, since they could be set in such a way as to trap the skier who did not use sound judgment. As skiing skill increased, slaloms became tighter and tighter, until today, in top national and international competitions, they are tests in maneuverability. Speed seldom exceeds 25 miles per hour, and it is conditioned by the racer's ability to weave his body through a series of up to 75 gates without falling or missing a gate. There is a minimum of 55 gates in a men's World Championship course, and a maximum of 75. For women it is 40 and 60. The winner is decided by two runs down two separate courses. No one has ever devised a more demanding obstacle course.

In slalom, the course consists of matching pairs of alternating colored flags, approximately ten feet apart, known by descriptive names. The poles used are solid blue, red, and yellow bamboo "trees" with correspondingly colored flags attached at the top, extending approximately seven feet over the snow. The imaginary line between the poles is horizontal in an open gate or vertical in a closed or blind gate, according to the direction of the descending skier. From these two basic sets other combinations are produced. Two blind gates in a line are called a hairpin. Three or more are termed a flush. Two blind gates set apart with an open gate between is an "H," or an offset "H" if any one pair is set out of line. All are tricky combinations meant to make it difficult when taken at maximum speed. A skillful course setter places the flags in such a way as to induce a skier to take chances in order to shave a fraction of a second off his time. The shortcut is often a trap, intended for just that purpose, and only a man eminently skilled in this event will be able, by superhuman effort, to avoid a time-consuming spill. The slalom course is set by the official "setter." It is his sole responsibility to use the terrain to the best advantage in testing the skills of the competition.

Taking a note from the official setter's handbook may give you a better idea of what

Layout of the Squaw Valley Olympic area.

sort of cunning this man must use. The rule states:

A slalom should not be a uniform succession of standardized combinations of gates but a technically clever composition of figures well related to the terrain and connected by single and double gates to form a fluent course requiring from the competitors accurate study, maximum skill and constant control. The test should be full of variety from the technical viewpoint of skiing, including changes of direction with very different radii. The gates shall in no case be placed only down the direct vertical line of a hill. They shall on the contrary be placed in such a manner that some full turns be required, interspersed with traverses.

A racer has only a limited time to study the course, and with 60 to 70 gates, this requires a well-trained and excellent memory. In fact, the slalom gates are not placed in final posi-

tion until the day of the race. Once they are set (this is not required until two hours prior to race time) the racers cannot ski on or by the side of the course under penalty of disqualification. They can only examine the course by climbing up on skis.

Gatekeepers are engaged to make certain that the racers ski between the matching pairs of flags. For example, a competitor can knock down flags with his arms or shoulders, but both feet must pass between the two poles. Should a racer not comply with these rules he is automatically disqualified unless he corrects the mistake by climbing back and skiing through the flags properly. Because it is sometimes difficult for the gatekeeper to call a penalty, many arguments occur. The race referee and jury, after considering all reports from the gatemen, make the final decision.

In most Alpine events (except for the Olympic and World Championship slalom—discussed later in this section), the starting

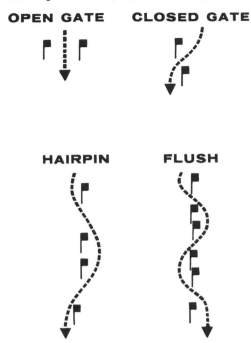

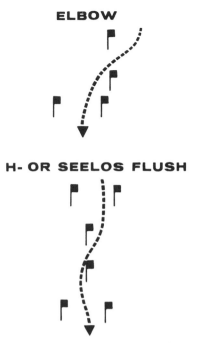

Open and closed gates are 10½ feet wide for competitive slalom, can be wider for recreational use. Allow 12 feet between single or H gates, 2½ feet between flush and hairpin gates, and 5 feet for elbows. Hairpin consists of two successive closed gates; third gate makes it a flush. Neither should be set so tightly that rhythm is broken, but both should require proper tech-

nique. Elbow is made up of a closed gate followed by an open gate set off to one side. As in all combinations, approach depends on the location and type of the next set of gates. The H or Seelos flush is a three-gate combination. Slalom gates can always be entered from either direction; choice is with the racer, and is determined by position and figures that follow.

order is dictated by the individual racer's position in an international ranking system based on what are called "FIS points." The racers with the lowest FIS points are seeded first and, therefore, receive the best starting positions. That is, the order in which racers appear on the master entrant list reflects their FIS ranking relative to other entrants and to the quality of the races in which they have participated.

The order is determined by a complex mathematical formula—for which a computer is used—which considers the best two finishes of each racer in the season. Penalty points are assigned to all races, with a higher number of points being assigned races which attract a weak field. In other words, the winner of a minor race, if this represents one of his best two finishes, would carry a high number of penalty points on the FIS list. The winner of a more important race would be penalized to a lesser extent.

All entrants at FIS-sanctioned Alpine races —and these include all major meets in the world—are broken into groupings, called "seeds," of 15 competitors apiece. On the basis of the aforesaid information it would seem that the racer ranked fifteenth at a given race would start in the first seed and the racer ranked sixteenth would start in the second. And this would be true were it not for a small-in-size but large-in-import FIS ruling which says that the first and second seeds (which historically produce the top finishers) shall not include more than four racers from any given country. The requirement is waived in the case of a national race or a race attracting competitors from three or fewer countries. For instance, let us suppose that an American girl, Mary Smith, is ranked sixteenth internationally in the slalom. But among those 15 racers ranking higher are 5 French girls. Applying the "nations clause," we find that the fifth-ranked French girl becomes ineligible for the first seed—though her name is set aside to head the second seed—and Miss Smith gaily moves into the first seed.

Once the seeds are determined, a racer in the first grouping is assured only of starting fifteenth or earlier. Actual selection within the seed or group is done by the less complex but time-honored method of drawing lots. That is, racers in the first-seeded group draw for starting positions from number 1 to number 15; racers in the second-seeded group draw for starting positions from number 16 to number 30. For the second run of a two-course event, the starting order is reversed in each seeded group. Thus the first racer from the first slalom run would race fifteenth in the second run; the second, fourteenth, and so forth down to one. Similarly, in the second-seeded group, the man who ran sixteenth in the first run starts from thirtieth position in the second run, and so on. The times for the two runs are added; you find out who won the race, and that is the end of it.

The problem, as any racer knows, is that a slalom course physically deteriorates after about 30 racers have gone through it, no matter how good the course preparation has been. (It should be noted that a number of new chemical preparations are creating more durable snow surfaces.) It is always better to have a course with a very hard surface, such as ice or near-ice, than a course that is very soft. A course set over soft, uncompacted snow will rut very easily, and most experienced racers agree that it is a relatively fairer test if the slalom race is held in firm snow conditions. But even on very hard-packed conditions, the course tends to become progressively more chatter-marked around the turns as more racers go through the course. The effect on a racer in a corner or turn is that the chatter marks tend to throw him to the outside. He loses his grip on the snow with his edges and tends to bounce to the outside of every turn. This means that he is not going where he wants to go. He is continually bounced to the outside of each turn so that he has to ski a much longer path through the course. The earlier racers, on the other hand, do not have this disadvantage. They can pretty much go where they wish without being troubled by chatter marks. In other words, if a racer is the best slalom

runner in the world, he would race first and thereby have an advantage over all the other racers. That advantage is in the fact that he does not have to contend with ruts on the course caused by other skiers. This advantage is short-lived, however, owing to the fact that on his second run he would be the last to race in his grouping of 15 racers. With the first racer on the course, the interval between competitors is at least 60 seconds in giant slalom and downhill only. The starter gives every competitor a warning, 10 seconds before the start: "Get ready." Five seconds before the start, he counts: "Five, four, three, two, one," followed by the start signal: "Go! Los! Allez!" The racer actually can start 3 seconds before or after the word "Go!" because the clock is started by his legs pushing aside a starting barrier which in turn starts the clock running. There may also be a series of four flashing yellow "on your mark" lights and a green "go" light, which is keyed into an electronic timing device.

Slalom Racing Rules. It would be almost impossible to list all the rules applicable to ski events. However, in this book we have selected excerpts from the major FIS rules that apply to the event being described.

According to the *International Ski Competition Rules* (FIS rules), "a slalom is a race in which competitors must follow a course defined by pairs of flags (gates). It must always be decided by two runs. For World Championships and Olympic Games two different courses must be used; if possible, two different courses should also be used for other international races. Courses for international Championships, Olympic Games and International Competitions included in the FIS Calendar shall be approved by the FIS."

The Course. The vertical drop of a Men's Slalom shall be between 180 meters (393.6 feet) and 220 (656.0 feet) meters for World Ski Championships and Olympic Winter Games, and between 120 and 180 meters for a Ladies' Slalom. For other International Competitions the vertical drop shall be between 120 and 200 meters. At World Ski Championships and Olympic Winter Games at least a quarter of the course shall be on slopes exceeding 30 degrees in gradient.

A slalom shall be held on hard snow. The snow should, if possible, be so hard that no

Slalom gate arrangement under competitive conditions (above). In recreational slalom, gates should not be as close together. A 35-second slalom (right) recommended for intermediates. Note that it is made up of all basic gate combinations, including a trap in the lower section.

In all racing, the start is most important. Today in major events the start and the timing are electronically controlled.

holes are made when competitors fall. If snow falls during the race, the Chief of the Course shall ensure that the newly fallen snow is stamped from time to time.

A slalom gate shall consist of two solid, round poles of the same color, 3 to 4 centimeters in diameter, and high enough to appear 1.80 meters above the snow. The poles shall not be more than 5 centimeters in diameter at the base. They shall be of wood that will not split or of similar material with the same qualities.

The poles must be painted blue, red, and yellow. Consecutive gates shall always be set in the order blue, red, and yellow. The poles shall carry a flag of the same color.

The gates shall be numbered starting from the top, and the numbers shall be fixed on the outside poles. No gate shall be less than 3.20 meters nor more than 4 meters wide. The distance from one gate to another shall not be less than 0.75 meters. This distance shall be observed between the poles of different gates as well as between the poles of one gate and those of another on the intended line. The position of the flagpoles must be marked on the snow with ink or some other substance in case they are knocked out of the snow. Number of gates for men: minimum 55, maximum 75. Number of gates for ladies: minimum 40, maximum 60.

Passing Gates. A competitor shall be deemed to have passed through a gate correctly only if both his feet have crossed the line between the poles. A competitor shall be disqualified if he does not correctly pass all gates as well as the Finish.

Disqualification. A competitor shall be disqualified for the following reasons:

If he is not qualified under the governing body's amateur rules.

If he enters the race under false premises.

If he trains on a slope that is closed to competitors or examines the course in a way that is not allowed.

If he is late at the start or makes a false start.

If he fails to complete the course on skis and to finish on at least one ski.

If he receives assistance in any form.

If he fails to pass through all the gates by crossing the line between the poles with both feet.

If he fails to finish the race by crossing the finish line with both feet.

Single-pole Slalom. While not used in international competitions, the single-pole slalom race course often is used in practice and many "local" events. In conventional two-pole slalom, the variety of gates the course setter can place to utilize the most interesting terrain contours forces the racer to execute and follow an exact line marked by the *second pole* in the gate. In addition, a course setter can make hundreds of combinations out of all the two-pole gates. From these he can produce the most delicate and intriguing championship slalom, or the simplest design for the skill and technique of a children's competition. At the same time, by using simple open and closed gates in rhythmical patterns, beginning racers can have fun while they are learning. These characteristics disappear with one-pole courses.

Most important is that every single pole set requires a turn around it. In other words, there is a continuous back-and-forth turning. For instance, a slalom of 65 single poles, properly spaced, will guarantee 65 turns. This eliminates many acrobatic fall-line maneuvers which are not necessarily pertinent to modern racing technique.

In the single-pole slalom, the main job of the racer will be to concentrate on absolute maximum speed, since he does not have to worry about missing a gate. All he must do is turn above every pole set, and he cannot go wrong. Potentially, the one-pole slalom eliminates some of the options and challenges that we identify with the slalom race. However, the competitor may favor the one-pole slalom because he can concentrate much more on his actual maximum skill and technique. It is easier for him to remember 65 poles than it is to remember 38 gates. Participants go "all out" for speed, producing keener competition.

Downhill

The essence of the downhill is speed. It is the most highly regarded of the Alpine events because it measures the courage, physical conditioning, and reflexes of the racer at speeds of more than 80 miles per hour over a course booby-trapped with bumps, rolls, gullies, and sudden changes in terrain. The only qualifying factor is judgment.

The downhill course is designed as a real test of the skier's ability. It is built from top down to take advantage of bumps, drop-offs, steep gulleys, and ditches. It is a course that offers a thrill a foot, but not a disaster a foot. The course is built fast, but within limits. That is why safety is built into the course almost everywhere. For instance, the little flags marking the sides of the course are directional flags—the green ones marking the right side, and the red ones tracing the left side.

FIS Downhill Rules. In order to direct the competitor over particular sections of the course or to protect him against the risks of accidents, the setter shall place obligatory gates. Such obligatory gates shall as far as possible be placed at right angles to the main direction of the course (open gates) and shall be not less than 8 meters wide. When setting such obligatory gates the setter shall bear in mind the standard of the competitor in relation to the risks of accidents.

Wood trails must be at least 20 meters wide. This, however, must not mean that all parts of the course must be well above 20 meters wide, as the effect of sun and wind can often cause considerable damage to the snow surface.

Starting Time and Training Hours. The starting time for downhill competitions must be fixed uncompromisingly for the time when the visibility is at the best. The light (light and shadow) as well as the effect of the sun on the course must be, in this connection, especially considered. Sections in full sun must not be immediately followed by sections in deep shadow. Organizers must realize that the choice of the official training hours and the starting time for downhill races, in consideration of the conditions of visibility, are to be taken as most important decisions.

Finish. Special attention must be paid to a long, wide, gently levelling and unobstructed run-out after the finish.

Men's Courses. Technical indications are as follows:

Minimum drop: 800 meters (in exceptional cases 750 meters).

Maximum drop: 1,000 meters.

Width of the obligatory gates: 8 meters (at least).

At Olympic Winter Games and World Ski Championships, the best time of men's downhill shall not be less than 2 minutes 15 seconds.

Ladies' Courses. Technical indications are as follows:

Minimum drop for Olympic Winter Games and World Ski Championships: 500 meters.

Maximum drop for Olympic Winter Games and World Ski Championships: 700 meters.

Minimum drop for other international races: 400 meters.

Maximum drop for other international races: 700 meters.

Width of the obligatory gates: 8 meters (at least).

At Olympic Winter Games and World Ski Championships, the best time of ladies' downhill shall not be less than 1 minute 50 seconds.

The downhill course for ladies shall be a "controlled course" taking the local conditions into account while its flagging is set by FIS standards. It shall not include technical slalom figures, but sufficient obligatory gates shall be placed on steep sections to eliminate excessive speed over difficult and bumpy terrain.

Ladies' downhill courses shall if possible be separated from men's.

Marking. The course shall be marked in the following manner:

1. *Direction flags.* In the sense of the downhill there shall be placed red direction flags on the left side of the course and green direction flags on the right side of the course in sufficient quantity, so that the competitor can recognize the course even in bad visibility.

2. *Obligatory gates.* An obligatory gate consists of two flags. Each flag must be a rectangular piece of cloth and shall be stretched between two vertically fixed poles of splinterproof and solid material, so that the lower edge of the flag's cloth remains about 1 meter above the snow. The poles shall be fixed in the snow, aligned in one direction at right angles to the racing line. On undulated terrains, which render the visibility more difficult, the lower edge of the cloth shall be more than 1 meter above the snow, in order to be recognized from far away. The gates

shall be numbered from start to finish.

The *men's downhill courses* shall be marked by red obligatory gates. Their flags are 1 meter wide and 0.70 meter high. The width of an obligatory gate must be at least 8 meters.

The *ladies' downhill courses* shall be marked alternately with red and blue obligatory gates. Their flags must be at least 1 meter wide and 0.70 meters high. The width of an obligatory gate must be at least 8 meters.

Giant Slalom

Giant slalom was originally developed just before World War II as a compromise event between downhill and slalom. Since that time, however, it has gained a distinct character of its own. Whereas downhill follows the fall line as closely as is practical within the limits of safety, and whereas slalom puts the emphasis on turning, giant slalom is essentially a test of traversing at high speed. The turn that follows the traverse should put the racer in such a position that he can traverse at high speed to the next gate. While there are gates in giant slalom, they are not put together in combinations.

Actually, a giant slalom race is a combination of the speed of a downhill and the agility of a slalom. That is due to the fact that the rules for setting the course state: "The course shall be prepared as for a Downhill race. The parts of the course where the control gates are placed and where competitors have to turn shall be prepared as for a slalom."

The gates are marked with red and blue flags in alternating order. Each gate has two flags with a minimum of 4 meters and a maximum of 8 meters separating them. The gates are open or closed, precluding the kind of configurations seen in the slalom. However, the crisscross pattern in which the gates are set out requires the racer to traverse and retraverse the fall line as he moves down the course.

Riding the edges of the skis is roughly analogous to taking an automobile turn on two wheels. Mastery of the technique is required for all racing turns. It is especially important in the giant slalom because so much time is spent on the ski edges in nego-

tiating the traverses. The racers are permitted to study the course for an hour or so prior to the race to determine their routes.

Giant Slalom Racing Rules. The FIS manual states that "a giant slalom is a race in which the competitors shall follow a course defined by control gates."

Men's Courses. When the giant slalom is carried out on only one run, the height difference must be at least 400 meters and must not surpass 600 meters. If the competition is carried out on two runs, the height difference for one run must be at least 250 meters.

Ladies' Courses. Giant slalom for ladies must be carried out on only one run. The height difference must be at least 300 meters and not more than 450 meters; with the exception of Olympic Winter Games and World Ski Championships, the height difference may be less than 300 meters in exceptional cases.

The Setting. A giant slalom shall have at least 30 gates including start and finish. The gates shall be at least 4 meters and at most 8 meters wide. The distance between the nearest poles of successive gates shall be not less than 5 meters. The gates shall be placed in such a manner that the competitors can distinguish them clearly and quickly even when running at high speed.

The setting of giant slalom gates is done as follows:

1. The poles are the same as those used for slalom (4 poles per gate). The rectangular cloths are at least 75 centimeters wide and 50 centimeters high. They are stretched between the poles in such manner that the lower edge of the flag is about 1 meter above the snow.

2. The gates will be red and blue, if possible with some distinctive marking, preferably white diagonal stripes.

3. The two flags of the gate should be placed perpendicularly to the direction of the course.

4. The gates shall be numbered starting from the top and the numbers fixed on the outside poles.

5. For blind gates, the flags shall be rolled to a width of 30 centimeters.

6. The position of the flagpoles must be marked on the snow with ink or some other substance in case they are knocked out of the snow.

In general a giant slalom course shall permit a judicious alternation of long, average, and small swings. The competitor should be free to choose his own track between the gates, which should not be set down the direct vertical line of a hill. When setting a giant slalom, the width of a hill should be used as much as possible.

The speed shall at all times be reasonable and shall normally not exceed 65 kilometers on a men's course and 45 kilometers on a ladies' course.

The average vertical drop between two gates should not be more than 13 meters on a men's course and 9 to 10 meters on a ladies' course. The width of the gates must be 4 to 8 meters; it is advisable to set them rather wide, especially where competitors are going fast, and in such a way that they can be easily anticipated.

In the case of giant slalom carried out on two runs, it is recommended that the setter sets the two courses in such a way that the best times of each run are close together (same table column) so that the classification of the two runs can be carried out by adding the times.

Disqualifications—Downhill and Giant Slalom

1. If he be not qualified under the governing body's amateur rules.

2. If he enters the race under false premises.

3. If he trains on a slope which is closed to competitors.

4. If he be late at the start or fail to return to the start after having made a false start.

5. If he fails to complete the course on skis, or fails to finish on at least one ski.

6. If he receives assistance in any form.

7. If he fails to give way to an overtaking competitor on first demand.

8. If he fails to pass all controls by crossing the line between the inner poles of the flags with both feet.

9. If he fails to finish the race by crossing the finish line with both feet.

Alpine Combined

According to FIS rules, the Alpine combination is the result of one slalom, one downhill race, and one giant slalom race in which the downhill is run first. While many in ski racing officialdom do not believe in the so-called "paper races," as combined events are sometimes called, they do give voice to a fundamental belief that it is wise and good to foster all-around skiing. The specialists—the downhill or slalom racers, for example—will, of course, top the list in any major competition. But that is not the point. Specialists will come up automatically from the ranks of young talented skiers. The point is that the specialists with a broad background in skiing will almost always be better than those who have restricted their development too early.

Since 1948, the Winter Olympic Committee does not award medals to the Alpine combined winners. (It does, however, to the Nordic combined—cross-country and jumping—winners.) In Olympic years when the Olympic Alpine events constitute the World Championship events for the FIS, the FIS has instituted a combined award based on the best overall performance in all three Olympic Alpine events. In even-numbered off-Olympic years when the FIS stages its own World Championships, it awards an Alpine combined title.

Watching Alpine Races

The skier who wants to be among the very best must be constantly alert to new refinements in equipment and technique. At least once or twice a season, he should make it a point to race with or watch the top skiers. If he knows how to watch, and knows exactly what he himself is doing and why he is doing it, he will quickly spot what is separating the top racers from the also-rans.

To make watching races more interesting, you must have the right equipment. This consists of the start order, a pencil, a stopwatch or two, and some knowledge about the event you are about to watch.

In the giant slalom and downhill events, the racers leave on an even-minute interval. With this piece of information and the right kind of stopwatch, it is possible to determine at any point on the course who is doing well, who is doing poorly, and by how much. The stopwatch you need for these events must have a split-second hand. The sweep should be in either half-minute or full-minute intervals, and the individual seconds should be calibrated down to tenths. A split-second hand allows the watch to be started and kept running, although a part of the second hand can be stopped at any individual time, the reading taken, and then reset without stopping the watch.

The way you use the watch is to position yourself alongside the course, starting the watch when the first racer goes by a gate, is silhouetted against a landmark, or any other way by which you can identify all the racers as they come to a specific point on the course. Now you know the second racer is starting exactly one minute after the first man. If the two racers have had exactly the same time down to the point where you are timing, then the second racer should appear at that point exactly one minute after the first racer. On the other hand, if the second racer appears at your checkpoint one minute and two seconds later than the first racer, you know that the second racer is already two seconds slower than the first. This is what you are interested in finding out: whether a racer reaches the point slightly ahead of or behind the even minute, and by how much. Your stopwatch with a split-second hand makes this possible because you can stop the split hand as each racer crosses the designated point, while the other second hand enables you to keep track of minute intervals.

The way you record times for each racer is going to be minus so many seconds or plus so many seconds, with the first racer being 00. At the end of five racers, you might have something that resembles this: first racer, 00; second racer, +1.1; third racer, −2.0; fourth racer, +3.0; fifth racer, −.5. At this point, you know that the fastest man past you is the third racer. The third racer is 1.5 seconds faster than racer number five, who is in turn a half-second faster than the first racer. The first racer is 1.1 seconds faster than the second racer, and the second racer is 1.9 seconds faster than the fourth. In other words, it is relatively easy to work out a placement of all racers at any given point in the race.

This form of timing is known as interval timing. It is used extensively by coaches and also by the European press, which will send whole timing teams to races, positioning them on major downhills, in order to come up with a comprehensive story covering an event. What they will do, for instance, is to place a reporter with a split-second stopwatch at the beginning of a long flat. They will place another reporter with a split-second watch at the end of that flat, and they will record times by this method all through the race. At the end of the race, they will get together, and by comparing the relative placement of all racers at the beginning and end of the flat, they can determine what teams did well through the flat. In other words, they can determine who had fast skis or who had good wax and so on. They can also do the same thing through a particularly steep or difficult portion of the race—the point being that many times the man who wins the race is not always the fastest on the toughest part of the course.

Skiing is a sport that is won in hundredths of a second, but these split seconds are gained and lost all the way down the course. It is interesting to try to find *where the race was won*. If you stand at the finish line, you can also use interval timing in order to determine your own order of finish. You will not, of course, know the absolute times of the racers, but you will be able to tell the relative order of finish.

The only thing to remember in using interval timing is that the major races nowadays are run with electronic timing. The racer in downhill or giant slalom does not have to leave exactly on the even minute in order to have his time recorded. The result is that the electronic timing can sometimes deviate slightly from the hand timing. As a practical matter, however, most racers will leave the starting gate as near to the even minute as possible so that interval timing is still valid. It is usually accurate to within two-tenths to three-tenths of a second, which in a long giant slalom or downhill gives great enough accuracy in order to draw meaningful conclusions.

Slalom races are usually easier to watch. You can usually see the start and finish of a slalom race, since it takes place in a more confined area than giant slalom or downhill, with shorter time spans.

On some hills it is impossible to see both the start and the finish of a slalom race from one vantage point. In this case you should use what is known as section timing, in which you pick a point where you begin to time the racer and another point farther down the course, still within sight, where you stop timing the racer. What you are doing is measuring the interval between the first point and the second point for all racers. This kind of timing will give you information on who is doing well in the race within that section of the course. This is a relatively simple kind of timing, and it is often very meaningful, particularly if the stretch that you are timing happens to be the most difficult on the course. In order to get meaningful information, the timed stretch should be at least 20 seconds long and preferably in excess of 30 seconds.

With these two methods of timing at your disposal—interval timing and section timing —it is possible for you to watch the race from literally any point on a race course and still have meaningful information on the relative order of racers as they go by you. You will find that this makes the race much more interesting than watching a great slew of race numbers go by with no idea of who is doing well or poorly. To see the best racing, you should be there at least five or ten minutes before the start, since the best racers run first because of their seeded order. In picking a spot from which to watch, bear in mind that the most important parts of the course are often not near the finish line, but are farther up the hill. That is, in selecting a spot to watch the race, ski alongside the course for the entire distance well before the race. Try to visualize the reason for gates and turns and how they fit in with the course above and below them. Do not ignore flats, particularly if they follow a turn. A flat may be the

crucial part of a course. Try to put yourself in the boots of the racer. If you are learning to race, you will see how far you still have to go. If you are merely a spectator, ski racing will come to mean a lot more than a progression of figures flashing by at high speed.

Head-to-Head Racing

In the past few years most of the professional ski races have a dual format in which two racers compete head to head. This dual competition is exciting. "No matter how much you concentrate on your own run," comments one of the top pros, "it is just not like a normal ski race. The temptation is always there to whip your head aside for a split second to see how the other fellow is doing."

Because no two courses over different terrain can be exactly alike, the racers switch in the second run, so that each competitor has a crack at both courses. For the spectator keen to spot where and how a racer has gained or lost time, the dual slalom is far more instructive. With two well-matched racers on duplicate courses, the eye quickly detects relative differences in line of approach, edging, and turning that add up to fractions of seconds on the clock.

The second run sees some tense, closely matched racing. Weaving, bobbing, and floating through the flags, the racers at times seem like two ballet dancers engaged in an intricate pas de deux on snow. Ten to fifteen gates from the finish, the cheering of the crowd rises to a pitch as spectators shout for their favorite to move faster and ahead. Often, a pair of pros will pole in a simultaneous wild dash to the finish line. This, indeed, is ski racing as the spectator wants to see it.

NORDIC SKI COMPETITION

The American ski heritage is essentially Alpine; we use lifts and ski downhill. In North American competition, downhill, slalom, and giant slalom are the premier events. It is only in the last few years that Americans have shown renewed interest in the Nordic competitive phase of the sport— cross-country racing and jumping.

Jumping

In 1866, Sondre Norheim "flew as if a bird on wing" and amazed all onlookers by outdistancing the competition at a meet in his native Telemark, a region of Norway. Inventive Norheim had put cables around his heels and had thus become the first man to exert precise control over his skis while in the air.

The excitement of split-second timing and birdlike soaring is such that ski jumping is the undisputed world king of winter spectator sports. As was stated earlier, skiing is usually thought of as a participation rather than a spectator sport. Consequently, most skiers would rather be on the hill carving their own Christies than standing in the cold and snow watching someone else perform. There is one phase of the sport, however, that consistently draws large spectator crowds who will stand in the cold and snow for hours, watching daring men glide through the air. Major jumping meets in Finland, Russia, Sweden, and Norway draw crowds of 50,000. Meets in the Midwest and at Bear Mountain in New York attract crowds of up to 20,000. Crowds of 100,000 watch at the oldest and most prestigious meet of them all, the Holmenkollen, in Norway.

The jumper's first concern is to jump farther than the competition; the other is to achieve an aesthetic style so perfect as to receive the maximum style points from the presiding judges. These goals are closely related. Other things being equal, the most perfect style results in the longest jump. On the other hand, given a big hill, a jumper may well outdistance the entire competition by 2 meters (about 6½ feet) every jump, yet lose the meet because one hand touched the snow every time he landed, costing him vital style points.

The first "big" jumping meet, at Husebybakken near Oslo in 1879, produced a winning jump of 23 meters (72 feet). Twenty years later, at the turn of the century, the world record was 35.5 meters (117 feet). In 1917, an American, Henry Hall, captured the record with 203 feet at Steamboat Springs, Colorado. As the heights of the hills grew larger, the jumpers were soon hitting 100 meters (328 feet). Because of cost and danger inherent on large hills, competition on giant, expensive hills (more than 90 meters) was made a separate sport, ski flying. The present ski-flying record is around 165 meters (542 feet). The "record" has been creeping up a few meters each year, although the jumping world feels that longer jumps are not humanly possible. However, ski jumping, not ski flying (described later), is the event at the Holmenkollen every year, at the FIS Nordic Championship every two years, and at the Olympics every four years.

Jumping style has an ideal form. On the inrun, a jumper starts by skating one step out onto the chute. Then he crouches in an "egg" position similar to that used in downhill. Early jumpers thought they could reduce wind resistance and prepare for powerful takeoff by crouching as low as possible. The half-crouch of the egg, however, is not only superior aerodynamically, but also is better for the takeoff. The modern jumper springs forward over his ski tips instead of hopping up at takeoff. The takeoff is crucial; it determines the success of the entire jump. To catch and ride the air from the very start, the jumper should leave the lip of the takeoff with his ski tips rising. If he springs before he reaches the lip of the jump, he will take off with his ski tips falling, and so lose part of his "lift."

If a jumper leaves the lip of the jump, his tips will *then* drop a bit because their support (the lip) has suddenly been removed. What happens in the next instant is important. If the jumper has sprung just slightly late, the ideal timing, his tips will come up again as he continues his flight, and he is on his way to a good jump.

To see why this is so, try a simple standing high jump. Notice that the more powerfully you jump, the more emphatically your feet point down toward the floor as you take off. The rapid straightening of your legs throws your weight onto the balls of your feet. This in turn triggers an ankle-straightening reflex. It is this reflex which results in the tips staying down for the ski jumper who takes off too early. Ideally the jumper times his takeoff so that his legs straighten fully just *after* takeoff. The tips then come up.

In the critical transition from inrun to flight, most jumpers swing their arms once or twice, forward and backward. As they spring over their skis, most jumpers carry their arms at their sides; a few carry them in front like divers. Both arm positions are equally correct. The arms-to-the-sides position is more prevalent because it is the easiest to hold while in flight. In flight, the skis are carried horizontal or a little above horizontal to ride the air current. "Tips down" not only looks awkward, but can be dangerous; wind pressure on the top of skis may drive a jumper down too early and too hard, turning him over in the air.

The jumper tries to hold a steady, controlled position as long as possible to receive the maximum number of points from the judges. Ideally, the jumper breaks his streamlined flight position just as the tails of his skis are about to touch the snow. Then he goes into the classic arms-relaxed, kneeling telemark landing. Dropping into the telemark to allow the knees and hips to absorb the shock of landing, the jumper can go from flight to snow in one continuous smooth movement. The telemark position is not simply a fancy style; it absorbs the landing shock on big jumping hills. The force of a landing is great; it flattens the shovels of the skis as the skis slam into the snow. (Jumpers often tape their ski tips to keep them from splintering on landing.) After the telemark landing is completed, the jumper straightens up and rides the hill to the end, snowplowing or turning to stop.

The modern aerodynamic style of jumping is not the result of any one single breakthrough. It represents a steady and constant development. The earliest jumpers based their technique on the standing high jump. They crouched as low as possible on the inrun and jumped straight up at the takeoff. In flight, they pulled their legs up as if trying to clear an imaginary barrier. Jumpers soon found that the legs-up position did not increase distance; it only increased the problems of absorbing the shock of landing. A nearly vertical body position became the accepted jumping style. By the 1930's, jumpers had discovered that jumping up could be combined with springing out over the skis. As the size of the hills jumped increased, jumpers began to lean farther and farther forward in the air. Pre-World War II Norwegian world champions, the Ruud brothers, developed the earliest "flying" style, a style which was to dominate for many years. The Ruuds used tight heel cables that kept their feet almost flat on the skis. They bent way forward from the ankles and forward from the hips until their torsos were almost parallel to their skis.

Then came the first of the modern "leaners," a new champion, Reidar Andersen. He used loose heel cables, to let his heels come farther off his skis. This meant more lean from the feet and less from the waist and hips; aerodynamically, it was more sound. Further refinements of Andersen's technique allowed the Norwegians to dominate international jumping until the 1954 FIS in Falun, Sweden. The Finns captured the Falun jumping and introduced the modern style. They jumped with bodies arched, arms pinned to their sides, and leaned farther toward their ski tips than anyone had thought possible. The Finns soared to victory at meet after meet and won the Cortina Olympics two years later.

The Finnish success unleased a flurry of inquiry. What did the Finns actually do, and why was it so successful? In Switzerland, an engineer, ex-jumper, and hill designer, Dr. Reinhard Straumann, analyzed jump films. He deduced that the Finns' arched profile enabled them to create "lift," just as the curved top of an airplane wing does. To test his theories, Straumann actually hung ski jumpers in a wind tunnel and measured their "flying" ability. The results of his measurements were conclusive. The more a jumper bent forward from his feet and arched his back and the more he "kissed his ski tips," the more "lift" he got from the air.

Straumann was not alone. In Norway, international ski jumping veteran and Olympic bronze medalist Coach Thorleif Schjelderup had taken thousands of feet of slow-motion film of the successful Finns. Schjelderup carefully analyzed every phase of movement from every angle, and then passed on his findings to his countrymen, including a promising young jumper named Toralf Engan.

The Finns continued to stay ahead. They went on to win at the 1958 FIS in Lahti. But then Helmut Recknagel of Germany caught on. Recknagel had learned the style well. He broke the Finns by an incredible five points in Squaw Valley's 1960 Olympics. By 1962 the Finnish winning streak was over. Recknagel and Engan won the jumping events at the FIS in Zakopane, Poland, in 1962.

Until 1963, the Finns, Norwegians, Swedes, Germans, and Russians never felt real competition from across the Atlantic. But 1963 was a year of change. At the Holmenkollen, 90,000 spectators gathered in the bitter cold with the full expectation that Toralf Engan would prove to be the master of the newly enlarged hill. Few took notice of two Americans far down on the list of some 90 starters. But after the second round was over, the Americans were no longer obscure. John Balfanz was in first place, and Gene Kotlarek had set a hill record with a jump of 82.5 meters (270 feet). Only a beautiful third jump, 6½ feet longer than Kotlarek's, by Norway's Torbjorn Yggeseth, saved the day for Norway. Finishing second and fourth, Balfanz and Kotlarek set an all-time team record for the hill.

The somewhat obscure process of awarding points for style theoretically measures how nearly a jump approaches the perfect, masterful control that is the real secret of long and safe flight. On big hills aerodynamics is extremely important. Indeed, it has been argued that the best style will result in the longest jump; thus, scoring on jump lengths alone should be adequate. For several years, the FIS had had just such a judging system as an option for big hills. Formulated by Dr. Reinhard Straumann of Switzerland, it is known as the S-method. Straumann postulated that the jumper who goes farthest compared to takeoff speed must have the best style. Speeds at takeoff time are electronically timed. Mathematical equations relate speed and jump length to arrive at style points. Elegant in concept, the S-method is complex in application and is not as applicable to smaller hills, where aerodynamics plays a smaller role. The lion's share of jumping meets is scored by judges in the classic method.

Instruments for measuring inrun speed and wind velocity may be used on jumping hills with critical points of more than 80 meters. Such instruments help judges decide inrun speeds. On an 80-meter hill most good jumpers will have inrun speeds of about 55 miles per hour.

In the classic system, the jumper starts with 20 points from each of five judges. After he has landed, each judge deducts points for style faults. The highest and lowest scores are then thrown out. The remaining three scores are added to give the style score. In principle, the judges deduct moderately for faults which shorten the jump, and heavily for faults

which are dangerous to the jumper. Style judging is not just a point system, but a key to safe jumps.

With keener and keener competition than in the past, finer judgments had to be made. By 1965, the FIS scale of fault penalties had grown like Topsy to include more than 30 separate faults divided up into inrun, takeoff, airborne, and landing faults. Some faults were rated at ½ to 2 points, others at ½ to 4 points, others at 1 to 3 points and so on. In all, there were 14 different categories of point penalties. The list was cumbersome, and judges found it increasingly difficult to give fair judgments on the basis of the few seconds they watched a jumper.

As if this were not enough, the FIS regulations had their hidden "blue laws." In flight, jumpers were required to keep their skis inclined at the same angle to the trajectory. This sounded logical in print, but meant that a jumper was forced to gradually lose lift by pressing his skis downward as the flight trajectory dropped. Few jumpers felt at all compelled to follow this illogical regulation—most good jumpers simply kept their skis horizontal, increasing the angle to the trajectory. Dissatisfied judges and nonconforming jumpers made it clear that the FIS style tables were due for revision. At the June, 1965, Mamaia meeting in Rumania, the FIS judging committee all but revolutionized judging.

The FIS decided that inrun and takeoff styles are so highly individual that they are almost impossible to judge properly. Thus it was decided not to begin scoring for style until the jumper reached the lip of the jump. The only penalty on the inrun would be a fall, which obviously costs a jumper all his points. In place of the many different point penalty categories during flight and landing, the following simplified scale was adopted:

In Flight. For small faults or for faults which begin early in flight and are quickly corrected: 1/2–2 points. For faults throughout the entire flight or for faults occurring in flight which are not corrected: 2–4 points. Faults are: bent knees, hips, or back; poor body position; and skis high, low, wide, waving, or crossed.

Landing. For small faults or more serious faults which are quickly corrected: 1/2–2

The seven phases of a jump. *Phase 1:* about to rise from egg position. *Phase 2:* at the lip. *Phase 3:* just off lip. *Phase 4:* jumper is in full flight position. *Phase 5:* getting ready to land. *Phase 6:* the skier lands. *Phase 7:* the full impact of landing.

points. For more serious faults or small faults which are not corrected: 2–4 points. Touching the snow or a ski with one hand: 2–4 points. Touching the snow or skis with both hands, but jumper rises quickly again: 8 points. Touching the snow or skis with both hands and not rising again counts as a fall: 10 points. Faults are: premature preparation for landing; body too stiff, too far backward or too bent; landing without telemark position; unsteadiness.

Because only the flight and landing are now judged, the judges' stand may now be located farther downhill: about one-half to two-thirds of the distance from the lip of the jump to the beginning of the transition. Because it is aerodynamically correct for a jumper to hold his skis horizontal while in flight, the old "same angle to flight trajectory" clause has been discarded. Jumpers now can keep their skis horizontal during flight until they prepare to land, when they will necessarily drop ski tips.

After the hill is prepared and before a meet begins, a metal measuring tape is fixed to the takeoff and is stretched down the landing slope. Lengths are then pegged out on each side of the landing slope with special signs every 5 meters, or the equivalent in feet. The length of a jump is measured to the nearest half-meter or nearest foot from the upper edge of the takeoff. The distance measured is to the midpoint between the feet of the jumper as he lands. Distance-marking officials standing at intervals of 3 meters (10 feet) along the landing slope sight across the hill and use the markers to measure length.

The measured jump lengths are converted into points according to the size of the jumping hill. In principle, style and length count equally; the perfect jump would get 60 points for the jump and 60 points for style.

Today, all international special jumping meets have three rounds of jumping. The first of these three rounds is a trial round in which all competitors are entitled, but not required, to jump. The first round does not enter in the meet results. The second and third rounds comprise the actual competition, and both are counted in the results. The total points for the two jumps determine the winner. The assignment of points per meter is according to the critical-point length of the jumping hill:

Hill Description	Critical-point Length	Points per Meter
Jumping	Under 40 meters	2.0
Jumping	40.5 to 60.0 meters	1.8
Normal jumping	60.5 to 70.0 meters	1.6
Big jumping	75.5 to 90.0 meters	1.4
Ski flying	90.5 meters and over	1.0

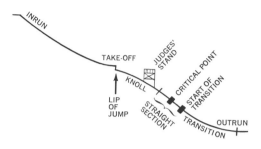

Before the start of a meet, 60 points are assigned to the rated length of the hill plus 10 per cent. For an 80-meter hill this means a standing jump of 88 meters receives 60 points. This guide can be used during the course of the meet and will accurately give the winner and the order of the other competitors. For the final official computations, the judges may, by unanimous decision, elect to assign 60 points to some other length.

The jumper is not judged until he reaches the takeoff. From that point on, he has 20 points from each of five judges (the number used for major competitions). The judges deduct points for various faults until the jumper has completed his landing. The highest and lowest scores are thrown out, and the jumper earns his points on the basis of scores of the three middle judges, 60 points being the maximum possible score for style. The jumper earns additional points, depending on the distance he jumps. On ski-flying hills with a critical point of 90 meters or more, he gets 1 point per meter; on jumps between 75 and 90 meters, which covers most of the internationally recognized ski jumps, he gets 1.4 points per meter, with more points per meter on smaller hills.

Every jumping hill used for international competition must have dimensions in such ratios and a profile in given curves, conforming to the precise designs worked out for the

FIS by Dr. Straumann. Between the convex knoll where the hill steadily gets steeper and the concave transition where it flattens out is a straight section where most jumpers will land. The "size" of the jumping hill is measured from the lip of the takeoff to a point slightly beyond the middle of the straight section. Called the "critical point," it is usually marked with a blue line or board and represents the point beyond which landing becomes increasingly difficult. The end of the straight section is usually marked with a red line or board and indicates the limit to safe landing. FIS regulations prohibit takeoff speeds which result in jumps with landings farther than halfway between the blue and red lines. Takeoff speeds are regulated by the location, higher or lower, of the starting platform on the inrun.

At all World Championships, two jumping hills must be used: a "normal" hill with a critical point of about 70 meters, and a "big" hill with a critical point between 80 and 90 meters, the difference between the two being about 15 meters. The "normal" hill is also used for the combined jumping. Thus, there can be two world jumping champions, plus a Nordic combined champion.

Ski Flying

Ski flying really has nothing to do with kites or airplanes; it is, in fact, very similar to ski jumping. The major difference between the two is the length of the jumps, based on the sizes of the hills themselves; a jumping hill is no more than 90 meters from the lip of the ramp to the norm point, while a flying hill measures 120 meters from lip to NP. This norm point, the end of the convex slope, is the optimum area on the outrun for a jumper to land.

According to FIS regulations, the longest jump in either flying or jumping should not be longer than roughly halfway between the norm point and the curve point (about 20 per

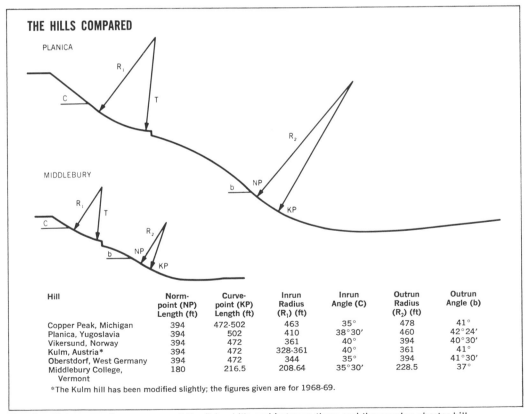

Hill	Norm-point (NP) Length (ft)	Curve-point (KP) Length (ft)	Inrun Radius (R₁) (ft)	Inrun Angle (C)	Outrun Radius (R₂) (ft)	Outrun Angle (b)
Copper Peak, Michigan	394	472-502	463	35°	478	41°
Planica, Yugoslavia	394	502	410	38°30'	460	42°24'
Vikersund, Norway	394	472	361	40°	394	40°30'
Kulm, Austria*	394	472	328-361	40°	361	41°
Oberstdorf, West Germany	394	472	344	35°	394	41°30'
Middlebury College, Vermont	180	216.5	208.64	35°30'	228.5	37°

*The Kulm hill has been modified slightly; the figures given are for 1968-69.

The chart lists comparisons among all the flying hills and between them and the regular, shorter hill.

cent farther down the hill). Rigid interpretation would enforce this, but it is obviously not the only measure, or all jumps on 120-meter hills would be near the formula: 120 meters plus 10 to 20 per cent. Form counts, too.

The secret to longer jumps lies in the profile of the hill. Jumpers should aim to land on an increasing or steady slope, not on a decreasing one. Thus, if the radius of the transition curve between the convex and the concave slopes is very large, the hill has virtually a flat slope beyond its curve-point length—making longer jumps both possible and likely. Thus, the real difference between flying and jumping is one of size and degree only.

Cross-country Racing

In the north European countries, where cross-country skiing is the natural way of walking in winter, cross-country racing is probably the most popular form of competition. In fact, cross-country racing is Scandinavian-type touring (see Section III) at speed. In major national and international meets, the distances are 15, 30, and 50 kilometers (9.4, 15.7, and 31.3 miles, respectively), although other distances are not unusual in Scandinavian meets. Juniors usually run less than 15 kilometers, while women race at 5 and 10 kilometers (2.6 and 5.2 miles, respectively). The longest and most unusual cross-country event is the Vasaloppet race in Sweden, which covers 85 kilometers (53 miles) between Sälen and Mora (see page 4 for details of this event).

The most exciting cross-country event is the relay, usually run in four legs of 10 kilometers and with the first runners from each team starting at the same time. The women's event usually consists of three legs of 5 kilometers. In the Olympic games the cross-country relay is considered the most exciting ski event, by both press and spec-

The start of a cross-country Olympic race.

Russia's Pavel Kolchin (left) relays to teammate Nikolai Anikin in the middle leg of the grueling 4 × 10-kilometer relay cross-country race at the 1956 Winter Olympics at Cortina. The Soviet victory in this event broke a long-standing Scandinavian monopoly on the event.

tators. In fact, in the first three Olympic Winter Games cross-country and jumping were the only ski events held. The Alpine races did not develop to a point where they qualified as Olympic competition until 1936.

Cross-country racing is conducted on "tracks" on well-prepared trails which ideally should cover terrain about one-third uphill, one-third downhill, and one-third on the level. The tracks, one for each ski, are set into the trail about 4 to 6 inches apart. Cross-country racers stick religiously to the tracks unless they are forced to yield to an overtaking runner, who has the right of way.

The training for cross-country racing is highly demanding. It requires year-around conditioning for speed, strength, and endurance and must be continued for years to build the necessary stamina. An Alpine racer's peak years are between the ages of twenty and twenty-eight; a cross-country racer's often between twenty and thirty-five. This peak period is being lowered somewhat by new training methods, but the fact remains that the best racers in the world are with few exceptions thirty years old and older.

Although it can take several hours to run off, a cross-country race is exciting sport and is followed avidly by the Scandinavians, who turn out by the tens of thousands to watch the major events. Most of them take their skis to the races and keep moving from key location to key location as the race progresses. Usually the tracks are laid on elliptical or figure-eight trails, and by means of shortcuts spectators can see their favorites several times in the course of a race.

Cross-country Rules. Here are some of the more important cross-country racing rules:

The Course. A cross-country course shall be so laid out as to be a true test of the competitor's strength, endurance, ski technique, and tactical knowledge.

The course shall consist of ever-varying sections of climbs, downhill, and flat parts. Climbs which are too long and steep, or very difficult and risky downhill sections, as well as monotonous open stretches, should be avoided. Artificial obstacles are not allowed.

In order to avoid undue strain as far as possible, the first section of the course should be comparatively easy. The most strenuous part of the course should occur about halfway or in the third quarter of the course.

The course shall be laid out naturally and vary as much as possible. Only when absolutely necessary should the ground be changed by cutting out traverses, etc.

The course may not be set on slopes that entail risk or danger to the competitor, who must be able to run at full speed without danger of accidents.

Changes of direction should not be allowed so close together that the rhythm of the competitor is broken and he is hampered in his stride.

In order to eliminate the risk of mistaking direction, outward and inward tracks must not run close to one another.

Courses for ladies should not be too flat or monotonous. They should be varied so that endurance and ski technique are put to the test.

Height Differences. The difference in height between the lowest and highest points of the course may not exceed: 100 meters on ladies' courses of 5 kilometers; 150 meters on ladies' courses of 10 kilometers; 200 meters on men's courses of 10 kilometers; 250 meters on men's courses of 15 kilometers and above.

The difference of height of any single climb (without intervening level ground or downhill of at least 200 meters), the so-called "maximum climb," must not exceed: 75 meters on ladies' courses; 100 meters on men's courses.

The course or part of it may be run twice.

Method of Start. The competitors start one or two at a time with a ½- or 1-minute interval between starts.

At Olympic Winter Games and World Ski Championships the competitors shall start one at a time with ½-minute intervals, and electrical timing should be utilized so as to provide the exact starting time for each individual competitor to the nearest one-tenth of a second.

Nordic Combined

Steeped in Norwegian tradition, this event is a combination of the two principal Nordic disciplines—jumping and cross-country racing. The combined cross-country distance is 15 kilometers, and the jumping is usually done on a 60- or 70-meter hill. The cross-country race is scored against the clock, with the various times accorded point coefficients. The jump is scored on distance and style for the best two out of three efforts. That is, the combined competitors are scored in jumping by the same system as in so-called normal jumping, and their cross-country time is converted into points. The jumping and cross-country points are then added for the combined score, the man with the most points being the winner. Needless to say, a Nordic combined competitor must have the special qualities of both the cross-country racer and the jumper, at least in good enough proportions to have a chance for victory, although most combined competitors are consistently stronger in one event. It is rare, indeed, at any level of combined competition, that the combined winner has won both the jumping and the cross-country. In fact, it is not at all unusual for the combined winner not to have won either individual event.

Biathlon

The biathlon is a quasi-military event involving rifle marksmanship and cross-country racing. The sport is highly esteemed by Nordic nations and the U.S.S.R. The United States Army operates a Biathlon Training Center in Alaska, but the event has caught on

The biathlon event at the 1964 Winter Olympics.

only in recent years in North America.

The Olympics biathlon is a 20-kilometer cross-country run spotted with four stationary targets set out at distances of 6, 10.5, 11.6, and 17.5 kilometers from the course. Contestants are required to fire a series of five rifle shots in a prone position at each of the first three targets from distances of 250 meters, 200 meters, and 150 meters. They must also fire five shots at the final target from a standing position at a distance of 100 meters. The targets are metallic disks, 8 to 12 inches in diameter. A hit is scored when the bullet strikes any part of the target. Time on the shooting range counts as part of the total race time, and each target miss carries a two-minute penalty.

The contestants leave the starting point at two-minute intervals, carrying an unloaded rifle and ammunition. Rifles are loaded at the range, and shots are delivered from a firing point assigned by a race official. No contestant is permitted to go on to the next range until he has unloaded his rifle. A first-rate biathlon racer can cover the distance, including time out for riflery, in about 85 minutes.

The skill and training that go into the biathlon can be only roughly appreciated by the layman. Even expert rifle marksmen and top skiers find the feat difficult to comprehend. It has been compared to hitting a thumb-sized target across the length of a baseball diamond while running 12 miles at top speed.

INTERNATIONAL SKI COMPETITION

Ski competition on an international scale is about as old as skiing itself—that is, skiing as a recognized sport. Almost from its very beginnings, skiing has had international participation, particularly in the Alpine events. The young Hannes Schneider, one of the most spectacular competitors of his day, used to cross over into Switzerland regularly to participate in races there. Downhill, of course, was his forte, but he also jumped and raced cross-country.

Even before Schneider's time, ski competition had an international flavor. The first ski competitions in central Europe invariably featured Norwegian students as well as local talent. The British, who had no skiing of their own to speak of, were regular competitors in Alpine races and until the mid-1930's were among the world's best. And Scandinavian-born jumpers and cross-country racers were invariably the favorites at American meets in the early days.

The oldest premier event in skiing is the Holmenkollen, held outside of Oslo, Norway. It started in 1892 and had foreign participation as early as 1909, the year before the first meeting of the International Ski Congress. The events at the Holmenkollen have evolved as the sport developed. However, although Alpine events were added in 1936, the emphasis is still on jumping and cross-country. In those years when there are no

Winter Olympics or FIS World Championships, the winners at the Holmenkollen are usually considered the best jumpers and cross-country racers in the world.

While ski competition was always international to some extent, the sport did not command major public interest until well after World War I, actually not until 1924, when jumping and cross-country racing were incorporated in the first Winter Olympic Games at Chamonix, France. That was also the year the International Ski Congress decided that skiing needed an international governing body. The result was the Fédération Internationale de Ski, which to this day makes the rules for the sport, compiles seeding lists, selects the sites for World Championships, and, through its officials, approves race courses and jumping hills for international competition.

It is indicative of the state of Alpine racing in 1924 that the FIS first refused to recognize downhill and the (then infant) slalom. It was not until 1928 that the group tentatively recognized the Ski Club of Great Britain rules for Alpine races, and not until 1932 that it sanctioned such races officially. As a result, Alpine events were not incorporated into the Olympic program until 1936.

Starting in 1925, the FIS organized so-called FIS Races on an annual basis, at first only in jumping and cross-country and beginning in 1931 for downhill and slalom. Although the winners of these races were called world champions, the title was not officially sanctioned until 1936, when the name of the races was changed to FIS World Championships. Except in the Olympic years of 1924, 1928, and 1932, they were held annually until 1939. Since World War II, World Championships have been held only on even-numbered years between Olympics.

The Olympics, the most important sports spectacle in the world, bring winners the greatest international renown. And the World Championships, while confined exclusively to skiing, run a close second. Although the medals at the Olympics and World Championships are the most highly prized in international ski competition, these two meets are not necessarily the ultimate ski racing tests. In these meets, the number of entries permitted each nation is limited: four in the case of the Olympics, five in the case of World Championships. As a result, the major ski nations may leave dozens of racers at home who are more than the equal of racers of lesser ski nations, who do enter teams in the Olympics and the World Championships. Thus the World Cup of Alpine Skiing has come to rival the Olympics and FIS Championships in importance. The World Cup is a season-long competition open to all racers. It had its beginning in the winter of 1967. For the first time in the history of the sport, the world's best racers were rated not on the basis of one or two headline races, but on a systematic accumulation of results over the whole season. The new system proved a smashing success, so much so that the World Cup of Alpine Skiing has become a permanent annual fixture of the sport, rivaling the Olympics and the FIS World Championships. Initially ignored by international ski officialdom, the World Cup won instant and enthusiastic acceptance by the two groups most important to the success of ski racing: the racers themselves and the press, radio, and television who must report the results to an eager public. The racers like the World Cup system because they instinctively know it is the fairest way to judge who are the truly top Alpine skiers of the world in a given year. The press and the public like it for the same reason. The World Cup point scoring is necessarily

complex because it seeks to be eminently fair in a complex situation. It starts by preselecting, before the start of the winter racing circuit, a series of meets in Austria, Germany, France, Switzerland, Italy, Japan, Sweden, and North America, and occasionally elsewhere, in which competitors can win World Cup points. The fairly large number of qualifying races offers many opportunities to compete as well as enabling top racers to miss races because of injuries or conflicting interests at home and school. It puts a high premium on first, second, and third places (25, 20, and 15 points) because it seeks ski champions, not racers who can accumulate a large number of points by consistently average performances. This feature of the World Cup is further accentuated by counting only the five best results of a racer in each Alpine specialty during the winter. It also prevents a competitor—who, for instance, is a specialized downhiller but only a mediocre slalom racer—from winning the overall World Cup by accumulating a huge total of points in one specialty. Under the present scoring system, a racer wins 25 points for first place in an event, and can therefore gather a maximum of 125 points or five first places in a specialty during the season.

The World Cup has not been without its critics who have complained about the complex scoring system. But the vindication of its fairness came one glorious March 26, 1967, in Wyoming when Nancy Greene had to fight her way down the second run in the final race of the World Cup season to wrest the title away by seven-hundredths of a second from Marielle Goitschel of France. It was an enormously exciting moment and proved just how close is the competition among women skiers in international racing today.

The next most important and oldest competition is the Arlberg-Kandahar, which is usually rotated among five key Alpine resorts—St. Anton, Austria; Mürren, Switzerland; Garmisch, Germany; Chamonix, France; and Sestriere, Italy. Started in 1928 by Sir Arnold Lunn and Hannes Schneider, it is to Alpine racing what the Holmenkollen is to Nordic competition—in effect, a world championship in the years when there is no World Championship or Olympics. Because they are likely to encounter the best competitors in the world at the Arlberg-Kandahar, many racers treasure an A-K pin as much as a World Championship or an Olympic medal.

National championships are rarely premier events. With the exception of the United States and Canadian championships, these races are open only to natives of the country. However, they are watched closely to determine the progress of each nation's second-string racers.

WINTER OLYMPIC GAMES

Although the ancient Greeks who staged history's earliest Olympic Games are not recorded as having displayed any interest in winter sports, the first site of the Games was an Alpine setting. The view from Mount Olympus was one of snow-clad peaks, wooded slopes, and wild valleys. Despite this prophetic setting, it was to take more than 3,000 years before winter sports became part of the Olympic ceremonial. The modern Olympic era began with the Summer Games at Athens in 1896, but another twenty-eight years elapsed until the first Winter Games were staged at Chamonix, France, in 1924. Since then, the Winter Games have become a brilliant ornament in the Olympic tapestry, laced with great moments, drama, pageantry, and spectacular individual performances.

The International Olympic Committee (IOC) makes no rules concerning any of the sports or individual events on the Olympic program. The rules of the international federation for each sport involved apply. Thus, the rules of the Fédération Internationale de Ski (FIS) govern the skiing events. However, the IOC does have rules defining amateurism (you are supposed to be one) and the number of entries permitted for each event. For skiing, that number is four per event per country, regardless of the number of high-ranking racers a nation may have. For this reason, the order of finish at Olympic races can be used only as an approximate indication of the ranking of the world's top ski racers and racing nations.

Here are the skiing champions and other records for the Winter Olympic Games from 1924 to 1972:

Nordic Events (Men)

Year	Champion	Runner-up	Third
	15-kilometer Cross-country		
1956	Hallgeir Brenden Norway	Sixten Jernberg Sweden	Pavel Kolchin USSR
1960	Hallgeir Brenden Norway	Sixten Jernberg Sweden	Veikko Häkulinen Finland
1964	Eero Mäntyranta Finland	Harald Grönningen Norway	Sixten Jernberg Sweden
1968	Harald Grönningen Norway	Eero Mäntyranta Finland	Gunnar Larsson Sweden
1972	Sven-Ake Lundback Sweden	Fedor Smaschov USSR	Ivar Formo Norway
	18-kilometer Cross-country		
1924	Thorleif Haug Norway	Johan Grøttumsbraaten Norway	Tapani Niku Finland
1928	Johan Grøttumsbraaten Norway	Ole Hegge Norway	Reidar Ødegaard Norway
1932	Sven Utterström Sweden	Axel Vikström Sweden	Veli Saarinen Finland
1936	Erik-August Larsson Sweden	Oddbjørn Hagen Norway	Pekka Niemi Finland
1948	Martin Lundström Sweden	Nils Östensson Sweden	Gunnar Eriksson Sweden

Year	Champion	Runner-up	Third
1952	Hallgeir Brenden Norway	Tapio Makela Finland	Paavo Lonkila Finland

30-kilometer Cross-country

1956	Veikko Häkulinen Finland	Sixten Jernberg Sweden	Pavel Kolchin USSR
1960	Sixten Jernberg Sweden	Rolf Rämgärd Sweden	Nikolai Anikin USSR
1964	Eero Mäntyranta Finland	Harald Grönningen Norway	Igor Voronckiken USSR
1968	Franco Nones Italy	Odd Martinsen Norway	Eero Mäntyranta Finland
1972	Vyacheslav Vedenin USSR	Paal Tyldum Norway	John Haroviken Norway

50-kilometer Cross-country

1924	Thorleif Haug Norway	Thoralf Strømstad Norway	Johan Grøttumsbraaten Norway
1928	Per Hedlund Sweden	Gustaf Jonsson Sweden	Volger Andersson Sweden
1932	Veli Saarinen Finland	Väinö Liikkanen Finland	Arne Rustadstuen Norway
1936	Elis Viklund Sweden	Axel Wikström Sweden	Nils Englund Sweden
1948	Nils Karlsson Sweden	Harald Erikkson Sweden	Benjamin Vanninen Finland
1952	Veikko Häkulinen Finland	Eero Kohlemainen Finland	Magnar Estenstad Norway
1956	Sixten Jernberg Sweden	Veikko Häkulinen Finland	Fydor Terentiev USSR
1960	Kalevi Hämäläinen Finland	Veikko Häkulinen Finland	Rolf Rämgärd Sweden
1964	Sixten Jernberg Sweden	Assar Rönnlund Sweden	Arto Tiainen Finland
1968	Ole Ellefsaeter Norway	Viatches Vedenine USSR	Josef Haas Switzerland
1972	Paal Tyldum Norway	Magne Myrmo Norway	Vyacheslav Vedenin USSR

15-kilometer Combined

1972	Karl Luck East Germany	Urban Hettich West Germany	Ulrich Wehling East Germany

Nordic Combined (Cross-country and Jumping)

1924	Thorleif Haug Norway	Thoralf Strømstad Norway	Johan Grøttumsbraaten Norway
1928	Johan Grøttumsbraaten Norway	Hans Vinjarengen Norway	John Snesrud Norway
1932	Johan Grøttumsbraaten Norway	Ole Stenen Norway	Hans Vinjarengen Norway
1936	Oddbjørn Hagen Norway	Olaf Hoffsbakken Norway	Sverre Brodahl Norway
1948	Heikku Hasu Finland	Martti Huhtala Finland	Sven Israelsson Sweden
1952	Simon Slattvik Norway	Heikku Hasu Finland	Sverre Stenerson Norway
1956	Sverre Stenerson Norway	Bengt Ericsson Sweden	Francis Gron-Gasienca Poland
1960	Georg Thoma Germany	Tormod Knutsen Norway	Nicolai Gusakov USSR

Year	Champion	Runner-up	Third
1964	Tormod Knutsen Norway	Nicolai Kiselev USSR	Georg Thoma Germany
1968	Franz Keller Germany	A. Kaelin Sweden	A. Kunz Germany
1972	Ulricn Wehling East Germany	Rauno Miettinen Finland	Karl Luck East Germany

Biathlon

Year	Champion	Runner-up	Third
1960	Klas Lestander Sweden	Antti Tyrvainen Finland	Alexandr Privalov USSR
1964	Vladimlr Melanin USSR	Olav Jordet Norway	Alexandr Privalov USSR
1968	A. Solberg Norway	V. Tikhonov USSR	A. Goundartsev USSR
1972	Maynar Solberg Norway	Hanyorg Knauthe East Germany	Lars-Goeran Arwidson Sweden

Jumping

Year	Champion	Runner-up	Third
1924	Jacob Tullin-Thams Norway	Narve Bonna Norway	Thorleif Haug Norway
1928	Alf Andersen Norway	Sigmund Ruud Norway	Rudolf Purkert Czechoslovakia
1932	Birger Ruud Norway	Hans Beck Norway	Kaare Wahlberg Norway
1936	Birger Ruud Norway	Sven Eriksson Sweden	Reidar Andersen Norway
1948	Petter Hugsted Norway	Birger Ruud Norway	Thorleif Schjelderup Norway
1952	Arnfinn Bergmann Norway	Torbjorn Falkanger Norway	Karl Holmstrom Sweden
1956	Antti Hyvaringen Finland	Aulis Kellakorpi Finland	Harry Glass Germany
1960	Helmut Recknagel Germany	N. Halonen Finland	O. Leodolter Austria

Jumping ("Normal" Hill, 70 Meters)

Year	Champion	Runner-up	Third
1964	Veikko Kankkonen Finland	Toralf Engan Norway	Torgeir Brandtzaeg Norway
1968	Jiri Raska Czechoslovakia	Reinhold Bachler Austria	J. Preiml Austria
1972	Yukio Kasaya Japan	Akitsugu Konno Japan	Seijii Aochi Japan

Jumping ("Big" Hill, 90 Meters)

Year	Champion	Runner-up	Third
1964	Toralf Engan Norway	Viekko Kankkonen Finland	Torgeir Brandtzaeg Norway
1968	Vladimir Beloussov USSR	Jiri Raska Czechoslovakia	Lars Grlnl Norway
1972	Wojciech Fortuna Poland	Walter Steiner Switzerland	Rainer Schmidt East Germany

40-kilometer (4 × 10 Kilometers) Cross-country Relay

Year	Champion	Runner-up	Third
1936	Finland	Norway	Sweden
1948	Sweden	Finland	Norway
1952	Finland	Norway	Sweden
1956	USSR	Finland	Sweden
1960	Finland	Norway	USSR

Year	Champion	Runner-up	Third
1964	Sweden	Finland	USSR
1968	Norway	Sweden	Finland
1972	USSR	Norway	Switzerland

30-kilometer (4 × 7.5 Kilometers) Biathlon Relay
(Each man skis 7.5 kilometers and shoots twice)

1968	USSR	Norway	Sweden
1972	USSR	Finland	East Germany

Alpine Events (Men)

Year	Champion	Runner-up	Third

Downhill

Year	Champion	Runner-up	Third
1948	Henri Oreiller France	Franz Gabl Austria	Karl Molitor Switzerland
1952	Zeno Colo Italy	Othmar Schneider Austria	Christian Pravda Austria
1956	Anton Sailer Austria	Raymond Fellay Switzerland	Andreas Molterer Austria
1960	Jean Vuarnet France	Hans Peter Lanig Germany	Guy Périllat France
1964	Egon Zimmerman Austria	Leo Lacroix France	Wolfgang Bartels Germany
1968	Jean-Claude Killy France	Guy Périllat France	Jean-Daniel Daetwyler Switzerland
1972	Bernhard Russi Switzerland	Roland Collombin Switzerland	Heinrich Nessner Austria

Slalom

Year	Champion	Runner-up	Third
1948	Edi Reinalter Switzerland	James Couttet France	Henri Oreiller France
1952	Othmar Schneider Austria	Stein Eriksen Norway	Guttorm Berge Norway
1956	Anton Sailer Austria	Chiharu Igaya Japan	Stig Sollander Sweden
1960	Ernst Hinterseer Austria	Mathias Leitner Austria	Charles Bozon France
1964	Josef Stiegler Austria	William Kidd USA	Jimmy Heuga USA
1968	Jean-Claude Killy France	Herbert Huber Austria	Alfred Matt Austria
1972	Francisco Fernandez-Ochoa Spain	Gustavo Thoeni Italy	Rolando Thoeni Italy

Giant Slalom

Year	Champion	Runner-up	Third
1952	Stein Eriksen Norway	Christian Pravda Austria	Toni Spiss Austria
1956	Anton Sailer Austria	Andreas Molterer Austria	Walter Schuster Austria
1960	Roger Staub Switzerland	Josef Stiegler Austria	Ernst Hinterseer Austria
1964	François Bonlieu France	Karl Schranz Austria	Josef Stiegler Austria
1968	Jean-Claude Killy France	Willi Favre Switzerland	Heinrich Messner Austria
1972	Gustavo Thoeni Italy	Edmund Bruggmann Switzerland	Werner Mattle Switzerland

Year	Champion	Runner-up	Third

Alpine Combined*

Year	Champion	Runner-up	Third
1936	Franz Pfnür Germany	Gustav Lautschner Germany	Émile Allais France
1948	Henri Oreiller France	Karl Molitor Switzerland	James Couttet France
1952	Not held		
1956	Anton Sailer Austria	Charles Bozon France	Stig Sollander Sweden
1960	Guy Périllat France	Chares Bozon France	Hans Peter Lanig Germany
1964	Ludwig Leitner Germany	Gerhard Nenning Austria	William Kidd USA
1968	Jean-Claude Killy France	Dumenc Giovanoli Switzerland	Heinrich Messner Austria
1972	Gustavo Thoeni Italy	Walter Tresch Switzerland	James Hunter Canada

Nordic Events (Women)

Year	Champion	Runner-up	Third

5-kilometer Cross-country

Year	Champion	Runner-up	Third
1964	Claudia Boyarsklkh USSR	Mirja Lehtonen Finland	Alevtina Koltjina USSR
1968	Toini Gustafsson Sweden	Galina Koulacova USSR	Alevtina Koltjina USSR
1972	Galina Koulacova USSR	Marjatta Kajosmaa Finland	Helena Sikolova Czechoslovakia

10-kilometer Cross-country

Year	Champion	Runner-up	Third
1952	Lydia Wideman Finland	Mirja Hietamies Finland	Siri Rantanen Finland
1956	Lyubov Kozyreva USSR	Radija Yeroshina USSR	Sonja Edstrom Sweden
1960	Maria Gusakova USSR	Lyubov Kozyreva USSR	Radija Yeroshina USSR
1964	Claudia Boyarsklkh USSR	Eudokia Mekshilo USSR	Maria Gusakova USSR
1968	Toini Gustafsson Sweden	Berit Mördre Norway	Inger Aufles Norway
1972	Galina Koulacova USSR	Alevtina Olunina USSR	Marjatta Kajosmaa Finland

15-kilometer (3 × 5 Kilometers) Cross-country Relay

Year	Champion	Runner-up	Third
1956	Finland	USSR	Sweden
1960	Sweden	USSR	Finland
1964	USSR	Sweden	Finland
1968	Norway	Sweden	USSR
1972	USSR	Finland	Norway

* No medals awarded after 1948; the FIS, however, makes awards to winners since 1956 of the best combined score of the three Olympic Alpine events (see page 242). The 1936 and 1948 Olympic Alpine combined events were based only on slalom and downhill races.

Alpine Events (Women)

Year	Champion	Runner-up	Third

Downhill

Year	Champion	Runner-up	Third
1948	Hedl Schlunegger Switzerland	Trude Belser Austria	Resi Hammerer Austria
1952	Trude Jochum-Beiser Austria	Annemarie Buchner Germany	Giuliana Minuzzo Italy
1956	Madeleine Berthod Switzerland	Frieda Dänzer Switzerland	Lucille Wheeler Canada
1960	Heidi Biebl Germany	Penny Pitou USA	Traudl Hecher Austria
1964	Christl Haas Austria	Edith Zimmermann Austria	Traudl Hecher Austria
1968	Olga Pall Austria	Isabelle Mir France	Christl Haas Austria
1972	Marie-Theres Nadig Switzerland	Annemarie Proell Austria	Susan Corrock USA

Slalom

Year	Champion	Runner-up	Third
1948	Gretchen Fraser USA	Antoinette Meyer Switzerland	Erika Mahringer Austria
1952	Andrea Mead Lawrence USA	Ossi Reichert Germany	Annemarie Buchner Germany
1956	René Colliard Switzerland	Regina Schöpf Austria	Yevgeniya Sidorova USSR
1960	Anne Heggtveit Canada	Betsy Snite USA	Barbi Henneberger Germany
1964	Christine Goltschel France	Marielle Goitschel France	Jean Saubert USA
1968	Marielle Goltschel France	Nancy Greene Canada	Annie Famose France
1972	Barbara Cochran USA	Daniele Debernard France	Florence Steurer France

Giant Slalom

Year	Champion	Runner-up	Third
1952	Andrea Mead Lawrence USA	Dagmar Rom Austria	Annemarie Buchner Germany
1956	Ossi Reichert Germany	Josefine Frandl Austria	Dorothea Hochleitner Austria
1960	Ivonne Rüegg Switzerland	Penny Pitou USA	C. Chenal-Minuzzo Italy
1964	Marielle Goltschel France	Christine Goltschel France Jean Saubert USA	
1968	Nancy Greene Canada	Annie Famose France	Fernande Bochatay Switzerland
1972	Marie-Theres Nadig Switzerland	Annemarie Proell Austria	Wiltrud Drexel Austria

Alpine Combined*

Year	Champion	Runner-up	Third
1936	Christel Cranz Germany	Kathe Grasegger Germany	Laila Schou-Nilsen Norway

* No medals awarded after 1948; the FIS, however, makes awards to winners since 1956 of the best combined score of the three Olympic Alpine events. The 1936 and 1948 Olympic Alpine combined events were based only on slalom and downhill races.

Year	Champion	Runner-up	Third
1948	Trude Belser Austria	Gretchen Fraser USA	Erika Mahringer Austria
1952	None held		
1960	Anne Heggtveit Canada	S. Sperl Germany	Barbi Henneberger Germany
1964	Marielle Goitschel France	Christl Haas Austria	Edith Zimmermann Austria
1968	Nancy Greene Canada	Marielle Goitschel France	Annie Famose France
1972	Annemarie Proell Austria	Florence Steurer France	Toril Foerland Norway

Winter Olympic Games Sites

I	Chamonix, France	1924
II	St. Moritz, Switzerland	1928
III	Lake Placid, New York, U.S.A.	1932
IV	Garmisch-Partenkirchen, Germany	1936
V	St. Moritz, Switzerland	1948
VI	Oslo, Norway	1952
VII	Cortina, Italy	1956
VIII	Squaw Valley, California, U.S.A.	1960
IX	Innsbruck, Austria	1964
X	Grenoble, France	1968
XI	Sapporo, Japan	1972

Ski Championships Won by Nations Year by Year

Year	Country	Men	Women	Total
1924	Norway	4		4
1928	Norway	3		3
	Sweden	1		1
1932	Norway	2		2
	Finland	1		1
	Sweden	1		1
1936	Norway	2	0	2
	Sweden	2	0	2
	Germany	1	1	2
	Finland	1	0	1
1948	Sweden	3	0	3
	France	2	0	2
	Switzerland	1	1	2
	Finland	1	0	1
	Norway	1	0	1
	Austria	0	1	1
	USA	0	1	1
1952	Norway	4	0	4
	Finland	2	1	3
	Austria	1	1	2
	USA	0	2	2
	Italy	1	0	1
1956	Austria	3	0	3
	Finland	2	1	3
	Norway	2	0	2
	USSR	1	1	2
	Switzerland	0	2	2
	Sweden	1	0	1
	Germany	0	1	1

Year	Country	Men	Women	Total
1960	Sweden	2	1	3
	Germany	2	1	3
	Finland	2	0	2
	France	2	0	2
	Switzerland	1	1	2
	Norway	1	0	1
	Austria	1	0	1
	USSR	0	1	1
	Canada	0	1	1
1964	USSR	1	3	4
	Finland	3	0	3
	Austria	2	1	3
	France	1	2	3
	Sweden	2	0	2
	Norway	2	0	2
1968	Norway	4	1	5
	France	3	1	4
	USSR	2	0	2
	Sweden	0	2	2
	Italy	1	0	1
	Germany	1	0	1
	Czechoslovakia	1	0	1
	Austria	0	1	1
	Canada	0	1	1
1972	USSR	3	3	6
	Switzerland	1	2	3
	Norway	2	0	2
	Germany	2	0	2
	Italy	1	0	1
	Japan	1	0	1
	Poland	1	0	1
	Sweden	1	0	1
	Spain	1	0	1
	USA	0	1	1

Medals Won by Nations 1924– 1972

Gold medals for first place, silver for second, a bronze for third. Relay medals count as one for nation.

Alpine Events	1st	2d	3d	Total
Austria	10	15	17	42

	1st	2d	3d	Total		Nordic Events	1st	2d	3d	Total
France	10	8	7	25		Norway	27	27	21	75
Switzerland	9	7	4	20		Finland	14	21	13	48
USA	4	6	3	13		Sweden	16	16	15	47
Germany	4	5	4	13		USSR	15	11	17	43
Italy	2	1	3	6		Germany	5	2	7	14
Canada	2	1	1	4		Austria	1	1	2	4
Norway	1	1	2	4		Czechoslovakia	1	1	2	4
Spain	1	0	0	1		Japan	1	1	1	3
Japan	0	1	0	1		Switzerland	0	1	2	3
USSR	0	0	1	1		Poland	1	0	1	2
Sweden	0	0	1	1		Italy	1	0	0	1

	Men				Women				Overall			
	1st	2d	3d	Total	1st	2d	3d	Total	1st	2d	3d	Total
Norway	27	27	20	74	1	1	3	5	28	28	23	79
Sweden	13	14	14	41	3	2	2	7	16	16	16	48
Finland	12	17	9	38	2	4	4	10	14	21	13	48
Austria	7	9	11	27	4	7	8	19	11	16	19	46
USSR	7	4	12	23	8	7	6	21	15	11	18	44
Germany	6	4	8	18	3	3	3	9	9	7	11	27
France	7	3	5	15	3	5	2	10	10	8	7	25
Switzerland	1	6	5	12	6	2	1	9	9	8	6	23
USA	0	1	1	2	4	5	2	11	4	6	3	13
Italy	3	1	1	5	0	0	2	2	3	1	3	7
Canada	0	0	0	0	2	1	1	4	2	1	1	4
Czechoslovakia	1	1	1	3	0	0	1	1	1	1	2	4
Japan	1	2	1	4	0	0	0	0	1	2	1	4
Poland	1	0	1	2	0	0	0	0	1	0	1	2
Spain	1	0	0	1	0	0	0	0	1	0	0	1

FIS SKI WORLD CHAMPIONSHIPS

At the 1924 Ski Congress in Chamonix, France, it was suggested that each year an international ski competition should be held which should be the most prominent event for the FIS members. During the first years these competitions were called FIS Races; later on they were named Ski World Championships. Up to 1930, the FIS was restricted to Nordic events; from then on, Alpine events were included. These world championships began to receive an extra boost of anticipation after 1950, when they were held every four years instead of yearly. Here are the winners in the various events from 1925 to date:

Men

Year	Event	Winner	Country
1925	18-km. cross-country	O. Nemecky	Czechoslovakia
	50-km. cross-country	F. Donth	Czechoslovakia
	Jumping	W. Dick	Czechoslovakia
	Nordic combined	O. Nemecky	Czechoslovakia
1926	30-km. cross-country	M. Raivio	Finland
	50-km. cross-country	M. Raivio	Finland
	Jumping	J. T.-Thams	Norway
	Nordic combined	J. Grøttumsbraaten	Norway
1927	18-km. cross-country	J. Lindgren	Sweden
	50-km. cross-country	J. Lindgren	Sweden
	Jumping	T. Edman	Sweden
	Nordic combined	R. Purkert	Czechoslovakia

Year	Event	Winner	Country
1929	18-km. cross-country	V. Saarinen	Finland
	50-km. cross-country	A. Knuttila	Finland
	Jumping	S. Ruud	Norway
	Nordic combined	H. Vinjarengen	Norway
1930	18-km. cross-country	A. Rustadstuen	Norway
	50-km. cross-country	S. Utterström	Sweden
	Jumping	G. Andersen	Norway
	Nordic combined	H. Vinjarengen	Norway
1931	18-km. cross-country	J. Grøttumsbraaten	Norway
	50-km. cross-country	O. Stenen	Norway
	Jumping	B. Ruud	Norway
	Nordic combined	J. Grøttumsbraaten	Norway
	Downhill	W. Prager	Switzerland
	Slalom	D. Zogg	Switzerland
1932	Downhill	G. Lantschner	Austria
	Slalom	F. Dauber	Germany
	Alpine combined	O. Fürrer	Switzerland
1933	18-km. cross-country	N. Englund	Sweden
	50-km. cross-country	V. Saarinen	Finland
	40-km. cross-country relay		Sweden
	Jumping	M. Reymond	Switzerland
	Nordic combined	S. Eriksson	Sweden
	Downhill	W. Prager	Switzerland
	Slalom	A. Seelos	Austria
	Alpine combined	A. Seelos	Austria
1934	18-km. cross-country	S. Nurmela	Finland
	50-km. cross-country	E. Viklund	Sweden
	40-km. cross-country relay		Finland
	Jumping	K. Johansen	Norway
	Nordic combined	O. Hagen	Norway
	Downhill	D. Zogg	Switzerland
	Slalom	F. Pfnür	Germany
	Alpine combined	D. Zogg	Switzerland
1935	18-km. cross-country	K. Karppinen	Finland
	50-km. cross-country	N. Englund	Sweden
	40-km. cross-country relay		Finland
	Jumping	B. Ruud	Norway
	Nordic combined	O. Hagen	Norway
	Downhill	F. Zingerle	Austria
	Slalom	A. Seelos	Austria
	Alpine combined	A. Seelos	Austria
1936	Downhill	R. Rominger	Switzerland
	Slalom	R. Matt	Austria
	Alpine combined	R. Rominger	Switzerland
1937	18-km. cross-country	L. Bergendahl	Norway
	50-km. cross-country	P. Niemi	Finland
	40-km. cross-country relay		Norway
	Jumping	B. Ruud	Norway
	Nordic combined	S. Röen	Norway
	Downhill	É. Allais	France
	Slalom	É. Allais	France
	Alpine combined	É. Allais	France
1938	18-km. cross-country	P. Pietikäinen	Finland
	50-km. cross-country	K. Jalkanen	Finland
	40-km. cross-country relay		Finland
	Jumping	A. Ruud	Norway
	Nordic combined	O. Hoffsbakken	Norway
	Downhill	J. Couttet	France
	Slalom	R. Rominger	Switzerland
	Alpine combined	É. Allais	France
1939	18-km. cross-country	J. Kurikkala	Finland
	50-km. cross-country	L. Bergendahl	Norway
	40-km. cross-country relay		Finland
	Jumping	J. Bradl	Austria
	Nordic combined	H. Beraur	Czechoslovakia

Year	Event	Winner	Country
	Downhill	H. Lantschner	Germany
	Slalom	R. Rominger	Switzerland
	Alpine combined	J. Jennewein	Germany
1950	50-18-km. cross-country	K.-E. Aaström	Sweden
	50-km. cross-country	G. Erikksson	Sweden
	40-km. cross-country relay		Sweden
	Jumping	H. Björnstad	Norway
	Nordic combined	H. Hasu	Finland
	Downhill	Z. Colo	Italy
	Slalom	G. Schneider	Switzerland
	Giant slalom	Z. Colo	Italy
1954	15-km. cross-country	V. Häkulinen	Finland
	30-km. cross-country	V. Kusin	USSR
	50-km. cross-country	V. Kusin	USSR
	40-km. cross-country relay		Finland
	Jumping	M. Pietikäinen	Finland
	Nordic combined	S. Stenerson	Norway
	Downhill	C. Pravda	Austria
	Slalom	S. Eriksen	Norway
	Giant slalom	S. Eriksen	Norway
	Alpine combined	S. Eriksen	Norway
1958	15-km. cross-country	V. Häkulinen	Finland
	30-km. cross-country	K. Hämäläinen	Finland
	50-km. cross-country	S. Jernberg	Sweden
	40-km. cross-country relay		Sweden
	Jumping	J. Kärkinen	Finland
	Nordic combined	P. Korhonen	Finland
	Downhill	A. Sailer	Austria
	Slalom	J. Rieder	Austria
	Giant slalom	A. Sailer	Austria
	Alpine combined	A. Sailer	Austria
1962	15-km. cross-country	A. Rönnlund	Sweden
	30-km. cross-country	E. Mäntyranta	Finland
	50-km. cross-country	S. Jernberg	Sweden
	40-km. cross-country relay		Sweden
	Jumping—70 meters	T. Engan	Norway
	Jumping—90 meters	H. Recknagel	Germany
	Nordic combined	A. Larsen	Norway
	Dowhill	K. Schranz	Austria
	Slalom	C. Bozon	France
	Giant slalom	E. Zimmerman	Austria
	Alpine combined	K. Schranz	Austria
1966	15-km. cross-country	G. Eggen	Norway
	30-km. cross-country	E. Mäntyranta	Finland
	50-km. cross-country	G. Eggen	Norway
	40-km. cross-country relay		Norway
	Jumping—70 meters	B. Wirkola	Norway
	Jumping—90 meters	B. Wirkola	Norway
	Nordic combined	G. Thoma	Germany
	Downhill	J.-C. Killy	France
	Slalom	C. Senoner	Italy
	Giant slalom	G. Périllat	France
	Alpine combined	J.-C. Killy	France
1970	15-km. cross-country	L. G. Aslund	Sweden
	30-km. cross-country	V. Vedenin	USSR
	50-km. cross-country	K. Oikarainen	Finland
	40-km. cross-country relay		USSR
	Jumping—70 meters	G. Napalkov	USSR
	Jumping—90 meters	G. Napalkov	USSR
	Nordic combined	L. Rygl	Czechoslovakia
	Downhill	B. Russi	Switzerland
	Slalom	J.-N. Augert	France
	Giant slalom	K. Schranz	Austria
	Alpine combined	W. Kidd	USA

Women

Year	Event	Winner	Country
1931	Slalom	E. M. Mackinnon	Great Britain
	Downhill	E. M. Mckinnon	Great Britain
1932	Slalom	R. Streiff	Switzerland
	Downhill	P. Wiesinger	Italy
	Alpine combined	R. Streiff	Switzerland
1933	Slalom	I. Wersin-Lantschner	Austria
	Downhill	I. Wersin-Lantschner	Austria
	Alpine combined	I. Wersin-Lantschner	Austria
1934	Slalom	C. Cranz	Germany
	Downhill	A. Rüegg	Switzerland
	Alpine combined	C. Cranz	Germany
1935	Slalom	I. Rüegg	Switzerland
	Downhill	C. Cranz	Germany
	Alpine combined	C. Cranz	Germany
1936	Slalom	G. Paumgarten	Austria
	Downhill	E. Pinching	Great Britain
	Alpine combined	E. Pinching	Great Britain
1937	Slalom	C. Cranz	Germany
	Downhill	C. Cranz	Germany
	Alpine combined	C. Cranz	Germany
1938	Slalom	C. Cranz	Germany
	Downhill	L. Resch	Germany
	Alpine combined	C. Cranz	Germany
1939	Slalom	C. Cranz	Germany
	Downhill	C. Cranz	Germany
	Alpine combined	C. Cranz	Germany
1950	Slalom	D. Rom	Austria
	Giant slalom	D. Rom	Austria
	Downhill	T. Jochum-Beiser	Austria
1954	10-km. cross-country	L. Kozyreva	USSR
	15-km. cross-country relay		USSR
	Slalom	T. Klecker	Austria
	Giant slalom	L. Schmith	France
	Downhill	I. Schopfer	Switzerland
	Alpine combined	I. Schopfer	Switzerland
1958	10-km. cross-country	A. Koltjina	USSR
	15-km. cross-country relay		USSR
	Slalom	I. Björnbakken	Norway
	Giant slalom	L. Wheeler	Canada
	Downhill	L. Wheeler	Canada
	Alpine combined	F. Dänzer	Switzerland
1962	5-km. cross-country	A. Koltjina	USSR
	10-km. cross-country	A. Koltjina	USSR
	15-km. cross-country relay		USSR
	Slalom	M. Jahn	Austria
	Giant slalom	M. Jahn	Austria
	Downhill	C. Haas	Austria
	Alpine combined	M. Goitschel	France
1966	5-km. cross-country	A. Koltjina	USSR
	10-km. cross-country	C. Boyarskikh	USSR
	15-km. cross-country relay		USSR
	Slalom	A. Famose	France
	Giant slalom	M. Goitschel	France
	Downhill	E. Schinegger	Austria
	Alpine combined	M. Goitschel	France
1970	5-km. cross-country	G. Kulakova	USSR
	10-km. cross-country	A. Oljunia	USSR
	15-km cross-country relay		USSR
	Slalom	I. Lafforgue	France
	Giant slalom	B. Clifford	Canada
	Downhill	A. Zyrd	Switzerland
	Alpine combined	M. Jacot	France

FIS Alpine Championship Medals

	Gold	Silver	Bronze	Total
Austria	40	41	40	121
Switzerland	27	31	27	85
France	30	33	18	81
Germany	20	19	25	64
United States	4	8	9	21
Italy	5	3	6	14
Great Britain	4	4	3	11
Canada	7	2	1	10
Norway	5	1	3	9
Sweden	0	0	5	5
Japan	0	1	1	2
USSR	0	0	1	1
Australia	0	0	1	1

FIS Nordic Championship Medals

	Gold	Silver	Bronze	Total
Norway	56	49	47	152
Finland	40	44	35	119
Sweden	32	31	36	97
USSR	26	22	22	70
Czechoslovakia	6	11	6	23
Germany	7	5	9	21
Switzerland	1	2	3	6
Italy	1	0	5	6
Austria	0	1	4	5
Poland	0	2	2	4
Japan	0	2	0	2

FIS Championship Sites

1925	Johannisbad, Czechoslovakia
1926	Lahti, Finland
1927	Cortina d'Ampezzo, Italy
1929	Zakopane, Poland
1930	Oslo, Norway
1931	Oberhof, Germany (Nordic events); Mürren, Switzerland (Alpine events)
1932	Cortina D'Ampezzo, Italy
1933	Innsbruck, Austria
1934	Solleftea, Sweden (Nordic events); St. Moritz, Switzerland (Alpine events)
1935	Strebski Pleso, Czechoslovakia (Nordic events); Mürren, Switzerland (Alpine events)
1936	Innsbruck, Austria
1937	Chamonix, France
1938	Lahti, Finland (Nordic events); Engelberg, Switzerland (Alpine events)
1939	Zakopane, Poland
1950	Lake Placid, U.S.A. (Nordic events); Aspen, U.S.A. (Alpine events)
1954	Falun, Sweden (Nordic events); Are, Sweden (Alpine events)
1958	Lahti, Finland (Nordic events); Bad Gastein, Austria (Alpine events)
1962	Zakopane, Poland (Nordic events); Chamonix, France (Alpine events)
1966	Oslo, Norway (Nordic events); Portillo, Chile (Alpine events)
1970	Strebski Pleso, Czechoslovakia (Nordic events); Val Gardena, Italy (Alpine events)

WORLD CUP

As stated earlier in this section, the World Cup point scoring is necessarily complex because it seeks to be eminently fair in a complex situation. It starts by preselecting, before the start of the winter racing circuit, a series of meets in Austria, Germany, Switzerland, Italy, Sweden, Japan, and North America, where competitors can win World Cup points. The fairly large number of qualifying races offers many opportunities to compete as well as enabling top racers to miss races owing to injuries or conflicting interests at home and school. It puts a high premium on first, second, and third places because it seeks ski *champions,* not racers, who can accumulate a large number of points by consistently average performances. This feature of the World Cup is further accentuated by counting only the three best results of a racer in each Alpine specialty during the winter. It also prevents a competitor—who, for instance, is a specialized downhiller but only a mediocre slalom racer—from winning the overall World Cup by accumulating a huge total of points in one specialty or discipline.

Under the *original* scoring system, a racer wins 25 points for first place in an event, and can therefore gather a maximum of 75 points or three first places in a specialty during the season. The maximum total of 225 World Cup points can be won by three victories in each of the specialties.

In 1970, in the men's portion of competition, "Formula 13" or "B" races were introduced. The "Formula 13" race awarded 13 points for first place and a correspondingly lesser number of points down to tenth place. But the "B" race experiment was dropped for the 1971 season.

In 1971 the World Cup Commission balanced the schedule of slaloms, giant slaloms, and downhills and allowed five instead of three races in each discipline counting for World Cup points. The theory behind the change is to make the World Cup a better test of the three-event skier. That is, for the standings within each Alpine discipline, only the best five results out of the total number are calculated into the standings. Thus, the maximum number of points per discipline is 5 races times 25 points, or a total of 125 points. World Cup points are still earned by competitors who finish in the first ten places in races on the World Cup schedule. They receive points as follows: first place 25 points; second, 20; third, 15; fourth, 11; fifth, 8; sixth, 6; seventh, 4; eighth, 3; ninth, 2; tenth 1. In case of ties, each racer receives the points allocated for the place finish.

The 1973 World Cup schedule was divided into three time periods: December, in which a racer can count his three best results, regardless of type of race; January, with five results; and February/March, with six results. For men, five races were scheduled in December, nine in January, and ten in February/ March, for a total of 24. For women, four races were planned for December, eight for January, and twelve for February/March, also for a total of 24. Trophies for downhill, slalom, and giant slalom were to be based on the five best results in the eight races scheduled in each discipline. Those who favor the new system say it allows the specialists at least one period in which to concentrate on their weaknesses without being distracted by worrying about their specialty. Furthermore, cancelations would no longer be as serious a matter as in the past. Those arguing against the change warn that the constant fiddling with the scoring system invites further fiddling in the future for some momentary advantage; that it makes performance comparisons meaningless; and above all, that it devalues one of the greatest racing accomplishments of all time—Killy's perfect World Cup season in 1967–68, in which he scored the maximum number of World Cup points possible (225), a feat that has never been matched.

Here are the winners of the World Cup since it was started in 1967:

Men

Year	Winner	Country	Slalom Points	Giant Slalom Points	Downhill Points	Total Points
1967	Jean-Claude Killy	France	75	75	75	225
	Heini Messner	Austria	51	32	31	114
	Guy Périllat	France	58	13	37	108
1968	Jean-Claude Killy	France	65	75	60	200
	Dumenc Giovanoli	Switzerland	70	43	6	119
	Herbert Huber	Austria	60	52	0	112
1969	Karl Schranz	Austria	37	70	75	182
	Jean-Noël Augert	France	65	58	0	123
	Reinhard Tritscher	Austria	47	61	0	108
1970	Karl Schranz	Austria	19	65	64	148
	Patrick Russel	France	75	70	0	145
	Gustavo Thoeni	Italy	65	75	0	140
1971	Gustavo Thoeni	Italy	70	70	15	155
	Henri Duvillard	France	22	60	53	135
	Patrick Russell	France	55	70	0	125
1972	Gustavo Thoeni	Italy	66	84	4	154
	Henri Duvillard	France	50	49	43	142
	Edmund Bruggmann	Switzerland	62	78	0	140
1973	Gustavo Thoeni	Italy	110	55	0	165
	David Zwilling	Austria	34	49	68	151
	Roland Collombin	Switzerland	11	0	120	131

Women

Year	Winner	Country	Slalom Points	Giant Slalom Points	Downhill Points	Total Points
1967	Nancy Greene	Canada	65	75	36	176
	Marielle Goitschel	France	70	46	56	172
	Annie Famose	France	70	50	38	158
1968	Nancy Greene	Canada	65	75	51	191
	Isabelle Mir	France	48	41	70	159
	Florence Steurer	France	70	60	23	153
1969	Gertrude Gabl	Austria	75	53	3	131
	Florence Steurer	France	41	51	20	112
	Wiltrud Drexel	Austria	12	34	65	111
1970	Michèle Jacot	France	65	70	45	180
	Françoise Macchi	France	31	70	44	145
	Florence Steurer	France	50	37	46	133
1971	Annemarie Proell	Austria	65	75	70	210
	Michèle Jacot	France	56	70	51	177
	Isabelle Mir	France	30	48	55	133
1972	Annemarie Proell	Austria	29	115	125	269
	Françoise Macchi	France	70	50	67	187
	Britt Lafforgue	France	76	52	0	128
1973	Annemarie Proell	Austria	6	94	125	225
	Monika Kaserer	Austria	67	110	28	205
	Patricia Emonet	France	110	52	0	162

WORLD CUP RACES

Men

Location	Slalom	Giant Slalom	Downhill
1967			
Berchtesgaden, Germany	Heini Messner Austria	Georges Maiduit France	
Adelboden, Switzerland		Jean-Claude Killy France	
Wengen, Switzerland	Jean-Claude Killy France		Jean-Claude Killy France
Kitzbühel, Austria	Jean-Claude Killy France		Jean-Claude Killy France
Mégève, France	Guy Périllat France		Jean-Claude Killy France
Madonna, Italy	Guy Périllat France		
Sestriere, Italy			Jean-Claude Killy France
Franconia, New Hampshire	Jean-Claude Killy France	Jean-Claude Killy France	Jean-Claude Killy France
Jackson, Wyoming		Jean-Claude Killy France	
Vail, Colorado		Jean-Claude Killy France	
1968			
Hindelang, Germany		Edi Bruggmann Switzerland	
Adelboden, Switzerland		Jean-Claude Killy France	
Wengen, Switzerland	Dumenc Giovanoli Switzerland		Gerhard Nenning Austria

Location	Slalom	Giant Slalom	Downhill
Kitzbühel, Austria	Dumenc Giovanoli Switzerland		Gerhard Nenning Austria
Mégève, France	Alain Penz France	Bernard Orcel France	
Chamonix, France	Reinhard Tritscher Austria		
Oslo, Norway	Patrick Russel France	Werner Bleiner Austria	
Grenoble, France	Jean-Claude Killy France	Jean-Claude Killy France	Jean-Claude Killy France

1969

Location	Slalom	Giant Slalom	Downhill
Val d'Isère, France (1968)	Karl Schranz Austria	I. Gerhard Nenning Austria II. Jean-Claude Killy France	
Berchtesgaden, Germany	Alfred Matt Austria		
Adelboden, Switzerland		Jean-Noël Augert France	
Wengen, Switzerland	Reinhard Tritscher Austria		Karl Schranz Austria
Kitzbühel, Austria	Patrick Russel France		Karl Schranz Austria
Mégève, France	Alain Penz France		Henri Duvillard France
St. Anton, Austria			Karl Schranz Austria
Cortina, Italy			Josuah Minsch Switzerland
Are, Sweden	Patrick Russel France	Jean-Noël Augert France	
Val Gardena, Italy			Jean-Daniel Daetwyler Switzerland
Kranjska Gora, Yugoslavia	Edmund Bruggmann Switzerland	Reinhard Tritscher Austria	
Squaw Valley, California	William Kidd USA		
Mont. Ste.-Anne, Quebec, Canada	Alfred Matt Austria	Karl Schranz Austria	
Waterville Valley, New Hampshire	Jean-Noël Augert France	Dumenc Giovanoli Switzerland	

1970

Location	Slalom	Giant Slalom	Downhill
Val d'Isère, France		Gustavo Thoeni Italy	Malcolm Milne Australia
Lienz, Austria	Jean-Noël Augert France	Patrick Russel France	
Hindelang, Germany	Gustavo Theoni Italy		
Adelboden, Switzerland		Karl Schranz Austria	
Wengen, Switzerland	Patrick Russel France		Henri Duvillard France
Morzine,* France	Gerhard Riml Austria		Bernard Grosfilley France
Villars-sur-Ollon,* Switzerland	Manfrid Jocoker Switzerland		Paul Mitterer Austria
Kitzbühel, Austria	Patrick Russel France	Dumenc Giovanoli Switzerland	
Kranjska Gora, Yugoslavia	Peter Frei Switzerland	Dumenc Giovanoli Switzerland	

Location	Slalom	Giant Slalom	Downhill
Mégève, France	Patrick Russel France		Karl Schranz Austria
Madonna, Italy	Henri Brechu France	Gustavo Troeni Italy	
Garmisch, Germany			Karl Schranz Austria
Val Gardena, Italy	Jean-Noël Augert France	Karl Schranz Austria	Bernhard Russi Switzerland
Saalbach,* Austria	Herald Rofner Austria		Kurt Huggler Switzerland
Jackson Hole, Wyoming	Alain Penz France		Karl Cordin Austria
Chamonix,* France			Rudi Saller Austria
Grouse Mt., B.C., Canada	Alain Penz France	Alain Penz France	
Leysin, Mosses,* Diablerets Swi.	Kurt Schnider Switzerland	Josef Loidl Austria	
Heavenly Valley, California	Alain Penz France	Patrick Russel France	
Voss, Bergen, Norway	Patrick Russel France	Werner Bleiner Austria	

1971

Location	Slalom	Giant Slalom	Downhill
Sestriere, Italy (1970)			Henri Duvillard France
Val d'Isère, France (1970)		Patrick Russel France	Karl Cordin Austria
Berchtesgaden, Germany	Jean-Noël Augert France	Jean-Noël Augert France	
Madonna di Campiglio Italy	Gustavo Thoeni Italy	Henri Duvillard France	
St. Moritz, Switzerland	Tyler Palmer USA		Walter Tresch Switzerland
Adelboden Switzerland		Patrick Russel France	
Kitzbühel, Austria	Jean-Noël Augert France		
Mégève, France	Jean-Noël Augert France		Jean-Daniel Daetwyler Switzerland
Mégève, France			Bernhard Russi Switzerland
Murren, Switzerland	Jean-Noël Augert France		
Mont. Ste.-Anne Quebec, Canada	Patrick Russel France	Bernhard Russi Switzerland	
Kingfield, Maine			Bernhard Russi Switzerland
Kingfield, Maine, USA		Gustavo Thoeni Italy	Stefano Anzi Italy
Heavenly Valley, California	Gustavo Thoeni Italy	Gustavo Thoeni Italy	
Are, Sweden	Jean-Noël Augert France	David Zwilling Austria	

1972

Location	Slalom	Giant Slalom	Downhill
St. Moritz, Switzerland (1971)			Bernhard Russi Switzerland
Val d'Isère, France (1971)		Erik Haker Norway	Karl Schranz Austria
Sestriere, Italy (1971)	Tyler Palmer USA		

Location	Slalom	Giant Slalom	Downhill
Berchtesgaden, Germany	Henri Duvillard France	Roger Rossat-Mignod France	
Kitzbühel, Austria (originally scheduled for Sestriere)			Karl Schranz Austria
Kitzbühel, Austria			Karl Schranz Austria
Wengen, Switzerland	Jean-Noël Augert France		
Adelboden, Switzerland		Werner Mattle Switzerland	
Banff, Alberta, Canada	Andrzej Bachleda Poland	Erik Haker Norway	
Sapporo, Japan	F. Fernandez-Ochoa Spain	Gustavo Thoeni Italy	Bernhard Russi Switzerland
Crystal Mountain, Washington			Bernhard Russi Switzerland Franz Vogler W. Germany
Heavenly Valley, California		Gustavo Thoeni Italy	
Val Gardena, Italy	Rolando Thoeni Italy	Edmund Bruggmann Switzerland	Bernhard Russi Switzerland
Pra Loup, France	Rolando Thoeni Italy	Edmund Bruggmann Switzerland	

1973

Location	Slalom	Giant Slalom	Downhill
Val d'Isère, France (1972)†		Piero Gros Italy	Reinhard Tritscher Austria
Val Gardena, Italy (1972)†			Roland Collombin Switzerland
Madonna di Campiglio, Italy†	Piero Gros Italy	David Zwilling Austria	
Garmisch, Germany‡			Roland Collombin Switzerland Roland Collombin Switzerland
Grindelwald, Switzerland‡			Bernhard Russi Switzerland
Wengen, Switzerland‡	Christian Neureuther W. Germany		
Adelboden, Switzerland‡		Gustavo Thoeni Italy	
Mégève, France‡	Christian Neureuther W. Germany	Henri Duvillard France	
Kitzbühel, Austria‡	Jean-Noël Augert France	Roland Collombin Switzerland	Roland Collombin Switzerland
St. Anton, Austria§	Gustavo Thoeni Italy		Bernhard Russi Switzerland
St. Moritz, Switzerland§			Werner Grissmann Austria
Mont. Ste.-Anne, Quebec, Canada§	Gustavo Thoeni Italy	Max Rieger W. Germany	
Alyeska, Alaska§		Hansi Hinterseer Austria	
Naeba, Japan	Jean-Noël Augert France	Erik Haker Norway	
Heavenly Valley, California§	Jean-Noël Augert France	Bob Cochran USA	

Women

Location	Slalom	Giant Slalom	Downhill
1967			
Oberstaufen, Germany	Nancy Greene Canada	Nancy Greene Canada	
Grindelwald, Switzerland	Annie Famose France	Nancy Greene Canada	Nancy Greene Canada
Schruns, Austria			Marielle Goitschel France
St. Gervais, France	Annie Famose France	Erika Schinegger Austria	
Monte Bondone, France	Brugl Farblner W. Germany		
Sestrlere, Italy			(T) Marielle Goitschel France Guistina Demetz Italy
Franconia, New Hampshire	Marlelle Goltschel France	Christine Beranger France	Isabelle Mir France
Jackson, Wyoming	Nancy Greene Canada	Nancy Greene Canada	
Vall, Colorado		Nancy Greene Canada	
1968			
Oberstaufen, Germany	Marielle Goltschel France	Fernande Bochatay Switzerland	
Grindelwald, Switzerland	Gertrud Gabl Austria	Nancy Greene Canada	
Badgasteln, Austria	Florence Steurer France		Olga Pall Austria
St. Gervals, France	Fernande Bochatay Switzerland		Isabelle Mir France
Chamonix, France	Nancy Greene Canada		Nancy Greene Canada
Oslo, Norway	Kiki Cutter USA	Fernande Bochatay Switzerland	
Grenoble, France	Marlelle Goltschel France	Nancy Greene Canada	Olga Pall Austria
1969			
Val d'Isère, France	Isabelle Mlr France	Florence Steurer France	
Oberstaufen, Germany	Gertrud Gabl Austria	Christina Cutter USA	
Grindelwald, Switzerland	Gertrud Gabl Austria		Wiltrud Drexel Austria
Schruns, Austria	Rosi Mittermaler W. Germany		Wiltrud Drexel Austria
St. Gervals, France	Ingrid Lafforgue France		Isabelle Mlr France
St. Anton, Austria			Olga Pall Austria
Viplteno, Italy	Judy Nagel USA	Michèle Jacot France	
Vysoke-Tatry, Czechoslovakia	Gertrud Gabl Austria	Gertrud Gabl Austria	
Squaw Valley, California	Bernie Rauter Austria	Florence Steurer France	
Mont. Ste.-Anne, Quebec, Canada	Christina Cutter USA	Mlchèle Jacot France	

Location	Slalom	Giant Slalom	Downhill
Waterville Valley, New Hampshire	Christina Cutter USA	Bernie Rauter Austria	

1970

Location	Slalom	Giant Slalom	Downhill
Val d'Isere, France	Michèle Jacot France	Françoise Macchl France	
Lienz, Austria	Judy Nagel USA	Judy Nagel USA	
Oberstaufen, Germany	Bernle Rauter Austria	Michèle Jacot France	
Grlndelwald, Switzerland	Michèle Jacot France		Isabelle Mir France
Badgastein, Austria	Ingrid Lafforgue France		Isabelle Mir France
Maribor, Yugoslavia	Barbara Cochran USA	Annemarie Troell Austria	
Saint Gervals, France	Kiki Cutter USA	Françoise Macchl France	
Garmisch, Germany			Françoise Macchi France
Abetone, Italy	Ingrld Lafforgue France	Britt Lafforgue France	
Val Gardena, Italy	Ingrid Lafforgue France	Betsy Clifford Canada	Anneroesli Zyrd Switzerland
Grouse Mt., B.C., Canada	Michèle Jacot France		
Voss, Bergen, Norway	Rosi Mittermaler Germany	Ingrid Lafforgue France	
Jackson Hole, Wyoming	Ingrid Lafforgue France		Isabelle Mir France

1971

Location	Slalom	Giant Slalom	Downhill
Sestriere, Italy (1970)			Françoise Macchi France
Val d'Isère, France (1970)	Betsy Clifford Canada		Isabelle Mir France
Maribor, Yugoslavia	Annemarie Proell Austria	Françoise Macchi France	
Oberstaufen, Germany	Michèle Jacot France	Michèle Jacot France	
Grindelwald, Switzerland	Britt Lafforgue France		
Montafon, Austria			Michèle Jacot France
Pra Loup, France	Annemarie Proell Austria		Wiltrud Drexel Austria
Murren, Switzerland	Britt Lafforgue France		
Mont. Ste.-Anne, Quebec, Canada	Marilyn Cochran USA	Isabelle Mir France	
Kingfield, Maine			Annemarie Proell Austria
Kingfield, Maine		Michèle Jacot France	Annemarie Proell Austria
Heavenly Valley, California	Barbara Cochran USA	Barbara Cochran USA	
Abertone, Italy		Annemarie Proell Austria	
		Annemarie Proell Austria	
Are, Sweden		Annemarie Proell Austria	

Location	Slalom	Giant Slalom	Downhill
1972			
St. Moritz, Switzerland (1971)			Annemarie Proell Austria
Val d'Isère, France (1970)			Jacqueline Rouvier France
Sestriere, Italy (1970)			Annemarie Proell Austria
Oberstaufen, Germany	Françoise Macchi France	Françoise Macchi France	
Maribor, Yugoslavia		Françoise Macchi France	
Bradgastein, Austria	Britt Lafforgue France		Annemarie Proell Austria
Grindelwald, Switzerland	Britt Lafforgue France		Annemarie Proell Austria
Saint Gervais, France		Annemarie Proell Austria	
Sapporo, Japan	Barbara Cochran USA	Marie-Theres Nadig Switzerland	Marie-Theres Nadig Switzerland
Banff, Alberta, Canada	Britt Lafforgue France	Annemarie Proell Austria	
Crystal Mountain, Washington			Annemarie Proell Austria Wiltrud Drexel Austria
Heavenly Valley, California	Florence Steurer France	Annemarie Proell Austria	
Pra Loup, France	Daniele Debernard France	Daniele Debernard France Annemarie Proell Austria	
1973			
Val d'Isère, France (1972)†	Pamela Behr W. Germany		Annemarie Proell Austria
Saalbach, Austria (1972)†		Annemarie Proell Austria	Annemarie Proell Austria
Maribor, Yugoslavia‡	Patricia Emonet France		
Pfronten, W. Germany‡			Annemarie Proell Austria Annemarie Proell Austria
Grindelwald, Switzerland‡	Minika Kaserer Austria		Annemarie Proell Austria
St. Gervais, France‡		Annemarie Proell Austria	
Les Contamines, France‡		Minika Kaserer Austria	
Chamonix, France‡	Marilyn Cochran USA		Annemarie Proell Austria
Schruns, Austria§	Rosi Mittiermaeir Austria		Annemarie Proell Austria
St. Moritz, Switzerland§			Annemarie Proell Austria
Abetone, Italy§		Minika Kaserer Austria	
Mont. Ste. Anne, Quebec, Canada§	Patricia Emonet France	Annemarie Proell Austria	
Alyeska, Alaska§		Bernadette Zurbriggen Switzerland	
Naeba, Japan§	Daniele Debernard France	Marilyn Cochran USA	

Location	Slalom	Giant Slalom	Downhill
Heavenly Valley, California§	Patricia Emonet France	Patricia Emonet France	

* B race. † First Period. ‡ Second Period. § Third Period.

THE NATIONS CUP

The Nations Cup, donated by *Ski Magazine,* is based on the aggregate of World Cup points earned by individual competitors—both men and women—from each Alpine skiing nation. While the World Cup goes to the top racers, the Nations Cup is presented to the coaches of the winning national team. The point totals reflect the work of the coaches in creating broad strength in their national teams.

Year	Country	Men's World Cup Points	Women's World Cup Points	Total World Cup Points	Year	Country	Men's World Cup Points	Women's World Cup Points	Total World Cup Points
1967	France	647	613	1,260		United States	148	433	581
	Austria	355	242	597	1971	France	510	823	1,333
	Switzerland	163	98	261		Austria	361	531	892
1968	France	500	665	1,165		Switzerland	388	8	396
	Austria	543	344	887	1972	France	374	771	1,145
	Switzerland	382	154	536		Austria	297	537	834
1969	Austria	654	466	1,120		Switzerland	534	126	660
	France	506	544	1,050	1973	Austria	635	891	1,526
	United States	150	392	542		France	230	486	716
1970	France	705	926	1,631		Switzerland	449	136	585
	Austria	593	296	889					

CANADIAN-AMERICAN SKI TROPHY SERIES

To help back up the World Cup circuit and to give more zip and continuity to the domestic program, the Canadian-American Ski Trophy Series was started in 1971 to fill the gap between the World Cup and the unrelated schedule of events in North America. The schedule, including dual-slalom events and head-to-head competitions, covers a series of races across North America. Scoring rules are similar to World Cup rules. Here are the winners of the Can-Am Trophy series from its inception:

Men

Year	Winner	Country	Slalom Points	Giant Slalom Points	Downhill Points	Total Points
1971	Lance Poulsen	USA	15	65	25	105
	Otto Tschudi	Norway	70	33	0	103
	Terry Palmer	USA	60	42	0	102
	Rod Taylor	USA	18	29	55	102
1972	Don Rowles	USA	46	70	38	154
	Steve Lathrop	USA	70	15	51	136
	Dave Irwin	Canada	70	27	0	97
1973	Cary Adgate	USA	55	65	60	180
	Heinz Weixelbaum	W. Germany	70	11	65	146
	Andy Mills	USA	5	15	61	81

Women

Year	Winner	Country	Slalom Points	Giant Slalom Points	Downhill Points	Total Points
1971	Karen Budge	USA	75	61	37	173
	Judy Crawford	Canada	70	65	36	171
	Carolyn Oughton	Canada	26	25	65	116
1972	Cheryl Bechdolt	USA	56	75	39	170
	Penny Northrup	USA	75	55	25	155
	Martha Coughin	USA	60	44	0	114

Year	Winner	Country	Slalom Points	Giant Slalom Points	Downhill Points	Total Points
1973	Betsy Clifford	Canada	70	70	44	184
	Cindy Nelson	USA	48	4	60	112
	Sheila McKinney	USA	45	30	26	101

EUROPEAN CUP

Created mainly to confer greater prestige on races that missed being chosen for World Cup points, the European Cup, started in 1972, provides an incentive for the racers who could not be included in the national World Cup Teams. The series also provides opportunities for national A Team members to keep in the competitive swing when for one reason or another they are not entered in a World Cup race. Another of its features is that it gives United States, Canadian, and Japanese competitors a chance to test themselves against European skiers rated just below the top level.

Points are awarded to the first ten finishers of races on the European Cup schedule, and the World Cup scale of 25-20-15-11-8-6-4-3-2-1 is used. The Cup is awarded to the man and woman compiling the highest total in five slaloms, five giant slaloms, and five downhills. Winners of the Cup are as follows:

Men

Year	Winner	Nationality	Points
1972	Ilario Pegorari	Italy	240
	Hubert Berchtold	Austria	222
	Renzo Zandegiacomo	Italy	163
1973	Fausto Radici	Italy	196
	Josef Loidi	Austria	112
	Heinz Weixelbaum	W. Germany	99
	Manfred Jakober	Switzerland	99

Women

Year	Winner	Nationality	Points
1972	Fabienne Serrat	France	212
	Anneliese Leibetseder	Austria	192
	Irmyard Lukasser	Austria	188
1973	Martine Couttet	France	213
	Martine Ducroz	France	177
	Ingrid Eberle	Austria	126

SAMSONITE NORDIC SERIES

The Samsonite Nordic Series (formerly known as the Trans-Am Trophy Series) is a circuit of Nordic competitions similar to the Can-Am Series for alpine skiers. With scoring based on the World Cup point system and points calculated for the best seven cross-country and best five jumps, the top finishers since the start in 1972 are:

Men's Cross-Country (Odyssey Cup)

Year	Winner	Nationality	Points
1972	Magne Myrmo	Norway	170
	Auelun Merland	Norway	145
	Fred Kelly	Canada	98
1973	Bob Gray	USA	130
	Mike Gallagher	USA	121
	Tim Caldwell	USA	96

Women's Cross-Country (Odyssey Cup)

Year	Winner	Nationality	Points
1972	Sharon Firth	Canada	205
	Shirley Firth	Canada	180
	Martha Rockwell	USA	141
1973	Mary Lee Atkins	USA	173
	Twila Hinkle	USA	157.5
	Kathy Anderson	USA	73
	Jana Hlavaty	USA	73

Jumping

Year	Winner	Nationality	Points
1972	Jim Miller	USA	48
	Patrick Morris	USA	38
	Arne Haugen	Norway	37
1973	Jerry Martin	USA	55

Year	Winner	Nationality	Points
	Greg Swor	USA	26
	Peter Kongsli	Norway	25
	Dane Norby	USA	25
	Vidar Nilsgaard	USA	25

OTHER MAJOR SKI EVENTS

It is impossible to give records on all the various ski events that take place each year in the world of ski racing. However, here are major events in existence before World War II.

Arlberg-Kandahar

Sir Arnold Lunn on a visit to St. Anton in 1927 organized a slalom race; the following year the Kandahar Ski Club held the first Arlberg-Kandahar. The race, also known as A-K now, takes place alternately in five famous European resorts. Here are the winners over the years:

Year	Winner (Men)	Nationality	Winner (Women)	Nationality	Locale of Race
1928	Benno Leubner	Austria	Lisbeth Poland	Austria	St. Anton
1929	Karl Neuner	Germany	Audrey Sale-Baker	England	St. Anton
1930	Walter Prager	Switzerland	Inge Lantschner	Austria	St. Anton
1931	Otto Fürrer	Switzerland	Audrey Sale-Baker	England	Mürren
1932	Otto Fürrer	Switzerland	Hedi Lantschner	Austria	St. Anton
1933	Walter Prager	Switzerland	Esmé Mackinnon	England	Mürren
1934	Otto Fürrer	Switzerland	Jeannetto Kessler	England	Mürren
1935	Arnold Glatthard	Switzerland	Anny Rüegg	Switzerland	St. Anton
1936	Friedl Pfeifer	Austria	Gerda Paumgarten	Austria	St. Anton
1937	Émile Allais	France	Christel Cranz	Germany	Mürren
1938	Race canceled				
1939	Rudolf Rominger	Switzerland	Marian Steedman	England	Mürren
1947	James Couttet	France	Celina Seghi	Italy	Mürren
1948	James Couttet	France	Celina Seghi	Italy	Chamonix
1949	Zeno Colo	Italy	F. Martell	France	St. Anton
1950	James Couttet	France	Marisette Agnel	France	Mürren
1951	Zeno Colo	Italy	F. Martell	France	Sestriere
1952	Fritz Huber, Jr.	Austria	Erika Mahringer	Austria	Chamonix
1953	Anderl Molterer	Austria	Trude Klecker	Austria	St. Anton
1954	Anderl Molterer	Austria	A. Buchner-Fischer	Germany	Garmisch
1955	Walter Schuster	Austria	Hilde Hofheer	Austria	Mürren
1956	Anderel Molterer	Austria	M. Berthod	France	Sestriere
1957	Karl Schranz	Austria	Lottl Blattl	Austria	Chamonix
1958	Karl Schranz	Austria	Putzi Frandl	Austria	St. Anton
1959	Karl Schranz	Austria	Anne Heggtveit	Canada	Garmisch
1960	Adrien Duvillard	France	Marianne Jahn	Austria	Sestriere
1961	Guy Périllat	France	Heidi Biebl	Germany	Mürren
1962	Karl Schranz	Austria	Traudel Hecher	Austria	Sestriere
1963	François Bonlieu	France	Traudel Hecher	Austria	Chamonix
1964	James Heuga	USA	Marielle Goitschel	France	Garmisch
1965	Gerhard Nenning	Austria	Marielle Goitschel	France	St. Anton
1966	Jean-C. Killy	France	Christl Haas	Austria	Mürren
1967	Jean-C. Killy	France	Marielle Goitschel	France	Sestriere
1968	Guy Périllat	France	Nancy Greene	Canada	Chamonix
1969	Karl Schranz	Austria	Gertrude Gabl	Austria	St. Anton
1970	Karl Schranz	Austria	Michele Jacot	France	Garmisch
1971	Jean-Noël Augert	France	Britt Lafforgue	France	Miirren
1972	Tyler Palmer	USA	Françoise Macchi	France	Sestriere
1973	Gustavo Thoeni	Italy	Marilyn Cochran	USA	Chamonix St. Anton

Hahnenkamm Races

The Hahnenkamm takes its name from the mountain which overlooks the town of Kitzbühel, Austria. Ever since this race started in 1933, it has drawn a maximum number of spectators and internationally famous racers.

Year	Winner	Country	Year	Winner	Country
1933	Walter Prager	Switzerland	1934	Émile Allais	France

Year	Winner	Country	Year	Winner	Country
1935	Siegfried Engl	Austria	1957	Josl Rieder	Austria
1936	Rudi Matt	Austria	1958	Anderl Molterer	Austria
1937	Willi Walch	Austria	1959	Anderl Molterer	Austria
1938	Franz Pallauro	Austria	1960	Andrien Duvillard	France
1939	Fritz Huber, Sr.	Austria	1961	Guy Périllat	France
1940–	Not held		1962	Gerhard Nenning	Austria
1945			1963	Egon Zimmerman	Austria
1946	Karl Koller	Austria	1964	Not held	
1947	Christian Pravda	Austria	1965	Ludwig Leitner	Germany
1948	Helmut Lantscher	Austria	1966	Karl Schranz	Austria
1949	Egon Schöpf	Austria	1967	Jean-Claude Killy	France
1950	Fritz Huber, Jr.	Austria	1968	Gerhard Nenning	Austria
1951	Christian Pravda	Austria	1969	Guy Périllat	France
1952	Not held		1970	Patrick Russel	France
1953	Anderl Molterer	Austria	1971	Jean-Noël Augert	France
1954	Christian Pravda	Austria	1972	Karl Schranz	Austria
1955	Anderl Molterer	Austria	1973	Bob Cochran	USA
1956	Toni Sailer	Autsria			

Lauberhorn

The Lauberhorn race always takes place in the second week of January. At first a purely British and Swiss affair, it quickly grew into one of Europe's most international races.

Year	Downhill	Country	Slalom	Country	Combined	Country
1930	Christian Rubi	Switzerland	Ernest Gertsch	Switzerland	Bill Bracken	Great Britain
1931	Fritz Steuri	Switzerland	Hans Schlunegger	Switzerland	Fritz Steuri	Switzerland
1932	Fritz Steuri	Switzerland	Fritz von Allmen	Switzerland	Fritz Steuri	Switzerland
1934	Adolf Rubi	Switzerland	Adolf Rubi	Switzerland	Adolf Rubi	Switzerland
1935	Richard Werte	Austria	Arnold Glatthard	Switzerland	Willi Steuri	Switzerland
1936	Hans Schlunegger	Switzerland	Hermann Steuri	Switzerland	Émile Allais	France
1937	Heinz von Allmen	Switzerland	Willi Walch	Austria	Willi Walch	Austria
1938	Heinz von Allmen	Switzerland	Rudl Cranz	Germany	Heinz von Allmen	Switzerland
1939	Karl Molitor	Switzerland	Pepi Jennewein	Germany	Willi Walch	Austria
1940	Karl Molitor	Switzerland	Karl Molitor	Switzerland	Karl Molitor	Switzerland
1941	Rudolf Graf	Switzerland	Marcel von Allmen	Switzerland	Marcel von Allmen	Switzerland
1942	Karl Molitor	Switzerland	Heinz von Allmen	Switzerland	Marcel von Allmen	Switzerland
1943	Karl Molitor	Switzerland	Heinz von Allmen	Switzerland	Marcel von Allmen	Switzerland
1944	Rudolf Graf	Switzerland	Marcel von Allmen	Switzerland	Marcel van Allmen	Switzerland
1945	Karl Moiltor	Switzerland	Otto von Allmen	Switzerland	Otto von Allmen	Switzerland
1946	Jean Blanc	France	Otto von Allmen	Switzerland	Karl Molitor	Switzerland
1947	Karl Molitor	Switzerland	Olle Dalman	Sweden	Edi Rominger	Switzerland
1948	Zeno Colo	Italy	Karl Molitor	Switzerland	Karl Molitor	Switzerland
1949	Rudlof Graf	Switzerland	Zeno Colo	Italy	Adolf Odermatt	Switzerland
1950	Fredy Rubi	Switzerland	Georg Schneider	Switzerland	Fredy Rubi	Switzerland
1951	Othmar Schneider	Austria	Stein Eriksen	Norway	Othmar Schneider	Austria
1952	Othmar Schneider	Austria	Stein Eriksen	Norway	Othmar Schneider	Austria
1953	Anderl Molterer	Austria	Anderl Molterer	Austria	Anderl Molterer	Austria
1954	Christian Pravda	Austria	Toni Spiss	Austria	Christian Pravda	Austria
1955	Tony Sailer	Austria	Martin Julen	Switzerland	Toni Sailer	Austria
1956	Tony Sailer	Austria	Anderl Molterer	Austria	Josl Rieder	Austria
1957	Tony Sailer	Austria	Anderl Molterer	Austria	Josl Rieder	Austria
1958	Tony Sailer	Austria	Josl Rieder	Austria	Bud Werner	USA
1959	Karl Schranz	Austria	Ernst Oberaigner	Austria	Ernst Oberaigner	Austria
1960	Willi Bogner	Germany	Hias Leitner	Austria	Pepi Stiegler	Austria
1961	Guy Périllat	France	Pepi Stiegler	Austria	Guy Périllat	France
1962	Not held		Adolf Mathis	Switzerland	Not held	
1963	Karl Schranz	Austria	Guy Périllat	France	Guy Périllat	France
1964	Egon Zimmerman	Austria	Ludwig Leitner	W. Germany	Gerhard Nenning	Austria
1965	Stefan Sodat	Austria	Guy Périllat	France	Karl Schranz	Austria
1966	Karl Schranz	Austria	Guy Périllat	France	Karl Schranz	Austria

Year	Downhill	Country	Slalom	Country	Combined	Country
1967	J.-C. Killy	France	J.-C. Killy	France	J.-C. Killy	France
1968	Gerhard Nenning	Austria	Dumenc Giovanoli	Switzerland	Gerhard Nenning	Austria
1969	Karl Schranz	Austria	Reinhard Tritscher	Austria	Heini Messner	Austria
1970	Henri Duvillard	France	Patrick Russel	France	Henri Duvillard	France
1971	Walter Tresch	Switzerland	Tyler Palmer	USA	Henri Duvillard	France
1972	Not held		Jean-Noël Augert	France	Not awarded	
1973	Bernhard Russi	Switzerland	Christian Neureuther	Germany	Henri Duvillard	France

Holmenkollen Competition: The Kings Cup

Nordic combined cross-country and jumping, the oldest ski competition in the world.

Winners are from Norway unless otherwise noted.

Year	Winner	Year	Winner
1892	Svein Sollid	1931	Johan Grøttumsbraaten
1893	Ingemann Sverre	1932	Oddbjørn Hagen
1894	Hans Johansen	1933	Hans Vinjarengen
1895	Victor Thorn	1934	Oddbjørn Hagen
1896	Sigurd Svendsen	1935	Oddbjørn Hagen
1897	Morten Hansen	1936	Olaf Hoffsbakken
1898	Canceled	1937	Sverre Brodahl
1899	Paul Braaten	1938	Emil Kvanlid
1900	Aksel Refstad	1939	Olaf Hoffsbakken
1901	Olaf Tandberg	1940	Emil Kvanlid
1902	Olav Bjaaland	1946	Olav Odden
1903	Karl Hovelsen	1947	Sven Israelsson, Sweden
1904	Per Bakken	1948	Simon Slattvik
1905	Thorvald Hansen	1949	Per Sannerud
1906	Johannes Grini	1950	Simon Slattvik
1907	Oistein Midthus	1951	Simon Slattvik
1908	Albert Larsen	1952	Gunder Gundersen
1909	Thorvald Hansen	1953	Heikku Hasu, Finland
1910	Lauritz Bergendahl	1954	Canceled
1911	Johan Kristoffersen	1955	Sverre Stenerson
1912	Lauritz Bergendahl	1956	Sverre Stenerson
1913	Lauritz Bergendahl	1957	Paavo Korhonen, Finland
1914	Lauritz Bergendahl	1958	Tormod Knutsen
1915	Lauritz Bergendahl	1959	Sverre Stenerson;
1916	Gregorius Garvlid		Gunder Gundersen
1917	Otto Aasen	1960	Gunder Gundersen
1918	Otto Aasen	1961	Nikolai Gusakov, USSR
1919	Thorleif Haug	1962	Ole Henrik Fageraas
1920	Thorleif Haug	1963	Georg Thoma, Germany
1921	Thorleif Haug	1964	Georg Thoma, Germany
1922	Harald Okern	1965	Georg Thoma, Germany
1923	Johan Grøttumsbraaten	1966	Georg Thoma, Germany
1924	Harald Okern	1967	Franz Keller, Germany
1925	Asbjorn Elgstoen	1968	John Bower, USA
1926	Johan Grøttumsbraaten	1969	Rauno Miettinen, Finland
1927	Ole Kolterud	1970	Karl-Heinz Luck, Germany
1928	Johan Grøttumsbraaten	1971	Rauno Miettinen, Finland
1929	Johan Grøttumsbraaten	1972	Ingols Mork
1930	Hans Vinjarengen	1973	Hans Schmid, Switzerland

UNITED STATES NATIONAL CHAMPIONS

Here are winners of the most important U.S. championships. The following abbreviations are used in these tables: (c) = closed; (o) = open; (*) = closed and open. Winners are from the United States unless otherwise noted.

National Men's Downhill

Year	Winner
1935	Hannes Schroll, Austria
1936	No race
1937	Dick Durrance
1938(*)	Ulrich Beutter, Germany
1939(c)	Dick Durrance
1939(o)	Toni Matt
1940(*)	Dick Durrance
1941(c)	William Redlin
1941(o)	Toni Matt
1942(c)	Barney McLean
1942(o)	Martin Fopp
1943–45	No race—World War II
1946	Steve Knowlton
1947	Karl Molitor, Switzerland
1948(*)	Jack Reddish
1949(o)	Yves Latreille
1950	Jim Griffith
1951(o)	Ernie McCulloch
1951(c)	Jack Nagel
1952(c)	Dick Buek
1952(o)	Ernie McCulloch

Year	Winner
1953(*)	Ralph Miller
1954	Dick Buek
1955(T)	Chiharu Igaya, Japan
	Bill Beck
1956	William Woods
1957	Bud Werner
1958	William Smith
1959	Bud Werner
1960	Oddvar Ronnestad, Norway
1961	None held
1962	Dave Gorsuch
1963	William Marolt
1964	Ni Orsi
1965	Loris Werner
1966	Peter Rohr, Switzerland
1967	Dennis McCoy
1968	Scott Henderson, Canada
1969	Spider Sabich
1970	Rod Taylor
1971	Bob Cochran
1972	Steve Lathrop
1973	Bob Cochran

National Men's Slalom

Year	Winner
1935	Hannes Schroll, Austria
1936	No race
1937(*)	Dick Durrance
1938(*)	Ed Meservey
1939(c)	Dick Durrance
1939(o)	Friedl Pfeifer, Austria
1940(c)	Dick Durrance
1940(o)	Friedl Pfeifer
1941(c)	Bill Redlin
1941(o)	Dick Durrance
1942(c)	Barney McLean
1943–45	No race—World War II
1946	Dick Movitz
1947	Karl Molitor, Switzerland
1948(*)	Jack Reddish
1949(*)	George Macomber
1950(T)	Jack Reddish
	Ernie McCulloch
1951(c)	Guttorm Berge
1952(o)	Jack Reddish
1953(c)	Raph Miller

Year	Winner
1953(o)	Stein Eriksen, Norway
1954	Chiharu Igaya, Japan
1955	Ralph Miller
1956	Tom Corcoron
1957	Tom Corcoron
1958	Charles Ferries
1959	Bud Werner
1960	Jim Heuga
1961	Rod Hebron, Canada
1962	Bill Barrier
1963	Charles Ferries
1964	William Marolt
1965	Rod Hebron, Canada
1966	Guy Périllat, France
1967	Jim Heuga
1968	Rick Chaffee
1969	Bob Cochran
1970	Bob Cochran
1971	Otto Tschudi, Norway
1972	Terry Palmer
1973	Bob Cochran

National Men's Giant Slalom

Year	Winner
1952	Gale Spence
1953	William Tibbits
1954	Darrell Robison
1955	Martin Strolz, Austria
	Jack Nagel (Open)
	Ralph Miller (Amateur)
1956(o)	Christian Pravda
1957	Toni Sailer, Austria
1958	Stanley C. Harwood
1959	Bud Werner
1960	Chiharu Igaya, Japan

Year	Winner
1961	Gordon Eaton
1962	Jim Gaddis
1963	Bud Werner
1964	Billy Kidd
1965	Bill Marolt
1966	Jean-Claude Killy, France
1967	Dumenc Giovanoli, Switzerland
1968	Rich Chaffee
1969	Hank Kashirva
1970	Tyler Palmer
1971	Bob Cochran
1972	Jim Hunter, Canada
1973	Bob Cochran

National Men's Alpine Combined

Year	Winner
1935	Hannes Schroll, Austria
1936	No race
1937(*)	Dick Durrance
1938(*)	Ulrich Beutter, Germany
1939(*)	Dick Durrance
1940(*)	Dick Durrance
1941(c)	William Redlin
1941(o)	Toni Matt
1942(c)	Barney McLean
1942(o)	Alf Engen
1943–45	No race—World War II
1946	Barney McLean
1947	Karl Molitor, Switzerland
1948(*)	Jack Reddish
1949(*)	George Macomber
1950(c)	Jack Reddish
1950(o)	Ernie McCulloch
1951(c)	Jack Nagel
1951(o)	Ernie McCulloch
1952	Jack Reddish
1953	Ralph Miller
1954	Chiharu Igaya
1955	Chiharu Igaya
1956	William Woods
1957	Tom Corcoran
1958	Gary Vaughn
1958	Frank Brown
1959	Bud Werner
1960	Oddvar Ronnestad, Norway
1961	Rod Hebron, Canada
1962	Gave Gorsuch
1963	Bud Werner
1964	Gordon Eaton
1965	Peter Duncan, Canada
1966	Guy Périllat, France
1967	Dumenc Giovanoli, Switzerland
1968	Scott Henderson, Canada
1969	Not held
1970	William McKay, Canada
1971	Bob Cochran
1972	Bob Cochran
1973	Bob Cochran

Note: 1935 through 1958 Alpine combined included only slalom and downhill. In 1958 an award was given to the winner of slalom, giant slalom, and downhill. From 1959 to date the Alpine combined includes slalom, giant slalom, and downhill.

National Women's Downhill

Year	Winner
1938	Marian McKean
1939(*)	Elizabeth Woolsey
1940(*)	Grace Carter Lindley
1941(c)	Nancy Reynolds
1941(o)	Gretchen Fraser
1942(c)	Shirley McDonald
1942(o)	Clarita Heath
1943–45	No Race—World War II
1946	Paula Kann
1947	Rhona Wurtele, Canada
1948(*)	Jannette Burr
1949(*)	Andrea Mead
1950(*)	Jannette Burr
1951	Katy Rodolph
1952	Andrea M. Lawrence
1953	Katy Rodolph
1954	Nancy Banks
1955	Andrea M. Lawrence
1956	Katherine Cox
1957	Linda Meyers
1958	Beverly Anderson
1959	Beverly Anderson
1960	Nancy Greene, Canada
1961	None held
1962	Sharon Pecjak
1963	Jean Saubert
1964	Jean Saubert
1965	Nancy Greene, Canada
1966	Madeleine Wuilloud, Switzerland
1967	Nancy Greene, Canada
1968	Ann Black
1969	Ann Black
1970	Ann Black
1971	Cheryl Bechdolt
1972	Stephanie Forrest
1973	Cindy Nelson

National Women's Slalom

Year	Winner
1938	Grace Carter Lindley
1939(c)	Doris Friedrich, Switzerland
1939(o)	Erna Steuri, Switzerland
1940(*)	Nancy Reynolds
1941(*)	Marilyn Shaw
1942(*)	Gretchen Fraser
1943–45	No race—World War II
1946	Rhona Wurtele
1947	Olivia Ausoni, Switzerland
1948	Ann Winn
1949	Andrea Mead
1950(c)	Norma Godden
1950(o)	Georgette T. Miller, France
1951	Katy Rodolph
1952	Andrea M. Lawrence
1953	Katy Rodolph
1954	Jill Kinmont
1955	Andrea M. Lawrence
1956	Sally Deaver
1957	Sally Deaver
1958	Beverly Anderson
1959	Linda Meyers
1960(T)	Anne Heggtveit, Canada
	Nancy Holland, Canada
1961	Linda Meyers

Year	Winner
1962	Linda Meyers
1963	Sandra Shellworth
1964	Jean Saubert
1965	Nancy Greene, Canada
1966	M. Goitschel, France
1967	Penny McCoy

Year	Winner
1968	Judy Nagel
1969	Not held
1970	Patty Boydstun
1971	Barbara Cochran
1972	Marilyn Cochran
1973	Marilyn Cochran

National Women's Giant Slalom

Year	Winner
1952	Rhona W. Gillis
1953	Andrea M. Lawrence
1954	Dorothy Modenese
1955	Jannette Burr Bray
1956	Sally Deaver
1957	Noni Foley
1958	Beverly Anderson
1959	Beverly Anderson
1960	Anne Heggtveit, Canada
1961	Nancy Holland, Canada

Year	Winner
1962	Tammy Dix
1963	Jean Saubert
1964	Jean Saubert
1965	Nancy Greene, Canada
1966	Florence Steurer, France
1967	Sandra Shellworth
1968	Marilyn Cochran
1969	Barbara Cochran
1970	Susan Corrock
1971	Laurie Kreiner, Canada
1972	Sandra Poulsen
1973	Barbara Cochran

National Women's Alpine Combined

Year	Winner
1938	Marian McKean
1939(o)	Erna Steuri, Switzerland
1940(*)	Marilyn Shaw
1940(*)	Marilyn Shaw
1941(c)	Nancy Reynolds
1941(o)	Gretchen Fraser
1942(c)	Shirley McDonald
1942(o)	Clarita Heath
1943–45	No races—World War II
1946	Rhona Wurtele, Canada
1947	Rhona Wurtele, Canada
1948	Suzzane Harris
1949(*)	Andrea Mead
1950(*)	Lois Woodworth, Canada
1951	Katy Rodolph
1952	Andrea M. Lawrence
1953(c)	Katy Rodolph
1953(o)	Sally Neidlinger

Year	Winner
1954	Nancy Banks
1955	Andrea M. Lawrence
1956	Katherine Cox
1957	Madi S. Miller
1958	Beverly Anderson
1959	Linda Meyers
1960	Elizabeth Greene, Canada
1961	Nancy Holland, Canada
1962	Linda Meyers
1963	Starr Walton
1964	Jean Saubert
1965	Nancy Greene, Canada
1966	Florence Steurer, France
1967	Karen Budge
1968	Judy Nagel
1969	Not held
1970	Rosi Forta
1971	Judy Crawford
1972	Stephanie Forrest
1973	Marilyn Cochran

Note: 1938 through 1958 combined included downhill and slalom; from 1959 to date it includes downhill, slalom, and giant slalom.

National Men's Cross-country

Year	Winner
1907	Asario Autio
1908–9	No record of event being held
1910	T. W. Glesne
1911	P. Blege Berg
1912	Julius Blegen
1913	Einar Lund
1914–15	No record of event being held
1916	Sigurd Overbye
1917–22	No events held
1923	Sigurd Overbye
1924	Robert Reid

Year	Winner
1925	Martin Fredboe
1926	Sigurd Overbye
1927	Johan Satre
1928	Magnus Satre
1929	Magnus Satre
1930	Magnus Satre
1931	No record of event held
1932	Hjalmar Hvam
1933	Magnus Satre
1934	D. Monson
1935	Ottar Satre
1936	Carl Sunquist
1937	Warren Chivers

Year	Winner	Year	Winner
1938	Dave Bradley	1960(30 km.)	Richard Taylor
1939	George Gustavson	1961(15 km.)	Norman Oakvik
1940	Peter Fosseide	1961(30 km.)	Norman Oakvik
1941	George Gustavson	1962(15 km.)	Mike Gallagher
1942	Howard Chivers	1962(30 km.)	Raimo Ahti
1943–46	No races—World War II	1963(15 km.)	Donald MacLeod
1947	Wendell Broomhall	1963(30 km.)	Ed Williams
1948	Trygve L. Nielsen	1964(15 km.)	Peter Lahdenpera
1949	Hans Holaas, Norway	1964(30 km.)	Ed Dermers
1950(18 km.)	Olavi Alakulpi	1965(15 km.)	David Rikert
1950(30 km.)	Theodore Farwell	1965(30 km.)	Bill Spencer
1951	Theodore Farwell	1966(15 km.)	Mike Gallagher
1952(18 km.)	Silas Dunklee	1966(30 km.)	Mike Elliott
1952(30 km.)	Richard Hale	1967(15 km.)	Mike Gallagher
1953(18 km.)	Tauno Pulkkinen	1967(30 km.)	Mike Gallagher
1953(30 km.)	Sheldon Varney	1968(15 km.)	Mike Gallagher
1954(18 km.)	Tauno Pulkkinen	1968(30 km.)	Mike Gallagher
1954(30 km.)	Ray Roy	1969(15 km.)	Clark Matis
1955(18 km.)	Tauno Pulkkinen	1969(30 km.)	Clark Matis
1955(30 km.)	Arne Borgness	1970(15 km.)	Mike Gallagher
1956	Norman Oakvik	1970(30 km.)	Mike Gallagher
1957(18 km.)	Sven Johansson	1971(15 km.)	Mike Elliott
1957(30 km.)	Oddvar Ask	1971(30 km.)	Mike Gallagher
1958(18 km.)	Leo Massa	1972(10 km.)	Mike Elliott
1958(18 km.)	Wayne Fleming	1972(30 km.)	Mike Elliott
1958(30 km.)	Leslie Fono	1972(50 km.)	Bob Gray
1959(15 km.)	Clarence Servold	1973(15 km.)	Tim Caldwell
1959(30 km.)	Leo Massa	1973(30 km.)	Bob Gray
1960(15 km.)	Clarence Servold	1973(50 km.)	Joe McNulty

National Nordic Combined

Year	Winner	Year	Winner
1932	Hjalmar Hvam	1956	Per Staavi
1933	Magnus Satre	1957	Bill Purcell
1934–36	No event	1958	Alfred Vincellette
1937	Warren Chivers		Frank Noel
1938	Dave Bradley	1959	Alfred Vincellette
1939	Alf Engen		Jon Mattson
1940	Peter Fosselde	1959	Norman Oakvik
1941	Alf Engen	1960	Al Vincellette
1942	Howard Chivers	1961	No event
1943–46	No event	1962	No event
1947	Ralph Townsend	1963	John Bower
1948	Robert Wright	1964	John Balfanz
1949	Ralph Townsend	1965	David Rikert
	Gorden Wren	1966	John Bower
1950	Robert Arsenault	1967	John Bower
1951	Ted Farwell, Jr.	1968	John Bower
1952	Corey Engen	1969	Jim Miller
1953	No event	1970	Jim Miller
1954	Norman Oakvik	1971	Bill Kendall
1955	No event	1972	Mike Devecka
		1973	Teyck Weed

National Men's Jumping

Year	Winner	Year	Winner
1904	Conrad Thompson	1908	John Evenson
1905	Ole Westgaard	1909	John Evenson
1906	Ole Fiering	1910	Anders Haugen
1907	Olaf Jonnum	1911	Francis Kempe

Year	Winner	Year	Winner
1912	Lars Haugen	1943–45	Championships canceled
1913	Ragnar Omtvedt	1946(o)	Alf Engen
1914	Ragnar Omtvedt	1946(c)	Arthur Devlin
1915	Lars Haugen	1947	Arnholdt Kongsgaard
1916	Henry Hall	1948	Arne Ulland
1917	Ragnar Omtvedt	1949	Petter Hugsted
1918	Lars Haugen	1950	Olavi Kuronen
1919	Canceled	1951	Arthur Tokle
1920	Anders Haugen	1952(c)	Clarence Hill
1921	Carl Howelson	1952(o)	Merrill Barber
1922	Lars Haugen	1953	Arthur Tokle
1923	Anders Haugen	1954	Roy Sherwood
1924	Lars Haugen	1955	Rudi Makl
1925	Alfred Ohrn	1956	Keith Zuehlke
1926	Anders Haugen	1957	Ansten Samuelstuen
1927	Lars Haugen	1958	Billy Olson
1928	Lars Haugen	1959	W. P. Erickson
1929	Strand Mikkelsen	1960	James Brennan
1930	Caspar Oimoen	1961	Ansten Samuelstuen
1931	Caspar Oimoen	1962	Ansten Samuelstuen
1932	Anton Lekang	1963	Gene Kotlarek
1933	Roy Mikkelsen	1964	John Balfanz
1934	Caspar Oimoen	1965	David Hicks
1935	Roy Mikkelsen	1966	Gene Kotlarek
1936	Gene Kotlarek	1967	Gene Kotlarek
1937	Sigmund Ruud	1968	Adrian Watt
1938(c)	Sig Ulland	1969	Adrian Watt
1938(o)	Birger Ruud	1970	Bill Bakke
1939	Reidar Andersen	1971	Jerry Martin
1940	Alf Engen	1972	Greg Swor
1941	Torger Tokle	1973	Jerry Martin
1942	Ola Aanjesen		

Women's Cross-country

Year	Winner	Year	Winner
1971(5 km.)	Sharon Firth, Canada	1972(10 km.)	Martha Rockwell
1971(10 km.)	Martha Rockwell	1973(5 km.)	Martha Rockwell
1972(5 km.)	Martha Rockwell	1973(10 km.)	Martha Rockwell

NATIONAL JUNIOR CHAMPIONSHIPS

These events are open to persons under nineteen years of age. Winners have been:

Boys' Downhill

Year	Winner	Year	Winner
		1960	Jack Morbeck
1948(T)	Muddy Numbers	1961	Ni Orsl
	Darrell Robison	1962	Ni Orsi
1949	Mac Miller	1963	Dale Miller
1950	Bud Morolt	1964	Rebel Ryan
1951	J. Lisac	1965	Rick Lounsbury
1952	Bud Werner	1966	Not held
1953	William Meyer	1967	Crandy Grant
1954	Frank Brown	1968	Dan Bell
1955	Marvin Moriarty	1969	Clifford Mann
1956	Dave Gorsuch	1970	Don Rowles
1957	Peter Ryan	1971	Alan Kildow
1958	D'arcy Marsh	1972	Greg Jones
1959	Bill Marolt	1973	Tom Simons

Boys' Slalom

Year	Winner
1948	Richard Ireland
1949	Darrell Robison
1950	Marvin Crawford
1951	R. Schwaegler
1952	R. Schwaegler
1953	Mel Hoaglund
1954	Bob Kinmont
1955	Frank Brown
1956	William Woods
1957	Van Card
1958	D'arcy Marsh
1959	Gary McCoy
1960	Jim Heuga
1961	Skip Bryan
1962	David Engen
1963	Ron Downing
1964	Greg Schwartz
1965	Greg Schwartz
1966	Mike Porcarelli
1967	Pat Simpson
1968	Eric Poulsen
1969	Steve Lathrop
1970	Brock Walker
1971	Kelly Drake
1972	McClain McKinney
1973	Phil Mahre

Boys' Giant Slalom

Year	Winner
1960	Bill Marolt
1961	Ni Orsi
1962	Roger Buchika
1963	Dale Miller
1964	Rebel Ryan
1965	Duncan Cullman
1966	Ray Miller
1967	Bobby Cochran
1968	Eric Poulsen
1969	Tim Skaling
1970	Craig Gorder
1971	Alan Kildow
1972	Bill Shaw
1973	Peter Jackson

Girls' Downhill

Year	Winner
1948	Dorothy Lynch
1949	Carolyn Teren
1950	Naomi Sandvig
1951	S. Werner
1952	Joyce Connor
1953	Teresa Schwaegler
1954	Teresa Schwaegler
1955	Penny Pitou
1956	Joan Hannah
1957	Joan Hannah
1958	Starr Walton
1959	Madeline Tschopp

Year	Winner
1960	Barbara Ferries
1961	Ingrid Simonson
1962	Cathy Nagel
1963	Cathy Nagel
1964	Vicki Jones
1965	Karen Budge
1966	No event
1967	Erica Skinger
1968	Cheryle Bechdolt
1969	Caryn West
1970	Becky Ellison
1971	Janet Turner
1972	Claire Blechmann
1973	Gail Blackburn

Girls' Slalom

Year	Winner
1948	Dorothy Lynch
1949	Charlotte Zumstein
1950	Skeeter Werner
1951	Naomi Sandvig
1952	Georgine Dunn
1953	Mary Litchfield
1954	Jill Kinmont
1955	Penny Pitou
1956	Patsy Walker
1957	Jean Saubert
1958	Sharon Pecjak
1959	Jean Saubert
1960	Sharon Pecjak
1961	Sandy Shellworth
1962	Karen Vance
1963	Karen Korfanta
1964	Cathy Allen
1965	Vicki Jones
1966	Marilyn Cochran
1967	Laurie Quest
1968	Jan Harvey
1969	Stephanie Forest
1970	Susan Corrock
1971	Gayle Susslin
1972	Lyndall Heyer
1973	Martha Coughlin

Girls' Giant Slalom

Year	Winner
1960	Karen Vance
1961	Ingrid Simonson
1962	Sandra Bower
1963	Cathy Nagel
1964	Cathy Nagel
1965	Ann Black
1966	Barbara Cochran
1967	Sandy Poulson
1968	Julie Wolcott
1969	Janet Turner
1970	Susan Corrock
1971	Paula Page
1972	Leslie Orton
1973	Lyndall Heyer

Boys' Cross-country

Year	Winner
1954	Arthur Demers
1955(T)	Phil Broomhall
	Martin Hale
1956	Bob Gray (Class I)
	William Ferguson (Class II)
1957	Karl Bohlin
1958	John F. Bower
1959	Michael Gallagher
1960	Mike Elliott
1961	Bruce Haskell
1962	Steve Chappell
1963	Jerry Varnum
1964	Clark Matis
1965	Pat Miller
1966	Ted Thompson
1967	Ted Thompson
1968	Malcolm Hunter
1969	Fred Kelly
1970	Fred Kelly
1971	Ron Yeager
1972	Bill Kock
1973	Dan Keenan

Boys' Nordic Combined

Year	Winner
1954	Arthur Demers
1955	Frank Brown
1956	Allan Lamson (Class I)
	William Ferguson (Class II)
1957	Danny Gatz
1958	John F. Bower
1959	Melvin A. Jodrey
1960	Thomas Upham
1961	Sam Barton
1962	John Darling
1963	Dave Rikert
1964	Randy Garretson
1965	Gary Giberson
1966	Jim Miller
1967	Ted Thompson
1968	George Perry
1969	Jason Densmore

Year	Winner
1970	Ron Yeager
1971	Bill Kock
1972	Joe Lamb
1973	Dan Keenan

Boys' Jumping

Year	Winner
1948	Marvin Crawford
1949	No event held
1950	Dean Polanka
1951	Jack Modahl
1952	John Cress
1953	John Cress
1954	Jerry Lewis
1955	Steve Rieschel
1956	Bill Brandenberg
1957	Gene Kotlarek
1958	Loris Werner
1959	Glenn Kotlarek
1960(T)	Jim Sechser
	Mike Hartig
1961	Robert Banovetz
1962	J. Martin
1963(T)	Robert Hedloff
	James Speck
1964	Randy Garretson
1965	Jerry Martin
1966	Jay Rand
1967	Bruce Cunningham
1968	Tim Kingsfield
1969	Matt Bimonte
1970	Bernard Wells
1971	Ron Steele
1972	Chris McNeil
1973	Dan Keenan

Girl's Cross-Country

Year	Winner
1971	Mary Lee Atkins
1972	Mary Lee Atkins
1973	Kathy Anderson

NCAA CHAMPIONSHIPS

Here are winners of the National Collegiate Athletic Association Ski Championships.

Year	Winner	College
Downhill		
1954	Pat Myers	Nevada
1955	Chiharu Igaya	Dartmouth
1956	Walt Taulbee	Washington
1957	Ralph Miller	Dartmouth
1958	Gary Vaughn	Norwich
1959	Marvin Melville	Utah
1960	Dave Butts	Colorado
1961	Gordon Eaton	Middlebury

Year	Winner	College
1962	Mike Baar	Denver
1963 (T)	Dave Gorsuch	Western Colorado
	Bill Marolt	Colorado
	Buddy Werner	Colorado
1964	John Clough	Middlebury
1965	Bill Marolt	Colorado
1966	Terje Overland	Denver
1967	Dennis McCoy	Denver
1968	Barney Peet	Fort Lewis
1969	Mike Lafferty	Colorado

Year	Winner	College
1970	Otto Tschudi	Denver
1971	Otto Tschudi	Denver
1972	Otto Tschudi	Denver
1973	Bob Cochran	Vermont

Slalom

Year	Winner	College
1954	John L'Orange	Denver
1955	Chiharu Igaya	Dartmouth
1956	Chiharu Igaya	Dartmouth
1957	Chiharu Igaya	Dartmouth
1958	Robert Gebhardt	Dartmouth
1959	Marvin Melville	Utah
1960	Rudy Ruana	Montana
1961	Buddy Werner	Colorado
1962	Jim Gaddis	Utah
1963	Jimmy Heuga	Colorado
1964	John Clough	Middlebury
1965	Rick Chaffee	Denver
1966	Bill Marolt	Colorado
1967	Rick Chaffee	Denver
1968	Dennis McCoy	Denver
1969	Paul Rachetto	Denver
1970	Mike Porcarelli	Colorado
1971	Otto Tschudi	Denver
1972	Mike Porcarelli	Colorado
1973	Peik Christensen	Denver

Alpine Combined

Year	Winner	College
1955	Chiharu Igaya	Dartmouth
1956	Chiharu Igaya	Dartmouth
1957	Ralph Miller	Dartmouth
1958	Dave Vorse	Dartmouth
1959	Marvin Melville	Utah
1960	Jim Gaddis	Utah
1961	Buddy Werner	Colorado
1962	Jim Gaddis	Utah
1963	Buddy Werner	Colorado
1964	John Clough	Middlebury
1965	Rick Chaffee	Denver
1966	Bill Marolt	Colorado
1967	Terje Overland	Denver
1968	Dennis McCoy	Denver
1969	Paul Rachetto	Denver
1970	Mike Porcarelli	Denver
1971	Otto Tschudi	Denver
1972	Mike Porcarelli	Colorado
1973	Peik Christensen	Denver

Cross-country

Year	Winner	College
1954	Marvin Crawford	Denver
1955	Larry Damon	Vermont
1956	Erik Berggren	Idaho
1957	Mack Miller	Western Colorado
1958	Clarence Servold	Denver
1959	Clarence Servold	Denver
1960	John Dendahl	Colorado
1961	Charles Akers	Maine
1962	James Page	Dartmouth
1963	Eddie Demers	Western Colorado
1964	Eddie Demers	Western Colorado

Year	Winner	College
1965	Mike Elliott	Fort Lewis
1966	Mike Elliott	Fort Lewis
1967	Ned Gillette	Dartmouth
1968	Clark Matis	Colorado
1969	Clark Matis	Colorado
1970	Ole Hansen	Denver
1971	Ole Hansen	Denver
1972	Stale Engen	Wyoming
1973	Steiner Hybertsen	Wyoming

Jumping

Year	Winner	College
1954	Willis Olson	Denver
1955	Willis Olson	Denver
1956	Willis Olson	Denver
1957	Alf Vincellette	Denver
1958	Oddvar Ronnestad	Denver
1959	Dave Butts	Colorado
1960	Dag Helgestad	Washington State
1961	Chris Selback	Denver
1962	Oyvind Floystad	Denver
1963	Tom Nord	Washington
1964	Frithjof Prydz	Utah
	Erik Jansen	Denver
1965	Erik Jansen	Denver
1966	Frithjof Prydz	Utah
1967	Bjorn Loken	Utah
1968	Peter Robes	Wyoming
1969	Odd Hammernes	Denver
1970	Jay Rand	Colorado
1971	Vidar Nilsgard	Colorado
1972	Odd Hammernes	Denver
1973	Vidar Nilsgard	Colorado

Nordic

Year	Winner	College
1955	Erik Berggren	Idaho
1956	Erik Berggren	Idaho
1957	Harold Riiber	Denver
1958	Clarence Servold	Denver
1959	Ted Farwell	Denver
1960	John Dendahl	Colorado
1961	John Bower	Middlebury
1962	Tor Fageraas	Montana State
1963	Aarne Valkama	Denver
1964	Erik Jansen	Denver
1965	Matz Jenssen	Utah
1966	Frithjof Prydz	Utah
1967	Matz Jenssen	Utah
1968	Jim Miller	Fort Lewis
1969	George Krog	Denver
1970	Teyck Weed	Dartmouth
1970	Jim Miller	Fort Lewis
1971	Bruce Cunningham	New Hampshire
1972	Bruce Cunningham	New Hampshire
1973	Pertti Reijula	Northern Michigan

Skimeister

Year	Winner	College
1954	Marvin Crawford	Denver
1955	Les Streeter	Middlebury
1956	John Cross	Denver
1957	Ralph Miller	Dartmouth

Year	Winner	College	Year	Winner	College
1958	Dave Harwood	Dartmouth	1966	Loris Werner	Western Colorado
1959	Dave Butts	Colorado	1967	Matz Jenssen	Utah
1960	John Dendahl	Colorado	1968	Eric Piene	Wyoming
1961	Art Bookstrom	Dartmouth	1969	Ed Damon	Dartmouth
1962	James Page	Dartmouth	1970	John Kendall	New Hampshire
1963	James Page	Dartmouth	1971	John Kendall	New Hampshire
1964	Jennings Cress	Denver	1972	Kim Kendall	New Hampshire
1965	Loris Werner	Western Colorado	1973	Kim Kendall	New Hampshire

Championship Results

Year	Site or Host	Champion	Points	Runner-up	Points
1954	Nevada	Denver	384.0	Seattle	349.6
1955	Norwich	Denver	567.050	Dartmouth	558.935
1956	Winter Park	Denver	582.01	Middlebury	541.77
1957	Ogden Snow Basin	Denver	577.95	Colorado	545.29
1958	Dartmouth	Dartmouth	561.2	Denver	550.6
1959	Winter Park	Colorado	549.4	Denver	543.6
1960	Bridge Bowl, Mont.	Colorado	571.4	Denver	568.6
1961	Middlebury	Denver	376.19	Middlebury	366.94
1962	Squaw Valley	Denver	390.08	Colorado	374.30
1963	Solitude, Utah	Denver	384.6	Colorado	381.6
1964	Franconia Notch, N.H.	Denver	370.2	Dartmouth	368.8
1965	Crystal Mt., Wash.	Denver	380.5	Utah	378.4
1966	Crested Butte, Colo.	Denver	381.02	West. Colo.	365.92
1967	Sugarloaf, Maine	Denver	376.7	Wyoming	375.9
1968	Mt. Werner, Colo.	Wyoming	383.9	Denver	376.2
1969	Mt. Werner, Colo.	Denver	388.6	Dartmouth	372.0
1970	Franconia Notch, N.H.	Denver	386.6	Dartmouth	378.8
1971	Lead, South Dakota	Denver	394.7	Colorado	373.1
1972	Winter Park, Colo.	Colorado	385.3	Denver	380.1
1973	Middlebury, Vt.	Colorado	381.9	Wyoming	377.8

Coaches of Team Champions

1954	Willy Schaeffler, Denver	1964	Willy Schaeffler, Denver
1955	Willy Schaeffler, Denver	1965	Willy Schaeffler, Denver
1956	Willy Schaeffler, Denver	1966	Willy Schaeffler, Denver
1957	Willy Schaeffler, Denver	1967	Willy Schaeffler, Denver
1958	Al Merrill, Dartmouth	1968	John Cress, Wyoming
1959	Bob Beattie, Colorado	1969	Willy Schaeffler, Denver
1960	Bob Beattie, Colorado	1970	Willy Schaeffler, Denver
1961	Willy Schaeffler, Denver	1971	Peder Pytte, Denver
1962	Willy Schaeffler, Denver	1972	Bill Marolt, Colorado
1963	Willy Schaeffler, Denver	1973	Bill Marolt, Colorado

NATIONAL SKI HALL OF FAME

The idea of a National Ski Hall of Fame and Ski Museum is an old one in American ski history. Visitors to Sweden and Norway told in glowing terms of the success of their two structures: the Skidmuseet in Stockholm, built first in Stockholm in 1912 by the Skidframjandet, and the Skimuseet at the Holmenkollen at Oslo, built in 1923 by the Foreningen Til Ski-Idrettens Fremme. Both buildings have been improved and expanded over the years.

Harold Grinden of Duluth first proposed the idea of a distinct structure while he was president of the National Ski Association—

now the United States Ski Association. Nothing concrete was done until the occasion of the fortieth anniversary of the National Ski Association in Ishpeming, Michigan, in February, 1944. The four great leaders during those years were Arthur J. Barth, Harold Grinden, Roger Langley, and John Hostvedt. They were all present and revived the idea with the suggestion that the building be located in Ishpeming, the birthplace of the NSA. Nothing could be done during the war years.

The idea smoldered in Ishpeming and was revived at the time of the National Jumping Championships in Ishpeming in February, 1947. The Ishpeming Ski Club appointed a special study group that year. Their enthusiasm was contagious. They brought their ideas to the Central Convention in Duluth, and their plan was adopted. A more detailed presentation was made to the National Convention in Chicago in November, 1948. A national committee was appointed. This committee worked over the next months until May, 1950, the time of the Sun Valley National Convention. On May 4, 1950, the National Convention both approved the plans and authorized the formation of the National Ski Museum Corporation. This was needed for tax purposes for donations.

During the period from 1950 to 1953, the greater part of the financial drive was conducted by the local committee from Ishpeming. The 1953 National Convention in New York City authorized the start of construction. Mr. William R. Atkins was in charge of construction. The building measures 34 by 52 feet, two full floors, fire resistant, complete with display areas and office. The building was dedicated at the time of the fiftieth anniversary, February 21, 1954, with a remarkable turnout of national and international officers and celebrities present.

The National Ski Hall of Fame Bronze Plaque Award is given only to competitors who have made a major contribution to the sport in competition. The National Ski Hall of Fame Certificate award is given to persons, whether competitor or non-competitor, making a major contribution to skiing as a diligent worker in and for the sport. Here are the people elected to the Hall of Fame:

1956

CARL TELLEFSEN, Ishpeming, Michigan, competed in first ski tournament in United States (1887) and was first president of National Ski Association (now USSA).

EDWARD F. TAYLOR, Denver, Colorado, Alpine racer and second director of National Ski Patrol System.

AKSEL HOLTER, Ashland, Wisconsin, competitor, official, editor of *American Ski Annual,* secretary of NSA 1904–18.

ARTHUR J. (RED) BARTH, Milwaukee, Wisconsin, NSA president and first American Olympic jumping judge in Europe. Barth died in 1956.

1957

FRED HARRIS, Brattleboro, Vermont, built first ski jump at Dartmouth College, NSA treasurer, 1929–31.

FRED H. MCNEIL, Portland, Oregon, newspaperman, first president of Pacific Northwest Ski Association.

1958

GORDON WREN, Jackson, Wyoming, Olympic jumper and Alpine racer, first American to jump more than 300 feet.

HAROLD GRINDEN, Duluth, Minnesota, organizer and longtime historian of Ski Hall of Fame, NSA president.

HANNES SCHNEIDER, North Conway, New Hampshire, "father of modern skiing," opened world's first ski school and developed Arlberg ski technique.

RICHARD DURRANCE, Aspen, Colorado, top American Alpine racer in 1930's, now moviemaker.

ROGER LANGLEY, Barre, Massachusetts, NSA president 1936–48, executive secretary 1948–54.

CHARLES M. (MINNIE) DOLE, Greenwich, Connecticut, founder of National Ski Patrol System and leader in organization of World War II ski troops.

MARTHINIUS STRAND, Salt Lake City, Utah, ski judge and Rocky Mountain skiing organizer.

ANDREA MEAD LAWRENCE, Rutland, Vermont, slalom and giant slalom gold medal winner in 1952 Olympics.

1959

TORGER TOKLE, record-breaking jumper who came to United States from Norway at the age of nineteen and was killed in action in 1945 with United States Army in Italy.

CHARLES N. PROCTOR, Yosemite, California, first four-way (jumping, cross-country, downhill, slalom) ski great.

DR. RAYMOND S. ELMER, Bellow Falls, Vermont, NSA president 1930–31.

ALF ENGEN, Salt Lake City, Utah, national jumping champion in 1940's and an Alpine racer.

ALEXANDER BRIGHT, Cambridge, Massachusetts, 1936 Olympic racer.

ROBERT (BARNEY) MCLEAN, Denver, Colorado, 1948 Olympic squad captain, jumper and racer.

1961

GRETCHEN FRASER, Vancouver, Washington, first American to win ski medals in Olympics, in 1948, gold medal in slalom and silver in combined.

1963

ARTHUR DEVLIN, Lake Placid, New York, 1952 and 1956 Olympic jumper, former national champion.

MAGNUS SATRE, Salisbury, Connecticut, cross-country champion, on 1932 Olympic team.

CASPER OIMOEN, Minot, North Dakota, national jumping champion in 1930's, on 1932 Olympic team.

LARS HAUGEN, Minneapolis, Minnesota, seven-time national jumping champion between 1912 and 1928.

ADERS HAUGEN, Yucaipa, California, four-time national jumping champion, on 1924 Olympic team.

1964

WALLACE (BUDDY) WERNER, Steamboat Springs, Colorado, 1964 Olympic racer, killed in Swiss avalanche, April 2, 1964.

ROY MIKKELSEN, Auburn, California, 1933 and 1935 national jumping champion, on 1936 Olympic team, also Alpine racer.

ROLF MONSEN, San Francisco, California, only jumper named to three Olympic teams, 1928, 1932, 1936.

1965

WALTER BIETILA, Iron Mountain, Michigan, one of the flying Bietila brothers, jumper on 1936 Olympic team, captain of 1948 team, now jumping official.

WENDELL ROBIE, Auburn, California, founder of Auburn Ski Club and first president of Far West Ski Association.

BURTON H. BOYUM, Timigami, Ontario, formerly of Ishpeming, former Hall of Fame curator, and ski administrator.

DR. AMOS R. LITTLE, JR., Helena, Montana, manager of Olympic teams and competition official.

EUGENE PETERSEN, Fox River Grove, Illinois, jumper and competition official.

1966

CONRAD THOMPSON, Ishpeming, Michigan, first national ski jumping champion (1904), won at Ishpeming.

HARRY S. WOOD, Warren, New Hampshire, first national downhill champion (1933), at Warren.

ASARIO AUTIO, Ely, Minnesota, first national cross-country champion (1907), at Ashland, Wisconsin.

MARIAN (MARGARET) MCKEAN WIGGLESWORTH, Beverly Farms, Massachusetts, first women's national downhill champion (1938), at Stowe, Vermont.

GRACE CARTER LINDLEY MCKNIGHT, Wayzata, Minnesota, first women's national slalom champion (1938), at Stowe.

DAVID LAWRENCE, California, first national men's giant slalom champion (1949), at Slide Mountain, California.

KATY RUDOLPH WYATT WEGEMAN, Las Vegas, Nevada, first women's giant slalom champion (1949), at Slide Mountain.

HANNES SCHROLL, San Francisco, California, first national men's slalom champion (1935), near Seattle.

ERLING HEISTAD, Lebanon, New Hampshire, organizer of New England high school skiing competition.

LAWRENCE MAURIN, Milwaukee, Wisconsin, ski jumper and international official, first American style judge at ski flying meet at Oberstdorf, Germany.

JOHN MCCRILLS, Newport, New Hampshire,

co-author of first American ski book and ski moviemaker.

CHARLES A. PROCTOR, Hanover, New Hampshire, with Sir Arnold Lunn of England helped introduce slalom racing in this country.

LOWELL THOMAS, Pauling, New York, radio commentator and longtime skier who promoted the sport.

1967

HENRY HALL, Farmington, Michigan, first American ski jumper to establish world distance marks: 203 feet in 1917 at Steamboat Springs, Colorado, and 225 feet in 1921 at Revelstoke, British Columbia, Canada; national champion in 1916.

RAGNAR OMTVEDT, Cary, Illinois, three-time national jumping champion, in 1913, 1914, and 1917, whose competitive career ended when he broke a leg while representing the United States in the first Olympic Winter Games in 1924.

JILL KINMONT, Los Angeles, California, former national women's slalom champion who has been paralyzed ever since her neck was broken in a racing accident in 1955.

TONI MATT, Pawling, New York, former national downhill champion of 1939 and 1941, and national combined winner of 1941; member 1950 FIS team.

HJALMAR HVAM, Portland, Oregon, winner of three gold medals during the 1932 nationals at Olympic Hill near Tahoe City, California; Class B jumping, the cross-country, and Nordic combined.

ED BLOOD, Durham, New York, Olympian of 1932 and 1936; intercollegiate ski coach and association official.

HANS (PEPPI) TEICHNER, Glen Arbor, Michigan, developer of recreational ski programs in lower Michigan; one time alpine competitor and veteran of the U.S. Mountain Troops.

DAVE MCCOY, Mammoth Mountain, California, coach of women ski racers; supporter of junior ski teams; veteran of thirty years of ski racing and winner of numerous championships; developer of the Mammoth Mountain ski area.

OTTO SCHNIEBS, Wilmington, New York, former coach at Dartmouth College and St.

Lawrence University, who developed ski talents of many Olympians and sloganized skiing as "More than just a sport, a way of life."

1968

SIR ARNOLD LUNN, Great Britain, drafter of the world's first downhill slalom competition rules, organizer of the first FIS Alpine world championships in 1931 at Mürren, Switzerland; set the first modern-day slalom course in 1922; founder of Kandahar Ski Club and events so named around the world; instrumental in getting the first U.S. women's ski team established in Europe. Perhaps more than any other individual, Sir Arnold stands as a giant in the early development of Alpine skiing.

JULIUS BLEGEN, Minneapolis, Minnesota, national cross-country champion of 1911 and 1912; Olympic team coach of 1932; NSA treasurer from 1937 to 1942.

JOHN ELVRUM, Running Springs, California, ski jumper who set the American distance record at 240 feet at Big Pines, California, and then stayed on to establish a ski school for children and eventually developed the Snow Valley Ski Area.

ALF HALVORSON, Hinsdale, New Hampshire, Nordic competitor and official who played major roles in establishing the United States Amateur Ski Association and the Canadian Amateur Ski Association.

OLE R. MANGSETH, Coleraine, Minnesota, top flight ski jumper in pioneering days of the NSA; this hall-of-famer served the NSA as treasurer from 1925 to 1928 and was active as a jumping coach until his death in 1952.

ROLAND PALMEDO, New York City, for more than half a century a contributor to affairs of the NSA and USSA at all levels; organizer of ski teacher certification; international competition official; founder of the Amateur Ski Club of New York.

CLARITA HEATH BRIHGT, Brookline, Massachusetts, former Californian who was a member of the first women's U.S. Olympic team in 1936; also contributed to skiing through efforts in instruction.

HELEN BENDELARI BOUGHTON-LEIGH MC-ALPIN, Convent, New Jersey, American-born skier who began her racing career as a British subject and as member of the British FIS teams of 1932, 1933, and 1934, but who subsequently returned home to captain the first U.S. international women's ski team in the 1935 FIS and the 1936 Olympics.

JOHN P. CARLETON, Manchester, New Hampshire, the leading intercollegiate skier from 1918 to 1925 (Dartmouth College and Oxford University); international Nordic and Alpine competitor; Olympian of 1924.

SELDEN J. HANNAH, Franconia, New Hampshire, North American ski great with championships won in Nordic and Alpine competitions of the NSA, Canadian Amateur Ski Association, Intercollegiate Ski Union, and USSA during a continuing fifty-year ski career.

EUGENE KOTLAREK, Duluth, Minnesota, winner of six national ski jumping championships: Boys' title in 1927, Class C in 1928, Class A in 1936, and Veterans in 1948, 1950 and 1954; named to 1944 All-American Ski Team.

ERNEST O. PEDERSON, West Springfield, Massachusetts, the University of New Hampshire's four-way ski great who won the American-Canadian all-round championships of 1927, 1928, and 1930; lengthy military career included Rifle Company Commander of 87th Mountain Infantry and then Executive Officer of the Mountain Warfare Training Center at Camp Hale in Colorado.

H. P. DOUGLAS, P.Q., Canada, founder and first president of the Canadian Amateur Ski Association (1921); native of Tarrytown, New York; played a leading role in ski sport's development throughout eastern North America; graduate of Cornell University, where he set out to master the sport on 8-foot skis in 1890.

1969

HARRY WADE HICKS, Lake Placid, New York, an organizer of 1932 Winter Olympic Games; served as president of United States Eastern Amateur Ski Association.

CARL HOWELSEN, Steamboat Springs, Colorado, considered father of competition and recreational skiing in Colorado; national ski jumping champion in 1921.

ALICE DAMROSCH WOLFE KIAER, New York, New York, assembled the National Ski Association's (NSA) first women's ski team for 1935 FIS World Championships and the 1936 Winter Olympics; initial promoter of international skiing competition for women of the United States.

COLONEL GEORGE EMERSON LEACH, Minneapolis, Minnesota, manager of NSA's first Olympic ski team in 1924; United States representative at founding of the Fédération Internationale de Ski.

GEORGE H. WATSON, Salt Lake City, Utah, deeded the surface rights to his vast mining claims in Alta region to the federal government for winter sports development.

DR. HAROLD C. BRADLEY, Berkeley, California, helped pioneer skiing in West; famous ski mountaineer.

JOHN HOSTVEDT, Wisconsin Rapids, Wisconsin, well-known ski competition official; cofounder of the National Ski Hall of Fame.

FRED PABST, Manchester, Vermont, ski jumping great who became noted ski-sport builder.

W. AVERELL HARRIMAN, Washington, D.C., founder of Idaho's Sun Valley as the nation's first ski resort planned from the ground up; founded Harriman Cup ski racing tourney.

SIEGFRIED STEINWALL, New York, New York, champion ski jumper in 1920's; ski coach at Dartmouth College 1927–28.

LEMOINE BATSON, Eau Claire, Wisconsin, membership on 1924 and 1932 Olympic teams; top-flight ski jumper for twenty years.

JOHN BOWER, Auburn, Maine, America's four-way Nordic ski great who in 1968 won the Holmenkollen's Kings Cup.

HARRY LIEN, Chicago, Illinois, membership 1924 Olympics; competitive career spanned both the professional and amateur eras of the NSA.

JACK REDDISH, Salt Lake City, Utah, spectacular fourteen-year competitive career included Olympic team in 1948, winner of Kandahar in 1948, three national combined championships, and many other events of national importance.

BETTY WOOLSEY, Wyoming, member of the first United States Women's Ski Team for the 1935 FIS World Championships and the first Olympic team of 1936.

NANCY GREENE, Rossland, British Columbia, Canada, rated the greatest woman competitor to date in North American ski history; in 1968 winner of the Olympic Gold Metal and

World Cup Championships; previous winner of numerous awards and races.

ERNIE MCCULLOCH, Mont Tremblant, Quebec, Canada, outstanding Canadian skier who in 1950 won the National Giant Slalom, the North American Championships, the National Downhill and the Harriman Cup; coached national ski team members of Canada and the United States, chief examiner of the Canadian Ski Instructors' Alliance.

HERMAN (JACK RABBIT) SMITH-JOHANNSEN, St. Sauveur and Showbridge, Quebec, Canada, a legend in his own lifetime; had a hand in cutting North America's most famous ski touring trails.

THE WURTELE TWINS, RHONA AND RHODA, Montreal, Quebec, Canada, the Wurtele twins won numerous championships representing clubs of both the Canadian and American ski associations.

1970

FRED BRUNN, Cary, Illinois, ski judge pioneer and former top jumping competitor.

PAUL BIETILA, Ishpeming, Michigan, the outstanding member of ski jumping's famous six-brother team "The Flying Bietilas" who died of injuries incurred during 1939 national tourney.

JOHN J. CLAIR, JR., New York, New York, ski association officer on divisional, national, and international levels.

GODFREY DEWEY, Lake Placid, New York, ski pioneer of the Adirondacks; Olympic official.

WILLIAM T. ELDRED, Hanover, New Hampshire, ski editor who published several ski magazines.

THOR C. GROSWOLD, Denver, Colorado, former competitor official; ski manufacturer.

OLE HEGGE, Lakeville, Connecticut, Norwegian Olympian who became an American ski-sport builder.

CORTLAND T. HILL, Monterey, California, ski racer and national Olympic and FIS Alpine official.

JANNETTE BURR JOHNSON, Sun Valley, Idaho, twice national downhill champion; bronze medalist of the 1954 FIS; ski instructor.

L. B. (BARNEY) MACNAB, Portland, Oregon, founder of the Mount Hood Ski Patrol, the forerunner to the National Ski Patrol System.

RICHARD MOVITZ, Salt Lake City, Utah, national slalom champion of 1946; ski association official.

GEORGE A. NEWETT, Ishpeming, Michigan, pioneer ski-reporting newspaperman who was among founders of NSA.

BIRGER AND SIGMUND RUUD of Norway, world championship Norwegian skiers and champions of the NSA.

LLOYD (SNOWBALL) SEVERUD, Chetek, Wisconsin, championship ski jumper and coach of American and Canadian teams.

JOHN ALBERET (SNOW-SHOE) THOMPSON, most famous and legendary skier in North America during last half of nineteenth century.

ARTHUR TOKLE, Lake Telemark, New Jersey, championship ski jumper and Olympic coach.

PAULA KANN VALAR, Franconia, New Hampshire, national downhill champion of 1946 as well as other racing events.

JOHN WICTORIN, Ridgefield Park, New Jersey, noted expert and official of Nordic skiing who began his career as a cross-country champion.

1971

REIDAR ANDERSEN, Oslo, Norway, one of the all-time Norwegian greats and rated among the best of Norway's jumpers to appear on the North American scene; won Holmenkollen classic three times and once held the world distance-jumping record.

WARREN CHIVERS, Saxtons River, Vermont, holder of numerous intercollegiate championships; member of 1936 Olympic team; national cross-country champion in 1937.

PAUL JOSEPH PERRAULT, Ishpeming, Michigan, one of the United States' best jumpers just after World War II; member of 1952 Olympic Team.

SALLY NEIDLINGER HUDSON, Olympic Valley, California, won Harriman Cup in 1948; member of 1952 FIS team and 1952 Olympic team; coach of juniors at national and international levels.

NELS NELSEN, Revelstoke, B.C., Canada, generally recognized as the man who did the most to promote the skisport in Western Canada; top-rated jumper in 1920's.

CHIHARU IGAYA, New York, New York, holder of six national collegiate titles plus five national Alpine championships; represented Japan in two Olympics.

JAMES R. HENDERICKSON, Eau Claire, Wisconsin, outstanding jumper who was a member of 1936 Olympic team.

NATHANIEL GOODRICH, Hanover, New Hampshire, one of the men most instrumental in introducing Alpine competition to America.

GUTTORM PAULSEN, Chicago, Illinois, noted ski jumper and ski jumping judge.

JAMES GRIFFITH, Ketchum, Idaho, winner of 1950 national downhill championship; member of 1950 FIS team; killed while training for 1952 Olympic team.

RON MACKENZIE, Lake Placid, New York, leader in the development of both recreational and competitive skiing as a teacher, coach, planner, builder, organizer, and promoter.

SIGI ENGL, Sun Valley, Idaho, former continental racing great and head of Sun Valley Ski School—the largest in the world—since 1952.

ALBERT E. SIGAL, Walnut Creek, California, former U.S. Ski Association president and noted skisport leader.

SVERRE ENGEN, Salt Lake City, Utah, jumping competitor, instructor, writer, resort operator, consultant on avalanche control in ski areas and maker of skiing movies.

OTTAR SATRE, Salisbury, Connecticut, a versatile competitor in cross-country, jumping, and combined during the period from 1930 to 1942; winner of 1935 national cross-country championship; member of the 1936 Olympic team.

1972

NANCY REYNOLDS COOKE, Armonk, New York, National Women's Closed and Open Slalom Champion of 1940; National Women's Closed Downhill and Alpine Combined Champion of 1941; holder of an enviable competition record throughout North America; named to the United States Ski Team for the 1940 Winter Olympics (canceled because of World War II); also member of the U.S. Team at the FIS World Championships of 1938; fund raiser for the U.S. Ski Team.

DONALD FRASER, Vancouver, Washington, world-famous early-day American downhill and slalom competitor; holder of a distinguished competitive career within the National Ski Association, the United States Ski Association, the Federation of International Skiing, and the Olympic movement; twice winner of the Silver Skis on Mt. Rainier, Washington, and an Olympian of 1936, and Pan American Slalom Champion of 1938.

DOROTHY HOYT NEBEL, Denville, New Jersey, FIS skier of 1938, PNSA Slalom Champion of 1939, Olympian of 1940, USEASA Alpine Champion of 1940 and 1941; winner of numerous top-rated competitions, including the Arnold Lunn Trophy and the Silver Skis at Mt. Rainier; numbered among America's earliest Class A rated internationalists; ski racing coach, ski instructor, and lifelong skisport builder.

WILLIS S. OLSON, Eau Claire, Wisconsin, outstanding ski jumper, better known as Billy (the Kid) Olson, began career as teen-ager with record-shattering performances and carried through to winning every class championship of the USSA: the Class C, the Class B, the Class A, and the Veteran's Class; member of two Olympic teams (1952 and 1956) and two FIS teams (1950 and 1954); undefeated University of Denver intercollegiate ski great and three times NCAA champion.

BIRGER TORRISSEN, Salisbury, Connecticut, a strong Nordic event competitor; Eastern Amateur's Nordic Combined Champion of 1934; an Olympian of 1936; a top performing ski jumper, excelling in the 18-, 30- and 50-km. cross-country competitions; attached to the 10th Mountain Division as a ski instructor; coach of numerous junior champions.

MAGNUS AND HERMOND BAKKE, brothers, skisport builders combined with ski athlete careers in support of skiing at the divisional, national, and international levels.

ERLING STROM, skisport builder and ski athlete career under three flags.

FRED ISELEIN, skisport builder and ski athlete.

SIGRID STROMSTAD LAMING, first woman to win a National Championship of the NSA and USSA: cross country of 1932.

EARLE B. LITTLE, skisport builder at the divisional, national, and international level.

JOHN E. P. MORGAN, skisport builder at all levels of the NSA in programs which placed American skiing into world-wide fame.

1973

HANNAH LOCKE CARTER, Los Angeles, California, member of four American Women's Ski Teams, 1936—1939, and the 1940

Olympic Ski Team; an international competitor who helped pave the way for increased skisport participation by American women; member of the Sun Valley Ski Club and Amateur Ski Club of New York.

HOWARD CHIVERS, Hanover, New Hampshire, National Nordic Combined Champion of 1942; Canadian National Cross-Country Champion of 1937; winner of numerous divisional and intercollegiate Nordic championships; an able Alpine competitor; named together with his brother, Warren, as the Number One Group to represent the U.S. in the 1940 Olympics and FIS Championships.

COREY ENGEN, McCall, Idaho, Nordic National Champion of 1942; National Veterans Alpine Combined Champion of 1959, 1962, and 1969; winner of more than 200 awards in Alpine and Nordic skiing; Captain of the 1948 Olympic Nordic Team; coach of national juniors and seniors.

SVERRE FREDHEIM, St. Paul, Minnesota, top-placing American ski jumper (11th) during the 1936 Winter Olympics; named to the 1940 Olympic Team, and an Olympic competitor in 1948 at age 41 when he placed 12th; winner of numerous divisional championships in Class A, B, and Veterans' divisions; often a runner-up in national tourneys, and at 44 years of age placing ninth in Olympic tryouts; an active competitor until 60.

CARL HOLMSTROM, Duluth, Minnesota, top-ranking national ski jumper and winner of numerous divisional and individual tournaments while representing the Duluth Ski Club and the Bear Mountain (New York) Winter Sports Association; member 1932 Olympic Team, also 1936 Team; now an internationally listed ski-jumping judge; fifty years of service to skisport—25 in competition and 25 as an official.

GEORGE MACOMBER, Concord, Massachusetts, Olympian of 1948 and 1952; FIS team member of 1950; National Combined Alpine Champion of 1949; National Veterans Champion of 1962; former president of the Eastern Amateur Ski Association and a driving force for many years in the development of Alpine competition.

HAROLD SORENSEN, Winter Park, Colorado, named to two All-American Ski Teams; captured numerous divisional crowns and twice runner-up in national tourneys; a career of six decades; winner in 1971 of the Russell Wilder Memorial for "outstanding activity in focusing the interests of America's youths on the sport of skiing."

LUGGI FOEGER, Incline Village, Nevada, international ski competitor and ski teacher; onetime number-one associate of Hannes Schneider, turned American ski area manager and developer; rated "one of the true mountain men of the world" and long involved in affairs of the USSA and its divisions.

ARTHUR G. KNUDSEN, Racine, Wisconsin, Ski Team Salesman and fund-raiser extraordinary; ski jumping competitor turned association official.

MALCOLM MCLANE, Concord, New Hampshire, long-time USSA officer; Blegen Awardee of 1959; captain of the Dartmouth ski team of 1949; international competitor and Rhodes Scholar.

J. STANLEY MULLIN, Los Angeles, California, able and articulate spokesman for organized skisport; a champion of the principle of amateurism; national leader against removal of the Ski Hall of Fame from Ishpeming.

Athlete-of-the-Year Awards

The National Ski Hall of Fame occasionally gives athlete-of-the-year awards to skiers for meritorious performances in ski competitions. Winners over the years are as follows:

Year	Winner
1959	Buddy Werner
1960	Penny Pitou
1964	Jean Saubert
	Bill Kidd
	Jimmy Heuga
1969	Adrian Watt
	Mike Gallagher
	Spider Sabich
	Marilyn Cochran
1970	Bill Kidd
	Barbara Cochran
	Greg Swor
	Bob Gray
	Jim Miller
	Martha Rockwell
1972	Barbara Cochran

UNITED STATES NATIONAL COMPETITIVE TROPHIES

Although the United States Ski Association was founded in 1904, most of its competitive trophies do not date back that far. The Beck International Ski Trophy is the oldest, dating back to 1931. In most cases, the trophies were not retroactive to the beginnings of the particular national competition they represent. One exception is the Gale C. Burton Memorial Trophy for the National 15- to 18-Kilometer Cross-country Race. This trophy dates back to 1907.

All of the national competitive trophies are housed in the United States Ski Hall of Fame at Ishpeming, Michigan. Matters pertaining to trophies and awards are administered by the United States Ski Association Board of Directors and the United States Ski Association National Ski Hall of Fame, History and Trophies Committee. Descriptions of the various trophies and lists of the winners follow.

Beck International Trophy

This trophy, presented by George Beck to the National Ski Association in 1930, is awarded annually to the outstanding United States skier in international performance. The International Committee selects the recipient and refers to the USSA Board of Directors for final approval.

Year	Winner
1931	Ottar Satre
1948	Gretchen Fraser
1952	Andrea M. Lawrence
1956	Buddy Werner
1957	Buddy Werner
1958	Buddy Werner
1959	Gene Kotlarek
1960	Penny Pitou
1961	No award
1962	Chuck Ferries
1963	No award
1964	Jean Saubert
1965	Dave Hicks
1966	Bill Kidd
1967	Jimmy Heuga
1968	John Bower
1969	Marilyn Cochran
1970	Bill Kidd
1971	Marilyn Cochran
1972	Barbara Cochran
1973	Tim Caldwell

Paul Bietila Trophy

This trophy was given in 1940 by Dr. and Mrs. H. C. Bradley of Madison, Wisconsin, as a memorial to be awarded annually to the American-born skier scoring highest in the National Ski Jumping Championships.

Year	Winner
1940	Merrill Barber
1941	Walter Bietila
1942	Art Devlin
1943–45	No award—World War II
1946	Art Devlin
1947	Joe Perrault
1948	Walter Bietila
1949	Art Devlin
1950	Art Devlin
1951	Art Devlin
1952	Clarence Hill
1953	Willis Olson
1954	Roy Sherwood
1955	Rudi Makl
1956	Keith Zuehlke
1957	Jerry Lewis
1958	Willis Olson
1959	W. P. Erlkson
1960	James Brennan
1961	Eugene Kotlarek
1962	Stephen Rieschl
1963	Gene Kotlarek
1964	John Balfanz
1965	Dave Hicks
1966	Gene Kotlarek
1967	Gene Kotlarek
1968	Adrian Watt
1969	Adrian Watt
1970	Bill Bakke
1971	Jerry Martin
1972	Greg Swor
1973	Jerry Martin

Julius Blegen Memorial Plaque and Medal

This award is presented to the National Ski Association (NSA) by the Central U.S. Ski Association in memory of Julius Blegen, Minneapolis, former treasurer of the NSA, 1937–42, former and first president of the CUSSA, American Olympic Coach in 1932. The award is given annually to the USSA member who contributed his or her outstanding service to the sport of skiing in the United States during the year.

Year	Winner
1946	Roger Langley

Year	Winner
1947	Arthur J. Barth
1948	Fred McNell
1949	John Hostvedt
1950	Fred C. Bellmar
1951	Douglas M. Burckett
1952	F. C. Koziol
1953	Albert E. Sigal
1954	Harold A. Grinden
1955	Burton H. Boyum
1956	John B. Carson
1957	Olav Ulland
1958	T. Lee McCracken
1959	Robert Johnstone
1960	Dr. Amos R. Little
	Malcolm McLane
1961	Sepp Ruschp
1962	J. Stanley Mullin
1963	Ralph DesRoches
1964	Robert Beattie
1965	Dr. Merritt H. Stiles
1966	Evelyn R. Masbruch
1967	Al Merrill
1968	Willy Scheaffler
1969	William Berry
1970	Earl D. Walters
1971	Gustav Raaum
1972	James Balfanz
1973	Charles T. Gibson

Year	Winner
1942	Howard Chivers
1947	Wendell Broomhall
1948	Trygve Nielsen
1949	Hans Holaas
1950	Olavi Alakulpi
1951	Ted Farwell, Jr.
1952	Silas Dunklee
1953	Tauno Pulkkinen
1954	Tauno Pulkkinen
1955	Tauno Pulkkinen
1956	Mack Miller
1957	Sven Johansson
1958	Leo Massa
1959	Clarence Servold
1960	Richard Taylor
1961	Robert Gray
1962	Mike Gallagher
1963	Donald MacLeod
1964	Peter Lahdenpera
1965	David Rikert
1966	Mike Gallagher
1967	Mike Gallagher
1968	No event
1969	Clark Matis
1970	Mike Gallagher
1971	Mike Elliott
1972	Mike Elliott
1973	Tim Caldwell

Gale Cotton Burton Memorial Trophy

This trophy was donated by the Burton family of Wayzata, Minnesota, for the winner of the National 15- to 18-Kilometer Cross-country Race, in memory of Gale C. Burton (1918–1943).

Year	Winner
1907	Asario Autio
1910	T. Glesne
1911	P. Blege Berg
1912	Julius Blegen
1913	Einar Lund
1916	Sigurd Overbye
1923	Sigurd Overbye
1924	Robert Reid
1925	Martin Fredboe
1926	Sigurd Overbye
1927	Johan Satre
1928	Magnus Satre
1929	Magnus Satre
1930	Magnus Satre
1932	Hjalmar Hvam
1933	Magnus Satre
1934	D. Monson
1935	Ottar Satre
1936	Carl Sunquist
1937	Warren Chivers
1938	David Bradley
1939	George Gustavson
1940	Peter Fosseide
1941	George Gustavson

Sally Deaver Award

This award is presented in memory of Sally Deaver to the National Women's Slalom Champion.

Year	Winner
1965	Nancy Greene
1966	Wendy Allen
1967	Penny McCoy
1968	Judy Nagel
1969	Barbara Cochran
1970	Patty Boydstun
1971	Barbara Cochran
1972	Marilyn Cochran
1973	Barbara Cochran

Finlandia Trophy

This trophy is annually awarded to the outstanding cross-country skier in the United States.

Year	Winner
1964	Mike Elliott
1965	Mike Elliott
1966	Mike Gallagher
1967	Mike Gallagher
1968	John Bower
1969	Barbara Britch
1970	Bob Gray
1971	Mike Elliott

Year	Winner
1972	Martha Rockwell
1973	Tim Caldwell

Paul Nash Layman, Jr., Trophy

This trophy is awarded to the winner of the National Nordic Combined Competition (jumping and cross-country).

Year	Winner
1932	Hjalmar Hvam
1933	Magnus Satre
1934–36	No event
1937	Warren Chivers
1938	Dave Bradley
1939	Alf Engen
1940	Peter Fosseide
1941	Alf Engen
1942	Howard Chivers
1943–46	No event
1947	Ralph Townsend
1948	Robert Wright
1949	Ralph Townsend
1949	Gorden Wren
1950	Robert Arsenault
1951	Ted Farwell, Jr.
1952	Corey Engen
1953	No event
1954	Norman Oakvik
1955	No event
1956	Per Staavi
1957	Bill Purcell
1958	Alfred Vincellette
	Frank Noel
1959	Alfred Vincellette
	Jon Mattson
	Norman Oakvik
1960	Alfred Vincellette
1961	No event
1962	No event
1963	John Bower
1964	John Balfanz
1965	David Rikert
1966	John Bower
1967	John Bower
1968	John Bower
1969	Jim Miller
1970	Jim Miller
1971	Robert Kendall
1972	Mike Devecka
1973	Teyck Weed

Sons of Norway Junior Jumping Trophy

This trophy was donated by the Supreme Lodge of the Sons of Norway for the best junior at the National Jumping Competition.

Year	Winner
1958	Gene Kotlarek
1959	Lyle Swenson

Year	Winner
1960	Butch Wedin
1961	Clyde Brodt
1962	Clyde Brodt
1963	J. Martin
1964	Ernie Ganz
1965	Adrian Watt
1966	Adrian Watt
1967	Gary Sparpana
1968	Ken Harkins
1969	Jerry Wetzel
1970	Joe Battig
1971	William Polanka
1972	Dave Tomten
1973	Scott Clayton

Torger Tokle Memorial

This award is given annually to the USSA Ski Jumping Champion by the Norway Club of New York.

Year	Winner
1948	Arne Ulland
1949	Petter Hugsted
1950	Olavi Kuronen
1951	Arthur Tokle
1952	Merrill Barber
1953	Arthur Tokle
1954	Roy Sherwood
1955	Rudi Maki
1956	Keith Zuehlke
1957	Ansten Samuelstuen
1958	Billy Olson
1959	W. P. Erickson
1960	James Brennan
1961	Ansten Samuelstuen
1962	Ansten Samuelstuen
1963	Gene Kotlarek
1964	John Balfanz
1965	David Hicks
1966	Gene Kotlarek
1967	Gene Kotlarek
1968	Jay Martin
1969	Adrian Watt
1970	Bill Bakke
1971	Jerry Martin
1972	Greg Swor
1973	Jerry Martin

United States Ski Club Award

This award is presented annually to the outstanding ski club in the United States. "A" category is for clubs with over 150 members; "B" is for clubs with less than 150 members.

Year	Winner
1964	Usequebaugh Ski Club—Salt Lake, Utah
1965	Ski Club of New Jersey
1966	Ramapo Mountain Ski Club, Nanuet, N.Y.

Year	Winner
1967	Brattleboro Outing Club, Brattleboro, Vermont
1968	Vagabon Ski Club, Wisconsin
1969	Ramapo Mountain Ski Club, Nanuet, N.Y.
1970	Fresno Ski Club, Fresno, California (A)
	Singles Ski Club, Los Angeles, California (B)
1971	Ramapo Mountain Ski Club, Nanuet, N.Y. (A)
	Singles Ski Club, Los Angeles, California (B)
1972	Westwood Ski Club, Los Angeles, California (A)
	Singles Ski Club, Los Angeles, California (B)
1973	Kansas City Ski Club, Kansas City, Kansas (A)
	Wachtung Ski Club, Wachtung, New Jersey (B)

White Stag Trophy

There are two identical trophies, one being for the winner of the Ladies Combined Downhill Slalom (and in 1958 the Giant Slalom was added) and the other for the Men's Alpine Combined.

Year	Winner (Women)	Winner (Men)
1949	Andrea Mead	George Macomber
1950	Lois Woodworth	Jack Reddish
1951	Katy Rodolph	Jack Nagel
1952	Andrea M. Lawrence	Jack Reddish
1953	Katy Rodolph	Ralph Miller
1954	Nancy Banks	Chiharu Igaya
1955	Andrea M. Lawrence	Chiharu Igaya
1956	Katherine Cox	Bill Woods
1957	Madi S. Miller	Tom Corcoran
1958	Beverly Anderson	Gary Vaughn
1959	Linda Meyers	Wallace (Bud) Werner
1960	Elizabeth Greene	Oddvar Ronnestad
1961	Nancy Holland	Rod Hebron
1962	Linda Meyers	Dave Gorsuch
1963	Starr Walton	Wallace (Bud) Werner
1964	Jean Saubert	Gordon Eaton
1965	Nancy Greene	Peter Duncan
1966	Florence Steurer	Guy Périllat
1967	Karen Budge	Dumenc Giovanoli

Year	Winner (Women)	Winner (Men)
1968	Judy Nagel	Scott Henderson
1969	Not awarded	
1970	Rosi Fortna	William McKay
1971	Judy Crawford	Bob Cochran
1972	Stephanie Forrest	Steve Lathrop
1973	Susan Corrock	David Currier

Wallace "Bud" Werner Award

This award is given to the skier who has made an outstanding contribution to international good will plus ski ability.

Year	Winner
1966	William Kidd
1967	Jim Heuga
1968	John Bower
1969	Adrian Watt
1970	William Kidd
1971	Rosie Fortna
1972	Eric Poulsen
1973	Bob Cochran

Ski Writers Award

This award is given for the year's most effective ski writing.

Year	Winner
1963	Bill Berry, Sacramento *Bee*
1964	Tom Place, Cleveland *Plain Dealer*
1965	Mike Beatrice, Boston *Globe*
1966	Bill Kattermann, Newark *Star Ledger*
1967	Burt Simms, Los Angeles *Herald-Examiner*
1968	Luanne Pfeiffer, Santa Monica *Evening Outlook*
1969	Dave Knickerbocker, Long Island *Newsday*
1970	Burt Simms, Los Angeles *Herald-Examiner*
1971	L. Dana Gatlin, *Christian Science Monitor*
1972	Bill Hibbard, Milwaukee *Journal*
1973	Ralph Thornton, Minneapolis *Star*

PROFESSIONAL RACING

Many skiers after a successful amateur racing career turn professional. In Europe, there are several racing events open to the pros, and there has been an increasing interest in having more professional contests. With this interest, there is a definite chance that there will be "open" events—both amateurs and professionals may take part—similar to those in golf and tennis.

In 1970, The International Ski Racers Association was founded. Its purposes are to promote the status of the qualified racer to the rank of professional, to promote interest in the sport of skiing, to protect the mutual interests of its members, to hold meetings and competitions, to assist deserving members to obtain employment in skiing, to promote better understanding with the ski area operators, and to establish a code of ethics for the future well-being of the sport. In 1970, the organization conducted three dual-format (head-to-head) meets and the pros won some $85,000 (the $50,000 Lange Cup was the big prize). The following season, 1970–71, the tour generated $127,000 in winnings at nine meets, and now there are some twelve events, and purses are ever increasing. In 1972 the ISRA tour became known as the Benson & Hedges 100's Grand Prix.

The format of Grand Prix is that the qualifying rounds for both slalom and giant slalom are held on Friday. The 16 qualifiers in each event then race on Saturday and Sunday in head-to-head elimination contest. Since most of the pro courses contain from 24 to some 30 gates, a racer who reaches the finals could run as many as 300-plus gates in one day. According to the Grand Prix system of awarding points, 25 is given for first, 20 for second, 15 for third, 10 for fourth, 7 for a racer who does not advance beyond the quarter-final rounds, and 5 for a racer who does not advance beyond the opening round. The five point winners at the end of the season divide the Special Grand Prix purse. At each meet, the racers are awarded prize money in accordance with points obtained in each of the two events—slalom and giant slalom. The leading money winners, since the ISRA was organized, are as follows:

1971		Earnings
1.	Spider Sabich	$21,189
2.	Hugo Nindl	14,319
3.	Terje Overland	7,875
4.	Erich Sturm	5,572
5.	Mike Schwaiger	5,474

1972		Earnings	Total Points
1.	Spider Sabich	$50,650	331
2.	Hugo Nindl	28,825	192
3.	Harald Stuefer	18,662	168
4.	Terje Overland	19,306	166
5.	Lasse Hamre	17,700	125

1973		Earnings	Total Points
1.	Jean-Claude Killy	$68,625	318
2.	Harald Stuefer	45,575	287
3.	Spider Sabich	36,550	268
4.	Hugo Nindl	31,100	248
5.	Otto Tschudi	21,750	202

The Lange Cup

The Lange Cup is a big prize on the pro tour. It is usually the last event on the tour and often determines the Grand Prix winner. The Lange Cup was also the first big event on the ISRA circuit. Winners are as follows:

Year	Winner
1970	Adrien Duvillard
1971	Spider Sabich
1972	Lasse Hamre
1973	Harald Stuefer

Professional Skier of the Year Award

The *Ski Magazine* Cup is awarded to the professional skier who is the leading money winner in the professional racing circuit. Winners are:

Year	Winner
1965	Ernst Hinterseer
1966	Hias Leitner
1967	Ernst Hinterseer
1968	Hias Leitner
1969	Adrien Duvillard
1970	William Kidd
1971	Vladimir Sabich
1972	Vladimir Sabich
1973	Jean-Claude Killy

THE FUN OF RACING

Have you ever been at the top of a hill and suggested to a friend that you race to the bottom? You probably have. And when it was all over, there was a lot of good-natured joshing and debate about why you won or lost. It was a great deal of fun, and, surprisingly, the next time you skied, you found yourself skiing a little bit better.

If you enjoy competition, skiing is the sport that can provide it—no matter how seriously you want to take it or how old you are. For instance, there is the National Standard Ski Race, Nastar, a relatively open-gated giant slalom classification for skiers over fifty. If you entertain hopes for this competition, you should be good. Few old-timers who ski consistently lose their skill (though they may lack endurance). Most of them ski better than they did in their racing heydays. Of course, this class of competition may be the furthest thing from your mind. You may want to race just for the fun of it, because you enjoy tying a racing bib across your chest, or because you enjoy collecting pins and medals, or because the hill you have to ski on week after week lacks a certain variety. Whatever your motives, there is a type of racing for you.

Techniques for Racing

The recreational skier may not be aware of it, but his basic information was developed out of ski racing. Since the early 1950's, advances in the sport can be traced to the ranks of the racers and the studies of men like Kruckenhauser, Joubert, and Testa in Europe. Analysis of racing technique by means of the camera may be expected to bring even more changes in recreational technique in future years.

Memorizing the Course. One of the most common problems with competitors is an inability to remember courses, particularly in slalom. The result is that the racer often does not know where he is going and resorts to the practice of following the tracks of the racers before him. Such a racer obviously is not able to give the course his maximum attention. But worse than that, he must depend on the racers before him to have chosen the correct line. Sometimes it has happened that a forerunner in opening the course misses a gate. The early racers subsequently follow his tracks and also miss the gate. This points out the hazard of merely following tracks.

It is not particularly hard to memorize a slalom course, but it is something that has to be done systematically, and requires discipline. In slalom, the racer should climb every course from the bottom. When he reaches the first gate before the finish line, he should look at the gate, figuring what his line should be in relation to the gates above, then close his eyes and mentally run the course from the last gate to the finish. Then he should climb one gate higher, looking to see how he plans to run that gate. He should close his eyes and run the course from the second to last gate, through the last gate, to the finish. At each gate, he should run the course two or three times in his mind before he moves to the next higher gate. If he finds he has forgotten a section below him, he should slip down the course to refresh his memory. He then moves back up the course, making sure he can run the entire course in his mind before moving higher. Many racers, when they are running

the course in their mind, will stand with eyes shut and weave through the course with an extended hand. When he reaches the top of the course, a racer with a good memory will find that he can run a 50- or 60-gate course in his mind in a matter of 10 or 15 seconds.

A good racer is concerned only with the position of the inside pole on every gate. This is the pole he must remember, since he wants to be tight on the inside pole of every turn. In fact, during his actual run down the mountain, a competent racer is probably completely unaware of the relative positions of the outside poles. This means that all he is really concerned about is the relative position of the inside pole of one gate to the inside pole of the next—the most direct line.

In studying the course, a racer should be continually looking for places where he might have to check. These are speed traps that the course setter lays out for unwary racers. The trap often consists of a sidehill hairpin. Here the racer has to go down into the gate and turn up against or out of the fall line, with gravity working against him, in order to make the second gate of the hairpin. Another speed trap is a tight hairpin after a long series of high-speed, open gates. The experienced racer, as he climbs the course, will be able to identify these portions of the course. From the condition of the snow, the steepness of the hill, and the relative position of the gates, he can judge approximately how fast he is likely to be entering any one gate from above. If a strong check is indicated, the racer should memorize the point where he must make it.

Course setters who are skilled in setting courses will often give the racer a choice of ways to run a particular combination. This means that when a racer approaches the combination, it is conceivable he will see tracks going straight into the combination or over the top. When the racer reaches this point, there can be no hesitation on his part as to which way he plans to run it.

After the racer reaches the top of the course and awaits the start, he should periodically, perhaps every four or five minutes, run the course several times in his mind to make sure he has not forgotten. Occasionally there is a gate in sight of the start concerning which there is a question in the racer's mind as to what is the best way to run it. He can learn by watching earlier racers run that section.

Above all, the decision of how to run any given section should be firmly made before the racer leaves the starting gate. We have seen many cases in which a racer has said before leaving, "I'll decide how to run it when I get there." But this almost invariably leads to hesitation and a lack of confidence on the part of the racer. On leaving the starting gate, a racer should stick to his race strategy and not deviate from it except in the most extreme circumstances.

In general, the same rules apply to giant slalom as to slalom, with the exception that usually a racer will learn a giant slalom course from the top down rather than from the bottom up. Giant slalom, because of the fact that the gates are fewer and farther apart with longer time intervals between, is generally easier to learn. Yet many racers make the mistake of thinking it is not particularly necessary to learn a giant slalom course. The fact is that the speeds are substantially higher than in slalom. A small mistake in line or a small mistake remembering where the racer actually *is,* and what is ahead of him, can cost the race. In downhill, the racer should descend the course very slowly, stopping and looking every 15 or 20 feet both up and down the hill, figuring out what his line will be and running the course in his mind down to that point from the top. He should try to remember particular landmarks or points of reference so that he. can stay on line. At the bottom of the downhill, the racer should be able to point out all of the difficult portions and what he plans to do about them. Later in downhill practice, he may decide to change his original thinking in regard to a section of the course. The important thing, however, is that he had a plan to begin with and merely was modifying it. In any Alpine event, a thorough knowledge of the course goes a long way toward building confidence.

Start Position. A proper start is one of the most critical—and least practical—parts of racing. The usual start is 5-4-3-2-1-go. Your feet cannot move until the word "go," but you are usually allowed to move your upper body during the countdown. If you are in doubt about what you can or cannot do, ask the starter; do not risk senseless disqualification, particularly since some regions have their own rules regarding starts. Watch earlier racers to get an idea of the exact starting method used, and to become accustomed to the rhythm of the starter's countdown. In general, you should be completely ready

Killy's Start. Step by step: (1) Just before countdown "5 . . . 4 . . . 3" starts, Killy gets set with feet 2 or 3 feet away from the starting bar, body slung back, poles raised, ready to plunge into the snow. (2) As count approaches zero or "go," Killy springs up, driving his poles into the snow with a catapulting effect, his body building speed before the clock has started to run. (3) Killy's pole push is so powerful that it has launched him into the air. In a split second his feet will strike the bar, starting the clock.

when the starter says "10 seconds," with both poles planted over the starting line and both feet just in back of it. Be careful that the poles are not planted in a spot that will give way when you push on them. At "two" you should drop down slightly, rising and reaching forward momentarily after the starter says "one." Hold the push-off until you actually hear the starter say "go."

Since in most races the first 20 or 30 feet after the starting gate are rather flat and slow, it is most important to reach high speed right from the starting gate. This can be done by taking the right body position. Both poles are planted in front of the starting gate. One ski boot tip is up to start line, the other not more than one foot behind, and feet are approximately one foot apart. Skis point exactly in the direction you have to go. Ankles, knees, and hips are bent in low, flexed position. Weight is on balls of feet, ready to spring forward using merely the power of the legs. The push with the poles is blended in with the legwork. One or two more powerful pole pushes will help to accelerate faster and bring you quickly to your racing speed.

Slalom Technique

The difference between a good and a great racer lies in very small actions, scattered down the length of a slalom course. The great racer moves precisely, while the good racer makes what are, by comparison, minute mistakes.

A racer has to make his skis go between the two poles of each gate; even if he knocks a pole down, he is still in the race as long as his skis go between the poles. If he misses a gate, the skier is marked DNF (did not finish).

Generally speaking a racer tries to ski the shortest distance between two gates—that is, the straight line from the inside pole of one gate to the inside pole of the next. The racer does not literally go straight for the inside pole of the next gate, but he goes as directly as he dares.

This brings up the concept of high line and low line. A high line puts a racer farther uphill of the coming gate than the low line. It is a longer but safer path; it gives him more time to start his turn, so he is less likely to miss the gate.

A low line is straighter and riskier. It slants more steeply toward the next gate and so gives the racer more speed. But he risks missing the gate because his turn has to be made more precisely, and he risks a skid because he is turning more sharply at a higher speed in the gate.

Always turn closest to the inside pole without skidding. The closer a racer turns to the inside pole, the shorter his path down the hill. If he skids, he may still be able to turn pretty close, but he will lose speed. He should carve his turn, make the edges bite.

Acceleration. Doing well in a race also depends—perhaps most important of all—on an almost indefinable sense by the racer of the fastest path down the hill; this is not necessarily being nearest to the inside pole of each gate, but rather sensing how to take advantage of the terrain to gain speed, how to know when the skis are sliding optimally and to know through a kind of mental clock how much extra risk and energy to expend to go faster.

To accelerate, you also can shoot your skis forward. To do this you must have strong stomach muscles and boots with good support in the back. As you come out of a turn, bend your knees and allow your feet and skis to advance until you are in a sitting-back position (avalement). Your upper body must be fairly erect; the relaxed shooting forward of the feet releases the edges and allows the skis to accelerate. You should feel your weight on the back of your skis.

Acceleration by skating or stepping varies according to the size of the turn and your speed. You need to have strong thigh muscles to skate. In slalom, the skate becomes a quick step. It is a motion to gain height (sometimes needed to enter a gate properly) as well as speed between gates. At the end of a turn you shift your weight from the outside ski to the inside or uphill ski and step it uphill slightly. (To get a shorter line, experienced racers often shift to this uphill ski before the turn is actually completed.)

Step Turn. Theoretically, the best way to take a gate and go across the hill to the next gate is to lose the least possible distance downhill at the open gate; stay high. This enables you to make your next turn well above the second gate so you can go through

Hard way

Fall line arrow

Easy way

If the placement of the gates above or below dictates the way you have to run the hairpin (i.e., on which side you will have to enter the hairpin), then you have to consider only the key turn in the middle of the hairpin by the two inside poles.

it at the most advantageous angle; also so you have time to make a smooth round turn rather than a hurried sharp one before the next gate. Skating through the first gate is the best answer. As you come into the gate you lunge forward off your downhill ski, picking up the inside ski and stepping uphill with it, in a skating step. Your weight goes fully on the uphill ski as soon as you can get the weight there. Then you straighten up, skiing on the one uphill ski for an instant as you pull the downhill ski up to it. Simultaneously start your turn to the next gate—a turn in which the uphill ski is the outside ski of the turn. Not only does the skating step keep you

from losing distance downhill, but it is an automatic way of shifting the weight to the outside ski of the coming turn as early and forcefully as possible. Also, if your timing is right, your skating motion imparts some speed to your run, especially on flat terrain.

Actually, in making comparative tests, it has been found that skating steps are used by almost 80 per cent of all racers of all calibers, but that very few get any advantage out of their skating attempt. The main reason is that they are not executing the skating step as it should be done. It should be applied just as it is by the speed skater, to throw and shift the weight of the body in a general forward direction, from one leg to the other, by using the inside edge for control and as a base for starting a powerful forward move. The poles play a very important part, too.

The skating step must be a completely coordinated movement of precision timing of body shift and leg action. Balance and timing will accelerate the racer very definitely, especially at lower speeds. The skating step can be used in flat starts and finishes and in slower sections of a slalom or giant slalom course.

In capsule form, here is an outline of the skated or step turn:

As you approach the inside pole of a gate with all your weight on the lower ski, pick up the tip of your unweighted upper ski and place it on a higher traverse, thus splitting the tips. Weight the uphill ski fully with a sharp up motion, usually with both hands swinging up in front at the same time. Continue to swing your weight up onto the uphill ski until it becomes momentarily unweighted. As the uphill ski is unweighted turn it into the fall line. Simultaneously place the unweighted lower ski beside it and drop into a moderate reverse as you pass the inside pole. Come to a square position on your skis as you come out of the fall line. Go straight toward the inside pole of the next gate and step up 5 to 25 feet before you reach the pole in the same way described above. The distance required is a judgment factor and varies with your speed and the sharpness of the turn.

Straddling. Straddling of slalom poles, which can lead to disqualification, may be avoided very simply by adopting a basic rule: finish a turn before entering the gate line and keep a distance from the pole of approximately 1 to 1½ feet. If a racer is any closer to the pole than this, he must dodge it, which can cause all kinds of trouble. This method of avoiding slalom poles puts the racer into a good starting position for his next maneuver and allows him to make steadier, surer, and safer slalom runs.

Braking. Braking is used by all racers who know it is no use being "fastest between falls." Of the several ways of braking or slowing down on skis—stemming, wind checking, sideslipping, and edging—stemming is hardly ever used by racers, because it is difficult to control at high speeds. In wind checking, which is used in downhill, a racer rises from

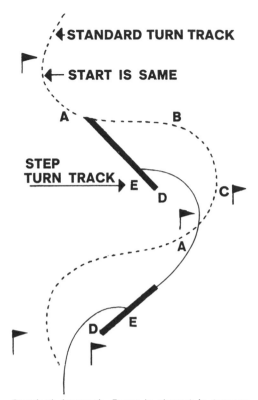

Standard Approach. Racer is slowest in traverse phase of turns (A to B) because he is on a high traverse, far out of fall line. From points B to C, racer turns well above inside pole of gate. From point C to inside pole, racer accelerates. This creates a problem. If acceleration is too great, racer will have to turn again at point A to remain in high line to next gate. In effect, this requires two turns, with two skids in one gate, a time-consuming maneuver. Racer is lowest during traverse, which is the easiest part and should be utilized fully. Racer is fastest as he approaches inside pole, where greatest control and least speed is needed.

his crouched position to create resistance to the wind.

The most common ways of slowing down in a race are sideslipping and edging. Good control depends a great deal on speed, strength, the type of turn, and the snow conditions. Only practice can teach you this, but generally speaking, the faster the speed and the harder the snow, the more edge pressure that must be applied by weighting the skis and increasing angulation. On soft snow and at slow speeds a more subtle pressure is best, so you will not lose too much speed.

Most racers practice slalom on fairly

smooth slopes and usually move the course as soon as foot-deep ruts appear. This is easy to understand, for ski area owners do not want a lot of ruts in their slopes. But unfortunately most racers actually race on deeply rutted courses which call for a technique quite different from that which they have practiced. Ideally, a racer wants to come as close as possible to the pole and to lean his upper body forward out over the hill. In ruts, however, he must aim not for the pole, but for the bank of the rut, and he should lean like a bobsled crew, against the bank of the rut—that is, up the hill. So that resistance of the bank will not throw him back, the racer should thrust his hands forward as he rounds the pole. Using this rut technique in a race will help you keep your balance and, in the long run, help you turn faster than the normal "flat slope" technique.

To summarize, here are several improvements to keep in mind when running a slalom course:

1. Strive for precision, not speed, at first.
2. Study the course. Climb it, memorize it, and plan your line of descent.
3. Make your turn before entering a gate, not while you are in it.
4. Enter a gate slowly, come out fast. Come into a gate high, even if you must use a skating step to gain height.
5. Keep your skis together and do not sit back. Do not overrotate. Use reverse shoulder to get past flags.

Recreational Racing

There is no truer test of a skier's ability and technique than a well-set slalom course, one that requires him to use all his resources, physical and mental, as he makes his way down through a maze of gates with rhythm and grace under perfect control. Slalom is a challenge for the advanced skier and competitor that can seldom be resisted. But slalom is not just for the experts. Many recreational skiers can find fun in it and an opportunity to improve their skiing.

Slalom requires timing, rhythm, edge control, and a firm grounding in the fundamental elements of technique. There is no better way for a recreational skier to develop these points than by practicing simple slaloms. A properly

set course can offer him a real challenge and can add the spice of competition to skiing with his friends.

Most intermediate skiers seem to believe that there is something very difficult about running a slalom course. This is true if one attempts to negotiate a slalom set for those of racing ability. Any expert course is set tightly, even closer on a practice course than on an actual competition run, so that reflexes and timing must be sharpened to the utmost. For a recreational skier to maneuver through such a course would be almost impossible, since he would not be able to move his skis rapidly enough or to check his speed sufficiently to follow the gates. As a result, he will lose control, slide past gates, straddle poles, break rhythm, and, usually, end up with a jarring spill. But a course need not be set so tightly. It does not even have to be difficult. It is possible, for example, to set an easy course of eight or ten gates, spaced sufficiently so that beginners who are mastering snowplow turns can negotiate it without fear or discouragement. They will have fun trying it and they will find that concentration on the course will relax them and relieve the tension that most beginners experience.

The same thing holds true for intermediate skiers learning stem Christies or parallel turns. Gates should be tighter, of course, and more interesting figures can be set. With intermediates, there is more opportunity to place gates so that the skier is required to use his fundamentals properly in order to pass from one gate to the next. The secret of slalom racing is to hold the shortest line from gate to gate without sacrificing rhythm or control. That means that weight distribution must be perfect and that edge control must be precise. It is often necessary to check speed from time to time so that the next gate can be entered from the proper direction and at the proper speed, but this must be done without losing the rhythm or fluidity of the skier's motion. This must also be kept in mind when setting a slalom. The whole point of slalom racing is to foster the use of skiing knowledge and technique in a continuous flowing succession of turns.

A course that requires this is a good one; a course that is overly difficult or that forces the skier to break rhythm defeats this purpose. An experienced course setter will deliberately set traps which will tempt the skier to enter a gate or combination from a direction or at a speed which will break his rhythm; the experienced racer is wary of these traps and chooses the correct alternatives in such situations.

A great many skiers would undoubtedly enjoy slalom practice and benefit from it, regardless of ability, but are prevented from doing so by the mistaken idea that a course that would be fun and within their ability is too difficult to set. Actually, keeping the philosophy of slalom racing in mind, all that is necessary to set up a course that would provide both fun and interest is a knowledge of three basic gate figures: the open gate, the closed gate, and the hairpin, which is actually two successive closed gates. These can be set in various combinations and sequences and at varying angles and pitches to yield the desired degree of difficulty and to keep speed within the ability of the skier. From these basic figures, it is easy to set combinations to form more advanced figures such as a flush, an elbow, or an H or Seelos flush.

When setting a course, a few simple considerations, aside from the gate combinations, should be kept in mind. The most important of these is the terrain. The relatively flat, even beginner's, slope presents no problem. Gates should be set in such a way that speed can be checked by traversing as well as by turning. After two or three gates more or less in the fall line, set the next gate some distance across it, making sure that the turns can be made smoothly. On more difficult terrain, when setting for intermediates, place the gates in such a way that the skiers are skiing across the fall line on the difficult pitches. Nothing is gained by scaring them to death. On the other hand, for advanced skiers an open gate on the fall line, particularly if the preceding gate is not too far offset, is a proper temptation to pick up speed, which, if not properly checked, will cause him to miss the next gate.

If the snow is not already packed, this should be done. A slalom course ruts easily and ceases to be fun when it does. Occasional repacking in the gates may also be necessary. And finally, set the course where it is out of the way of the other skiers.

According to international rules of competition, set by the Fédération Internationale de Ski (FIS), the minimum distance between flags in any gate is 10 feet 6 inches. For recreational skiers, however, we would recommend that you allow between 12 to 16 feet for open gates and between 15 to 16 feet for closed gates; the steeper the hill, the wider the gates. If you are not sure of distance when you are setting up a course, you can measure quite accurately with your ski.

With these basic combinations, you can gradually cut down the distance between gates and the width of gates until, using proper terrain, you can eventually set a slalom of racing caliber. Of course, it takes expert knowledge and experience to set a championship slalom, but you should have no difficulty in laying out a course that will hold the interest of your friends and yourself and will yield benefits in improved ability and sharper technique.

To summarize, here are some tips for setting a slalom course for recreational use that you should keep in mind:

1. Do not set gates too tight; 12 to 15 feet for open gates, 10 to 15 feet for closed gates, is sufficient.
2. Set gates to maintain smooth, flowing run. Do not set sharp corners that will break rhythm.
3. Allow natural check points or gate combinations to hold down speed.
4. Utilize terrain to require variation in technique and permit alternate lines of approach to gates.
5. Set gates to test total technique, keeping in mind the skier's ability. Slalom is a test of ability, not endurance.

Sneak Gate. When experienced racers are climbing up and looking at slalom courses, one of the things they are looking for is a "sneak gate." A sneak gate is found in a combination where the gates are set close together and can be run several different ways. Characteristically, the sneak gate has one route that is slightly longer and requires a greater turn, but is relatively "safe." There is often, however, a way in which the gates can be run in a straight line. This way can be substantially faster, but because of the tightness of the gates, the risk is proportionately higher. Some course setters relish setting courses that require the racer to choose several times between the slow, safe line and the faster, more risky line, thus putting a premium on a racer's judgment.

Hairpins on a flat provide typical examples of a sneak. When looking at gate combinations that offer the possibility of a sneak, the racer should weigh the relative advantages and disadvantages of taking the sneak. He should try to calculate roughly how much faster the sneak would be, figuring out by sighting down the sneak how much room he would have between the inside poles for both his skis and his shoulders and whether the snow preceding the sneak is smooth enough so that his skis will track into the sneak without difficulty. Ordinarily, he should have at least 12 inches between the sneak gates in order to get by, but sometimes better racers can make it with less space. He should figure out whether he will have time and space to get lined up for the sneak and whether he will have to use a check before he hits the sneak. He should also try to determine whether his competition in the race is going to attempt the sneak, which might affect his decision. Regardless of what others do, however, never attempt a sneak that you are not confident of making. Nine times out of ten you will not.

One last piece of advice: as you hit the sneak, be sure your skis are close together so that you do not hook a tip, and make sure your arms are close to your body so that you do not hook an arm around a pole as you go by.

Giant Slalom Technique

As was stated previously, the difference between giant slalom and slalom is that the giant slalom gates are farther apart, making a much faster course, and usually only closed and open gates are used. It is also longer and covers more difficult terrain. A giant slalom is similar to a tightly controlled downhill course.

The important thing to remember when skiing a giant slalom is to regulate your speed so that you are high in all the gates and not caught low in some of the more difficult combinations. We wince, however, every time we hear a racer explain a slow run in giant slalom by saying, "I didn't have a flat enough ski," or, "I edged too much." These quota-

tions reveal either that the speaker has forgotten some basic skiing tenets (or never knew them) or that he does not have much of an idea about giant slalom (GS)—or both.

Let us look at some fundamentals. The beginning skier learns that an edged ski enables him to traverse a slope. He also learns that when the edge is released and the ski is flattened, the ski slides sideways down the hill. He next learns that when the ski is sliding sideways it goes slower than when it is sliding forward. He then finds out that the more the skis slide sideways or skid in a turn, the slower the turn is.

The racing applications are obvious. If you want to go fast, you have to go straight. If you want to go straight across a traverse, you have to edge. As a practical matter, you cannot vary the amount of edging too much; you can only roll the knee and ankle of the lower ski in so far. The degree of edging, generally, is not critical. Then, why talk about overedging in turns? A more common—and more valid—complaint would be over-turning. Over-turning means that a turn is longer in circumference than it needs to be due to overskidding of the tails. Why did the tails skid? Probably because the skis were not edged enough. This is a far cry from over-edging.

Giant slalom is actually a series of connected traverses, with the accent on the traverse. The turns are important only in that they connect your traverses efficiently or inefficiently.

Is this a question of semantics? No, it is not. It is a question of approach, and how you answer this question will dictate how you run GS. We maintain that you cannot win consistently unless you emphasize the traverse phase. You cannot win in the turns; you *can* win in the traverses.

The racer who goes straightest between gates is going the fastest. If he can hold the corners, he is bound to win. How do you "go straight"? You pick a traverse line *below* the tracks of your competitor and you edge; you do not sideslip. This guarantees that you reach the next gate before he does. When you reach the gate you step uphill for space, turn strongly, edge hard, scramble, and start to head straight for the next gate as soon as possible. If it sounds rough, that is the way it is. Long, smooth turns may look pretty, but they do not necessarily win races.

The most efficient turn for GS is a "square turn," a change of direction with no slide at all and without a loss of momentum and speed. The only way this is possible is by a step, which is limited to the degree of arc in which you can swing your tips. Beyond that point your skis have to skid somewhat; a carved turn with plenty of edging will minimize the skid. It helps if your inside edges are razor sharp. As you come out of the fall line,

a sharp up motion momentarily increases the weight and pressure on the lower ski's inside edge, checking chattering. As the up motion continues, the skis become unweighted, allowing you to step onto the uphill ski which is on a higher traverse and tangent. Hopefully you are then heading for the next gate. At least part of the turn has been made without a skid; the rest of the turn has been made with minimum skid.

The step described above can be at the be-

Giant slalom, serpentine turn.

ginning of the turn (uphill to gain some altitude) or at the end or both. In between, a carved, jammed turn is the best you can hope for. In execution, the whole thing is often sloppy and requires strength.

The Strategy of the Second Run

The second run is involved in two out of three of the Alpine events—slalom and giant slalom—in skiing. There are a great many Alpine competitors who have a terrible time putting two standing runs together for a respectable total elapsed time, and more often than not, it is on the second run that they make the serious mistake.

What is the key to a successful competitive strategy in the second run? The answer is to understand and never lose sight of the fact that skiing is a sport in which you do not compete against the course but you compete against other ski racers. An experienced ski racer, above all, has the ability to evaluate a course in terms of his own skiing ability. Before he races he should have a clear idea of how fast he can run the course and stand up. It is a very rare course, particularly in slalom, where a racer can proceed with full speed all the way down the course and expect to make it. This does not mean that experienced racers always throw in obvious checks. Occasionally they will, depending on the conditions. But if a check is needed, more often than not it is incorporated in the previous turn, where the edges are hit a little harder than necessary, or the turn is lengthened slightly, or the racer allows his skis to skid a little more than necessary, or he turns farther away from the inside pole.

The point is that the experienced racer recognizes there is a maximum speed at which he can run any given course. Coupled with this is his knowledge that if he cannot put two standing runs together, he will not even show up in the results sheets. In short, the experienced racer recognizes his own limitations.

How does all this relate to the second run? Purely and simply, it establishes an upper limit on what a racer can do. And that may be something less than his maximum. On the first run, most racers will, for instance, try to finish in a competitive position. Ideally, they

hope to be in the lead or at least close enough to the leader to have a chance to catch him on the second run. In most cases, the racer does not take his first run at his absolute maximum, but races at something like 90 to 95 per cent of maximum. In the easy parts, where there is little likelihood of catching a tip or making a mistake, he will run at 100 per cent. In the hard parts, he will aim to stand up.

Occasionally a racer will increase the tempo by running at 100 per cent maximum on the first run, and stand up. If this fact is known by the other racers, it forces them to try to run the course at 100 per cent too, so that no one has an insuperable advantage at the end of the first run. Generally, however, most racers take their first run at something less than 100 per cent, relying on the second run to make their move if necessary.

If the strategy of the first run is rather clearly defined, the strategy of the second run can vary enormously. On the first run, everyone starts equally. At the start of the second run, the standings of the racers, the time gaps between them, and the starting order are all significant in determining strategy. Take the starting order, for instance. The early racers in the second run have an advantage of running on a better course. But the later racers have the advantage of knowing what has happened to the earlier ones. Did they fall? What was their time? And so on.

The performances of the principal competitors running before you on the second run, combined with your standing at the end of the first run, dictate strategy. Sometimes it will be necessary to make a 100 per cent effort in order to do well in the overall time. On other occasions, if you had a slight lead after the first run, and your nearest competitors have had only mediocre times on their second runs, you will know it is unnecessary to run at 100 per cent of your maximum. You will be able to afford to ski safely and still win.

If you have to run before your principal competitors in the second run, and they have the advantage of watching you, then your strategy will be different. If you are in the lead, and depending on the size of your lead, you may decide that your closest competitors cannot catch you and that a run at 90 per cent of your maximum will be good enough to win. On the other hand, if your lead is small, you may feel obliged to run the course at 100 per cent. If you are behind, you will have no choice but to run it 100 per cent. Again, if you are running ahead of your nearest competitors in the second run, it is usually advisable to try for a fast start, running the gates near the top at 100 per cent maximum. This is a sound strategy no matter what your first-run placing was, because it creates psychological pressure on the other competitors who are watching you from the starting gate. Often it will force them into assuming that your run is better than what it may actually be. Thus it can force them to take unnecessary chances by trying to ski over their heads—a tactic that usually leads to mistakes.

The most important thing to keep in mind on the second run is that you are racing against other racers, not against the course. The three things that determine your strategy are: your standing at the end of your first run; the time interval between you and your nearest competitors; your starting position in the second run.

These are the factors which determine how fast or slow you have to go on your second run. Finally, you may further modify your second-run strategy on the basis of what happens to the racers who run before you.

Make up your mind before you start how fast you have to go. If you have a chance to win, you should go fast enough for that. If, however, you can win by having a second run that is 90 per cent of your maximum, then it is foolish to have a second run that attempts to be 100 per cent.

Between two racers of equal technical ability, the one with a strategic sense will consistently do better than the one who always simply goes as fast as he can. The racing record of the former will be a mounting success, while the second will often find himself listed under DNF (did not finish) and DQ (disqualified).

Downhill Technique

Of the three Alpine events, downhill is by far the most exciting and the least understood, despite its seeming simplicity. It is unquestionably the hardest event to excel in. It has been called by many "the premier event of skiing." Few American racers have ever mastered downhill, and in the long run, United States results in international downhill have been significantly poorer than American results in slalom and giant slalom.

The public conception of downhill is that it takes little skill, strong legs, and no brains. In reality, it requires skills which are harder to acquire than those of either slalom or giant slalom, more experience than either of the other two events, and, undoubtedly, more judgment than either of the others. There is no question that it requires a high level of conditioning and the strongest possible legs. The importance of courage or sheer guts has

Recreational skiers find the downhill racing position useful to gain speed through a long runout.

Three ways to check your speed while racing: (A) the sharp, hard edge set; (B) a lengthening of the previous turn; (C) the snowplow check.

been somewhat overemphasized. It is axiomatic that personal courage is required. But there have been times in the past when American racers have tried, with some success, to make up in courage what they lacked in technical skill.

Downhill technique in itself is a rather ephemeral thing to come to grips with. In the parlance of the trade, it requires the ability to ride a fast ski. This in turn, requires total body relaxation at high speeds; excellent body control and balance either on the snow or in the air; intuitive and continual weight shift to keep the skis planing as much as possible; and a combination of judgment and experience to determine the fastest line to follow at any given time. Downhill also involves the ability to hold an aerodynamically correct tuck position as much of the time as possible, the knowledge of what makes one pair of skis intrinsically faster than another pair of skis, a knowledge of waxing, great confidence, and a genuine liking for the event.

There are two basic crouches used in downhill. One is a very low crouch—often called the "egg position"—for the greatest speed. The other is similar except that the body is a little higher to allow more knee action and better balance over rough terrain. It might also be used in a long race to rest the skier's legs for a second or two.

The most important aspect of a good downhill egg position is to have your back level at all times. In this position, it is difficult to see ahead; therefore, some neck exercises are important, or you will find your shoulders raising, thereby catching some wind.

Of nearly equal importance is that your knees remain as far apart as your feet. If knees are too far apart or too close together, your skis will edge. Your feet should be from 6 to 12 inches apart, and you should try to keep skis on the flat at all times. Above all, relax.

The wrong idea of training for a downhill is to go to the top and run it immediately as fast as you can, which is bound to lead to a lot of high-speed falls. This, in turn, leads to lack of confidence, resulting in a tightening up on the part of the racer, worse falls, and inevitably more injuries.

In fact, the aim is to maintain and increase the racer's confidence in himself at all costs. This means starting to train for downhill at relatively low speeds, with a gradual build-up under conditions carefully controlled to avoid the risk of confidence-shattering falls. The big downhills are examined minutely before any training runs are taken. The individual racer determines what speeds he is likely to attain and what speeds he feels he can hold. Training begins by running individual sections of the trail. As a section of the trail is mastered, speed on it is increased, and the section is overlapped.

In downhill, it is an unfortunate fact that the course is rarely in good condition for training in the early part of the week. As race day comes closer, the organizers put more effort into course preparation so that by race day it is in excellent condition. Training at high speed during the early part of the week on poorly prepared courses is often an invitation to injury. It is usually better to build up speed as the course is put in better condition. Once the course is in good shape and the racer has put his sections together and made his nonstop run, he should go into the starting gate confident of his own capabilities, knowing he has run all parts of the course at speeds which he will attain during the race. After the actual race, he should feel he has made a run better than any he made in practice.

NORDIC COMPETITION

As previously stated, competition in the Nordic phase of the sport—cross-country and jumping—is a great deal older than the Alpine events. It has often been said that of the four different events characterizing the competitive side of skiing you might say that jumping is the most spectacular, downhill the fastest and most dangerous, slalom the most graceful, and cross-country the most demanding.

Cross-country Racing

This is really a demanding sport, since the body and mind of the skier must be trained for the rigors of the event.

The techniques employed in cross-country racing are essentially the same as those described in Section III for ski touring. There are, of course, some special techniques for various uphill and downhill situations. However, most of these are learned by the racer by experience and are performed in his own style. Thus, a would-be cross-country racer should first learn the basic principles of cross-country touring, and then increase his stamina and speed. The rest will all fall into place as one practices.

Jumping

Ski jumping is perhaps the most brief and intense of sporting events. Fifteen seconds pass between leaving the top of the inrun and the swing at the bottom; actual flight may last two or three seconds. Jumping is a spectacular sport. It looks dangerous. Actually, however, jumping is quite safe, provided the hill is ready for jumping and the skier ready for a hill of that size.

Jumping can be learned only on small hills where the speed, height, and shock of landing can be reduced to a minimum. You would not expect a young diver to begin on a 10-foot board; neither should young jumpers start on anything larger than a 20-meter hill. Moreover, the hills should be of proper trajectory design, for a hill which is too high and too flat, or a hill that pitches the skier out into space, will establish a train of bad jumping habits and may permanently and needlessly scare a young jumper. Two hills, side by side, one 15 to 20 meters, the other 30 to 40 meters, each with its proper speed, height, and trajectory curve, make an ideal setup for learning to jump, and a place where youngsters from age six to sixty can "train."

Jumpers must keep to their own hills. It is necessary during practice and all too often during tournaments. But small hills are easy to maintain, and by working on the hill the young jumper learns to connect the "look" of the hill with the "feel" of it, so that in time he will be able to estimate just what a hill will do to him and how to make his jump accordingly.

1. Tramp out the landing whenever it needs it. Boot-tramp it first if it is soft, for a fall in soft snow is the quickest way to twist an ankle.

2. Always leave the hill well tramped out.

3. Do not jump in rain or hard thaw. Actually, ice, deep new snow, and wet new snow also present special problems. In any case, pay particular attention to the condition of the takeoff and the dip. These are the danger areas.

Blue soap powder or spruce boughs alongside the takeoff and dip are valuable guides to the jumper, especially in flat light or falling snow. A strip of bluing across the "break of the hill" is also a great help in showing jumpers the limits to which they can stretch.

Takeoff. The takeoff extends from the time the jumper rises from his inrun position (chest still pressed against his knees), through the arm swing and jump, into the air, and continues until he has attained his flight position. It is not a matter of just jumping hard on the lip. The purpose of the takeoff is to launch the jumper out over his skis where he can "get on the air" as quickly as possible. It is a forward rolling motion, ending in a snap timed to hit the lip of the jump. The proper takeoff is the same whatever the size of the hill. There is a fundamental physical problem here, however.

1. On a small hill: distance is largely the result of a sharp, strong jump.
2. On a big hill: distance is a matter of getting into an aerodynamic flight position as quickly as possible and riding the air as long as possible.

The dilemma here is due to the difference in wind pressure, which is not a significant force at slow speeds, but which, on a big hill, is the controlling factor. The young jumper is likely to learn to jump straight up, and then jack over, rather than to roll out of his inrun position into a snap. Such a takeoff will give him good distance now, but will be wrong when he gets on a hill 40 meters or larger.

Concentrate on the lip of the jump; get your timing right. Jump so that your weight goes out over your tips, and, at the same time, flip your tips up so they will catch the wind pressure. Jump steady and straight ahead; if you twist in the air, you are probably trying too hard.

At this stage, poise, timing, and a good lean from the ankles are more valuable to you than distance. And most important: Do not fight your jump in an effort to place your hands on your hips. Let your arms move as your body calls on them to maintain balance. When your weight is out over your tips, your arms will come to rest easily and naturally in the air.

Flight. A good jump is one beautiful motion from top to bottom; the flight is only the most apparent part. On big hills the jumper actually rides a curve of wind—much as a surfboarder rides down the crest of a Pacific roller. Men begin to get the feeling of catching the air on a 40-meter hill; from 60 meters up they ride it. Youngsters, being light, begin to catch the air on a 20-meter hill.

The judges, whose job it is to compare the jumper against an ideal standard, mark the whole jump from top to bottom but place more weight on the flight than on any other

part. They watch for the four signs of a good jumper in the air: courage and quickness in leaving the takeoff; a sense of drive out over the tips; poise and control in the air; quick adjustments to minor imperfections. A good judge can determine not only a skier's skill and timing but also his state of mind by watching what he does in the air. If the jumper is inexperienced or frightened, there is no way he can hide it: his takeoff shows no zip; he hangs back in the air either standing straight up or doubling over in a horrendous jackknife; he lands any old way, feet apart, cowboy style.

Inevitably a jumper's landing shows in everything he does from the inrun down. If he has no confidence in what will happen to him when he hits, how can he lean out on his skis and pull for distance? How can he make a strong takeoff that will put him out there over the bottom of the hill?

The takeoff controls the jump, but timing controls the takeoff. Timing, an instinct essential to all sports, can be developed only through much practice. In jumping you should work for timing first, strength of takeoff later; for nothing is more apt to make you jump too early or too late than trying to jump too hard. Body positions in the air always reveal what happened on the takeoff:

1. *Jumping too early.* Your tips tend to suck the takeoff, throwing your skis down in the air and your body forward.

2. *Jumping too late.* (a) *On a small hill* you may jump with the heels of your skis still on the lip. This throws the tips way down, in danger of sticking in the knoll. (b) *On a big hill,* the heels of your skis go down and you get the tips in your face.

Landing. The landing extends from the latter part of the flight, down through the transition of hill to the outrun. It is often called the "telemark position," but it is not a telemark and even less a "position." It is a complete rhythmic action designed to cushion the shock, catch the weight, and take the pressure of the dip.

A landing, of course, must begin in the air—at that point when you decide where you want to "put them down." You stop pulling for distance and straighten up your body. (Your arms come forward, your head and chest are raised in order to increase the drag of the wind so that you can straighten up.) Straightening up like this is very important. Without it you will lose the spring action at the hips and leave your knees to absorb the whole shock. Your tips are held a little up so that the limberness of the skis will absorb the first part of the shock of landing. Then, as you take the snow, you shoot one leg ahead to catch your weight. At the same instant you let your hips roll down, and under, and forward. The action of the hips is like the turning of a cam on a camshaft, deflecting a straight shock into a smooth, easy motion. And as part of the same motion you come back up partway, to the recovery position, to take the pressure of the dip.

Every jumper falls many, many times. Through hard experience, he learns to fall without getting hurt. The main thing is to avoid a twist, a roll, or a somersault. Here are a few suggestions to prevent injury:

1. You get both skis on the same side and hold them together, flat on their sides, or they will not dig in and catch.
2. You get down flat on the snow and skid.
3. You relax "just like dead" with your arms out, holding your body in a skid.

Landings are the great watershed in learning to jump. It is the takeoff which controls your entire jump: grace in the air, courage, distance, are all determined by what you do on the takeoff. But during the learning process it is largely the success in mastering a landing which decides whether you will ever be anything more than a mediocre performer. It is fair to say that 75 per cent of the jumpers in this country never get beyond the beginning stages. Fewer than 10 per cent know what a good landing is. No more than 30 or 40 jumpers can make one. The trouble is that most jumpers, seeking the thrill of long jumps on big hills, never stop to learn a first-rate landing. They learn, instead, some makeshift method for getting down out of the air, and standing. It works. It becomes habit. Such a landing will cost the skier points (see pages 248–250 for full information on how judges rate a jump), but he still feels that to return to a small jump for practice is not necessary. Things you should remember when landing are:

1. *Keep forward* "on them," as the Nor-wegians say. Do not sit back or pull back or back-paddle. You cannot make any landing with your weight back. If you are overjumping the hill, you still need your weight forward, for if you pull back then, the dip will take your skis right out from under you.

2. *Straighten up in the air.* If you land head down in a jackknife position, you have lost the spring action at the hips. You may pitch forward for a hard fall in the dip, or, overcompensating, you may flip back and fall.

3. *Skis together under you.* Even if you are not quite in balance over your skis, keep them together. A slight downhill turn after taking the snow will bring your skis under you. But spreading wide may mean a caught inside edge and a bad fall.

In the air consciously straighten up the head and arch the shoulders as you approach your landing. On the snow, as you take your "split," consciously let your hips drop down and then drive them forward. One point worth noting about a good landing is that, if an unexpected fall occurs, the jumper is down close to the snow where he will not get hurt. Were he standing up straight, or jacked over at the waist, he would fall like a tree.

In junior skiing circles (those under nineteen years of age) today, there is a tendency to consider as passé the practice of training a youngster in all four of the sport's main events—downhill and slalom (Alpine), and cross-country and jumping (Nordic). Opponents of four-event skiing argue that if a junior wants to become good, he must concentrate on either the Alpine events or the Nordic events; he cannot do both.

It is our opinion that the average junior not only can do both Alpine and Nordic, but should do both. Despite the evident dissimilarities, the fact is that both sets of events tend to complement and strengthen each other. Cross-country is an excellent means of building up endurance in young downhill racers who almost invariably are physically weaker and have less endurance than they should have.

In cross-country skiing, only the toe of the boot is attached to the ski, so that fore and aft balance is much more critical than on slalom skis, which have more rigid bindings. Cross-country skis are usually moved individually and turns are often stepped; these are two characteristics also used by the best slalom runners. Instead of limiting a junior's slalom running, cross-country often can help.

Jumping is also beneficial to Alpine skiers. By starting with small jumps and building up gradually, the skier learns to relax when he is airborne and not tighten up.

There is also a psychological advantage in doing four events. When juniors have an opportunity to ski almost every day throughout the winter and concentrate solely on Alpine, they tend to become bored and stale. They go through the motions and put in the training hours, but seem to have observably less eagerness and less enthusiasm than juniors who have trained in four events.

Many of our greatest Alpine skiers have been excellent in the Nordic events also. And without exception they credit Nordic skiing with helping their Alpine. Bud Werner was a precocious jumper as a boy and always maintained that his early jumping training taught him more than anything else about running downhill. Ernie McCulloch started as a jumper. Ralph Miller was great in all four events. Chiharu Igaya, who won a silver medal in the 1956 slalom, was also a fine jumper.

There are some less obvious advantages in Nordic competition, and they have to do with college scholarships. If a boy is thinking about a skiing scholarship, he should know that the woods are full of pretty fair Alpine skiers. Any college coach will tell you that it is much harder to find a good Nordic skier than to find a good Alpine racer. And many juniors who take up Nordic strictly as a sidelight to Alpine, or with thoughts of improving their Alpine, have found to their surprise that colleges were interested in them—because of their Nordic ability. Many juniors have tried Nordic and found that they like it and have a talent for it that was totally unexpected. Furthermore, an Alpine racer who can run or jump adequately gives a college team coach flexibility, enabling him to switch a man from Alpine to Nordic, or the reverse, as the need arises. Thus if two men are roughly equal in downhill and slalom, but one can also run cross-country or jump, the latter more often than not will get the nod from the coach in selection of the final ski team.

The relative ease with which a Nordic skier can make a college team also finds a parallel in the selection of United States and Canadian Olympic and FIS teams. The plain fact is that most juniors consider Alpine skiing more glamorous than Nordic. So they concentrate on Alpine. This increases the competition for Alpine team berths and makes it that much tougher to make the team. In Nordic, on the other hand, there is only a relatively small number of dedicated skiers, and the competition for places on a Nordic Olympic team, while intense, is much less than for Alpine. Moreover, the Olympic men's team requires more Nordic than Alpine competitors. Team berths must be filled for the special cross-country team, special jumping team, a Nordic combined team, and a biathlon team. Thus fewer people are trying out for more team positions in Nordic competition.

HOW TO START RACING

So you want to race. Probably the first thing to consider is whether you really like to compete and whether you are now a good enough skier. These questions might come as a surprise, but there are many people who force themselves, or their children, into ski racing when they are not naturally competitive. We cannot believe that ski racing does these people much good, and in some cases the results have been tragic—physiologically and psychologically.

The same applies to skiing ability. It should be apparent that you ought to be a good skier if you want to take up racing, but some people, curiously, regard racing as an alternative to formal ski instruction, and take up racing literally before they can turn each way. These people, at worst, will have a serious accident; at best, they will never really learn to be good skiers. It is very difficult to learn how to ski properly when you are racing. It is not surprising that the best skiers reach the top in racing much more easily and quickly than poorer skiers.

One of the best ways of becoming a racer is to attend one of the many race camps that are available.

Other prerequisites are physical strength and self-discipline. You do not have to be a strongman to enjoy racing and do it safely—but it helps. You should realize that you will be required to ski hard for three minutes or more, with no stand-up coasting in between continually pushing and working through to 60 to 70 continuous turns, a large part of the time in a bent-over (tuck) position. Even the best of racers in superb condition generally finish races exhausted. Your effort and condition may not have to be as great, but you cannot be a weakling either. In most races the strength required is gained by concentrated practice and by exercises. The better racers put themselves through some kind of all-conditioning program and do daily calisthenics during the ski season. When they ski and are not racing, they work either on improving technique or on gaining strength and endurance. For the latter they might make nonstop runs staying in a tuck position for long periods of time or making as many complete turns as possible down the length of the mountain. Physical strength *is* important, and it bears a close relationship to safe racing.

Self-discipline is probably the last major prerequisite. Everyone sees the magnificent performances that good racers can turn in on occasion, and it sometimes appears to the uninitiated that the whole thing does not look that hard. We have heard excellent skiers depreciate the difficulty of racing, and later watched the same good skiers flounder pathetically through the simplest slalom. The truth is, racing requires a great deal of practice before and between races that is totally unglamorous, often discouraging, and a lot of work. And, to make it worse, your friends will continually urge you to skip practice and join them for romps in the powder, etc. It takes will power and a sacrifice of much "fun skiing" to be a good racer.

The first thing you should know is how racing is organized and run in this country. All amateur racing is controlled by the U.S. Ski Association (USSA). The USSA is divided into eight geographical regions. In each region, a division of the USSA runs the racing program. What you should do is find out what division you are located in and contact that division for membership, classification, a schedule of races, a rule book, and any other information they have for new competitors. To find out what division you are located in, write: Executive Secretary, U.S. Ski Association, 1726 Champa Street, Denver, Colorado 80202. Then, write your division headquarters for information on:

Membership. Before you can race you must be a current member of a divison of the USSA (see page 329).

Classification. Racers under nineteen are called juniors; from nineteen through twenty-six, seniors; and from twenty-seven on, veterans. In junior and veteran competition, there are subclassifications according to various age brackets. In senior competition, there are three classes based on ability: A, B, and C. Classification procedures for new racers vary among divisions. Some divisions use "classification races" in the early season so that would-be racers can run and show if they are good enough to be given a class C race card. In other divisions, a class C card is granted automatically to new racers. In others, an "unclassified" race card is given to new racers, entitling them to race in certain races and qualify for a class card. In one division there is a class D for new racers, and a system of examiners to study applicants and decide if they should be given a class C card. The point is that beginning classification procedures vary greatly among divisions, and only by writing your division can you find out exactly what you must do. In most divisions there are also ability classifications for junior racers, similar to the senior classification system, with class C for the poor racers.

Schedule of Races. Each division compiles a list of races and sends it to all competitors in its regions. Most racers plan at the beginning of the season what races they will attend.

FIS Rule Book. As stated previously, the international governing organization in skiing is the Fédération Internationale de Ski. The FIS puts out the official rule book for skiing, and all skiing events in the United States are run in accordance with these rules. Of particular interest to racers are the racing rules relating to disqualifications and starts. An FIS rule book can be purchased through your division, and you should read and re-read it.

Other Divisional Information. Find out from the division about their promotional policies. In all divisions promotion from class C to class B is based on some kind of point system. In some divisions the points are based on placings; in others, on FIS points, which are allocated to each racer depending on how far behind the winner he was in time.

Ask your division about racing instruction schools or camps that they may be organizing as an aid to new racers. These schools and camps are often run over part of the Christmas holidays and occasionally on weekends. The cost for such division-sponsored camps is not great, and they will give you a chance to have your race technique criticized by competent coaches. You will also learn about waxing, equipment, and racing strategy. Some regions have commercial racing schools and camps run by ski areas, ski schools, or individuals. Some of these are excellent, but it is best to check on the reputation of these schools through your divisional office.

FIS POINT SYSTEM

Unlike any other timed individual sport, Alpine ski racing is not conducted on a carefully dimensioned course. In the three disciplines of downhill, slalom, and giant slalom, only general guidelines are given to govern the setting of race courses. To compensate for variations in courses, the FIS has established scoring tables to normalize each competitor's standing behind the winner's time. The resulting points are called FIS points and actually are a more realistic way of comparing two racers than using the "seconds behind winner" criterion.

In any ski race, the winner is credited with zero FIS points and each succeeding racer is given points based on the FIS tables. Lower points mean better performance. If two races are run at adjacent areas on a given day, one a World Cup event with the recognized best international racers and the other a junior competition for regional racers, both race results will show a winner who obtains zero FIS points. Obviously the two cannot be ranked as equals.

A handicapping system, the Bob System, is

used to calculate additional points to be added to each racer's FIS points in a race to compensate for the difference in level of competition. From each race, each racer is credited with a result which is the sum of his FIS points in the race and the handicap calculated for that race.

The racer's seeding points are basically the average of his two best results in a season for each discipline. The system is progressive. Consequently, as he obtains better results during the season, his seeding points will continue to improve. Once again lower points mean better ranking.

The FIS usually publishes its Blue Book of racers' international seeding points twice a year, in November and February. The United States Ski Association maintains a computerized seeding and ranking system in Denver which recalculates a racer's new seeding points following each race in which he competes. New seeding lists are published and dis-

tributed nationwide at scheduled intervals during the competition season.

In order to equalize the differences in the caliber of competitors and races, the FIS points of each racer are increased by a penalty. According to a decision of the Downhill/ Slalom Committee, these penalty points are calculated according to the Bob System, as follows:

1. Determine which five of the first ten competitors finishing have the best seeding points in that event from the most recent seeding list and add their seeding points together.

2. Add together the difference between the seeding points from the most recent list and the race points received in the respective race for the five competitors under (1).

3. Add the results of (1) and (2) above and divide by 10. The result is the race handicap and should be printed on the race results.

Here are the results of an imaginary giant slalom as an example:

Place	Racer	Seeding points from last list	Best five seeding points	Race FIS points	Difference of seeding points minus FIS points	
					—plus—	—minus—
1	Dave John	11.00	11.00	0.00	11.00	
2	Bill Smith	19.04	19.04	12.50	6.54	
3	John Doe	34.52		15.05		
4	Don Black			15.44		
5	Dick Anderson	36.49		15.82		
6	Russ Jolin	40.79		17.07		
7	Pete Eaton	23.89	23.89	19.28	4.61	
8	Jack Thompson	10.68	10.68	20.14		9.46
9	Tom Jones	31.15	31.15	23.31	7.84	
10	Rick Brown	40.21		23.74		
			95.76		29.99	9.46

From the plus column, 29.99
subtract the minus −9.46
_____
20.53

To this, add the total from 20.53
the best five seeding points: 95.76
_____
116.29

Divide this by 10: 11.63 is the race handicap.

Only races which fulfill the following conditions count for FIS points:

1. The race must be listed on the FIS calendar and held on an approved course.

2. At the time of the race, at least five of the competitors from the first ten places must have less than 80 points according to the valid FIS point list.

3. The result list must contain all relative technical details and must be printed on the color prescribed by the FIS (downhill, yellow; slalom, blue; giant slalom, pink).

4. The subsequent FIS points must be printed next to the times taken for the race.

5. At least two countries must be represented at the race.

6. The organizer and the technical delegate must see that the results are transmitted to the appropriate USSA offices. The USSA offices will forward them to the FIS.

Races in other seeding point systems, such as the USSA and divisional systems, have different criteria for qualification.

There is also an alternate method of penalty point calculation called the Short Method.

To figure points by the Short Method:

1. Determine which five of the first ten competitors finishing have the best seeding points in that event from the most recent seeding list, add their seeding points together, and multiply by 2.

2. Add the race points of the five racers determined in (1) above.

3. Subtract the total in (2) from the total in (1) and divide by 10.

Using the same imaginary giant slalom as before, we now have:

Place	Racer	Seeding points from last list	Best five seeding points	FIS Race points	Race points of the five racers with best seed points
1	Dave John	11.00	11.00	0.00	0.00
2	Bill Smith	19.04	19.04	12.50	12.50
3	John Doe	34.52		15.05	
4	Don Black			15.44	
5	Dick Anderson	36.49		15.82	
6	Russ Jolin	40.79		17.07	
7	Pete Eaton	23.89	23.89	19.28	19.28
8	Jack Thompson	10.68	10.68	20.14	20.14
9	Tom Jones	31.15	31.15	23.31	23.31
10	Rick Brown	40.21		23.74	
			95.76		75.23

Multiply 95.76 times two = 191.52, subtract 75.23 = 116.29, divide by 10 = 11.63, which is the race handicap.

In general, seed points are based on the best two results in one event over an established period, usually a full ski season. If there is only one result, an adjustment is made.

NATIONAL SEEDING SYSTEM

The National Seeding System is an implementation of the philosophy and procedure approved by the 1969 USSA convention. All the top amateur alpine ski racers in the country are ranked according to this system on the National Ranking List. Many divisions also extend the system down into their program to include even beginning racers. The purpose of this system is to select promising racers for national training camps and inter-divisional events more fairly and to provide a means by which racers can be seeded equitably in events both in and out of their division. During the season, each division is responsible for keeping national points using a formula common to all divisions and using a common starting point. This formula is the Bob System, and the National Seeding List published in the fall, known as the Fall List, is the common starting point.

The USSA in Denver maintains a National Seeding List during the season of the competitors from each division starting the season with fewer than 100 points in any one event.

Divisions may elect to process their own file of their competitors scored according to the National Seeding System, or they may participate with the USSA in its Alpine seeding list service and have their file processed in Denver. For a race to qualify for national points in the National Seeding System, the following conditions must be met:

1. The race must be a complete race; a single run of slalom does not count as a race.

2. There must be no fewer than six finishers for the event to count. If one or more of the five best finishers does not already have national or international points, he is assumed to have the maximum points for seeding system purposes.

3. The winning time must be at least 50 seconds for the race to be scored. Preferably, all events will be considerably longer than that. There are further technical requirements for nationally sanctioned races to meet.

4. Only the winning time shall be used to determine the appropriate FIS table for the computation of race FIS points for everyone

of the same sex who competed on the same race course. Even if different ability classes or age classes of competitors participate, only one winning time is recognized as the base.

5. Scoring shall be by the latest edition of the FIS tables or their equal. Racers who DNS, DSQ, or DNF receive no points. Likewise, racers whose times are greater than the sum of the winning time plus the maximum tabulated difference time in the applicable table receive ño points.

6. Race committees should calculate an unofficial handicap at the race and print this on the results for the benefit of the racers. For races on the international calendar, the computation of the official handicap must be shown on an attached page.

7. One copy of every race result that is included in the National Seeding System is to be sent to the USSA office in Denver within one week of the date of the race. For races on the divisional calendar only, but which are to be scored on the USSA Alpine seeding list service, two copies of the results are required. For races on the international calendar, 12 copies of the results in the proper format and on the proper colored paper must be sent to the USSA in Denver.

The seeding lists maintained by each division can be updated as frequently or as seldom as is desired, although there is a distinct advantage to the division's racers to have a current seeding list. The USSA alpine seeding list service updates the seeding points after each event.

The seeding list will be kept by sex and by event. Seeding points should be listed vertically by competitor and in order of DH, SL, and GS across the page. The race result (handicap points plus race FIS points) is the input to the seeding system. For each event, the seeding list points will be computed as the average of a racer's best two results in that event according to the following schedule. The seeding points shall be the better (lesser) of:

1. The average of the best two results from the current season; or

2. The Fall List points until March 1. After March 1, the Fall List points increased (decreased) by supplemental points of 20 percent of the Fall list points; or

3. The average of the best results from the current season and the Fall List points taken as one result. Again, after March 1 the Fall List points are increased by the supplemental points.

Supplemental points are used as an incentive for every racer to be active and to penalize a racer who has not improved his standing by mid-season.

The Fall List each year consists of the season-end seeding points calculated as shown below, to which corrections and adjustments may be made to bring the National Seeding List in line with the FIS international points listing. In a similar manner, the division-maintained lists may be corrected to make them correspond with the National Seeding List. Both of these corrections are intended to minimize the effect of using different update schedules. The adjustment becomes necessary whenever the FIS forces their points to zero. The Fall List will have points for each racer which are the better of:

1. The racer's current international Fall List points; or

2. The corrected and adjusted average of the best two results from the immediately completed season; or

3. The corrected and adjusted Fall List points from the previous year increased by supplemental points of 50 percent, or

4. The corrected and adjusted average of the best result from the immediately completed season and the previous year's Fall List points increased by supplemental points of 50 percent and taken as a single result.

Points for racers injured during a season are "frozen" and carried forward as following-season Fall points upon approval of a petition from the competitor through his division office.

Use of the Seeding List. Seeding should be done in the following sequence:

1. Racers with international points less than 80.

2. Racers with national points.

3. Other racers.

In division-sanctioned events, item (3), other racers, may be further divided into subcategories to permit seeding by systems other than the National Seeding System.

Racers entering races outside their division are to be seeded by their earned points from their division's most current seeding list, provided that division has followed the rules of the National Seeding System. It is the responsibility of the racer to transmit to the race secretary prior to the race seeding his up-to-date seeding points if he will be outside his division. He is likewise responsible for sending a copy of the out-of-division race results to his home division in a timely fashion.

HOW THE UNITED STATES NATIONAL ALPINE TEAM IS SELECTED

The United States A and B Teams and Talent Squad is selected largely on the basis of international and national FIS point profiles. The national staff feels that the selection criteria will make the United States a true contender in international competition while at the same time increasing emphasis on domestic competition and development of a broad base of racers at all levels.

The goal of the United States Alpine program for the 1970's is to create and maintain a broad base of competitive skiing in America so that thousands of skiers will have the opportunity to have successful experience in competition and reach their competitive potential in ski racing as quickly, safely, and efficiently as possible.

The United States A Team. The men's A team for 1973–74 consisted of those skiers seeded in the first or second international group in any discipline. Therefore, any racer ranked in the top 30 internationally in one discipline is named to the A team. The FIS list used for this ranking can be corrected to reflect retiring or injured competitors. Additional men may be named to the A team by the national staff based on outstanding international performance.

The women's A team must be seeded in the first group internationally in any discipline. The women have to be among the top 15 on the corrected international FIS list. Additional women may be named during the season by the national staff based on outstanding international performance. In other words, both the men's and women's A team was selected solely on international FIS points.

The United States B Team. The B team is selected on the basis of domestic results, national points and international seeding. For example, in 1974, the first selections were those Americans with the best rankings in each discipline in the final Can-Am Series standings. For instance, the best American male in slalom points on the 1973 Can-Am circuit was named, and so forth for men and women in giant slalom and downhill, regardless of FIS points.

As just described, the first 5 competitors in total slalom points and in total giant slalom points from the International Spring Race Series were also automatic selections for the 1974 B team. The first 5 competitors in national downhill points from the 1972–73 season were also named to the B team.

These approximately 13 automatic selections are the core of the B team. The balance of the team is chosen on international FIS groupings with requirements differing for men and women.

Any male competitors in the third, fourth, or fifth international group selected by the event, and not previously selected by the domestic criteria, are named to the B team from the corrected FIS list. This includes male competitors within the top 75 racers in seeding in the world in any discipline.

Women competitors in the second or third grouping internationally in any discipline and not previously selected by domestic criteria are named to the B team. This includes all women competitors seeded within the top 45 on the corrected international FIS list.

Additional members of the men's and women's B team may be selected during the season by the national staff based on outstanding performance or potential.

The United States Talent Squad. This group was established to recognize outstanding developing racers who have not yet compiled FIS points or a competitive record required of the national staff to identify the most promising young competitors in the nation. The maximum age limit is 21 for men and 19 for women.

The initial racers named to the talent squad are those skiers who place first, second, and third in each event at the Junior National Championships, if they are not already members of a national team. Thus, a maximum of

9 men and 9 women automatically qualify for the talent squad based on performance at the junior nationals.

The men's talent squad for the 1973–74 season, for example, had a minimum size of 20 racers and a maximum of 25. From the national FIS list, the top 15 men, jumping from discipline to discipline, were named to the talent squad. The next 5 spots were filled by national staff option. The remaining 5 spots were filled during the season by the national staff as young racers distinguish themselves in competition.

The women's talent squad had a minimum of 15 and a maximum of 20 competitors during the 1973–74 season. The first 10 members were named from national seeding lists in each discipline after the A and B team were named. Following the 10 selected by points, 5 were selected by the national staff. The remaining 5 spots were filled during the season by the national staff based on outstanding performances of young competitors.

World Cup Team. Usually, 10 men and 10 women are selected to compete in World Cup and B races in Europe. The team is selected from low international FIS point rankings in downhill and slalom. World Cup entry re-

quirements specify under 30 points for men and under 50 for women. Racers who appear to be developing quickly and competing well and who show marked FIS point improvement may be sent to Europe by national staff selection for competition on the European B race circuit for a given period of time.

Cam-Am Series. The top 35 men and 25 women in the United States in current international FIS points are automatically qualified for all Can-Am races held in the United States. The remaining spots in the field of 70 men are filled by 12 Canadians, one racer selected by each USSA division and 15 racers determined by divisional percentages. The women's field of 50 is filled out by 8 Canadians, 1 racer from each division, and 9 selected on a divisional basis. All United States entries must be among the top 100 competitors on the international FIS point lists. If the fields are not filled by entry deadlines, the national staff may pick 2 competitors and the division may fill the remaining spots.

For the Can-Am meets held in Canada, the United States usually has a quota of 15 men and 15 women, who are selected by the national staff prior to each event.

NASTAR

In 1968, *Ski Magazine* introduced the National Standard Ski Race (Nastar) to a limited number of ski areas. The idea behind Nastar is that you can ski down an open, flagged giant slalom course on an easy hill on any day of the winter under any conditions and still wind up with a performance time comparable to that of another skier on a different day. It does not matter if you skied a Nastar course in Vermont and the other fellow did it in Colorado. As with golf, Nastar awards you a handicap rating, uniform for all skiers.

To be sure that everyone who runs a Nastar race is competing on an equal footing, each area sends a pacesetter to a rating meet in December. At these meets, one held in the East and one in the West, each pacesetter runs the course 10 times. The fastest pacesetter gets a zero rating, every other pacesetter

receives a handicap. For instance, if the fastest time for all 10 runs is 20 seconds and the Mt. Snow pacesetter runs the course in 21, he gets a 5 per cent handicap. Each time you run Nastar, the pacesetter's actual time is corrected by his handicap, so that you race against par. In other words, if the Mt. Snow pacesetter's time on a given day is 25 seconds, it is speeded up by a factor of 5 per cent to set par for the course.

Whatever your time is, it is recorded at the area along with the class you are running in and sent on to headquarters at Boulder, Colorado. There your time and classification are checked out and if you come within the right percentage of par, you win a gold, silver, or bronze pin. Here you will find a chart showing you what it takes for each class of skier to win a pin:

HANDICAPS

	GOLD		SILVER		BRONZE	
Age	Men	Women	Men	Women	Men	Women
9 & Under	30	35	45	50	60	65
10–11–12	25	30	40	45	55	60
13–14–15	20	25	35	40	50	55
16–17–18	15	20	30	35	45	50
19–29	15	20	30	35	45	50
30–39	20	35	35	40	50	55
40 & over	25	30	40	45	55	60

After you have skied down a Nastar course, the ski area will tell you your time and your Nastar rating. If you had a previous Nastar rating, you are eligible for the area's weekly award, given to the skier who has registered the greatest improvement in his Nastar rating.

Skiers 18 years and older are eligible for the Nastar finals. Usually the 60 best men and women from 5 regions are invited to the finals, all expenses paid. Their handicaps often range from zero to 43. The entry fee is $2 with a $1 fee for each rerun.

There is also a junior Nastar program for boys and girls in four age groups: nine and under, 10 to 12, 13 to 15, and 16 to 19.

Nastar time standards in these groups will enable an 11-year-old boy, for instance, to compare how well he is skiing with other 10- to 12-year-olds across the country.

Nastar courses are easy-to-ski giant slalom runs with about 20 flagged gates on a smooth open slope. Nastar is an incentive program for the recreational skier to improve his ski ability as well as to be able to judge how he compares with recreational skiers in other parts of the country.

Buddy Werner League

The Buddy Werner League was founded several years ago to foster ski racing for both boys and girls in the 9 to 13 age bracket. Often called the "little league of skiing," it was organized to provide the opportunity for children to compete against other children of the same age and/or ability. Full information on the program may be obtained by writing the United States Ski Association or the Divisional office. Addresses are given in Section VI of this book.

Skiers in the professional championship tour racing head-to-head down the slope.

HOW TO ORGANIZE A SKI COMPETITION

Each year the importance of efficient ski race management grows as the number of races increases. Every winter there are about 500 sanctioned races in the United States and 250 in Canada, to say nothing of a host of unclassified club races. The sanctioned races alone take in about 20,000 competitors in downhill, slalom, giant slalom, cross-country, jumping, and biathlon (shoot and ski). Fortunately, organizations like the United States Ski Association and the Canadian Amateur Ski Association (the groups which govern and give official status to races in North America) have established some guidelines for holding ski races. Under USSA rules, a sanctioned race is one that affects a racer's class rating—A, B, C, junior, veteran. Each division has slightly different requirements for classification. But generally a racer must attend a specified number of sanctioned races to qualify for a class card and move up to a higher rating. All the divisions use the FIS (the international governing body of ski racing) point system to rate the racers and results. In this way, a competitor can travel from one division to another and race in his established class.

A club or group of clubs interested in sponsoring a *sanctioned* race should start planning six months to one year before the event. The first step is to select a race chairman. He is the key person in organizing and administering the race. Certainly he should be familiar with racing, but if the division officials feel that he needs assistance, they may assign a technical adviser to work with the club. There is often a charge for the adviser's time spent at meetings and the race.

Some time early in the planning, the site of the race must be selected by the sponsoring group. Because ski races are usually held on weekends when areas are most crowded, it is important to consider only those areas that have sufficient trails to be devoted exclusively to the race.

Other factors to consider in selecting the area are: availability of the trails for practice prior to the race; adequate lifts or snow vehicles to take racers uphill between runs; proper snow equipment and vehicles to prepare the course; facilities for the extra ski patrol needed for the race; and nearby housing accommodations for racers, officials, and spectators.

When a site is selected, the group can apply to the competitions committee of the local USSA division for official sanctioning of the proposed race. Tournament rules and regulations vary slightly from division to division, but usually you will need to provide detailed information on the who, what, when, and where of the race. There is also a fee, usually ranging from $25 to $100.

Once the application is approved, the committee chairman can start gathering personnel to prepare and run the race. Several race officials may be appointed by the competitions committee. For instance, in the Rocky Mountain Ski Division of USSA (whose rules and regulations are drawn upon for much of this discussion), the referee, chief of course, course setter, chief timer, and jumping judges must be certified officials. This means that they have special training or experience for handling these jobs.

Officials drawn from the organization sponsoring the race are: chief starter, start judge, start secretary, judge of finish, and forerunners. You will need many other people to gather equipment for the race, handle entry blanks, supervise gatekeepers, and recruit course police and ski patrol. At the race itself, people will be needed to distribute number bibs, collect number bibs, record results, calculate results, operate radios and telephones and public address systems, assist starters and timers, and serve refreshments. Many of these posts will require one or more relief men, especially if it is very cold.

Subcommittees must be appointed to handle prizes, programs, publicity, housing, entertainment, and the banquet after the race. Keep in mind that more people will be needed after the race is finished to clean up the course and remove ruts and hazards, return borrowed equipment, write thank-you notes, and so on. Prior to the race, however, one of the most critical jobs is gathering equipment. Items of equipment start with slalom poles, which should be bamboo, 8 or 9 feet long, 1¼ inches in diameter, and painted red, blue, and yellow. You should have two spare poles for every three gates set on the course. Blank express-type tags can be used to number the gates from the top of the course to the bottom. Tape the tag on the outside gate. Slalom flags should be the same color as the poles. Other special items of equipment include: four phones or radios and spare batteries, six timing watches, officials' arm bands, pinnies or number bibs for each racer and for the forerunners and postrunners. (Incidentally, arrange with the area to have some identifying insignia for racers to wear during the practice period before the race. Area management and lift operators should also be supplied with a list of racers and officials who will be using lift facilities.) You will need vegetable coloring or other water-soluble fluid to mark the slalom gate positions for the first run (blue) and changes for the second run (red). To handle poor snow conditions, such as extremely wet snow or cold sugar snow, have several hundred pounds of rock salt and ammonium chloride available. Of course, first aid equipment and toboggans should be available at three positions on a downhill course and two positions on all other courses. Each gatekeeper will need a rake or shovel to repair the course. They should also be outfitted with fluorescent-colored vests (which may be obtained at army surplus outlets) to signify their positions as gatekeepers.

Paperwork and office supplies needed at the race include: entry blanks, racing order sheets, time sheets and cards, gatekeeper's cards, at least five clipboards with plastic top cover sheets, two typewriters, an adding machine, a computer, paper, pencils, carbon paper, paper clips, a stapler, Mimeograph machine with stencils and paper. Signs needed are: start and finish markers, a blackboard and chalk to mark race results, a blackboard and chalk for last-minute information for racers and officials, cardboard and felt-tipped markers for posting announcements. Some of these items, such as official forms, watches, and arm bands, can be bought or rented from your division office. Others may be borrowed from other clubs or the area management.

The starting area should have a shack for officials and racers. If one is not available, you will need to bring a tent for this purpose.

The area around the start should be level and elevated. If crowds are likely to be a problem, have extra bamboo poles and rope or snow fences to hold them back. If the area does not have a starting gate, use two-by-fours set 2 feet apart and about 2½ feet above the snow. The finish gate should be large and highly visible. Plan to construct snow chutes 2 or 3 feet high on either side of the finish to protect fallen skiers.

Between the start and finish is the weightiest problem for the officials—safety. This is where the advice of a technical adviser or experienced racer will be most valuable. The International Ski Competition Rule Book gives specific descriptions of the terrain requirements for all the races. Trail and snow preparation is spelled out thoroughly. Follow this advice closely and go beyond it by exaggerating the possibility of open or hidden dangers on the trails. Wherever an obstacle might pose a safety problem, build a snow or straw safety wall, barrier, or net.

Certain safety factors of a race are, however, left to the judgment of the racing officials. For instance, the rule books say nothing about a downhill race in weather 35 degrees below zero or winds up to 50 miles per hour or fog, flat light, or poor visibility. These are problems which rest on the shoulders of the key people who run the race. They need to have the courage to cancel a race or stop or delay a race to remove hazards or allow time to make it safe rather than take a chance on accidents. A course that can break up or become hazardous or rutty after only 15 or 20 racers is inadequate. Rolling equipment, tramping, and chemicals properly used on a race course should enable it to hold up for 80 or more competitors.

Weather conditions and course preparations are particularly important in junior races. Older competitors are seasoned to the difficulties of racing. One bad experience may be enough to make a youngster drop out for good. For junior races, take extra safety precautions and keep the atmosphere happy.

One safety feature to check on the day of the race is protective headgear. All competitors in downhill and giant slalom events must wear a race helmet bearing the approval decal of the Snell Foundation. This means it has been tested for impact safety.

Announce and post unofficial results as soon as they are available. While these may be changed later, you will make the race more exciting by giving racers and spectators some reference immediately. You will need two or three people to work out these calculations. Be prepared to act promptly on protests. The referee and his committee should use the FIS rules as a guide in disqualifications. Whenever there is a doubt about a dispute, allow the racer a rerun. You can make the final decision later.

Always have some kind of an award ceremony, a banquet if you have time, or presentations immediately after the race near the course or in the base lodge. Prizes may be trophies, medals, or diplomas and should not cost more than $5 to $8.

A final word on holding a better ski race. Even if you follow all of the above advice to the letter and carry out every procedure, your image will be muddied if the race does not *start on time*. The time schedule below will guide a race chairman to that critical moment when he gives the signal to *go*.

Check List for Ski Race Planning

Six months before race

1. Name race committee chairman.
2. Select committee members who are potential race officials.
3. Investigate sites for race.
4. Prepare application for sanctioned race.
5. Appoint subcommittees.
6. Assign duties.

Six weeks before race

1. Check equipment available.
2. Distribute press releases.

Four weeks before race

1. Check arrangements with area.
2. Check progress of committees.
3. Mail entry blanks to clubs and other potential racers.

Three weeks before race

1. Notify all officials and committee chairmen of time schedule and duties at the race. Be sure they contact all workers.
2. Check snow cover at race site.
3. Check equipment procurement.

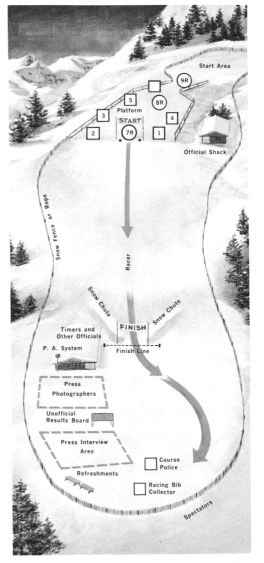

The organization of a typical race course. Personnel on the platform include: (1) chief starter, (2) assistant starter, (3) start judge, (4) and (5) radio or phone men, (6) start recorder, (7) racer in gate, (8r) and (9r) next two racers on deck.

4. Install wiring for phones.
5. Obtain prizes.

Two weeks before race

1. Check progress of all officials.
2. Mail second press release.
3. Check arrangements for spectator control and first aid.
4. Check office supplies, race forms.

One week before race

1. Arrange to pick up equipment borrowed from division headquarters or other ski clubs.
2. Transport some equipment to the area.
3. Check on press representation.

Two days before race

1. Check snow report.
2. Arrange for preparation of the course with snow vehicles and/or chemicals.
3. Arrange to mark the course and the practice areas.
4. Hold a meeting to have draw for positions in the first event. Print race order sheets.
5. Check the order of time cards.

One day before race

1. Hold a meeting of the racers.
2. Check course conditions.
3. Arrange for distribution of the numbers either at the draw for second and third events or at the start.

Day of race

1. Recheck communications system several hours before.
2. Recheck condition of course.
3. Check classification cards and distribute numbers.
4. Check helmets for Snell O.K.
5. Check on refreshments.
6. An hour and a half before race, brief officials.
7. Half an hour before race, officials in positions and police the course.
8. Ten minutes before race, forerunners on the start.
9. Start the race—on time.

10. Have five racers lined up and ready to go at all times. In a giant slalom and downhill, allow one to two minutes' interval between racers. In a slalom the course should be cleared before another racer starts. In cross-country, racers can start every 30 seconds.
11. Announce and post results as soon as they are available. Post disqualifications and reruns.
12. Be prepared to act promptly on protests.
13. Have bibs collected at finish.

After the race

1. Check gatekeepers' cards.
2. Make final computation of results and post them.
3. Distribute press releases.
4. Clean course, collect equipment.
5. Hold banquet and awards.
6. Mail results to clubs, papers.
7. Return borrowed equipment.
8. Send thank-you notes to all who assisted.
9. Hold post-race meeting of officials to get suggestions for future races.

For a rule book on ski racing, write to your local division headquarters. The International Ski Competition Rule Book is available from the United States Ski Association, 1726 Champa Street, Denver, Colorado 80202. The National Collegiate Skiing Rules can be obtained from the National Collegiate Athletic Association Bureau, Box 757, Grand Central Station, New York, New York 10017. For information about Nastar, write *Ski Magazine,* 235 East 45th Street, New York, New York 10017.

JOINING THE USSA

The United States Ski Association is the governing body for the sport of skiing in this country. It has responsibility for recreational skiing as well as amateur ski competition. It sends delegates to the International Ski Federation and the United States Olympic Committee.

The cost of membership is only a few dollars, and the benefits are many. The USSA is divided into eight geographical divisions (see page 424); and although each division's membership fee varies slightly, it always includes an opportunity to purchase accident insurance at a low rate. In addition, you may receive an annual directory of ski officials, instructors, and fellow members with whom you can strike up friendships. You will also get a handsome ski patch, discounts on leading ski magazines such as *Ski,* and discounts at some ski areas. But most of all, you will also know that your dues support the junior ski programs which are so vital to the development of American skiing.

SECTION V

Where to Ski

The ideal ski area would be hard to define. Naturally, mountains should be big, have a variety of terrain, and be adequately supplied with lifts and other base facilities. But size, either of ski terrain or of facilities, is not always decisive. In the Midwest, for instance, Boyne Mountain, which is less than 500 vertical feet, consistently draws thousands from six-hour-distant Detroit. And amid some of the grandest peaks in the Canadian Rockies, Sunshine Village had an enthusiastic group of followers when it could offer only two relatively modest T-bars.

Of course, some skiers are limited to what is closest at hand. For most, however, a choice is possible, particularly when it comes to ski vacations of a week's duration or longer. To decide on where you want to go, you may want to take into account the general characteristics of several ski regions, their principal subregions, and what some of their major resorts have to offer. Details on individual ski areas within a given region or state are given later in this section, but for now, let us consider your ski trip in general.

PLANNING A SKI TRIP

Any ski trip must be planned, whether it is for one day at a nearby slope, for a long weekend at a famous ski area, or for a three-week vacation in Europe. Planning is, essentially, getting information. This may involve simply asking questions of a skiing friend or, at the other extreme, writing for folders, reservations for all manner of things, a study of timetables, and painstaking pencil work to make sure not only that the itinerary works, but also that you can afford it. Of course, one can draw heavily on summer experiences in planning trips, but it should be remembered that winter imposes some special conditions. Lack of a properly confirmed reservation may

not be a serious matter in summer, but it can be close to a catastrophe in winter, particularly if children are involved.

As ski resorts continue to boom, it is more important than ever not only to get information, but also to make sure it is up to date. Your skiing friend may indeed have skied in Austria for less than $5 a day, but that may have been four or five years ago, before the Austrians themselves caught up with the economic times. Similarly, the area you thought two years ago was "not much" may in the meantime have developed into a full-fledged resort with all conveniences.

There is a well-established skiers' grapevine

that will relay the message that a particular area is the place to go—sometimes sight unseen. You soon learn to recognize grapevine reports, and they should be treated with caution, especially if the resort is a new one. Particularly helpful in providing you with a starting point for planning are the ski publications, state and national tourist offices (addresses given later in this section), and commercial airlines.

Some ski publications have buying and travel guides, which contain listings of resorts and areas, their skiing facilities, the available number of beds, addresses, and telephone numbers. While limited in detail on any one area—close to a thousand areas are listed for the United States and Canada—they do provide a basis for comparing resorts throughout North America and in any particular region. Guides put out by state and national tourist offices make generous use of pictures and quite frequently contain the names and addresses of lodges, motels, and hotels. More specific still are the brochures of the resorts themselves or, if the resort is a large one, the local Chamber of Commerce.

Depending on whether your plans are for a weekend or a ski vacation, here are some basic factors to keep in mind: Does the resort offer enough variety and challenge for the length of the stay? If novices are in your party, does it have adequate beginner terrain? Are the ski facilities easily accessible from the lodges in the event you use public transportation to get to the resort? Is evening entertainment available? Does it have such services as a ski school, baby sitting, equipment rentals, medical facilities beyond first aid, and anything else you may particularly require? And, above all, what does all this cost?

The answers to these questions are reasonably easy to determine from brochures and with a letter of inquiry. Somewhat more difficult to find out is whether the resort's character will be to your liking. Strangely enough, brochures, although they are designed to show the resort's best face, often provide true clues to the resort's character. If the brochure is cluttered, fussy, and dwells excessively on the beginners' slope, you can be reasonably sure you will find an area that is cluttered, fussy, and with only limited expert terrain. Conversely, if the brochure stresses the challenges, its immense lifts, and the depth of the snow, the chances are good that the area will appeal to the better skier. Unconsciously, brochures give the show away. If you find the brochure appealing you will probably enjoy yourself.

Equally instructive is the resort's program of events. If the area is promoting a large number of costume races, this will give an idea of the social life of the resort. If there is a strong schedule of bona fide races, including regional and national championships, you can be sure that a large portion of the terrain will appeal exclusively to the better skier. Only a small number of resorts are so large and diverse that they can encompass the full range of desirable terrain, snow conditions, accommodations, after-ski diversions, and atmosphere.

BASIC COSTS

There is a wide range of prices for lifts, lodging, and food, a slightly smaller range for equipment rentals, ski lessons, and other services. Lift tickets, for example, run from $4 a day at a small rope tow area to over $15 a day at major resorts with chairlifts, gondolas, and aerial tramways. Many areas charge less on weekdays than on weekends. Others have multiple-day ticket plans with reductions of 25 per cent or more. There are a number of other ticket plans, including coupon books which require the skier to surrender a certain number of coupons per lift ride, the number depending on the size of the lift; half-day tickets, usually obtainable in the afternoon only; interchangeable tickets good at any one of a number of areas in a given vicinity; and season tickets.

If you ski a lot at one area, a season ticket may be your most economical way to ski. Furthermore, there are usually discounts for additional members of the family. The more you ski, the lower the per-day cost of skiing. However, it should be kept in mind that you are risking paying for snowless days and that the cost precludes your trying other areas. See

Section III for information on ski schools.

Unless you are on a day trip and pack a lunch, there is the cost of food.

Expect to pay at least 15 per cent more at a ski area than you would at a local restaurant or cafeteria. If you are on an overnight trip, remember to budget for meals, unless you plan to stay at an American-plan lodge. Several of the larger resorts have outstanding restaurants. You will probably want to try at least one of these, and in that event you should add a little more to the food budget.

Lodging runs from dormitory bunks to highly expensive suites, apartments, and cottages. Cost is partly determined by the plan under which the lodge operates: the European plan (no meals or breakfast only), the American (all meals), or modified American (breakfast and supper only).

DAY, WEEKEND, AND VACATION SKIING

Generally speaking, the American skier does most of his skiing on weekends, particularly on long holiday weekends. This creates a pattern with some unfortunate effects: it results in long weekend lift lines and makes skiing more expensive than it needs to be. Without going deeply into the economics of ski areas, it should be obvious that if only two out of seven days bring in substantial revenue, the per-day, per-skier cost for using lifts and other area facilities is going to be substantially higher than if attendance were to be distributed equally over the entire seven days. As long as lifts and lodges costing hundreds of thousands of dollars have to be built to accommodate weekend crowds only, the charges are going to be relatively high.

A more economical way to ski on weekends is to make day trips to nearby areas. Those fortunate enough to live in such cities as Seattle, Denver, Portland, Salt Lake City, or Montreal have the advantage of finding major ski areas within one to two hours' drive. Those in other cities in the northern half of the country, however, are not as deprived as they might think they are. Owing in part to skiing's tremendous expansion over the last decade, in part to the spread of superhighways, and in part to developments in snowmaking, most metropolitan areas have skiing within easy driving distance. These ski areas are rarely spectacular, but they are usually more than adequate.

The most economical plan is to ski during the week. In many cases, weekday lift rates are lower, and since the areas are less crowded one can get in a great deal more skiing. Many metropolitan ski areas also have night skiing, making it possible to get in a few runs in the evening after a day at the office.

A ski vacation is usually the most satisfactory way to go skiing. The choice of where to ski is larger, there is greater flexibility in cost, and the frantic aspects of weekending are avoided. You are certain to get more skiing and other kinds of recreation on a vacation than you will on weekends or on day trips. But the very fact that a ski vacation affords a great deal of skiing should give pause to some. Of course you do not have to ski every day, but you will want to. Are you in shape to do so? Two weeks in Aspen may sound idyllic, but it may be more than you are up to. This is an important consideration for those just learning to ski. A moderate amount of preconditioning is essential if you want to take maximum advantage of a ski vacation.

Regardless of the type of resort, your vacation will be cheaper if you avoid the high season. High season is when the resorts are busiest because of holidays or school vacations or both. This includes the two-week period starting the Sunday before Christmas; the period from mid-February to mid-March; and Easter, if it comes before April 7. As far as the quality of the skiing is concerned, these high-season periods have no particular advantage. The snow cover may be a little thin before the Christmas period, but with today's groomed slopes this means little. January has the reputation for being cold, but particularly in the Rocky Mountain resorts it is also the month with the lightest, driest snow. Strangely enough, skiing after mid-March is often the best. The snow at lower elevations may get a little mushy toward mid-afternoon, but the days are longer and the chances of getting sun are much better.

One of the disadvantages of high-season ski vacations is that they limit the choice of accommodations. Those lodges offering the best value are sometimes booked years ahead, and if they do have a vacancy, they may require a stay of two weeks over Christmas-New Year's and at least a week during other high-season periods. One solution to the problem of a high-season vacation is to visit a number of smaller, nonlodge resorts within reasonable driving radius of home and use accommodations to be found in towns along the way.

TYPES OF TRIPS

Having decided where you will go, and when, you must next decide how you will get there. Most skiers prefer to travel in company. The company may be predetermined—your family. In that case you must make all arrangements, from lodge reservations to transportation. If you are taking young children, allow enough time for rounding them up, tracing lost mittens, and similar chores.

Many skiers band together in small groups to share the expenses of a trip. Such groups work out well if all members have about the same skiing ability, are reasonably punctual, and are generally agreeable. Unless exempt by special invitation, members are expected to share equally in the costs, male and female alike.

Package trips can be arranged through ski shops, travel agents (some of whom specialize in skiing), railroads, airlines, and bus companies. Some of them, specifically tailored for the beginner, offer everything—rentals, bus fare, lift tickets, meals, instruction, and lodging—but most are not that inclusive.

Another type of money-saving arrangement is a "learn-to-ski week," which can be enjoyed by beginner and expert alike. Most of the larger areas have such programs. They may offer only a simple lift ticket-ski lesson combination, but frequently they also include meals and lodging. Many of these learn-to-ski weeks are actually shorter than a week, running only from Sunday night to Friday afternoon, but they are available at very reasonable prices. During certain parts of the season the cost is so low as to make living cheaper than it would be at home. For most learn-to-ski weeks you must make your own transportation arrangements.

Ski Clubs

Particularly in the larger cities, there are ski clubs that sponsor trips to ski areas one or more times a season. Clubs have great advantages of economy and convenience. The trip chairman is usually the one responsible for making all arrangements, including bargaining with area managers and lodge owners for reductions in rates. Clubs generally travel by charter bus, which further reduces the cost of a trip. Some clubs also have at least one member qualified to give lessons, or occasionally will hire a certified instructor as an incentive for people to join.

Ski clubs also provide companionship, since skiing generally is a gregarious sport. Some serve as a clearing house of information about snow reports, road conditions, good places to stay, new equipment, and other aspects of the sport. Many clubs sponsor ski swaps where skis, boots, etc., can be traded. These are particularly advantageous with growing children in the family. Many clubs have heavy schedules including ski films, ski schools, conditioning clinics, races, and parties—lots of parties. Some clubs cater to single men and women, others to families; others are a congenial group of all types of skiers.

For ski clubs in your area, check the local papers for notices of meetings or call the sports department of the paper. Inquire at ski shops. If all else fails, write the U.S. Ski Association, 1726 Champa Street, Denver, Colorado 80202, and ask for the ski club located nearest you.

SNOW REPORTS

You can get reasonably accurate advance information on what snow conditions are going to be like at a ski area. Here are some points to keep in mind about snow reports:

1. Use snow reports in a newspaper as a last resort. They are the least up to date, and because of the reluctance of many newspapers to give skiing much space, they lack sufficient detail.

2. Do listen to radio and television snow reports. They are not perfect by a long shot, but they are usually based on information that is only a few hours old and that is usually more complete than what you will find in the papers.

3. Call the ski area for a snow report. (You can call some areas collect, free of charge). If you get a tape-recorded report on the phone, the chances are it is more up to date than one you would get on the radio. If you are lucky, you will get one of the area people in person, and you can do some interrogating.

4. Do check the weather bureau for long-range forecasts. If the snow is wet on Friday, and the temperature is going to drop to zero on Saturday, the conditions will be icy. If it is icy on Friday and the temperature is going to rise above freezing tomorrow, the skiing will be good. These are just two instances of how long-range weather predictions can help you anticipate weekend snow conditions.

5. Unless you know something about the integrity of the area personnel issuing a snow report, ignore the adjectives in the descriptions of ski conditions. Rather, look for descriptions of the actual snow—terms like "light powder over a hard base," "six inches of fresh snow," "hard, granular surface."

6. Unless snow has been meager through the season, ignore overall snow depths. It is what is on top that counts.

7. Snowmaking and good snow-maintenance machinery at an area can often spell the difference between marginal ski conditions and fairly good skiing. Remember, however, that snowmaking equipment is not always a guarantee that skiing is available. Temperatures lower than 32 degrees are necessary to make snow.

8. Experience and grapevine gossip will acquaint you with those areas which have the best reputation for understanding the quality of their skiing. Their reports will give you a good relative judgment on how the snow is at other areas. Another good bet: In the East, state-run areas like Belleayre, Gore, and Whiteface in New York and Cannon Mountain in New Hampshire issue "straight" reports. The state-run areas are under less commercial pressure than private enterprises to issue overoptimistic appraisals of ski conditions. Besides, the taxpayers would not stand for anything less.

9. Warning: A big fall of snow does not always mean superior ski conditions. Many big snowstorms are immediately followed by violent winds and plunging temperatures that can turn a ski slope into a nightmare of ice patches and drifts. Much of that new snow may wind up in the woods.

10. Big falls of heavy, wet snow—particularly in California and the Pacific Northwest—do not always spell good ski conditions. The stuff must be packed out, which means that a ski area must have plenty of rolling machinery to guarantee good skiing.

And a final word to the wise: When you get to the ski area, check out your own mental attitude. If you have already decided that the conditions are bad, then nothing is going to change your mind, and you will almost certainly not ski well or enjoy yourself. The best approach is to psyche yourself into a frame of mind which enables you to be pleasantly surprised the moment you get off the chair lift. In the last analysis ski conditions are what you will them to be, and a good skier should be capable of enjoying anything from ice to deep powder.

Making Snow

More and more ski areas depend on snowmaking equipment each year. This revolutionary process is breathing new life into areas with little (or no) early snowfall. All it takes to work is some water, compressed air, and a subfreezing dip in the thermometer. In fact, snowmaking apparatus will work prop-

A snowmaking machine at work.

erly only when the air temperature is no more than 32 degrees. To be effective, the temperature should be below 25 degrees, at least. While the snow is man-made, it is not artificial; although it is manufactured, it is, in effect, real snow. Preparing it is infinitely less complicated than the process appears. Snowmakers are an intricate network of pipes, hoses, and nozzles. The operation, briefly, goes something like this: Air from huge compressors is forced through a pipeline. Water, usually from a nearby well, is then forced through another pipe running parallel to the air pipe. Both pipes are joined by a single, spraying nozzle, forming a giant atomizer. As the water from one pipe is bombarded by the compressed air from the other, a spray is formed at the nozzle which turns to snow the instant it hits the atmosphere.

Different consistencies of snow, ranging from the wet, dense variety to dry powder, can be made simply by varying the ratio of air and water. Generally, the preferred ratio is about 7½ gallons of water for every 100 cubic feet of air. The ideal temperature is anywhere from 5 to 15 degrees, with low humidity and no wind, but such conditions rarely occur.

Even under the best weather conditions, it still takes many hours to make as much as one foot of snow in a given area. Areas which use snowmaking equipment literally roar with activity late at night. With the last skier bedded down, and the night air providing the desirable temperature, the snow machines can work without interruption, assuring a fine blanket of snow for the next day's skiing.

It has been proved that man-made snow lasts longer than natural snow, because the man-made stuff is denser and therefore builds up a greater base. Even in areas where there has been a fairly heavy snowfall, the manufactured snow comes in handy. The machines can be used to cover ruts and bare spots created by a full day of skiing. Turning the sprayers on overnight replenishes the snow for the following day's traffic. Once considered a gimmick, snow manufacturing today has emerged as a booming industry which provides new life to skiing, with more

The pond next to the fairway at the left supplies the water for the snowmaking in the winter (right) at Boyne Country, Michigan.

and more areas installing the special equipment each year. And although the machines are now in operation all across the country, the East and Midwest, owing to their more unpredictable weather, remain the regions that are serviced by the most snowmaking apparatus.

WHAT TO TAKE ALONG

There is nothing quite so annoying or needlessly expensive as to arrive at a ski area only to find that you have forgotten some essential item of equipment or clothing. And while of less consequence, it can also be embarrassing to find yourself unprepared for certain if infrequent social occasions calling for something more formal than stretch pants and sweater.

It may seem too obvious a point to stress, but boots, skis, bindings, and poles are essential for a day of skiing; a good portion of a rental shop's business is with people who have forgotten one or more of these essentials.

A vacation requires a good deal of clothing, not so much for skiing as for after-skiing. While informality is acceptable at even the largest resorts, there are some hotels and restaurants which require suits and ties for men and dresses for women. And there are some social occasions calling for formal dress. You may also want to take along a bathing suit if the lodge you are going to has a heated swimming pool. The rule to apply is: when in doubt, take it with you. Everything is invariably more expensive at a ski resort than at home.

SKIER'S TRIP LIST

To help you make sure that you have all the equipment and clothing for a ski trip—whether short or long—check the following list. If you are driving to the slopes and have an unlimited amount of space, you may want to take the maximum number of clothing and equipment items suggested here. When flying, check special baggage regulations in effect for ski equipment.

Ski Equipment for All Trips

Skis with bindings
Poles
Boots
Boot tree
Wax and repair kit
Ski ties or carrier

Day Trip

Parka

Sweater
Jump suit
Turtleneck shirt
Stretch pants
Long johns
Light socks
Heavy socks
Car coat
Hat/Headband
Face mask
Mittens/Gloves
Goggles/Glasses
Après-ski boots
Lip and sun cream
Driving gloves

Resort Wear

To any of these lists, add:

Women	Men
Dressy blouse	Flannel slacks
Festive slacks or skirt	Blazer or sport jacket
Dressy flat shoes	Colored shirts
Nylon stockings	Tie or ascot

Weekend Trip

Items listed for day trip, plus:

Second sweater
Second turtleneck shirt

Second stretch pants
Second pair light socks
Second hat/Headband
Light sweater
Shirt/Blouse
Slacks
Shoes
Socks
Underwear
Pajamas
Slippers
Toilet kit

Ski Week

Same as weekend list, plus:

Light parka
More turtleneck shirts
Additional sweaters
More stretch pants
Second set long johns
Extra light socks
More hats/Headbands
Sport jacket/Dressy sweater
Two or three shirts
Blouses
Second pair of slacks
Additional underwear
Camera

HOW TO GET THERE

Although the skier travels a great deal, he is somewhat different from the usual tourist. His principal concern is to get to the slopes; scenery along the way, while it may be pleasant, is secondary. One problem he finds is that few ski areas are on the main lines of railroads, airlines, or even buses.

The automobile, despite its limitations, is undoubtedly the skier's best means of transportation. It gives him the largest leeway in choice of route and time of departure. Although day and weekend bus and railroad trips are available and probably somewhat cheaper (at least for the owner of the automobile), going by car costs less in terms of direct cash outlay and avoids the inconvenience of lugging equipment and suitcases to the station and from the depot to the lodge. A car also has the advantage of being a portable locker. Its limitations are its relatively low speed over longer distances, its vulnerability to weather conditions, and its lack of comfort on long trips.

The next choice is among bus, train, or plane, and sometimes it takes all three to get there. With the general decline of railway passenger service in North America, the opportunity for train travel to most ski areas has become limited, particularly to Eastern and Midwestern areas. But for, say, the Midwestern skier planning a leisurely trip to Colorado, New Mexico, or Montana, the train offers a good alternative, sometimes with attractive excursion rates.

Packaged bus tours operated by ski clubs, travel services, and ski shops are one of the best ways of introducing new skiers to weekend skiing. The "package" usually includes the round-trip bus ticket, lodge accommodation, equipment rental, and ski lessons given by an instructor accompanying the tour. Some packages also include lift tickets or a special ticket discount. While economical and frequently convivial, these bus tours can be disappointing if you are not in good hands. Try to check on the reputation of the people operating the tour. When renting equipment through a tour operator, do not settle for simply giving your foot size and weight by telephone; have your boots and bindings fitted and adjusted personally. This will also give you a chance to examine the quality of the skis and equipment being offered. Condition of equipment can tell you much about the operation of a tour. It is also advisable to obtain specific information from the tour director on lodge and hotel reservations; you may want to check out the reservations yourself. And you might ask about that "instructor" on the bus, whether he is actually certified.

Older ski hands who have become weary of driving long distances to ski areas in their own cars, and who wish to avoid the bunny-oriented bus tours, now make increasing use of special bus services. This kind of arrangement charges only for the bus. You board the bus on your own. Once you reach the area (frequently nonstop), you are free to stay where you want, eat what you want, and get to the mountain when you want. New York, San Francisco, and Detroit are among the cities which have such "super ski bus" services.

Flying by plane is generally the quickest way to go to distant ski areas. With jumbo jets, STOLcraft, air taxis, helicopter service and private planes, service to ski resorts is improving and the long-range prediction is that fares will go down. There are several domestic flight fare plans that skiers should be acquainted with:

1. First class means you can fly whenever you want to; the cost differential between first and tourist is not so great that you might not consider grabbing a first-class seat if coach seats are unavailable. The straight coach fare also means you can fly any day, any hour, and return whenever you wish.

2. The special airlines excursion fare applies basically to coach flights any time except 12:01 to 11:59 P.M. Fridays or 12:01 P.M. Sunday to 11:59 A.M. Monday and some holidays. The return trip must be made after more than seven days but not after thirty. This is also known as the thirty-day excursion fare and is about three-fourths of the regular coach fare.

3. The Family Plan rate may or may not be cheaper than the special airlines excursion rate, depending on how many children of what ages are accompanying you. (For two adults, special excursion rates are usually cheaper than Family.) For Family Plan, the head of the family pays the regular coach or first-class fare. The spouse (or first child under 21, if no spouse is going) pays three-quarters of the regular rate. A second child pays one-half, if he is between 12 and 21, or one-third, if he is between 2 and 11, and so do subsequent children. One infant under 2 is carried free. Unaccompanied children pay full fare. The rate is not available on certain peak days and is not available from 12:01 P.M. Sunday to 11:59 A.M. Monday and from 12:01 P.M. to 11:59 P.M. Friday.

4. The youth fare is available to anyone with a Youth Fare Identification Card, providing he is at least 12 but less than 22. Certain high-traffic holidays are restricted, but otherwise he travels on a standby basis (i.e., he gets a seat only if there is no full-fare passenger for it) and pays 50 per cent of the coach fare.

In traveling other than by car, the skier's major problem is the baggage and equipment he has to carry. Every baggage transfer is an unpleasant chore, particularly with a party. Furthermore, each transfer runs the risk of loss or misplacement, and there is the additional strain of making connections. Thus an overnight sleeper that takes you close to the resort may be more satisfactory than a plane, which will get you to the nearest major city in the fastest time, but may require several additional transfers to limousines, buses, and/or trains before you finally arrive in your remote mountain valley. It is therefore a good idea to study all the schedules—rail, bus, and airlines—before settling your plans.

In making travel plans, one of the more important considerations is the size of the party. A group of ten or more traveling to the same destination may be eligible for discounts up to 30 per cent on most domestic airlines and on a number of overseas carriers. This has been standard for several years. An airlines sales representative (not a reservations clerk) or a knowledgeable travel agent should be consulted when such a group trip is being considered. Eligibility requirements change periodically, and group fares may not be available at certain peak travel periods, such as Christmas and Washington's Birthday.

From a purely economical point of view, there is no better way to go than by charter, whether by bus, train (seldom available), or plane. To give an example, regular winter jet, round-trip, economy fare from New York to Munich is more than $400. For a charter plane, this fare is reduced to $250. Airline charters operate under the Civil Aeronautics Board (CAB) and the International Air Transport Association (IATA), both of which have been known to crack down on illegitimate charters.

To be eligible for an airline charter you must be a member of the sponsoring organization for at least six months prior to the date of departure. The sponsoring organization itself must be a local group organized for purposes other than cut-rate travel. Almost any ski club, employee group, alumni association, or lodge can run a winter charter. If your membership has lapsed, you can still qualify by paying back dues. If you sign up for an illegitimate charter, you run the risk that it will be exposed and canceled. It is best to stay with airlines with established reputations and groups that have run successful charter flights in the past.

Although charter groups work with travel agents who make up special packages, you have to remember that charters only fly you there and back; once there you are on your own. Usually you have to make your own arrangements for accommodations and ground transportation.

Charters have other drawbacks. You must leave and return when the group does, possibly on dates not to your liking. The object of your trip may be a tour of the French resorts. If the plane lands in Munich, the trip's economy and convenience will be reduced. A more drastic problem is the possibility of a shortage of passengers. If the price for the trip is based on 100 passengers and fewer actually sign up, you may well be asked to make up the difference on a prorated basis. And even legitimate charters have been canceled at the last minute. In such a case you would either have to pay the full fare to protect the deposits you have made or stay home. You can protect yourself against this eventuality by buying insurance that covers the regular fare in both directions. This insur-

ance also protects you in the event injury prevents you from returning with the group.

Strange as it may seem, domestic charter flights are much more difficult to arrange than overseas charters. Transatlantic airlines have more planes than they can use on scheduled runs during the winter. Also domestic airlines are in a better position to shift their equipment to routes busier in winter than in summer. And domestic charter flights are likely to end up with propeller-driven planes instead of jets. However, this situation has been improving with the growth of American resorts.

Travel between ski areas can be a chore, and is often more complicated than getting to a resort from your hometown. With a few notable exceptions, most major American resorts are situated discouragingly far apart. European resorts, while closer to each other, require more traveling time. For instance, it is about 350 miles from Aspen to Salt Lake City, a seven-hour drive. That is about the same length of time it takes to go from Chamonix to Zermatt by train, although the two are only 45 miles apart.

How to Use a Travel Agent

A travel agent is a specialist who represents the traveler in negotiating with carriers and hotels. He can save you time, money, and effort—if he is good, and if you do your homework. He can help you find your ideal goal, plan your itinerary, get your travel and room reservations (often, reservations available to pros alone), and take care of rental cars, insurance, and financing. If he is ski-wise, he can give you firsthand advice on trails, after-ski conditions, when to go, and what to bring. His services cost you relatively little. Most of his compensation comes from commissions, which are fairly uniform, so that his preference for one airline or resort over another is usually based on honest judgment.

The fact that an agency belongs to the American Society of Travel Agents is supposed to guarantee minimal professional ethics, but many are the crimes committed by even the most ethical agents because they do not know a gondola from a rowboat. The dangers have lessened, thanks to the recent rise of IT (Inclusive Tour) ski vacations put together by specialized wholesalers, resorts, or specific lodges and various carriers. Even if your neighborhood travel retailer is a ski ignoramus, he can utilize the knowledge built into the IT packages. Regardless of the retailer's personal familiarity with the ski scene, maintain a sharp and skeptical eye. Here are some tips for dealing with him:

1. Be completely honest with him about your budget, your interests and your qualms.
2. Think about your needs and assign priorities. Only you can say whether liftside location is more important than a swimming pool or a short flight out-

weighs après-ski opportunities.
3. Be specific in describing what you want. "Any old room" will not do, if you prefer ultramodern or rustic.
4. Do your homework, so you can at least ask the right questions. Ask for and read all the promotional literature. Look at timetables, maps, and rate cards. Find out what competitive resorts offer. Check guidebooks and back issues of skiing publications.
5. At each step make sure which items are covered in the deal and which will cost extra.
6. Get everything in writing and take the documents with you—receipts, letters of confirmation, specifics on what is in the deal.

WINTER DRIVING TIPS

The legislatures of states in ski regions are very aware of the value of the skier's dollars and have been fairly generous in awarding good roads to ski areas. In addition, state highway departments do an excellent job in keeping roads open. But good skiing weather is often bad driving weather. Therefore, it behooves the skier to be a good bad-weather driver.

First, about your car. It is meant to be a convenience, but if it causes you one moment of delay or concern, it is not serving the purpose. You can help it most before you even head for the snow country by keeping it in good general repair and paying particularly close attention to four things: battery, oil, antifreeze and tires.

Battery

You cannot imagine how much cold weather cuts into the efficiency of a battery. One that gives instant starts in the city will sound that heart-stopping "ur-ur-ur-ur" when the temperature drops a few degrees. Water in it, of course, terminals checked for clean, sure contact, but, if it is aging, it might save you a morning of skiing if you get a new one. Remember that tow charges in ski areas are usually *outrageous*.

At the time your battery is checked, make

sure that the entire electrical system is functioning perfectly. Old spark plug cables, points, plugs, and loose connections may keep your car from starting even if it has a first-rate battery.

Oil

Oil is another item which reacts sharply to cold weather. Absolutely essential is a light oil—either a combination 10-30-weight oil or a straight 10-weight. In extreme cold weather, many experts suggest a low-viscosity oil such as 5W-20.

Antifreeze

If you are an Eastern skier, particularly, be sure to take the safety in your radiator down to 40 below zero. And, speaking of antifreeze, do not forget your windshield washer. Use the stuff specially made for it. The radiator variety is often death on paint.

Traction

Traction depends on several factors. Let us look at tires first.

Radial-ply Tires. Their construction is such that they will resist skidding in cornering. In straight-ahead driving, the rear wheels will have less tendency to slither to one side, which is often a major part of the problem in getting up a hill. While they cost more, they deliver more miles per buck. They do not have quite the traction of snow tires, but you can use them all year.

Snow Tires. As an all-around solution, they are hard to beat. Caution: Snow tires priced to sell fast are all too common, and the result often is a quick trip to the nearest ditch or skidding in wet weather even when there is no snow or ice.

People in the business whose word we trust say that the rib effect at the edge of a snow tire tread provides a sort of paddle-wheel effect, and that is where most of the pull comes from. This is best accomplished by a tire with expensive rubber. This same expensive rubber in the tire discourages skids on wet pavement—and that is the kind used in premium snow tires. If you find the right dealer, the premium snow tire is not all that much more expensive, and nothing cheaper than a premium tire is worth buying.

Studs help, too, but some people have complained they chew up macadam driveways, or wear off after several thousand miles of driving.

Chains. Full chains are still the final answer when the going gets really tough. In many situations, however, emergency strap-on chains are just as good. Before you buy

either, make sure your tires will take them. Plan to use at least two straps, one for each wheel. Reinforced-link chains cost a little more, but do a better job. It used to be that underinflating a tire was thought to be the best way to get traction out of it. Now opinion has swung the other way, the reasoning being that a slightly overinflated tire will bite down through the snow and find solid stuff.

The Limited-slip Differential. It is almost a must in snow country. It causes both rear wheels to power the car when you get in the snow, rather than just one wheel spinning. You can have it as an optional installation on many cars.

Miscellaneous Equipment

To be prepared for the worst, your car should carry the following items: spray cans of antimist and deicer to treat windshield and other windows; pieces of carpet or wire mesh as traction aids; flares and flashlights (the stand-up type that can act as a blinker is particularly helpful); a bag of sand or cinders; a sheet of plastic for lying or kneeling on when you work around the car; a strong windshield scraper with a brush on the other end; and jumper cables.

SKI RACKS

Outside ski racks are essential for any car being used to transport skiers. Skis carried inside the car not only can damage the interior, but they can be dangerous in the event of a hard stop, even hurtling through the windshield.

There are two basic types of racks: those that fasten to the roof and those that attach to the trunk. The roof type is more convenient, if the design of your car allows it. Trunk racks have the drawback of limiting access to the trunk or engine. Most of them require that the skis be removed to make access possible, and some require that the whole rack be removed.

When putting the skis in the rack, be sure to secure all straps and cables. If these are

allowed to flutter in the wind they will scratch and even dent the car. The most important requirements of a rack are that it be sturdy and capable of secure fastening. These points should be carefully checked before purchase.

After purchase, perhaps one of the most neglected pieces of equipment in a skier's possession is his automobile rack, and yet it takes only a few minutes to make it as good as new. Many racks come with rubber attachment devices or suction cups. Since rubber deteriorates, it is always wise to replace these parts every few years, if necessary, to provide trouble-free service. Another cause for irritation can be the sponge rubber used for padding on many racks, which often has a habit of coming unglued.

Three popular types of car ski racks.

TECHNIQUES OF WINTER DRIVING

The two important points to remember in driving on ice and snow are (1) conserve what little friction is available to you, and (2) if you lose it, do not panic.

Drive on ice the same way you drive on a clear road—except do everything easier and sooner. Ice has a way of magnifying your every move. (Rather like skiing in deep powder, which shows up your skiing faults much the same way ice shows up your driving faults.) Actually, there is this paradox in glare-ice driving—you must be much quicker in anticipating trouble than on a clear road, and your reactions must be much faster in point of time, but they must be executed more slowly. Steer gently. A sudden jerk at the wheel means there is a jerk at the wheel, all right. And most likely off in the ditch. Brake gently, too, and accelerate with a feather foot.

Control of your car depends for all practical purposes on *rolling* wheels. If your wheels are not rolling in the direction of your car's principal momentum, the result will be a skid—loss of friction between tires and road surface. While harsh and sudden braking will lock wheels, control of the car is lost until the wheels start to roll again. It is therefore always advisable to apply brakes gently in a series of pumping motions. This dissipates the momentum of the car slowly, keeps the wheels rolling, and thereby prevents loss of control.

The commonly stated rule about skids is: "Turn in the direction of the skid." This means that if the car's back end skids to the right, you turn to the right. If it skids to the left, you turn to the left. What you are doing is keeping the front end of the car in line with the back end. Your action should be a smooth, gentle steer in the direction of the skid accompanied by a gradual easing of pressure on the gas pedal.

If you find yourself unable to stop short of an obstacle, remember that you must retain your maneuverability at all costs. Slow the car down, by gentle braking and/or shifting to a lower gear, but avoid locking your wheels. If your car remains steerable, you may be able to dodge the trouble, or at least reduce the seriousness of the impending accident. If you cannot avoid a collision, yet still have some sort of steering option, it is better to hit something soft than something hard, better to hit something going your way than something stationary, and better to hit something stationary than something coming toward you. The point is to keep thinking and working, not to give up. Control is usually not so much lost as it is surrendered.

Here are a few do's and don'ts that you should keep in mind when in snow country:

1. Do not leave your parking brake on overnight. It might freeze on.
2. Try parking your car with its engine end toward the east; no religious significance, but if the sun does have any warmth, it might as well be on your engine.
3. When you stop on a hill, angle the wheels away from the road and leave the car in gear or in "park" with a rock blocked against a tire for extra safety. (Some "snow" states have specific rules on parking a car, so check at the lodge if you are not familiar with them.) Always try to park in authorized areas. It is risky to park alongside the road, where snowplows may bury the car, block your reentry to the highway, or accidentally smash a snow-covered fender.
4. Avoid parking where tree branches or a sloping roof may shed a snow load on your unprotected car. Stop facing downhill, if you can, for an easy getaway.
5. When you return to the car, clear all snow and ice from the windows. If your door lock is frozen, open it by heating the key with matches or a cigarette lighter before pushing it into the lock.
6. Pump your accelerator before you try to start some car models. Do not grind and grind; you will only run your battery down. Remember that it is possible to "deflood" most late-model cars by holding the gas pedal to the floor.
7. Idling speed warm-up may not be the best thing for your engine, but it is better than pulling out into traffic with your car one cough away from extinction.
8. Use low-beam lights during bad weather, and turn them on for daytime snow, rain, or fog. You may not see any better, but it will help approaching cars see you.

CAR RENTALS

The easiest way to get a skierized car (i.e., one with rack and snow tires) is to reserve it from one of the big national chains when buying transportation or ski week packages. That is not necessarily the cheapest way, but it is not necessarily the most expensive, either. National, local, and regional companies offer intricate rates which may or may not be bargains for the individual customer. The only way to tell is to get all the offers and figure out how they apply to you. Consider:

1. *What kind of car do you want?* A typical rate for a simple but full-sized American car is $11 a day and 11 cents a mile, gas and oil included. This is far from standard, however. Some services charge 50 per cent less, but only for Volkswagens or other small cars, which are not always available as ski cars. Foreign or sports cars are also not always ski-equipped, but they fetch a premium price when they are. Station wagons, compact or larger, can usually be found, though often at higher rates than sedans.

2. *Do you need the car within the resort?* The nationwide services usually allow for drop-off in top cities but not in ski towns, though the situation is improving.

3. *Is free mileage really free to you?* Some ski weeks include rental cars to be used for several hundred miles without further charge. Do not think of the car as free, however. You are paying for it one way or another.

4. Are you better off with free gas? Prices pegged to free gas are best if you plan a lot of driving.

5. On one-way car rentals, can you get a car with its home port close to your goal?

6. At a counter, are you getting the best deal? The clerks are empowered to bargain.

7. Bring three things to a rental counter: written confirmation of your reservation; renter's credit card or a national charge card, to avoid paying a $50 deposit; identification showing that you work for a company entitled to volume discounts.

WHERE TO STAY

At most ski areas, lodging can range from luxurious suites with fireplace, ample baths, and comfortable furniture to a dorm with outhouse facilities. It is important when selecting a lodge to remember that a good one can more than make up for an area's skiing shortcomings or even poor weather. Conversely, a poor lodge can make a stay at an otherwise ideal resort a miserable experience.

Lodges, over a period of time, get reputations for certain types of atmosphere and attracting certain types of clientele. Although price is a fair indication, some detective work may be needed to determine exactly what you will be getting into. If a choice is available, make telephone calls to the managers. And by all means, consult friends and acquaintances who have stayed there in the past, making sure that the management has not changed since they have been there (or perhaps that it has).

Types of Accommodation

At major American and Canadian ski areas (European resorts are discussed later in this section) accommodations can range from simple dormitories to luxury condominium apartments. Although the range of accommodations may be narrower at smaller resorts, this does not mean that they offer less in every respect. Luxury features may be missing, but many hosts go out of their way to make up in organized entertainment and hospitality whatever their resort or lodge may lack in swimming pools and precipitous slopes. If lodges in the smaller resorts can be faulted at all, it is in their tendency to be oversolicitous.

If you are young, single, not overly concerned about privacy, and determined to get the maximum skiing mileage out of your dollar, a dormitory bed is the answer. Dormitories can be almost anything—extra attic space (bring your own sleeping bag), bunk rooms holding ten to fifteen members of the same sex, or even an entire lodge. Some dormitory lodges are remarkably elaborate, offering a two-to-a-room bunk arrangement with semiprivate bath. The one disadvantage is that you have no choice of roommate unless you are in a group large enough to take over completely whatever dormitory space is available.

In any event, expect to find a young crowd almost totally dedicated to skiing. Families with older children may actually find it an advantage to put their youngsters in dormitories. This will not only save money; it will also throw children together with others their own age, something they are bound to enjoy.

With separate rooms you have the widest latitude, both in conveniences and in cost. The cost depends on a number of factors that should be taken into account before making a selection. It makes little sense to pick the lowest priced lodge only to find that you have to spend money for cab fares to the slope or for a night on the town. Similarly, if a daily sauna is your heart's desire, it is better to pay a dollar a day more for a lodge with this facility.

For stays of over a week, you may want to consider renting a house or a condominium apartment, especially if there are several in your party. The per-day cost will be less— though not a great deal less—than at a lodge, but the responsibilities are somewhat greater. Minor breakages have to be paid for; the walks shoveled; there is no manager to provide little services; and you have to seek your own entertainment. Management agencies, rental services, or resort associations can make all the rental arrangements for you.

If you are single, you will have difficulty finding single rooms at most areas. If you cannot find someone to share a room with you (you have to provide your own roommate) or insist on being alone, you will be expected to pay the double rate, at least in high season.

Most lodges have both in and off season rates. The latter, of course, are cheaper. Also remember that the American plan is the cheapest way to eat at a resort, but it does not give you much choice of food. Many lodges offer food family style with very limited choice; others have three or four items on a menu from which you must choose your dinner before leaving the lodge in the morning. Only a few offer a complete menu at the time of the meal. The wider the choice of food, the more costly the accommodations.

Reservations and Deposits

It is the height of folly not to make reservations, particularly during high season. Make your reservations early, starting in midsummer for Christmas, in late fall for February and early March. At the more popular resorts, it may take quite a few letters to get what you want. Many skiers who go to the same resort year after year make their reservations for the next year prior to leaving.

Once you have made a reservation, confirm it with a deposit. Deposit policies vary from resort to resort, but anticipate paying about 30 per cent of the total cost of the stay if it is for a week or more, or the equivalent of two days if the stay is for less than a week. Deposits are usually refunded in full upon thirty days' notice (this also varies). Increasing percentages are deducted as the cancellation approaches the reservation date. This may seem like an unreasonable policy, but it has to be recognized that the lodge owner has only a limited time in which to realize his income. Because of your reservation, he may have turned down dozens of others (who have then gone somewhere else), and it may no longer be possible to fill the space at that late date.

Lodge Life

Most well-designed ski lodges have a lounge with a big fireplace; a dining room; a rumpus room with various games, including the inevitable Ping-pong table; perhaps a small dance floor and a bar; and a ski room where skis, poles, and boots are stored. (Remember that because metal toe and heel plates damage floors and carpets, proprietors discourage their wear indoors.) Private rooms and sleeping areas are usually upstairs.

Apparel is always informal at American lodges. Female après-ski wear may consist of sweaters and pants or long skirts, but is always informal in appearance. Although most lodges now have city-type bars and cocktail lounges, a few still provide free ice, setups, and cocktail snacks, and serve to the guest with his own bottle (which has been marked with his name).

The hard work of catering to the guests' needs is performed in many lodges by young people who like to call themselves ski bums. These boys and girls, of college age or just beyond, work for their room and board by waiting on tables and helping to clean up.

Tipping has infiltrated the ski economy. Some old-time lodges still have a ski bum kitty. Your problem is solved if you put in 10 per cent of your bill at an informal or modest establishment and 15 per cent at a more pretentious, service-oriented spot. In the Laurentians, a 10 to 12.5 per cent service charge is added to your hotel bill, but you still must cross the more obvious palms on your way out. The same is true in Europe, where service charges are included to the tune of 10 to 15 per cent in Austrian hotels or restaurants, 12 to 15 per cent in their Swiss counterparts, and 15 to 22 per cent in French or Italian ones.

In North America you are likely to be on your own. Be guided by the basic rule: Tip anyone who wears a uniform and looks you in the eye while performing his service, plus chambermaids, who do most of their chores for you unseen. Since ski-country employees frequently wear ordinary sports clothes, this rule applies to employees who would be wearing uniforms if they had the job in a city.

The specific amounts depend on how long you stay, how much special service you get, and most important, the kind of establishment. Motel employees really do not expect tips, unless they are bellboys doing specific errands, or waitresses or bartenders. In dorms

Après-ski life can range from just sitting around an open fireplace (left) to paid entertainment (right).

tips are required only if there is a kitty or if you stay for a week or longer. In the hotel, lodge, or inn categories, the level of tipping ascends with flossiness. In a middle-bracket establishment, count on $3 per week to the chambermaid, $5 to a regular waiter or waitress, $5 for a captain or a maître d'. Tip at the end of your stay, except for bartenders, who should be tipped at the end of each session (15 per cent, but never less than 25 cents), and anyone who helps with baggage (50 cents per bag, on the spot). Owners are never tipped, but their children are, if they serve as staff. A ski instructor is tipped after a private lesson or after a week of group lessons; $5 is suitable from a ski weeker.

Owning Your Own Ski Home

After adding up the season's lodge receipts, the cost of telephone calls for reservations and all the headaches, you may find it wise to consider purchasing a home in your favorite ski area—especially if you are in the process of raising a family.

The economics and advantages of a ski home depend to a degree on the size of your family, the type of accommodations you want, how often you will use it, the amount of the mortgage payments, taxes, and other costs. Depreciation and the amounts paid out for interest, taxes, and improvements of course are legitimate tax deductions. Under certain conditions, a ski house can qualify as a business operation; and as such, any losses can be written off for taxes. In addition, a ski house, under certain circumstances, can be a source of cash profit. At the most popular resorts, you can finance your entire ski budget by renting your ski home in high season and using it yourself during low season and the summer.

Providing you have chosen the site and the building wisely, and have maintained them properly, the chances are much better than even that the property will increase in value. Remember that even though there may have been a boom in a particular ski area's development for periods of time, chances are that it is nowhere near at its peak yet. Every time a lift is built in the vicinity, your ski property increases in value.

The major reason for owning a ski home is the convenience. You can eat and drink when you please. You never have to worry about the quality of accommodations or their availability. You will generally have all the necessary storage space you need. And you are free to choose your fellow guests. In some ski resort areas, the management is in the real estate business, or rather is in the ski area business in order to be in the real estate business. As an incentive to buying real estate, some managements will offer reduced-cost skiing privileges with each sale.

As any homeowner knows, there are, of course, disadvantages to owning a ski home. And the drawbacks of a vacation house are the same as in your primary home, plus a few extra. For instance, maintenance costs are going to be high. A plumber or furnace repairman is difficult enough to get in the city. In the country, he may be virtually nonexistent.

Problems are reduced to a minimum if you use the house only for yourself and your own family. You can expect to find it as you left it, and you can leave it as you wish. But if

Ski homes may range from a simple A-frame type of house (left) to a modern condominium (right).

you expect to rent it, you will have to keep it neat and tidy, or pay to have this done. And while it is possible to do the renting yourself, it usually requires the services of an agent, who charges 10 to 25 per cent of the rental fee. But if you rely on rental income to pay for part of the mortgage, a bad snow year can be disastrous. And even if you do not depend on rental income, the house may be useless to you during such a year. There is nothing quite as exasperating as a ski house during a snowless winter.

Unless you have money to burn, the very ownership of a ski home tends to commit you to one ski area, or at best to a limited selection. It is rather foolish to own property in one area and then drive a distance to another area. Better to find a site equidistant from several areas, both as a hedge on snow conditions and to assure skiing variety. And finally, there are the problems of construction. What may be an ideal site from a ski point of view may have major drawbacks in terms of labor availability, access, utility hookups, and other services.

Rather than a house, you may wish to consider a condominium apartment. Most major resorts have a number of these available for sale. They offer the advantage that upkeep, heating, road plowing, and so forth, are taken care of by management of the resort. This overcomes one major drawback of ski home ownership.

MONEY-SAVING TIPS

Saving money on ski trips—both for the family group and for the individual—is something that definitely can be accomplished provided you plan ahead. Planning ahead means more than starting to think on Wednesday about how you will economize on the following weekend. Your plans, after all, are rather complex—transportation, food, lodging, skiing, ski equipment, and après-ski entertain-

ment all have to be taken into consideration. If you are planning for a family, the complexity seems to increase roughly 96.4 per cent for each child included in the party. If there are any children younger than three, the planning includes a vast amount of paraphernalia that must accompany the child. The smaller the child, the bigger the mound of luggage that travels with him.

Money-saving Tips for the Family

1. *Transportation.* Consider skiing in the purchase of your next car. Station wagons and bus-type vehicles can be economical on gas, and many models are now equipped for camping or sleeping. If the car you are buying will be your all-purpose car, then obviously the pickup truck with an attached camper unit would be out of the question. (Who wants to go rolling off to a dinner engagement in a pickup truck?) If, however, you are in a position to purchase something along these lines, its uses are manifold and not limited to skiing.

2. *Save Phone Calls.* A single long-distance call to the area's accommodations booking center can save you a lot in the long run. Even if you know the lodge, and the owner is your brother—if they are full, they are full. The central booking agency can save you several phone calls and will usually be able to find you the accommodations you need.

3. *Farmhouses, Motels.* If you are prepared to eschew the luxuries of the larger, more elaborate ski lodges, the private home or farmhouse-type accommodation will save you money. It is usually comfortable and quiet—and who wants the kids hanging around the bar all night, anyway? Locate these places during summer travels if you are in the area or consult the area's accommodations center. Many areas also have housekeeping cabins or motel units with cooking facilities. If food is bought at home, the cost for weekend eating is no greater than if the family stayed home.

4. *Extra Beds.* Take a folding cot or travel bed for children. If you can set it up in your room, or put all the children in one room, it cuts down costs.

5. *Rent a House?* If you are going to all the fuss and bother of traveling about with your own food and your own beds, why not set up your own headquarters at your favorite ski area? There are many points which must be considered, however, before one gaily assumes that this arrangement would be perfect. Unless your family is large and you spend every weekend and school vacation skiing, the cost may be prohibitive. On the other hand, it can work well if you are willing to share with another family, alternating weekends and vacations. All of you together may be a vast mistake. (Then again, it may not.)

6. *Buy Real Estate?* If you like the area well enough and spend enough time there, consider building or buying your own weekend house. A strategic location can result in accessibility to three or four ski areas more easily than staying at one of them. With this variety, the location ought to appeal for years —enough to make the initial investment worthwhile. Select an area which offers summer vacation use as well. But again, weigh the pros and cons carefully before going ahead. Ask yourself these questions: Will I use it in the summer? Can it be considered an investment? (Land at many ski areas is multiplying in value.) Should I build a new house? Is it possible to buy and renovate an old farmhouse? How much will I utilize it? Remember that the average American skier skis only twelve days a year.

7. *Equipment Pool.* A neighborhood buying and selling pool saves on equipment for children who often outgrow skis, boots, and poles before they wear them out. If you live near ski country, most homes have at least a couple of pairs of spare boots "that Junior has outgrown, and we are waiting for Susie to grow into." Check your local ski club to see if they sponsor such a pool. Possibly the child's school does. If there is no pool organized, but you think the field looks promising, organize your own. Simply set aside a cellar for a Saturday in November and invite the neighbors to bring along their children's ski equipment.

8. *What Kind of Area?* Pick your area carefully before embarking on a weekend or vacation. Decide whether you will settle for a T-bar or rope area to shave the price of uphill transportation. If you want to go to a chairlift area, expect lift ticket prices to be higher. Smaller areas are generally less crowded, and you may get more skiing for less money.

9. *Family Season Tickets.* Some areas have family ski plans which (among other benefits) entitle one to lower lift rates (about 10 per cent). Others have family season passes at considerable savings if you are doing much skiing. Membership in organized skiing may also entitle you to lower lift rates at some areas.

10. *Touring.* Cross-country touring, while involving the initial cost of adjustable bindings, presents no other additional costs. It is away from the stamping hordes; it opens up whole new vistas of previously unseen territory and affords a glimpse of wildlife. In the age of fast lifts, well-groomed slopes, and the urge to schuss, cross-country touring can be a pleasantly relaxing variation for the whole family.

11. *Children's Lift Tickets.* Do not waste the cost of a day ticket on a small child, one who is just beginning to ski or one who feels the cold easily. They will be better off with individual ride tickets and, in the case of the cold children, much happier. They will feel free to go in the warming hut more frequently. A certain amount of climbing will also keep children physically fit and warm, and will save on the cost of tickets besides.

Fifteen Money Savers for the Single Skier

1. *For Beginners.* If you are a beginner, do not worry about getting to that glamorous, far-off ski resort yet. The closer, less sophisticated areas will do until you get your skis under you. Then you can get your money's worth of enjoyment when you travel to the big-name areas. Also, rent your equipment until you are sure if you like the sport. In many instances, the rental fee can be applied toward the purchase of your own equipment.

2. *Skiing Vacation.* Consider a winter vacation. A whole week of skiing (even if not a learn-to-ski week) can cost less than three weekend trips—less money, less travel time, less wear and tear on you.

3. *Single Area.* Consider skiing one area all winter. It can cost less than if you switch areas every weekend. You can buy a season pass, and you will become familiar with one town's characteristics, costs, and people.

4. *Food.* Make your own lunches—but know your area. Some places frown on "brown-baggers"; others set aside a special place in the warming hut for those who bring their own lunch. A word of warning: Buy your food before you come. Resort prices sometimes approximate those of a gold-rush town. Do not leave food to freeze in the car on a very cold day. If everything works out well, you can save money and avoid the line in the cafeteria.

5. *Join a Ski House?* Joining a ski club or an informal group of friends who are planning to rent a lodge on a seasonal basis at an area may be an advantage. But there are many angles to consider. Your lodging and food costs are cut appreciably if the group is large enough. Even après-ski costs are diminished with the probability of Saturday evening parties right at your lodge. Still, if it is going to cost you $100 to join the ski house, this amount is equivalent to twenty-five nights at $4 per in a lodge, or a total of twelve weekends. Are you going to ski this much? Weigh all points. Examine what you are getting for the price. Some summer homes—with no insulation and poor heating—are rented at exorbitant fees. You may be more comfortable in a lodge.

6. *Ski Bum on Weekends.* Many lodges increase their staff on weekends to handle the larger crowds. This arrangement usually takes care of room and board, if not lift tickets or a pass (usually only the full-time ski bum gets a pass).

7. *Dormitories.* If you are looking for less expensive lodgings, consider the dormitories. They are not as costly as more elaborate lodges, and they provide a "get-acquainted" atmosphere for the single skier. Many lodges have several rooms set aside for dormitory-style quarters.

8. *Sleeping Bag.* Your initial investment in a sleeping bag can be recovered by enabling you to obtain less expensive dormitory lodging or even to camp out on friends' sofas. An air mattress is an added expense, but added comfort. Both items can also be used for summer camping.

9. *Ski Lessons.* Generally, beginner classes do not utilize the lifts. Do not spend money on day tickets or a book of individual rides until you discover what the requirements for your class will include.

10. *Individual Lift Ride versus All-Day Ticket.* Attempt to figure in advance how much skiing you will do in a day—then calculate if the number of individual lift rides involved would be less than a day ticket. You can also check on areas that offer a half-day ticket.

11. *Bus Tours.* Bus tours include trans-

portation, lodging, and most meals. Some tours take their own instructors; but check to determine if these instructors are as competent as those employed by the area. Some areas (particularly in the East) do not welcome tour groups. You yourself have to decide whether you want to spend the weekend with a possibly uncongenial tour group. A less restricted, yet economical, variation is the bus which takes the skier to the area but does not tie him tightly to a tour. Bus transportation offers a safety factor which is worth considering if you have ever made the Sunday night drive home drooping with sleep and driving on an icy road.

12. *Automobiles and Car Pools.* If you drive yourself, consider a small economy car. AAA figures show a definitely lower operating cost for domestic and foreign compacts. If you have no car, try to get in a car pool. Some car owners merely elect to charge their riders for gas and oil. But a fairer arrangement for the owner is payment on a basis that covers not only these costs, but also maintenance, depreciation, tires, insurance, etc.

13. *Hitchhike.* If not from your home point (chancy these days), you may at least hitchhike from the lodge to the mountain. At ski areas, it is even respectable for girls to hitchhike.

14. *Use Bulletin Boards at Lodge or Area.* Many single skiers with room in the car will take passengers for little more than gas and oil costs. This is not, strictly speaking, a car pool, since it is generally a one-time trip. Still, many motorists appreciate the company enough to accommodate you at a very low cost. Bulletin boards are also handy to check for used equipment. And should you break one ski, do not spend money on a whole new pair before trying to locate a mate via the bulletin board.

15. *The Going-home Supper.* An increasing number of lodges will willingly provide the home-bound skier with a box lunch to take on the trip back. The expense of eating on the way home is reduced, and the time you would spend stopping for something to eat is eliminated.

UNITED STATES

There are more than 1,200 ski areas in at least forty states. These spots range from small metropolitan hills operating on artificially made snow to lively ski towns with several mountains. For all practical purposes, however, skiing in the United States can be roughly divided into four skiing regions: East, Midwest, Rockies, and Far West.

Each of these regions has its own ski character, influenced largely by geography. Snow conditions and ski slopes within each region also vary greatly, depending on such factors as altitude, exposure, and how far north the hill is located. As a rule, the best skiing snow is found at the higher altitudes in the more northerly locations, especially when the slopes face northward so that they are protected from the sun's melting rays.

East

"Eastern skiing" can range from Beech Mountain Ski Slopes in North Carolina's Blue Ridge country in the South, to Mars Hill, Maine, in the North, and to Oglebay Park, near Wheeling, West Virginia at the East's western extremity. Not surprisingly, considering this geographical spread, skiing in the East offers enormous variety in its snow and conditions.

Most of the skiing in the East is at modest altitudes—between 1,500 and 4,500 feet. This, and the pattern of weather pressure—center movements, plus the proximity of the sea—tend to cause instability of temperature and, hence, of snow conditions. That is, snow conditions are relatively unpredictable from day to day as well as from year to year. Periods of extreme cold alternate with devastating thaws, and a major snow drought can be reasonably expected every five years or so. Winds are occasionally strong, too. In addition, because the mountains are generally fairly heavily wooded, most of the ski trails have had to be carved from the forests. This tends to make them narrower and, because of use, packed hard. But despite these drawbacks, Eastern areas offer some of the most

*Mount Mansfield chair lifts and Smugglers'
Notch.* The first chair lift to be built in the East
(1940) was supplemented twenty years later with a
double chair lift on Mount Mansfield. The lifts
carry 1,350 skiers per hour to twenty different runs
for all degrees of skiing ability.

interesting and stimulating skiing in the
United States, jokes about "Eastern powder"
(heavy, wet snow) notwithstanding.

The most intensive ski terrain in the East is
along the spine of Vermont that is parallel to

the state's Route 100. It is within a few miles
of this highway that some of the East's most
popular ski areas are located—reading from
south to north: Mount Snow, Stratton Mountain, Big Bromley, Magic Mountain, Killington, Sugarbush Valley, Glen Ellen, Mad
River Glen, Stowe, Madonna Mountain, and
Jay Peak. Throughout the state there are
other fine ski areas, too.

In neighboring New Hampshire and Maine,
snow conditions are similar to Vermont and
so are their major ski resorts. Cannon Mountain, Mount Cranmore, Waterville Valley,
and Wildcat Mountain in New Hampshire are
among the most challenging areas in the East.
It is significant that these spots were not
skiable until relatively recently. Fortunately
some of the more rugged aspects of Eastern
skiing "like it used to be" are still to be found
at these areas. Also overlooked until recently
was Sugarloaf in Maine. Not only does this
area offer an impressive number of lifts and
excellent amounts of snow, but it also sports
a distinctive Down East flavor, which it re-
fuses to surrender despite its growing regional
and national fame.

New York State has really one "big mountain" area—Whiteface near Lake Placid, but
there are more than 90 smaller ski areas

Waterville Valley is portrayed in this drawing, with the multi-million-dollar development seen on Mount
Tecumseh on the right, and the old and smaller ski area on Snow's Mountain on the left.

scattered throughout the state all the way to the Pennsylvania border, some only an hour's drive from New York City. Until a few years ago, these areas had no particular distinction. Today, however, they have made up in atmosphere, service, and accommodations for what they lack in terrain. As a result many skiers prefer them to the big-mountain skiing in the West or in Europe. Not all these areas are small. Some, like Belle Ayr, Hunter, Windham, and Gore have challenging trails and can offer a full weekend of top-rate skiing.

Pennsylvania provides fine skiing at such well-known resorts as Camelback, Blue Knob, Elk Mountain, and Seven Springs. Even Laurel Mountain, near Pittsburgh, offers good skiing, though usually on machine-made snow. As previously stated in this section, many areas, even in "good" ski country have installed snowmaking machinery. Except in unusual warm spells, this enables most of them to continue operating even though the surrounding ground is bare. Unfortunately, the cost and water demands of snowmaking are such that it is only suitable for small areas or for small sections of large areas.

The other northeastern states—Massachusetts, Rhode Island, Connecticut, and New Jersey—have a few good areas and are building several new ones. But one of the serious problems of most Eastern ski areas is that they are overcrowded on weekends and undercrowded during the week. Liftline waits of a half hour or longer are not unusual, particularly at the more popular resorts. The ski areas are not unaware of this problem. One of the features of Eastern skiing is that you can get a bargain-rate Sunday afternoon to Friday afternoon vacation. What is more, ski school classes are small during the week. There are more good schools in the East than anywhere else, so it is a good place to learn. If you can ski well in the East, Easterners claim, you can ski well anywhere else.

Midwest

The "flatland" skier, as the Midwest skier is often called, is a breed apart from fellow sportsmen of other regions of the country. In terms of enthusiasm, there are few groups who can match the Midwestern passion for skiing, yet its ski areas are something less than impressive; one wonders how the small hills could generate any enthusiasm for the

A "snow belt" created by Clear Fork makes this area near Butler, Ohio, a ski oasis.

Midwest enthusiasts enjoying fresh powder-snow skiing at the Midwest's highest ski area, Indianhead Mountain in Michigan's Upper Peninsula. In an average year, Indianhead receives more than 250 inches of the "white gold."

sport. A maximum vertical drop of 200 to 600 feet is the best that can be expected in this region. Here, as on Eastern slopes, the trails are generally cut through wooded areas.

Midwestern ski spots compensate for their deficiencies first by featuring good ski schools; second, by lifts and tows by the dozens; and third, by plenty of after-ski activities. Nor are most Midwest ski area owners bashful about lack of vertical drop.

Boyne Country has always been "first" in the Midwest. In 1949, Boyne Mountain began its career with a warming hut and second-hand chair lift—the first chair lift in the Midwest. Today, the Boyne complex—consisting of Boyne Highlands, Boyne Mountain, Thunder Mountain, and Walloon Hills—is not only first in the Midwest, but first in the world to have a quadruple chair lift. But Boyne is by no means unusual in the number of lifts and tows it offers. Mount Telemark, near Hayward, Wisconsin, has a double chair lift, three T-bars, and ten rope tows; Sugar Hills, at Grand Rapids, Minnesota, is similarly equipped; Alpine Valley, at East Troy, Wisconsin, has seven double chair lifts and six rope tows; and Caberfae, near Cadillac, Michigan, holds the record with two chairs, five T-bars, and sixteen rope tows on 340 vertical feet.

Midwesterners have been aided in their passion for practice by growing clusters of ski areas in the suburbs of Detroit, Chicago, Milwaukee, and Minneapolis–St. Paul. Thanks to snowmaking and the bone-chilling cold to be found throughout much of the Midwest in December, January, and early February, these areas offer reliable skiing if not massive mountains. Although the hills as such may offer little real challenge to the expert skier, for learners they can be ideal. For one thing, neither the skier's friends nor his own foolishness will tempt him to slopes and trails beyond his capabilities; for another, having traversed a given slope a number of times, he is likely to find practicing on one slope more appealing than simply going up on one of the high-speed lifts and schussing down again. Thus, what is lacking in impressive terrain in the Midwest is more than made up for by enthusiasm and dedication to the sport of skiing.

The Jackson Hole aerial tram soars to the top of Rendezvous Peak at the Jackson Hole ski area. The aerial tram, one of the world's major tramway installations, rises a total of 4,135 vertical feet over a distance of 2.4 miles from the valley floor and Teton Village to the top of the ski area. Each of the two tram cars holds sixty-three passengers.

Rocky Mountains

The skiing in this region is chiefly between the 5,000-foot and the 11,000-foot levels, some resorts being based as high as 8,000 feet. The longer descents have a vertical drop of up to 3,000 feet, partly over open slopes, but largely on trails through the forest. Many of these trails, however, resemble attenuated open slopes, as they are 300 feet wide or more. The ski season is longer and the snow conditions in the Rockies are usually better than in the East or in the Midwest.

Looking at a map of the Rockies, you will note that these mountains run in a long chain of ranges from New Mexico into Canada, traversing in the process New Mexico, Colorado, Utah, Wyoming, Idaho, Montana, and the Canadian provinces of Alberta and British Columbia. These mountains divide a largely arid plain and are the major source of water for thousands of square miles of land and millions of people. They are the only barrier to intercept the vast storms generated in the North and prevent them from sweeping to the East and South. As a result the Rocky Mountains not only get vast quantities of snow, but owing to the general aridity of that part of the continent, the snow has a particular quality which makes it ideal for skiing. The dry powder of the Rocky Mountains, however, is not uniformly dry. The southern Rocky Mountain states—Utah, Colorado, and New Mexico—are more arid than the northern states, and as a consequence their powder is drier. On the other hand, snow depths are greater in the northern Rockies. Such differences between subregions are not substantial, however, and matter only to dyed-in-the-wool powder enthusiasts. The quality of this snow is legendary. Not even Europe can match its

Just a half hour's hiking from the world-famed resort of Alta brings a group of ski tourers to a number of magnificent glacial cirques surrounded by serrated ridges such as Cardiac Ridge. This ridge is over 11,000 feet high, and crossing it leads Utah ski tourers into a ski run nearly 5 miles long, with a vertical drop of about 4,500 feet.

consistency. Even when packed, it rarely packs into hard snow or ice.

The Rocky Mountains were the site of America's first real ski resort—Sun Valley. Since the opening of Sun Valley in 1936, the region has added such famous names as Alta, Aspen, Jackson Hole, Park City, Taos Ski Valley, and Vail to its growing list of well-known resorts. This by no means exhausts the list. There are others with more than adequate slopes and lifts for several days of interesting and challenging skiing: Winter Park, Arapahoe Basin, Loveland Basin, Steamboat Springs, Purgatory, and Breckenridge in Colorado; Red River, Sierra Blanco, and Santa Fe Ski Basin in New Mexico; Solitude, Brighton, and Sundance in Utah; Bogus Basin, Brundage Mountain, and Schweitzer Basin in Idaho; and Red Lodge, Big Mountain, and the Missoula Snow Bowl

in Montana are all areas that would be more prominent were it not for the reputations of glamor spots of Aspen, Sun Valley, Vail, and other "big" Rocky Mountain resorts.

Part of the Rocky Mountain ski legend maintains that it snows only at night and that the sun shines every day. Were it only so. It is true that overall the region has more sunny winter days than other ski regions in the United States, but this is no guarantee that the weather is always bright. With a lot of skiing done on relatively open slopes at high altitude, there are occasional whiteouts when skiers find themselves actually skiing in the clouds. So-called flat light is not uncommon in other ski regions, but it is more of a problem for the skier in the Rockies because of the absence of reference points on the open slope. This makes it difficult to judge the steepness of the slope and the character of the

A panorama of Sun Valley Village, Idaho.

terrain. These drawbacks aside, Rocky Mountain skiing is American skiing at its best. It is not surprising that the region contains the country's most prestigious resorts and that even its smaller resorts match the largest resorts of other regions in size, if not necessarily in facilities.

Far West

This region covers the Pacific Coast from the southern Sierra Nevada, north into Canada and Alaska.

As far as skiing altitudes, the Pacific Coast mountain chains are about the same as the Rockies. The trail conditions are similar, too. Snow falls in the High Sierra region of California are unusually reliable, so reliable in fact that there is more apt to be too much snow than too little. At least once a year, the Sierra resorts are overwhelmed by a massive snowfall that may drop as much as two feet

an hour for days at a time. So there is always a certain risk that you will get snowed in. There is also a good likelihood that the snow will be on the wet side. Warmed by the brilliant Sierra sun, it can make for sticky going, particularly in the latter part of the season.

The snow in the Pacific Northwest is frequently on the damp side; but like the skiers, it is of a hardy variety, perfectly capable of resisting an occasional downpour. Moreover it comes early, stays late, and is deep. In fact, Pacific Northwest skiers hardly know when one season ends and the next one begins.

Skiing in California is concentrated in two relatively small sections of the state. Within 100 miles of Los Angeles, there is a cluster of about a dozen areas catering mostly to residents of that city. The other cluster is to be found in the Donner Pass–Lake Tahoe region in the center of the High Sierra. The most famous of this group is Squaw Valley, site of the 1960 Olympic Winter Games. The '60

Squaw Valley, California, was the scene of 1960 Winter Olympic Games.

At Alpine Meadows, California, a solitary skier makes his way down Ward Peak and into Ward Bowl.

Games focused attention on this region, and things have never been the same since. Where there was nothing in 1950, there is now a completely self-sustained village with a lively nightlife. Although nightclub entertainment is available at nearby Reno and Stateline, the crowd that stays in the Valley evenings is an active one. Other ski resorts in the Donner Pass–Lake Tahoe region include Heavenly Valley, Alpine Meadows, and Sugar Bowl. South of this region, but still in High Sierra, are the two well-known resorts of Bear Valley and Mammoth Mountain.

Standing alone in the northern part of California is Mount Shasta. High above timberline Shasta offers open bowl skiing with many different routes of descent and a season that runs from late November to the beginning of June. Panoramic skiing, friendly people, and informal living all help make Shasta a prime ski area in the Far West.

Pacific Northwest skiing has the advantage

Timberline Lodge, located 60 miles east of Portland, Oregon, on the south slopes of Mount Hood.

of being eminently available. The Seattle or Portland skier merely has to throw his skis in the car and drive for an hour or so to get all the skiing he wants—a choice of three areas on the flanks of Mount Hood if he lives in Portland; a choice of three areas in Snoqualmie Pass if he lives in Seattle. Other major ski spots include White Pass, Mount Bachelor, Crystal Mountain, and Mount Baker.

Alaska and Hawaii

Although our forty-ninth state has a reputation as the land of snow and ice, Alaska was late in its ski arrival. Rapid strides have been made since snow shoes were the favored mode of winter transportation. Alyeska, not far from Anchorage, is a major area by any measure and has lots of snow, a long season, and surprisingly mild temperatures. It has many open slopes and dramatic vistas. The sourdough atmosphere is prevalent, but there is also a considerable international flavor since Anchorage is a stop of several transpolar flights.

Speaking of our new states, our fiftieth also has skiing. True, Hawaii, with its mild and

Scene from the Thundermug Jumping Contest at Mount Baker held each July 4.

Varied ski runs start from the Sun Deck at the top of Alyeska's double chair lift. Turnagain arm of the Pacific Ocean is far below.

balmy climate which varies little from season to season, is far from being a winter sports resort. However, the two big volcanic peaks of "The Big Island," as Hawaii is called, sweep from the sea to well over 13,000 feet into the mid-Pacific skies, and the tops of the cones are white during several months of the year. Thus skiing is definitely an exotic sport in the Islands. The dyed-in-the-wool skier who is willing to cope for the arduous climb and the five-figure altitude can find slopes big enough for really long runs among spectacular surroundings when conditions are right— which is most likely in February or early March.

SKI AREAS: UNITED STATES

More than 800 ski areas are listed in the following guide. Space limitations do not permit listing of the many smaller rope-tow areas. Therefore, all areas included here have a minimum of four rope tows, or at least one T-bar, platterpull, or other lift device. The areas listed in italics type have two or more chair lifts or a tramway or gondola lift, while those marked with an asterisk are major ski resorts. North American tourist bureaus are listed separately on page 388.

Name of Area	Location (nearest town or postal address)	Kinds of Lifts						Total Vertical Descent (in feet)	Snow-making
		Gondolas, tramways	Chair lifts	T-bars	Platterpulls	J-bars	Rope-tows		
Alaska									
Alyeska	Girdwood		x		x		x	2,200	
Arctic Ski Valley	Anchorage		x	x			x	990	
Cleary Summit	Fairbanks			x		x	x	1,200	
Skiland	Fairbanks			x			x	1,200	
Ullrhaven	Fairbanks						x	400	
Arizona									
Arizona Snow Bowl	Flagstaff		x		x		x	2,100	
Big Cienega	McNary			x			x	450	
Mt. Lemmon	Tucson				x		x	875	
Mt. Williams	Williams				x		x	400	
Sunrise Park	Pinetop		x	x	x			650	
California									
*Alpine Meadows**	Tahoe City		x	x	x			1,600	
Badger Pass	Yosemite Nat'l Park		x	x			x	700	
*Bear Valley**	Arnold		x				x	2,500	
Blue Ridge Ski Area	Wrightwood		x				x	1,100	
Boreal Ridge	Truckee		x	x			x	600	
China Peak	Huntington Lake		x	x			x	1,450	
Cottage Springs	Camp Connell				x		x	200	
Dodge Ridge	Long Barn		x		x		x	1,050	
Donner Ski Area	Norden		x		x		x	826	
Echo Summit	South Lake Tahoe				x		x	400	
Granlibakken	Tahoe City				x		x	450	
Green Valley Snow Bowl	San Bernardino				x		x	350	
*Heavenly Valley**	South Lake Tahoe	x	x	x			x	3,600	
Holiday Hill	Wrightwood		x		x		x	1,600	
Homewood Ski Area	Homewood		x	x	x	x	x	1,200	
June Mountain	June Lake		x	x			x	2,535	
Kirkwood Meadows	Carson Pass		x				x	3,000	
Kratka Ridge	Angles Crest		x				x	800	
Lassen Park	National Park				x		x	500	
*Mammoth Mountain**	Mammoth Lakes	x	x	x				2,000	
Moonridge	Bear Lake				x		x	900	x
Mt. Baldy	Upland		x		x	x		2,100	
Mt. Shasta Ski Bowl	Mt. Shasta		x	x			x	1,933	
Mt. Waterman	La Canada		x				x	600	
North Star	Truckee		x					1,500	
Papoose Ski Area	Tahoe City				x		x	150	x
Peddler Hill	Jackson			x		x	x	700	
Pla-Vada Hills	Soda Springs			x	x		x	370	
Plumas Eureka Ski Bowl	Portola				x		x	600	
Powder Bowl	Deer Park				x		x	1,000	
Rebel Ridge	Big Bear Lake			x	x		x	400	x
Sierra Ski Ranch	Twin Bridges		x		x		x	860	
Snow Forest	Big Bear Lake		x		x		x	700	x
Snow Summit	Big Bear Lake		x				x	1,300	x
Snow Valley	Running Springs		x		x		x	900	x
Soda Springs	Soda Springs		x	x		x	x	650	
*Squaw Valley**	Tahoe City	x	x		x			1,850	
*Sugar Bowl**	Norden		x	x			x	1,600	
Table Mountain	Wrightwood				x		x	800	
Tahoe Ski Bowl	Tahoe City		x				x	750	

Name of Area	Location (nearest town or postal address)	Gondolas, tramways	Chair lifts	T-bars	Platterpulls	J-bars	Rope-tows	Total Vertical Descent (in feet)	Snow-making
Wolverton Ski Bowl	Sequoia Nat'l Park						x	1,000	
Colorado									
*Arapahoe Basin**	Dillon		x		x			3,300	
Aspen/Ajax	Aspen		x					3,282	
*Aspen Highlands**	Aspen		x		x			3,800	
*Aspen Mountain**	Aspen		x					3,300	
Berthoud Pass	Idaho Springs		x	x				685	x
Breckenridge	Breckenridge		x	x	x			1,900	
*Buttermilk**	Aspen		x	x				2,250	
Cooper Hill	Leadville			x	x			1,200	
Copper Mountain	Vail		x		x			2,436	
Cranor Ski Hill	Gunnison				x			262	x
Crested Butte	Crested Butte	x	x	x		x		2,100	
Cuchara Ski Basin	Cuchara				x			346	
Fun Valley	Littleton		x		x		x	550	x
Geneva Basin	Grant		x	x			x	1,150	
Glenwood	Glenwood Springs		x					200	
Grand Mesa	Mesa			x			x	800	
Hesperus Ski Center	Durango			x			x	600	
Hidden Valley	Estes Park			x			x	850	x
Holiday Hills	Woodland Park					x	x	400	
Howelsen Hill	Steamboat Springs			x			x	800	
Keystone	Dillon		x		x			2,400	
Lake Eldora	Nederland		x	x				1,200	
Loveland	Georgetown		x	x	x		x	1,050	
Meadow Mountain	Minturn		x		x			900	
Monarch	Salida		x	x	x			890	
Mt. Werner	Steamboat Springs		x		x			2,850	
Pike's Peak	Colorado Springs				x		x	350	
Powderhorn	Grand Junction		x		x			200	
Purgatory	Durango		x		x		x	1,500	
Silver Hills	Wetmore				x		x	200	
Ski Broadmoor	Colorado Springs		x					640	x
Ski Dallas	Norwood			x				800	
Ski Idlewild	Winter Park		x		x			400	
*Snowmass**	Aspen		x	x				3,500	
Squaw Pass	Denver			x			x	700	
Stagecoach	Steamboat Springs		x					1,850	
Steamboat	Steamboat Springs			x			x	500	
Stoner	Cortez			x			x	1,225	
Sunlight Ski Area	Glenwood Springs		x		x			1,800	
Telluride	Montrose		x					3,200	
*Vail**	Vail	x	x		x			3,050	
*Winter Park**	Winter Park		x	x				1,700	
Wolf Creek	Monte Vista				x		x	1,050	
Connecticut									
Mohawk Mountain	Cornwall		x		x		x	750	x
Mt. Southington	Southington		x	x			x	425	x
Powder Hill	Middlefield		x	x			x	475	x
Satan's Ridge	New Hartford		x	x			x	554	x
Ski Sundown	New Hartford		x	x			x	570	x
Tapawingo	Woodbury			x			x	225	x
Idaho									
Bald Mountain	Pierce			x			x	700	

Name of Area	Location (nearest town or postal address)	Gondolas, tramways	Chair lifts	T-bars	Platterpulls	J-bars	Rope-tows	Total Vertical Descent (in feet)	Snow-making
		Kinds of Lifts							
Bear Gulch	Ashton		x	x			x	725	
Blizzard Mountain	Moore				x		x	800	
Bogus Basin*	Boise		x		x		x	1,500	
Brundage Mountain	McCall		x		x		x	1,550	
Caribou	Pocatello		x				x	715	
Cottonwood Butte	Cottonwood			x			x	875	
Jackass Ski Bowl	Kellogg		x				x	1,900	
Kelly Canyon	Ririe		x				x	866	
Grand Targhee	Driggs		x				x	2,000	
Lookout Pass	Wallace				x		x	750	
Lost Trail Pass	Salmon				x		x	770	
Hitt Mountain	Cambridge			x			x	500	
Magic Mountain	Twin Falls			x	x		x	1,000	
Moscow Mountain	Moscow			x			x	400	
North-South Ski Bowl	Harvard			x	x		x	500	
Payette Lakes	McCall				x		x	900	
Pine Basin	Swan Valley				x		x	1,000	
Pomerelle	Albion		x		x		x	1,000	
Rotarun	Hailey					x	x	400	
Rupert	Albion		x		x		x	1,000	
Schweitzer Basin*	Sandpoint		x	x			x	2,000	
Skyline	Pocatello		x		x		x	1,650	
Soldier Mountain	Fairfield				x	x	x	800	
Sun Valley*	Sun Valley		x	x				3,282	
Tamarach	Troy			x			x	900	
Taylor Mountain	Idaho Falls		x		x		x	780	
Illinois									
Buffalo Park	Algonquin						x	200	x
Chestnut Mountain	Galena		x				x	465	x
Four Lakes	Lisle						x	125	x
Fox Trails	Gary						x	135	x
Gander Mountain	Spring Grove				x		x	200	x
Holiday Park	Fox Lake		x				x	200	x
Indiana									
Mt. Wawasee	New Pairs	x		x			x	175	x
The Pines	Valparaiso						x	110	x
Ski Valley	LaPorte						x	120	x
Tamarack	Angola		x		x		x	270	x
Iowa									
Crescent Ski Hills	Council Bluffs				x		x	200	x
Holiday Mountain	Estherville				x		x	175	x
Winter Playland	Humboldt						x	125	x
Ski Pal	Mount Vernon						x	250	x
Nor-Ski Runs	Decorah						x	250	x
Kansas									
Greenwood Heights	Beaumont		x	x				158	
Mont Bleu	Lawrence			x			x	230	x
Maine									
Baker Mountain	Bingham			x				400	
Bald Mountain	Dedham		x	x			x	800	
Camden Snow Bowl	Camden			x			x	900	
Chisholm Winter Park	Rumford			x				900	

Name of Area	Location (nearest town or postal address)	Gondolas, tramways	Chair lifts	T-bars	Platterpulls	J-bars	Rope-tows	Total Vertical Descent (in feet)	Snow-making
Colby College Ski Area	Waterville			x			x	265	x
Eaton Mountain	Skowhegan		x				x	500	
Enchanted Mountain	Jackman		x	x				1,000	
Lost Valley	Auburn		x	x			x	236	x
Mars Hill Ski Area	Mars Hill				x		x	610	
May Mountain	Island Falls			x				400	
Mt. Abram	Locke Mills			x				940	
Mt. Agamenticus	York		x	x			x	500	x
Mt. Hermon	Hermon			x			x	300	
Mt. Jefferson	Lee			x			x	410	
Northmen	Caribou			x				350	
Pleasant Mountain	Bridgton		x	x				1,200	
Poland Spring	Poland Spring			x			x	350	
Saddleback Mountain	Rangeley		x	x				1,400	
Sky-Hy Park	Topsham			x			x	215	x
Snow Mountain	Winterport			x			x	800	
Spring Hill	South Berwick					x	x	700	
Squaw Mountain	Greenville			x	x			1,750	
Sugarloaf	Kingfield	x		x	x			2,406	
Sunday River Skiway	Bethel			x				1,400	
Titcomb Memorial	Farmington				x		x	400	
White Bunny	Fort Fairfield			x				300	

Maryland

Name of Area	Location	Gondolas, tramways	Chair lifts	T-bars	Platterpulls	J-bars	Rope-tows	Total Vertical Descent	Snow-making
Braddock Hts. Ski Way	Braddock Heights			x			x	120	x
Deep Creek Lake	Cumberland				x		x	500	x
Oregon Ridge	Cockeysville		x					300	x
Wisp	Oakland		x	x	x		x	600	x

Massachusetts

Name of Area	Location	Gondolas, tramways	Chair lifts	T-bars	Platterpulls	J-bars	Rope-tows	Total Vertical Descent	Snow-making
Amesbury	Amesbury				x		x	220	x
Avaloch	Lenox			x			x	200	
Beartown State	South Lee						x	100	
Benjamin Hill	Shirley			x			x	105	x
Berkshire Snow Basin	West Cummington			x			x	551	x
Blanchard Hill	Dunstable			x			x	205	x
Blue Hills	Canton		x			x	x	350	x
Boston Hill	Andover					x	x	250	x
Bousquet's	Pittsfield		x	x	x		x	750	x
Brodie Mountain	New Ashford		x	x			x	1,250	x
Butternut Basin	Great Barrington		x	x			x	1,000	x
Catamount	South Egremont		x	x			x	1,000	x
Chickley Alp	Charlemont			x			x	230	
Eastover	Lenox		x				x	200	x
Groton Hills	Groton						x	145	x
Hansen Ski Slope	Waltham			x			x	100	x
Hartwell Hill	Littleton						x	175	
Indian Head	East Pepperell			x			x	320	
Jiminy Peak	Hancock		x	x			x	1,120	x
Jug End	South Egremont			x			x	500	
Innsbruck Ski Area	Franklin		x				x	500	x
Leominster	Leominster			x		x		225	x
Locke's Ski Tows	Amesbury						x	350	
Mohawk Mountain	Greenfield			x			x	450	
Mt. Tom	Holyoke		x	x	x	x	x	840	x
Mt. Wachusett	Princeton			x				625	
Mt. Watatlc	Ashby			x			x	550	
Nashoba Valley	Littleton						x	240	x

Name of Area	Location (nearest town or postal address)	Gondolas, tramways	Chair lifts	T-bars	Platterpulls	J-bars	Rope-tows	Total Vertical Descent (in feet)	Snow-making
Otis Ridge	Otis			x	x	x	x	345	x
Page Hill	Peabody			x			x	210	
Pheasant Run	Leominster			x			x	225	x
Petersbury Pass	Williamstown		x		x		x	950	
Sea View	Rowley		x				x	166	
Snow Hill	Athol		x				x	200	
Springfield Ski Club	Blandford						x	400	
Thunder Mountain	Charlemont		x	x		x	x	1,000	x
Wachusett	Westminster			x			x	625	x
Ward Hill	East Shrewsbury			x			x	200	x

Michigan

Name of Area	Location	Gondolas, tramways	Chair lifts	T-bars	Platterpulls	J-bars	Rope-tows	Total Vertical Descent	Snow-making
Alpine Valley	Pontiac		x	x			x	200	x
Apple Mountain	Freeland						x	160	x
Au Sable Ski Club	Gaylord				x		x	300	
Barn Mountain	Boyne City		x		x		x	355	
Bear Mountain	Grayling		x	x	x		x	195	x
Big-M	Manistee		x	x			x	315	x
*Big Powderhorn**	Bessemer		x	x			x	200	x
*Boyne Highlands**	Harbor Springs		x	x	x			568	x
*Boyne Mountain**	Boyne Falls		x				x	500	x
Brady's Hill	Lakeview						x	200	x
Briar Hill	Mesick						x	300	x
Brule Mountain	Iron River		x	x			x	400	x
*Caberfae**	Cadillac		x	x			x	340	x
Cannonsburg	Grand Rapids			x			x	210	x
Carousel Mountain	Holland		x	x		x	x	311	x
Chimney Corners	Frankfort						x	250	
Cliff's Ridge	Marquette			x			x	435	x
Crystal Mountain	Thompsonville		x		x		x	370	x
Dryden	Rochester						x	150	
Eskar	Middleville						x	325	x
Glacier Hills	Bellaire		x				x	265	
Gladstone	Gladstone						x	140	
Grampign Mountain	Oxford			x	x		x	150	x
Grand Haven	Grand Haven						x	130	
Grayling Winter Park	Grayling			x			x	150	x
Hickory Hills	Traverse City						x	525	
Houghton Lake	Houghton						x	300	
*Indianhead Mountain**	Wakefield		x	x	x		x	638	x
Irish Hills	Clinton			x			x	165	x
Iroquois Mountain	Brimley		x				x	400	
Lansing Ski Club	Lansing						x	125	x
Major Mountain	Clare						x	205	
Maplehurst	Elk Rapids				x		x	250	
Mio Mountain	Mio						x	250	
Mont Ripley	Houghton			x			x	408	
Mott Mountain	Farwell						x	200	x
Mt. Brighton	Southfield		x			x	x	218	x
Mt. Christie	Oxford			x			x	180	
Mt. Frederick	Frederick			x			x	200	x
Mt. Holly	Pontiac		x	x			x	200	x
Mt. Mancelona	Mancelona			x	x		x	300	
Mt. Maria	Lincoln				x		x	265	x
Nub's Nob	Harbor Springs		x		x		x	427	x
Ogemaw Hills	West Branch		x				x	110	
Pando	Grand Rapids						x	100	x
Pine Knob	Clarkston		x				x	130	x

Name of Area	Location (nearest town or postal address)	Gondolas, tramways	Chair lifts	T-bars	Platterpulls	J-bars	Rope-tows	Total Vertical Descent (in feet)	Snow-making
*Pine Mountain**	Iron Mountain		x				x	375	x
Pinnacles	Gaylord		x				x	235	x
Porcupine Mountain	Ontonagon			x			x	600	
*Schuss Mountain**	Mancelona		x				x	400	x
Shanty Creek	Bellaire		x	x	x		x	387	x
Sheridan Valley	Lewiston				x		x	250	
Silverbell	Pontiac						x	225	x
Skyline	Graybury		x				x	220	
Snow Snake Mountain	Clare						x	200	
Sugar Loaf	Traverse		x			x		400	
Swiss Valley	Three Rivers						x	200	
Sylvan Knob	Gaylord				x		x	250	
Teeple Hill	Pontiac						x	100	
Thunder Mountain	Boyne Falls		x	x	x		x	450	x
Timberlee	Traverse City		x	x			x	380	x
Timber Ridge	Plainvell						x	212	
Traverse City Holiday	Traverse City				x		x	275	x
Walloon Hills	Walloon Lake		x	x	x		x	400	x
Ward Hills	Baldwin						x	200	

Minnesota

Name of Area	Location (nearest town or postal address)	Gondolas, tramways	Chair lifts	T-bars	Platterpulls	J-bars	Rope-tows	Total Vertical Descent (in feet)	Snow-making
Afton Alps	Afton		x	x	x		x	270	x
Breezy Point	Breezy Point		x				x	130	
Buck Hill	Minneapolis		x	x		x	x	310	x
Buena Vista	Bemidji						x	225	
Buffalo Valley	Buffalo				x		x	225	
Cedar Hills	Shakopee						x	150	x
Detroit Mountain	Detroit Lakes				x		x	230	x
Giant's Ridge	Biwabik				x		x	440	
Hallaway Ski Hill	Pelican Rapids						x	200	
Hidden Valley	Ely					x	x	145	
Hyland Hills	Minneapolis						x	200	x
Inver Hills	St. Paul				x		x	218	x
Lookout Mountain	Virginia		x				x	305	x
Lutsen	Lutsen		x	x			x	630	x
Mont Du Lac	Duluth				x		x	310	x
Moon Valley	Shakopee				x		x	196	x
Mt. Frontenac	Red Wing				x		x	420	x
Pine Bend	St. Paul					x	x	258	x
Powder Ridge	Kimball		x	x			x	250	x
Quandna Mountain	Hill City				x		x	375	x
Ski Devil	Fertile						x	150	
Ski Gull	Brainerd				x		x	285	
Ski-Tonka	Minneapolis						x	225	x
Sugar Hills	Grand Rapids		x	x			x	350	x
Theodore Wirth	Minneapolis						x	125	
Timberlane	Red Lake Falls						x	110	
Val Chatel	Park Rapids		x				x	275	x
Val Croix	Taylor Falls				x		x	258	
Welch Village	Red Wing		x	x			x	330	x

Missouri

Name of Area	Location (nearest town or postal address)	Gondolas, tramways	Chair lifts	T-bars	Platterpulls	J-bars	Rope-tows	Total Vertical Descent (in feet)	Snow-making
Ski Tan-tar-a	Camdenton				x		x	175	x

Montana

Name of Area	Location (nearest town or postal address)	Gondolas, tramways	Chair lifts	T-bars	Platterpulls	J-bars	Rope-tows	Total Vertical Descent (in feet)	Snow-making
Bear Paw	Havre				x		x	800	

Name of Area	Location (nearest town or postal address)	Kinds of Lifts						Total Vertical Descent (in feet)	Snow-making
		Gondolas, tramways	Chair lifts	T-bars	Platterpulls	J-bars	Rope-tows		
Beef Trail	Butte			x			x	680	
Belmont	Marysville				x		x	1,500	
Big Mountain	Whitefish		x	x	x		x	2,000	
Big Sky	Gallatin Gateway		x	x	x			2,230	
Bridger Bowl	Bozeman		x	x	x			1,530	
Butte Ski Club	Butte			x			x	800	
Deep Creek	Wise River			x			x	900	
Ennis	Ennis				x			1,500	
Grass Mountain	White Sulphur Spring				x		x	565	
King's Hill	Neihart			x	x		x	1,000	
Chief Joseph Snow Bowl	W. Yellowstone		x	x			x	2,175	
Lookout Pass	Wallace				x		x	780	
Cooke City	Cooke City				x		x	2,000	
Corona Lake	Plains			x			x	800	
Lost Trail	Hamilton				x		x	600	
Marshall Mountain	Missoula			x	x		x	800	x
Missoula Snow Bowl	Missoula		x	x	x		x	2,600	
Rainy Mountain	Dillon		x		x		x	1,600	
Red Lodge Mountain	Red Lodge		x	x				910	
Sundance	Red Lodge		x				x	700	
Turner Mountain	Libby			x			x	2,165	
Teton Pass	Chateau				x		x	800	
Wraith Hill	Anaconda						x	500	
Z-T Ski Area	Butte			x	x		x	1,000	
Nevada									
Lee Canyon	Las Vegas		x				x	1,000	
Mt. Charleston	Las Vegas	x					x	500	
Mt. Rose	Reno		x	x			x	1,500	
Ski Incline	Reno		x	x				700	x
Slide Mountain	Reno		x					2,000	x
Tannenbaum	Reno			x	x		x	535	
New Hampshire									
Arrowhead	Claremont				x		x	650	
Attitash	Bartlet		x	x				1,525	
Black Mountain	Jackson		x	x		x		850	x
Bretton Woods	Twin Mountain		x	x				625	
Brookline	Brookline			x			x	600	x
*Cannon Mountain**	Franconia	x	x	x				2,210	x
Copple Crown	New Durham			x			x	500	
Crotched Mountain	Francestown		x	x				800	x
Dartmouth Skiway	Lyme		x	x	x			900	
Fitzwilliam	Fitzwilliam				x		x	240	x
Gunstock	Laconia		x	x			x	1,400	
Highlands	Northfield			x			x	700	
Intervale	Intervale			x	x			600	
King Pine Ski Area	East Madison		x			x	x	300	
King Ridge	New London				x		x	495	
Loon Mountain	Lincoln	x	x					1,800	
Meriden	Meriden				x		x	300	
Mittersill	Franconia		x	x				800	x
Moose Mountain	Brookfield		x	x			x	940	
*Mount Cranmore**	North Conway	x	x		x			1,360	x
Mt. Rowe	Gilford			x				370	x
Mt. Sunapee	Newbury		x	x	x			1,500	

Name of Area	Location (nearest town or postal address)	Kinds of Lifts						Total Vertical Descent (in feet)	Snow-making
		Gondolas, tramways	Chair lifts	T-bars	Platterpulls	J-bars	Rope-tows		
Mt. Whittier	West Ossipee	x		x			x	1,650	
Onset Mountain	Bennington		x	x				800	
Pat's Peak	Henniker		x	x			x	700	
Pinnacle Mountain	Keene					x	x	350	
Purity Springs	East Madison		x			x	x	350	
Ragged Mountain	Danbury		x	x				1,200	
Snowcrest	Lebanon			x				500	
Snow's Mountain	Waterville Valley			x				600	
Spruce Mountain	Jackson				x			210	
Temple Mountain	Peterborough			x	x		x	450	x
Tenney Mountain	Plymouth		x	x				1,300	
Tyrol	Jackson		x	x	x			700	
*Waterville Valley**	Waterville Valley		x	x		x		2,020	x
*Wildcat**	Pinkham Notch	x	x	x				2,050	
Wilderness	Colebrook		x	x				1,000	
New Jersey									
Belle Mountain	Lamberville			x			x	190	
Camp Gaw Mt.	Ramsey		x	x				265	x
Craigmeur	Danville			x			x	205	x
Great Gorge	McAfee		x		x		x	1,033	x
Jugtown Mountain	West Portal		x				x	305	x
Mt. Peter	Greenwood Lake		x				x	325	x
Pine Hill	Pine Hill			x				127	
Ski Mountain	Pine Hill			x			x	500	x
Snow Bowl	Dover			x			x	205	x
Thompson Park	Jamesburg			x			x	110	x
Vernon Valley	Vernon		x	x			x	198	x
New Mexico									
Ançel Fire	Eagle Nest		x					2,100	
Pajarito	Los Alamos		x	x			x	1,140	
Powder Puff Mountain	Red River		x		x		x	100	
Raton Ski Basin	Raton			x				223	
Red River	Red River		x	x				1,600	x
Sandia Peak	Albuquerque	x	x	x	x			1,750	
Santa Fe Ski Basin	Santa Fe		x		x			1,800	
Sierra Blanca	Ruidoso	x	x	x	x		x	1,700	
Sipapu	Taos				x			437	
Ski Cloudcroft	Cloudcroft			x				460	x
*Taos Ski Valley**	Taos		x		x		x	2,580	
Val Verde	Eagle Nest			x			x	138	
New York									
Adirondack Center	Saratoga Springs			x				274	
Andes Ski Center	Andes		x				x	850	
Bald Hill	Farmingville			x			x	180	x
Belleayre Mt.	Pine Hill		x	x		x		1,200	
Big Basin	Salamanca				x		x	208	
Big Bear	Vega			x		x	x	1,000	
Big Tupper	Tupper Lake		x	x				800	
Big Vanilla at Davos	Woodridge		x	x			x	500	x
Birch Hill	Brewster		x	x			x	300	x
Brantling	Newark			x			x	215	x
Bristol Mountain	Canandaigua		x	x		x		1,050	x
Catamount	Hillsdale		x	x			x	1,000	x
Catskill Ski Center	Andes			x				911	

Name of Area	Location (nearest town or postal address)	Gondolas, tramways	Chair lifts	T-bars	Platterpulls	J-bars	Rope-tows	Total Vertical Descent (in feet)	Snow-making
Cockaigne	Sinclairville		x			x		425	x
Colgate Outing Club	Hamilton			x				348	x
Columbia Ski Resort	Hurleyville			x			x	410	x
Concord	Monticello			x			x	300	x
Delaware Ski Center	Andes			x				1,050	
Drumlins	Syracuse					x	x	100	
Dry Hill	Watertown		x	x			x	250	x
Dutchess Ski Area	Beacon		x					588	x
Eagle Mountain	Sloatsburg		x	x			x	380	x
Eagle Ridge	Westfield		x	x				300	
Easton Valley	Greenwich		x			x		420	x
Fahnestock	Carmel			x	x		x	240	x
Fawn Ridge	Lake Placid				x			150	
Frost Ridge	LeRoy			x			x	134	x
Garnet Mountain	North Creek			x				400	
Glenwood Acres	Glenwood			x			x	517	x
Gore Mt. Ski Center	North Creek	x	x	x		x		2,100	
Greek Peak	Cortland		x	x	x		x	750	
Grossinger Ski Valley	Liberty			x			x	190	x
Grosstal	Allegany		x	x			x	813	x
Gunset Ski Bowl	Richfield Springs				x		x	300	
Harvey Mountain	North Creek			x				405	
Hickory Hill	Warrensburg			x	x		x	600	
Hidden Valley	Lake Luzerne			x				120	x
Highmount	Highmount			x			x	975	
Holiday Mountain	Monticello		x		x	x	x	235	x
Holiday Valley	Ellicottville		x	x			x	700	
Holimont	Ellicottville		x	x			x	560	
Homestead	Pattersonville			x			x	450	
Honey Hill	Warsaw			x			x	130	
Hunter Mountain	Hunter		x	x	x		x	1,600	x
Innsbruck USA	Binghamton			x		x		480	x
Intermont	Solon	x	x					800	x
Ironwood Ridge	Cazenovia			x				550	x
Juniper Hills	Harrisville			x		x		200	
Kissing Bridge	Glenwood	x	x				x	490	x
Kutsher's Country Club	Monticello			x	x		x	75	
Labrador Mountain	Truxton			x			x	680	x
Lake Placid Ski Center	Lake Placid				x			200	
Marcy Lake Center	Lake Placid				x			100	
McCauley Mountain	Old Forge		x					600	
Moon Valley	Malone	x	x					460	
Mt. Cathalla	Ellenville	x	x				x	500	x
Mt. Otsego	Cooperstown			x			x	400	
Mt. Peter	Warwick	x					x	340	x
Mt. Pisgah Ski Center	Saranac Lake			x			x	300	
Mt. Storm	Stormsville			x	x		x	600	x
Mystic Mountain	Cazenovia			x				590	
North Creek Ski Bowl	North Creek			x				900	
Oak Mountain	Speculator			x			x	650	
Orange County Ski Area	Montgomery			x				150	x
Paleface Ski Center	Wilmington	x	x					730	
Parkway	Utica			x			x	220	
Peek'n Peak	French Creek	x	x		x			340	
Petersburg Pass	Petersburg	x						800	
Phoenicia Ski Center	Phoenicia					x		450	
Pine Ridge	Salisburg					x		150	
Pines Ski Center	South Fallsburg	x					x	159	

Name of Area	Location (nearest town or postal address)	Gondolas, tramways	Chair lifts	T-bars	Platterpulls	J-bars	Rope-tows	Total Vertical Descent (in feet)	Snow-making
Plattekill Mountain	Roxbury		x				x	970	
Poverty Hill	Ellicottville		x	x				435	
Rock Candy Mountain	Troy		x				x	250	x
Royal Mountain	Johnstown		x				x	550	
St. Lawrence Snow Bowl	South Colton		x				x	300	
Scotch Valley	Stamford	x	x				x	750	x
Scott's Cobble	Lake Placid				x			380	
Seven Springs	Parishville		x				x	300	
Shayne's	Highmount					x		2,200	
Silver Bells	Wells		x				x	400	
Silvermine	Bear Mountain		x		x		x	210	x
Sitzmarker Ski Club	Colden		x				x	385	
Skiland	East Berne					x	x	300	
Ski-Minnewaska	New Paltz		x			x	x	360	x
Ski Valley	Naples		x			x	x	560	x
Snow Ridge	Turin	x	x					500	
Song Mountain	Tully		x			x		600	x
Sterling Forest	Tuxedo	x			x		x	400	x
Stony Point	Stony Point	x			x			300	x
Swain	Nunda		x					607	x
Tall Timber	Van Etten		x		x			400	x
Toggenburg	Fabius		x		x			580	x
Val Bialas Ski Center	Utica	x	x				x	300	x
Van Cortland Park	The Bronx						x	100	x
Villagio	Haines Falls				x		x	125	x
Wallkill Park	Goshen		x					133	
Western Chautauqua	Clymer		x			x		410	
West Mountain	Glens Falls		x		x		x	1,010	x
White Acres	Utica		x				x	350	
*Whiteface Mountain**	Wilmington	x	x			x		2,400	x
Willard Mountain	North Easton		x				x	456	
Windham	Windham	x	x				x	1,500	x
Win-Sum	Ellicottville	x	x				x	400	
Woods Valley	Rome		x				x	410	

North Carolina

Name of Area	Location	Gondolas, tramways	Chair lifts	T-bars	Platterpulls	J-bars	Rope-tows	Total Vertical Descent	Snow-making
Appalachian Ski Mt.	Blowing Rock		x	x			x	350	x
Beech Mountain	Banner Elk	x	x			x		1,200	x
Catalooche	Waynesville		x	x			x	740	x
Hound Ears Ski Club	Boone		x	x				100	x
Sapphire Valley	Cashiers		x				x	325	x
Seven Devils	Boone		x		x		x	700	x
Sugar Mountain	Banner Elk		x				x	1,200	x

North Dakota

Name of Area	Location	Gondolas, tramways	Chair lifts	T-bars	Platterpulls	J-bars	Rope-tows	Total Vertical Descent	Snow-making
Twilight Hills	Bismark				x		x	407	x
Villa Vista	Grand Forks						x	105	

Ohio

Name of Area	Location	Gondolas, tramways	Chair lifts	T-bars	Platterpulls	J-bars	Rope-tows	Total Vertical Descent	Snow-making
Apline Valley	Chesterland		x				x	240	x
Boston Mills	Peninsula	x	x				x	240	x
Brandywine Ski Center	Sagamore Hills		x				x	200	x
Clear Fork Valley	Butler	x	x			x	x	325	x
Mont Chalet	Chesterland		x				x	110	x
Snow Bowl	Cadiz		x				x	300	x

Name of Area	Location (nearest town or postal address)	Gondolas, tramways	Chair lifts	T-bars	Platterpulls	J-bars	Rope-tows	Total Vertical Descent (in feet)	Snow-making
Snow Trails	Mansfield		x	x			x	275	x
Sugarcreek Ski Hills	Dayton				x		x	150	x
Valley High	Bellefontaine		x				x	375	x
Oregon									
Anthony Lakes	Baker		x		x		x	950	
Arbuckle Mountain	Heppner		x				x	500	
Hoodoo Ski Bowl	Sisters		x				x	1,025	
Mt. Ashland	Ashland		x	x	x			1,500	
Mt. Bachelor	Bend		x	x	x		x	2,000	
Mt. Hood Meadows	Government Camp		x	x			x	1,200	
Multorpor Ski Bowl	Government Camp		x	x			x	1,200	
Spout Springs	Elgin		x	x			x	520	
Summit Ski Area	Government Camp			x			x	200	
*Timberline**	Government Camp		x		x		x	5,000	
Tomahawk Ski Bowl	Klamath Falls				x		x	625	
Williamette Ski Area	Eugene				x		x	800	
Pennsylvania									
Apple Hill	Allentown			x			x	240	x
Bear Rocks Ski Slopes	Mt. Pleasant	x					x	350	
Big Boulder	White Haven	x	x			x	x	450	x
Black Moshannon	Philipsburg				x			250	
Blair Mountain	Dillsburg			x			x	400	x
Blue Knob	Bedford	x			x	x	x	1,000	x
Boyce Park	Monroeville			x				169	x
Buck Hill	Stroudsburg			x				300	x
Camelback	Tannersville	x			x	x		750	x
Camp T. Frank Soles	Somerset		x					400	
Charnita	Fairfield	x					x	592	x
Denton Hill	Coudersport	x			x			570	x
Dol Mountain	Topton	x	x				x	467	x
Elk Mountain	Union Dale	x	x			x		1,000	x
Hickory Ridge	Honesdale			x			x	357	x
Hidden Valley	Somerset				x		x	400	x
Highland	Muncy				x	x	x	275	x
Indian Lake	Somerset				x			250	
Jack Frost	Blakeslee	x				x		540	x
Laurel Mountain	Ligonier	x	x	x			x	910	x
Mt. Summit	Uniontown	x	x				x	400	x
Paper Birch	Hawley			x			x	400	x
Pine Forge	Pottstown				x		x	268	x
Plateau De Mount	Somerset	x					x	240	x
Pocono Manor	Pocono Manor					x	x	220	x
Poco-North	Hawley	x	x				x	416	x
Richmond Hill	Fort Laudon			x			x	125	x
Seven Springs	Champion	x		x			x	634	x
Sharp Mountain	Pottsville	x	x			x		400	x
Ski Blue Knob	Bedford	x		x	x			1,000	x
Skimont	Boalsburg		x				x	390	x
Ski Roundtop	Lewisberry	x		x			x	540	x
Ski Sno-Hill	Lake Como		x				x	400	
Spring Mountain	Schwenksville	x					x	280	
Timber Hill	Canadensis		x	x				400	x
White Mountain	Champion		x	x			x	380	
Wolf Hollow	Stroudsburg			x			x	350	x
York Mountain	Youngsville			x			x	500	

Name of Area	Location (nearest town or postal address)	Kinds of Lifts						Total Vertical Descent (in feet)	Snow-making
		Gondolas, tramways	Chair lifts	T-bars	Platterpulls	J-bars	Rope-tows		
Rhode Island									
Diamond Hill	Cumberland		x	x			x	275	x
Pine Top	Escoheag			x			x	280	x
Ski Valley	Woonsocket				x		x	180	x
Yawgoo Valley	Wickford		x				x	175	x
South Dakota									
Terry Peak	Lead		x		x			1,200	
Tennessee									
Gatlinburg Ski Resort	Gatlinburg		x				x	800	x
Renegade Ski Resort	Crossville		x	x			x	400	x
Utah									
Alta*	Salt Lake City		x				x	2,000	
Beaver Mountain	Logan		x	x				1,700	
Blue Mountain	Monticello				x		x	800	
Brian Head	Parowan		x	x				600	
Brighton Ski Bowl	Salt Lake City		x	x			x	525	
Gerzoga	Salt Lake City		x	x			x	430	
Grizzly Ridge	Vernal			x			x	400	
Mountain Empire	Salt Lake City		x	x				1,350	
Park City*	Park City mine train		x			x		2,460	
Park West	Park City		x				x	2,000	
Snow Basin	Ogden Canyon		x				x	2,600	
Snowbird*	Salt Lake City	x	x	x				3,100	
Snow Park	Park City		x					600	
Solitude	Big Cottonwood		x	x				1,900	
Sundance	Provo		x			x		1,800	
Timp Haven	Provo		x	x	x		x	1,400	
Vermont									
Birdseye	Castleton		x	x			x	500	x
Bolton Valley*	Bolton Valley		x					1,100	
Bromley*	Manchester		x		x	x		1,360	x
Burke Mountain	East Burke		x	x	x			1,600	
Burrington Hill	Whitingham				x		x	240	
Carinthia	West Dover		x				x	800	
Dutch Hill	Heartwellville		x			x	x	570	
Glebe Mountain	Windham		x					302	
Glen Ellen*	Fayston		x				x	2,645	x
Goodrich	Northfield		x		x		x	1,000	
Haystack Mountain	Wilmington		x	x				1,400	
High Pond	Brandon			x			x	300	
Hogback	Brattleboro			x	x		x	500	
Jay Peak*	North Troy	x	x	x	x			1,950	x
Killington*	Sherburne	x	x		x			2,020	x
Living Memorial Park	Brattleboro			x				204	
Lyndon Outing Club	Lyndonville			x			x	800	
Madonna Mountain	Jeffersonville		x		x			2,150	x
Mad River Glen*	Waitsfield		x	x			x	1,985	
Magic Mountain	Londonderry		x	x				1,600	x
Maple Valley	Brattleboro		x	x				940	x
Middlebury Snow Bowl	Hancock				x			900	
Mt. Ascutney	Windsor		x	x				1,470	x
Mt. Mansfield–Spruce Peak*	Stowe	x	x	x				2,300	x
Mt. Snow*	West Dover	x	x	x			x	1,900	x

Name of Area	Location (nearest town or postal address)	Kinds of Lifts						Total Vertical Descent (in feet)	Snow-making
		Gondolas, tramways	Chair lifts	T-bars	Platterpulls	J-bars	Rope-tows		
Mt. Tom/Suicide Six	Woodstock				x			600	x
Okemo Mountain	Ludlow		x		x			1,950	
Pico Peak	Rutland		x	x		x		1,967	
Pinnacle Skiways	Randolph				x			550	
Prospect Mountain	Bennington		x				x	676	
Round Top Mountain	Ludlow		x		x			1,250	
Skyline	Barre				x			500	
Snow Valley	Manchester		x			x		586	
Sonnenberg	Barnard					x		500	
Stratton*	South Londonderry		x	x				1,200	
Sugarbush*	Warren	x	x	x				2,400	x
Timber Ridge	Londonderry				x			300	
Underhill Ski Bowl	Underhill Center					x	x	140	
Virginia									
Bryce Mountain	Mount Jackson		x				x	590	x
The Homestead	Hot Springs	trestlecar	x				x	500	x
Massanutten	Harrison		x			x		300	x
Rappahannock	Washington		x				x	650	x
Shawnee-land	Winchester			x			x	400	x
Washington									
Alpental	North Bend		x				x	2,400	
Badger Mountain	Waterville						x	1,000	
Chewelah Peak	Chewelah		x				x	1,600	
Crystal Mountain*	Enumclaw		x	x			x	2,400	
Hurricane Ridge	Port Angeles						x	500	
Hyak Ski Bowl	North Bend		x		x		x	1,260	
Loup Loup Ski Bowl	Okanogan				x		x	1,380	
Mission Ridge	Wenatchee		x				x	2,140	
Mt. Baker	Bellingham		x				x	1,000	
Mt. Pilchuck	Granite Falls		x				x	1,217	
Mt. Spokane	Spokane		x				x	1,523	
Paradise Valley	Longmire						x	400	
Status Peak	Goldendale			x			x	500	
Ski Acres	Snoqualmie Summit		x	x			x	900	
Snoqualmie Summit	Snoqualmie Summit		x		x		x	850	
Squilchuck	Squilchuck State Park				x		x	300	
Stevens Pass	Leavenworth		x				x	1,800	
White Pass	White Pass		x		x		x	1,500	
West Virginia									
Canaan Valley	Davis		x		x		x	315	x
Chestnut Ridge	Morgantown						x	345	
Oglebay Park	Wheeling				x		x	250	x
Snaggy Mountain	Terra Alta		x				x	300	x
Wisconsin									
Alpine Valley*	East Troy		x				x	288	x
Birch Haven	Sauk City						x	275	
Birch Park	Stilwater		x	x			x	235	
Bruce Mound	Merrillan						x	325	x
Calumet Park	Appleton						x	180	
Camp 10	Rhinelander		x				x	225	
Cascade Mountain	Portage		x	x		x	x	460	x
Deepwood	Colfax		x				x	293	x
Delafield Lodge	Delafield						x	200	

Name of Area	Location (nearest town or postal address)	Gondolas, tramways	Chair lifts	T-bars	Platterpulls	J-bars	Rope-tows	Total Vertical Descent (in feet)	Snow-making
Devil's Head	Merrimao		x				x	358	x
Eight Flags of Birch Park	Houlton		x	x			x	200	x
Englewood	Osceola			x		x	x	340	
Gateway Ski Area	Land O'Lakes			x			x	200	
Hardscrabble	Rice Lake			x			x	350	x
Hidden Valley	Monitowac		x				x	200	
Hilly Haven	DePere						x	100	
Kettlebowl	Antigo						x	200	
Little Switzerland	Slinger		x				x	200	x
Lockhaven	Spooner						x	250	x
Majestic Hills	Lake Geneva						x	250	x
Manitou Valley	Superior						x	125	
Mont Du Lac	Duluth			x			x	310	
Mt. Ashwabay	Bayfield			x			x	317	
Mt. Fuji	Lake Geneva	x	x				x	240	x
Mt. LaCrosse	LaCrosse		x		x		x	516	x
*Mt. Telemark**	Cable		x	x			x	370	x
Mus-Ski Mt.	Sayner					x	x	200	
Nor-Ski Ridge	S. Fish Creek			x			x	226	x
Northercaire Valley	Three Lakes				x		x	200	
Paul Bunyan Ski Hill	Lakewood			x			x	120	x
Rib Mountain	Wausau		x	x			x	680	x
*Playboy Club Hotel**	Lake Geneva		x					850	x
Sheltered Valley	Three Lakes				x		x	200	
Ski-Mac	Somerset						x	268	
Skyline	Friendship		x				x	335	x
Squirrel Hill	Minoqua						x	200	
Timberline	Madison			x			x	300	x
Trollhaugen	Dresser			x			x	256	x
Tyrol Basin	Mt. Horeb		x	x			x	380	x
View Ridge	New London						x	120	
White Cap Mountain	Hurley		x	x			x	350	
Wilmot Mountain	Wilmot		x	x			x	230	x
Wintergreen	Spring Green		x			x	x	400	x
Wunderberg	West Bend			x			x	200	x

Wyoming

Name of Area	Location	Gondolas, tramways	Chair lifts	T-bars	Platterpulls	J-bars	Rope-tows	Total Vertical Descent	Snow-making
Antelope Butte	Greybull			x	x			650	
Eagle Rock	Evanston		x				x	467	x
Fun Valley	Greybull			x	x			650	
Happy Jack	Laramie			x			x	300	x
Hogadon Basin	Casper			x			x	600	
*Jackson Hole**	Jackson	x	x					4,135	
Meadowlark	Worland				x			600	
Medicine Bow	Centennial			x	x			700	
Pinedale	Pinedale				x		x	900	
Sleeping Giant	Cody			x			x	500	
Snow King Mt.	Jackson Hole		x				x	1,571	
Snowy Range	Saratoga		x	x				750	

CANADA

Skiers find their winter fun most everywhere, but the sport comes fully into its own in British Columbia, Alberta, Ontario, and Quebec.

British Columbia is probably favored with more top skiable terrain than any other area of similar size in the world. The mountains, plus a superabundant snowfall, make ski con-

Looking down to the lodge, Sunshine ski area in Banff has that comfortable yet interesting look.

ditions fast and fluffy from the Coastal Range to the Monashees in the interior, and eastward to the Rocky Mountains on the Alberta border. In the Okanagan Valley of British Columbia, the slopes of Black Night Mountain, overlooking Kelowna and the Okanagan Lake, offer admirable ski conditions from December to March. There are nursery hills, jumps and slalom hills, and one of the most exciting downhill runs in Canada.

There is plenty of good skiing near Vancouver, British Columbia's largest city. Only eight miles away, Mt. Seymour towers 4,700 feet. Short, steep downhill runs abound, and there are many miles of scenic trails over mountainside meadows. Skiing at the higher elevations may last till July 1. Snow depth at the peaks sometimes reaches 30 feet. Twenty miles northeast of Vancouver is spacious Garibaldi Park, where the season sometimes stretches from November to June. Diamond Head Chalet, on a lofty plateau, is the assembly point for Garibaldi skiers. The mile-high chalet is above timber line.

Mount Revelstoke National Park in the Selkirk Mountains, high in the clouds, offers jumping to test the mettle of the most skilled skiers, and there are many ski trails open during the long winter season there. The Nels Nelsen Jumping Hill at Revelstoke is internationally known.

That is not all of British Columbia's ski country, for there still remain Hollyburn Ridge and Grouse Mountain, as well as the Forbidden Plateau, Bralorne, and Wells. Through those areas the ski conditions are superb. Grouse Mountain, facing Vancouver from the north shore of Burrard Inlet, has two twin-seat chair lifts and a cablecar, with a 2,300-foot vertical rise and a combined length of 9,000 feet. Hollyburn has a chair lift and six ski tows. The peak of the mountain is 3,974 feet.

One of the principal gateways to the ski spots of Alberta is Banff, opening on a winter playground that ranges beyond Jasper, on the Athabasca River. A giant chair lift, supported by thirteen steel towers, lofts skiers and their friends up the eastern slopes of Mount Norquay, only five miles from Banff itself. Floodlights operate when darkness comes, and a school for ski beginners is conducted at the 6,000 foot level.

Three fine high-country skiing areas are at

Mount Assiniboine, the Sunshine district, and in the Skoki Valley. All are about 8,000 feet above sea level and have rolling, open country with varied mountain scenery. At Jasper there is a downhill course that drops 4,600 feet in three miles, and 100 miles of trails through wooded valleys. Most spectacular of all sports in the Canadian Rockies is ski mountaineering, which European visitors especially enjoy. Just a few miles northwest of Lake Louise is ideal country for the sport, and also at Mount Balfour and Snow Dome; the last crowns the Columbia Icefield. Marmot Basin, at Jasper, the most northerly of Alberta's Rocky Mountain ski giants, is a varied complex of sheltered bowls and marathon runs from the 8,557-foot summit of Marmot Peak. Motel and hotel accommodation in Jasper is eight miles from the Marmot lifts. High bowl skiing is a feature here.

There is an Alpine accent to Western Canada's ski fun, but skiing in Eastern Canada is Scandinavian-type. North America's most concentrated ski development covers 2,000 square miles of the Laurentian area of Quebec, serviced by railways, airlines, and highways to spare. Some Laurentian ski resorts have their own airfields, with regular daily plane schedules for visiting sportsmen. The Laurentians, Eastern Canada's best known ski slopes, begin about 40 miles north of Montreal, largest city in Canada.

In the Shawbridge district is the start and finish of the original Maple Leaf Trail, and in the Piedmont–St. Sauveur district is a valley with myriad ski tows, the famed Hill 70, and many miles of cross-country trails. Other noted ski sections of Quebec include Mont Rolland, Ste. Adele, Ste. Marguerite, Val Morin, Val David, Sun Valley, Lac Paquin, Ste. Agathe, Mont Tremblant, and Mont Ste. Anne. The Eastern Townships, in the southeast part of Old Quebec, offer long and excellent skiing, especially at Mount Orford, which lies in a charming provincial park. The Gatineau Hills, just a few miles from the neighbor cities of Hull and Ottawa, are among the oldest ski zones in Quebec. The medium-size rolling hills of the Gatineau are particularly appealing to the average skier.

Winter accommodation can be found in Quebec to suit any skier's purse. The larger resorts have their own ski professionals, and facilities usually include electrically operated tows or T-bar lifts. The cuisine at Quebec winter resorts is particularly good. It has been said one cannot get a poor meal in the Laurentians.

The central and eastern sections of Ontario are the best ski locales in that province, from Ottawa in the east to Port Arthur and Fort William in the west. Ski clubs function in most large Ontario cities and towns, as well as in more than a few of the smaller communities. Chief problem in recent years has been unusually light snowfalls.

Ontario's ski terrain is varied enough for any skier's taste. There's downhill running, slalom racing over middle-size hills, woodland trails and gentle valleys, and a wide range of jumps. Just 12 miles from Toronto is the Toronto Ski Club's 1,000-acre property. The club has over 7,000 members. For scenic skiing in Ontario, the Muskoka Lakes district is unsurpassed. Lying about 150 miles north of Toronto, its hundreds of square miles of hilly lake country afford fine ski sport and at Huntsville one can ski over excellent slopes right in the town.

Even the remote Atlantic island province of Newfoundland has broken into the ski business with a T-bar lift at Cornerbrook, midway up the western coast. The city of Saint John's, New Brunswick, is opening a new ski area right inside its city limits. Not only will Rockway Park have a T-bar humming in time for the Christmas holidays, but they are equipping their slopes with automatic snowmaking equipment.

Mount Martock at Windsor, Nova Scotia, equipped with a 2,700-foot T-bar and two rope tows, has added snowmaking equipment this season. The largest Atlantic Province ski club is at Wentworth Valley, 26 miles from Truro, Nova Scotia, on the Trans-Canada Highway. The club is open to the public and has a 3,800-foot T-bar, plus three rope tows, fifteen trails, and a 730-foot vertical drop.

Overall, Canadian skiing offers dependable snow at the occasional risk of very cold weather. Take an extra sweater, also your driver's license for border identification. Otherwise you will need nothing extra to enjoy Canadian skiing.

SKI AREAS: CANADA

The areas listed in italics have two or more chair lifts or a tramway or gondola lift.

Name of Area	Location (nearest town or postal address)	Gondolas, tramways	Chair lifts	T-Bars	Platterpulls	J-Bars	Rope-tows	Total Vertical Descent (in feet)	Snow-making
Alberta									
Camrose	Camrose						x	130	
Canyon Ski Lodge	Red Deer			x				465	x
Devon	Edmonton			x			x	200	x
Edmonton Ski Club	Edmonton						x	200	x
Happy Valley	Calgary				x		x	300	x
Lake Louise	Banff	x	x	x	x			2,850	
Marmot Basin	Jasper		x	x				1,800	
Mt. Norquay	Banff		x	x	x		x	1,350	
Paskapoo	Calgary			x			x	300	x
Pigeon Mountain	Cranmore				x			800	x
Snowridge	Kananaskis Valley		x	x				1,100	
Sunshine Village	Banff		x	x				675	
Valley Ski Club	Castor			x			x	200	
Whistler Mountain	Jasper				x			1,500	
West Castle	Alta			x				2,500	
Whitehorn-Temple	See Lake Louise								
British Columbia									
Apex Alpine	Penticton			x	x		x	1,200	
Bear Mountain	Dawson Creek			x			x	410	
Big White	Kelowna			x				1,350	
Borderline Ski Club	Osoyocs			x			x	700	
Fernie Snow Valley	Fernie			x			x	2,100	
Forbidden Plateau	Courtenay			x			x	1,500	
Garibaldi's Whistler Mountain	Vancouver	x	x	x				4,300	
Gibson Pass	Princeton		x	x			x	732	
Green Mountain	Vancouver						x	1,900	
Grouse Mountain	Vancouver	x	x	x			x	1,200	
Hollyburn Ridge	Vancouver		x	x				1,800	
Kimberly Ski Club	Kimberly			x				2,500	
Lac Le Jeune	Kamloops			x				800	
Last Mountain	Kelowna		x	x				575	
Little Squaw Valley	Williams Lake			x			x	740	
Mt. Becher Ski Club	Courtenay		x			x		3,100	
Mt. McKenzie	Revelstoke			x			x	600	
Mt. Seymour	Vancouver		x	x	x		x	500	
North Star Mt.	Kimberly			x				1,600	
Panorama Ski Hill	Invermere			x			x	1,800	
Red Mountain	Rossland		x		x		x	2,790	
Revelstoke Ski Club	Revelstoke				x		x	500	
Ridge Mountain	Kamloops			x			x	800	
Silver King Ski Club	Nelson			x				1,000	
Silver Star Mt.	Vernon			x	x			1,000	
Snow Valley	Fernie			x			x	2,000	
Tabor Mountain	Prince George			x			x	800	
Tod Mountain	Kamloops		x	x				3,100	

Name of Area	Location (nearest town or postal address)	Gondolas, tramways	Chair lifts	T-bars	Platterpulls	J-bars	Rope-tows	Total Vertical Descent (in feet)	Snow-making
Manitoba									
Falcon Lake	Falcon Beach						x	140	
Holiday Mountain	La Riviere			x			x	300	x
Mt. Agassiz	McCreary			x			x	500	x
Newfoundland									
Marble Mountain	Corner Brook			x			x	550	
Smokey Mt. Ski Club	Labrador City				x		x	500	
Nova Scotia									
Alpine Ski Trails	Wentworth Valley				x		x	600	
Ben Eoin	Sydney			x			x	492	
Mount Martock	Windsor			x			x	600	
Wentworth Valley	Route 4			x			x	860	
Ontario									
Alice-Hill Park	Pembroke			x			x	210	
Alpine	Collingwood			x			x	530	
Bay Motor Hotel	Owen Sound	x	x					400	x
Beaver Valley	Flesherton-Markdale			x		x	x	550	
Blue Mountain Winter Park	Collingwood	x	x	x			x	800	x
Britannia Hotel	Huntsville			x			x	175	
Caledon Ski Club	Caledon			x			x	300	
Candiac Skiways	Dacre			x			x	550	
Caswell Ski Club	Sundridge			x	x		x	175	x
Cedar Springs	Burlington			x			x	300	x
Chedoke	Hamilton			x				150	x
Chicopee	Kitchner						x	185	
Corwhin Ski Slopes	Guelph						x	169	
Craigleith	Collingwood			x			x	700	
Dagmar Ski Club	Claremont						x	240	
Devil's Elbow	Bethany			x			x	325	
Devil's Glen	Glen Huron			x			x	500	
Don Valley	Toronto				x		x	100	
Espanola Ski Club	Espanola		x				x	200	
Fonthill	Fonthill				x		x	105	
Fort William	Fort William		x				x	110	x
Georgian Peaks	Thornbury	x	x	x			x	810	x
Glenn Abbey	Oakville			x			x	140	
Glen Eden	Milton			x			x	220	
Haliburton Highlands	Haliburton			x				237	
Happy Valley	Walkerton			x	x			210	
Hidden Valley	Huntsville	x	x				x	360	x
Hockley Valley	Orangeville				x		x	142	x
Honey Pot	Maple				x		x	130	x
Horseshoe Valley	Craighurst	x	x					187	
Hotel Bernard	Sundridge				x		x	175	
Kamiskotia	Timmins			x			x	350	
Kingston Ski Club	Kingston						x	120	
Kirkland Lake	Swastika					x		220	
Laurentian	North Bay			x			x	325	
Limberlost Ski Hills	Huntsville			x			x	250	
Little Norway	Fort William			x			x	675	
Loch Lomond	Fort William			x			x	775	x
London Ski Club	London						x	100	x
Loretto	Alliston			x			x	180	x

Name of Area	Location (nearest town or postal address)	Gondolas, tramways	Chair lifts	T-bars	Platterpulls	J-bars	Rope-tows	Total Vertical Descent (in feet)	Snow-making
		Kinds of Lifts							
Mansfield Skiways	Alliston			x				375	x
Moose Mountain	Beardmore			x				375	
Mt. Baldy	Port Arthur		x				x	600	
Mt. Evergreen	Kenora			x			x	200	
Mt. McKay	Fort William		x	x			x	625	x
Mt. Pakenham	Pakenham			x			x	300	
Mt. St. Louis	Barrie			x			x	318	
Mt. Wawa	Wawa		x				x	500	
Mountain View	Midland				x		x	150	
Muskoka Sands	Gravenhurst			x				800	
Nacona	Napanee				x		x	160	x
Nipissing Ridge	Powassan			x			x	448	
Nordic Hills	Sudbury			x			x	260	
Oak Hills Ski Club	Belleville			x			x	193	
Old Smokey	Kimberley			x			x	265	
Onaping	Onaping			x			x	280	
Oshawa	Oshawa			x			x	300	x
Pinery Park	Grand Bend				x			200	
Port Arthur	Port Arthur		x				x	550	
Rainbow Ridge	Bracebridge			x			x	225	x
Raven Mountain	Kirkland Lake			x				525	
St. Bernard	Haileybury				x			400	
Saulte Ski Club	Saulte Ste. Marie				x		x	225	
Searchmont Valley	Saulte Ste. Marie			x	x		x	650	
Skee-Hi Ltd.	Thamesford			x			x	150	x
Snow Valley	Barrie			x			x	350	
Sundridge	Sundridge				x		x	175	
Talisman	Kimberley		x	x			x	600	x
Tally-Ho Winter Park	Huntsville				x		x	210	
Timmins Ski Club	Timmins			x			x	350	
Toronto Ski Club	Richmond Hill						x	80	
Twin Hearths	Orangeville			x			x	200	
Valley Schuss	Orangeville			x	x		x	350	
Quebec									
Avila Ski Center	Piedmont	x	x			x		590	x
Ayers Ski Centre	Brownsburg	x	x					400	
Belle Neige	Val-Morin			x				480	x
Bellevue	Morin Heights			x		x		300	
Bromont	Bromont	x	x					1,100	x
Camp Fortune	Ottawa	x	x	x	x		x	600	x
Centre Le Ralais	Quebec	x	x	x				725	x
Chanteclair	Ste. Adèle-en-Haut				x	x		280	x
Chateau Lac Beauport	Lac Beauport		x	x			x	550	
Club Mont Bellevue	Ste. Anne Desmonts				x			185	
Cochand's Swiss Valley	Ste. Marguerite	x	x	x			x	400	x
Devil's River Lodge	St. Faustin	x	x					1,760	
East Angus	East Angus				x			325	
Edelweiss Valley	Wakefield		x	x				600	x
Far Hills Inn	Val Morin			x			x	265	
Glen Mountain	Knowlton	x	x					1,050	
Grey Rocks Inn	St. Jovite			x				550	x
Hills 40 & 80	Ste. Adele			x				350	
La Marquise	Montreal			x				500	
La Reserve	St. Donat	x			x			1,000	
La Tuque	La Tuque		x					475	
Laurentide Inn	Ste. Agathe	x	x	x				425	

Name of Area	Location (nearest town or postal address)	Kinds of Lifts						Total Vertical Descent (in feet)	Snow-making
		Gondolas, tramways	Chair lifts	T-bars	Platterpulls	J-bars	Rope-tows		
Manoir St. Castin	Lac Beauport		x	x				550	x
Manor House	Ste. Agathe		x					150	
Marquis Hill	St. Sauveur		x				x	250	
Montagne du Manior	Lac Beauport	x	x				x	215	
Morin Heights	Morin Heights		x			x		300	
Mt. Adstock	Thetford Mines	x	x				x	1,100	
Mt. Alouette	Ste. Adèle		x					500	
Mt. Avalanche	Ste. Agathe		x					450	
Mt. Blanc	St. Faustin		x	x				715	
Mt. Carmel	Valmont		x				x	225	x
Mt. Castor	Ste. Agathe		x					270	
Mt. Chevreuil	Ste. Agathe	x	x					757	x
Mt. Chich-Chocks	Cap Chat		x	x				500	
Mt. Christie	St. Sauveur		x				x	400	x
Mt. De Lanaudiere	Joliette		x	x				300	
Mt. Echo	Sutton	x		x				1,500	
Mt. Fortin	Kendgami		x				x	480	
Mt. Fugere	Ste. Agathe		x	x				400	
Mt. Gabriel	Mt. Gabriel		x					560	x
Mt. Garceau	St. Donat	x	x	x				950	
Mt. Habitant	St. Sauveur		x					550	x
Mt. Kanasuta	Rouyn		x					510	
Mt. Mars Ski Club	Port Alfred		x				x	525	
Mt. Olympia	Piedmont		x					600	
Mt. Orford	Magog	x	x					1,600	
Mt. Plante	Val David		x					100	
Mt. Ste. Agathe	Ste. Agathe		x		x			710	
Mt. Ste. Anne	Quebec City	x	x	x				2,050	
Mt. Ste. Castin	Lac Beauport		x	x				950	x
Mt. Ste. Marie	Lac-Ste.-Marie	x	x					1,100	
Mt. Sutton	Sutton	x	x					1,500	
Mt. Tremblant	Mt. Tremblant	x	x	x			x	2,400	x
Mt. Video	Barraute	x						400	
Mt. Villa	Alma		x				x	180	
North Hatley	North Hatley				x			545	x
Owl's Head	Mansonville	x	x					1,330	
Petit Chamonix	Matapédia		x					400	
St. Sauveur des Monts	St. Jerome	x	x			x	x	700	
Stoneham	Stoneham	x	x	x				1,250	
Summit Sauvage	Val Morin		x					420	
Sun Valley	Ste. Adèle	x	x	x				475	x
Tobo-Ski	St. Felicien		x				x	250	
Up-Hill	St. Sauveur	x	x					700	
Vallee-Bleue	Val David		x	x				360	
Victoria Ski Club	Victoriaville				x	x		375	
Vorlage	Ottawa		x					450	x

LATE-SEASON SKIING IN NORTH AMERICA

Defiant of comprehension, along with the universe and psychology of woman, is the depopulation of ski hills in the months when they offer their greatest pleasure. No one has satisfactorily explained this perverse decline of skiers in March and the ensuing weeks. All that is certain is that it occurs at a time when sun, snow, and mountain air are most intoxicating. Happily, these spring ski pleasures are finding more adherents. Knowledgeable Eastern skiers, for instance, are well aware of hills with northern exposures that hold snow long after it has disappeared from other slopes; or of lift operators who maintain midstations and tows for skiing on upper slopes. The West has weeks of skiing long after snow has disappeared in other parts of the continent. Result? Many Easterners and Midwesterners now take a two-week spring skiing vacation in the West.

Here is a guide for spring and summer skiing. Information was supplied to *Ski Magazine* by the areas; the closing dates for lift and base lodge facilities are, in all cases, projected dates and are necessarily contingent on weather and snow conditions. Skiers, therefore, are advised to check by phone in advance with these areas before making travel plans.

Open June or Later

Area	Name	Dates
Alaska	Alyeska	Through May (midsummer glacier skiing)
California	Mammoth Mountain	Early July
Colorado	Arapahoe Basin	After June
Oregon	Mount Hood Meadows	Early June
	Timberline Lodge	August 1
Washington	Alpental	June 15
	Crystal Mountain	Closes late May; reopens for June and July
	Mount Baker	Mid-July
British Columbia	Whistler Mountain	Open year around; in summer, lifts operate weekends only

Closing in May

Area	Name	Closing Date
California	Alpine Meadows	Early May
	Bear Valley	Late May
	Boreal Ridge	Mid-May (weekends only after mid-April)
	Heavenly Valley	Late May (weekends only after April 20)
	Mount Shasta	Late May
	Squaw Valley	Early May
Colorado	Loveland Basin	Early May
Idaho	Jackass Ski Bowl	Mid-May
Maine	Sugarloaf	Early May
New Hampshire	Wildcat	Early May
New Mexico	Taos	Mid-May
Oregon	Mount Bachelor	May 31 (weekends only after mid-April)
Utah	Alta	Early May
	Brighton Ski Bowl	Mid-May
Vermont	Jay Peak	Mid-May
	Killington	Mid-May
Washington	White Pass	Early May
Alberta	Marmot Basin	Late May
	Sunshine Village	Late May

Closing Middle to Late April

Area	Name	Closing Date
California	June Mountain	Late April
	Lassen Park	Mid-April
	Sugar Bowl	Late April
Colorado	Aspen Highlands	Mid-April
	Crested Butte	Late April
	Mount Werner	Late April
	Snowmass	Mid-April
	Vail	Late April
	Winter Park	Mid-April
Idaho	Bogus Basin	Mid-April
	Schweitzer Basin	Late April

Area	Name	Closing Date
Maine	Squaw Mountain	Late April
Michigan	Indianhead Mountain	Mid-April
	Iroquois Mountain	Mid-April
	Schuss Mountain	Mid-April
Montana	Red Lodge/Grizzley Peak	Late April
Nevada	Ski Incline	Late April
	Slide Mountain	Mid-April
New Hampshire	Loon Mountain	Mid-April
	Waterville Valley	Late April
New York	Hunter Mountain	Mid-April
	Windham	Mid-April
South Dakota	Terry Peak	Mid-April
Vermont	Bolton Valley	Mid-April
	Glen Ellen	Late April
	Madonna Mountain	Mid-April
	Mad River Glen	Mid-April
	Mount Snow	Mid-April
	Pico Peak	Mid-April
	Stow	Late April
	Stratton	Mid-April
	Sugarbush	Late April
Washington	Ski Acres	Mid-April
Wyoming	Jackson Hole	Mid-April
Alberta	Lake Louise	Late April
Quebec	Camp Fortune	Mid-April
	Grey Rocks	Late April
	Mount Ste. Anne	Mid-April
	Mount Ste. Marie	Mid-April
	Mount Sutton	Late April
	Owl's Head	Mid-April

NORTH AMERICA'S MOST CHALLENGING SKI RUNS

The North American continent has in its enormously varied mountain terrain ski runs second to none in the world. *Ski Magazine*'s editors, after consulting with its nationwide staff of correspondents, has selected the following trails as being the most challenging fifty ski runs in North America. Some of the trails are famous, while others are known only locally, but they all offer great skiing. They are given here in alphabetical order—not in degree of difficulty.

Area	Trail
Eastern	
Cannon Mountain, New Hampshire	Paulie's Folly
Dutch Hill, Vermont	Windmill
Jiminy Peak, Massachusetts	Whirlaway Trail
Killington, Vermont	East Fall Run
Mad River Glen, Vermont	Chute
	Fall Line
Madonna Mountain, Vermont	FIS
Magic Mountain, Vermont	Twilight
Pico, Vermont	Sunset Schuss Run
Squaw Mountain, Maine	Penobscot Trail
Stowe, Vermont	Nose Dive
	National
	Goat Path
	Starr Run
Stratton, Vermont	North American
Sugarbush, Vermont	Stein's Run
	The Glades
	Rumble

Area	Trail
Mont Tremblant, Quebec	Ryan's Run
Mount Washington, New Hampshire	The Inferno Run
Whiteface, New York	Wilderness
Wildcat Mountain, New Hampshire	Wildcat Trail

Western

Area	Trail
Alta, Utah	Chartreuse Trail
	Wildcat
Arapahoe Basin, Colorado	Palavacinni Run
Aspen, Colorado	Ruthie's Run
Aspen Highlands, Colorado	Stein Eriksen
Crystal Mountain, Washington	Green Valley
	Exterminator
Heavenly Valley, California	Gun Barrel
Jackson Hole, Wyoming	Rendezvous
Loveland, Colorado	Avalanche
Mount Alyeska, Alaska	National
Mount Norquay, Alberta	North American
Park City, Utah	Payday
Red River, New Mexico	Massacre Run
Slide Mountain, Nevada	John Frémont Run
Snoqualmie, Washington	Powderbowl Run
Snowmass-at-Aspen, Colorado	Big Burn
Squaw Valley, California	KT-22
Sugar Bowl, California	Silver Belt Run
Sun Valley, Idaho	Baldy-Exhibition Run
	Warm Springs Run
Taos Ski Valley, New Mexico	Al's Run
Timberline, Mt. Hood, Oregon	Magic Mile
Vail, Colorado	Ruebezahl
	Seldom
	International
	Riva Ridge

Nose Dive Trail at Stowe, Vermont.

THE 25 STEEPEST SKI TRAILS IN NORTH AMERICA

Rating the steepest ski trails in North America presented a number of difficulties. There is, for instance, no answer to the question: "What is the steepest ski trail in the country?" because you must then ask: "How long is the trail?" A number of hills in the Midwest have very short pitches of more than 30 degrees, but they hardly compare with a 2,500-foot run like Exhibition at Sun Valley. In rating the steepest trails, *Ski Magazine* created two categories: lift-served slopes more than 3,000 feet long, having a steepness greater than 40 per cent (21.8 degrees); and slopes more than 4,000 feet (over three-quarters of a mile) long, having a steepness

greater than 30 per cent (16.7 degrees). This eliminated a number of very steep trails—like those at Suicide Six and Cannon Mountain, Bradley's Bash at Winter Park, the Slalom Glade at Mount Snow, and slopes at Loveland, Arapahoe, and Tremblant.

The following are the steepest, lift-served, nonavalanche ski slopes in North America. Steepness is given in both degrees and percentages, although the percentage method is the one most universally in use by ski areas. Percentages are computed by dividing the vertical drop of the slope by the horizontal length, and multiplying by 100.

Trails of More than 40 Per Cent Steepness and More than 3,000 Feet Long

Area	Trail	Vertical Drop—Feet	Slope Length—Feet	Grade—Degrees	Average—Per Cent
Jackson Hole, Wyo.	South Hoback Ridge	2,200	4,750	27.7	52.5
Taos Ski Valley, N.M.	Al's Run	1,792	4,000	26.6	50.0
Aspen Highlands, Colo.	Stein Eriksen	1,600	3,200	30.0	57.7
Sugarbush Valley, Vt.	Ruthies Run	1,380	3,000	27.4	51.8
Stowe, Vt.	Goat Trail	1,350	3,000	26.8	50.4
Squaw Valley, Calif.	KT-22	1,850	4,785	22.8	42.0
Heavenly Valley, Calif.	Gun Barrel	1,650	4,000	24.3	45.2
Alta, Utah	High Rustler	1,330	3,300	23.3	42.9
Sugarbowl, Calif.	Silverbelt	1,400	3,200	26.0	48.7
Crystal Mt., Wash.	Exterminator	1,250	3,200	23.0	42.5
Mt. Norquay, Alberta	Memorial Bowl	1,240	3,045	24.0	44.6
June Mt., Calif.	Slalom	1,300	3,000	25.7	48.1
Vail, Colo.	International	1,280	3,000	25.3	47.2

Trails of 30–40 Per Cent Steepness and More than 4,000 Feet Long

Area	Trail	Vertical Drop—Feet	Slope Length—Feet	Grade—Degrees	Average—Per Cent
Sun Valley, Idaho	Warm Springs	3,200	11,100	16.8	30.1
Glen Ellen, Vt.	Upper FIS	2,675	9,000	17.3	31.1
Aspen, Colo.	Ruthies Run	2,500	8,500	17.1	30.9
Solitude, Utah	Race Course	2,500	7,900	18.3	33.3
Madonna Mt., Vt.	FIS	2,018	6,900	17.0	30.5
Mad River Glen, Vt.	Fall Line–Grand Canyon	2,000	6,000	19.5	35.3
Stowe, Vt.	National	1,850	5,500	19.6	35.7
Slide Mt., Nev.	Gold Run	1,500	4,800	18.2	32.9
Whiteface, N.Y.	Wilderness	1,460	4,600	18.5	33.5
Stowe, Vt.	Starr Trail	1,650	4,500	21.5	39.4
Sugarloaf, Me.	Upper Winter's Way	1,500	4,250	20.6	37.7
Killington, Vt.	Cascade	1,350	4,100	19.2	34.9

THE 18 EASY SKI TRAILS IN NORTH AMERICA

Ski Magazine's editors, after consulting with its nationwide staff of correspondents, have selected 18 easy trails spanning the country.

They are tricky and fun, but if you can do a stem turn, you can ski these. They are challenging for the novice, but not scary. They all are respectably long, so they will spare you that feeling of being a "yo-yo" instead of a skier which plagues those forced to stick to beginners' slopes.

Area	Trail
Belle Ayr, New York	Roaring Brook
Big Bromley, Vermont	Lower Boulevard
Big Powderhorn, Michigan	Bovidae
Buck Hill, Minnesota	Teacher's Pet
Holiday Valley, New York	Holiday Run
Killington, Vermont	Snowshed Run

Area	Trail
Mt. Rose, Nevada	Ponderosa
Mt. Snow, Vermont	Long John
Mt. Telemark, Wisconsin	Christiana Run
Mt. Tremblant, Quebec	Beauchemln
Park City, Utah	Claim Jumper
Schuss Mountain, Michigan	Mellow Yellow
Sugarloaf, Maine	Tote Road Run
Sun Valley, Idaho	Dollar Mountain
Taos Ski Valley, New Mexico	Idiotenhugel
Timberline, Mt. Hood, Oregon	Wingle's Wiggle
Wildcat, New Hampshire	Polecat
Winter Park, Colorado	Crammer Trail

SELECTING SKI AREAS FOR CHILDREN

The ideal vacation place for a skiing family is one where the parents can have the fewest worries about their offspring. More and more ski areas are turning themselves into family vacation developments, but even at resorts that specialize in adults' skiing, parents can now look for and expect to find:

1. Resorts that have minimized the threat of traffic hazards to wandering children.
2. Accommodations with cooking facilities and play space.
3. Accommodations near the lifts, so that the kids can easily warm up, put on another sweater, or have a cup of cocoa.
4. Trails that funnel back to a central meeting point.
5. Good novice and intermediate facilities, preferably not used by fast-moving skiers, yet not too far from where parents ski.
6. Lifts easily ridden by small children.
7. Special classes for children and, if there are some in the family too young to ski, a nursery.
8. Baby-sitters available.
9. A bar or recreation room at the lodge so that the parents can have some after-ski activity without always needing a baby-sitter.
10. After-ski activities specifically for children.
11. A break on lift and room prices.

Below are good vacation bets for families with ski-age children:

Alta
Bear Valley
Big Boulder
Big Bromley

The Big Mountain
Boyne Country
Camelback
Chantecler
Cranmore
Crystal Mountain
Garibaldi's Whistler
Glen Ellen
Grey Rocks Inn
Heavenly Valley
Hunter Mountain Ski Bowl
Killington Ski Area
Jackson Hole
Jay Peak
Loon Mountain
Mad River Glen
Madonna Mountain
Magic Mountain
Mammoth Mountain
Mittersill
Mont Tremblant
Mount Hood
Mount Snow
Park City
Pico Peak
Schuss Mountain
Snowmass-at-Aspen
Steamboat Springs
Stratton
Sun Valley
Sunshine Village
Taos Ski Valley
Vail
Whiteface Mountain
The Wilderness
Waterville Valley

Note
Stowe has one plush motel at Toll House beginner slope.

Aspen has lodges near slopes and nurseries but is a giant town.

Sugarbush: nursery near one hotel some distance from major lift; total area is large.

Alta lodges are near slopes, but area is rugged and vast, with no real nursery.

OTHER BEST BETS IN SKI AREAS

Abby Rand, *Ski Magazine*'s travel editor, with the cooperation of our editors, has selected the following ski areas—from her book *Ski North America*—as best bets for:

Early and Late in the Season

Alta
Arapahoe Basin
Aspen
Bear Valley
The Big Mountain
The Bugaboos
Crystal Mountain
Garibaldi's Whistler
Heavenly Valley
Jackson Hole
Jay Peak
Killington Ski Area
Lake Louise
Mammoth Mountain
Mount Hood
Mount Washington
Park City
Snowmass-at-Aspen
Steamboat Springs
Stowe
Sugarbush Valley
Sugarloaf
Taos Ski Valley
Tuckerman Ravine
Waterville Valley
Wildcat Mountain
Vail

Social Celebrities

Aspen
Mammoth Mountain
Mittersill
Mont Tremblant
Snowmass-at-Aspen
Squaw Valley
Stowe
Stratton
Sugarbush Valley
Sun Valley
Vail
Waterville Valley

Students and New Alumni

Alta
Arapahoe Basin
Aspen

The Big Mountain
Cannon Mountain
Crystal Mountain
Grey Rocks Inn
Mad River Glen
Mammoth Mountain
Mount Snow
Mount Washington
Squaw Valley
Steamboat Springs
Stowe
Sugarloaf
Taos Ski Valley

Midweek Night Life

Aspen
Grey Rocks Inn
Heavenly Valley
Mont Tremblant
Park City
Playboy Club-Hotel
Snowmass-at-Aspen
Squaw Valley
Sun Valley
Vail

Weekend Night Life

Aspen
Boyne Country
Cannon Mountain
Cranmore
Grey Rocks Inn
Grouse Mountain
Haystack
Heavenly Valley
Hunter Mountain Ski Bowl
Killington Ski Area
Mittersill
Mont Tremblant
Mount Snow
Mount Washington
Park City
Snowmass-at-Aspen
Sugarbush Valley
Stowe
Sun Valley
Wildcat Mountain
Vail

Budget Watchers

Arapahoe Basin
Banff
Big Boulder

The Big Mountain
Camelback
Cannon Mountain
Chantecler Crystal Mountain
Garibaldi's Whistler
Grey Rocks Inn
Heavenly Valley
Hunter Mountain Ski Bowl
Jay Peak
Mont Tremblant
Mount Washington
Park City
Steamboat Springs
Sugarloaf
Tuckerman Ravine
Whiteface Mountain

Slopeside Resort Village

Alta
Arapahoe Basin
Aspen
Bear Valley*
The Big Mountain
The Bugaboos
Chantecler
Crystal Mountain
Garibaldi's Whistler
Grey Rocks Inn
Jackson Hole
Lake Louise*
Loon Mountain
Mittersill
Mont Tremblant
Mount Hood
Mount Snow
Playboy Club-Hotel
Schuss Mountain
Snowmass-at-Aspen
Squaw Valley
Stratton
Sun Valley*
Sunshine Ski Village
Taos Ski Valley
Vail
Waterville Valley*
The Wilderness*

* Shuttle service; lodges within 3 miles.

Expert Skiers

Alta
Arapahoe Basin
Aspen
Bear Valley
The Bugaboos
Cannon Mountain
Crystal Mountain
Garibaldi's Whistler
Heavenly Valley
Jackson Hole
Lake Louise
Mad River Glen
Mammoth Mountain
Mont Tremblant
Mont Norquay

Mount Snow
Mount Washington
Squaw Valley
Steamboat Springs
Stowe
Sugarbush Valley
Sun Valley
Taos Ski Valley
Tuckerman Ravine

Intermediate Skiers

Arapahoe Basin
Aspen
Big Bromley
The Big Mountain
Boyne Country
Cranmore
Crystal Mountain
Glen Ellen
Heavenly Valley
Hunter Mountain Ski Bowl
Jay Peak
Killington Ski Area
Lake Louise
Loon Mountain
Madonna
Mammoth
Mont Tremblant
Mount Hood
Mount Snow
Park City
Snowmass-at-Aspen
Squaw Valley
Steamboat Springs
Stowe
Stratton
Sugarbush Valley
Sugarloaf
Sun Valley
Vail
Waterville Valley
Whiteface Mountain

Beginning Skiers

Big Boulder
Boyne Country
Camelback
Chantecler
Grey Rocks Inn
Haystack
Jay Peak
Killington Ski Area
Loon Mountain
Madonna
Magic Mountain
Mittersill
Playboy Club-Hotel
Schuss Mountain
Squaw Valley
Stowe
Stratton
Sunshine Ski Village
Vail
Waterville Valley

Night skiing at Mount Tom in Massachusetts.

NORTH AMERICAN TOURIST BUREAUS

The following state-administered or state-supported agencies help promote the sport of skiing through advertising or public service programs:

Alaska	Economic Development & Planning, Travel Division, Box 2391, Juneau, Alaska 99801
Arizona	Arizona Development Board, 1500 West Jefferson Street, Phoenix, Arizona 85007
California	Department of Parks & Recreation, State Capital Building, Sacramento, California 92511
Colorado	Department of Commerce & Development, 600 State Services Building, Denver, Colorado 80203
Connecticut	Connecticut Development Commission, P. O. Box 865, State Office Building, Hartford, Connecticut 06115
Idaho	Department of Highways, Box 879, Boise, Idaho 83701
Illinois	Division of Parks and Memorials, Room 100, State Office Building, Springfield 62706
Indiana	Department of Conservation, State Office Building, Indianapolis, Indiana 46209
Iowa	State Conservation Commission, East 7th and Court Avenue, Des Moines, Iowa 50309
Kansas	Kansas State Park and Resources Authority, 801 Harrison, Topeka, Kansas 66612

Skiing at White Pass, Washington.

Maine	Maine Department of Economic Development, State Office Building, Augusta, Maine 04330
Maryland	Department of Economic Development, State Office Building, Annapolis, Maryland 21404
Massachusetts	Department of Commerce, 150 Causeway Street, Boston, Massachusetts 02108
Michigan	Department of Conservation, Stevens T. Mason Building, Lansing, Michigan 48929
Minnesota	Minnesota Tourist Information, 212 State Office Building, St. Paul, Minnesota 55101
Missouri	Division of Resources & Development, 1206 Jefferson Building, Jefferson City, Missouri 65102
Montana	State Highway Commission, Helena, Montana 59601
Nevada	Nevada State Park Commission, State Capitol, Carson City, Nevada 89701
New Hampshire	Office of Vacation Travel, P. O. Box 856, Concord, New Hampshire 03301
New Jersey	Department of Conservation and Economic Development, Division of Resources Development, Bureau of Commerce, State Promotion Section, P. O. Box 1889, Trenton, New Jersey 08625

New York	State Department, Department of Commerce, 112 State Campus Site, Albany 12207		North Main Street, Providence, Rhode Island 02903
North Carolina	Department of Conservation & Development, Division of State Parks, Raleigh, North Carolina 27607	South Dakota	Department of Game, Fish and Parks, Pierre, South Dakota 57501
		Tennessee	Department of Conservation, 203 Cordell Hull Building, Nashville, Tennessee 37219
North Dakota	State Historical Society of North Dakota, Division of State Parks, Liberty Memorial Building, Bismarck, North Dakota 58501	Utah	Utah Travel, Council Hall, Capitol Hill, Salt Lake City, Utah 84114
Ohio	Ohio Division of Parks & Recreation Department of Natural Resources, 913 Ohio Department Building, Columbus, Ohio 43212	Vermont	Development Commission, Montpelier, Vermont 05602
		Washington	Department of Commerce & Economic Development, General Administration Building, Olympia, Washington 98502
Oregon	Travel Information Division, Oregon State Highway Department, Salem, Oregon 97310	West Virginia	Industrial & Publicity Commission, State Office Building, Charleston, West Virginia 25305
Pennsylvania	Travel Development Bureau, Department of Commerce, South Office Building, Harrisburg, Pennsylvania 17120	Wisconsin	Conservation Department, Box 450, Madison, Wisconsin 53701
Rhode Island	Department of Natural Resources, Division of Parks & Recreation, 100	Wyoming	Travel Commission, 2320 Capitol Avenue, Cheyenne, Wyoming 82001

CANADIAN TOURIST BUREAUS

Canadian Government Travel Bureau, Ottawa, Canada or 680 Fifth Avenue, New York, New York 10019

			Box 1030, Fredericton, New Brunswick
		Newfoundland	Tourist Development Office, Confederation Building, St. John's, Newfoundland
Alberta	Alberta Government Travel Bureau, 1629 Centennial Building, Edmonton, Alberta	Nova Scotia	Nova Scotia Travel Bureau, Department of Trade and Industry, 5670 Spring Garden Road, Halifax, Nova Scotia
British Columbia	British Columbia Travel Bureau, Department of Travel Industry, Victoria, British Columbia	Ontario	Department of Tourism and Information, 185 Bloor Street East, Toronto 2, Ontario
Manitoba	Tourist Branch, Department of Tourism and Recreation, Legislative Building, Winnipeg, Manitoba	Quebec	Tourism Branch, Department of Tourism, Game and Fisheries, Parliament Buildings, Quebec City, Quebec
New Brunswick	New Brunswick Travel Bureau, Department of Natural Resources, P. O.		

SKIING IN EUROPE AND THE REST OF THE WORLD

There is no day of the year—any year—when skiing is not being done somewhere on the continent of Europe. In August, when Sicily is scorched by the Mediterranean sun and the siesta in Palermo stretches through the day, Italian skiers find hard-packed, fast slopes on the flanks of volcanic Etna. Spanish skiers (their number is growing) from Madrid, Barcelona, and Malaga run the Sierra Nevada almost any day in July. On the other side of the Mediterranean, in Morocco, one of the hottest countries on the planet in the summer, the European colony in Rabat and Tangiers skis the long, shallow, but high runs of the Atlas Mountains, where a few hours away the temperature touches 125 degrees. More on this later in the section, but for now let us see about planning a ski trip to Europe.

PLANNING A SKI TRIP TO EUROPE

Once you decide to ski Europe, your decision making has just begun, for there are so many mountains, so many ways to reach them.

To point you toward the most enjoyable European ski vacation with the fewest headaches, there are twenty-eight things you should think about, preferably right away. These are not laws, but suggestions, based on the experience of skiers and travel professionals.

Let us assume that like most people, you will fly over the ocean, stay three weeks, and sample more than one area. Your basic budget—fares, rooms, meals, lifts—can be rock-bottom or freewheeling. How you invest it should be weighed against two standards: is it what *you* like, and is it feasible? Only you know whether you crave tough skiing or easy night life. But in checking feasibility, there are good sources.

Where to Get Information

The various national tourist agencies (given later in this section), airlines, and foreign railroads have offices in major cities. If you live beyond visiting range, write to their New York headquarters (not overseas). Go back as often as necessary. Do not be afraid to ask "silly" questions. If you want to know where to see royalty or learn curling, you will get a serious answer. Ask friends, and friends of friends, about their trips. But be wary of information you get from non-pros, unless you know their tastes and trust their judgment. Be even warier of travel agents, unless they are ski specialists or are recommended by satisfied *ski* customers. A good ski-oriented agent can be a godsend, with access to reservations you would never get on your own. His services will be free, except for cables and such. Like general travel agents, general guidebooks are useless. Their data is like "Davos has skiing in winter."

If you hate homework, but do not know a travel agent, ask an airline about package trips. They do not save money, but they save research time by getting all your reservations and making all your arrangements. Packagers have leverage in booking choice hotels.

Information You Will Need

From the tourist offices, get descriptive folders on individual villages that interest you. These specify ski terrain, facilities, prices, hotels, ways of getting there. The best ones have trail maps and street maps.

From tourist offices and carriers, get travel maps and timetables. No, you do not need to pick departure times now, but you do need to estimate the length, complexity, and cost of a trip between resorts. Caution—tourist officials will read you timetables by the hour rather then let you take a copy home to study. Insist.

From everybody, get prices on everything. Ask if there are special rates for groups, for certain dates, for buying tickets here, for any reason whatsoever. Always check the date the information was issued and the period it covers. Do not despair. This literature is beautifully prepared, free, and makes great autumnal reading. It is vital that you read it all, simultaneously, including the footnotes. Those annoying asterisks signify things like "not until June" or "surcharge 15 per cent."

Charter Trips

If you are eligible, a charter trip is hard to beat for price. Most of the information given on page 339 holds true for European charter trips, too.

Precautions for Charter Members. For a few dollars, you can buy insurance that covers the regular fare in one or both directions. This protects you if your charter does not take off, or if injury prevents you from returning with the group. To recoup the return fare, you will need a doctor's certificate proving you could not fly with the group.

If You Cannot Go Charter. Careful scheming might offset the higher regular fares. For instance, midweek flights (Monday through Thursday) are usually cheaper than those on weekends.

Other Budget Savers

Avoid the high season and save 10 to 15 per cent on hotels. Definitions vary by vil-

lages, but high season usually includes the Christmas holidays, plus February 1 to March 15. Low season means lower prices, but it also means riskier snow and less jollity. Even during the high season, new and offbeat resorts compensate for their lack of development by offering bargains.

Wherever and whenever, dollars can be stretched by traveling second class on trains and staying in second- and third-class hotels, pensions (boarding houses), or private homes. Private homes can be lonely, but inexpensive hotels can swing. Joining the local ski club might also cut your costs.

Buying tickets in the U.S. can also save you money. The Swiss offer a Holiday Ticket, a made-to-your-order package for internal surface transportation, with various bonuses and reduced fares.

Skiing Ability

European skiing is not tough. Even the hairiest mountains, with the possible exception of Chamonix, have easy ways down. At Gstaad, Cervinia, and elsewhere, there are entire beginners' Alps. All resorts have facilities and classes for intermediates and novices. If the mountains intimidate you—and they should, a little—join a class.

Picking Your Resorts

Consider first the places you have heard about most. There are reasons why resorts get famous. Then consider your own tastes. St.

A brilliant Alpine sun at La Plagne, France, supplies radiant heating to gondola cars shaped like modernistic telephone booths. Much of the skiing at the new French resort, designed by Émile Allais, is on easy beginner terrain. But there are timed race courses and steep couloirs, such as the one at left, to challenge even the expert skiers.

Moritz and Gstaad are terribly social, but if you are not terribly social, there are merely magnificent resorts with a lot of pretty girls. Klosters attracts the literati, but there is no guarantee you will ski into a famous author without an appointment. Davos, Zermatt, St. Anton, Zürs, and Chamonix are classic choices for superior skiers. Kitzbühel is famed for its night life as well as its infinite variety of slopes. Lech-am-Arlberg is the epitome of picture-postcard charm. Switzerland and France tend to be more expensive than Austria or Italy, but you can reverse the tendency by your choice of hotels.

Offbeat Resorts

As noted previously, new, minor, or faraway places have lower price scales. They tend to be more informal, friendlier, and less crowded. A major attraction is the thrill of discovery. A major disadvantage is the relative lack of varied ski facilities. Unless you have a minimal budget do not spend your whole vacation discovering Alps.

Prevalence of Americans

Ask not how to avoid your countrymen, unless you can ask it in three languages. At least, settle for a resort with a big British clientele. Areas with few English-speaking customers might lack English-speaking instructors. Europeans, hereinafter known as The Real People, are less prone to make friends if they have trouble communicating. One index to the proportion of English-speaking guests is the quality and quantity of our language in the resort's brochure.

Many skiers going to Europe find it makes sense to pick three areas that offer different atmospheres and spend one week in each. Any more than this leaves you little chance to get acquainted with slopes or people, and consumes money as well as time.

To get the "all-in" rate at hotels (full board, room, heat, taxes), you must stay at least three days. The best lift-ticket buys are *Abonnements,* unlimited tickets for seven days or longer.

In composing a resort itinerary, the amount of effort needed to get from one place to another is a basic consideration. This is where maps and timetables can save you grief.

Tips on Interarea Travel

Villages in two different countries might be closer together or easier to travel to than villages at opposite ends of the same country. To save ski time, leave one area late in the afternoon, spend the night at a town en route, and head for your next mountain in the early morning. The best travel day is Sunday, when even the biggest resorts are clogged with weekenders. It is also when the most trains and buses run. If your heart is set on skiing two far-apart resorts, consider flying between cities, despite higher costs.

Driving

Assuming the pass you want is open in the winter—many, such as the Simplon and Furka are not—European roads are good, if not exactly thruways. Check the footnotes on your map about passes and tunnels, and check the road conditions before you start out.

It is easy to rent a car in big resorts and big cities. European rental rates are not bad, but check the gas tank before you get in and drive away. If you are going to start driving on arrival day, reserve your car before you leave home.

If you are going to Europe and plan to drive, you should get an international driver's license before leaving. The AAA can handle this for you if you show them your domestic license and give them two passport photos and $3. If you happen to be in the market for a new foreign car, buying one in Europe is appreciably cheaper than buying it in the U.S. Your own foreign car dealer can provide you with details.

They Drive It

You can often arrange to be driven to railheads, nearby airports, and resorts by taxi, jitney, or chauffered car. Ask at your hotel. If you ever miss connections on public transportation, try a taxi. A few dollars might save a long delay.

Hotels

Categories of quality and price quotations are safeguarded by law. The brochures quote price ranges; when you reserve, ask for the specific cost of your room. In general, the rate structure in most resorts looks like this—for one person, room, bath, three meals, trips, and assorted surcharges: deluxe, $10–$27; first class, $9–$22; second class, $6–$18. Pension, guest house, and third class, $5–$12.

If you stay less than three days, the rates are higher. If you forgo a private bath, you save a few dollars. If you eat out you cut a little from your hotel bill. But unless you are planning to live on crackers, you will end up paying more in restaurants.

Remember that some French hotels, even in high season, have *Forfait* packages that include lift tickets if you stay seven days.

European hotels are hotels, not ski lodges. Remember that European ski resorts were resorts long before they catered to skiers. Their facilities and services reflect a tradition going back centuries. You will find liveried porters and chambermaids even in cheaper establishments, where the style and service surpasses all but North America's poshest places. You will not find bunk rooms or room-sharing with strangers. Many older hotels, even expensive ones, have few rooms with private baths. Going without a bath does not mean going dirty. It means you ask the chambermaid to draw you a bath and you tip her for each tubful.

Choosing Hotels

If you like things lively, look for a hotel with lots of rooms, an orchestra, and dancing—or a cheaper hotel next door to it. If you want to save yourself for skiing, check the brochure street map to make sure your hotel is near the principal lifts. If your budget is limited, pick a second- or even third-class hotel and settle for running water.

Getting Reservations

Please do not dash off without reservations, at least for your first area. You can end up sleeping in a bathtub, or taking the train back down the valley. The resorts are self-contained. There are no highways to drive down, seeking motels.

Write to several hotels at the same time. Some have three-year waiting lists. Give your exact arrival and departure dates, number in

your party, the kind of room you want, and the kind you will settle for. Do not send money yet. Ask for the specific rate on the room being offered you.

Enclose an international postal coupon, which you get at any post office, to cover the cost of their reply. Use airmail. When you get word that they have room, send the deposit requested, usually several nights' rent. If you are applying late, write the village tourist office and ask them to find you a room in one of several hotels, stating your price range and preferences. Take the letter confirming your reservation with you.

When you arrive, if you loathe your hotel, move! You will lose money, but it will be a small percentage of what you have invested in a good time.

Meals

Eating in is much less expensive and more convenient than in America, obviously. If you do not want to come down the mountain to get lunch, they will give you a picnic lunch in a shopping bag. Restaurants will give you water with meals, if you ask for it. Wine, ordered from the waiter or wine steward, is best ordered by the bottle, which is brought back to your table until you finish it, or as "open wine," lesser vintages served in carafes and also brought back each meal until it is gone. The Real People (Europeans) also order bottled mineral water to go with the wine. Except with breakfast, coffee costs extra.

Do not expect to be seated at a jolly table with ten strangers. You are assigned a table for the precise number of people you registered with. Changes require permission of the maître d'.

Buying Equipment

If you are planning to buy new stuff, at least take your old boots with you. Do not expect universal bargains, or stateside stocks. The boots carried in a single shop back home might be made in ten different villages. Strolz in Lech can make you Strolz boots, but for custom-made Molitors you must go to Wengen. Bootmaking can take anywhere from one to five days.

Taking Equipment

Figure that skis, boots, and poles weigh 20 pounds. On charters, you usually get 55 pounds of baggage free. On regular economy flights, you get 44, but one set of equipment is counted as 4.4 pounds, whatever its actual weight. Only if your gear puts you over the free limit will you pay excess penalties.

You can rent anything you need when you get there, but most of us are too fussy to enjoy rental boots or clothes. As a compromise, skis, which are easy to fit but hard to lug, might be rented and everything else brought along. Rentals are expensive. Yes, most places will have American metallics and safety bindings on rental. Write ahead to reserve equipment through your hotel.

If you are going off to sightsee, check your gear at a hotel, station, or airport (free, if you leave them with customs as you enter the country) or ship them ahead to yourself via the equivalent of Railway Express.

Ski Schools and Guides

If you stick to the main pistes (that is international for trail; even on open slopes there is often a beaten track), you can simply follow the crowd. If you want to explore, get a guide or join a class. Classes are a great way to meet people and to learn the areas. Even at low intermediate levels, classes go on interesting day trips.

Guides and private instructors get tipped; class instructors get treated to a drink by the entire student body.

Pacing Yourself

Jet flying makes for a grueling trip, and the time change will leave you unglued for several days; so will the high altitude. It takes all of Disembarkation Day, and possibly longer, to reach your first area.

Go native. None of the Real People hit the slopes before 10 A.M. If the dining room is empty at breakfast, it is because "They" are breakfasting in bed. Everyone, including the lift operators, knocks off for a long lunch. If you stick to stateside schedules, you will avoid long lines, but you will be one tired American. When the weather gets bad enough, many Europeans stop skiing. They often are right.

Differing Customs

Adopting local folkways can be intriguing, but there is no need to make yourself miserable. They do not drink orange juice for breakfast, but if you must, order it, or buy oranges to keep on your windowsill. Americans are so determined to be Good Ambassadors that we drive Europeans crazy by refusing to say what we want. If you think you are not getting a square deal, first check your facts, then complain.

You can get by with your stateside sports clothes, but girls should be aware that Europe has gone very dressy—stretch suits by day, pants suits by night, and no holds barred on cut or fabric. In posh places, men will need jackets and ties; and girls, fancy pants or long skirts. In informal establishments, ski pants will do for the evening. On slopes you will not need to bundle up New England style. European hotels, however, tend to be chillier than ours. Wear an extra sweater.

The only truly gauche thing you can do is ask for a typical native drink. The bartender's stock in trade is knowing your typical native drink, no matter where you are from.

Do not let tipping be a nightmare. When in doubt, ask. Most hotels and restaurants put a 15 per cent service charge on your bill. If you are not sure it is there, ask. Even with a service charge, you should give a small additional amount directly to anyone who performs a personal service—the waiter, wine steward, concierge, porter, chambermaid. How much? Ask the manager, or a European guest. One word of warning—no one will swoon with joy because you have arrived. Not that you will be picketed. You will merely be nodded to, for the first 72 hours. Europeans, particularly older people, do not rush to get acquainted with their fellow guests.

Language Barrier

Ignore it. If you do not already know foreign languages, it is too late to learn before you leave. Take a phrase book.

Sightseeing

If this is your first trip, consider spending part of it looking at cities. A popular compromise is two weeks skiing, one week sight-seeing. Keep your dream cities in mind when choosing your dream mountain. If you ski first, you will be in better physical shape.

Après-ski

What will you have? Casinos with roulette, orchestras and black-tie patrons? Or disco-theques where no one needs a tie or shirt? You will find as much action as you are looking for. Still popular is tea dancing, be-tween 5 and 7 P.M. Go in your ski clothes.

At your hotel, do not expect an American-Alpine lounge with fireplace. Do not expect the innkeeper to introduce you around, or to be talked to by strangers, but do not let that stop you. Just remember to shake hands with any nonservant over sixteen, whenever you meet or part.

Before You Leave Home

Write for reservations; buy tickets; write to reserve cars and equipment; buy small amounts of foreign currencies you will use; take extra passport photos for lift tickets; check your passport and smallpox papers; buy traveler's checks; pack your timetables, maps, and letters of confirmation; check the weight of your luggage and gear (on a bath-room scale, weigh yourself, weigh yourself holding your baggage, then subtract); resolve to be flexible.

When You Arrive

Double-check all arrival and departure times. Cash your traveler's checks at banks or currency exchanges when possible; you will get better rates than at hotels. Reserve some single dollar bills, to change when you need only a small amount of foreign currency (and to get you out of the airport when you come home).

At All Times

Despite the planning, trains get missed, baggage gets lost, and digestive tracts get homesick. But—all those Europeans who ignore you when you seem to be okay will scurry to your aid at the first sign of trouble. Above all else, remember, if you do not know what to do, or do not see what you want—ask.

EUROPE'S ALPS

Europe has a very special kind of mountains —the most accessible big mountains in the world. The slopes you ski on there are no higher than ski areas in our own Sierra and Rocky Mountains, and the snowfall is often not nearly so great. What makes the Alps so different is the fact that they have been lived in for millenniums, whereas our own high mountains are comparatively wild.

For 3,000 years cattle have been grazing on the slopes of the Alps. (Thus the name of the most famous ski region of the world, the Parsenn of Switzerland, is derived from the Latin word for pasture: *pratum*.) Even high above the timber line—except on bare rock, ice fields, and avalanche tracks—the cattle have fertilized and mown a lush carpet of turf. The mountains are girdled with forests which are no wild, accidental growth, but a woodland garden cultivated by people who think in terms of decades and centuries in-stead of minutes and hours. The floor of these forests is kept free of undergrowth, and in many places to this day are picked clean of fallen branches by wood gatherers. Foresters prune the lower branches of the trees, and remove windfalls and mature timber.

There, skiers have inherited an almost limitless variety of skiing terrain. Once on top of a medium-sized mountain, you can ski down in practically any direction over the snowfields. If there is no trail, you can ski right through the woods with perfect ease. The runs in the Alps are sometimes planned to avoid obstacles and uninteresting detours; often they are quite arbitrary routes to the bottom, from which you may depart at will. Deep snow, smoothly packed slopes and trails, woods slalom, endless touring possibil-ities—as well as the inevitable mogul mazes on the more popular steep runs—all of these are yours in the Alps.

The "lived-in" aspect of the European Alps benefits skiers in other ways. The region is crisscrossed with good roads and railroad tracks running between, around, over, and through the mountains. You can go anywhere quickly and conveniently. Every valley, however "remote," has its town or villages, with at least a place to stay and eat, and usually much more than that. Many Alpine resorts were thriving a hundred years before skiing became popular, and could provide accommodations for thousands and all the civilized comforts from the very start. For Americans used to long drives to ski areas, rope tows, long waits at the lift, a diet of soggy hamburgers and stale coffee in paper cups, and crowded accommodations, skiing in Europe is a luxury—for only a few of the best-known Alpine resorts become overcrowded at the height of the season.

Because the mountains are easily accessible, and because comparatively little needs to be spent on improving slopes and cutting trails, European ski entrepreneurs can afford to construct more and bigger lifts. Some of

Street scene in the ski resort of Lech, Vorarlberg, Austria.

The skiing area around Innsbruck, Austria.

The "Bräma-Büel" cable airway at Davos, Switzerland.

the funiculars and tramways were originally built for summer tourists and have been taken over by skiers in the winter. Many more lifts were built specifically for skiers, particularly since the past wars. Today, more than 1,000 ski lifts of all kinds are concentrated in a region the size of New England, and in some places you can ski all day and never ride the same lift twice.

Thus, European ski areas serve as a model for the rest of the world. By dint of enormous labor and expense, skiing and vacationing of the Alpine variety has been made possible at top American resorts like Aspen and Sun Valley. But Europe has a long head start, and it is almost inconceivable that we should ever catch up. Why try, when it is so easy to hop a plane? And of course, with its Old World atmosphere and scenic and cultural attractions, Europe has so much more to offer besides *just* skiing. In fact, it is off the slopes that Europe comes into its own. The development of American-type ski resorts has reduced somewhat the glamour of the European ski village, but it has not changed its service. It is not so much *what* is done as *how* it is done that accounts for European flair. From the chef and maître d' hôtel down, the

employees are professionals, dedicated by tradition and training to serving you. Dinner under these circumstances is not a meal, but an occasion. One experiences a sense of luxury, even at an ordinary hotel.

Galas, balls, costume parties, torchlight parades, midnight sleigh excursions, church festivals, races, ski school parties, Tyrolean evenings, skating exhibitions, ice hockey games—each Alpine resort has special events on top of its regular after-ski life. These are scheduled irregularly, and the trick is to find out all the possibilities. Look at posters around town; study the magazine or calendar of events put out by almost every Tourist Information Office. Do not wait for someone to tell you. Ask the concierge at your hotel. Ask at the Tourist Office. Ask your ski instructor or the people in your class. If some event interests you, book a table or buy a seat in advance.

Europeans, especially Europeans who go to ski resorts, are a sophisticated people. This sophistication is reflected in their after-ski life. Quite possibly because Europeans are not as leisure-oriented as Americans and look to their vacation as a chance to splurge for the season, they expect more from their resorts in

Winter days at St. Moritz, Switzerland, where the frozen lake is a famous site for horse races.

the way of after-ski entertainment. Music and entertainers will be first rate, and the evening meal, as already noted, will be superb. The nightclub you go to for a finishing liqueur will be sparkling and gay. You will leave an Alpine resort feeling that you have lived.

Europeans, particularly the older people, tend to be very formal. They love to exchange calling cards; bring some along. Fellow hotel guests do not rush to become friends. Not that they are hostile; they simply do not share most Americans' across-the-board gregariousness. Usually they nod to you. Nod back. Remember to shake hands with any non-servant adult when being introduced, when meeting, or when parting. Men shake hands with women and women shake hands with other women—constantly. Despite what you have heard about how much Europeans appreciate Americans trying to speak their language, they hate to hear us mangle it. If you start out in French, and the other person answers in perfect English, that means you have lost the game and should switch to English, too.

No matter how standoffish Europeans seem when everything goes well, they rush to your rescue at the first sign of trouble. They are more than generous about giving directions, often grabbing your arm to guide you to the bus stop or to lead you to someone who speaks English. If you have questions that need on-the-spot answers—questions about who gets tipped or whether you need a tie—do not hesitate to ask the nearest European. As a matter of fact, a small crisis can be an excellent ice-breaker.

Most of the big European winter resorts close about the end of March. A few run through May. At some of the most popular, like Val d'Isere in France, ski schools operate through July and August. As stated previously, there are more than a dozen major summer ski resorts in Europe—in Austria, France, Germany, Italy, and Switzerland. Germany is not, however, an important factor in summer skiing. One German ski glacier qualifies as a late-season ski center. This is Zugspitze, 9,700 feet over Garmisch.

You will find European Alpine skiing

The giant slalom course at Val Gardena, Italy, which was the scene of the 1970 FIS championships.

different. The Continental resorts are organized in a way that simplifies the struggles of a rank beginner. Classes and slopes usually are in the heart of the village. The weather is less cruel and the quality of after-ski life more soothing than it is back home. At the end of a week, the initiate is going on excursions to the top of the mountain with his class. And, if it turns out he hates skiing, well—he has had a trip to Europe.

Those less than devout about the sport can be right at home on the Continent. Europeans tend to be more relaxed about skiing than Americans. Their resorts offer ample facilities for such non-ski pleasures as window shopping, promenading, and terrace sitting. If the mountains intimidate you—and they should, a little—join a class. You will get a great fringe benefit, the chance to acquire European friends.

Despite all the hoopla, you need not be a social lion or a dilettante to enjoy Europe. After-ski frenzy is not mandatory. You can bed down early, just like the homegrown diehards. If you are taking youngsters along, you will find baby-sitters, ski kindergartens, and even children's ski camps and hotels. Because of the time of the year and the costs, most Americans going over are well beyond student age. The Europeans you encounter will be too, except during Christmas, Carnival, Easter, and mid-February school break.

Guide to Major Alpine European Ski Areas

Austria

For information and travel folders, write: Austrian National Tourist Department, 545 Fifth Avenue, New York, New York 10017; 332 S. Michigan Avenue, Chicago, Illinois 60604; 3440 Wilshire Boulevard, Los Angeles, California 90005; 2433 N.W. Lovejoy Street, Portland, Oregon 97210.

Name of Area	Nearest Major City	Base Altitude	Number of Lodges	Number of Beds	Number of Lifts
Voralberg					
Brand	Bregenz	3,401	9		4
Grosswalsertal & Fontella	Faschinajoch Bregenz	3,756	9		5
Riezlern	Bregenz	3,556	58		17
Lech-Oberlech am Arlberg	Innsbruck	4,740–5,580	30		18
Schruns	Bregenz	2,264	55		8
Tschagguns	Bregenz	2,264			
Gaschurn	Bregenz	3,210			
Gargellen	Bregenz	4,670	8		4
Partenen	Bregenz	3,450			
St. Anton Im Montafon		3,139			
Zürs am Arlberg	Innsbruck	5,655	8		8
Tyrol					
Ehrwald, Lermoos	Innsbruck	3,265	56		8
Gerlos & Gmünd	Salzburg	4,090	11		5
Hopfgarten	Innsbruck	2,200	20		5
Igls	Innsbruck	2,970	215		17
Mutters	Innsbruck	2,950			
Axams-Lizum	Innsbruck				
Kitzbühel	Kitzbühel	2,500	134		21
Hintertux	Innsbruck	4,900	16		6
Lienz	Lienz	2,225	20		4
Mayrhofen	Innsbruck	2,070	63		5
Ober-Gurgl	Innsbruck	6,320	17		7
St. Anton am Arlberg	Innsbruck	4,280	162		12
St. Christoph am Arlberg	Innsbruck	5,905	5		5
St. Johann	Kitzbühel	2,160	121		29
Kirchberg		2,750			
Seefeld	Innsbruck	3,870	135		10
Sölden-Hochsölden	Innsbruck	4,470–6,790	34		11
Wildschönau	Innsbruck		36		10
Niederau		2,870			
Oberau		3,070			
Zell am Ziller	Innsbruck	1,890	30		5
Salzburg					
Bad Gastein	Salzburg	3,550	123		11
Bad Hofgastein	Salzburg	2,850	130		6
Dieten am Hochkönig	Salzburg	3,540	5		2
Krimml, Gerlosplatte	Salzburg	3,520–5,580	43 plus 300 private beds		6
Mitterbergalp am Hochkönig		4,930			Summer skiing on glacier
Mittersill, Pass Thurn	Salzburg	2,590–4,180	29 plus 100 private beds		
Muhlbach	Salzburg	2,820	12		8
Obertauern	Salzburg	5,705	41		16
Saalbach	Salzburg	3,290	78		28
Zell am See	Salzburg	2,490	103		9
Carinthia					
Heiligenblut	Klagenfurt	4,270	6		9
Kanzelhöhe Gerlitze	Villach	4,920–6,260	17		4
Styria					
Bad Aussee	Salzburg	2,130	59		4
Haus im Ennstal	Salzburg	2,530	17		7

Name of Area	Nearest Major City	Base Altitude	Number of Lodges	Number of Beds	Number of Lifts
Mariazell	Vienna	2,850–4,260	65		5
Ramsau	Salzburg	3,940	32		7
Schladming	Salzburg	2,460	25		8
Tauplitz-Tauplitzalm	Salzburg	2,920–5,440	27		9
Upper Austria					
Ebensee am Traunsee	Salzburg	1,460	27		7
Feuerkogel		5,248			
Hallstatt		6,890			
Hinterstoder	Salzburg	2,130	13		6
Obertraun	Salzburg	1,680–	24		9
Spital am Pyhrn	Linz	2,120	15		5
Lower Austria					
Lilienfeld	Vienna	1,230	15		6
Puchenstuben	Vienna	2,850	17 plus 390 private beds		8
Semmering	Vienna	2,750			

France

For information and travel folders, write: French Government Tourist Office, 610 Fifth Avenue, New York, New York 10020; 9418 Wilshire Boulevard, Beverly Hills, California 90210.

Haute Savoie

Name of Area	Nearest Major City	Base Altitude	Number of Lodges	Number of Beds	Number of Lifts
Avoriaz	Geneva	5,900			7
Chamonix-Mont Blanc	Geneva	3,415–12,605	112	3,000	26
Châtel	Geneva	3,960	17	300	8
Flaine	Geneva	5,000			12
Les Contamines	Geneva	3,841	22	500	8
La Clusaz	Geneva	3,432	30	1,000	19
Les Gets	Geneva	3,867	30	650	18
Megève	Geneva	3,672	93	1,875	24
Les Houches	Geneva	3,326	35	600	5
Morzine	Geneva	3,300	55	1,200	16
St. Gervais	Geneva	2,970	65	1,205	15
Samoëns	Geneva	2,706	23	800	6

Savoie

Name of Area	Nearest Major City	Base Altitude	Number of Lodges	Number of Beds	Number of Lifts
Courchevel	Geneva	6,105	60	4,500	25
La Plagne	Geneva	6,200	7	4,000	5
Méribel	Geneva	5,280	26	382	8
Notre Dame de Bellecombe	Geneva	3,742	12	250	10
Pralognan-la-Vanoise	Geneva	4,653	8	580	7
Tignes	Geneva	6,930	19	298	12
Val d'Isère	Geneva	6,105	60	7,500	28
Valloire	Grenoble	4,719	21	380	11

Dauphine Region

Name of Area	Nearest Major City	Base Altitude	Number of Lodges	Number of Beds	Number of Lifts
Alpe d'Huez	Grenoble	6,128	42	1,000	9
Chamrousse	Grenoble	5,445	16	750	12
Les Deux Alpes	Grenoble	5,478	24	300	14
Montgenèvre	Briançon	6,138	12	290	7
Le Sauze	Grenoble	4,620	13	320	7
Serre-Chevalier	Briançon	4,455	20	350	15
Villard-de-Lans	Grenoble	3,465	29	500	10

Name of Area	Nearest Major City	Base Altitude	Number of Lodges	Number of Beds	Number of Lifts
Côte d'Azure Region					
Auron	Nice	5,280	13	279	9
Valberg	Nice	5,610	10	183	7
Les Pyrénées					
Barèges	Lourdes	4,092	17	410	6
Font-Romeu	Toulouse	5,940	19	700	6
Superbagneres	Luchon	5,940	2	195	14
Le Massif Central					
Le Mont-Dore	Clermont-Ferrand	3,465	60	1,200	11
Le Jura					
Métabief	Geneva	3,333	18	300	12
Les Rousses	Geneva	3,795	15	315	16

Italy

For information and travel folders, write: Italian Government Tourist Office, 630 Fifth Avenue, New York, New York 10020; 333 North Michigan Avenue, Chicago, Illinois 60611; St. Francis Hotel, Post Street, San Francisco, California 94119.

Name of Area	Nearest Major City	Base Altitude	Number of Lodges	Number of Beds	Number of Lifts
Dolomites					
Belluno Nevegal	Milan	4,839–5,192			5
Turin					
Sauze D'ouix	Turin	4,920–7,000	5		12
Sestriere	Turin	6,000	15		20
Ala di Stura	Turin	3,608	8		3
Bardonecchia	Turin	4,303	19		7
Cesena	Turin	4,429	15		3
Chiomonte	Turin	2,453	3		4
Claviere	Turin	5,774	8		3
Alessandria					
Limone Piemonte	Genoa	3,608	21		6
Vercelli					
Alagna Belvedere	Milan	3,906	10		4
Alpe Mera	Milan	5,151	6		8
Breuil-Cervina	Milan	6,574	20		7
Novara					
Macugnaga	Milan	4,353	25		4
Bergamo					
Foppolo-Montebello	Milan	4,970	7		6
Sondrio					
Aprica	Milan	3,874	20		6
Bormio	Milan	4,019	32		6
Madesimo	Milan	5,032	11		6
Ponte di Legno	Brescia	4,127–6,100	3		
Aosta					
Cervinia	Milan	6,700	30		17
Cogne	Aosta	5,032	10		

Name of Area	Nearest Major City	Base Altitude	Number of Lodges	Number of Beds	Number of Lifts
Courmayeur	Milan	4,029	67		4
Gressoney La Trinité	Milan	5,337	6		1

Trento

Canazel alla Marmolada- Alba Penja	Trent	1,465– 5,220	31		10
Madonna di Campiglo	Trent	4,993	29		6
San Martino di Castrozzo	Trent	4,737	28		8
Vigo and Pozza di Fassa	Trent	4,330	18		4

Bozen

Alpe di Siusi-Selseralm	Milan	6,135	22		17
Corvara-Kurfar	Milan	5,144	13		7
Val Badia (3 Villages)	Milan	4,921	22		9
Monte San Vigilio	Milan	5,000	5		4
Ortisei-St. Ulrich (Val Gardena)	Milan	4,048	31		7
Passo Gardena- Grödner Joch	Bolzano	6,958	3		4
Santa Cristina	Milan	4,685	10		5
Selva (Val Gardena)	Milan	5,127	37		15
Solda	Milan	6,233	22		5

Belluno

Cortina d'Ampezzo	Belluno	4,016	71		20
Dobbiaco	Belluno	4,045	4		4
Penavena-Belvedere and Croce D'Aune	Belluno	3,412	4		4
Sappada	Belluno	4,101	28		6

Vicenza

Asiago	Vicenza	3,283	26		6

Udine

Tarvisio-Camporosso	Udine	2,463	14		4

Pistoria

Abetone-Monte Gomito	Florence	6,207	22		7

Frosinone

Campocatino	Rome	5,905	2		6

Rieti

Terminillo	Rome	5,577	11		6

Germany

For information and travel folders, write: German Tourist Information Office, 500 Fifth Avenue, New York, New York 10036; 11 South La Salle Street, Chicago, Illinois 60603, 323 Geary Street, San Francisco, California 94102.

Upper Bavaria

Garmisch-Partenkirchen	Munich	2,400– 9,250	60	8,870	30
Berchtesgaden Land	Munich	5,600– 7,200	54	10,500	12
Ruhpolding	Munich	1,950– 5,100		800	5
Bayrischzell	Munich	2,406– 5,400		1,226	8

Name of Area	Nearest Major City	Base Altitude	Number of Lodges	Number of Beds	Number of Lifts
Rottach-Egern	Munich	2,220–5,400		605	5
Schliersee	Munich	2,400–3,700		2,600	6
Grainau	Munich	3,000–8,400		600	4
Mittenwald	Munich	2,760–7,200		1,000	3
Obergammergau	Munich	2,550–5,400		2,600	4
Bad Reichenhall	Munich	1,410–7,500		3,000	4
Allgau Region					
Oberstdorf	Munich	2,529–7,215		1,650	8
Hindelang-Bad Oberdorf	Munich	2,550–6,740		4,000	9
Kleinwalsertal (Riezlern, Hirschegg, Mittelberg)	Munich	3,300–6,600	206	6,000	14
Pfonten	Munich	2,700–6,000		1,600	6
Upper Valley (Bavaria)					
Reit im Winkl	Munich	2,600–6,400		1,700	7
The Harz					
St. Andreasberg	Hannover	2,250–2,692		391	3
Sauerland					
Winterberg	Bonn or Cologne	2,010–2,526		303	4
Black Forest					
Feldberg-Schwarzwald	Freiburg	3,000–4,500	34	800	5
Todtnauherb	Freiburg	3,063–4,500		200	2

Switzerland

For information and travel folders, write: Swiss National Tourist Office, 608 Fifth Avenue, New York, New York 10020; 661 Market Street, San Francisco, California 94105.

Name of Area	Nearest Major City	Base Altitude	Number of Lodges	Number of Beds	Number of Lifts
Adelboden	Berne	4,452–7,216	18	7,500	13
Andermatt	Lucerne	4,738–9,842	22	700	8
Anzère	Geneva	5,000	4		10
Arosa	Zurich	6,200–9,166	66	3,804	10
Champéry	Geneva	3,460–6,000	14	513	9
Château-d'Oex	Geneva	3,300–5,800	20	500	8
Montana-Crans	Geneva	4,987–7,800	60	3,000	16

Name of Area	Nearest Major City	Base Altitude	Number of Lodges	Number of Beds	Number of Lifts
Davos and surroundings	Zurich	5,120–9,262	110	5,000	21
Les Diablerets	Geneva	3,816–10,000	10	500	5
Engelberg	Lucerne	3,347–7,500	20	2,000	11
Flims	Zurich	3,800–8,775	30	1,300	12
Grindelwald	Berne	3,468–11,342	34	4,000	17
Gstaad	Geneva	3,450–7,080	15	937	25
Kandersteg	Berne	4,000–6,050	20	850	5
Klosters	Zurich	3,967–7,553	30	1,500	9
Lenzerheide-Valbella	Zurich	5,000–7,970	13	850	9
Leysin	Geneva	4,050–7,100	40	2,000	13
Mürren	Berne	5,450–7,100	16	750	17
Pontresina	Zurich	6,000–10,013	28	2,000	11
Saas-Fee	Geneva	5,906–13,000	30	1,500	9
St. Moritz	Zurich	6,135–10,013	52	4,176	11
Verbier	Geneva	4,921–9,000	25	1,100	20
Villars-Chesières-Bretaye	Geneva	4,300–7,300	30	1,500	10
Wengen	Berne	4,260–11,342	28	1,500	17
Zermatt	Geneva	5,315–10,284	76	4,000	17

OTHER SKI AREAS

If skiing is your reason for traveling, there are almost unlimited opportunities throughout the world. Even in Europe, your ski-travel plans need not be confined to the Alpine region. True, they may not be as spectacular as the Alps, their facilities may be less glamorous, but they have a degree of native flavor no longer present in the tourist-conscious Alps.

Pyrenees

The Pyrenees that form the boundary between France and Spain, for example, are reminiscent of the Alps in profile and formation, although they are on a smaller scale and have perhaps a friendlier and more intimate atmosphere. There are many fine ski slopes in the range, although the mountains have been only sparsely developed, and, on the average, the runs are shorter and less steep than in the French Alps.

Scandinavian Countries

We should not forget where the sport of skiing got its start—the Scandinavian countries. Norway, Sweden, and Finland offer thousands of miles of touring trails. True, these countries have developed slopes in an Alpine European fashion. The real charm of skiing in these countries is to go touring. It is the national sport in these countries, and the visitor has no problem in joining a touring

Cross-country skiing near the Pyhölunturi Fall in the Finnish Lapland.

party. The natives think nothing of going 30 to 40 miles on a day's outing. Although this may seem an incredible distance to travel on skis, it is not once you get the hang of the art. Most of the trails are over easy, rolling terrain. If refreshments are needed, they come out of your own rucksack, and there are lots of warming huts along the trail. Language in the Scandinavian countries is no problem, since most Scandinavians speak English.

Yugoslavia and Greece

Yugoslavia and Greece offer some fine skiing, although facilities in both countries are not yet up to "modern" resort standards. If you do not mind going through forbidding paperwork, there is excellent skiing in the Iron Curtain countries of Bulgaria, Czechoslovakia, Rumania, Russia, and Poland. You will find that resorts in these countries have native, if not sophisticated, charm and that you are genuinely welcome there.

Scotland

There is skiing in Scotland, although it is of a rather rugged nature, combining some of the worst elements of the American East,

Midwest, and Pacific Northwest. Nevertheless the Scots claim to enjoy it. Actually, the popularity of skiing in Scotland has grown steadily, especially in recent years, since the first handful of enthusiasts formed the Scottish Ski Club in 1907. The ski areas are located in central Scotland, north of Glasgow, Edinburgh, and Dundee. Tows and chair lifts have been slow in coming but are likely to proliferate with the increasing popularity of the sport. In fact, it is virtually impossible to go anywhere in Europe without finding skiing somewhere within easy train or driving distance.

Middle East and North Africa

There is skiing even in the Middle East and North Africa. True, skiing in North Africa cannot compare with that of the Alps, of course, for length and variety of runs, magnificence of scenery, length of season, uphill facilities, or any other essential element. Nevertheless, the skiing can be very good in the Atlas Mountains, and those who appreciate contrasts will enjoy approaching the ski areas through semitropical desert country, with mosques, and palm trees, and Berbers,

An ice palace sprouts in downtown Sapporo, Japan, site of the 1972 Winter Olympics.

and camels in evidence. Although there is no resort life at the ski areas, there are many fine hotels in other parts of Morocco and Algeria, especially in the larger cities and at the many seashore resorts.

Skiing has grown rapidly in popularity in Iran since it was introduced about thirty years ago, and Iranian teams have competed in Olympic winter games and world ski championships since 1956. There is also some in the other Middle East countries of Lebanon and Turkey.

Far East

In the Far East, the Japanese are fanatical skiers. In recent years, they have been sending highly disciplined ski teams to major world events in both Alpine and Nordic competition, and the teams have done remarkably well. The 1972 Olympic winter games were held at Sapporo, on Japan's northern island of Hokkaido. Actually, in no country in the world has skiing enjoyed a greater and more enthusiastic upsurge than in Japan. Popular participation has increased by leaps and bounds, so that now there are estimated to be over six million skiers in the country, far more than in the United States. In all, there are over 200 ski areas. However, only a few can as yet be regarded as full-fledged resorts for skiers from abroad.

If you want to reverse your season—in other words have a real ski vacation during the North American summer—South America, Australia, and New Zealand offer the answer.

South America

Portillo, Chile, is without doubt the most sophisticated skiing area in the Southern Hemisphere. Located below Mount Aconcagua in the Andes, Portillo is reached from Santiago by train. But once you arrive, accommodations, instruction, and slopes are first rate; you will find the atmosphere more St. Moritz than South American.

Skiing involves such things as the "Garganta Run," experts-only terrain that begins with a 30-degree headwall. The same lift-served area offers an intermediate's delight—a mile-long curved run through fluff. One can also run to the famed Lake of the Incas and to Juncal station, (four miles) with the hope of a Kristi-Kat ride back, or a slow freight.

Chile offers, in addition to Portillo, two other major resorts—Farellones-La Parva and Llaima. The latter is unique since skiing is done at the base of a smoking volcano near Temuco, which is in Chile's southern zone. Farellones-La Parva, located near Santiago, is more representative of the country, but the facilities are of the clubby variety.

In Argentina there is Bariloche, a first-class resort by any standard. Accessible by direct flight from Buenos Aires, one skis on the semi-open of the Cerro Catedral on runs that are long, but not steep. At Bariloche, you have

The Gran Hotel Portillo, at 10,000 feet, lies at the heart of Chile's spectacular ski country.

Skiing in Australia has become increasingly popular over the last few years.

your pick of luxury hotels and Swiss-type lodges.

There is also limited skiing in Colombia and Bolivia. Although these countries have no lack of mountains with snow, there are few lifts and fewer facilities.

Australia

While the sport Down Under is historically older than it is in the United States (see Section I), it was not really until 1960 that many ski vacationists began feeling the urge to head for the Australian Alps with their many-hued sno-gums and their plummeting snowfields. In Australia one skis at an elevation of 5,000 to 7,000 feet in temperatures that remain consistently warmer than they do during North American skiing seasons.

The time to come is between June 1 and October 15; all facilities are running, all lodges are open. The places to go are in either of two areas, one in New South Wales, the other across the Murray River Valley in Victoria. By far the largest section of the Alps lies in New South Wales with Mount Kosciusko at 7,314 feet looming above its neighbors Mount Townshend, Mount Ramshead, and Mount Twynam. The latter's western face provides a swift, uninterrupted run without peer, even in its European Alpine counterparts.

Victoria's ski fields, although not as extensive, are interesting and sometimes exciting, with one of them, Mount Buller (the racing fraternity's favorite), lying only 150 miles from Melbourne.

There is skiing, too, in Tasmania, a short sea voyage or air hop from the mainland. The snow line (the island is below the 40th parallel) is at 3,000 feet, and the entire aspect awakens a feeling of having been transported to Switzerland.

Uphill facilities are reasonably extensive. Thredbo and Perisher Valley, in New South Wales, have highways into the ski areas. Housing is going up, but not in proportion to the growing number of skiers. A man with an Aussie skiing friend is fortunate, espe-

New Zealand's high mountains are excellent for skiing.

cially if he can use the facilities of his friend's club. For others, at Thredbo there are village accommodations, and at Perisher there are such new hotels as The Sundeck and one delightfully named The Man from Snowy River.

New Zealand

Smoking active volcanos, steaming crater lakes, verdant subtropical foliage—and treeless, 6-mile runs through corn-filled snowfields; these are the contrasts that characterize skiing in New Zealand, certainly one of the unique settings in the ski world.

New Zealand is comprised of two islands; both feature spectacular skiing regions with seasons running from mid-July to mid-November on the North Island, from mid-June to mid-October on the South Island. In several high-peak and glacial areas, perpetual snows provide year-around playgrounds for adventure-loving skiers.

North Island skiing centers around Mount Ruapehu in the Tongariro National Park, not too far from Rotorua, where primitive Maori villages such as Whakarewarewa offer vivid contrasts to stretch-panted skiers. Ruapehu, 9,175 feet high, boasts three chair lifts, a T-bar, pomalift, and rope tows. Partway up the mountain, but below its snow line, is the government-operated Chateau Tongariro, a deluxe hotel in the true Alpine sense. From there, a highway leads to the lifts, where one can ski the National Downhill run or several other pistes, some more than 6 miles long. Near the summit, skiers sometimes stop for a dip in the large crater lake which bubbles up through the snow and sometimes boils.

Ruapehu and neighboring Mount Tongariro and Mount Ngauruhoe are all classed as semi-active volcanos and exhibit varying degrees of geothermal activity. Ngauruhoe, in fact, is very much alive and constantly spouts steam and smoke from its cone-shaped summit. It last erupted in 1954 in full view of spectators riding the Ruapehu lifts. Tongariro, Ngauruhoe, and Mount Egmont, 90 miles to the west, all offer excellent, though not as well-developed, facilities for ski-adventuring and downhill runs.

On the South Island, the flavor varies, for here facilities are primarily club-sponsored rather than commercially operated. Touring and ski-climbing arouse as much if not more interest than downhill skiing. In the Southern Alps, Coronet Peak, near Queenstown, offers commercial facilities and excellent skiing through nearby glacier country. Mount Cook, New Zealand's highest peak (12,349 feet), has superb runs and the Hermitage, a palatial Alpine hotel. To the north, Arthur Pass offers additional popular snowfields.

As you can see, there is skiing almost everywhere there is snow. It is up to you—and your budget—where you ski.

For more information on other so-called ski areas you may want to contact one of the following sources:

Argentina Argentine Airlines, 9 Rockefeller Plaza, New York, New York 10020.

Australia Australian Tourist Commission, 630 Fifth Avenue, New York, New York 10020.

Bulgaria Bulgarian Tourist Office, 50 East 42nd Street, New York, New York 10017.

Chile Chilean Consulate General, 809 UN Plaza, New York, New York 10017.

Czechoslovakia Czechoslovak Travel Bureau, 10 East 40th Street, New York, New York 10016.

Finland Finnish National Tourist Offices, 505 Fifth Avenue, New York, New York 10017.

Greece Greek National Tourist Organization, 601 Fifth Avenue, New York, New York 10036.

Iceland Icelandic Consulate General, 420 Lexington Avenue, New York, New York 10017.

India India Government Tourist Office, 19 East 49th Street, New York, New York 10017.

Iran Iranian Consulate General, 630 Fifth Avenue, New York, New York 10020.

Israel Israel Government Tourist Office, 574 Fifth Avenue, New York, New York 10036.

Japan Japan National Tourist Organization, 45 Rockefeller Plaza, New York, New York 10022.

Lebanon Lebanon Tourist and Information Office, 527 Madison Avenue, New York, New York 10022.

Morocco Moroccan National Tourist Office, 597 Fifth Avenue, New York, New York 10017.

New Zealand New Zealand Travel Commissioner, 630 Fifth Avenue, New York, New York 10020. (Packages to Australia and New Zealand available through Qantas Airways, 542 Fifth Avenue, New York, New York 10036.)

Norway Norwegian National Travel Office, 505 Fifth Avenue, New York, New York 10017.

Poland Polish Travel Office, 500 Fifth Avenue, New York, New York 10017.

Scotland British Information Services, 845 Third Avenue, New York, New York 10022.

Soviet Union Intourist, 45 East 49th Street, New York, New York 10017.

Spain Spanish Consulate General, 964 Third Avenue, New York, New York 10022.

Sweden Swedish National Travel Office, 505 Fifth Avenue, New York, New York 10017.

Yugoslavia Yugoslav State Tourist Office, 509 Madison Avenue, New York, New York 10022.

SECTION VI

Glossary, Lexicon, and Ski Associations

GLOSSARY OF SKIING TERMS

Skiers have their own special language—about technique, about equipment, about competition, about the ski area. To converse with them, know what they are talking about—on the slopes, at the bar, and in the magazines—then, as they say, "dig the action" in this section and you are practically guaranteed to become a better listener, a better talker, and maybe even a better skier. Here are the terms most used in skiing:

Abstem. A turn in which the lower ski is stemmed.

Acrobatics. Ski tricks or stunts.

Advanced. Skiers who are able to make parallel turns.

Aerial tramway. An uphill ski lift utilizing two aerial cabin cars that move in opposition to each other.

Airplane turn. An airborne turn off a large bump.

Alpine. All competitive events whose basic element is down-mountain skiing; downhill slalom, giant slalom.

American plan. A method followed by some lodges and hotels in which the per-day cost includes both meals and lodging.

American Ski Technique. Official sequence of instruction forms fostered by the Professional Ski Instructors of America and taught by its member instructors.

Angulation. A body position in which the knees and hips are rolled into the hill in order to edge the skis. The upper body is angled outward and down the hill to compensate for this action. Also called *comma position.*

Anodizing. A finishing process for aluminum used in poles. Through electrochemical means, a hard, scratch- and corrosion-resistant coating is put on the aluminum. Coating can take dyes of various colors.

Anticipation. Rotation of the upper body in the direction of the turn prior to unweighting and edge change. Distinguished from rotation inasmuch as anticipation can be followed by counterrotation or a reversing of the shoulders as the turn is carved.

Après-ski. Social activity at a resort after skiing.

Arlberg. A mountain region in Austria.

Arlberg strap. A leather strap attached to the ski and wrapped around the boot to prevent the ski from running away when the binding releases.

Arlberg technique. The first organized system of skiing and teaching. Developed by Hannes Schneider in the Arlberg region of the Austrian Alps in the early thirties. Noted for its use of entire body rotation, lift, forward lean, and the stem. Has been replaced by the new Austrian method.

Attack. Racer's phrase for all-out assault on course.

Austrian method. The basis for present-day modern skiing, this system was developed in the Arlberg region in the mid-fifties. It emphasizes economy of movement, a more erect stance, and use of the legs in turning. Because the legs turn first, the upper body appears to be in a slight "reverse-shoulder" position most of the time. The entire body is in a comma position.

Avalanche. A mass of snow and ice falling swiftly down a mountainside.

Avalanche control. Evaluation of high-altitude steep terrain with heavy accumulation of snowfall, and necessary preventative measures, such as artificially stimulating potential avalanches by dynamite.

Avalement. French term describing ability of skier to absorb or swallow irregularities in terrain or to promote turning by projecting feet forward with result that skier momentarily sits back.

Axial motion. Motion about the body's axis. This includes both rotation and counterrotation.

Backward lean. A body position in which the skier's center of gravity is behind the bindings.

Banking. The leaning of the entire body toward the imaginary center of a parallel Christie turn.

Base. The running surface of a ski; also, the amount of packed snow underlying a snow surface; also, the bottom of a hill or ski area; also, a protective layer of lacquer or plastic covering the running surface of the ski and designed to make the ski slide easier.

Base lacquer. A hard lacquer put on the bottoms of skis to protect the wood. Most skis now have plastic bottoms.

Base lodge. Central customer facility at ski area, usually at hill bottom.

Basket. The part of the ski pole which prevents the point or tip from going too deeply into the snow.

Bathtub. The hole in the snow made by the body of a skier who has fallen. Skiers who fail to fill in their bathtubs create unnecessary hazards for others.

Bear trap. Any nonrelease binding, specifically toe irons.

Biathlon. A Nordic event combining cross-country racing and rifle marksmanship.

Binding. A device which keeps the boot fastened to the ski.

Bite. To put pressure on the edges of the skis so that they grip the snow.

Block, blocking. A contraction of any or all of the rotary muscles of the body which transmit the turning power generated in one portion of the body to another part.

Boiler plate. A hard, frozen surface formed by a freeze following a warming period or rain.

Bomber. A skier who prefers speed to turning.

Bootlock. A type of binding which grips the boot by spring pressure and usually consists of both a toe and a heel unit. The springs are adjustable and usually require metal boot plates for proper functioning.

Boot press. A mechanical device to hold the soles of ski boots flat.

Bottoms. The running surface of skis.

Bounce. A motion used to unweight the skis.

Bowl. Large bowl-shaped mountainous area.

Breakable crust. Snow covered with a crusty surface that will not support a skier.

Buckle boots. Boots which close with a system of buckles or snaps rather than laces.

Bunny. A beginning female skier who is usually overdressed, wears too much makeup, and is not yet oriented to skiing. Same as *snow bunny*.

Bunny hill. Gentle beginner's slope.

Camber (bottom). The built-in arc of the ski as seen from the side view; designed to distribute the skier's weight more evenly on the snow.

Camber (side). The built-in arc on each side of the ski as seen from the top view, designed to enable the ski to carve a turn in the snow when it is edged and weighted while moving forward.

Carved turn. A turn which the skier manages to carve as finely as possible on the edges of the skis and in which there is a minimum of skidding or sideways slipping.

Catching an edge. Accidental catching of the edge of a ski, often resulting in a fall.

Catwalk. Narrow road for vehicular traffic up a mountain, which doubles as a ski trail, characterized by long traverses, often joining two ski trails.

Certification. The method used in the United States and Canada to distinguish fully competent instructors. A certified instructor has passed both written and practical examinations administered by a board of examiners who are experienced ski instructors. In order to remain certified, an instructor must repass the certification examination every couple of years.

Chair lift. A means of uphill transportation consisting of a series of moving chairs suspended from a moving cable. A chair can accomodate one to four skiers.

Change of lead. On a traverse the upper ski always leads. Therefore, as a Christie progresses, the inside ski of the turn must advance, either automatically or deliberately, to change the lead.

Charter flight. A flight (usually to Europe or a major resort) in which a bona fide group charters a plane for the purposes of skiing. Charter flights can result in a per-seat cost about 40 per cent lower than the lowest regular air fare.

Chatter. Vibration of a ski or ski tip as it moves over a snow surface; a generally undesirable feature of some skis.

Check. Any maneuver to slow down the skis.

Chord length. The length of the ski on the

straight line between the tail and the tip.

Christiania léger. French for "light Christiania"; a turn of the French National Ski School. It consists of four phases: flexion, extension, *projection circulaire,* and flexion.

Christie. A contraction of the word "Christiania"; any turn in which the skis are in a parallel position as the turn is completed.

Chute. Steep, narrow descent.

Climbing skins. Strips of sealskin or synthetic fiber which can be temporarily attached to the running surface of the skis. The position of the hairs permits the skis to slide forward with the grain, yet keeps the skis from slipping back when the movement is against the grain. Used for high Alpine ski touring where there are no lifts.

Closed gate. A gate with its two poles set vertically down the fall line of the hill; thus it is closed rather than open to the descending racer approaching it.

Combined. The result of two or more races arrived at by converting the results of each into points and then adding them together. Also see *FIS points.*

Comma position. See *angulation.*

Control gates. Sets of two flags placed on a down-hill course through which the racers must pass. Used to control the racers' line at potentially dangerous parts of the course.

Corn. A snow type found in spring or warm weather, formed by alternate freezing and thawing. Its honeycombed structure permits easy turning.

Cornice. An overhanging ledge of snow or ice.

Corridor. A flag combination used in slalom racing.

Counterrotation. A turning motion of the upper part of the body which results in an equal but opposite action in the lower part of the body. This occurs while the skis are unweighted.

Course marker. Small flag, twig, or evergreen bough used to delineate outside limits of a downhill race course.

Crash helmet. Protective headgear worn by racers in downhill competition, also used in giant slalom.

Crevasse. A deep crack found in glaciers.

Cross-country. A race in which competitors cover a set distance 5, 10, 15, 30, or 50 kilometers. The terrain usually consists of one-third uphill, one-third downhill, and one-third on the level.

Crud. Undesirable snow conditions consisting mostly of breakable crust. Same as *junk snow.*

Crust. Glazed surface formed on the top of snow caused by thaw-freeze cycles.

CSIA. Canadian Ski Instructors Alliance, the association of ski instructors.

CUSSA. Central United States Ski Association.

Damping. When a ski is flexed or subject to impact, the internal working or movement of materials absorbs energy so that the ski does not vibrate forever. Damping time refers to the period required for vibrations in the ski to disappear. A highly damped ski does not have as much bounce, liveliness, and flutter as a lesser-damped ski. A ski without sufficient damping, on the other hand, tends to flutter and does not track or carve as well.

Damping layer. An additional layer of rubber or other materials molded into the ski to provide additional internal damping to the ski.

Deep powder. A blanket of soft, dry, light powder of a foot or more in depth. Many purists consider this the ultimate skiing experience.

Direct parallel. A method of teaching skiers from the beginning to ski with skis and feet parallel, not in stem or V position.

Dope. Special wax preparations applied to the skis primarily by early California skiers.

Double boot. A ski boot with a soft inner boot built into a stiff outer boot which provides control over the skis and support for the ankle.

Double chair lift. Form of uphill transportation carrying two skiers at a time on one chair.

Double stem. A running position in which the tails of both skis are pushed out into a V position. Commonly called snowplow.

Downhill. Fastest and most dangerous of the three forms of Alpine racing. The racer is directed only by control gates.

Downhill ski. The lower ski or the one that will become the lower ski in any ski turn.

Down-unweighting. Reducing the body's weight on the snow by "dropping" the body sharply.

Drift. Another word for *sideslipping.*

Drop. The rapid lowering of the body to unweight the skis, making it easier for the skis to be turned. Also refers to the vertical distance between the top and the bottom of a mountain.

Drop-off. An abrupt change to a steep slope from a flat one.

Edge (one piece, continuous). The full-length piece of steel built into the running edges of the ski to provide bite on the snow when the ski is edged, and to resist wear or damage.

Edge (segmented). Shorter sections of steel placed end to end along the lower corner of the ski. Segmented and continuous steel edges affect the flexural properties of the ski differently.

Edge control. The ability to flatten the skis or put them on edge as required by circumstances.

Edge offset. The amount the steel edge extends beyond the side of the ski as seen in the top view; required for subsequent repair by sharpening.

Edge set. Increasing the holding action of the edges. The skier may set edges or create a "platform" before the turn by increasing the weight applied to the edges by rising quickly.

Edging. A means of controlling the sideward slippage of the skis by setting the skis at an angle to the snow so that they "bite" the surface.

Elbow. A slalom figure in which a closed gate is followed by an open gate set off to one side.

Epoxy. A very large class of resins characterized by great adhesion, strength, and ability to be modified by various reinforcing materials or fillers.

European plan. A method followed by most lodges and hotels in which the per-day cost includes only lodging, meals (if available) are to order and charged separately.

Excursion fare. A fare usually lower than economy fare, but which requires that the passenger return within a set period of time, usually two to three weeks.

Expert. A skier whose speed is always under control and who can handle any type of terrain, however difficult, under any snow or ice conditions.

Extension. A French term describing the rising motion of the body to unweight the skis and start the turn.

Face. The steepest part of a mountain, exposed front of a slope.

Fall line. A hill's steepest line of descent.

Fanny pack. A pack resting around the hips, used to carry excess ski paraphernalia or, in the case of ski patrolmen, first aid equipment.

Fiberboard core. A wood core of a metal-wood ski made up of pressed-together wood fibers or small chips.

Fiberglass. Various types of hairlike pieces of glass used to reinforce a resin matrix or body. Resins for skis are usually epoxy or polyester. The fiberglass reinforcing could be chopped, woven, or monofilament randomly distributed or oriented.

Fiberglass skis. Skis whose main strength-bearing element is glass fibers in a plastic mat.

File. A tool used to trim edges and bottom of skis.

Finish. End of a race course.

FIS. Fédération Internationale de Ski, the world ski federation that supervises organized skiing and regulates international competition.

FIS points. A mathematical system both to determine a racer's ranking in the combined standings and to determine his seeding or starting position. Basically points are determined by the percentage by which competitors trail the winner.

Flat light. Visual condition, usually in haze or cloudy weather, that obscures delineation of terrain.

Flat ski. A ski held flat on the snow without any edging.

Flex. The bending properties of the ski.

Flex distribution. The variation in stiffness or bending properties throughout the length of the ski; a ski is usually stiffer near the midsection, where bending is greatest. Other variations in flex distribution throughout the length of the ski adapt it to a specific type of skier and skiing. An advanced skier's ski, for instance, may lose flex distribution that makes it soft in front, stiff in tail.

Flexion. The lowering of the knees, hips, and upper body in a down motion preceding or ending the turn.

Flexural strength. The resistance of the ski to breaking or permanent damage as it is flexed (bent) to extremes.

Flush. A combination of gates used in a slalom race which forces the racer to make a series of tight turns on the fall line.

Foehn. A warm wind that brings thaw conditions. Often called *chinook* in the western parts of the United States.

Foot steering. Changing the direction of the skis by turning the feet and legs. A primary source of turning power in modern skiing.

Foot swivel. A form of turning power in which the strength of the lower legs is used to swing both ends of the skis, so that they swivel or pivot around directly underfoot. Often used to initiate parallel Christies. Same as *foot pivot*.

Forebody. That section of the ski ahead of the area where the boot is normally positioned.

Forerunner. Noncompetitive first runner on a race course. Used to evaluate acceptability of conditions.

Foreward lean. A body position in which the skier's center of gravity is ahead of the bindings.

Four-way competition. Ski competition that involves downhill, jumping, slalom, and cross-country.

Free skiing. Skiing other than in competition.

Frozen granular. Condition of snow which is composed of frozen crystals or granules compacted into a hard, often solid surface.

Full turn. A turn from a traverse into the fall line and then out of the fall line again, to a traverse.

FWSA. Far West Ski Association.

Garland. A teaching exercise in which the skis are alternately slipped downhill and traversed across the hill, but not fully turned.

Gate. Any arrangement of two flags or poles through which a skier must pass in a race.

Gatekeepers. Referees on the course to confirm racer's successful passage of the course.

Gegenschulter. A German term meaning reverse shoulder.

Geländesprung. A jump over a bump or an obstacle, using both poles for support.

Geschmozzle start. A start in Alpine racing, no longer used, in which all racers started at once.

Giant slalom. A form of Alpine racing in which the racer passes through a series of gates which are connected by relatively long traverses. Giant slalom combines elements of both slalom and downhill.

Glade. Wooded portion of a ski slope used by skiers.

Glissement. French term meaning sliding—particularly a racer's sense of how fast his skis can be made to slide on varying snow terrain.

Glühwein. A hot spiced wine drink, popular after skiing.

Godille. Linked parallel turns performed in the fall line; French equivalent to Austrian wedeln.

Gondola. An uphill ski lift that carries several skiers in each of a series of enclosed aerial cars suspended from a moving cable.

Grade. The pitch or angle of a slope.

Gradient. Pitch of a slope.

Graduated-length Method (GLM). A system of ski teaching in which the pupil progresses through a series of successively longer skis.

Granular snow. Snow consisting of big, coarse crystals which look like rock salt. Usually found in the springtime.

Grip. Handle on a ski pole.

Groove. The indentation in the base of the ski, running nearly the length of the ski to provide straight-line stability in running.

Hairpin. A slalom figure made up of two successive closed gates.

Hardpack. Powder snow that has been packed by many skiers passing over it.

Head-on-head race. More than one competitor starting on the same course at the same time, but more commonly on two parallel flagged courses down the mountain.

Heel of the ski. The tail or back end of the ski.

Heel plate. Reinforcing layer molded into the ski to provide additioinal strength as required in the binding heel-screw area.

Heel release. A device that enables the heel to release from the ski in the event of a fall directly over the tips of the skis.

Heel thrust. Pushing of the ski tails sideways across the snow, which changes their direction. For the average pleasure skier it means the same as foot steering, since the skis change direction through leg action.

Herringbone. Climbing a hill with the skis in a V position, with pressure being exerted against the inside edges.

H-gate (Seelos flush). A three-gate slalom figure in which a closed gate is sandwiched between two open gates.

High season. A time of the year when the resorts are busiest, specifically the two weeks over Christmas–New Year's, from mid-February to mid-March, and over Easter if Easter falls within the ski season. European hotels usually raise their rates during these periods.

Hogback. A sharply ridged bump.

Homologation. Preparing a race course according to regulated procedures.

Hop. A means of up-unweighting.

Hop Christie. One of the advanced skidding turns, which starts when the skier lifts the tails of both skis at the same time and changes their direction in air.

Hotshot. Expert skier, sometimes a show-off.

Inrun. The steep slope, frequently set on a high scaffolding, from which a ski jumper picks up speed prior to jumping.

Inside ski. The ski which is, or will become, the one on the inside of the arc in a turn.

Instructor. Professional who teaches skiing, generally sanctioned by certification of country or region where he teaches.

Interval timing. Timing racers over sections of a course.

ISA. Intermountain Ski Association.

J-bar. An uphill ski lift on which a single skier is pulled up the slope by each of a series of J-shaped sticks suspended from a moving cable.

Jet turn. Technical racing turn where skier rocks back on his skis at end of a turn, releasing pressure on skis and jetting out of a turn faster than when he went into it.

Jumping. A Nordic form of competition in which competitors jump on a specially prepared hill both for distance and for style.

Jump turn. An aerial maneuver, used when going at slow speed, during which the skier makes a complete turn in the air.

Kandahar. Arlberg Kandahar. Premier international class ski meet that rotates annually among major European resorts.

Kanone. A German word meaning "cannon," a somewhat dated designation of a "hot" skier.

Kick turn. A 180-degree turn made usually on level ground, moving one ski at a time.

Knee crank. A strong turning force exerted by the knees, either singly or together, when they are pushed in toward the center of an intended turn.

Kneeling. Bending the knee at a slight angle to receive the oncoming weight and create an edge.

Kofix. Trade name for a polyethylene (plastic) mixture bonded into a cloth and then permanently bonded on to the skis. Preferred by better skiers. Comes in several grades. Racers prefer softer grade because it holds wax better, others harder grade because it resists chipping and scratching. Other trade names of similar materials: P-Tex and Blue Nalten.

Lace boots. Rigid ski boots that utilize laces or thongs to control fit.

Laminate. Fabric bonded to a thin, almost weightless polyurethane foam lining with exceptional insulating properties. The new linings can be used with all materials, including knitted goods, and still allow fabrics to drape. Made possible the racer's look in parkas. Can be cleaned, or washed without losing shape.

Laminated core. A wood core of a metal-wood or fiberglass-wood ski made up of multiple pieces of wood for better consistency of properties.

Langlauf. The German word for "cross-country."

Leverage. The effect produced in ski turns by a skier moving his weight forward or back in relation to the centers of the skis. This principle applies primarily at advanced levels of skiing.

Lift. A method of unweighting the skis, making it easier to turn them, by an up motion of the body—a straightening-up of the legs. Also refers to the mechanical means of pulling or lifting a skier to the top of the mountain.

Lift line. Queue at bottom terminal of a lift. Also, the actual line followed by the lift in its progress up hill.

Line. Fastest ideal path down any race course. Racer determines in advance best line for him to follow. How well he has judged and how closely he held line generally determines how well he did in a race.

Line (flex curve). This is the smoothness or quality of the arc formed by the ski running surface or edge as it is flexed to any reasonable deflection.

Linked turns. A series of consecutive turns, in which the end of one turn is the start of the next.

Long thong. A long leather strap attached to binding and wrapped around skier's boot.

Loop. The leather circular strap at the top of the ski pole through which one puts his hand to prevent it from sliding down the shaft of the pole.

Low season. That part of the ski season when most resorts are relatively quiet, usually before Christmas, in January, and in late spring.

Mambo. A series of rhythmic turns in which the skier's upper body leads the legs around the turn, producing a serpentine effect. Usually done on smooth snow conditions, this maneu-

ver has many individual variations.

Mashed potatoes. Heavy, wet snow.

Meadow. Large, open skiable slope, usually gentle.

Metal skis. Skis whose primary strength-bearing element is metal (generally aluminum alloy).

Modified American plan (MAP). Hotel accommodation which includes room, breakfast, and dinner, but not lunch. Favored at many ski resorts.

Mogul. A bump in the terrain usually caused by many skiers turning on the same spot and pushing the snow into a mound.

Nastar. National Standard Race. A *Ski Magazine* racing program whereby recreational skiers can compare their abilities on a nationwide basis.

Nations Cup. Trophy awarded to national team that amasses greatest number of World Cup points during season.

Natural position. A position in which the skier is at a natural angle to his skis. This assures that the body weight will be carried by the skeleton, rather than by the muscles. A basic principle of American Technique.

Nonstop. Final practice run over actual course prior to a downhill race. (Note: racer is not permitted to practice on course in giant slalom or slalom; only permitted in downhill.)

Nordic combined. Competition involving both jumping and cross-country racing, the winner being determined by adding the point totals earned in each event.

Nordic events. The cross-country races and ski jumping.

Notching. Two vertical notches in front of the boot sole spaced to engage two projections in the binding toe unit so that there is sufficient grip to assure release only at proper time.

Novice. A skier who has mastered the snowplow and the snowplow stop.

NRMSA. Northern Rocky Mountain Ski Association.

NSA. National Ski Association, the parent organization of organized skiing in America. A member of the FIS, it has seven regional divisions throughout the country.

NSPS. National Ski Patrol System, a nationwide organization of volunteer skiers, trained in first aid and winter rescue procedures. It promotes ski safety and administers aid to disabled skiers on the slopes.

Offset flush. A flag combination used in slalom racing.

Open gate. A gate whose line between the two poles is across the fall line. (See *closed gate*.)

Optraken. See *prejump*.

Outrun. A flat stretch at the bottom of the

jumping hill where the jumper loses speed and makes his stop.

Outside ski. The ski which goes around the outside arc of a turn.

Package tour. An arrangement whereby the skier pays for everything—transportation, lifts, rooms, and meals—at one time. Some package tours are somewhat less comprehensive.

Packed powder. Snow condition in which the surface snow has been compacted into a firm but yielding mass. It will accept an edge and provides good skiing.

Painting. Applying wax to bottom of skis.

Parallel. Skis parallel and together. Also means an ability on skis.

Parallel Christie. The advanced, most graceful form of the skidded turn, in which the skis are pressed together and kept parallel throughout the entire turn.

Parallel skiing. A technique in which the skis are kept parallel to each other at all times.

Patrolman. Trained and certified volunteer or paid ski patrol member. (See *NSPS*.)

Piste. A ski trail.

Pivoting. Twisting the ski in a new direction by turning the ball of the foot.

Platform. An imaginary plane on the surface of the snow on which preparatory motions for a turn are performed.

Platterpull. A ski lift consisting of disks at the ends of bars which are suspended from a moving overhead cable. Similar to a *pomalift*.

PNSA. Pacific Northwest Ski Association.

Pole plant. A quick jab into the snow with the inside ski pole, to serve as a pivot for a turn.

Poling. Using the poles to move along over flat terrain.

Polyethylene. A plastic available in various degrees of hardness and used for the running surfaces of skis. It is very fast on snow. Usually on skis under the trade names of Kofix or P-Tex.

Pomalift. A ski lift consisting of disks at the end of bars which are suspended from a moving overhead cable. Similar to a *platterpull*.

Postrunner. Noncompetitive skier designed to clear course after a race.

Powder. A snow type, usually found in cold weather after a fresh snowfall, composed of light, dry flakes.

Powderhound. A skier who loves and seeks out deep-powder skiing.

Prejump. A maneuver, similar to a gelände-sprung, in which the skis are lifted into the air on the uphill side of a bump or mogul, before the crest is reached. Prevents the skier from being hurled excessively in the air by the bump.

Projection circulaire. The actual turning phase of the *Christiania léger,* characterized by a forward extension of the outside arm and shoulder leading the hips and lower body through the turn.

PSIA. Professional Ski Instructors of America, association of ski instructors in America.

PSRA. Professional Ski Racers of America, professional ski racing league.

Race circuit. A series of races, generally a series of key races throughout the season in which ambitious racers are expected to participate.

Racing edges. Edges made of somewhat softer steel than those usually found on recreational skis. The steel is softer so that the edges can be sharpened more readily.

Rattlesnake turn. Otherwise known as a *turn within a turn,* an expert maneuver in which a skier makes a small turn during the course of a larger turn.

Release binding. Any heel or toe release or a combination thereof that releases the skis from the boot in the event of a bad fall.

Reverse shoulder. The legs turn in one direction while the upper body moves in the opposite direction or remains relatively stationary. The shoulders are reversed rather than square to the skis. The amount of reverse is determined by the steepness of the slope, the speed of the skier, and his path. Exaggerated reverse shoulder, once a vogue, is no longer the mark of an advanced skier.

Ridge-top ski. An older type of ski with a ridge, rather than flat surface, along the top.

Rock garden. A group of uncovered rocks on a slope or trail.

Rope tow. A moving rope used to pull skiers uphill.

Rotation. Motion of the body or part of the body around an imaginary axis in the direction of the turn. The old Allais method used shoulder rotation; the classic Arlberg involves entire body rotation; and the new Austrian method emphasizes leg rotation as the force which turns the skis.

Royal Christie. An advanced turn performed on the inside ski, with the outside ski lifted off the snow.

Ruade. A turn performed by lifting the ski tails off the snow, and pivoting around on the tips.

Rücklage. Literally, a "backward leaning" or shifting of the weight.

Rucksack. An over-the-shoulder carrying bag used by touring skiers to carry supplies.

Running position. See *posture.*

Running surface. The bottom of the ski.

Ruts. System of relatively deep man-made tracks on a slope or trail.

Safety binding. A mechanism which aims at releasing the foot from the ski automatically under dangerous pressure.

Sandwich construction. The traditional ski construction utilizing lightweight, high-strength aluminum or fiberglass-epoxy in upper and lower skins with wood or filler in between.

Schmieren. A style of skiing in which relatively flat skis are pushed from side to side on the snow to effect a turn.

Schuss. Skiing straight down the fall line, without turns or checks.

Schussboomer. A skier who skis recklessly and indiscriminately.

Seeding. A method of classifying racers in a given race according to ability. Racers are usually seeded in groups of fifteen, each racer's group being determined by his number of FIS points. Within each group, a racer's starting number is determined by draw. Racers in first seed have choice starting positions from 1 to 15.

Setting the edges. Applying the edges on the snow by pressing the knees toward the hill with an upward thrust of the body. See *platform*.

Shaft. The tubular or straight section of the ski pole.

Shell boot. Ski boot consisting of a soft inner boot attached to a rigid outer shell, usually fiberglass.

Shimmy. The tendency of the skis to wander from side to side when skiing straight and with the skis flat on the snow.

Short ski. An adult ski of less than the normal length.

Short swing. The basic appearance of modern wedeln, so called because of the short, swinging motion of ski tails from side to side during the maneuver. (See *wedeln.*) Also known as *kurzschwingen*.

Shovel. The forward half of the forebody through the widest part of the ski and up into the tip.

Side-sliding. Same as *sideslipping*.

Sideslip. A slipping of the skis sideways down a slope by flattening the skis.

Sidestepping. Climbing by stepping skis sideways at right angles to the hill.

Single chair lift. Means of uphill transportation in which moving cable carries chairs that take one person each.

Sinking motion. A slow down motion used as a preparation for an up or rising motion.

Sitzmark. A depression made in the snow by a fallen skier. Same as *bathtub*.

Skating. Skiing on one ski at a time. A pleasurable exercise for improving your balance, for learning to ski on one ski, and for learning to keep your weight forward.

Ski! A cry to warn others of a loose runaway ski hurtling down a slope. Also, device used to glide over snow.

Skidded turns. Any turns where skis slip partially sideways.

Ski flying. A form of jumping on hills where distances of 100 meters or more can be reached.

Ski heil! A skier's salute expressing good luck or good-bye.

Skimeister. A German term meaning "ski master"; also, in four-way competition the competitor who has the best combined score in downhill, slalom, jumping, and cross-country.

Skins. See *climbing skins*.

Ski postion. Relative position of one ski to the other: closed, opened, stemmed, or advance.

Ski school. An organized body of ski instructors.

Slalom. An Alpine form of competition in which the racer must run a course designated by a series of relatively tightly set gates set in various combinations to test his technique, speed, and agility. Failure to pass properly through the gate results in disqualification. Slalom courses may have as many as 70 gates on a relatively steep hill.

Slipped turn. A turn with the skis relatively flat through the greater part of the turn.

Slope. Generic term for ski terrain, generally applied to a specific part of a hill.

Snaking. The ability of a ski to follow terrain variations smoothly.

Snow bunny. See *bunny*.

Snowcat. Actually a trade name used generally by skiers to designate all over-the-snow, tracked vehicles.

Snowmaker. System of combining water and compressed air at freezing temperatures to produce a blanket of man-made snow.

Snowplow. To ski with your skis in an inverted V, tips close, heels apart. A maneuver used to control speed, especially for beginners. Useful for learning muscular coordination and edge control.

Snowplow turn. A simple turn performed from the snowplow position by shifting the weight onto one ski.

Soft. See *flex distribution*.

Split rotation. Combining rotation and reverse shoulder in one turn.

Spring conditions. A catch-all phrase used in snow reporting to designate constantly variable conditions owing to freezing temperatures at night and above-freezing temperatures throughout most of the day.

SRMSA. Southern Rocky Mountain Ski Association.

Standard race. A race for rank-and-file skiers

over a standard course, trying to equal or beat a standard time that has been set by a forerunner.

Start. Beginning of a race. A gate which triggers an electronic timing device as skier passes through it. An electric eye at finish stops timer.

Steered turn. Maneuver in which skier uses pressure only on one ski to cause him to turn.

Steering. Snowplow and stem turns are often spoken of as steered turns because the strength of the legs and feet are used to steer them.

Steering action. To maneuver by ski position and weight transfer, or by leverage.

Stem. Opening the tail of one ski into a V position. Stemming the downhill ski is called an *abstem*.

Stem Christie. Turn initiated by stemming one ski, after which the skis are brought into the parallel position for the duration of the turn.

Stem turn. Turn initiated by stemming one ski into the V position, which is maintained during the turn; the skis are brought parallel after the conclusion of the turn.

Step-in binding. Usually, a release binding consisting of an integral toe and heel unit which snaps the boot in place as the skier steps on the ski.

Step turn. A change in direction usually accomplished as skier steps from downhill onto uphill ski, which then starts to carve turn.

Steilhang. Very steep section of hill.

Stiffness. See *flex distribution*.

Straightness. In ski terminology, straightness refers to the quality of the contact line formed when the two running surfaces of a pair are clamped tightly together— bottom to bottom.

Straight running. Descending a hill with parallel skis.

Style. The individual interpretation of technique.

Swallow terrain. A slope with deeply forked or cut ridges.

Swingweight. Resistance of an unweighted ski to being turned. Light skis have lower swingweight.

Tail. That section of the ski behind the area where the boot is normally positioned.

Tail protector. An additional metal piece molded into or tacked onto the tail of the ski to protect against delamination or external blows against the ski in this area.

Takeoff. The lip of the inrun where the ski jumper takes off into the air.

T-bar. A lift consisting of a series of T-shaped bars suspended from a continuously moving cable. The T accommodates two skiers who lean against the bar and are pulled uphill.

Technique. A formal exposition of ski instruction from the beginning stages to the advanced maneuvers. Also called a teaching system or a teaching method. Hence American Technique.

Téléférique. See *aerial tramway*.

Telemark. A steering turn for deep snow that used to be popular years ago. Named after a region in Norway, the telemark was performed by pushing one ski ahead of, and across at an angle to, the other ski. The leading ski carried most of the skier's weight, with the opposite knee sharply bent until it almost touched its ski.

Terrain. The configuration of skiable surface of any mountain.

Three-sixty. Airborne maneuver in which skier does one complete rotation about a vertical axis before landing.

Tip. Front portion of the ski.

Tip protector. An additional metal piece molded into or tacked onto the tip of the ski in the area most susceptible to damage by bumping the skis together during skiing.

Tip splay. The open distance back from the tip before the skis contact each other when they are tightly clamped together, bottom to bottom.

Tip thrust. The skier thrusts or pulls ski tips to induce a quick change of direction. Same as *tip pull*.

Toe irons. A nonrelease binding which holds the toes of the boots rigidly by means of two metal brackets fastened to a base plate.

Toe release. Any unit which holds the toes of the boot to skis but releases in the event of a serious twisting fall.

Top edge. A strip of harder plastic or metal along the top edges of the ski to protect against damage; can also affect flexural properties of some skis.

Torsion. The resistance of a ski to being twisted as forces are applied to the ski as seen from the end view.

Torsional deflection. The amount the ski twists as twisting forces are applied to it. The ski is normally held from twisting at the center by the skier's foot and boot. The bite of the wide points of the ski at the two ends thereby introduces twisting forces, and the ski responds by twisting along its cross section.

Total motion. A basic principle of American Technique which states that muscle action is a product of the entire body, rather than of one part only.

Touring. Recreational cross-country and Alpine skiing using light skis and boots.

Touring adapter. Special metal plates used to adapt a release binding for cross-country touring, allowing free heel movement.

Track. Path a skier has taken.

Tracking. A performance characteristic of a good pair of skis. The ability to hold a straight course on every type of snow surface.

"Track left" or "track right." A warning a descending skier shouts to someone in his path whom he intends to pass, "left" or "right" indicating on which side the skier will pass.

Tram. An enclosed car suspended from a moving cable, used as a ski lift in some areas.

Transition. The relatively flat or level area before, after, or between steep sections.

Traverse. Skiing straight or diagonally across the fall line.

Traverse position. The special body position used when skiing diagonally down a hill.

Turn. Any curved path on the slopes made by the skis.

Turn downhill. Same as turn into the fall line.

Turning. The act of changing direction on skis.

Turning power. Any of the many sources of force used to initiate or continue a turning movement of the skis.

Turn into the fall line. A turn that goes from a traverse into the fall line.

Turn out of the fall line. Same as uphill Christie.

Turntable. A swiveling heel binding for attaching long thongs that enables the toe release to function. There are also turntables which allow for release in a forward fall.

Twisting. The pivoting of the foot and lower leg which turns the ski.

Unweighting. A means of reducing the weight on the skis prior to turning so that the skis turn more easily.

Uphill Christie. A turn "into" the hill with skis parallel. The completion phase of all Christie turns.

Uphill ski. The upper ski or the one that will become the upper ski in any ski turn.

Up-unweighting. Unweighting by means of rising sharply. When the rising motion slows or stops, the skis are unweighted.

USEASA. United States Eastern Amateur Ski Association.

USSA. U.S. Ski Association, the national federation of American skiers and a governing body of the sport in the United States.

Vorlage. Forward lean or shifting the weight forward prior to a turn.

Waist. The narrowest part of the ski as seen from the top view; usually the area beneath where the boot is normally positioned.

Warp. A lateral twist in a ski.

Wax. A preparation applied to the running surface of a ski to facilitate its movement and to reduce friction with the snow.

Wedeln. A series of close parallel turns made in the fall line with a minimum of edge set. Means literally "tail wagging."

Weighting. The application of weight to the skis in order to set the edges. Usually accomplished by angulation or by rising sharply.

Weight shift. A transfer of weight from one ski to the other, specifically from the downhill ski to the uphill ski in the initiation phase of steered turns.

Weight transfer. The shifting of weight from one ski to the other, or onto both edges, usually during a turn. A basic principle of American Ski Technique.

Wide track. Skier skis with skis parallel but feet apart by as much as a foot to 18 inches.

Wind-slab. Snow packed by the wind.

Windup. Akin to counterrotation, except that a windup is used only before a turn is initiated and not to initiate it. Windup is a preparatory movement—somewhat like in tennis or golf—of a ski pole or arm or shoulder or hip, or all of these, to permit a swing of great power and amplitude.

Wood skis. Skis whose primary strength-bearing material is wood.

World Cup. Annual FIS ski competition, started in 1967, in which racers earn points in a series of major international meets during the winter. Racer with greatest number of points at season end wins World Cup.

THE INTERNATIONAL SKIER'S LEXICON

What to say on the skiing slopes of Europe when the translator is not around—in English, German, French, and Italian.

English	German	French	Italian
après-ski	après-ski	après-ski	après-ski
avalanche	Lawine	avalanche	valanga, slavina
base	Unterlage	couche de fond	base, suola
base of ski, sole	die Sohle	la semelle de ski	la suola de ski
basket	Schneeteller	rondelle, disque	rotella
belt	Gürtel	ceinture	cintura
binding	Bindung	attache, fixation	attacco

English	German	French	Italian
boiler plate	Eisplatte	neige tolée	neve glinecciata
boot tree	Stiefelstrecker	porte-chaussures	tendi scarpone
buckle boot	Schnallenstiefel	chassures à crochets	scarpone a fibbia
bump	Buckel	bosse	cunetto
cable	Kabel	câble	cavo
cable car	Seilbahn	téléférique	funivia
camber	Spannung	flêche	balestra
chair lift	Sessellift	télésiège	seggiovia
check	abschwingen	contrôle	controllo
Christie	Christiania	christiania	cristiania
coach	Trainer	moniteur	allenatore
cogwheel railway	zahnradbahn	crémaillère	cremagliera
corn	Firn	neige de printemps	neve granulosa
crash helmet	Sturzhelm	casque	casco
cross-country	Langlauf	ski de fond	fondo
downhill	Abfahrt	descente	discesa
earband	Stirnband	bandeau	para orecchi
edges	Kanten	carres	laminature
fiberglass	Fiberglas	fibres de verre	fibra sintetica
finish line	Ziel	arrivée	traguardo
forward lean	vorlage	position avancée	pendura in avanti
funicular	drahtseilbahn	funicular	funicular
gate	Tor	porte	porta
gentle slope	Flaschang	pente legere	modesta pendenza
giant slalom	Riesenslalom	slalom géant	slalom-gigante
glacier	Gletscher	glacier	ghiacciaio
gloves	Handschuhe	gants	guanti
goggles	Schneebrille	lunettes en coque	occhiali da neve
gondola	Gondel	telecabine	gondola
groove	die Laufrille	la rainure	il canale centrale
helicopter	hubschrauber	helicoptère	elicòttero
herringbone	Grätschritt	enciseaux	spina di pence
inn	Gasthaus	auberge	rifugio
instructor	Ski Lehrer	moniteur	istrutorre
jumping	Sprung, Ski Springen	saut	salto
kick turn	Spitzkehre	demi tour de pied ferme	mezzo giro su se stresso
knee socks	Kniestrümpfe	bas	calzettoni
knickers	Bundhosen	pantalons de montagne	calzoni alla zuava
lace boots	Schnürstiefel	chaussures à lacets	scarponi a lacci
leotard	Strumpfhosen	collants	calzamaglia
lift line (waiting)	Lift-Schlange	ligne d'attente	fila d'attesa
lift line (trail under)	Lift-Hang	piste sous le teleski	pista di funivia
lodge	Pension	logis, chalet, pension, hôtel	pensione
long thong	Langriemen	lanière	cinghia lunga d'attacco
long underwear	lang Unterwäsche	caleçon long	mutande lunghe
metal	Metall	métal	metallo
mittens	Fausthandschuhe	mitaines	guanti da neve
mogul	Buckel	bosse	gobba
mountain	Berg	montagne	montagna
new snow	Neuschnee	neige fraîche	neve fresca
parallel	Parallel	parallèle	parallelo
parka	Anorak	anorak	giacco a vento
pass	Joch	col	passo, colle
patch	Stoffabzeichen	badge, écusson	insegna
pin	Anteckzeichen-nadel	médaille	distintivo
plastic	Plastik	plastique	plastica
platterpull (poma)	schlepplift (schleppbahn)	télé-ski	
poles	Stöcke	batons, cannes	bastoni
powder snow	Pulverschnee	neige poudreuse	neve farinosa
railroad	eisenbahn	chemin de fer	ferrovia
race	Rennen	course	gara

English	German	French	Italian
release binding	Sicherheitsbindung	fixation de sécurité	l'attacco di sicurezza
reverse shoulder	Gegenschulter	avancé de l'épaule	spalla contraria
room to let	Fremdenzimmer	chamber a louer	trampolino
rope tow	Schlepplift	(none in France)	sciovia
rotation	Rotation	rotation	rotazione
rücklage	Rücklage	position de recul	pendenzo indietro
rucksack	Rucksack	sac de montagne	zaino
safety strap	Sicherungsriemen, Fangriemen	courroie de sécurité	la cinghietta di sicurezza
schuss	Schuss	schuss	schuss
shoe lace	Schuhband	le lacet de soulier	laccio
short swing	Kurtschwung	petit virage	raggio cordo
side slip	Seitrutschen	dérapage	scivolare
ski	Ski	ski	sci
ski hat	Skimütze	bonnet de ski	berretto da sci
ski rack	Skihalter	porte-ski	porta sci
ski shop	Ski Gescheft	boutique de ski	negozio di sci
ski tail	Skiende	talon du ski	coda
ski tip	Skispitze	spatule	punta
slalom	Torlauf	slalom	slalom
sledge lift	Aufzugschlitten	téléluge	slittovia
slope	Hang	pente	pendío
slush	Matsch	neige fondue	neve sciolta
snowplow	Schneepflug	chasse-neige	spazza neve
socks	Socken	chausettes	calzettoni
spring conditions	Frühjahrsschnee	condition de printemps	neve primaverile
station	Bahnhof	gare	stazione
steep slope	Steilhang	pente raide	pendio ripido
stem	Stemmbogen	stem	stem
stretch pants	Elastic-Hosen	fuseaux	pantaloni elastici
sunglasses	Sonnenbrille	lunettes de soleil	occhiali da sole
sun lotion	Sonnenoel	crème solaire	lozione solare
sweater	Pullover	pull, chandail	pullover, maglione da sci
T-bar	Bügellift	téléski double	sciovia a T
trail	Weg	piste	pista
traverse	Hangschrägfahrt	traversée	diagonale, mezza costa
turn	Umdrehung	virage	curva
turntable	Drehteller	talonniere tournante	la piastra girevole
turtleneck	Rollkragen	à col roulé	a collo rivoltato
unweighting	entlasten	allègement	allegerimento
uphill ski	Bergski	ski amont	salita
vertical	vertical	vertical	verticale
V-neck	V-Ausschnitt	chandail en pointe	collo a V
wax	Wachs	fart	sciolina
wedeln	Wedeln	godille	wedeln
weighting	belasten	appui	applicare il peso
wood	Holz	bois	legno
wool	Wolle	laine	lana

SKI ASSOCIATIONS OF THE WORLD

United States

United States Ski Association (USSA), 1726 Champa Street, Suite 300, Denver, Colorado 80202

United States Eastern Amateur Ski Association (USEASA), 20 Main Street, Littleton, New Hampshire 03561

Central Division, USSA, PO Box 66014, Chicago, Illinois 60666.

Northern Division, USSA, 1111 North 7th, Bozeman, Montana 59715.

Rocky Mountain Division, USSA, 1463 Larimer Street, Denver, Colorado 80202.

Intermountain Division, USSA, 3584 South West Temple, Salt Lake City, Utah 84115

Far West Ski Association (FWSA), 812 Howard Street, San Francisco, California 94103

Pacific Northwest Division, USSA, P. O. Box 6228, Seattle, Washington 98188

Alaska Division, USSA, P. O. Box 4–2126, Anchorage, Alaska 99503

International

Compiled by the Fédération Internationale de Ski (FIS), Stora Nygatan 20, 11127 Stockholm, Sweden.

Algeria	Fédération Algerienne de Ski, 30 boulevard Zirout Youcef, Alger
Andorra	Esqui Club d'Andorra, Carrer Mn. Cinto Verdaguer, 4 ler, Andorra la Vella
Argentina	Federación Argentina de Ski y Andinismo, Viamonte 1560, 30 piso, Buenos Aires
Australia	The Australian National Ski Federation, 10 Farleigh Avenue, Beaumaris, Victoria
Austria	Österreichischer Skiverband, Maria-Theresien-Strasse 53, Innsbruck
Belgium	Fédération Belge de Ski, 37 Rue des Drapiers, Bruxelles
Bolivia	Federación Boliviana de Ski y Andinismo, Av. 16 de Julio 1473, La Paz
Brazil	Clube Alpino Paulista, Rua Xavier de Toledo 316–13° andas, São Paulo
Bulgaria	Section Bulgare de Ski, Bld. Tolboukhine 18, Sofia
Canada	Canadian Amateur Ski Association, Room C–15, 306 Place d'Youville, Montreal 125, Quebec
Chile	Federación de Ski de Chile, Casilla 9902, Compania 1630, Santiago
China. Republic of	Republic of China National Ski Association, No. 3, Lane 153, Chang An East Road, Section 2, Taipei, Taiwan
Cyprus	The Cyprus Ski Club, P. O. Box 2185, Nicosia
Czechoslovakia	Ceskoslovenská sekce lyzovaní, Na. Porící 12, Praha 1
Denmark	Dansk Skiforbund, Vester Voldgade 11, København V
Finland	Suomen Hiihtoliitto, Topeliuksenkatu 41A, Box 25202, Helsinki 25
France	Fédération Française de Ski, 119 rue Courcelles, Paris XVII
German Democratic Republic (DDR)	Deutscher Skiläuferverband, Storkower Strasse 118, 1055 Berlin NO 18
German Federal Republic (BRD)	Deutscher Skiverband, Brienner Strasse 50, D–8 München 2
Great Britain	The National Ski Federation, 118 Eaton Square, London S. W. 1
Greece	Club Alpin Hellénique, Karageorgi Servias 7, Athens 126
Holland	Nederlandse Ski Vereniging, Wassenaarseweg 220, B. P. 2200, Gravenhage
Hungary	Magyar Si Szövetség, Rosenberg Hazaspar u. 1, Budapest
Iceland	The Icelandic Ski Association, Ithróttamidstödin, Laugardal, Reykjavik
Iran	Fédération Iranienne de Ski, Kakhe Varzesh, Teheran
Israel	Israel Ski Club, P. O. B. 4031, Tel Aviv
Italy	Federazione Italiana Sport Invernali, Via Cerva 30, Milano
Japan	National Ski Association of Japan, Kishi Memorial Hall, 4–6 Surugadai, Chiyoda-ku, Tokyo
Korea	Korean Ski Federation, P. O. B. 106, Seoul

Lebanon	Fédération Libanaise de Ski, Rue d'Alger—Imm. Khiani, BP 3626, Beyrouth		Avenida da Roma 7 A, Lisbonne
Liechtenstein	Liechtensteinischer Ski-verband, Vaduz	Rumania	Federatia Romina de Schi, Str. Vasile Conta, 16, Bucurest
Mongolia	Mongolian Ski Federa-tion, 55, Boga Toirog, Ulanbator	Spain	Federación Española de Esqui, Modesto La-fuente 4, Madrid 10
Morocco	Fédération Royale Ma-rocaine de Ski, Avenue de France 3, Fès	Sweden	Svenska Skidförbundet, Stora Nygatan 20, 11127 Stockholm
New Zealand	The New Zealand Ski Association, P. O. Box 2213, Wellington	Switzerland	Fédération Suisse de Ski, Luisenstrasse 20, Bern
Norway	Norges Skiforbund, Stortingsgt 4, Oslo 1	Turkey	Fédération Turque de Ski, Kayak Federa-syonu, Ulus, Ankara
Pakistan	Pakistan National Ski Association, Goffer Chambers, Victoria Road, Karachi 3	USSR	The Ski Federation of the USSR, Skatertnyi pererlok 4, Moscow G–69
Poland	Polski Zwiazek Narci-arski, Sienkiewicza 12/14, Warszawa 1	Yugoslavia	Fédération Yougoslave de Ski, Case postale 316, Beograd
Portugal	Ski Club de Portugal,		

Abbreviations of FIS National Associations

The following is a listing of the abbrevia-tions of the FIS member nations. These ab-breviations are often used to designate the nationality of the winner of ski competitions.

Algeria	ALG	Iran	IRA
Andorra	AND	Israel	ISR
Argentina	ARG	Italy	ITA
Australia	AUS	Japan	JPN
Austria	AUT	Korea	KOR
Belgium	BEL	Lebanon	LIB
Bolivia	BOL	Liechtenstein	LIC
Brazil	BRA	Mongolia	MON
Bulgaria	BUL	Morocco	MAR
Canada	CAN	Netherlands	NED
Chile	CHI	New Zealand	NZE
Republic of China	ROC	D.P.R. Korea	NKR
Czechoslovakia	CSF	Norway	NOR
Cyprus	CYP	Pakistan	PAK
Denmark	DAN	Poland	POL
Finland	FIN	Portugal	POR
France	FRA	Rumania	RUM
German Democratic Republic	DDR	Soviet Union	SOV
		Spain	SPA
German Federal Republic	BRD	Sweden	SWE
		Switzerland	SUI
Greece	GRE	Turkey	TUR
Great Britain	GBR	United States of America	USA
Hungary	HUN		
Iceland	ISL	Yugoslavia	JUG

Illustration Credits are listed by page numbers. All other illustrations courtesy of Universal Publishing and Distributing Corp.